GRACE

Commentary on the *Summa theologica* of
St. Thomas, Ia IIae, q. 109-14

By
REV. REGINALD GARRIGOU-LAGRANGE, O.P.

Translated by
THE DOMINICAN NUNS
Corpus Christi Monastery
Menlo Park, California

B. HERDER BOOK CO.
15 & 17 SOUTH BROADWAY, ST. LOUIS 2, MO.
AND
33 QUEEN SQUARE, LONDON, W. C.
1952

NIHIL OBSTAT

Innocentius Swoboda, O.F.M.

Censor Librorum

IMPRIMATUR

✠ *Joseph E. Ritter*

Archiepiscopus

St. Ludovici, die 25a mensis, Julii, 1952

Vail-Ballou Press, Inc., Binghamton and New York

To the holy Mother of God,
Mother of divine Grace,

WHO SWEETLY AND SUBLIMELY TEACHES TO LITTLE
ONES THE MYSTERIES OF SALVATION,
THE AUTHOR DEDICATES THIS WORK
IN TOKEN OF GRATITUDE AND FILIAL OBEDIENCE

PREFACE

WE have already explained at length in the treatise on the one God the doctrine of St. Thomas about the knowledge and will of God, providence and predestination, and likewise in the treatise on God the Creator his doctrine on evil. Now it remains to apply the principles already expounded to the questions of grace, so that these may be considered in relation to man, and also in relation to God, the author of grace, who is the subject of sacred theology. Indeed this science considers all things in relation to God, as optics does in relation to color and light, mathematics in relation to quantity, metaphysics in relation to being as such.

Hence the present treatise *On grace* depends on the treatise about the divine will in which we have already set forth the will for universal salvation and the distinction between antecedent will and consequent will, which is the ultimate basis, as we shall see, of the distinction between sufficient grace and efficacious grace.

We presuppose, likewise, St. Thomas' doctrine on the intrinsic and infallible efficacy of the divine decrees, presented in Ia, q. 19, a. 8, which we have explained at length in the treatise on the one God, refuting the objections based on the violation of freedom, on insufficiency of help, and on affinity with Calvinism.

Our treatise on grace is especially connected with question 20, Part I, on the love of God: 1. whether love exists in God; 2. whether God loves all things; 3. whether God loves all things equally; 4. whether God always loves better things more. In explanation of this last article, we show the value of the principle of predilection: "Nothing would be better than anything else (as an act, easy or difficult, natural or supernatural, initial or final) unless it were more loved and sustained by God." "What hast thou that thou hast not received?" (I Cor. 4:7.) As we shall see, this principle throws a light from on high upon all questions of predestination and grace. It is likewise the basis of Christian humility and of our gratitude to God, "who hath first loved us."

At the same time, no less emphasis must be placed on another principle of St. Augustine, formulated and cited at the Council of Trent (Denz., no. 804): "God does not command the impossible, but by commanding He incites thee to do what thou canst and to ask what thou canst not, and He assists thee so that thou mayst be able." These two principles taken together prevent opposing deviations, preserve balance of thought and the harmony of the divine word in regard to these most difficult questions.

AUTHORS TO BE CONSULTED

1. The teaching of the Fathers on grace

Schwane, *Histoire des Dogmes,* tr. Degert, 1904.

J. Tixeront, *Histoire des Dogmes.* Vol. I: Théologie antérnicéenne, 1905; Vol. II: S. Athanase à S. Augustin, 1909; Vol. III: La fin de l'âge patristique, 1912, p. 274 ff.

Héfele, *Histoire des conciles,* tr. Leclerq (Paris, 1908), II, 168.

St. Augustine, *De natura et gratia; De gratia Christi; Enchiridion; Sex libr. adversus Julianum; De gratia et libero arbitrio; De correptione et gratia; De praedestinatione sanctorum; De dono perseverantiae.*

St. Prosper, *PL,* LI, 155–276.

St. Fulgentius, *De gratia et libero arbitrio.*

St. Bernard, *De gratia et libero arbitrio.*

Peter Lombard, *Sent.,* Bk. II, d. 26–28: *De gratia.*

St. Bonaventure and St. Albert the Great, *In II Sent.*

2. Works of St. Thomas and of Thomists on grace

St. Thomas, *In II Sent.,* d. 26–28; *Ia IIae,* q. 109–14; *Contra Gentes, Quaest. disput.*

Principal commentators: Capreolus, *In II Sent.,* d. 26; Cajetan, *In Iam IIae,* q. 109 ff.; Medina, John of St. Thomas.

Sylvius, Gonet, the Salmanticenses, Gotti, Billuart.

Soto, *De natura et gratia,* 1551.

Thomas Lemos, *Panoplia gratiae,* 4 vols., 1676.

Alvarez, *De auxiliis divinae gratiae,* 1610.

Gonzalez de Albeda, *In Iam,* q. 19, 1637.

Goudin, *De gratia,* 1874.

Reginaldus, O.P., *De mente Conc. Trident. circa gratiam seipsa efficacem,* 1706.

Among recent works by Thomists: Dummermuth: *S. Thomas et doctrina praemotionis physicae,* Paris, 1886; *Defensio doctrinae S. Thomas,* 1895. N. Del Prado, O.P.,: *De gratia et libero arbitrio,* 3 vols., Fribourg (Switzerland), 1907. Garrigou-Lagrange, O.P.: *La prédestination des saints et la grâce,* 1936; *Dict. théol. cath.,* arts., "Prédestination," "Prémotion." Schaezler: *Natur und Gnade,* Mainz, 1867.

3. Outside the Thomistic School

Molina, *Concordia,* Paris, 1876.

Suarez, *De gratia.*

St. Robert Bellarmine, *De controversiis* (Prague, 1721), Vol. IV.

St. Alphonsus de Liguori, *De modo quo gratia operatur; De magno orationis medio.*

Scheeben, *Natur und Gnade,* Mainz, 1861. Strongly inclines toward Thomism.

Billot, S.J., *De gratia Christi,* 2nd ed., 1921.

Van der Meersch, *De divina gratia* (Bruges, 1910) and *Dict. théol. cath.,* art., "Grâce."

J. Ude, *Doctrina Capreoli de influxu Dei in actus voluntatis humanae,* Graz, 1905. This author favors Thomism.

TREATISE ON GRACE

Ia IIae, q. 109–114

In the first place something must be said about the position of this treatise in the *Summa theologica.* St. Thomas treats of grace in the moral part of his *Summa,* for, after the questions of human acts themselves, must be considered the principles of human acts; first, the intrinsic principles, namely, good and bad habits, or virtues and vices; secondly, the external principles of human acts, namely, God's teaching us by means of His law, and His assistance to us by His grace.[1]

Hence the treatise on grace belongs to the moral part of theology

[1] Cf. Ia IIae, q.90, introd. With regard to this heading, it should be noted that God assisting by His grace is an extrinsic principle. Grace, however, is not a principle extrinsic to man, but inhering in him, as will be explained later.

no less than the treatise on law. Moral theology is not a science distinct from dogmatic theology, since the formal object (*objectum formale quod et quo*) is ever the same: God under the aspect of His Deity so far as it falls under virtual revelation. It would be surprising if the moral part of sacred theology did not treat of the necessity of grace for doing good conducive to salvation and of the effects of grace, i.e., justification and merit. Indeed, if moral theology is deprived of these treatises, it will be reduced almost to casuistry, which is only its lowest application, as asceticism and mysticism are its highest applications.

Division of the Treatise on Grace

The grace of God itself
{ the necessity of grace for our final end, q. 109.
the essence of grace, q. 110.
the divisions of grace, q. 111.

The cause of grace: q. 112, the efficient cause and the prerequisite disposition.

The effects of grace
{ justification, q. 113.
merit, q. 114.

Among Thomistic commentators the following, along with Cajetan, are especially to be read: Soto (*De natura et gratia*), John of St. Thomas, the Salmanticenses, Gonet, Gotti, Billuart. Cf. also among modern theologians, Scheeben (*Natur und Gnade*).

This division of the whole treatise is methodical, corresponding to the division into four causes. 1. Grace is considered beginning with the definition of the word and with reference to its necessity for the end of eternal life and to its existence. 2. Thus, in regard to its end, grace, as it is the seed of glory, is defined as a participation in the divine nature and is determined by the subject in which it resides, that is, the essence of the soul. 3. After the definition of grace, its subdivisions are given. Then its efficient cause and its effects are discussed. Thus all those things which belong to it *per se* are taken into consideration.

A brief comparison may be made between this division of St. Thomas and the division made by various modern writers. Many modern scholars, such as Tanquerey, divide this treatise into three parts, but this division is rather material than formal.

Grace		
	Actual grace	Its necessity for supernatural works and good acts in the natural order.
		The dispensation of actual grace and its nature, including sufficient and efficacious grace (Thomism, Molinism).
	Habitual grace, or the grace of justification	The nature of justification and the dispositions it requires.
		The essence of grace.
		Its properties, namely, the virtues and gifts.
		The graces *gratis datae*.
	Merit: its nature, conditions, and object.	

This division is less correct; in treating of the necessity of grace the necessity of habitual grace is also treated. And in the order of knowledge it is better to deal with justification, which is an effect of grace, after considering the essence of grace. Hence Father Billot, S.J., after his preliminary remarks, rightly divides his treatise on grace according to St. Thomas. Father Hugon, O.P., does the same, as do many others. Nor may it be said that St. Thomas did not distinguish clearly between habitual and actual grace; this distinction is made time and time again in the articles, and thereby is made evident how St. Thomas perfected the Augustinian doctrine, regarding grace not only from the psychological and moral aspects, but ontologically: 1. as an abiding form, and 2. as a transitory movement.

This entire treatise is a commentary on the words of our Lord in John 4:10: "If thou didst know the gift of God," and our Lord's discourse by which they are elucidated, according to St. John. At the same time it may be said that St. Paul was the apostle of grace who opened to us the deep things of God, predestination and grace. And the two great doctors of grace are Augustine, who defended divine grace against Pelagius, and St. Thomas, of whom the liturgy sings:

> "Praise to the King of glory, Christ,
> Who by Thomas, light of the Church,
> Filled the earth with the doctrine of grace."

This work is a translation of *De gratia* by Father Garrigou-Lagrange, O.P.

Contents

Contents

GRACE

CHAPTER I

▲▲▲

B RIEF introductory remarks are necessary so as to avoid repetitions:

1. On the various meanings of the word "grace" and presupposed notions from the treatise on God;

2. On the errors involved in this subject.

MEANINGS OF THE WORD "GRACE"

The various meanings are indicated by St. Thomas (Ia Iae, q. 110, a. 1), but it is fitting that we say something of them at the beginning so that the connection may be apparent between the present question and the questions relating to God's love for us.

First, there are of course three acceptations of this word "grace" even used in human affairs. For grace (χάρις) originally refers to something which is not due or is freely bestowed; this meaning is very common in both profane and biblical writings. Hence even in purely human matters the term "grace" has a threefold application, as follows:

1. The love of benevolence conferring a gift which is not due; for example, we say: This soldier has the grace of the king.

2. The gift itself freely bestowed; thus we say: I grant you this grace.

3. Gratitude for a benefit received; thus: I render you thanks for your benefits.[1]

Moreover, these three significations may be transferred to the supernatural order, whereupon the word grace applies to the following.

1. The love of benevolence on the part of God, conferring supernatural life. This love of God is uncreated grace.

---

[1] In Latin the word for "thanks" is *"gratiae."* Hence the third meaning of *gratia.* (Tr.)

2. The supernatural gift of grace itself, freely bestowed and ordained to eternal life; this is created grace, of which we are now treating, whether it is interior or exterior, such as the preaching of the gospel.

3. Our gratitude to God.

Between the human and the supernatural meanings of the word "grace" there lies a great difference which is principally based upon the fact that God's love of benevolence for us, as stated in Ia, q. 20, a. 2, infuses and creates goodness in things, whereas the love of benevolence of one man for another presupposes something lovable in that other. But "God's love for the creature is twofold, the common love whereby natural being is bestowed on created things, and the other special love by which God raises the rational creature above the state of nature unto a participation in the divine good. Thus grace is the effect of the love of God in us and signifies the supernatural gift freely granted by God to an intellectual creature ordained to eternal life" (Ia IIae, q. 110, a. 1).

Thus the whole treatise on grace in the *Summa theologica* of St. Thomas depends upon the treatise on the love of God (Ia, q. 20), in which are expressed and explained two supreme principles which throw a light from above upon all the articles of the treatise on grace and virtually contain them.

Hence St. Thomas says: "It is demonstrated above (q. 19, a. 4) that the will of God is the cause of all things; so it must be that so far as a thing possesses being or any good whatever, to that extent it is willed by God. Therefore God wills some good to whatever exists. And since loving is nothing else but wishing well to someone, it is clear that God loves all things that are, not however in the same way as we do. Our will is not the cause of the goodness of things. But the love of God infuses and creates goodness in things" (Ia, q. 20, a. 2). Accordingly the will of God is also the cause of the goodness of our acts, while preserving their liberty. As St. Thomas says: "If the will of God is most efficacious, it follows not only that those things will be done which God wills to be done, but that they will be done in the way God wills them to be done. Thus God wills certain things to be necessary, others to be contingent, that there may be order among things for the perfection of the universe" (Ia, q. 19, a. 8).

From this first principle thus understood the second follows: "Since the love of God is the cause of the goodness of things, nothing is in any respect better, if God does not will one thing to be better than another" (Ia, q. 20, a. 4, 5). This is the principle of predilection which is valid for every created being and for the facility or difficulty of each of its acts: No created being is in any respect better if it is not preferred by God. St. Thomas deduces from this that "in God love precedes election . . . for His will, willing good to whatever it loves, is the cause of its possessing this good from Him beyond others" (*ibid.*, q. 23, a. 4).

This principle of predilection presupposes that the divine decrees in regard to our future acts conducive to salvation are infallibly efficacious of themselves and not from a foreknowledge of our consent (Ia, q. 19, a. 8). Otherwise, of two men equally loved and assisted by God, one would be in some respect better. He would be better of himself and not so far as preferred by God; and therefore the free determination in him to be saved would be something good which would not proceed from the source of all good, contrary to the words of St. Paul: "For who distinguisheth thee? Or what hast thou that thou hast not received?" (I Cor. 4:7.)

These are the principles already laid down and explained in the treatises on the will and on the love of God; they virtually contain what is now to be said concerning grace, both habitual grace and actual grace.

Finally, it must be remarked that the Pelagians, not wishing to recognize the love of God as being the first cause of all our good choices, were equally averse to distinguishing the natural from the supernatural meanings of this word "grace." They therefore misused it in a broad, incorrect sense and applied the word "grace" to any free gift of God whatever; thus creation, preservation, and even free will are called by them graces.

Likewise created grace properly so called is defined in a variety of ways:

1. As external grace, such as the preaching of the gospel, the example of Christ; and the Pelagians admitted this grace.

2. As internal grace, namely, that which is received in the interior of the soul, ennobling it.

Moreover, this internal grace may be either that which makes one pleasing (*gratum faciens*), which is divided into habitual or sanctifying grace, and actual grace, or charismatic grace (*gratia gratis data*), which is principally or primarily for the benefit of others.

Grace
- internal
  - which renders pleasing (*gratum faciens*)
    - habitual or justifying or sanctifying.
    - actual, which includes sufficient and efficacious.
  - charismatic (*gratis data*): for example, the gift of prophecy, the discernment of spirits, the gift of tongues.
- external: e.g., the preaching of the Gospel

Since grace is indeed supernatural, and frequently in this treatise there will be question of the distinction between what is supernatural substantially and what is supernatural modally, it will be well to recall the definition and division of supernaturalness itself as it has already been set forth in fundamental theology. The supernatural, according to the Catholic Church, is that which is above all created nature; which, although it exceeds the powers and requirements of any nature created or capable of being created, does not exceed the passive capacity of perfectibility and aptitude of our nature. (Cf. Denz., nos. 1790, 1795, 1808, 1816; Garrigou-Lagrange, *De revelatione*, I, 193, 197, 202.)

Moreover, according to the Church, supernaturalness is at least twofold, namely:

1. The supernaturalness of miracles, which surpasses the efficient powers and requirements of any created nature, but not, however, the cognitive powers of human nature. (Denz., nos. 1790, 1818.)

2. The supernaturalness of mysteries strictly speaking and of the life of grace and glory is that which surpasses not only the efficient powers and requirements of any created nature, but also the cognitive and appetitive powers (or natural merit) of any intellectual nature created or capable of being created.

Such is the declared doctrine of the Church as follows from the condemnation of naturalism, rationalism, semi-rationalism (which deviates in the matter of the powers), Baianism (an excess as to requirements), and agnosticism (denying that miracles are ascertainable). Cf. Denz., nos. 1795, 1808; cf. *De Revelatione*, I, 193.

This division of supernaturalness may be otherwise expressed according to the terminology rather generally accepted among theologians, thus:

THE ABSOLUTE SUPERNATURAL exceeding the powers and requirements of any created nature	with respect to substance or to the formal cause	uncreated, substantial of itself.	God in the most intimate sense of His Deity and Trinity. The uncreated person of the Word subsisting in the human nature of Christ.
		created (accidental)	Habitual and actual grace, the infused virtues, the gifts of the Holy Ghost (supernatural by virtue of their formal object).
	with respect to the manner or to the extrinsic causes, that is, in the manner both of its extrinsic disposition and of its production	in regard to the end	Natural act, such as acquired temperance, as supernaturally ordered by charity to a supernatural end.
		in regard to the efficient cause (Ia, q. 105, a. 8)	The miraculous substantially (the glorification of the body or prophecy). The miraculous subjectively (nonglorified resurrection, the knowledge of the secrets of hearts). The miraculous modally (sudden cure of a fever, the gift of tongues).

This is found in John of St. Thomas, the Salmanticenses, and Suarez. Cf. *De revelatione,* I, 205, for the explanation of this division and its reduction to the division of the four causes. The miraculous substantially is not to be confused with the supernatural substantially.[2]

[2] The supernatural substantially (such as sanctifying grace) is said to be formally so (*formaliter quoad substantiam*), for it is essentially supernatural. The substantially miraculous (such as the glorious resurrection) is said to be supernatural effectively

ERRORS CONCERNING GRACE

In the introduction a brief reference must be made to the history of this doctrine of grace in relation to the mutually opposing errors on the subject: that is, Pelagianism and Semi-Pelagianism on the one hand, Baianism and Jansenism on the other. For at the appearance of these contrary errors, the Church solemnly defined its doctrine on grace. It is therefore advisable to determine at the start at least the principal opposing theses which have been condemned; thus will be brought to light the problems still disputed among Catholic theologians. It will be easier in explaining the articles later to show how St. Thomas' arguments prevail over such and such a heresy.

Since St. Thomas preceded Baius, he could not have before his eyes, as we have, several definitions of the Church which clearly determined how the excess contrary to Pelagianism was to be avoided; yet St. Thomas was acquainted with predestinationism from the Council of Lyons (475) and its subsequent condemnation at the Council of Quierzy against Gottschalk, who prepared the way for Lutheranism and thereby for Baianism and Jansenism.

Generally, it is true, when great problems must be solved, there arise almost from the beginning mutually opposing theses, and only by degrees, under the inspiration of God, does the mind attain to the summit of truth whereon diverse aspects of reality are reconciled. St. Thomas reached this summit and escaped the excess of future Jansenism no less than the defect of Pelagianism.

As we observed in *De revelatione* (I, 398), the two extremes that are to be avoided may be termed naturalism and pseudo-supernaturalism.

Naturalism denies that the Christian life is beyond natural powers; in other words, it declares that what is in reality achieved by it can be achieved without interior grace. Indeed it maintains that the human intellect in its natural development is capable of attaining to the possession of every truth and good, even to the intuition of God. (Denz., no. 1808.)

Pseudo-supernaturalism denies that the Christian life is above the requirements of nature; in other words, human reason is so weak that it necessarily stands in need of revelation, which accordingly is

---

(*effective quoad substantiam*) but not formally; that is, on the part of the agent, but not as to the exercise of the effect produced.

not properly supernatural, and its exaltation to a participation in the divine nature was due to it for the integrity of its original state.

In both errors there is a confusion of the two orders, but the first confusion sins by exaggerated optimism in regard to the powers of human nature, and the second by exaggerated pessimism in regard to the destitution of nature.

Pelagian naturalism differs, as a matter of fact, from modern rationalism so far as it does not reject the external revelation of the Gospel confirmed by miracles, holding it to be divine, as did the Semirationalists (Froschammer, Gunther, and Hermes), who nevertheless wished to prove every mystery. But in all these doctrines the tendency is the same, namely, to deny the necessity of grace.

Particularly it should be noted that naturalism proceeds historically from the pagans or Gentiles; many of their philosophers thought that moral powers came from man alone and not from God, and they besought God only for fortune or a happy outcome. Thus, in particular, Cicero and Seneca who agreed that "there is one good, which is the cause and foundation of a blessed life: to have faith in oneself" (Letter 31, 3). Such is the opinion of naturalists today, whether atheists or deists, who deny that providence extends to every individual thing, or theists, who admit providence in the natural order but not in the supernatural. Liberal Protestants adhere to this teaching in a greater or less degree.

On the other hand, Judaism inclined toward naturalism in another way, for Judaism, contrary to the evident testimony of Holy Scripture, made justice or justification dependent, not on the supernatural grace of God, but on the external observance of the law and the physical origin of the children of Abraham. Against this, cf. Council of Jerusalem, Acts of the Apostles, A.D. 50 (Acts, 15), and St. Paul (Rom. 2-4; Gal., 3-5).

Likewise the Origenists and Theodore of Mopsuestia did not recognize sufficiently the necessity of grace.

Pelagianism, the chief heresy of this kind, gathered together the preceding errors of like tendency into something of a system and spread it throughout the world in the fifth century. Historically speaking, there were three phases to the doctrine of the Pelagians.

1. It denied original sin, the necessity of baptism and interior grace for obtaining ordinary eternal life. It declared, however, that baptism and grace are necessary for entering the kingdom of God, which is

something excelling ordinary eternal life. Hence, to attain to eternal life as commonly accepted, no grace was necessary, not even the grace of faith or the knowledge of external revelation. But, said Pelagius, God gave us a power or faculty, i.e., free will; moreover, willing and doing are eminently proper to us. Grace would be only an unnecessary adornment, just as some souls have visions and ecstasies, without which, however, a man can be saved.

2. Later, to refute the objections drawn from Holy Scripture, Pelagius admitted the term "grace" and the necessity of grace, but by this name he designated free will, and subsequently the external grace of revelation or the preaching of the gospel.

3. Finally, Pelagius, not knowing how to reply to the objections of Catholics, admitted internal grace, but first in the intellect alone, that is, as enlightenment; secondly, he recognized some habitual grace, but not as plainly gratuitous (he maintained that it was given according to the merits of nature) nor strictly supernatural; thirdly, the Pelagians ultimately admitted as more probable actual grace in the will, not however plainly gratuitous (but granted according to natural merits) nor necessary for doing good, but only for working more easily and perfectly. Cf. Billuart (*De gratia,* diss. I), who cites many texts of St. Augustine on the subject.

Hence there are in Pelagianism two heresies in particular regarding internal grace.

1. If internal grace is given, it is not simply gratuitous, but is bestowed according to natural merit.

2. It is not necessary for merely acting as is needful for salvation, but for doing so with greater facility or for accomplishing some more excellent works.

Thus without the internal grace of faith we can arrive at the formal motive of Christian faith.

This is the teaching of Pelagius and of his principal disciples, Caelestius and Julian of Eclanum, against whom Augustine and Jerome wrote. Cf. Tixeront, *Hist. des dogmes.*

This heresy was condemned by twenty-four separate councils, notably by the first and second councils of Carthage, that of Milevum, and finally by the ecumenical Council of Ephesus, 431; cf. Denz., nos. 101 ff., 126, 129, 142, 174 ff., 138.

The Semi-Pelagians admitted not only external revelation but properly supernatural internal grace, although they erred in two respects, namely, in regard to initial grace and final grace.

They said: 1. The beginning of salvation depends on man's petitioning for it, so far as man, without grace, by desiring through a pious disposition to believe, by knocking, by asking, can prepare himself for grace, which is bestowed on account of this natural preparation. Hence initial grace was not simply gratuitous. Likewise they all maintained that the consent to the initial grace offered is entirely ours.[3]

2. The last grace, namely, of final perseverance, is not strictly gratuitous but may be obtained by our merits; nay rather, they said, "man perseveres to the end, so far as he abides in that consent to the grace offered him, bestowed at the moment of justification" (Billuart, *loc. cit.*).

From these two errors it followed that predestination, whether to grace or to glory, is not strictly gratuitous for, according to this teaching, the first grace is conferred on account of the merits of nature, broadly speaking, and the term of salvation depends upon the preceding merits which have been foreseen. (See the canons of the Council of Orange; Denz., nos. 176 ff.)

It would be well to have a thorough knowledge of the history of Semi-Pelagianism so as to understand correctly what was condemned in it and in what respect Molinism differs from it.

It is clear, as Billuart demonstrates (*ibid.*), that the Semi-Pelagians taught that predestination, whether to grace or to glory, was not gratuitous, but that God accompanied all men, the reprobate as well as the predestinate, with equal love, and offered grace and glory to all

---

[3] Not all the Semi-Pelagians understood in the same way that the initial step to salvation comes from us and not from God. Some who approached nearer to Pelagius placed the beginning of salvation in some acts performed, such as the act of believing, desiring, asking, seeking grace and salvation. Others, convinced by the arguments of Catholics, that every work conducive to salvation is from God, limited this initial movement to the consent to that grace which God offered each one that it might cooperate in a good act. On this beginning, whatever it might be, and on perseverance in it they based their argument for predestination. (Cf. Billuart, *op. cit.*) They maintained that this beginning of salvation, proceeding from us and not from God, merits the first grace, at the favorable moment, so to speak. This is evident from Faustus, who, as Gennadius relates in his life, used to say: "Whatever freedom of the will may acquire of honest reward for labor is not, properly speaking, merit." Likewise Cassian in his *Collationes,* chap. 14: "God is ready in the event of the offering of our will to bestow all these things upon it."

equally; hence, according to the Semi-Pelagians, of two men to whom grace is offered equally by God, he possesses grace who consents to it of himself, he receives no greater help, and he receives glory who, of himself, perseveres in the grace received.

Consequently the Semi-Pelagians declared in respect to foreknowledge: "God, from eternity, predestined to grace those who He foresaw would consent and utilize it well, and He predestined to glory those who He foresaw would similarly persevere in grace, of themselves." Thus the knowledge of God is not the cause of things, at least it is not the cause of our determination toward the good, which is first in the affair of salvation. Hence men rather save themselves than are saved by God; in other words, God would not bestow our consent to good, but would expect it of us. (Denz., no. 177; *Summa theol.*, Ia, q. 23, a. 5, 2nd error.)

Indeed the Semi-Pelagians hit upon mediate knowledge (*scientia media*) before Molina, as the Thomists in general clearly show, particularly, among the more recent, Father del Prado (*De gratia et lib. arb.*, III, 312). And this is also evident from the epistles of St. Prosper to St. Augustine and from the book on the *Predestination of the Saints,* (chaps. 14 and 17).

As a logical conclusion to their theory, the Semi-Pelagians necessarily arrived at mediate knowledge, at least in regard to the salvation of infants. They were therefore obliged to solve this objection: among infants, some, without any merit on their part, are predestined to baptism and eternal life. But not being willing to admit gratuitous predestination even in this case, the Semi-Pelagians replied: God knows even the conditional future, and predestined to baptism those infants who He foresaw would have consented to grace and persevered if they had reached the age of adults.[4]

Similarly, they maintained, in regard to infidels: God foresaw what they would have done, of themselves, if the preaching of the gospel had been proposed to them.[5] Moreover, this foreknowledge of conditional future events or of events possible in the future, independent of divine decree, is the foreknowledge which is now called *scientia media.* But Molina admitted, above and beyond this, prevenient grace.

[4] And, on the other hand, infants who die without baptism would be punished for sins which they would have committed if they had lived for a long time. Thus they would be punished for sins that were not real but only conditional, which is unjust.

[5] Cf. *Summa theol.*, Ia, q.23, a.5, 3rd error.

From this theory they further deduced many corollaries, for instance: Christ died equally for all, and dispenses the price of His death equally to all, so that the vessels of mercy receive no more of benefit than the vessels of wrath, whatever St. Paul may say (Rom. 9:22). Otherwise, as they said, God would be an unjust respecter of persons if, without previous merit or disposition, He were to give grace to one and deny it to another. And, they added, this would lead to fatalism, would deprive reproof and prayer of their usefulness, and would lead to despair.

Moderate Semi-Pelagians, such as Cassian (13th Conference), although they admitted initial grace, whenever it was given gratuitously without any merits, allowed that it was more often bestowed on the basis of merit. Further, certain Semi-Pelagians openly declared that perhaps prevenient grace was truly gratuitous in respect to initial acts, and was indeed conferred by God, although He expects our consent. And, as Billuart remarks (*loc. cit.*): "This was the last stand of this heresy, so far as its concessions are concerned, namely: it depends upon us to accept or reject grace, so that in those who accept it their consent does not depend on the grace of God, but on themselves. In this sense they withdrew from grace the initial step toward salvation as well as perseverance, and attributed them to free will."

The advocates of Semi-Pelagianism were certain monks of Hadrumetam, as well as Cassian, Gennadius of Marseilles, and Faustus of Riez.

The Semi-Pelagianism of Cassian is found particularly in his thirteenth Conference entitled: "Of God's Protection," in which he teaches: "Grace and free will certainly concur in the matter of salvation to the extent that the initial good will and pious disposition to believe, that is, the first step toward salvation, is ordinarily from man alone, and not from God, although in exceptional cases the beginning of salvation and good will comes from God, as in the vocations of St. Matthew and St. Paul."

The adversaries of Semi-Pelagianism were the aged St. Augustine [6]

---

[6] *De civ. Dei*, Bk. XII, chap. 6: "If the efficient cause of bad is sought, none will be found. . . . If two individuals similarly constituted as to soul and body, both perceive the beauty of the same body; if, having seen it, one of the two is moved to illicit enjoyment, whereas the other perseveres firmly in a virtuous will, what shall we consider to be the cause of bad will present in one and not in the other? . . . If both are tempted by the same temptation and one yields and consents, while the other remains unmoved, what else is evident but that one willed and the other did not will to fail

and St. Prosper, St. Fulgentius, Hilary, and Caesarius of Arles.

This heresy was condemned by Pope Celestine (432), Pope Gelasius (494), who denounced the books of Faustus and Cassian, and finally by the Second Council of Orange (529), which had the special approbation of Boniface II.

In regard to the condemnation of Semi-Pelagianism, Denzinger records the entire Second Council of Orange (529), that is, twenty-four canons; see especially 3–12, 18–22, 25.

Molinism differs from Semi-Pelagianism in three respects: 1. in regard to prevenient grace; 2. in regard to the covenant entered into between God and Christ the Redeemer; 3. in regard to the circumstances of the life of the predestinate. Cf. Molina, *Concordia.*

1. Molina admits prevenient grace inclining to the initial movement to salvation, or consent to good, but he says: the distinction between the will consenting to this grace offered and the will rejecting it depends on man's liberty alone. Cf. Molina, *op. cit.,* pp. 230, 459.

The Thomists object that before this distinction, there is not yet any initial step toward salvation, because it is not found in those who resist first grace, as in Lessius, *De gratia efficaci,* chap. 18, no. 7.

2. Molina maintains that, if anyone does whatever he can by means of mere natural powers, God does not refuse grace; but he avoids Semi-Pelagianism by saying: God does not confer grace on account of this good natural disposition, but because of the covenant entered into between Himself and Christ the Redeemer. Cf. *infra,*

---

in chastity? . . . The same beauty was seen equally by the eyes of both; the same interior temptation solicited both equally; what, therefore caused that particular bad will in one of them? . . . Nothing presents itself. Can (human) nature be the cause of evil will in that it is human nature? No, for it is found in both individuals. But so far as it is drawn from nothingness, it is deficient in one and not in the other." (St. Thomas says: that which is defectible in itself can be reasonably expected to fail in some respect, with divine permission.) Chap. 7: "Let no one, therefore, seek the efficient cause of bad will, since it is not efficient, but deficient; for this is not an effect, but a defect. To fall away then, from what is greater to what is less is to begin to have an evil will." Chap. 9: "These angels, who were created with the good, and are yet bad, bad by their own will, either received less grace of divine love than those who persevered in it, or if they were both created equally good, when the former fell from evil will, the latter, receiving greater help, attained to that fullness of beatitude."

Whence the same Augustine says, commenting on St. John (tr. 26): "If you do not wish to fall into error, do not attempt to judge why God draws this one and does not draw that one." Likewise St. Thomas (Ia, q.23, a.5), when the Semi-Pelagians said: "God draws this person because He sees the initial step to salvation naturally in him and not in another."

q. 109, a. 6; q. 112, a. 3; Molina, *op. cit.,* pp. 43, 564; Index, "Faciens quod in se est."

3. Molina says (pp. 51, 565): help being equal, it is possible for one of those called to be converted and another not converted. With less assistance from grace it is possible for the one assisted to make progress, while another, with greater help, does not improve, and hardly perseveres. They are not aids established as efficacious in themselves which distinguish between the predestinate and the non-predestinate. However, according to Molina, the predestinate receives greater help than the reprobate from the standpoint of the situation in which he is placed by the divine good pleasure, for indeed he is placed in circumstances in which God foresees by mediate knowledge that he will consent to grace.

Hence, from the viewpoint of circumstances, the gift of final perseverance depends solely on the divine good pleasure; thus, to a certain extent at least, the gratuity of predestination, denied by the Semi-Pelagians, is preserved; but, as the Thomists declare, this is seen to be gratuity of predestination only in regard to the circumstances which are more or less appropriate or suitable.

THE PSEUDO-SUPERNATURALISM OF PREDESTINATIONISM, PROTESTANTISM, BAIANISM, AND JANSENISM

This pseudo-supernaturalism is the error opposed to naturalism; it sins by excess, that is, it affirms the necessity of grace even for all natural good works, so that all the works of infidels are sins. But in reality, as we have said, it further confuses the order of grace with the order of nature, as it holds that grace is not above the exigencies of our nature, which it considers entirely impotent even in its own order. Whence it can be seen that it extolls grace, while it proclaims its necessity beyond measure, but it actually destroys the supernatural-ness of grace and depreciates nature. It is pessimistic in regard to nature as Pelagianism is optimistic in its estimate of nature.

This pseudo-supernaturalism appears in predestinationism (cf. Denz., nos. 316 ff., 320 ff.). The doctrine is attributed to Lucidus, a priest of the fifth century, who retracted his error. But the heresy is found especially in the writings of Gottschalk, in the ninth century (cf. Denz., nos. 316 ff.; *Dict. théol, cath.,* "Predestination," section on the Middle Ages, ninth century).

According to predestinationism, grace and predestination are necessary for doing good; whence those who are not predestined to eternal life sin necessarily, just as the predestinate are necessarily saved. Thus no real liberty remains after original sin. According to predestinationism, there is not only predestination to eternal life, but also predestination to evil for the reprobate.

All these errors were condemned, in 853, at the Council of Quierzy at which the following was defined (Denz., no. 317): "There is no predestination to evil. . . . We have a free will for good, aided by prevenient grace. . . . We have a free will for evil, deprived of grace." Likewise Denz., no. 318: "Almighty God wills that all men without exception should be saved (I Tim., 2:4) although all are not saved. That some are saved is due to the gift of salvation; that some are lost is due to the lack of merit in the reprobate." Denz., no. 319: "There never was and never will be a man . . . for whom Christ did not suffer . . . ; that all are not redeemed by the mystery of His passion pertains to the working of infidelity . . . , unless they drink, they cannot be cured."

This error was revived by Luther and Calvin. Luther maintained that grace and integrity were due to nature in the state of innocence; whereas in the state of fallen nature, free will is so corrupted that it is a mere name without a reality, and therefore requires grace, to such an extent that whatever is done without faith and grace is sin. Whence it follows that all the works of infidels and sinners are sins. Sanctifying grace is, in fact, only an external imputation of the merits of Christ, and man is justified by faith alone without works; man is justified by a "fiduciary" faith by which he believes that his sins are forgiven.

Calvin agrees with Luther in this, and adds that God predestined some to hell, and the faithful who believe themselves predestined are saved by this very faith. Further, children born of predestinate parents are by that very fact children of God and can be saved without baptism.

Thus it is apparent how, in this pseudo-supernaturalism, nature is greatly depreciated and even grace is only apparently extolled, since it is due to nature and reduced to a mere extrinsic denomination or to an external imputation of the merits of Christ. The way was prepared for this teaching by Ockham and the Nominalists of whom Luther was a disciple at the University of Wittemberg, as Denifle shows in his *Luther und Luthertum,* 1904. For the Nominalists, habitual grace is not intrinsically supernatural, but only by extrinsic denomination, as a bank note is not gold.

Baianism is again a somewhat attenuated Protestantism. It teaches in particular three doctrines:

1. The grace accorded to Adam was due to nature, and hence did not exceed the requirements of nature.

2. Faith is therefore necessary even for natural good, so that all the virtues of infidels are vices.

3. Sanctifying grace is so necessary that all the works of sinners are sins. (Denz., nos. 1001 ff.) Baianists almost identify grace and natural probity.

Jansenism retained these same errors in substance, as is evident from the five propositions of Jansen. (Denz., no. 1092.) It suffices to note the first of these to make it clear how widely Thomism differs from Jansenism, whatever else may be sometimes asserted. This first Jansenist proposition is, in fact, thus expressed: "Some precepts of God to just men who are willing and striving, are, in the present state of their powers, impossible; grace is wanting to them, also, by which such precepts may become possible." Augustine declared the contrary, as cited by the Council of Trent: "God does not command the impossible, but by commanding He incites thee both to do what thou canst and to ask what thou canst not, and He assists thee that thou mayest be able" (Denz., no. 804).

Likewise, 101 propositions of Quesnel were condemned in the bull *Unigenitus* (1713) (Denz., nos. 1351, 1451); lastly the synod of Pistoia was condemned by Pius VI in the bull *Auctorem fidei*. (Denz., nos. 1516 ff.)

As can be seen, Baianists and Jansenists agree in some respects with Pelagianists, that is, in denying the gratuity and therefore the true supernaturalness of the state of innocence. Jansen also said that in the state of innocence efficacious grace in itself was not necessary. (He was a Molinist in this regard.) In line with the same tendency, the immanentism of the Modernists, for example, Laberthonnière, asserts that grace is demanded by nature, and thus they destroy its supernaturalness (cf. Denz., no. 2103, and Hugon, *De gratia,* p. 212).

Finally, it should be remarked that, just as Molinism withdraws from Semi-Pelagianism, so Thomism recedes from Calvinism and Jansenism, as the Sovereign Pontiffs, Clement XI, Benedict XIII, and Paul V have declared. (Denz., p. 342 note.) Benedict XIII forbade anyone to condemn the doctrine of St. Thomas and his school or to traduce it as condemned by the bull *Unigenitus*. Subsequently Clement XII forbade "the branding of this doctrine by any note or theological censure by the schools holding diverse opinions . . . until the Holy See should pass judgment by some definition or pronouncement in regard to such controversies." Cf. Denz., no. 1097 note.

Thomism differs particularly from predestinationism and Jansenism in the following respects.

1. It denies predestination to evil and the opinion that God is the author of sin.

2. It teaches that predestination to glory does not destroy, through intrinsically efficacious grace, the freedom necessary for meriting, but rather brings it into play.

3. It admits that God wills the salvation of all men and gives to all adults truly sufficient graces; but if a man resists them, he deserves to be deprived of the efficacious graces which he would otherwise receive. Hence God does not ask the impossible and wills the salvation of all men, but He does not will the salvation of all equally, contrary to what the Semi-Pelagians maintain.

And herein lies a great mystery, namely, that God often but not always gives to sinners the efficacious grace of conversion; indeed, He always bestows it upon the predestinate to whom He has determined to grant the gift of final perseverance; often He even confers the grace of conversion upon others, but later denies them, for reasons of justice, on account of repeated sins, the grace of perseverance, which, absolutely speaking, He could grant them for reasons of mercy. Whence it becomes evident that in this treatise the following two principles are reconciled.

1. God does not ask the impossible, and sincerely wills the salvation of all, contrary to predestinationism, Protestantism, Baianism, and Jansenism.

2. "Without Me ye can do nothing" in the order of salvation. "What hast thou that thou hast not received?" (I Cor. 4:7); or, as St. Thomas says (Ia, q. 20, a. 3), "Since the love of God is the cause of the goodness of things, nothing is in any respect better if God does not will greater good to one than to another."

These two principles are most certain, but their intimate reconciliation remains hidden, for it is the intimate reconciliation of infinite mercy, infinite justice, and supreme liberty in the sublime depth of the Deity. I have presented this matter in the volume entitled, *La prédestination des saints et la grâce,* pp. 49–51, 132 ff.

The relative position of the various doctrines can thus be indicated.

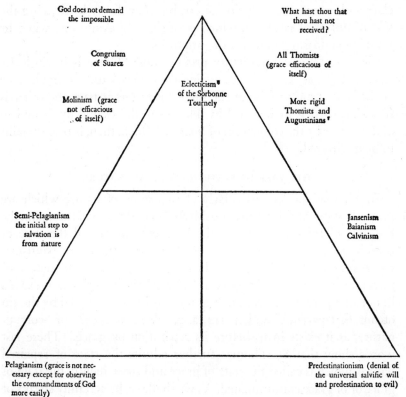

God does not demand the impossible

What hast thou that thou hast not received?

Congruism of Suarez

All Thomists (grace efficacious of itself)

Eclecticism⁸ of the Sorbonne Tournely

Molinism (grace not efficacious of itself)

More rigid Thomists and Augustinians⁷

Semi-Pelagianism the initial step to salvation is from nature

Jansenism Baianism Calvinism

Pelagianism (grace is not necessary except for observing the commandments of God more easily)

Predestinationism (denial of the universal salvific will and predestination to evil)

Finally, it must be observed that two contradictory propositions cannot be true at the same time or false at the same time; one is true, the other false. On the other hand, Pelagianism and predestinationism are doctrines simultaneously false; they are not contradictory in this, but in other respects. For instance, Pelagianism and Semi-Pelagianism erroneously maintain that "God wills equally the salvation of all men,

---

⁷ The more rigid Thomists and Augustinians seem to minimize the will for universal salvation by saying that negative reprobation, which precedes the prevision of demerits, consists not only in permitting sins that will not be absolved, but in positive exclusion from glory as a benefit which is not due. This is justifiably rejected by Billuart and many Thomists.

⁸ The eclecticism of the Sorbonne maintains that grace is efficacious of itself for difficult acts conducive to salvation (such as contrition), but that grace is not efficacious of itself for easy acts conducive to salvation (such as attrition).

namely, the elect and the reprobate." The contradictory proposition: "God does not will equally the salvation of all men," is true. This indeed is what the predestinationists, Calvinists, and Jansenists declare and in so doing they do not err, but they do err by denying the will of universal salvation, which is affirmed by Augustine when he says: "God does not demand the impossible."

Likewise these contradictory propositions: "Grace is intrinsically efficacious," and "Grace is not intrinsically efficacious," cannot be true at the same time or false at the same time; one is true, the other is false. The first is maintained by Thomism, the second by Molinism and likewise by the congruism of Suarez. Which, then, is true remains to be discovered.

THE VARIOUS STATES OF HUMAN NATURE

St. Thomas speaks particularly of two states of nature which are properly states of this nature considered formally as a nature, namely, the state of original nature in the innocent Adam and the state of corrupt nature after the sin of our first parents, before baptismal regeneration. Cf. Ia, q. 94, a. 2; Ia IIae, q. 109, a. 2.: "The nature of man may be considered in two ways, either in its integrity, as it existed in our first parents before sin, or as it exists in us, corrupted by the sin of our first parents," and q. 114, a. 2, where he speaks of "corrupt nature, as it exists in us before its reparation by grace." These last words show that St. Thomas further admits the state of repaired nature, which is called the state of grace and subsequently the state of glory or of grace consummated. As we shall see, he certainly speaks of the possibility of another state merely natural or of pure nature, and in the state of innocence he distinguishes the integrity of nature itself from the grace which elevated it. Cf. IIIa, q. 53, a. 2.

Theologians now, more or less generally, distinguish five states of nature.

State, as a general term, is the condition proper to man with a certain stability and permanence. (Cf. IIa IIae, q. 184, a. 1.) That which human nature possesses of itself as ordained to its final end is here taken as a stable condition and mode. Five such states are differentiated: 1. the state of pure nature, 2. the state of incorrupt nature, 3. the state of original justice, 4. the state of fallen nature, 5. the state of restored nature. We might add the state of glory and the state of damnation, but we are not concerned with these, since we are now directing our attention to nature only so far as, with divine help, it tends toward its final end.

The state of pure nature or the merely natural state. St. Thomas speaks of it, *II Sent.,* d. 31, q. 1, a. 2 ad 3. "In the beginning when God created man, He could also have formed another man from the slime of the earth and have left him in the condition of his nature, that is, mortal and passible, and experiencing the struggle between concupiscence and reason; nothing of human nature would have been removed thereby, for this condition follows from the principles of nature. Nor would this defect in it be a reason for blame or punishment, since the defect would not be caused by its own will."

Again, St. Thomas alludes to this state of pure nature as being possible: "Humankind in general suffers diverse pains, corporal and spiritual . . . (death, hunger, thirst . . . weakness of intellect . . . from which there results an inability to overcome animal appetites entirely). Nevertheless, one may say of such defects, corporal as well as spiritual, that they are not punitive, but rather natural defects consequent upon the requirements of matter. For instance, the human body, since it is composed of unlike substances, must of necessity be corruptible . . . , and the intellect . . . on account of the ease with which it may deviate from the truth through phantasms" (*Contra Gentes,* Bk. IV, chap. 52). St. Thomas adds, however, that, considering the sweet providence of God, it was fitting that man at his creation should be delivered from these defects by supernatural gifts.

How is the state of pure nature to be defined? The state of pure nature means precisely nature with its intrinsic constituent principles and such as follow from them or are due to them; in other words, it implies all those notes which are included in the definition of man, a rational animal, and further the properties of man and the natural aids due to human nature that it may attain its final natural end. Aristotle thought that men are actually in this merely natural state.

Hence in this state man would have a body and a rational soul, lower and higher faculties of the soul, would know the natural law, and would accept the helps of a natural order for arriving at his final natural end, which consists in the abstract knowledge of God and in the natural love of God above all things. However, since what is naturally deficient sometimes fails, in this state also God would permit sin against the natural law in one individual more than in another who received more assistance, and therefore, in this state, there

would be given sufficient helps of the natural order to all, but efficacious helps to certain ones. These efficacious natural helps would be
due, not to this individual in particular, in whom God could permit
sin, but due to human nature as a whole; for God would be creating
human nature incompetent for its final end if no individual of the
species attained its end.

This state of pure nature may thus be considered in accordance
with the four causes: 1. formal cause: the rational soul with its faculties; 2. material cause: the body; 3. efficient cause: God, the author
of nature, from whom proceed the natural law and the helps of the
natural order, whether sufficient or efficacious; 4. final cause: God, the
author of nature, known abstractly and loved above all things. This
is the order that philosophy speaks of when it abstracts from both
original sin and grace.

First corollary. Neither habitual grace nor the infused virtues and
gifts nor actual grace of the supernatural order belong to this state of
pure nature.

Second corollary. Moreover, man, like any other animal, would
be subject to pain, death, and so also to ignorance and concupiscence.
Thus four unhappy natural consequences would follow. He would
be subject to pain and death; for, as his body is composed of elements
capable of suffering from exterior causes and often at war with one
another, old age and death normally come upon man as upon other
animals. Likewise man would be subject to ignorance because our
intellectual knowledge, having its source in the senses, is very apt
to deviate from the truth on account of its disordered phantasms, for
example, by interpreting in an excessively material sense things which
are spiritual and which are known only as through a glass in the
natural manner of the senses. (Cf. *ibid.*) Similarly he would be subject to concupiscence, for the sensitive appetite naturally obeys right
reason only as a subject, not as a slave; indeed, it can be carried toward
its own proper object, that is, toward a delectable good or toward a
sensible good difficult of attainment, according to the suggestion of the
senses and imagination without any rational direction. (Cf. Ia IIae,
q. 17, a. 7.)

Hence the subject may be divided thus:

God, author of nature, { soul, faculties, natural final end;
directing and aiding   { body.

Four unhappy natural   { ignorance   { did not exist in Christ
consequences   { concupiscence {   or B. V. M.
                        {   { present in Christ and
                        {   {   in B. V. M. as a con-
                        {   {   sequence of nature,
                        { pain   {   not as a consequence
                        { death   {   of original sin, and
                        {   {   Christ willed to en-
                        {   {   dure them as means
                        {   {   of redemption.

All theologians agree that this state of pure nature never existed. Baius and the Jansenists denied its possibility; we shall see later the refutation of this error.

The state of incorrupt nature consists in the perfect subjection of the body to the soul and of the sense appetites to the reason; therefore it implies exemption from the four unfortunate natural consequences, that is, from ignorance, concupiscence, pain, and death. If only the sense appetites are subject to reason without the subjection of the body to the soul, the perfection of nature is only partial, not total, since the defects of old age and death will appear.

In this integrity of nature Adam was created, according to revelation, which declares that "through sin death entered the world" (Rom. 5:12); and before sin, Adam and Eve, although naked, experienced no shame; but only after sin, as we read in Gen. 2:25, since before sin no inordinate passion of which they might be ashamed, could arise.

This gift of integrity, according to St. Thomas (Ia, q. 97, a. 1 c. and 3 ad 2; Ia IIae, q. 91, a. 1), resided in a certain force of a natural order, just as we find even now that certain people possess greater health and sturdiness. In the beginning God made man perfect, for the works of God Himself are perfect, and as every agent produces something like himself, a most perfect agent produces a perfect work; for example, when God wills to establish a new religious order, He sends to the Church a holy founder, in whom all the perfections of this new order are at least virtually present. Hence, with all the more reason, when He created the first man He created him perfect, with full natural perfection; in other words, He created him in the adult state, with those virtues capable of being acquired although sometimes accidentally infused. Thus is explained this force in which the gift of natural integrity consisted.

This gift of integrity in Adam sprang *de facto* from sanctifying grace, by which the higher reason was subjected to God. From this primary harmony there followed, as St. Augustine and St. Thomas maintain, two others, namely, between right reason and the sensitive appetite and between body and soul. Moreover, natural integrity belonged to the natural order (like the acquired virtues) and thus was differentiated from grace which elevated to the supernatural order. The gift of integrity did not constitute man an adopted son of God, a participant in the divine nature, an heir to the kingdom of heaven; all of these were bestowed by sanctifying grace. Hence nothing prevented God from being able to create man in the state of incorrupt nature without original grace; for, although these two states were combined in Adam, the Fathers and theologians often speak of them as if they were one.

The state of original justice or of innocence is described by St. Thomas (Ia, q. 95, a. 1). It consists: 1. in the perfect subjection of the reason to God by grace and charity; 2 in the perfect subjection of the sense appetites to reason; 3. in the perfect subjection of the body to the soul.

As long as the soul adhered to God by grace, the rest were perfectly subject to it; however, it was capable of failing in this perfect subjection to God through sin, for the will was not yet confirmed in goodness.

Some say, Father Kors among them, that, according to St. Thomas, sanctifying grace in Adam was not an endowment of nature but only a personal gift, as it is in us; and accordingly grace would be the external root of original justice, which would be nothing else but integrity of nature.[9]

Generally, in fact, Thomists hold that, according to St. Thomas, sanctifying grace was in Adam an endowment of nature: first, because it was to be transmitted with nature by way of generation; for if Adam had not sinned, his children would have been born with grace, receiving at the same time the spiritual soul and grace, at the time the

---

[9] We examined this opinion in our treatise *De Deo trino et creatore*, 1944, pp. 430–38.

body is ultimately disposed to receive the soul (Ia, q. 100, a. 1 ad 2). Thus sanctifying grace is the intrinsic root of original justice, as the root is an intrinsic part of a tree.[10] Secondly, because original sin is, as declared by the councils (Denz., no. 175, Council of Orange), the death of the soul. But the death of the soul is the privation not only of the integrity of nature, but of sanctifying grace or spiritual life. Thirdly, thus is explained the remission of original sin by baptism, although this sacrament does not restore the integrity of nature.

Accordingly, to this state of original justice the following pertain: 1. sanctifying grace, the infused virtues whether theological or moral, the gifts of the Holy Ghost, actual graces; 2. exemption from the four lamentable consequences to nature, namely, ignorance, concupiscence, pain, and death. The first two consequences are also called wounds; two other wounds are malice and weakness. These are the six punishments of this life (Ia IIae, q. 85, a. 3).

Corollary. If original justice is understood adequately, it includes several habits, such as habitual grace, infused virtues, and preternatural privileges, namely, exemption from ignorance, concupiscence, pain, and death. In fact the root of all these perfections was habitual grace, or the union of the soul with God, the author of grace.

Problem. Whether the sanctifying grace of the state of innocence was of the same kind as the sanctifying grace which is granted to us now unto justification. We answer in the affirmative that it was the same kind as to substance, since its formal effect was the same, to make man pleasing to God, an adopted son, a friend, and an heir to the kingdom of heaven. However, in regard to the manner of its being communicated to the subject, there is a twofold difference between the two.

1. On the part of the principle: the grace of the state of innocence as an endowment of nature proceeded from God as Creator establishing nature in its natural as well as in its supernatural being. On the contrary, habitual grace now proceeds from God as Redeemer, not as establishing nature but as restoring persons to health.

2. On the part of the subject, the grace of the original state regarded nature directly as an endowment of nature, and persons by reason of

---

[10] At the Council of Trent it was declared (Denz., no. 789) that Adam "lost for himself and for us the sanctity and justice received from God"; therefore he received it for himself and for us as an endowment granted to nature, not merely as a personal gift.

their nature, in other words it was communicated at the same time with nature, and fully, entirely communicated itself to nature in respect to all its operations (Ia, q. 100, a. 1; Ia IIae, q. 81, a. 1 and 2).

On the contrary, habitual grace now regards, primarily and directly, the person to be restored by means of humility and penance; it does not look primarily and directly to nature, and accordingly it is no longer communicated with nature. Thus the son of Christian, even saintly, parents is now born in original sin, and the punishments of this life remain after baptism, as opportunities for struggle and merit (IIIa, q. 69, a. 3 and 49, a. 5 ad 1).

The state of fallen nature is described at length in the treatise on original sin. It is the state of nature despoiled of sanctifying grace, of the virtues attached to it, and of the gift of integrity, in other words, subject to pain and death as well as the four wounds of ignorance in the intellect, malice in the will, concupiscence in the concupiscible appetite, and weakness in the irascible (cf. Ia IIae, q. 85, a. 3, 5, 6, on the four wounds and also pain and death).

Thomists generally hold that man in the state of fallen nature not yet restored has less strength for moral good than he would have had in the state of pure nature. The principal reason is that in the state of fallen nature, man is born with his will directly opposed to his final supernatural end and indirectly opposed to his final natural end, because every sin against his supernatural end is indirectly against the natural law, according to which we ought always to obey God, whatever He commands us. On the contrary, in the state of pure nature, man would be born with his will directed neither toward nor away from his final natural end, but with a capacity for directing himself either toward or away from this end.

The state of restored nature. It belongs properly to the treatise on grace to deal with this state, and the whole of question 109 is a discussion of it, as well as of the state of fallen nature considered as its contrary.

At the outset, however, certain general observations should be made to avoid repetition. This expression, "the state of restored nature," is not actually found in St. Thomas, who rather speaks of the state of grace after justification or of the healing grace, but not expressly of the state of restored nature. Perhaps the reason is that after sin, habitual grace regards primarily and directly the person to be cured and nature by reason of the person. Moreover, nature is not fully or perfectly restored; there remain the four wounds, which are only in process of being healed in the baptized; besides, pain and death remain. Therefore the state of restored nature will not be perfect except in heaven. Cf. IIIa, q. 49, a. 5 ad 1, and 69, a. 3.

However, this expression may be accepted in treating of these different states of nature, as grace is the seed of glory and as grace is now considered as healing the person and, by reason of the person, the nature.[11]

This state is expressed by various names in Holy Scripture; it is termed redemption, liberation, (spiritual) resuscitation, regeneration, vivification, reconciliation, renovation. Thus in I Tim. 2; Ephes. 2; II Cor. 5.

This state resembles the state of innocence inasmuch as sanctifying grace is present in both, identical as to substance and similarly ordered to the supernatural beatitude of heaven.

But there are several differences.

1. From the standpoint of their end: the remote end of the grace of the state of innocence was the manifestation of the divine liberality, whereas the end of the state of restored nature is the manifestation of mercy and now, certainly, the gift is greater, namely, the only-begotten Son of God: God so loved the world as to give His only-begotten Son. To be sure, God does not permit evil to be done except that He may bring good even out of evil, as St. Augustine says (*Enchir.*, chap. 11), that is, except on account of a greater good. The Church sings: "O happy fault which merited to have such and so great a reparation!" And St. Paul also said (Rom. 5:20): "Where sin abounded, grace did more abound." Hence, according to several Thomists (for example, the Salmanticenses): God permitted the sin of Adam and original sin for the sake of the redemptive Incarnation, as for a greater good; cf. IIIa, q. 1, a. 3 ad 3. Likewise He permitted the threefold denial of Peter for the sake of the greater humility of the Apostle. Thus in the life of the predestinate the divine permission of sin is indirectly the working out of predestination, namely, that the elect may attain to greater humility.

[11] In this sense, St. Thomas says (IIIa. q. 49, a. 5): "Christ by His passion opened to us the gate of Heaven"; the souls of the just under the Old Testament could not have the beatific vision before the Passion, because, although they had a certain grace "in respect to the purifying of their own persons," there still remained "an impediment which was an arraignment of all humanity, and which indeed is removed at the price of the blood of Christ."

Hence Billuart (*De gratia*) rightly says that in the state of restored nature the charity of God toward us is greater, for it is a greater charity to do good to enemies and especially the gift itself is greater, namely, the only-begotten Son of God. The new Adam is infinitely above the first Adam, and the Blessed Virgin Mary far surpasses Eve in excellence; the worship of the Eucharist is higher than the worship in the Garden of Eden.

Moreover, the proximate end of the grace of the state of innocence was the imprinting of the image of God the Creater upon man; now it is, above and beyond this, the imprinting of the image of the redeeming Christ as well, according to the words in Rom. 8:29: "whom . . . He predestinated to be made conformable to the image of His Son"; and all things in the present state of restored nature are referred to the glory of Christ.

2. The second difference lies in the efficient cause, according as the order of action should correspond to the order of ends. God is the efficient cause of the state of innocence immediately, but of the state of restored nature through Christ, since Christ merited this restoration for us and is its efficient instrumental cause, as an instrument indissolubly united to the divinity.

3. The third difference is on the part of the subject. The subject in the state of innocence was nature possessing no right to the gratuitous gifts of this state, but with nothing, on the other hand, that would resist them. The subject of the state of restored nature is nature which must be cured of sin or, preferably, already cured and adorned with virtue.

Problem. Whether in the state of restored nature man has less powers for doing good conducive to salvation than he had in the state of innocence.

It is not easy to reply because innocent nature, healthy and vigorous, was in itself more capable of doing good and persevering in it than nature restored but still weak and harassed by many temptations; therefore the sin of Adam was all the more grave inasmuch as it could more easily have been avoided. But on the other hand, "Where sin abounded, grace did more abound," "and with Him plentiful redemption." Besides, the Redeemer, head of the Church, substantially present in the Eucharist, is infinitely higher than Adam, head of elevated nature in the state of innocence. Eucharistic Communion which offers sustaining grace is infinitely above the tree of life, the proper effect of which was to preserve the vegetative faculty against the infirmity of old age.

Hence, unless I am mistaken, the question must be solved by making a distinction, thus: in the state of restored nature, still weak and vexed by many temptations, man has less strength on the part of nature than in the state of innocence.[12] But on the part of Christ the Redeemer, present in the Eucharist, good Christians who generously strive after intimacy with Christ and attain it seem, in spite of temptations, to receive greater graces, at least in the unitive life, than they would have had in the state of innocence, on account of their greater union with God through Christ the Redeemer. Nature, indeed, even in the unitive way is not yet fully restored; there remain pain, old age, death, a certain disorder in the feelings. But the life of the saints, after achieving the victory, is higher, most assuredly in the Blessed Virgin Mary and very probably, if not certainly, in St. Joseph, the apostles, and the great saints. As a matter of fact, in every fervent Eucharistic Communion it seems that the union with God through Christ is greater than it was in the earthly paradise. And in the Sacrifice of the Mass the consecration is infinitely above the worship rendered in the state of innocence.

Objection. St. Thomas says (Ia, q. 95, a. 4): "The works of man would be more efficacious for meriting in the state of innocence than after sin, if the amount of merit is estimated from the standpoint of grace; for this latter would then have been more plentiful, finding no obstacle in human nature. Likewise, also, if the absolute quantity of his work be considered, for if man were possessed of greater powers, he would do greater works. But if the amount is considered proportionately, the reckoning of merit after sin is found to be greater, on account of the weakness of man, for a work of less magnitude done under difficulty greatly exceeds a work of greater magnitude performed without any difficulty."

---

[12] Thus Billuart declares: "In the state of innocence grace, conferred as an endowment of nature, encountered nothing contrary to itself in integral nature, and accordingly communicated itself fully to nature, with regard to all its effects, primary as well as secondary." Now, grace regards directly (*per se*) and primarily the justified person, who previously was unworthy and finds in nature four wounds which are only in process of being healed: ignorance, malice, weakness, concupiscence, and, in addition, pain and death. Hence grace does not now communicate itself fully to nature. But the justified person ought to fight manfully and continually to implore the help of Christ.

Reply. In this text St. Thomas seems to compare the merits of man in general in these two states. He is not really comparing the merits of Adam with the merits of any great saint of the New Testament; for, most certainly, the merits of the Blessed Virgin Mary are much higher than the merits of Adam. Moreover, when he says, "grace would be more plentiful, finding no obstacle in human nature," he is speaking of grace in relation to incorrupt nature in general, not in relation to such and such a person.

Hence this article (Ia, q. 95, a. 4) is indeed true of men as a whole, and on the part of nature, but he does not compare Adam with the saints of the New Testament who, after the victory over all temptations, seem, by the power of Christ the Mediator, through the Sacrifice of the Mass and Communion, to attain a greater union with God. Cf. on this subject St. Thomas' Commentary on the words of St. Paul: "And where sin abounded, grace did more abound" (Rom. 5:20); "grace, which hath superabounded in us in all wisdom" (Ephes. 1:8); "Now the grace of our Lord hath abounded exceedingly with faith" (I Tim. 1:14); "I exceedingly abound with joy in all our tribulation" (II Cor. 7:4). These words could never be said of Adam.

Commenting on the Epistle to the Romans (5:20), St. Thomas says: "Sin abounded, that is, in the human race, and especially in the Jews (more enlightened and more ungrateful), but grace superabounded, that is, in Christ remitting sin. Hence it is said (II Cor. 9:8): 'God is able to make all grace abound in you.'" But two reasons may be assigned to what is said here. "One from the operation of grace, . . . for it required abundant grace to cure an abundance of sins; 'many sins are forgiven her, because she hath loved much' (Luke 7:47)." The other reason is derived from the disposition of the sinner, for whenever through divine assistance he is rendered more humble by the consideration of his sins, he attains to greater grace, according to these words of Ps. 15:4: "Their infirmities were multiplied: afterward they made haste." Thus St. Peter after his conversion; thus, among mankind, the saints after the redemption of the human race by Christ. Besides, with God there is plentiful redemption, as has already been said regarding the Psalm *De profundis* and, in truth, redemption through Christ was superabundant. Cf. also IIIa, q. 1, a. 3 ad 3: "Nothing prevents human nature from being advanced to something greater after sin, for God permits evil to be done that He may draw something better therefrom. Hence it is said in Romans (5:20):

'Where sin abounded, grace did more abound,' and in the blessing
of the paschal candle we find the words: 'O happy fault, which deserved to have such and so great a Redeemer!' "

In the article on whether God would have become incarnate had
man not sinned, St. Thomas uses the above words ("O happy fault,"
etc.) to refute the following objection: "Human nature did not,
through sin, become more receptive of grace; therefore even if man
had not sinned God would have become incarnate." Because of this
reply of St. Thomas, I cannot doubt the proposition held by many
Thomists, though not by all of them, namely, that according to St.
Thomas and according to the true state of things, God permitted original sin that He might draw something better therefrom, the redemptive Incarnation. Thus there is mutual causality: merits dispose
for the reception of glory, in the way of a disposing cause, but glory
is the cause of merits, as a final cause (Ia, q. 23, a. 5).

Another difficult problem in regard to the various states is this:
What is the order of these states according to the decrees of divine
providence? There is not complete agreement even among Thomists
on this problem (cf. Billuart, De incarnatione, d. II, a. 3), just as
some (the Salmanticenses, Godoy, Gonet) admit that original sin
was permitted by God for the sake of a greater good, that is, the
redemptive Incarnation, whereas others do not (Biluart, John of St.
Thomas).[13]

For the solution of this question particular stress must be laid on
the text of St. Thomas already quoted (IIIa, q. 1, a. 3 ad 3): "Nothing prevents human nature from being advanced to something greater
after sin, for God permits evil to be done that He may draw something
better therefrom. Hence it is said in Romans (5:20): 'Where sin
abounded, grace did more abound,' and in the blessing of the paschal

[13] John of St. Thomas, Cajetan, and Billuart refuse to reply to this question: Why
did God permit the sin of Adam, for what greater good? And they thus multiply the
divine decrees, asserting that: 1. God willed the order of nature with the intention of
manifesting His goodness; 2. He ordered intellectual creatures to a supernatural end:
3. foreseeing the sin of Adam and original sin, He decreed the restoration of the human
race by Christ the Redeemer; 4. in Christ He chose some more especially and efficaciously and left others. Thus these various decrees would be virtually distinct, and
this question would remain unsolved: For what greater good did God permit the sin
of Adam and original sin, so as to make this permission holy? The reply would be
exceedingly general: God permitted this in order to manifest His mercy and His
justice. But it must be admitted that this supreme manifestation of mercy and justice
was made through the redemptive Incarnation.

candle we find the words: 'O happy fault, which deserved to have such and so great a Redeemer.' " Likewise IIIa, q. 46, a. 1 ad 3.

We consider the solution advanced by the Salmanticenses (*Cursus theol.,* "De motivo incarnationis") as well as by Goday and Gonet, to be true. They maintain the following views.

1. God, through the knowledge of simple intelligence, knows all things possible, among which is this possible world in which the order of nature, the order of grace with the permission of original sin, and the order of hypostatic union, or the redemptive Incarnation, are subordinate the one to the other.

2. God intends to manifest His goodness outside Himself.

3. God judges the aforesaid possible world to be a very suitable medium for manifesting the divine goodness.

4. God chooses this disposition of things (this is the determination of His will).

5. God commands the execution of these means to be set in action in time (this is, formally, providence).

6. For the operation of the aforesaid disposition of things God moves the universe by directing it. Thus by a single decree God simultaneously willed this possible world with all its parts; in the same way, a builder does not first design the foundation of the house and afterward the roof, but first he designs a suitable dwelling place and, with this in view, the whole house and all its parts in harmony. This interpretation seems profound because of its superior simplicity according as it answers the question: Why did God permit the sin of Adam? Hence it is more and more accepted by modern Thomists.

THE POSSIBILITY OF THE STATE OF PURE NATURE

To complete these preliminary observations in regard to the five states of nature, something must be said against Baius and the Jansenists and also against certain Modernists about the state of pure nature. Certainly this state never existed; and Augustine, writing against Pelagius, shows that Adam in the state of innocence received more than natural gifts. But Jansen maintained that the state of pure nature is impossible. This thesis is well explained by Billuart, who should be read; here it suffices to present his principal arguments.

Augustine says (*Retract.,* Bk. I, chap. 9.): "Ignorance and difficulty belong to the wretchedness of just damnation . . . although, even if they were the natural beginnings of man, God is not to be blamed on this account, but rather praised." Likewise (*De dono persever-antiae,* chap. 11) : "Even if it were true that ignorance and difficulty, without which no man is born, were not the original penalties of nature, still the Manichaeans would be refuted." That is, not on this account is the Author of nature to be blamed.

St. Thomas is in agreement with this (*II Sent.,* d. 31, q. 1, a. 2 ad 3; text cited above on the definition of pure nature. Cf. p. 21).

Proof from reason. The state of pure nature is not contradictory either from the part of man or from the part of God; hence it is simply possible. On the part of man, neither sanctifying grace nor the gifts of integrity and immortality are due to human nature regarded in itself, but are merely gratuitous. Hence the state of pure nature without these gifts is not contradictory from the side or part of man.

The antecedent is evident from the very notion of grace; if it is due, it is no longer a grace; nor is the adoption of sonship due to us, for adoption is made by the free will of the one adopting; and neither to our nature nor to the angelic nature is due the elevation to a participation in the divine nature, as the Church declared against Baius (Denz., nos. 1021, 1026, 1055, 1078, 1079) and against Quesnel (Denz., nos. 1384 ff.). Thus Augustine (*De civitate Dei,* Bk. XII, chap. 9) says of the angels: "God created them, at the same time creating nature in them and bestowing grace upon them."

Nor is the gift of integrity and immortality due to our nature; for ignorance, concupiscence, passibility, and mortality proceed from the elements of human nature, as St. Thomas teaches (*Contra Gentes,* Bk. IV, chap. 52).

Thus man, created in a purely natural condition, would possess all those things that coincide with his nature, in both his physical and his moral being; in other words, he would have a body and rational soul with their properties and powers, spiritual as well as sensitive, that is, with free will and the potentiality of achieving his natural end. The proximate end of man in the state of pure nature would be an honorable good, and his final end God as the author of nature, known abstractly and loved above all things with a natural love. In this state all the sufficient aids of a natural order would be given to all, and to some certain efficacious helps which are indeed not due to any particular individual, but are necessary to human nature so that, in some individuals it may attain the end for which it was created by God.

Likewise this state of pure nature is not contradictory on God's part; for God could have denied gratuitous gifts to man without detriment to His justice, goodness, or wisdom, just as, without any injustice, He did not prevent the sin of Adam, which He most easily could have prevented. Hence even by His ordinary power God could have created man in the state of pure nature.

Against the possibility of the state of pure nature there is a particular objection which deserves to be considered: man cannot have even perfect natural happiness without a body, that is, without resurrection after death. But resurrection is a miracle and therefore would not be possible in the state of pure nature. Therefore this state is impossible. As a solution of this objection theologians propose three opinions.

1. In this state of pure nature there would not be the resurrection of bodies; and yet at the end of their way the just would be essentially happy, just as now, in the supernatural order, the souls of the saints are essentially happy before the resurrection of the body, which imparts only an accidental happiness. This first opinion is probable.

2. In this state of pure nature there would be a resurrection; and this is not unlikely, for the resurrection of the body is supernatural only as to mode (or modally), not as to substance (or substantially) as grace is. Therefore this state of pure nature in its term, for the just would have a certain perfection of integral nature. Moreover, God could perform a miracle in the state of pure nature to confirm the natural truths of religion. This second opinion is also probable.

3. In this state the just man would not die to be beatified; God would transfer him, body and soul, to the place of beatitude. This third opinion seems least probable; perhaps the second opinion is the more probable. In order to defend the possibility of a state of pure nature, it is not necessary to prove conclusively by what means man would attain to beatitude, just as, to demonstrate the immortality of the soul, it is not necessary to determine categorically the particular way by which the separated soul derives its knowledge. This will suffice, then, in regard to the possibility of the state of pure nature. The other objections of the Jansenists are of less consequence and may easily be found in the writings of Thomists.

THE VARIOUS DEGREES OF DIVINE MOTION

This is the last preliminary note to the understanding of our treatise. It is to be interpreted in the light of what has been said above (Ia, q.

105, a. 5 and 6; Ia IIae, q. 9, a. 6; q. 10, a. 4; q. 79, a. 1 and 2).[14]
As explained by Father del Prado, O.P. (*De gratia,* II, 240, 253–57),
according to the terminology of St. Thomas there are three degrees
of divine motion in the natural order and three corresponding degrees
in the supernatural; for in both the natural and the supernatural
order divine motion is either before our deliberation or after it or
above it.

Before our deliberation, as long as we naturally desire to be happy,
we are moved to desire happiness in general. For, since this desire is
the first act of our will, we are not moved to it by virtue of a previous
act of deliberation. There is something similar in the supernatural
order when we are moved to our final supernatural end, for we cannot be moved to it by virtue of a previous higher act by way of deliberation.

After deliberation, or at its end, we are moved toward some good
(on which we have deliberated) by virtue of a previous act; for by
intending the end we are moved to choose the means to the end
under divine cooperating concursus; this, indeed, whether in the natural order or in the supernatural by the exercise of the infused virtues.

Above deliberation we are moved toward some object which surpasses our powers. Thus, in the natural order, under special inspiration of God, the author of nature, great geniuses in the philosophic,
poetic, or strategic sphere, as well as great heroes are moved. There
is something similar and even more frequent in the supernatural
order, when a just man is moved by special inspiration of the gifts
of the Holy Ghost; this is properly above discursive deliberation and
the human mode of operation. St. Thomas often refers to the matter.[15] Whence the following synopsis may be drawn, reading from
below in an ascending order.

[14] Cf. Billuart, *De gratia,* diss. III, a.1.

[15] If these various degrees of divine motion are carefully studied according to St.
Thomas, it will be easy to reply to several difficulties recently proposed by Father
H. Bouillard, S.J., *Conversion et grâce chez S. Thomas d'Aquin,* 1944.

Divine motion by which the mind is moved in respect to its exercise

In the supernatural order

6) to acts of the gifts of the Holy Ghost.

Here the will does not move itself but freely consents to the motion, as a faithful pupil or obedient inferior (operating, but not really justifying grace, for the man is already justified).

5) to determining to use the infused virtues (cooperating grace, in a human manner). Here it moves itself by virtue of a previous act.

4) to direct itself toward its final supernatural end (operating and justifying grace). Here it does not move itself by virtue of a previous act, but freely consents.

Under these three motions, if they are efficacious, the will never sins, although it can refuse if it so wills, but it never does.

In the natural order

3) to the good and also to the best without deliberation; this is an inspiration of particularly good fortune; thus, in the order of philosophy, poetry, strategy, or even of morals, great geniuses, heroes. Here the will does not move itself, but freely consents to the motion of God (as obeying).

2) to determine itself to {a real good or an apparent good

> Here the will is moved, and moves itself freely by virtue of a previous act; it may be a sin.
>
> 1) to the good in general; I will to be happy (an entirely general aid): the will is moved but does not move itself by virtue of a previous act; however, it elicits the act vitally, but not indeed freely as to specification; in this act there can be no sin.

These six degrees are reducible to the three which St. Thomas speaks of (Ia IIae, q. 9, a. 6 ad 3; q. 109, 1, 2, 6, 9).

The will is moved
> before deliberation, properly speaking, by counsel (no. 1 and also no. 4, since one does not deliberate, properly speaking, about the ultimate end);
> After deliberation, properly speaking, by counsel (nos. 2 and 5);
> above deliberation properly speaking (nos. 3 and 6).[16]

(N.B. Father del Prado distinguishes only five degrees, since he does not mention our third degree separately, but reduces it to the sixth.)

The first mode is explained in Ia IIae, q. 9, a. 6 ad 3, q. 10, a. 1, 2, 4.

The second mode is explained in Ia IIae, q. 9, a. 6 ad 3; Ia, 63, a. 1 ad 4 and 5; Ia IIae, 79, a. 1 and 2, and whether the will may move itself, Ia IIae, q. 9, a. 3.

The third mode is explained in Ia IIae, q. 68, a. 1, where the *Ethics*, attributed to Aristotle, is cited, Bk. VII, chap. 14: "On good fortune."

The fourth mode is explained in Ia IIae, q. 111, a. 2 c and ad 2, operating grace before an interior act, especially when the will, which previously willed evil, begins to will the good. The will does not properly move itself, since the efficacious act is not given beforehand in respect to the final supernatural end, by virtue of which it could move itself toward that end. Further (IIa IIae, q. 24, a. 1 ad 3): "Charity, whose object is the ultimate end, should rather be said to

[16] These six modes of divine motion are explained at greater length in our *Christian Perfection and Contemplation*, pp. 286–99. Cf. below, p. 89 ff.

reside in the will than in free choice," for choice properly applies
to the means to the end (Ia IIae, q. 13, a. 3).

The fifth mode is explained in Ia IIae, q. 111, a. 2, cooperating
grace (cf. Cajetan); and Ia, 63, a. 1, 5, 6, concerning the second instant in the life of the angels when they were able to sin.

The sixth mode is explained in Ia IIae, q. 68, a. 1 ff.

To these may be added
the miraculous mode
{ as in the instantaneous conversion of St.
Paul; or as in prophetic illumination and
various graces *gratis datae* (cf. Ia IIae, q.
111, a. 4 and 5).

GENERAL HELP AND SPECIAL HELP

St. Thomas and nearly all theologians employ this terminology,
and commonly apply the term "general help" to that which is given
for operations in accordance with the universal or common mode of
acting. "Special help" is that which is given for operations above the
aforesaid universal or common mode, and this in a variety of ways;
for example, either because a particular difficulty is to be overcome,
or because this mode is properly extraordinary or miraculous. Hence
there are many more or less special degrees. At the outset the principal degrees should be noted (cf. John of St. Thomas, *De gratia,*
index under *"gratia specialis";* also the Salmanticenses, Gonet, and
Lemos).

1. The most general help is that by which the will is moved toward
the universal good, as described above in the synopsis (no. 1); without this help the will can will nothing, nor, in fact, can it sin.

2. General help often signifies the motion indicated in no. 2, as
when the will is moved in the natural order toward some real good,
for instance, honoring one's father. In fact this "general help" is
sometimes called grace in a broad sense because, although it is due
to human nature in general, it is not due to this individual whom God
may permit to sin by his not honoring his father; so in a certain
sense this help is special in relation to this individual who does not
sin (cf. also *De veritate,* q. 24, a. 14); [17] see also the Salmanticenses

---

[17] Ia, q. 21, a. 1 ad 3: "It is due to every created thing that it should have that which
befits it, as for a man to have hands and to be served by the other animals, and thus
again God exercises His justice when He gives to anything that which is due to it
according to the purpose of its nature and condition." Rather does God owe it to
Himself to give to creatures whatever is necessary so that at least many of such and
such a nature may attain their end.

on q. 109, a. 2, as well as Gonet, d. 1, a. 3, nos. 148, 170, Cajetan, Billuart, *De gratia,* diss. I, a. 1, and Suarez.

Indeed, "general help," sometimes by many theologians of almost all schools, signifies the entirely common actual grace of the supernatural order, indicated in our synopsis as no. 5, provided that there is no special difficulty to be overcome. For example, it is said that, for overcoming slight temptations against supernatural precepts, general help of the supernatural order suffices, and that this help is due to elevated nature in general, but not to this just one in particular. John of St. Thomas (*De gratia,* disp. 21, a. 1, no. 11) thus distinguishes between general and special help and also uses the terms "ordinary" and "extraordinary help," but this extraordinary does not here signify miraculous.

3. The term "special help" is usually applied by theologians to that which is included under nos. 3, 4, and 6 of our synopsis, that is, to a special inspiration, particularly of the supernatural order, an operating grace either in the moment of justification or later in accordance with the exercise of the gifts. Sometimes "special help" signifies, although less properly, actual grace even cooperating necessarily in overcoming a great difficulty. Thus it is almost commonly said that to overcome grave temptations special help, or special grace, is required. (Billuart, diss. III, a. 6). Such help is not due to this just man, nor proximately due to elevated nature, but is particularly to be obtained by praying for it.

Corollary. In respect, not to nature, but to individual persons, all supernatural help is special, according to John of St. Thomas (Ia IIae, q. 109, disp. 21, a. 1, no. 11), for aid given to one person and not to another is special to the person to whom it is given; yet that aid can be called general in relation to common elevated nature, e.g., in the overcoming of temptations.

The following speak in like manner: Billuart, *De gratia,* beginning;

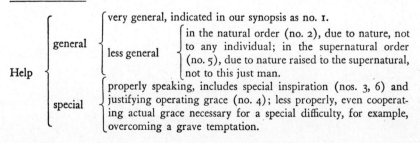

Help
- general
  - very general, indicated in our synopsis as no. 1.
  - less general
    - in the natural order (no. 2), due to nature, not to any individual; in the supernatural order (no. 5), due to nature raised to the supernatural, not to this just man.
- special
  - properly speaking, includes special inspiration (nos. 3, 6) and justifying operating grace (no. 4); less properly, even cooperating actual grace necessary for a special difficulty, for example, overcoming a grave temptation.

the Salmanticenses, *De gratia,* Ia IIae, q. 109, disp. II, dub. II, nos. 27, 34, and disp. V, dub. VII, no. 171; Gonet, *De gratia,* disp. I, a. 3, § 5, nos. 157, 170, 172; Lemos, *Panoplia,* t. IV, p. Ia, q. 85, no. 162. Lemos here maintains that general help is twofold; one is sufficient, bestowing the power to conquer a slight temptation, and this is given to all, the other is efficacious, bestowing the conquest of this slight temptation, and this is not given to all; it is necessary to pray in order to receive it.

This division corresponds to the division of the divine will into antecedent and consequent as explained in Ia, q. 19, a. 6, where it is stated that "whatever God wills absolutely, happens; although what He antecedently wills may not happen. He wills absolutely or simply when He wills a thing considering all its particular circumstances, here and now, as a just judge wills absolutely that a murderer be hanged, although in a certain sense he wills him to live inasmuch as he is a man." Likewise in Ia, q. 20, a. 4, it is said that God always loves better men more, but they would not be better were they not loved more by God. (Cf. *De veritate,* q. 6, a. 2; Ia IIae, q. 109, a. 9, at the end of the body of the article.)

CHAPTER II

QUESTION 109

The Necessity of Grace

▼▼▼

IN this question there are ten articles, methodically arranged in progressive order, beginning with the lesser actions for which grace is necessary (for example, knowing some truth) and ending with the last supreme good work, that is, final perseverance. (Cf. titles.) There are three parts, as Cajetan observes at the beginning of article 7:

$$\text{necessity of grace} \begin{cases} \text{for fallen man} \begin{cases} \text{for doing good (a. 1–6).} \\ \text{for avoiding evil (a. 7 and 8).} \end{cases} \\ \text{for the just (a. 9 and 10), acting and persevering.} \end{cases}$$

ARTICLE I. WHETHER WITHOUT GRACE MAN CAN KNOW ANY TRUTH

Statement of the question. It seems that grace is required for knowing any truth whatever, for it is said in II Cor. 3:5: "Not that we are sufficient to think anything of ourselves as of ourselves." And St. Augustine maintained this answer in a certain prayer, but he himself retracted later (*Retract.*, I, 4), as is said in the argument to the contrary and declared that it could be refuted thus: "Many who are not sinless know many truths," for example, those of geometry.

The first conclusion is the following. To know any truth, man requires at least natural help from God, but he does not require a new supernatural illumination for it. The aforesaid natural help is due to human nature as a whole, but not to any individual.

Proof of the first part. Since every created agent requires divine premotion in order to pass from potency to act, "however perfect the nature of any corporal or spiritual being, it cannot proceed to act unless moved by God." [1]

[1] Thus the Council of Orange (can. 22, Denz., no. 195): "No one has anything of his own but lying and sin. But if man has something of truth and justice, it comes

Proof of the second part. Because many truths do not surpass the power proper to our intellect, they are easily knowable naturally (cf. ad 1, ad 2, ad 3).

It should be noted that the natural concurrence called here by St. Thomas "motion" (*motio*) is not mere simultaneous cooperation.[2] Likewise, contrary to Suarez, the virtual act of the will cannot, without divine motion, be reduced to a secondary act, for St. Thomas said: "However . . ." (cf. Suarez, *Disp. met.,* disp. 29, sect. 1, no. 7, on virtual act). We reply: there is more in the secondary act than in the virtual act, which in reality differs from the action, nor is it its own action. Already in this first article it is evident that St. Thomas withdraws nothing from divine motion.

The second conclusion is the following. For attaining a knowledge of supernatural truths, our intellect stands in need not only of the natural concurrence of God, but of a special illumination, namely, the light of faith or the light of prophecy and of a proportionate motion. The reason is that these truths surpass the power proper to our intellect.

OBJECTIONS

Objection to the first conclusion. Vasquez presents several objections. In the first place, he says:

The intellect, indifferent to truth and falsehood, is determined by grace toward any truth.

But our intellect is indifferent to truth and falsehood.

Therefore our intellect is determined by grace toward any truth.

Reply. I distinguish the major: by grace, broadly speaking, granted; properly, denied. Let the minor pass, although the intellect is not so indifferent to truth and falsehood as not to incline naturally to truth. It is called grace broadly since, for example, it is given to Aristotle rather than to Epicurus.

I insist. Grace properly speaking, is required in this case, at least after original sin, according to the fideists, such as Bautin, Bonetti.

---

from that source after which we should thirst in this desert land." At least natural concurrence is required.

[2] In simultaneous concurrence, admitted by Molina, God and the secondary cause are like two men rowing a boat, that is, like two coordinated causes. On the contrary, for St. Thomas, God's premotion and the secondary cause thus moved are two causes of which the second is subordinated to the supreme first cause, with reference both to causality and to being.

Grace, properly speaking, is required that the wounded intellect may be healed.

But when it knows any truth, our intellect is at least partially healed.

Therefore grace, properly speaking, is required for knowing any truth.

Reply. I distinguish the major: for knowing the whole body of natural truths, I concede; for any one truth, I deny. The intellect would thus be not merely darkened but extinct, were it incapable of knowing even the least truth without healing grace. Let the minor pass. I distinguish the conclusion in the same way as the major— I say *transeat* in regard to the minor but I do not concede since the intellect is not properly healed when it knows a truth of geometry but rather when it knows the truth of natural religion.

Instance: But the intellect is extinct or almost extinct, according to the Jansenists.

Ignorance is opposed to knowledge as being a total deprivation.

But the wound of ignorance is in the intellect, according to tradition. Therefore.

Reply. I distinguish the major: total ignorance, granted; partial ignorance, denied. I contradistinguish the minor; explanation: the wound of ignorance affects principally the practical intellect wherein prudence resides; but there remains in the practical intellect a synderesis, and the speculative intellect is less wounded, since it does not presuppose rectitude of the appetites.

Objection to the second conclusion.

Whatever does not surpass the object of our intellect can be known without grace.

The mysteries of faith do not surpass the object of our intellect.

Therefore.

Reply. I distinguish the major: a proportionate object, granted; an adequate object, surpassing a proportionate object, denied. I contradistinguish the minor.

I insist. But the mysteries of faith do not surpass the proportionate object.

That which is known habitually to the senses does not surpass the proportionate object.

But the mysteries of faith are known habitually to the senses. Therefore.

Reply. I distinguish the major: whatever is so known without revelation, granted; after revelation, I distinguish further: they do not surpass the remotely proportionate object, granted; proximately proportionate, denied.

I insist. But at least, after external revelation, the mysteries of the faith do not surpass the proximately proportionate object.

That which is known by its species abstracted from the senses and through external signs does not surpass the proximately proportionate object.

But the mysteries of faith are thus known.

Therefore.

Reply. I distinguish the major: if this is known from a human motive, granted; and then it does not require supernatural grace; and contrariwise if it is known from a supernatural motive, that is, on the authority of God revealing in the order of grace (cf. below, Corollary 4).

I insist. But man is made in the image of the Trinity.

And he is naturally capable of knowing this image.

Therefore.

Reply. I distinguish the minor: so far as man is the image of God, the author of nature, granted; so far as he is the image of the Trinity, denied, since the term of this relationship is of a higher order. Thus if someone is given an image of an entirely unknown man, he cannot say whose image it is. (For a correct treatment, cf. Salmanticenses, *De gratia,* disp. III, dub. IV, no. 40, and Billuart, *De gratia,* diss. III, a. 2). Thomists have drawn several corollaries from this article, using more modern terminology.

Corollary 1. Fallen man, without grace, with natural concurrence alone, is capable of knowing certain natural truths, namely, the first speculative and practical principles of reason and the conclusions which are easily drawn from them. This is contrary to some ancient writers who do not distinguish sufficiently between grace and natural concurrence; it is also contrary to Vasquez who, following the ways of the nominalists, disparaged the powers of reason excessively, as did Baius and the Jansenists, Quesnel and the nineteenth-century fideists, such as Bautin and Bonetty. With regard to this conclusion, cf. the following condemned propositions.

Denz., no. 1022. This one of Baius is condemned: "Those who consider, with Pelagius, the text of the Apostle to the Romans (2:14): 'The Gentiles, who have not the (written) law, do by nature those things that are of the law,' understand it to apply to the Gentiles who have not the grace of faith." For it is certainly contrary to Baius that, without grace, man by natural reason can know the first precepts of the natural law: good ought to be done, thou shalt not kill.

Denz., no. 1391. This proposition of Quesnel is condemned: "All knowledge of God, even natural, even in pagan philosophy, can come only from God, and without grace it produces nothing but presumption, vanity, and opposition to God Himself, in place of sentiments of adoration, gratitude, and love." Thus had spoken previously Luther and Calvin (I *De Inst.,* chaps. 1 and 2), as if peripatetic philosophy had come from diabolic inspiration. The natural reason of Aristotle was capable of discovering the theory of potency and act, of the four causes, and this without any opposition to God.

Denz., no. 1627. The following may probably be attributed to Bautin: Although reason is obscure and weak through original sin, there still remains in it enough lucidity and power to lead us with certainty to (the knowledge of) the existence of God, to the revelation made to the Jews by Moses and to the Christians by our adorable God-man."

The Vatican Council defined the following (Denz., no. 1806): "If anyone says that the one true God, our Creator and Lord, cannot certainly be known by the light of natural human reason, let him be anathema." This is contrary to the traditionalists, Kant, and the Positivists. Finally, in the oath against Modernism: "I acknowledge in the first place and of a truth, that, by the light of natural reason through the things which have been made, that is, through the visible works of creation, God, the beginning and end of all things, can be certainly known and even demonstrated." Likewise in regard to miracles confirming the Gospel it is similarly declared that they are "most certain signs that the Christian religion is of divine origin . . . and even in the present time especially adapted to the intelligence of all men." Moreover, the reason for this conclusion is the one given in the article, that is:

Every power infused in created things is efficacious in respect to its own proper effect.

But our intellect is a power infused into us by God and, granted that it is darkened by sin, yet it is not extinct.

Therefore it can of itself, with natural concurrence, arrive at a knowledge of certain natural truths.

Otherwise intellectual power would be, in its own order, much more imperfect than are the powers of bodies, of plants and animals, in respect to their own objects, sight and hearing, for example.

As a matter of fact, the natural concurrence required for the knowledge of any truth may be called grace in the broad sense, inasmuch as it is not due to any individual but to human nature in general; (cf. Ia, q. 21, a. 1 ad 3): "It is due to any created thing that it should have that which is ordained to it, as to a man that he have hands and that the other animals serve him; and thus again God works justice when He gives to anything that which is due to it by reason of its nature and condition." God owes it to Himself to give to the various kinds of plants and animals and to humankind the natural concurrence enabling them to reach their final end on account of which they were made. But, on the other hand, it is not to be wondered at that what is deficient should sometimes fail, and God is not bound to prevent these defects, since, if He prevented them all, greater goods would not come about, and it is on account of these many goods that He permits the defect. Hence, as our intellect is defective, there is due to it, according to the laws of ordinary providence, that it should at least sometimes be moved toward the truth and not always fall into error. But the fact that Aristotle, for example, rather than another, let us say Epicurus, may be moved in the direction of truth, this is not due to him; it is by a special providence and benevolence, and in this sense such natural concurrence is called "grace" broadly speaking. And it is proper to pray that one may obtain this grace in the wide sense of the term.

Corollary 2. Fallen man, without a special added grace, cannot, at least with any moral power, know either collectively or even separately all natural truths, speculative or speculative-practical, or, for still greater reason, practical-practical; since for these last, as for prudence, rectitude of the appetite is required.

Many hold, not without probability, that without special grace man can know all natural speculative truths, by physical power, since these truths do not exceed the capacity of a man possessing a keen mind. But in the present corollary it is a question of moral power, that is, such as may be rendered active without very great difficulty. And it is certain that this moral power is not given in regard to all the aforesaid kinds of truth taken together. Rather, it was on this account that the Vatican Council declared (Denz., no. 1786) revelation to be morally necessary "so that those things concerning divine matters which are not of themselves impenetrable to human reason may nevertheless, in the present condition of the human race, be readily known by all with a firm certainty and no admixture of error." This is explained by St. Thomas (Ia, q. 1, a. 1; IIa IIae, q. 2, a. 3 and 4; *Contra Gentes,* Bk. I, chaps. 4 and 6; Bk. IV, *Gentes,* chap. 52). For the impediments are manifold: the shortness of life, the weakness of the body, domestic cares, the disorder of the passions, etc. It is clearly evident that, with all these impediments, fallen man without grace has not the moral power to attain to the knowledge of all natural truths together; nor even, as a matter of fact to the separate knowledge of them: 1. because the wound of ignorance is in the intellect, preventing especially that ease of understanding necessary to prudence, for prudence presupposes rectitude of the appetite; 2. because many speculative natural truths are very difficult, demanding long and rigorous study for a certain and complete knowledge of them and therefore a constantly good will, burning love of truth, a relish for contemplation, undisturbed passions, a good disposition of the senses, leisure uninterrupted by cares. All of this cannot be arrived at easily before regeneration by healing grace; indeed even afterward a special grace is required for it.

Among natural truths, according to Billuart, there are some so extremely difficult that no man has thus far been able to attain a certain knowledge of them, for example, the ebb and flow of the tides, the essence of light, electricity, magnetism, the inner development of the embryo; similarly, the inner nature of sensation, the active intellect and its functioning, the intimate relationship between the last practical judgment and choice, etc.; likewise the reconciling of the attributes of God as naturally knowable, although the knowledge of the existence of God, supreme Ruler, is easily arrived at by common sense from the order of the universe.

Doubt. Whether this special grace required for a knowledge of all these natural truths is properly supernatural.

Reply. It suffices that it is supernatural in respect to the manner of its production, by a special providence; these is no real need of a grace which is supernatural in respect to its substance, because the knowledge of which we are speaking is ontologically natural.

Corollary 3. Supposing the existence of an external revelation, fallen man, with natural, general concurrence alone and without a special added grace, is able to know and enlarge on supernatural truths, from some human or natural reason.

Thus the demons believe naturally, by a faith not infused but acquired, on the evidence of compelling miracles, as is demonstrated in IIa IIae, q. 5, a. 2. And formal heretics retain certain supernatural truths, not from the supernatural motive of divine revelation (otherwise they would believe all that is revealed), but from a human motive, that is, on the bases of their own judgment and will; for example, because they consider this faith to be honorable or useful to themselves, or because it seems to them very foolish to deny certain things in the Gospel. The reason for this is that, although a true supernatural is in itself entitatively supernatural, yet, as depending upon a human or natural motive, it is not formally supernatural.

Why? Because an object, not as a thing, but by reason of object, is formally constituted by the formal motive through which it is attained. Thus when a formal heretic from a human motive and by human faith believes in the Incarnation, while rejecting the Trinity; then the object believed, as a thing, is supernatural, but, as an object, it is not supernatural. Therefore it may thus be attained by the natural powers, and then the supernatural truth is attained only materially because it is not attained formally in its supernaturalness, as it is supernatural.

That a demon should naturally believe the mysteries of faith is analogical, all proportions being maintained, to a dog's materially hearing human speech as sound but not really hearing formally the intelligible meaning of this same speech. Similarly, "the sensual man (for example, a heretic retaining certain mysteries of faith) perceiveth not these things that are of the Spirit of God; for it is foolishness to him, and he cannot understand" (I Cor. 2:14); cf. also St. Thomas' Commentary on this Epistle. We might draw another comparison with the case of one who listens to a symphony of Beethoven or Bach, possessed of the sense of hearing but devoid of any musical sense; he would not attain to the spirit of the symphony (cf. our *De revelatione*, I, 478, based on IIa IIae, q. 5, a. 3).

Corollary 4. Man cannot believe supernatural truths from the supernatural motive of divine revelation without a special interior grace, both in the intellect and in the will.

This is contrary, first, to the Pelagians, who say that external revelation is sufficient for the assent of faith (cf. Denz., nos. 129 ff.) and, secondly, to the Semi-Pelagians, who would have it that the beginning of faith comes from us (cf. Denz., nos. 174 ff.; Council of Orange, c. 5, 6, 7); therein it is declared that the inspiration and enlightenment of the Holy Spirit is required in this matter (Denz., nos. 178–80).

These definitions of the Church are based upon several texts of Sacred Scripture cited by the Council of Orange, for example, Ephes. 2:8: "for by grace you are saved through faith, and that not of yourselves, for it is the gift of God; not of works, that no man may glory." This does not refer to external revelation, for it is further said in the same Epistle (1:17 f.): "That . . . God . . . may give unto you the spirit of wisdom and of revelation, in the knowledge of Him: the eyes of your heart enlightened, that you may know what the hope is of his calling"; and (Acts 16:14): ". . . Lydia . . . whose heart the Lord opened to attend to those things which were said by Paul."

Again, this fourth corollary is opposed to Molina and many Molinists who declare that fallen man can, without supernatural grace, believe supernatural truths from a supernatural motive, but then he does not believe as is necessary for salvation, for which grace is required. And therefore Molina holds that the assent of faith is supernatural not in respect to substance by virtue of its formal motive, but only in respect to mode, by reason of the eliciting principle and by reason of its extrinsic end. (Cf. *Concordia*, q. 14, a. 13, disp. 38, pp. 213 ff., and our *De revelatione*, I, 489, where Molina and Father Ledochowski are quoted.)

This question has been treated at length and fully by the Salmanticenses in their Commentary on our article, *De gratia*, disp. III, dub. III, and I have quoted their principal texts in *De revelatione*, I, 494, 496, showing that therein they are in accord with all Thomists from Capreolus to the present day (pp. 458–514). Their conclusions, here cited, ought to be read.

The argument put forth against Molina and his disciples is found in IIa IIae, q. 6, a. 1, "Whether faith is infused in man by God": "For, since man, assenting to the things which are of faith, is raised above his nature, it is necessary that this be instilled into him by a supernatural principle impelling him interiorly through grace," for an act is specified by its formal object (*objectum formale quo et quod*); if, therefore, the latter is supernatural, the act specified by it is essentially supernatural and cannot be elicited without grace. Further, St. Thomas affirms this to be true even of faith lacking form (*informus*), that is, faith without charity (IIa IIae, q. 6, a. 2); even faith lacking form is a gift of God, since it is said to lack form on account of a defect of extrinsic form, and not on account of a defect in the specific nature of infused faith itself, for it has the same specifying formal object.

Thus Billuart comments on our article: "the formally supernatural object as such cannot be attained except by a supernatural act. This upsets the basic assertion of Molina, who maintains that the assent to faith from the motive of divine revelation is natural in respect to its substance, and supernatural in respect to its mode. . . . This opinion does not seem to us sufficiently removed from the error of the Semi-Pelagians." (Likewise, the Salmanticenses, *loc. cit.*)

Confirmation. The Council of Orange (c. 5, 6, 7; Denz., nos. 178–80) defined grace to be necessary for the initial step toward faith and for the belief necessary to salvation.

But to believe on account of the formal supernatural motive of infused faith itself is already to believe in the way necessary to salvation; what more formal belief can then be required?

Therefore, to believe on account of this supernatural motive is impossible without grace.

Many difficulties would arise from any other opinion.

1. An act cannot be specified by an eliciting principle, for this eliciting principle itself requires specifying, and it is specified by the act toward which it tends, as the act is specified by its object. Otherwise specification would come from the rear rather than from the front, as if the way from the College "Angelicum" to the Vatican were specified by the terminus from which, and not by the terminus toward which.

2. An act of faith would be no more supernatural than an act of acquired temperance ordered by charity to a supernatural end; it would be less supernatural than an act of infused temperance, as referred to by St. Thomas (Ia IIae, q. 63, a. 4). This supernatural in respect to mode is the supernatural almost as applied from without, like gold applied over silver for those who cannot afford to buy pure gold jewelry: it is "plated," "veneered."

3. What Molina says of the act of theological faith, could equally be said of the act of hope, and even of the act of charity, for the substance of which natural good will would suffice, and the supernatural

mode would be added to make it what is required for salvation. But then the charity of the *viator* thus specified by a formal object naturally attainable would not be the same as the charity of the blessed, which must be, like the beatific vision, essentially supernatural. Hence charity would be something different in heaven from what it is now, contrary to the words of St. Paul, "charity never falleth away" (I Cor. 13:8). Thus even Suarez vigorously opposes Molina in this matter. There would be innumerable other consequences as indicated in *De revelatione,* I, 511–14.

We cannot therefore admit the following two theses of Cardinal Billot on the subject as put forward in his book, *De virtutibus infusis* (71, 87, 88): "Supernatural formality, causing acts to be proportioned to the condition of objects conformable to themselves, does not proceed from the object in that it performs in respect to us the office of an object, nor, namely, either from the material object which is believed, hoped, or loved, or from the formal object on account of which it is believed, hoped, or loved, but solely from the principle of grace by which the operative faculty is elevated." "Supernatural habits are not necessarily distinguished from natural habits according to their objects" (p. 84).

In opposition to our thesis, cf. the objections in *De revelatione,* I, 504–11. The principal one is the following.

The demons believe (Jas. 2), and they believe without grace.

But they believe from the motive of divine revelation.

Therefore grace is not necessary to believe from a motive of divine revelation.

Reply. I concede the major. I distinguish the minor: that the demons believe formally from the motive of divine revelation according as it is supernatural in respect to substance in itself and on that account, I deny; that they believe materially on the evidence of the signs of revelation, I grant; to this evidence their faith is ultimately reducible. (Cf. IIa IIae, q. 5, a. 2 ad 1, 3.) They believe, says St. Thomas, as it were under constraint from the evidence of miracles, for it would be exceedingly stupid for them to reject this evidence. They therefore attain to God the author of nature and of miracles, but not really to God the author of grace, nor to revelation as it proceeds from God the author of grace. On the contrary, revelation as proceeding from God, the author of grace, specifies infused faith which is of a higher species than would be a faith, supernatural in respect to mode, based upon the revelation of God, author of nature. (Cf. Salmanticenses quoted in *De revelatione,* I, 496, 471.)

ARTICLE II. WHETHER MAN CAN WILL TO DO ANY GOOD WITHOUT GRACE

State of the question. It seems that man can do some good without grace: 1. for his acts are in his power, since he is ruler of his acts; 2. for everyone can do better that which pertains to him by nature than that which is beyond him by nature; but man can sin by himself, which is acting beyond and even against nature; therefore with even greater reason can he do good of himself. This objection raises the question whether not sinning, or persevering in good, is itself a gift of God; whether of two men, equally tempted and equally assisted, it can happen that one sins and the other does not. 3. Just as our intellect can, of itself, know truth, so our will can, of itself, will the good.

This question concerns: 1. a morally or ethically good work in the natural order (such as proceeds from the dictates of right reason and is not vitiated by any circumstances) so that it is not a sin; and 2. good works conducive to salvation, such as are ordained to a supernatural end, not indeed always as meritorious acts presupposing habitual grace, but as salutary acts disposing to justification and presupposing actual grace.

Reply. In respect to these two problems, certain truths are articles of faith. 1. It is of faith that not all the works of infidels or sinners are sins (against Wyclif, Denz., no. 606; John Hus, no. 642, Baius, nos. 1008, 1027 ff.; Quesnel, nos. 1351, 1372, 1388). Therefore without the grace of faith a man can do some morally or ethically good works. 2. It is of faith that supernatural good cannot be effected by fallen man without grace. Cf. Council of Orange (Denz., no. 174), can. 6, 7, 9, 11, 12–20, 22; and Council of Quierzy (Denz., no. 317), c. 2. These two articles of faith are based on many passages in Holy Scripture.

1. Holy Scripture does indeed praise certain works of infidels and testifies that they were rewarded by God; for example, it praises the kind-heartedness of the Egyptian midwives who did not wish to kill the children of the Hebrews in conformity with the iniquitous command of Pharaoh (Exod., chap. 1); the hospitality of Rahab the har-

lot, who refused to betray the men sent by Josue (Josue, chap. 2), is also praised; likewise God gave the land of Egypt to King Nabuchodonosor, that he might wage a successful war against the inhabitants of Tyre, according to the command of God (Ezech. 29:20). St. Augustine says (*De civ. Dei,* Bk. V, chap. 15) that God granted a vast empire to the Romans as a temporal reward of their virtues and good works. But God neither praises nor rewards sins, but rather punishes. Therefore. Similarly it is said in Romans (2:14): "The Gentiles, who have not the law, do by nature those things that are of the law"; in other words, they do at least some good works, as St. Augustine shows (*De spiritu et littera,* chap. 27).

2 The other proposition of faith, that supernatural good works cannot be performed by fallen man without grace, is also based on many texts from Scripture cited by the Council of Orange: "A man cannot receive anything, unless it be given him from heaven" (John 3:27). "This is the work of God, that you believe in Him whom He hath sent" (John 6:29). "Without Me you can do nothing" (John 15:5). "I am the vine; you the branches" (*ibid.*). "It is not of him that willeth, nor of him that runneth, but of God that showeth mercy" (Rom. 9:16). "It is God who worketh in you, both to will and to accomplish, according to His good will" (Phil. 2:13). "What hast thou that thou hast not received?" (I Cor. 4:7.) "No man can say the Lord Jesus, but by the Holy Ghost" (I Cor. 12:3). "Not that we are sufficient to think anything of ourselves, as of ourselves: but our sufficiency is from God" (II Cor. 3:5). "Every best gift, and every perfect gift, is from above, coming down from the Father of lights" (Jas. 1:17). There are innumerable texts from St. Augustine; for example, the one quoted in the *Sed contra.* In the body of the article are found four conclusions, which should be consulted in the text itself.

1. To accomplish any good whatever, man, in any state, requires the general concurrence of God, whether in the state of incorrupt or of corrupt nature (or even in the state of pure nature of which St. Thomas does not speak here, but the possibility of which he admits, as stated in *II Sent.,* d. 31, q. 1, a. 2 ad 3, and Ia, q. 95, a. 1). The reason for this is that every creature, since it neither exists nor acts of itself, is in potency regarding action, and needs to be moved from without that it may act, as said in article 1. This efficacious concurrence toward a naturally virtuous good is due, as we have said, to human nature in general, not to any individual, in whom God may permit sin.

2. In the state of integral nature, man did not require special added grace, except for performing supernatural works, not, that is, for morally good works commensurate with nature. For nature was then in a perfect state and needed only general concurrence, which is, of course, to be understood in the sense of a concurrence which is prior and efficacious in itself, not in the sense accepted by Molina.

3. In the state of fallen nature man requires supernatural grace not only to perform a supernatural work, but to observe the whole natural law (as will be made more evident later in article 5).

4. Fallen man can do some morally good work in the natural order with general concurrence alone, for example, build houses, plant vineyards, and other things of this kind; and he can do this on account of a duly virtuous end, so that this act may be ethically good from the standpoint of its object, its end, and all its circumstances; for instance, that a man build a home for the good of his family, that is, in such a way that there is no sin involved. This is particularly evident from the fact that, for St. Thomas, there are no indifferent acts in regard to an individual (Ia IIae, q. 18, a. 9; cf. above, Ia IIae, 65, a. 2): "Acquired virtues, according as they are operative of good ordained to an end which does not exceed the natural faculty of man, can be deprived of charity," but they are so on the part of the subject in the circumstance of his disposition, not in the circumstance of a virtue difficult to set in motion, nor closely connected actually. Thus not all the works of infidels and sinners are sins. The reason is that, since human nature "is not totally corrupted" by sin so as to be entirely deprived of natural good, therefore it can, through the power which remains, easily do some morally good works with general concurrence, just as a sick man may have some power of movement in himself, although he is not able to move perfectly unless he is cured.

REFUTATION OF OBJECTIONS (cf. *De veritate,* q. 24, a. 14)

First objection. That is in the power of a man of which he is master. But a man is master of his acts.

Therefore it is in the power of a man to do good.

Reply. I distinguish the major: without the concurrence of God, denied; with the concurrence of God, granted. I grant the minor. I distinguish the conclusion in the same way as the major. (Read St. Thomas' answer.)

Second objection. Everyone can do better that which pertains to him by nature than that which is beyond his nature. But man can sin of himself, which is beyond nature. Therefore man can do good of himself. (See a similar objection in *De veritate,* q. 24, a. 14, objections 3 and 4, also objection 2 and the body of the article toward the end.) Likewise some say that of two men, tempted in the same way and equally assisted, it may be that one perseveres in attrition or in an easy, imperfect prayer, whereas the other, on the contrary, sins by not continuing this easy act.

St. Thomas' reply to objection 2 is as follows: "Every created thing needs to be preserved in the goodness proper to its nature by something else (that is, by God), for of itself it can fall away from goodness. At least, he who does not sin is divinely preserved in the goodness proper to his nature, while God does not preserve the other, but, on the contrary, permits sin in him; therefore they are not equally assisted. However, nature is not completely corrupt; it is able to do some good but with the help of God, which is due to nature in general, but not indeed to this individual. Therefore, as Augustine says, we ought to thank God inasmuch as we avoid sins which were possible to us, for the very fact of not sinning is a good coming from God; it is, in other words, being preserved in goodness.

In reply to the third objection it is noted that "human nature is more corrupted by sin in regard to its appetite for the good than in regard to its knowledge of the truth." This is because original sin first causes an aversion of the will directly from the final supernatural end, and indirectly from the final natural end; and consequently a disorder in the sensitive appetite tending toward sensible goods, not according to the dictates of right reason.

Doubt. How is this general concurrence, necessary for fallen man to accomplish any moral good, to be understood?

Reply. The Molinists understand it as a natural, general, indifferent concurrence which the will, through its own volition, directs toward the good. But the Thomists reply that in that case God, by moving one as far as the exercise of the will is concerned, would be no more the author of a good work than of a bad one (contrary to the Council of Trent, Denz., no. 816).[3] Therefore they insist upon a prevenient, determining, and effective concurrence enabling a man to do good rather than evil. The early Thomists called this a special concurrence,

---

[3] "If anyone should say . . . that bad works as well as good are done by God, and not merely by His permission . . . let him be anathema."

since it is not due to this or that individual; but later Thomists call it a general concurrence, because it is, in a certain sense, due to human nature, even in its fallen state, for nature is not totally corrupt or confirmed in evil, but only weakened. However, it is not due to one individual rather than to another, and from this aspect it is special.

In the same way various texts from Scripture, the councils, the Fathers, and St. Thomas, which seem to be contradictory, are reconciled. For example: "No one has anything of himself but sin and lying," says the Council of Orange (can. 22). That is to say, no one tells the truth with honest intent without at least the natural assistance of God, which is a grace, broadly speaking, with respect to this man on whom it is bestowed rather than on another; otherwise it would have the meaning which Baius gives to it when he says: "Man's free will, without the grace and help of God, is of no use except to commit sin." Baius means not only natural assistance, or grace broadly speaking, but grace in the proper sense, which comes from Christ, hence sanctifying grace and charity.

ARTICLE III. WHETHER MAN CAN LOVE GOD ABOVE ALL THINGS WITHOUT GRACE, BY HIS MERELY NATURAL POWER

We are especially concerned, in this article, with the love of God, author of nature, above all things, although there is still a reference in the reply to the first objection to the love of God, author of grace, which proceeds from infused charity. St. Thomas had already dealt with this subject (Ia, q. 60, a. 5) in respect to the angels, and later (IIa IIae, q. 26, a. 3), where he distinguishes more explicitly between natural and supernatural love of God. (Likewise on I Cor., XIII, lect. 4; *De virtutibus,* q. 2, a. 2 ad 16; q. 4, a. 1 ad 9; *Quodl.* I, q. 4, a. 3.)

In the statement of the question he sets down the objections to the possibility of a natural love of God above all things. Later, Baius and Jansen again voice the same objections. This natural love of God above all things seems impossible: 1. because loving God above all things is proper to the act of infused charity; 2. since no creature can rise above itself, it cannot naturally love God more than itself; 3. because grace would be added to no purpose. Let us examine: 1. the doctrine of St. Thomas; 2. its confirmation by the condemnation of Baius and Quesnel; 3. the controversy of modern theologians on this subject.

I. THE TEACHING OF ST. THOMAS

This teaching can be reduced to three conclusions treating of

1. the love of God, author of nature, above all things in the state of integral nature;

2. the love of God, author of nature, above all things in the state of corrupt nature;

3. the supernatural love of God, author of grace, above all things.

We shall see later, in reference to a particular problem, whether man in the state of pure nature would be able to love God, author of nature, above all things. This question is not solved by the *Sed contra,* because in it the expression "by merely natural powers" does not refer to pure nature but to integral nature. The article itself should be read.

Conclusion 1. In the state of integral nature, man did not require an added gift of grace to love God, the author of nature, above all things efficaciously; he required only the help of God moving him to it, or natural concurrence. This is proved as above, in regard to the angels, that is, in forms.

Loving God, the author of nature, above all things is natural to man and to every creature, even irrational, in its own way; for, as the good of the part is for the sake of the good of the whole, every particular thing naturally loves its own good on account of the common good of the whole universe, which is God.

But man in the state of integral nature could have performed, by virtue of his nature, the good which was natural to him.

Therefore man in the state of integral nature could, by virtue of his nature without any added grace, efficaciously love God the author of nature above all things.

The major is explained above (Ia, 60, a. 5) and later (IIa IIae, q. 26, a. 3). According to Ia, 60, a. 5: "The natural inclination in those things which are without reason throws some light upon the natural inclination in the will of the intellectual nature. But in natural things, everything which, as such, naturally belongs to another, is principally and more strongly inclined to that other to which it belongs than toward itself. For we observe that a (natural) part endangers itself naturally for the preservation of the whole, as the hand exposes itself without any deliberation to receive a blow for the safeguarding of the whole body. And since reason imitates nature, we find an imitation of this manner of acting in regard to political virtues. For it is the

part of a virtuous citizen to expose himself to the danger of death
for the safety of the whole nation. And if a man were a natural part
of this state, this inclination would be natural to him. Since, therefore, the universal good is God Himself, and angels and men and all
creatures are encompassed by this goodness, and since every creature
naturally by its very being belongs to God, it follows that even by
a natural love angels and men love God in greater measure and more
fundamentally than they do themselves. Otherwise, if they naturally
loved themselves more than God, it would follow that natural love
was perverse and would not be perfected by charity but rather destroyed." These last words imply that in the state of pure nature
man would be able to love God naturally above all things, otherwise
natural love would be perverse; but we shall see in the second conclusion that this is not so in the state of fallen nature on account of
its wounds.

The major of the present argument is entirely fundamental and a
most beautiful concept. It is thus explained (Ia, q. 60, a. 5 ad 1):
"Every (natural) part naturally loves the whole more than itself.
And every individual member naturally loves the good of its species
more than its own individual good." Hence onanism, preventing fer-
tility, is a crime against nature, against the good of the species. A good
Thomist, then, loves and defends the doctrine of St. Thomas more
than his personal opinions. However, in the exposition of this major
the excess of pantheism must be avoided, for then the creature would
love God more than self naturally in such a way that sin would be
impossible. This impossibility of sinning only follows confirmation
in goodness, and especially the beatific vision.

The contrary excess would be a pessimism arising from dualism,
which would lead to Manichaeism, that is, the doctrine of two principles. As Father Rousselot demonstrates in his thesis, "Pour l'histoire
du problème de l'amour au Moyen Age," [4] there are various theories
between these two mutually opposing excesses. There is already,
therefore, in our nature an inclination to love God, the author of nature, more than ourselves.

Conclusion 2. In the state of fallen nature, in order to love God,
the author of nature, above all things efficaciously, man requires the
help of grace restoring nature. (Cf. the end of the article's conclusion.)

---

[4] *Beiträge zur Geschichte der Phil. des Mittelalters,* Münster, 1908. (ed. Cl.
Baeumker).

The proof given in the words of St. Thomas is as follows: "because, on account of the corruption of nature, the will adheres to a private good, unless cured by the grace of God." In other words, unless cured by grace, man does not refer to God, efficaciously loved as an end, his love of self and of all other things; thus, unless cured by grace, man does not love God more than himself with a natural love. And inasmuch as this disordered inclination is perverse, it is called an inordinate love of self, self-love, or egoism. By original sin, man's will is directly averse to his final supernatural end and indirectly to his final natural end. For every sin against the supernatural law and end is indirectly against the natural law which prescribes that God is to be obeyed, whatever He commands. Hence fallen man is averse to God as his final end even naturally.

Conclusion 3. Man in any state requires the help of special grace to love God, the author of grace, with an infused, supernatural love (cf. ad 1). This is of faith, contrary to Pelagianism and Semi-Pelagianism (Council of Orange, can. 17, 25; Denz., nos. 190, 198; Council of Trent, Sess. VI, can. 3; Denz. no. 813). It was declared that "if anyone should say that, without a prevenient inspiration of the Holy Ghost and His assistance, man can believe, hope, love, or repent in such a way that the grace of justification would be conferred on him, let him be anathema." This definition of faith is based on the texts of Sacred Scripture quoted at the Council of Orange as follows: "The charity of God is poured forth in our hearts, by the Holy Ghost, who is given to us (Rom. 5:5). "No man can say the Lord Jesus, but by the Holy Ghost" (I Cor. 12:3). "The fruit of the Spirit is charity, joy, peace" (Gal. 5:22). "Peace be to the brethren and charity with faith, from God the Father, and the Lord Jesus Christ" (Ephes. 6:23). "Dearly beloved, let us love one another, for charity is of God. And everyone that loveth, is born of God, and knoweth God. He that loveth not, knoweth not God: for God is charity" (I John 4:7 f.); that is, he does not know, as it were, experimentally, with an affective knowledge. Baius and Quesnel said that he does not know in any way.

In regard to the explanation of this third conclusion, see the reply to the first objection, which was quoted against Baius. St. Thomas says: "Nature loves God above all things since God is the beginning and end of natural good; charity, however, loves God since He is the object of (supernatural) beatitude and since man has a certain spiritual fellowship (by grace) with God." From which is to be intimated what man would be capable of even in the state of pure nature. Cf. IIa IIae, q. 26, a. 3, where it is declared that: "We can receive a two-fold good from God, the good of nature and the good of grace. More-over, natural love is based upon the communication of natural goods made to us by God. . . . Hence this is much more truly evident in the friendship of charity, which is based upon the communication of the gifts of grace." Again in the reply to the second objection: "Any part loves the good of the whole according as it is becoming to itself, not however in such a way as to refer the good of the whole to itself, but rather so as to refer itself to the good of the whole." And in reply to the third objection: "We love God more with a love of friendship than with a love of concupiscence, for the good of God is *in se* greater than the good which we can share by enjoying Him." And thus, ab-solutely, man loves God more in charity than himself. And he loves the God who is to be seen more than the beatific vision or the created joy following upon this vision. Thus, it may be said (IIa IIae, q. 17, a. 6 ad 3): "Charity (inasmuch as it surpasses hope) properly causes a tending toward God, uniting the affections of a man with God, so that man does not live for himself but for God." This is pure love properly understood, that is, above hope; but not excluding hope, as the Quietists would have it.

Doubt. Whether in the state of pure nature man would be able to love God the author of nature, above all things, with a natural love.

Reply. Thomists generally reply in the affirmative.

1. On account of the universality of the principle invoked by St. Thomas (Ia, q. 60, a. 5, and in the present article): "Every creature according to its being as such, is of God, and therefore it loves God with a natural love more than self." This principle is valid for any natural state in which there is no disorder. But in the state of pure nature there would be no disorder.

2. In *Quodl.*, I, a. 8, St. Thomas enunciates the principle of our article in a very comprehensive way, so that it would be valid for any natural state in which there is no perversion.

3. Since it is said (Ia, q. 60, a. 5) that, "if (man) were to love him-self naturally more than God, it would follow that natural love would be perverse, and that it would not be perfected by charity but de-stroyed." But this natural love would not be perverse in the state of pure nature. Therefore.

4. Since man in the state of pure nature would not be born, as now,

habitually averse to his final supernatural end directly and to his final natural end indirectly. There would be no aversion to the final natural end, but the possibility of conversion or aversion.

Corollary. Man has less powers in the state of fallen nature for naturally doing what is morally good than he would have in the state of pure nature. This is contested by several authors of the Society of Jesus.

II. CONFIRMATION OF THIS DOCTRINE OF ST. THOMAS FROM
THE CONDEMNATION OF BAIUS (cf. Denz., nos.
1034, 1036, 1038) AND QUESNEL (Denz.,
nos. 1394-95) [5]

The entire solution may be reduced to the following:

The love of God above all things
{
(supernatural) is impossible without grace in any state.
(natural) is possible without grace in the state of integral nature and also in the state of pure nature, but not in the state of corrupt nature.
}

Hence it must be firmly maintained that the natural love of God above all things is the supreme precept of the natural law, and with still greater reason does this hold in the supernatural order, as it was already formulated in Deut. 6:5: "Thou shalt love the Lord thy God with thy whole heart"; but there it was proclaimed as a law of the supernatural order as well, as also in Matt. 22:27, Mark 12:30, Luke 10:27. But the natural law is neither abolished by sin nor given by grace, since it is naturally stamped upon creatures.

III. CONTROVERSIES AMONG MODERN THEOLOGIANS ON THIS SUBJECT

The controversy is twofold, first on natural love and secondly on supernatural love. The first problem is whether fallen man can, without repairing grace, love God the author of nature above all things with a love that is affectively efficacious. (Cf. Billuart, *De gratia*, diss. III, a. 3.) The second problem is whether the act of the love of God, author of grace, considered substantially, is impossible without grace.

---

[5] The excess of Jansenism is found to a certain extent in the argument proposed by Pascal as "the wager," in which he says: a choice must be made between the Christian life which is set before us as the way to heaven, and the life of the libertine which is said to be the way of damnation. Some might add a third alternative: natural virtue. But in practice, the argument proposed by Pascal holds good, since the fullness of natural virtue is not present in fallen nature without grace.

Molina denies this. First of all the terminology must be explained as follows:

> **Natural love**
>
> - **innate;** before any knowledge whatever it is the faculty of the will which naturally is inclined to love God, author of nature, above all things (Ia, q. 60, a. 5).
> - **elicited**
>   - **necessary:** the love of happiness in general, by which God is loved in a somewhat confused way, but not really distinctly above all things.
>   - **free (in regard to God distinctly known as the highest good)**
>   - **inefficacious:** simple complacency in the goodness of God, not employing the means of pleasing God or withdrawing from mortal sin.
>   - **efficacious (by force of the means put forth)**
>   - **affectively:** simple act of love of God above all things with the intention of pleasing Him in all things and withdrawing from mortal sin.
>   - **effectively:** practice of the aforesaid intention by the actual observance of the natural law.

1. It is certainly true that without grace there can be: a) an innate love or natural inclination to love God above all things; this is the faculty of the will itself; b) a necessary, elicited love of God vaguely loved in happiness in general, which all desire; in this case God is not loved above all things, since He is not considered as distinct from all other goods; c) a free inefficacious love, or simple complacency in the goodness of God, not going so far as to adopt means of pleasing God nor of withdrawing from mortal sin, for which natural concurrence would be adequate. Thus many poets have written beautiful poems on the goodness and wisdom of God, ruler of the world, but without the intention of reforming their voluptuous lives.

2. We shall see in the following article that effectively efficacious love, at least absolutely, or the practice of all the commands of the natural law which are gravely obligatory, cannot now be possessed without a special healing grace.

3. The controversy, therefore, concerns affectively efficacious love, by which God, author of nature, distinctly known, is loved with esteem above all things, with the intention of pleasing Him in all things and of withdrawing from mortal sins against the natural law.

Thomists maintain that this affectively efficacious love cannot exist in fallen man without healing grace.[6] And in this regard they differ especially from Molina, who teaches that fallen man can, by his natural powers, thus love God, the author of nature, with an affectively efficacious love, and even, after having been instructed in the teaching of faith, can, likewise by his natural powers, love God as author of grace substantially, although not in respect to supernaturalness of mode, which is bestowed by charity.[7] Molina adds to this that the affectively efficacious natural love of God, author of nature, is not meritorious of grace (that would be Semi-Pelagianism) but, on account of the covenant between God and Christ the Redeemer, if man thus does what in him lies through his natural powers, God will not refuse sanctifying grace.[8] With still greater reason, for Molina, if anyone imbued with the doctrine of faith undertakes an act, natural substantially, of affectively efficacious love of God, author of grace, God infuses charity, and this love become supernatural in respect to mode and thus available for salvation. Scotus, Gabriel, and certain others are cited as holding the same opinion.

Against the first of these teachings of Molina on the possibility of an affectively efficacious love of God, author of nature, above all things without grace, Thomists declare that: 1. This doctrine does not seem to preserve sufficiently the sense of the words of the Council of Orange (can. 25; Denz., no. 199): "We must believe that by the sin of the first man free will was so inclined and weakened that no one subsequently is able either to love God as he ought, . . . or to do for the sake of God what is good, unless the grace of mercy anticipates him." The Molinists reply that the Council says, "as he ought with regard

[6] It is a question of the consequent power. Cf. Salmanticenses, De gratia, disp. II, dub. IV, no. 135, where other important Thomists are quoted; cf. also John of St. Thomas, Gonet, Billuart.

[7] Cf. Molina, Concordia, Paris ed., 1876, pp. 31, 34, 68 ff., 73, 255.

[8] Ibid., pp. 43, 73, 564.

to salvation," and hence refers only to supernatural love. To this the Thomists answer that the Council is not referring to supernatural love alone, since it repeats that the impotence to love God above all things arises not from the supernaturalness of the act but from the infirmity of fallen nature; therefore it refers to natural love as well, since the impotence arising from the supernaturalness of the act was already present in the state of innocence. This also seems to be the meaning of the Council of Trent (Sess. VI, can. 3; Denz., no. 813): "If anyone should say that without the inspiration of the Holy Ghost and His assistance man can believe, hope, love, or repent as is required in order that the grace of justification should be granted to him, let him be anathema."

Nevertheless, the Thomists add, it is not possible for the grace of justification not to be conferred upon one who loves God, the author of nature, above all things with an affectively efficacious love. (Cf. below, q. 109, a. 6, on whether man, without grace, can prepare himself for grace, and q. 112, a. 3.)

Moreover, the aforesaid teaching of Molina is contrary to the final proposition of the body of the present article of St. Thomas, where he contrasts the state of fallen nature with that of integral nature: "In the state of corrupt nature, man requires the help of grace healing nature, even for loving God naturally above all things." There is no doubt but that St. Thomas is speaking also of affectively efficacious natural love, that is, with the intention of pleasing God in all things and of withdrawing from mortal sin. This is confirmed by what has been said above (Ia IIae, q. 89, a. 6): "When man begins to have the use of reason . . . (he should) deliberate concerning himself. And if anyone orders his life toward the proper end (that is, to God even as author of nature), he will obtain the remission of original sin by grace. In the present article St. Thomas is not yet speaking of effectively efficacious love, that is, of the fulfillment of every natural precept; but he refers to it in the following article.

Finally, the opinion of Molina is thus refuted by theological argument: A weak power, inclined to selfish good opposed to the divine, cannot produce the superior act of a healthy power with reference to God, unless it is healed. But man in the state of fallen nature has a weak will, inclined to a selfish good. Therefore he cannot produce a pre-eminent work with reference to God. This act is pre-eminently that of a healthy power, since it virtually contains the fulfillment of the whole natural law, for the actual accomplishment of the law follows from the efficacious will to fulfill it. Hence grace is necessary not only for the actual observance of the whole natural law, but also for the intention of fulfilling it. Nor is the efficacious natural volition granted for accomplishing anything which is now naturally impossible.

This weakness of the will consists in its "following a selfish good unless healed by the grace of God," as stated in the article. In other words, it is turned away from God and even its natural final end; for sin offends God even as author of nature. Moreover, it is a disorder of the concupiscence which the demon augments and enkindles.

First doubt. What, then, of the natural love of God in the separated souls of children who die without baptism, of whom St. Thomas speaks (IIa, d. 33, q. 2, a. 2 ad 5)?

Reply. There is, first of all, an innate love and a necessary, elicited love of God, confusedly, as in happiness in general, for this love remains even in the demons (Ia, q. 60, a. 5 ad 5). Secondly, there is a free, imperfect, inefficacious love, or love of complacency, toward God as principle of all natural good, but not really an efficacious love. Otherwise we should have to deny the last proposition in the body of the present article.

In this connection it seems that, as stated in a. 2 ad 3, "Nature is more corrupted in regard to the appetite for good than in regard to the knowledge of the truth." For the mind of fallen man is able by its own powers to judge speculatively that God is the highest good, lovable and worthy of love above all things; but without healing grace, he is incapable of recognizing this with his practical judgment, impelling him to action. Hence the words of Medea spoken of by the poet: "I see what is better, and I approve it (speculatively), but I follow what is worse." Man, then, is more deeply wounded in his will by which he sins than in his intellect. If, therefore, a child, reaching the full use of reason, loves God, the author of nature, above all things with an affectively efficacious love, this can only be by means of healing grace.

Objection. Fallen man can, without grace, love his country, or his friend, or his chastity more than his own life; therefore, with still greater reason can he so love God, the author of nature.

Reply. I reply by distinguishing the antecedent: fallen man does this without the special help of God, if it is done from a worldly motive, such as the desire for fame or glory, granted; but if from the pure motive of virtue, denied; for this requires the special help of God, as conceded to many pagans, according to Augustine. Moreover it is more difficult to love God, the author of nature, above all things in a manner that is affectively efficacious than to love the attractiveness of any particular virtue more than one's life; for this is, at least virtually, to love all the virtues beyond all sensible feelings. This is more difficult; for instance that a soldier, ready to die for his country, is not willing to spare his enemy when he should.

Second doubt. What grace is required for this affectively efficacious love of God, author of nature above all things?

Reply. Of itself, by reason of its object, it requires only help of a natural order, but accidentally and indirectly, by reason of the elevation of the human race to the supernatural order, it requires supernatural help, that is, healing grace (as declared in the article). This is because the aversion to a final natural end cannot be cured without the aversion to a final supernatural end being cured; for this latter contains indirectly an aversion to the final natural end, for every sin against the supernatural law is indirectly against the natural law: God is to be obeyed, whatever He may command. Moreover, as we shall state in the following article, the love of God virtually includes the fulfillment of the whole natural law, for which supernatural healing grace is required.

The Thomists also reject the other opinion of Molina, that man imbued with the teaching of faith can without grace love God, the author of grace, in respect to the substance of this act, although not in respect to its mode as proper to salvation. Contrary to this, the Thomists generally hold, as for the act of faith, that the act is specified by its formal object; but the formal object of the aforesaid act is God, the author of grace; therefore this act is essentially supernatural, or supernatural in respect to substance and not merely in respect to mode (cf. Salmanticenses, *De Gratia,* disp. III, dub. III; and our *De revelatione,* I, 498, 511). A natural act in respect to substance would be an act specified by a natural object, such as an act of acquired temperance, which might yet become supernatural in respect to mode, according as it is commanded by charity and ordered by it to the reward of eternal life.

ARTICLE IV. WHETHER MAN, WITHOUT GRACE, BY HIS NATURAL POWERS,
CAN FULFILL THE PRECEPTS OF THE NATURAL LAW

State of the question. In this article, as is evident in the body, we are especially concerned with the precepts of the decalogue which already belong to the natural law and can substantially be fulfilled without charity; indeed, even the acts of faith and hope can be accomplished in the state of mortal sin. Let us examine:

1. St. Thomas' conclusions and arguments;
2. How they are based on Holy Scripture and tradition;
3. The refutation of the objections. (The article should be read.)

I. ST. THOMAS' CONCLUSIONS

His first conclusion is that in the state of corrupt nature, man cannot, without healing grace, fulfill all the precepts of the natural law with respect to the substance of the works, while on the contrary he would be able to do this without grace in the state of integral nature (supposing, however, natural concurrence). From these last words, which are found in St. Thomas, it is evident that he is concerned in this instance with the precepts of the natural law in respect to the substance of the works, for the substance of a work correlative with a supernatural precept is supernatural and cannot, even in the state of integral nature, be produced without grace. In fact, precepts are called supernatural because they enjoin acts which surpass the powers of nature. In article two it is stated that "grace was necessary to man in the state of integral nature in order to perform or will a supernatural work."

The argument supporting this conclusion is the same as in the preceding article for the impossibility of loving God, author of nature, with an affectively efficacious love; indeed the argument now holds with still greater reason, that is, in the case of effectively efficacious love or the fulfillment of all the precepts of the natural law.

In other words, a weak man cannot of himself perform the very superior work of a healthy man, unless he is first cured. Nor can a will turned away from even its natural final end be properly oriented in regard to all the means to that end. It would be rash to deny this first conclusion or to maintain that effectively efficacious love of God, author of nature, above all things can be attained without grace. This is conceded by the Molinists.[9] It would be rash because the Council of Orange (Denz., nos. 181 ff., 199) refers not only to impotence arising from the supernaturalness of the work, but from the weakness of fallen nature.

The second conclusion is that in no state can man without grace fulfill the commands of the law with respect to the mode of acting, that is, performing them from charity. This is of faith. St. Thomas makes the assertion without proof, for he has already said, in article two, that man even in the state of incorrupt nature required "grace added to nature in order to perform or will supernatural good," and particularly to elicit a supernatural act of charity. For acts are specified by their objects and therefore the act specified by a supernatural object is essentially supernatural.

II. THE BASES OF TRADITION

They are as indicated by Billuart, in addition to many texts of St. Augustine.

1. *The Council of Milevum* (Denz., no. 105), against the Pelagians who declared that without grace man can keep all the commandments of God, but with difficulty; with grace, however, he can do so with facility; it is defined that "if anyone should say . . . that grace . . . is given to us that we may more easily fulfill the divine commands, and . . . that, without it, we are able to fulfill them, although not easily, let him be anathema." From this it is deduced that the commandments of God cannot be fulfilled as is necessary for salvation, that is, from charity, without grace.

St. Augustine always defends this truth against the Pelagians in his *De spiritu et littera, De gratia Christi, De libero arbitrio;* in the book *De haeresibus* (heresy 88), speaking of the Pelagians, he says: "They are such enemies of the grace of God that they believe a man can accomplish all the divine commands without it." Likewise, St. Augustine on Ps. 118, conc. 5, and in Sermon 148 (*de tempore*), chap. 5, where he is concerned with the precepts of the decalogue.

The opposite error in Baius (Denz., nos. 1061, 1062) was condemned because it rejects the distinction between fulfilling the commandments in respect to substance and in respect to mode, supernaturally.

[9] St. Thomas' first conclusion on the necessity of grace to fulfill substantially all the precepts of the natural law is commonly accepted by theologians, although it was formerly denied by Scotus (II, d.28, a.1), Gabriele, and Durandus; to deny it would be rash or erroneous and savors of Pelagianism. Cf. Hugon, *De gratia,* p. 259.

2. *The Council of Orange* (II, c. 25; Denz., no. 199) declared: "We must believe that through the sin of the first man free will was so inclined and weakened, that no one has since . . . been able to perform what is good for the sake of God unless the grace of divine mercy precedes him." Hence St. Thomas' second conclusion is of faith; that is, without grace, men cannot fulfill the commandments with respect to supernaturalness of mode, namely, so as to be performed out of charity. And the Molinists admit this.

Doubt. Whether grace is necessary for the fulfilling of any supernatural precept, in respect to its substance. Herein lies the controversy with the Molinists. Scotus and the Molinists hold that without grace men imbued with the teaching of faith can fulfill, substantially, even interior works correlative to the supernatural precepts of faith, hope, and charity.

Reply. The Thomists reply that it is not possible, since precepts are called supernatural because they enjoin acts which, in themselves, essentially surpass the powers of nature, and these acts are such, in fact, because they are specified by a supernatural formal object. Thus, for example, an act of Christian faith differs from an act of acquired temperance.

Insistance by Molina, Lugo, and Billot, that diversity of the activating principles (that is, of habits) alone is sufficient to cause acts to differ in species, even when they attain the same formal object.

Reply. 1. These very activating principles, that is, habits and powers, should be specified by the formal object. 2. The Salmanticenses reply (*De gratia,* disp. III, dub. III, no. 60): "I deny the antecedent, for if it were true, as our adversaries contend, nothing in true philosophy but would waver (or be overturned) in regard to species and the distinction of powers and habits; we should be compelled to establish new bases such as were not taught by Aristotle, Master Thomas, or the leaders of other schools. Although younger writers would easily grant this, we should have no leader from among the ancients. The result would indeed be to the highest detriment of true wisdom; wherefore it is essential in this respect to hinder their proclivity with all our powers." Cf. other texts of the Salmanticenses quoted in our *De revelatione,* I, 495.

To the same effect Thomas de Lemos, O.P., replied in the celebrated discussions of the Congregatio de Auxiliis, on May 7 and 28, 1604, before Clement VIII (cf. *De revelatione,* I, 491). He challenged

the opinion of Molina in the following words: "By which system he
would overturn faith as well as philosophy; faith, certainly, because
thus God is feared and loved by the powers of nature, as the end is
supernatural; philosophy indeed since, in this way, the formal object of a superior habit is attained by the inferior powers." And on
May 28, 1604, session 54 settled a problem proposed according to the
interpretation of the Thomists explained by Lemos. Lemos expresses
the same opinion in his *Panoplia gratiae* at the beginning of Bk. IV,
nos. 24 f. (Cf. *De revelatione,* I, 491; Del Prado, *De gratia,* I, 48;
Suarez expresses agreement with us in *De gratia,* Bk. II, c. 11, nos.
22 f., quoted in *De revelatione, ibid.*) Thus Suarez, as well as Lemos
and the Salmanticenses considers it rash to deny the aforesaid traditional teaching of theologians. In respect to this matter many Jesuits
follow Suarez, including the Würzburg school (*De virtutibus theologicis,* disp. II, c. III, a. 3); Bellarmine is also cited and, among more
recent writers, Wilmers (*De fide divina,* 1902, pp. 352, 358, 375);
Mazzella, in the first two editions of *De virtutibus infusis,* and Pesch
(*De gratia,* nos. 69, 71, 410).

Objection. The Molinists object, referring to Ia IIae, q. 54, a. 2,
where it is stated that "the species of habits are distinguished in
three ways: 1. according to the activating principles of such dispositions, 2. according to nature, 3. according to objects." Therefore, declare the Molinists, habits are not specified only by their objects.

Reply. All of these are to be taken together and not separately.
An act cannot be essentially supernatural from the standpoint of its
eliciting principle and according as it presupposes habitual grace unless it is at the same time supernatural from the standpoint of its object. Moreover, we contend in *De revelatione,* I, 506, in agreement
with the Salmanticenses and other Thomists, that from St. Thomas'
context it is clearly evident that, when he says habits are specified
according to their active principles, he means according to their objective, regulating, specifying principles; for he says in the answer to
the second objection of the same article: "The various means (of
knowledge) are like various active principles according to which the
habits of science are differentiated." And in answer to the third objection: "Diversity of ends differentiates virtues as diversity of active
principles" or motives according as the end is the object of a prior
act of the will, in other words, the intention.

Similarly in Ia IIae, q. 51, a. 3, St. Thomas shows that the regulat-

ing reason is the active principle of the moral virtues, and the understanding of principles is the principle of knowledge, that is, as
proposing the formal object (*objectum formale quo*) or motive. Moreover, when he says that habits are specified according to nature, this
is according as the habit is good or bad, suitable or not suitable to the
nature; or according as it is suitable to human nature as such, or suitable to the divine nature in which man participates; but it cannot be of
itself suitable to a higher nature, unless at the same time it has a formal
object proportionate or of the same order; otherwise it would be an
accidentally infused habit, such as infused geometry. Father Ledochowski, General of the Society of Jesus, further acknowledges that
the teaching of Molina we are discussing is not that of St. Thomas (cf.
De revelatione, I, 489).

III. REFUTATION OF THE PRINCIPAL OBJECTIONS AGAINST THE
NECESSITY OF GRACE FOR OBSERVING SUBSTANTIALLY
ALL THE PRECEPTS OF THE NATURAL LAW

The first classical difficulty is indicated by St. Thomas in the first
objection, taken from the text of St. Paul to the Romans (2:14):
"The Gentiles who have not the (written) law, do by nature those
things which are of the law."

Reply. According to St. Augustine, followed by St. Prosper, St.
Fulgentius, and by St. Thomas here in his refutation, these words
are to be understood of the Gentiles acting from grace; and then "by
nature" is not interpreted according as it is opposed to grace, and
according as it is equivalent to "the powers of nature," but according
as it is opposed to the Mosaic law, so that the meaning is: "The Gentiles who have not the written law, do naturally those things which
are of the law," in other words, without the law of Moses, but not
without the spirit of grace. Thus Augustine in *De spiritu et littera,*
Bk. I, c. 27, quoted here by St. Thomas; likewise St. Chrysostom.[10]
But other interpreters understand this of the infidel Gentiles and
hence "by nature" of the powers of nature; but this disposes of the

---

[10] St. Chrysostom, in his fifth homily on the Epistle to the Romans, declares: "The
Apostle refers not to the idolatrous Greeks but to those who by worshiping God and
obeying the natural law, practiced all those things that pertain to piety, even prior to
the Jewish observances; such were those who lived with Melchisedech, such was Job,
such were the Ninivites, such finally was Cornelius." St. Chrysostom, in his thirteenth
homily on the same Epistle, commenting on the words "miserable man that I am,"
teaches that the law without grace does not suffice.

objection just as well, for the meaning is that the Gentiles by their own natural powers perform certain works of the law, but not all.

The second difficulty is as follows: if the observance of the whole natural law, in respect to the substance of the works, is impossible to fallen nature, then the Jansenist heresy follows logically, that is, that certain of the precepts of God are impossible to fallen man. Luther and Calvin held the same opinion.

Reply. "What we can do with divine assistance is not altogether impossible for us"; and we avoid Jansenism by declaring that the grace necessary to accomplish the commandments is not wanting to anyone except by reason of his own fault. All adults receive graces at least remotely sufficient for salvation, and if they did not resist them, they would obtain further graces. The error of Luther and Calvin is apparent from this: according to them, Christ did not come to form observers of the law, but to redeem the faithful from the obligation of observing the law, in accordance with Luther's words: "Sin strongly and believe more strongly," in other words, believe firmly that you are freely elect, and you are saved, even if you persevere in crimes and the transgression of the law until death.

The Jansenists erred similarly by maintaining that certain commands of God are impossible not only to fallen man, but even to the just man. This is manifest from the first proposition of Jansen (Denz., no. 1092): "Other precepts of God are impossible to just, willing, zealous men with the powers which they now possess; they also lack the grace which would make them possible"; in 1653 this was condemned as heretical.

The Council of Trent had previously defined (Denz., no. 804): "God does not command the impossible, but by commanding He urges you both to do what you can and to ask what you cannot, and He assists you that you may be able." Also in the corresponding canon (Denz., no. 828). The foregoing words of the Council are taken from St. Augustine, and, according to them, sufficient grace to pray is never wanting, and by it man has at least the remote power of observing the divine precepts, for "by commanding, God urges you to do what you can and to ask what you cannot, and He assists you that you may be able."

I insist. God cannot demand that a blind man see, although he may see by a miracle; therefore, neither can He demand that fallen man observe the law, although he may do so by means of grace.

Reply. The disparity lies particularly in the fact that the blind man is not offered a miracle which would cure him; but fallen man is offered grace by which he may observe the law, and he would receive it if he did not voluntarily set obstacles in the way. Hence one must pray as did Augustine, saying: "Lord, grant what Thou commandest and command what Thou wilt," that is, give us grace to fulfill Thy commands and command what Thou wilt.

First doubt. Which grace is required by fallen man for the keeping of the whole natural law?

Reply. As in the explanation of the preceding article: of itself, by reason of its object, help of the natural order would suffice, since the object is natural. Accidentally, however, and by reason of the elevation of the human race to a supernatural end, supernatural grace is required, which under this aspect is called healing grace. This is because in the present economy of salvation man cannot be converted to God, his final natural end, and remain estranged from God, his supernatural end, since this aversion is indirectly opposed to the natural law, according to which we ought to obey God, whatever He may command.

Second doubt. To observe the whole natural law for a long time is supernatural actual grace sufficient, or is habitual grace required?

Reply. According to ordinary providence, habitual grace is required, by which alone man is solidly well disposed toward his final end. And this firm disposition toward his final end is itself required that man may keep the whole natural law enduringly and perseveringly. Nevertheless, by an extraordinary providence, God can fortify a man's will in regard to the observance of all the natural precepts by means of continuous actual graces; but if a man does what lies within his power by the help of actual grace, God will not withhold habitual grace from him. As we shall see below (a. 9), over and above habitual grace, actual grace is required for the just man to perform any supernatural good work, and even to persevere for long in the observance of the whole natural law, in spite of the rebellion of the sense appetites against reason, and the temptations of the world and the devil.

Third doubt. Whether in the state of pure nature man would be able to observe enduringly the whole natural law without special help of the natural order.

Reply. I reply in the negative with Billuart: Since to do so demands constancy of the will in good against the temptations that arise, a constancy which man established in the state of pure nature would not have had, of himself, with the aid of ordinary concurrence alone; hence, to persevere he would have had need of special natural help which God would have given to many, but not to those in whom He would have permitted the sin of impenitence of this natural order in punishment for preceding sins.

Cajetan's opinion. In his commentary on the present article, which preceded the disputes aroused by Molina, at a time when the terminology of this subject was not yet fully established, Cajetan spoke less accurately in explaining the answer to the third objection. He says, "man, by nature, can believe, hope, love God, with respect to the substance of the act," and he cites the example of a formal heretic who adheres to certain dogmas. He expresses himself similarly in regard to IIa IIae, q. 171, a. 2 ad 3. But it is evident from the context and from this example that Cajetan is referring to the generic substance of the acts, not to the specific substance, not to the formal object itself (*objectum formale quod et quo*); for a heretic believes formally, not by divine, but by human faith.

Later Cajetan corrects his terminology (commenting on IIa IIae, q. 6, a. 1, no. 3), declaring that "it should be said, therefore, that the act of faith springs forth as a result of no natural knowledge, of no natural appetite, but from the appetite for eternal beatitude and from an adherence to God supernaturally revealing and preserving His Church." Cajetan likewise defends the common opinion of Thomists against Scotus and Durandus (Ia IIae, q. 51, a. 4): "Infused habits are of themselves essentially supernatural." Also, q. 62, a. 3; q. 63, a. 6, and IIa IIae, q. 17, a. 5, no. 1, where he defends the opinion that without infused virtue there would be no act "proportionate to the supernatural object," nor to the supernatural end. (Cf. Del Prado, *De gratia*, I, 50 and our *De revelatione*, I, 484 f., note 1.)

ARTICLE V. WHETHER MAN CAN MERIT ETERNAL LIFE WITHOUT GRACE

After considering the observance of the divine commands in themselves, St. Thomas considers it in relation to eternal life. The question is here posed generally and indefinitely; later, in q. 114, a. 1, 2, 3, where he is dealing with merit properly speaking, the question will be more particularly treated as to whether man without grace can merit *de condigno* eternal life. The answer is negative and is of faith, against the Pelagians.

1. It is proved from authority in the argument *Sed contra* (Rom. 6:23): "the grace of God life eternal," which is thus explained by Augustine, here quoted: "that it may be understood that God, in His compassion, leads us unto eternal life." St. Augustine is also quoted in the answer to the second objection. (Cf. Council of Orange, II, can. 7, Denz., no. 180; and Trent, Sess. VI, can. 2, Denz., no. 812.)

2. It is thus proved by theological reasons: Acts leading to an end must be proportionate to the end. But eternal life is an end exceeding the proportion of human nature (cf. Ia IIae, q. 5, a. 5, on supernatural beatitude). Therefore man cannot by his natural powers produce works meritorious of eternal life. Read the answer to the third objection with respect to the distinction between final natural end and supernatural end (cf. *Contra Gentes,* Bk. III, chap. 147, and *De veritate,* q. 14, a. 2). These references are clear, and whatever is to be said on this subject is reserved for consideration in q. 114, a. 1 and 2, that is, whether man can merit anything *de condigno,* and so merit eternal life.

ARTICLE VI. WHETHER MAN CAN PREPARE HIMSELF FOR GRACE BY HIMSELF WITHOUT THE EXTERIOR HELP OF GRACE

State of the question. The external help of grace with which we are here concerned, is not only the preaching of the gospel itself, confirmed by miracles (the Pelagians admitted this), nor is it only the natural concurrence of God for the performance of a naturally good act, the necessity of which the Semi-Pelagians did not deny, but, as the body of the article explains, it refers to actual supernatural help.

That the difficulty of this question may be more manifest, St. Thomas considers the following. 1. The arguments maintained by the Pelagians or Semi-Pelagians, namely· it seems that without actual grace man can prepare himself for habitual grace, for, we read (Zach. 1:3): "Turn ye to Me . and I will turn to you." 2. It is frequently said. "To him who does what he can, God does not deny grace"; and (Luke 11:13): "If you then, being evil, know how to give good gifts to your children, how much more will your Father from heaven give the good Spirit to them that ask Him?" 3. It would be an infinite process, since to prepare himself for a prior grace, man would require another, and so on *ad infinitum*. 4. In the Book of Proverbs (16:1) it is said that "it is the part of man to prepare the soul," according to the Vulgate; but in many codices this verse is lacking and in the Greek codices in which it occurs, the sense is: "It is the part of man to form a proposal in his heart," as if to say: man proposes and God disposes.

On the other hand we find in the Gospel according to St. John (6:44): "No man can come to me, except the Father, who hath sent Me, draw him." How are these quotations to be reconciled? Let us examine 1. The errors on this subject which have been condemned; 2. the disagreement among Catholic theologians; and 3. the opinion of St. Thomas.

I. The condemned errors. The Pelagians, denying original sin, maintained, at least at the beginning of their heresy, that man by his own powers, without grace, can prepare himself for grace so as to merit the first grace. This was condemned by the Councils of Neo-Caesaria and Milevum (Denz., nos. 104 ff., 133 ff.).

The Semi-Pelagians said that fallen man, without grace, can have of himself the beginning of salvation and can prepare himself for grace, by asking, desiring, knocking, seeking; thus he does not merit grace, but he disposes himself for it by himself alone, and God seizes upon this beginning of salvation as an occasion for conferring grace, otherwise He would be an acceptor of persons if He conferred grace upon one rather than another without any reason on the part of man.[11] This was condemned by the Council of Orange (II, can. 3 and 6, Denz., nos. 176, 179). The same declaration was made by the Council of Trent (Sess. VI, can. 3, Denz., no. 813).

II. Among Catholic theologians, notwithstanding the condemnation of the Semi-Pelagians, Molina, following the lead of Durandus, Scotus, and Gabriel Biel, maintains in his *Concordia* (disp. 10), that if one does what one can by merely natural powers, God never denies actual grace, and at last bestows sanctifying grace; not that man may prepare himself positively for grace, but he prepares himself negatively by not placing obstacles to it and by removing impediments.[12] And in order to avoid Semi-Pelagianism, Molina declares

[11] The Semi-Pelagians held that the preparation for grace could be made naturally in three ways: 1) by positively disposing oneself for grace; 2) by meriting it, at least *de congruo;* or 3) by asking it through prayer.

[12] Molina holds: To him who does what in him lies by his natural powers in easier matters, and by the powers of medicinal grace (which is natural from the standpoint of its being) in more difficult matters, God does not deny actual grace and, eventually,

that God confers actual grace and subsequently habitual grace, not on account of the merit of a natural act, but on account of the covenant between God and Christ from the beginning. Christ indeed presented His merits to the Father, and the Father promises that He will bestow grace upon anyone who does what is possible to his natural powers or who uses well the goods of nature.

III. The doctrine of St. Thomas, as is clear from the last lines of the article and from the answer to the second objection, is that fallen man cannot prepare himself for habitual grace except by the help of prevenient actual grace, and "when it is said that man does what he can, the meaning is that this is within the power of man, as he is moved by God." These words in the answer to the second objection are contrary to the opinion proposed subsequently by Molina. Stated more briefly the thesis of St. Thomas is: Fallen man can in no way dispose himself either for habitual or for actual grace by his natural powers alone.

Scriptural proof. It is proved from the authority of Scripture in the argument *Sed contra:* "No man can come to Me, except the Father, who hath sent Me, draw him" (John 6:44). But if man could prepare himself, there would be no need of his being drawn by another. "Convert us, O Lord, to Thee, and we shall be converted" (Lam. 5:21). See also Jer. 31:18. "The will is prepared by the Lord" (Prov. 8:35, according to the Septuagint, but the Hebrew text is not so clear). St. Augustine here and there puts it forward against the Semi-Pelagians, and it is quoted by the Council of Orange, Denz., no. 177). "Without Me you can do nothing" (John 15:15); therefore neither can one prepare oneself for grace, since that is doing something ordained to salvation. "Who hath first given to Him, and recompense shall be made him? For of Him, and by Him, and in Him, are all things" (Rom. 11:35 f.). According to the contrary opinion a man could reply: I first gave him my effort and disposition. "Who distinguisheth thee?" (I Cor. 4:7.) Man may answer: my striving. "What hast thou that thou hast not received?" (*ibid.*) Man may reply: I have my effort and my disposition. "You have not chosen Me: but I have

---

He grants sanctifying grace, on account of the covenant entered into with Christ. Molina does not give sufficient attention to the fact that man alone, by himself, can set up some obstacle, but he cannot, by himself, avoid setting up an obstacle, for this latter is a good act proceeding from the source of all good: "What hast thou that thou hast not received?"

chosen you" (John 15:16). The Semi-Pelagians would say: I chose Thee first by disposing myself for grace. This text is addressed to the apostles, of course, but in that they are the friends of God, and therefore it also applies to other friends of God.

The Council of Orange (can. 3, Denz., no. 176), according to the obvious meaning of the words, declares that all preparation for grace is of itself prevenient grace; there is no reference to a covenant entered into between God the Father and Christ. Read canons 3, 4, 5. Likewise the Council of Trent (Sess. VI, chap. 5, Denz. 797, and chap. 6).

St. Augustine (*De peccatorum meritis,* Bk. I, chap. 22), especially in the three arguments against the Semi-Pelagians, maintained the following.

1. In the affair of salvation nothing at all must be withdrawn from divine grace; but something would be withdrawn if the disposition for grace were not from grace.

2. The Church prays God not only to help those who will and strive after good, but also that those who will it not be made to will it.

3. It is said in II Cor. 3:5: "Not that we are sufficient to think anything of ourselves, as of ourselves." But the slightest preparation for grace is a good thought. Therefore. Hence the words of Augustine on St. John, at the beginning of tract 26: "Why does God draw this man and not that man? Do not attempt to judge if you do not wish to err."

Theological proof. By theological argument St. Thomas thus proves his thesis in the body of the article in form.

Since every agent acts on account of a proportionate end, the order of agents corresponds to the order of ends, and the disposition toward a supernatural end cannot be produced except by God, the supernatural agent.

But man prepares himself for grace according as he disposes himself for it as for a proximate supernatural end, and according as he turns to God as to his final supernatural end.

Therefore man cannot prepare himself for grace except by the supernatural help of God, moving him. St. Thomas does not fear to repeat this principle often; these repetitions are a kind of leitmotiv in theology, like St. John's often repeated: "Beloved, let us love one another" (I John 4:7).

The major of this argument is based on the principle of finality, not that from this metaphysical principle the dogma may be rationally demonstrated, but that the dogma cannot be contrary to the principle of finality. For the corollary of this principle is: the order of agents corresponds to the order of ends; hence it is necessary that man be converted to his final end by the motion of the prime mover, just as the will of the soldier is directed toward striving for victory by the motion of the leader of the army, and toward following the standard of some battle by the motion of the commander. Moreover, according to this principle, the disposition toward a supernatural end cannot be produced except by a supernatural agent, that is, except by God according as He moves toward something which exceeds all nature created or capable of being created.

The minor of this argument, however, is explained later in more detail, but it is already self-evident (cf. q. 112, a. 3). More briefly, the argument can be stated thus:

Every disposition, whether remote or proximate, should have a certain proportion to the form for which it disposes; otherwise it would not dispose for it.

But merely natural acts have no proportion with supernatural grace; they do not attain to the life of grace nor do they in any way require it.

Therefore man by his own natural powers cannot prepare himself even remotely for grace, without supernatural help; it is not only morally impossible, but physically and absolutely as well.

Confirmation. In order to dispose himself, man would at least need to have a good thought from himself.

But, according to II Cor. 3:5: "Not that we are sufficient to think anything of ourselves, as of ourselves," in the order of salvation.

Hence, with still greater reason, to desire, ask, merit even *de congruo,* or dispose ourselves in any way. For merit *de congruo* already pertains to salvation; it is a right, based on friendship, to a supernatural reward. And if man without grace could pray and thus obtain grace, the first step to salvation would be attributable to nature. Hence this is condemned by the Council of Orange, c. 7.

The whole proof, therefore, is reducible to the infinite distance between the order of nature and the order of grace, since grace as essentially supernatural surpasses the powers and the requirements of any intellectual nature, created or capable of creation. God from all eternity might at any time create angels of greater and ever greater perfection so that they would have an ever loftier natural intelligence and an ever more steadfast will; but never could these superior angels naturally dispose themselves for grace, which is of a higher order.

Thus the imagination may become ever better endowed in its own order but it will never arrive at the dignity of the intellect; thus the sides of a polygon inscribed in a circle may be ever multiplied but, however small each side, it will never be equivalent to a point. With still greater reason, when it is a question of the impossibility of disposing oneself naturally for the life of grace, natural good works can be ever increased, but they will never amount to a disposition proportionate to grace, which is essentially supernatural, whether for man or for any angel capable of being created, and they can always be created with greater perfection, since no limit of possibility can be named which would exhaust divine omnipotence.

How beautiful, how wonderful; how great a light there is in this doctrine! "All bodies, the firmament and the stars, the earth and its kingdoms, are not worth the least of spirits, for it is conscious of all that and of itself; and bodies are conscious of nothing. All bodies and all spirits together and all their productions are not worth the slightest movement of charity, for that is of an infinitely higher order" (Pascal, *Thoughts*).

Confirmation from the refutation of the objections.

First objection. But it is said in Zach. 1:3: "Turn ye to Me . . . and I will turn to you."

Reply. It is indeed prescribed for man that he turn to God freely, but the free will cannot turn to God unless God Himself converts it to Himself, according to the words of Jer. 31:18: "Convert me, and I shall be converted." Likewise Augustine and the Council of Trent (Sess. VI, chap. 6; Denz., no. 797).

Second objection. But it is generally said that to him who does what he can God does not deny grace.

Reply. Contrary to what Molina says, to him who does what he can, with God's help; and it is a question of supernatural help granted through Christ the Redeemer, since the following words of Christ are quoted: "Without Me ye can do nothing." Nor does natural help suffice to produce a disposition which is supernatural in form, since the order of agents should correspond to the order of ends. And God, as author of nature, cannot move one to a supernatural end.

Third objection. But this would be an infinite process, for man would need some grace to prepare himself for grace, and so on indefinitely.

Reply. A disposition is required only for habitual grace, for every form requires a disposition capable of receiving it. But for actual grace a disposition is not required, since a disposition is not necessary for yet another disposition.

Fourth objection. But in Prov. 16:1 it is written: "It is the part of man to prepare the soul and of the Lord to govern the tongue"; and further: "The heart of man disposes the way, but it is the Lord who directs his steps."

Reply. Certainly, because man does this through his free will, but he does not therefore do it without the help of God moving and drawing him. The meaning of Holy Scripture here is that it does not suffice to consider what thou wilt say or do, unless God directs the tongue and the work so that thou mayest succeed. And this is also a very common saying: Man proposes and God disposes. St. Thomas teaches this doctrine in several other places as well. (Cf. *Quodl.*, Ia, a. 7; in *Ep. ad Rom.*, c. 10, lect. 3; III *C. Gentes,* chap. 150; *De verit.*, q. 24, a. 15.)

Doubt. Whether according to St. Thomas, following the doctrine which he maintains in Ia IIae, q. 89, a. 6, to all who arrive at the use of reason sufficient help is given for fulfilling the precept, there and then urgent, of loving God efficaciously above all things.

Reply. The Salmanticenses reply in the affirmative (*In Iam IIae,* q. 89, a. 6, no. 65); God gives efficacious help only to those whom He at the same time decided to justify and with the aforesaid efficacious help He gives them sanctifying grace and explicit faith concerning the things which are necessary as means essential to salvation.

Whether this sufficient help which is then given to all is supernatural. It is at least supernatural modally through the merits of Christ; but it may also be said that it is supernatural substantially since it gives the proximate power of accomplishing an efficacious act of the love of God above all things, beyond the powers of fallen nature. This supernatural help should result in a certain supernatural enlightenment for the intellect and, if man would not resist this enlightenment, he would receive the grace of faith with respect to the things necessary to salvation. (Cf. below, what is said on justification and the salutary but not meritorious acts which precede it; also Billuart, *De gratia,* diss. VII, a. 4, nos. 2, 3.)

It should be remarked that Quesnel's proposition was condemned: "No graces are given except through faith" (Denz., no. 1376); "Faith is the first grace and the source of all the others" (Denz., no. 1377); "The first grace which God grants to the sinner is the remission of sins" (Denz., no. 1378); likewise the Synod of Pistoia was condemned, denying grace preceding good will and faith.

Concerning the Molinist interpretation of the common axiom: "to him who does what he can, God does not refuse grace." Cf. *Concordia,* disp. X, latest edition, Paris, pp. 43 and 564: "God always confers the helps of prevenient grace on him who strives with natural powers to accomplish what in him lies." Molina, as we have said, maintained that: to him who does what he can by his natural powers alone, God never denies actual grace, and later He gives habitual grace. To avoid Semi-Pelagianism, he continues, 1. claiming that this is done not on account of the value of a natural good work, but for the sake of a convenant entered into between God and Christ the Redeemer, a covenant for thus certainly conferring grace; and 2. claiming that man thus naturally prepares himself negatively only, that is, by not raising obstacles, not sinning at least for some little time; but always, or as it were infallibly, actual grace is then conferred upon him.

What is to be thought of this covenant and of this natural, negative preparation? In regard to the covenant, we may say with the Thomists that it lacks a basis in tradition; on the contrary, it seems to be opposed to the testimony of tradition and to the principles of sound theology.

1. This pact has no basis either in Scripture or in the councils or in the Fathers. Hence it is clearly fictitious. Certainly the Council of Orange does not speak of it, although it would have been most useful for recalling the Semi-Pelagians to the faith, had this theory been true. The Semi-Pelagians would very easily have admitted it, since they did not deny Redemption through Christ nor did they deny that the primary grace was conferred on account of the merits of Christ upon those who prepared themselves naturally for it. The Semi-Pelagians did not contend that the primary grace was given on account of natural merit, but by the occasion of natural good works. Neither does Pius IX (Denz., nos. 1648, 1677) refer to this covenant.[13]

[13] Pius IX declares (Denz., no. 1677): "Those who labor under invincible ignorance in regard to our most holy religion, and who observe conscientiously (this presupposes

As a matter of fact, Valentia, S.J., attempted to demonstrate this pact at the Congregatio de Auxiliis from Augustine (*The City of God,* Bk. XIX, chap. 13) but to obtain this proof, in reading the text of Augustine he changed the particle *scilicet* to *et*. Immediately, however, Thomas de Lemos, recognizing the text of Augustine, replied: "The text is not being rendered correctly," and taking up Augustine's book he read the text as it was. (Cf. Billuart, d. III, a. 7, and Serry, *Histoire de la Congregatio de Auxiliis,* Bk. III, chap. 5.) It is said in Scripture and tradition only that God wills the salvation of all men, that Christ died for all, and that, accordingly, graces sufficient for salvation are conferred upon all adults.

2. Not only is this covenant not affirmed by tradition, but it seems to be contrary to the Council of Orange (can. 6, Denz., no. 179) which condemned anyone who should say that, "Without the grace of God, mercy is bestowed upon those who believe, will and desire it." But supposing the aforesaid covenant, the mercy of Christ and of God would thus be conferred upon men naturally desiring it. (Likewise can. 4.) [14]

3. This pact is opposed to the teaching of Augustine, who declared against the Pelagians (*De peccatorum meritis,* Bk. I, chap. 22) that there are among infidels and sinners some who observe many precepts of the law and are less wicked, more modest, temperate, and merciful, and yet grace passes them by and converts the most infamous; in other words, those who are converted are not always those who do more naturally good works. Moreover, according to St. Augustine, the judgment of God is inscrutable, for He draws one and does not draw another; as he says in regard to St. John (at the begin-

---

the help of grace) the natural law whose precepts are inscribed by God in all hearts, and are ready to obey God, can lead an honorable, righteous life, by virtue of the operation of divine light and grace, and arrive at eternal life." Pius IX has no recourse to the Molinistic pact, but speaks as does St. Thomas.

[14] According to the Council of Orange (can. 4, Denz., no. 177): "If anyone maintains that God waits upon our will in order to cleanse us from sin, and does not rather acknowledge that even our willing to be cleansed is brought about in us through the infusion and operation of the Holy Ghost, such a one is resisting the same Holy Ghost." And yet, according to Molina's theory, God waits upon our will, that is, our natural effort, which He foresees by *scientia media,* and which is produced simultaneously with only the concurrence of God, before the conferring of prevenient actual grace. Thus this natural effort precedes prevenient grace itself, and thus it seems to be the first step to salvation, which is therefore natural. On the contrary, it is God who knocks first, according to the words of the Apocalypse (3:20): "I stand at the gate and knock."

ning of tract 26) : "Why does He draw this man and not that one? Do not attempt to judge if you do not wish to err." St. Thomas refers to this in Ia, q. 23, a. 5 ad 3. But assuming the existence of the aforesaid covenant and the resulting law, God's judgment would not be inscrutable, rather could it be easily explained, for indeed God draws this man and not another because this one does what he can by his own powers and the other does not.

4. This pact seems to be contrary to the principles of sound theology based on revelation. For, according to this hypothesis, man would have something of himself to distinguish him, in which he would glory, in other words, something ordained to salvation he would not receive from God, namely, a good work of nature which, according to the law established, would lead to salvation, and to which grace would infallibly be attached.

Hence it is incompatible that Christ should merit the establishment of this law on the part of God the father, by which the reason for grace would be destroyed. For if this pact were formed and this law established, grace would be given on account of works, and thus would no longer be grace, prevenient grace would be anticipated by the free will, the first place would be given to man, the last place to God, and thus the doctrine of grace defended by St. Augustine would be overthrown. With this law in effect, a natural good work possesses some proportion and some right to the help of grace. All these suppositions seem to be contrary to the words of St. Paul (I Cor. 4:7): "Who distinguisheth thee? Or what hast thou that thou hast not received? And if thou hast received, why dost thou glory, as if thou hadst not received it?"

Particularly opposed to these words is the teaching of Molina which holds that man thus naturally disposes himself for grace with the aid of simultaneous natural concurrence only determinable by human liberty alone. But this doctrine is not very much developed by admitting general, indifferent premotion, ultimately determinable by man alone, since one man would thus distinguish himself from another who was not converted. Moreover, as we have said, intrinsically efficacious, predetermining premotion of a natural order does not suffice as a preparation for grace; the supernatural help of grace is required, because the order of agents should correspond to the order of ends. Here indeed the end, whether proximate (grace) or remote (glory), is supernatural.

It is therefore not to be wondered at that the French clergy, in a general assembly, in 1700, condemned this teaching in regard to a covenant, declaring that "it restores Semi-Pelagianism, merely changing its language. . . . The pact which is held to exist between God and Christ, is an audacious, erroneous invention brought forth, not only under the silence of Holy Scripture and the tradition of the Holy Fathers, but even under their contradiction." (Cf. Billuart, *De gratia,* diss. III, a. 7.)

What, then, is to be said of the negative natural preparation, that is, not setting up obstacles to grace, which being accomplished, God infallibly confers grace, according to Molina?

Reply. 1. Not to set up any obstacles at all is to observe the whole natural law, avoiding every sin against it, and this cannot be done without healing grace, as we have already shown. 2. Not to set up obstacles in some respects, observing certain precepts, avoiding certain sins, with general natural help, does not infallibly dispose one for grace; since, as we asserted with Augustine and as experience demonstrates, some men observe many commandments, and yet grace is denied them which, at one time or other, is granted to the most profligate, who have no regard for any law, according to the words of Isaias (65:1), as quoted in Rom. 10:20: "I was found by them that did not seek Me: I appeared openly to them that asked not after Me."

3. Nowhere is there a basis for this principle: upon him who does not set up obstacles to grace through his powers of nature alone, God infallibly confers grace.

4. All the aforesaid objections reappear; thus it would no longer be inscrutable why God confers grace upon one and not upon another; one could distinguish himself and glory over another; the beginning of salvation would not be the compassion of God alone, but the willing of man as well; and other conclusions opposed to the words of St. Paul: "It is not of him that willeth, nor of him that runneth, but of God that showeth mercy" (Rom. 9:16).

How, then, are we to understand the common axiom: to him who does what he can, God does not deny grace? I answer as St. Thomas here interprets it (q. 109, a. 6 ad 2), namely, "to him who does what he can, with the help of actual grace, God does not deny further grace." We are concerned with supernatural help, which comes from Christ the Redeemer, for the words of Christ are quoted here: "Without Me you can do nothing." And (q. 112, a. 3) St. Thomas shows that this preparation, since it is from God moving supernaturally, has an infallible connection with the infusion of sanctifying grace. Hence, as Father Hugon indicates (*De gratia,* p. 267), this axiom is threefold: 1. the necessity of a certain preparation for justification on the part of an adult man, 2. the infallibility of its connection with sanctifying grace, 3. the gratuity of justification, which is accomplished by God alone. "No one can come to Me unless the Father who sent Me draw him." Therefore the meaning is: to him who does what he can by the power of actual grace, God does not deny sanctifying grace. This opinion is also held by Cardinal Billot, but with indifferent concurrence.

The axiom thus explained is only the theological formula of the dogma of God's will to save. For, once it is admitted that God wills the salvation of all, it follows that sufficient grace necessary for salvation is conferred upon all; and if man does not resist this grace, he will receive a higher grace and thus arrive at justification. Man indeed resists by himself, but not to resist is already a good and proceeds from God preserving him in good and helping him, for at that moment God can permit resistance, as happens in the case of many. (Cf. Council of Trent, Sess. VI, chap. 5, Denz., no. 797.) "Hence," says the Council, "when it is written in Holy Scripture: 'Turn ye to Me, . . . and I will turn to you' (Zach. 1:3), we are reminded of our liberty; when we reply: 'Convert us, O Lord, to Thee, and we shall be converted' (Lam. 5:21), we acknowledge that we are anticipated by the grace of God."

Corollary. The real clarity of the principles of superior reasoning leads to a translucent obscurity of mysteries, while, on the contrary, the false clarity of the fiction of inferior reasoning, withdrawing from the principles of superior reasoning, shuns supernatural mysteries, denying their sublimity.

This is particularly evident in the present question; thus, the true clarity of the principle, that the order of agents corresponds to the order of ends, leads to the translucent obscurity of the mystery: "No one can come to Me, unless the Father, who sent Me, draw him." This obscurity is fully preserved by the contemplation of Augustine, when he says: "Why does He draw this man and not that one? Do not attempt to judge if you do not wish to err."

And the mysteries, which are the object of contemplation, are all the more obscure the higher they are, with this obscurity which is not incoherence or absurdity below the level of understanding, but light inacessible beyond understanding, with respect to us who are wayfarers. Therefore it is said that Thomism fears neither logic nor mystery, but, fearlessly following the logic of first principles, arrives at the highest and most profoundly inscrutable mysteries, which are the true object of infused contemplation.

On the other hand, the false clarity of the fictions of inferior reasoning is evident in these words: to him who does what he can by his natural powers alone, God does not refuse grace; in other words, man can naturally prepare himself for supernatural grace. But this assertion of inferior reasoning withdraws from the principle: the order of agents should correspond to the order of ends, and a supernatural agent to a supernatural end.

And thus withdrawing from this principle, this false clarity ignores the inscrutable mystery: "No one can come to Me, unless the Father, who sent Me, draw him." Nor indeed is it true any longer to say: "Why does He draw one man and not another? Do not attempt to judge if you do not wish to err." But on the contrary, all things are clearly explained by the fiction: "this man is drawn by God because he disposed himself naturally." The mystery is removed, and with it is taken away the highest object of contemplation; we descend to an inferior order of reasoning by rational subtleties, and inordinately so, which leads not to the obscurity of a mystery, but to the absurd denial of a principle: that the order of agents should correspond to the order of ends, every agent acts on account of a proportionate end. Hence false clarity must not be confused with true clarity. The purification of the spirit by the gift of understanding dispels such deceptive clearness and purifies "from phantasms and errors" (IIa IIae, q. 8, a. 7).

REFUTATION OF THE PRINCIPAL OBJECTIONS OF THE MOLINISTS

1. In Holy Scripture many are mentioned who attained to grace by a natural good work, such as the Egyptian midwives moved by natural compassion for the Hebrew children, Rahab the harlot receiving and not exposing the scouts sent by God, Zachaeus welcoming Christ to his house, Cornelius practicing almsgiving and prayer before he believed in Christ.

Reply. These natural good works do not exclude the necessity of interior grace, but remain inadequate unless God disposes the heart interiorly by His grace; in other words, these naturally good works as such do not infallibly prepare for grace, and it is erroneous to declare that "to him who of himself does natural works, God does not deny grace." Moreover, as Augustine says, among infidels and sinners, those who are converted are often not those who at first were less wicked. And at the Council of Orange (can. 25) it was stated that in the good thief, in Zachaeus and Cornelius, their pious disposition to believe was the result of a gift of God. But it is true that the occasions by which some seem to reach grace were procured for them by the special favor of providence disposing external matters in such a way that they would combine to lead these rather than others to grace. Thus in the cases of Zachaeus and Cornelius.

I insist. St. Paul says (I Tim. 1:13): "I obtained the mercy of God, because I did it ignorantly in unbelief." Therefore he disposed himself negatively infallibly.

Reply. Ignorance is alleged not as a negative and infallible disposition for grace, but as matter more appropriately calling forth mercy, since indigence as such is involuntary, such as ignorance, and for this reason induces mercy. On the other hand, sin, inasmuch as it is voluntary, does not call forth mercy, but avenging justice, and this all the more so in proportion to its gravity. Thus St. Augustine explains in his eighth, ninth, and tenth sermons on the words of the Apostle. The meaning is the same as when Christ says: "Father, forgive them for they know not what they do." Estius is also thus interpreted.

I insist. But at times Cyril of Jerusalem, Chrysostom, and Clement of Alexandria, quoted in this regard by Billuart, seem to teach that grace does not anticipate our wills but awaits them.

Reply. 1. In these quotations they are speaking either of habitual grace or of the increase of actual grace for more perfect works, but they are certainly not speaking of the first actual grace, through which a beginning of good will is attained. Hence their meaning is: God awaits not our bare will, but our will supported by grace. These Fathers also deny that this first grace is an imposition of necessity, in opposition to the Manichaeans who would deprive man of free will (cf. Ia, q. 23, a. 1 ad 1). This interpretation is confirmed by the fact that the aforesaid Fathers teach in various places the Catholic dogma on prevenient grace, when they explain the words of St. Paul: "What hast thou that thou hast not received? What then distinguisheth thee?" Nor is it remarkable if they at times spoke less accurately on the need for prevenient grace, when the Pelagian heresy had not yet broken out flagrantly, particularly since they desired to defend free will against the Manichaeans. At that time no one was attacking grace. St. Augustine replied similarly in his *De praedestinatione sanctorum* (chap. 14).

I insist. But St. Thomas himself says (IIa, d. 5, q. 1, a. 1): "For the eliciting of an act of conversion free will suffices, which prepares and disposes itself for obtaining grace through this act." Similarly (IIa, d. 28, q. 1, a. 4) he declares: "Since the preparation made for grace is not by acts which are commensurate to grace itself with an equality of proportion, as merit is commensurate to its reward, therefore it is not necessary that the acts by which man prepares himself for grace should exceed human nature."

Reply. 1. If such were the meaning of these passages quoted, we should have to admit that St. Thomas had subsequently retracted his own words, changing the opinion which he had held when he was younger. He wrote on the Sentences at Paris when he was only twenty-five years of age. 2. But St. Thomas did not change his opinion, for in the Commentary on the Sentences he rejects the opinion of certain others who held that man, to prepare himself for habitual grace, requires a habitual supernatural light, preamble to sanctifying grace. (Cf. II, d. 28, q. 1, a. 4.) St. Thomas denies this, maintaining that this would go on into infinity, but he does not exclude actual grace which he clearly affirms in the *Summa* and in *Quodl.,* 1, a. 7, even more clearly: "It pertains to the Pelagian error to say that man can prepare himself for grace without the help of divine grace." (Likewise Ia, q. 23, a. 5, on the beginning of good works.) Indeed certain theologians attacking this opinion fell into the opposite excess and thus prepared the way for Molina. Nor did St. Thomas say that a preparation is not required "proportionate to grace," but proportionate in the way in which merit is commensurate with reward. This is true since merit demands nature elevated by sanctifying grace; merit is a right to a supernatural reward. (Cf. *Quodl.,* 1, a. 7 ad 1.) The distance is greater between the sinner and the just man than between the just and the blessed, for grace is the seed of glory, but nature is not really the seed of grace.

I insist. But of what use, then, are natural good works performed at the dictate of reason alone without any grace?

Reply. They are meritorious *de congruo* of temporal good, to the extent that it is appropriate for divine liberality in consideration of them, to grant certain temporal benefits. Hence Christ says: "They have received their reward" (Matt. 6:2). And on the other hand, good works done outside of charity, but with the help of actual grace, are a disposition to habitual grace; St. Thomas refers to them in *IV Sent.*, q. 14, a. 4, and also in *De veritate,* q. 14, a. 11 ad 1, when he says: "If a person brought up in the wilderness follows the guidance of reason (with actual grace), it can be held for a certainty that God will either reveal to him by inspiration the things that are necessary to believe or will send some preacher of the faith to him, as he sent St. Peter to Cornelius."

I insist. Nevertheless, natural good works done without the help of actual grace seem to be at least a negative disposition to actual grace.

Reply. An infallible negative disposition, excluding every impediment to grace: denied. A fallible negative disposition, excluding some impediment: let it pass.

I insist. But man of himself can refrain from setting up an obstacle, at least at the moment when the grace is offered to him.

Reply. At that moment, of himself, with general concurrence which is in some way special for this individual, he can do so partially: granted. Completely: denied; that would be loving God the author of nature above all things.

I insist. St. Thomas (*Contra Gentes,* Bk. III, q. 159) declares: "Fallen man can hinder or not hinder the reception of grace."

Reply. Not hinder, in part (and this with the concurrence of God preserving Him in good whereas He could permit sin): granted; totally: denied, because of himself he cannot avoid every sin, observing every precept of the natural law (cf. *ibid.,* c. 160).[15]

Another objection. In Ia, q. 62, a. 6, it is taught that God conferred grace and glory upon the angels in proportion to their nature; hence there is no incompatibility in His conferring grace upon men who do what they can by natural powers alone.

Reply. St. Thomas himself replies to this objection (*ibid.,* ad 2): "The acts of a rational creature are from itself; but the nature is im-

---

[15] Man alone of himself can resist grace (and this is sin permitted by God), but "not to resist grace" is itself a good which proceeds from God who preserves him in good whereas He might have permitted resistance. Cf. our *La prédestination des saints et la grâce,* 1936, p. 381.

mediately from God. Hence it seems rather that grace is given according to the rank of the (angelic) nature than according to its works." For thus man would single out himself, and God would be moved objectively by another, which is not the case when He gives grace to the angels at the instant of their creation according to the quantity of their nature, which He alone created. To the same effect it is said that "it is reasonable for the angels, who have a better nature, to be converted to God even more powerfully and efficaciously," since in them nothing retarded the movement of the intellect and will. There is, moreover, an analogy between converted angels and men, for "according to the intensity of their conversion is greater grace given."

I insist. But the disposition can be of an inferior order, as, for example, the disposition of the embryo to a spiritual soul.

Reply. But then they belong to the same nature, which is not true of grace.

Objection. God owes it to Himself to bestow His gifts upon those who are more worthy. But he is more worthy who does many natural good works of himself than he who does less. Therefore God should confer grace upon the former.

Reply. I deny the minor: he is not more worthy because natural works have no proportion with grace; they are of an inferior order.

I insist. Nevertheless he who sets up less impediments is less indisposed.

Reply. Let it pass. But he is not more disposed and worthy; thus a worm and a dog are certainly unequal; yet the dog is not more disposed to rationality. Therefore it is not unusual for God to draw to Himself those who are worse.

Thus we are back again at what we said at the end of the exposition of this thesis.

ARTICLE VII. WHETHER MAN CAN RISE FROM SIN WITHOUT THE HELP OF GRACE

State of the question. This article, following upon the preceding ones, may seem a useless repetition. Such is not the case, however, for, as Cajetan remarks: "thus far St. Thomas was dealing with the necessity of grace for doing good; now he is concerned with evil," and in the last two articles with the necessity of grace for the man who is already just.

What is meant by rising from sin? It is not the same as ceasing from the act of sin, as Protestants claim, but it is man being restored to what, by sinning, he had forfeited. Now, by sinning, man incurs a threefold loss: the stain (habitual sin, privation of the ornament of grace), the incurring of punishment, and the decrease of the natural inclination to virtue, as stated previously (q. 85–87). The reply to the question thus posed is negative; that is certain, so that Pelagius himself did not deny it but only insisted that grace should be bestowed on account of merits.

The answer is of faith, defined at the Council of Orange, can. 4, (Denz., no. 177) also can. 14 and 19; and at the Council of Trent, Sess. VI, can. 1 (Denz., no. 811), can. 3 (Denz., no. 813). The teaching of the Fathers is clear; cf. the words of Augustine quoted in the argument *Sed contra;* otherwise "Christ died for nothing," if man can rise from sin without the help of grace.

This conclusion is proved by theological argument as follows:

To rise from sin is for man to be restored and liberated from the evils which he incurred by sin.

But by sin he incurred a threefold loss which cannot be repaired except by grace.

Therefore.

The minor is proved thus: 1. The stain is a privation of the ornament of grace, therefore it cannot be repaired except by grace itself. 2. The decrease in the inclination of the will toward virtue cannot be repaired unless God draws the will to Himself. 3. The incurring of punishment cannot be remitted except by God against whom the offense was committed. Nevertheless there can be an imperfect resurrection without habitual grace, by actual grace which is present in attrition when the sinner aspires after reconciliation. Cf. on this subject the sixty-fourth proposition of Baius (Denz., no. 1064).

ARTICLE VIII. WHETHER WITHOUT GRACE MAN CAN AVOID SIN

State of the question. From the second article wherein it is said that fallen man can, with the natural concurrence of God, perform some good works, it is to be supposed likewise that with this natural concurrence he can, for a certain length of time, avoid sin and overcome slight temptations. For it is not necessary that he should continually sin by act, by a sin of commission, such as blasphemy, or of omission, such as never praying when he ought to pray, since the good of reason is not entirely extinct in him. As a matter of fact, this natural concurrence, although it is in a way due to human nature in general, may, as we have said, be called gratuitous in a certain sense with respect to this man to whom it is given here and now rather than to another in whom God permits sin; from this standpoint it may be called grace, broadly speaking. This observation is necessary in order to reconcile various texts of the councils and of the Fathers on this question. Hence the problem, properly stated, is: whether man without grace, strictly speaking, can, over a long period of time, avoid mortal sins. Cf. above, Ia IIae, q. 109, a. 2 ad 2, and *De veritate,* q. 24, a. 14 ad 2 and 3.

That such is the proper statement of the question is evident from the objections or difficulties which are raised against the first article: it seems that man can, without grace, avoid sin: 1. because no one sins in that which is unavoidable; 2. because otherwise the sinner would be blamed without cause, if he could not avoid sin; 3. because a person who sins does not cease to be a man, and it is within his power to choose good or evil; for human nature after the fall is not totally corrupt.

However, as stated in the argument *Sed contra,* St. Augustine declared that: "Whoever denies that we ought to pray, lest we enter into temptation, ought to be removed from the ears of all and anathematized by the mouth of all, I have no doubt."

In the body of the article there are two principal conclusions, which, all things considered, can and ought to be proposed thus: 1. concerning fallen man avoiding mortal sin; 2. concerning the just man avoiding venial sins.

The first conclusion, which is proved in the second part of the article is as follows: Fallen man being in the state of mortal sin, cannot, without the addition of healing, habitual grace, continually avoid all mortal sin against the natural law and overcome all temptations. In this regard, St. Thomas seems to correct what he had said in *II Sent.,* d. 28, q. 1, a. 2.

1. This is proved first of all from Holy Scripture: "By Thee I shall be delivered from temptation" (Ps. 17:30). "Being pushed I was overturned that I might fall: but the Lord supported me" (Ps. 117:13). "Unhappy man that I am, who shall deliver me from the body of this death? (And he replies): The grace of God, by Jesus Christ" (Rom. 7:24 f.). This is true with still greater reason of fallen man before

justification. "And God is faithful, who will not suffer you to be tempted above that which you are able: but will make also with temptation issue, that you may be able to bear it" (I Cor. 10:13). Likewise the Council of Neocaesarea (chap. 11) against the Pelagians condemned the following proposition of Pelagius: "Our victory is not by the help of God." Similarly the Council of Milevum (Denz., nos. 103 f.), Pope St. Celestine (Denz., no. 132), and the Council of Orange against the Semi-Pelagians (Denz., nos. 184, 186, 192, 194).

2. The conclusion is proved, secondly, from theological argument which is the corollary of articles 3 and 4 (explained here in the second part of the article): fallen man cannot, without healing grace, efficaciously love God the author of nature above all things nor observe all the precepts of the natural law; therefore neither can he avoid every mortal sin, for they are committed by transgression of the commandments.

The basis of this argument lies in the fact that man in the state of mortal sin has his will turned away from even his natural final end; therefore he is already inclined toward some mortal sins. In order, then, continually to avoid all mortal sins and overcome all temptations, he must have his will directed toward his final end, adhering to God so firmly that he will not be separated from Him for the sake of anything created; cf. the end of the body of the article.[16] In short, an infirm nature cannot efficiently produce an act of healthy nature. St. Thomas says that this requires healing grace, that is, habitual grace; for without it man is not firmly established in good dispositions with regard to his final end.

Three principal objections are made to this first conclusion.

First objection. Some pagans have withstood very serious temptations for the sake of virtue.

Reply. As we have already said, perhaps they did so from a human motive of glory or pride, and, in that case, without the special help of God, or else they did so for love of virtue, in which case it was not without the special help of God. (See Augustine, Bk. IV against Julian, chap. 3.)

Second objection, which St. Thomas mentions first as follows: if

---

[16] Here the words of Aristotle are cited: "In unexpected circumstances a man acts according to a preconceived objective and a pre-existing habit"; hence one who is in the state of mortal sin cannot long remain without mortal sin, especially in sudden temptation. Even if he should wish to act rationally, he cannot long maintain this intention on account of his habitually bad disposition.

man in the state of mortal sin cannot avoid sin, then by sinning he does not sin, for sin is always avoidable.

Reply (ad 1): "Man (in the state of mortal sin) can avoid individual acts of (mortal) sin, but not all, except by means of grace. Nevertheless man is not excused, since the fault is his own that he does not prepare himself to possess grace . . ."; in other words, grace is offered to him and is not lacking except through his fault. (Cf. above, a. 4 ad 2.)

Third objection. But then it would follow that man in the state of mortal sin is bound to repent instantly, for otherwise he will always be in danger of committing sin again.

Reply. He is bound to repent instantly when the danger of sinning is certain and definite; otherwise there is no grave obligation to repent instantly.

Second conclusion. The just man, by the ordinary assistance of grace without any special privilege, can continually avoid all mortal sins, but not however, over a long period of time, all venial sins, although he can avoid individual venial sins.

The first part of this conclusion is that the just man can, without very special help, continually avoid all mortal sins (to avoid them actually and continually until death, however, requires the gift of final perseverance, as we shall explain in article 10). In support of this first part of the conclusion the following scriptural texts are quoted: "If anyone love Me, he will keep My word, and My Father will love him, and We will come to him, and make Our abode with him" (John 14:23). "My grace is sufficient for thee" (II Cor. 12:9). Also the Council of Trent (Denz., no. 804): "For God will not forsake those who are once justified by His grace, unless He is first abandoned by them"; cf. below, q. 112, a. 3.

The theological argument is the opposite of the reasoning in the preceding conclusion: since the just man firmly adheres to his final end, therefore he can avoid all mortal sin; he has even the proximate power to do so; whether he actually perseveres or not is another matter. Neither does the just man actually avoid sins of omission unless he performs a good work, with the help of actual grace. And that he should actually persevere in the state of grace until death, is still another question (cf. a. 10, and q. 114, a. 9).

The second part of this conclusion is as follows: The just man cannot avoid all venial sins collectively. It is proven from Holy Scripture: "There is no man who sinneth not" (III Kings 8:46). "There is no just man upon earth, that doth good, and sinneth not" (Ecclus. 7:21). "In many things we all offend" (Jas. 3:2). "If we say that we have no sin, we deceive ourselves, and the truth is not in us" (I John 1:8). This second part of this conclusion is also declared by the Council of Milevum (can. 6 and 7, Denz., nos. 106, 107) and of Trent (Sess. VI, can. 23, Denz., no. 833), where it was stated that it was the special privilege of the Blessed Virgin Mary that she could avoid all venial sin. Likewise, against the Beghards and several propositions of Michael Molinos (from 55 to 63, Denz., nos. 471, 1275–83).

The second theological argument for this conclusion is proved in the body of the argument as follows:

Although sanctifying grace heals a man with respect to his spirit, there still remains a disorder of the sensitive appetite, so that inordinate movements often arise.

But allowing that his reason can repress individual movements (thus they have an element of involuntary act) yet not all, because while he is endeavoring to resist one, perhaps another will arise and also because the reason cannot always be vigilant.

In other words, the reason itself can be watchful to avoid some inordinate movement, but not all. But in order that this movement be voluntary it is essential that the reason have the power and duty of considering this movement in individual cases. To continue in goodness without venial sin presents great difficulty the surmounting of which requires a very special grace, by which the instability of the will is stabilized, infirmity healed, weariness refreshed, and disgust overcome.

It is a disputed question in mystical theology whether the soul that arrives at transforming union can continually avoid all venial sins collectively. It is admitted that it can avoid all fully deliberate venial sins, but not all semi-deliberate ones, except while it is under the influence of the actual grace of union. But this actual union is not absolutely continuous, saving always the exception of the Blessed Virgin Mary. (Cf. St. Theresa, *Interior Castle,* Seventh Mansion, chap. 4.)

The fact remains that resisting sufficient grace is an evil, and man is sufficient unto himself to do so; but not resisting grace is a good, which proceeds from God, the source of every good.

ARTICLE IX. WHETHER THE JUST MAN CAN PERFORM GOOD WORKS
(AVAILING TO SALVATION) AND AVOID SIN WITHOUT ACTUAL GRACE

The state of the question appears from the objections at the beginning of the article. Some hold with Molina [17] that natural concurrence suffices (cf. Hugon, *De gratia*, p. 282).

St. Thomas' answer is: The just man needs the help of actual grace
to act aright supernaturally.

1. This is proved from authority; Augustine is quoted in the argument *Sed contra*, which should be read.

a) *Holy Scripture*: "As the branch cannot bear fruit of itself, unless it abide in the vine, so neither can you, unless you abide in Me"
(John 15:4); as the branch cannot bear fruit without a continual infusion from the vine, neither can the just man without a continual
infusion of Christ. Therefore does He say: "Without Me ye can do
nothing," and "You must pray always." (Cf. Council of Orange, can.
10, Denz., no. 183.)

b) *Pope Zozimus* (*Epist. tractoria, PL*, XX, 693, quoted by Denz.,
nos. 135 ff.) says: "Therefore our aid and our protector should be
appealed to in all acts, causes, thoughts, and movements." Also Council of Orange (can. 10 and 25, Denz., nos. 183, 200) and Pope Celestine
I (Denz., no. 132).

c) *Council of Trent* (Denz., no. 809): "Since indeed this same
Christ Jesus, as head in the members and as the vine in the branches,
continually infuses power into justified souls, which power always
precedes, accompanies, and follows their good works, and without
which they cannot be pleasing to God or meritorious in any way." [18]
Also Trent, Sess. VI, can. 2.

2. *The theological proof* is twofold: by title of dependence and by
title of infirmity.

a) The first proof is general, by title of dependence. St. Thomas
states only the major, but the syllogism is easily completed from what
has previously been said, thus:

No created thing can proceed to any act except by the power of
divine motion (a. 1).

[17] Molina, *Concordia*, q. 14, a. 13, disp. 8, p. 36; also quoted by Billot, *De virt. infusis*,
1905, p. 176.

[18] This cannot all be regarded as applying to habitual grace, which is not a subsequent but a permanent aid; hence it must refer to actual grace.

But for any supernatural act in a just soul a proportionate motion is required, since the order of agents should correspond to the order of ends (as has been said in a. 6).

Therefore the just man requires supernatural, actual grace for any supernatural act.

A certain law of metaphysics, namely, the principle of finality, requires that the introduction of the agent which is to make the transition from potency to act must be of the same order as the act and the end toward which it moves. As stated in the reply to the first objection, even in the state of glory man requires commensurate actual help (cf. ad 2). Hence natural concurrence does not suffice, as Molina would have it (*op. cit.,* p. 36), and as Cardinal Billot sometimes seems to imply (*Virt. infusis,* 1905, thes. VII, p. 176). Thus even Pesch declares (*De gratia,* no. 109): "Should it be denied that any supernatural help is required (for any work conducive to salvation), this doctrine is most generally and deservedly rejected by theologians." Similarly Mazzella (*De gratia,* disp. II, a. 2, prop. 8,) declares: "The opinion maintaining the necessity of actual grace for individual acts conducive to salvation, even in a man trained to supernatural habits, seems altogether to be held more consistently, considering the authority of Holy Scripture, the constant teaching of the Fathers, and the decrees of the Church."

b) The second proof from theology is somewhat special: "by reason of infirmity" applies to the condition of human nature, not as fallen, since we are concerned with a just man, but as not fully regenerated, thus:

He who is not perfectly cured requires external assistance in order to act properly.

But, allowing that the just man is cured by sanctifying grace, he is still subject to inordinate concupiscence and the obscurity of ignorance.

Therefore, for this special reason, the just man requires the help of God to direct and protect him; hence he should say daily: "and lead us not into temptation."

First corollary. This second argument should be distinguished but not separated from the first as if it were interpreted thus: infallibly efficacious concurrence is required only for difficult acts conducive to salvation, but not for easy ones. This is false for, according to the first argument, in every state, general concurrence, at least, is required, but infallibly efficacious concurrence for any good act proposed here and now.[19]

Second corollary. In connection with this article Billuart brings forward a new distinction which may be admitted but it is not necessary, that is: the just man requires the general help of God, as author of the supernatural, for any easy supernatural acts, and this general help, although, in a sense, due to nature raised to the supernatural, is yet not due to this individual rather than to another, since free will remains defectible and God is not always bound to profer a remedy for this defectibility, even for the just. But the just man requires special help for more difficult acts and also for constant perseverance.

Thus, Billuart maintains, several texts of the Fathers are more easily reconciled. And C. Billot, referring to the thesis that general concurrence is sufficient in the just man for individual supernatural acts (which are not difficult), seems to mean, in agreement with Billuart, general supernatural concurrence or ordinary actual grace; this is admissible. But Billot is more probably referring to general supernatural concurrence with respect to mode, whereas we refer to it with respect to substance. Cf. above, p. 51, his theory on the supernaturalness of faith.

ARTICLE X. WHETHER MAN IN THE STATE OF GRACE REQUIRES THE HELP OF GRACE TO PERSEVERE

State of the question. We are not concerned here with perseverance taken as a virtue inclining one to elicit the intention of persevering

---

[19] Cf. *De malo,* q.6, a.1 ad 3. "In all things divine providence works infallibly, and yet effects to proceed from contingent causes dependently to the extent that God moves all things proportionately, each according to its own mode."

For, as St. Thomas declares (Ia, q.19, a.6 ad 1): "Whatever God wills absolutely is done, even if what He wills antecedently is not done." But all the good which takes place here and now, even the least, was from eternity the object of the consequent divine will, which concerns, as stated in the same place, not the absolute good, as it were abstractly, with which the antecedent will deals, but the good here and now clothed in all its circumstances; for no good comes about except by the intention of the consequent will. And the antecedent will never produces any good, even the slightest and easiest here and now, except by virtue of the accompanying consequent will, which is concerned with the good regarded here and now and infallibly produces it. Cf. our *La prédestination des saints et la grâce,* 1936, pp. 381-94. In thus explaining metaphysically the distinction of Damascene, reconciling it with the dogmas of divine omnipotence and predestination, St. Thomas shows the supreme, fundamental distinction between efficacious grace, which proceeds from the consequent will of God, and sufficient grace, which proceeds from His antecedent will.

(cf. IIa IIae, q. 137) nor with the intention of persevering itself, but with the actual exercise of perseverance in good conducive to salvation until the end of one's life. That this is the sense in which it is used is evident from the body of the article, at the very beginning of which St. Thomas eliminates the consideration of the acquired virtue of perseverance, discussed by Aristotle, and of the infused virtue of temperance, annexed to fortitude, which are infused with sanctifying grace. Here it is rather a question "of the continuation in good until the end of life."

Moreover, perseverance thus defined is capable of a twofold acceptation: 1. the enduring continuation in grace and good works until death, as attained to by many predestined adults; and 2. the coincidence of habitual grace and death, without prolonged continuation, as occurs in children who die after their baptism [20] and also in adults who die shortly after obtaining justification,[21] for example, the good thief; and thus it becomes the grace of a happy death.

Reply. To the question thus stated, the Church, as we shall presently see, replies that a special gift of perseverance is required. But in what does this special gift consist? Is it a habitual gift or an actual grace? This is the statement of the question which is quite complex. Let us examine: 1. the errors involved, 2. the teaching of Holy Scripture and the Church, 3. St. Thomas' conclusion, and 4. the problems to be solved.

I. ERRORS ON THIS SUBJECT

The Pelagians, at least in the beginning, attributed perseverance to the powers of nature alone. The Semi-Pelagians maintained that grace was required for it, but not a special gift distinct from sanctifying grace, and, according to them, grace is given to those who possess the beginning of salvation through their natural effort. Hence the grace of final perseverance is always given to those who persevere in this natural effort. In opposition to them, St. Augustine proved that the gift of final perseverance is a special gift and not subject to merit. Certain theologians, such as Duval and Vega, hold that a special gift is required for perseverance which is active and protracted over a long

---

[20] Then it is final passive perseverance, requiring no cooperation, since an infant is not capable of cooperation.

[21] Then it is perseverance not only passive but active, including at least a certain brief cooperation.

period of time, but not for a brief perseverance during which no special difficulties occur.

II. THE TEACHING OF SCRIPTURE AND THE CHURCH

In Scripture our perseverance in good until the end is attributed to God. "I set the Lord always in my sight: for He is at my right hand, that I be not moved" (Ps. 15:8). "Perfect Thou my goings in Thy paths: that my footsteps be not moved" (Ps. 16:5). "Be Thou my helper, forsake me not; do not Thou despise me" (Ps. 26:9). Likewise Ps. 37:22. "When my strength shall fail, do not Thou forsake me" (Ps. 70:9). "And unto old age and gray hairs: O God, forsake me not" (Ps. 70:18). Christ says to His disciples in the Garden of Gethsemane: "Watch ye, and pray that ye enter not into temptation. The spirit indeed is willing, but the flesh weak" (Matt. 26:41). "And now I am not in the world, and these are in the world, and I come to Thee. Holy Father, keep them in Thy name whom Thou hast given Me; that they may be one, as We also are" (John 17:11). "He that thinketh himself to stand, let him take heed lest he fall" (I Cor. 10:12). "With fear and trembling work out your salvation. For it is God who worketh in you, both to will and to accomplish, according to His good will" (Phil. 2:12 f.).

The doctrine of the Church. It is of faith that final perseverance is something gratuitous, not due to the powers of nature, and more a gift distinct from the grace of justification. This was defined against the Pelagians and Semi-Pelagians whom St. Augustine specifically refuted in his book on the gift of perseverance.

Cf. Denz., no. 132, the letter of Pope Celestine I: "No one, even among the baptized, is sufficiently restored by grace to triumph over the wiles of the devil and overcome the temptations of the flesh unless by the daily help of God he receives perseverance in the frequent practice of good."

Also the Council of Orange, can. 10 (Denz., no. 183): "The help of God, even for the redeemed and sanctified, is ever to be implored, that they may come to a good end or continue in good works." (Likewise can. 25, Denz., no. 200.)

The Council of Trent (Sess. VI, can. 16, Denz., no. 826) declares: "If anyone should say with absolute and infallible certainty that he surely will have the great gift of perseverance to the end, unless he learns it from special revelation, let him be anathema." Likewise (can. 22, Denz., no. 832): "If anyone should say either that a justified soul can persevere in the justice it has received without the special help of God, or that with it it cannot do so, let him be anathema."

Father Hugon (*De gratia,* p. 286) asks whether this canon also includes perseverance for a short space of time (for instance, between justification shortly before death and death itself) and passive perseverance (of infants dying after baptism). The Council does not distinguish; several authorities consider that a real distinction is not to be excluded from the sense of the definition. At least, it is of faith that for the active perseverance of adults over a long period of time a special aid is required distinct from habitual grace.

Among the Fathers, Augustine in particular is cited (*De dono perseverantiae,* chap. 2); he refutes the objections of the Pelagians, to which may be added those which are presented by St. Thomas at the beginning of the article, as follows:

1. Perseverance in virtue is something less than the virtue of perseverance itself which can be acquired by repeated acts. 2. Christian perseverance is a certain moral virtue, annexed to fortitude, and infused at the same time as grace. 3. Adam in the state of innocence would have been able to persevere, but those who are justified by Christ are not in a less perfect state with respect to grace.

Against these difficulties, St. Thomas explains, in the body of the present article, that the term "perseverance" is used in a threefold sense:

1. Acquired perseverance, described by Aristotle (*Ethics,* Bk. VII, chap. 7). This is a moral virtue attached to fortitude which consists in a certain firmness of the reason and will, so that a man may not be dissuaded from the path of virtue by the onslaught of melancholy. This perseverance maintains itself against such an onslaught as continence does against the temptations of the flesh. Cf. IIa IIae, q. 137, a. 2 ad 2.

2. The infused virtue of perseverance. By this virtue man has the intention of persevering in good until the end. But many had this intention during their lives and yet, in fact, did not persevere to the end. This virtue gives the power of persisting in the first act in spite of the difficulty which arises from the long duration of the act itself. Cf. IIa IIae, q. 137, a. 3 and 4.

3. Perseverance in the sense of a continuation of a certain good work until the end of one's life. For this, the just man requires a

special grace, not habitual but actual, directing and protecting him against the impelling force of temptation. This follows from the preceding article in which it was proved that the just man needs the help of actual grace to do good and avoid evil and therefore, with still greater reason, to do good and avoid evil until the end of his life. This is the perseverance of which we are now speaking.[22]

Similarly, in IIa IIae, q. 137, a. 4, the question, whether perseverance requires the help of grace, is answered thus: 1. the infused virtue of perseverance presupposes habitual grace; 2. for the act of perseverance lasting until death "man requires not only habitual grace, but also the gratuitous help of God preserving a man in good until the end of life." "Since, with free will, man himself is changeable, and this condition is not altered by habitual grace in the present life, it is not within the power of free will, even restored by grace, to remain fixed in the good, although it is in its power to choose to do so. For the most part, election falls within our power, but not execution" (*ibid.*).

III. ST. THOMAS' CONCLUSION

The conclusion is thus proved. The just man requires the help of actual grace to do the good necessary for salvation and to avoid evil (preceding article).

But perseverance is the continuation of a certain good work until the end of life.

Therefore, for this perseverance until the end a special actual grace is required, distinct from habitual grace and even from the preceding actual graces, such, that is, as precede the moment of death. (Cf. ad 3.)

This argument thus proposed is metaphysical: no one is preserved in good works until death unless specially preserved by God. Some authors state this argument in a slightly different way, so that its metaphysical necessity is less evident. They say that for perseverance until the end there is a great threefold difficulty for the surmounting of which a special actual gift is required. Thus they rather proceed inductively.

It is a great threefold difficulty: 1. to shun evil, 2. to fulfill every commandment continually and enduringly, and 3. to have death coincide with grace, or to die at the opportune time. But all these taken together require a special favor from God, distinct from ha-

[22] Cf. *Tabulam auream,* s.v. Perseverantia.

bitual grace. Since man cannot, without additional help, overcome
temptations and elicit supernatural acts, for still greater reason does
he require aid to practice these until the end. Moreover, only God,
who is master of grace and of death, can cause grace to coincide with
death; in doing so He manifests a special providence toward the elect.
Therefore final perseverance (at least such as endures for a long time
before death) requires a special favor distinct from habitual grace.
This point, at least, in the question, is of faith and is confirmed by
this argument based upon still higher principles of faith. This argument is good, but is better formulated by St. Thomas, inasmuch as
he shows more clearly why an utterly special actual gift is required
for surmounting this great difficulty in fact, that is, preservation in
good.

IV. DOUBTS

First doubt. Whether a special grace, distinct from ordinary,
actual helps, is required for long-continued, active final perseverance.

At present theologians generally reply in the affirmative, which is
thus proved by the following arguments. a) From authority, since
Christ prayed especially for the perseverance of His disciples, who
were already just: "Holy Father, keep them" (John 17:11–15). Likewise the Church thus prays in particular: "Enable us always to obey
Thy commandments" (Tuesday after the Second Sunday of Lent).
"Never permit me to be separated from Thee" (prayer before Communion). The Council of Trent calls the gift of perseverance, "that
great, special gift." b) From theological argument. (Cf. ad 3.) Long-
continued, active final perseverance, that is, with our cooperation,
demands not only sufficient grace, but efficacious grace, nay rather the
most important of all efficacious graces which consummates the state
of wayfarer and brings about an infallible coincidence between the
state of grace and death. This efficacious grace confers the final act
of the wayfarer connected with the attainment of the final end and
therefore proceeds from a very special infusion by which God is the
mover. And this, too, certainly depends upon the merits of Christ
who merited for us all the graces, both sufficient and efficacious, which
we receive and also all the effects of our predestination.

Second doubt. Whether a special gift distinct from the ordinary
aids is required for final perseverance over a short space of time, either

in adults or in infants who die soon after their justification. At present theologians more generally reply in the affirmative.

a) Since this seems to be the obvious meaning of the Councils of Orange and Trent (Denz., nos. 183, 200, 806, 826, 832, 805 ff.), although this was not expressly defined. The Council of Orange declared (no. 183). "The help of God is to be implored even by the redeemed and sanctified, that they may arrive at a good end or may continue long in good works." In speaking thus, as Billuart remarks, the Council distinguishes perseverance taken as the attainment of the end from perseverance taken as a continuation of good over a long period of time, and for both of these require a special help which is to be implored by those who are living a holy life. Likewise the Council of Trent requires a special help for perseverance simply and without any limitations.

b) Theological argument. The very special effect of predestination, which has an infallible relationship to glory, is a very particular gift. But the coincidence of grace with death is an effect of this kind, conferred only on the predestinate. Therefore it is a very special gift, surpassing ordinary aids, which are attributed to ordinary providence.

This is confirmed from the consideration of death. Death may come about, for those who persevere, in a twofold manner: 1. Beyond the natural course of events, according to divine decree, the time of death is hastened or delayed; then it is manifestly a special favor. 2. Or it occurs according to the natural order, but even then providence had disposed natural events from all eternity so that they would bring about death at an opportune time, when a man is in the state of grace. And this indicates a special care on the part of providence, which extends to all things, ordains means to their end, and in particular to the glory of God and of the elect. Therefore the coincidence of the state of grace with death is a special favor from God, who alone can cause these two to coincide, since He is the master of grace and of death. At least, this disposition of circumstances is in some respects a special favor; this is admitted by Molina when he maintains that God foresees through mediate knowledge that, if a certain person at the moment of death were placed in such and such circumstances, he would elicit an act of contrition. (Cf. *Concordia,* ed. cit., p. 548.)

Third doubt. In what does this special gift of final perseverance consist? A distinction must be made between adults and infants.

a) In baptized children who die before attaining the use of reason, this special gift does not require internal actual grace but consists in an external grace, that is, in a special providence by virtue of which the infant dies when in the state of grace.

b) In adults, however, the gift of final perseverance does not consist in any one indivisible thing, but comprises a great many, thus: 1. on the part of God it is the special providence causing grace to coincide with death; 2. on the part of man it consists in a series of helps by which he is preserved from temptation, or overcomes temptations, or, if he falls, he rises again at the opportune time; finally, it includes the last efficacious grace, connecting the last meritorious act with the end, which, as it is an efficacious grace, is called by antonomasia "the great and signal gift of God."

But whether this last grace is intrinsically efficacious, as the Thomists hold, or extrinsic through the prevision of the *scientia media,* Billuart (diss. III, a. 10) cites texts from Scripture and from St. Augustine in which it is attributed to the grace of final perseverance that man does persevere. "What hast thou that thou hast not received?" (I Cor. 4:7.) Therefore election "is not of him that willeth, nor of him that runneth, but of God that showeth mercy" (Rom. 9:16). That is, divine election does not depend on the will or the effort of man, but on God who shows mercy. "For it is God who worketh in you, both to will and to accomplish" (Phil. 2:13).

St. Augustine's references to the subject include the following: They receive "grace which is not rejected by any hard heart, since it is first granted to them to have their hardness of heart taken away" (*De praedestinatione sanctorum,* chap. 8). "God has the wills of men in His power to a greater extent than they themselves have" (*De correptione et gratia,* chap. 14). "We are speaking of that perseverance which perseveres until the end; if it is granted, one perseveres until the end; but if one does not persevere until the end, it is not granted" (*De dono perseverantiae,* chap. 6). "Therefore the weakness of the human will is assisted, so that it may be moved invariably and inevitably by divine grace, and hence, although weak, it may not fail nor be overcome by any adversity" (*De correptione et gratia,* chap. 12). Cf. R. de Journel, *Enchir. patr.,* no. 1958; read also the reply to the third objection of the present article.

The question is whether this grace is efficacious because God wills it to be so or because man wills to render it so. In the answer to the third objection St. Thomas says: "By the grace of Christ many receive the gift of grace by which they can persevere and also it is further granted to them that they do persevere." Hence if, of two equally obdurate sinners, one is converted rather than the other, this is the effect of a special mercy toward him. With still greater reason, if anyone perseveres in good throughout the whole of his life, this is the effect of a special mercy of God toward him.

Fourth doubt. Whether perseverance was a very special gift for the angels. The Jansenists reply negatively, both for angels and for man in the state of innocence. The answer of St. Thomas and the generality of theologians is affirmative. Cf. *III C. Gentes,* chap. 155, and IIa IIae, q. 137, a. 4.

a) The foregoing arguments are also valid for the angels and for man in the state of innocence, in whom free will was capable of defection.

b) Moreover, for the angels, final perseverance is the proper effect of predestination, and not all the angels were predestined. Further, this is implied by the Council of Orange (Denz., no. 192) when it declares: "Human nature, even had it remained in that state of integrity in which it was created, would by no means have preserved itself without the aid of its Creator." And St. Augustine, in *The City of God* (Bk. XIII, chap. 9) maintains: "If in both cases (the angels) were created equally good, some fell through bad will, while others, receiving more help, attained that fullness of beatitude, whence they were made absolutely certain that they will never fall."

Fifth doubt. Whether the gift of final perseverance is identical with the gift of confirmation in grace. Cf. Salmanticenses, *De gratia,* q. 110, disp. III, dub. XI, no. 259. The answer is in the negative, since the gift of final perseverance is common to all the predestinate, but not the gift of confirmation in grace, which was conferred upon the apostles on the day of Pentecost and upon souls that arrived at the intimate union with God which is called the transforming union. In what respects do they differ? In this: the gift of confirmation in grace preserves one from mortal sin and also generally from deliberate venial sin, according to the mode in which it is given, that is, by a certain participation in the impeccability of the blessed, and the intrinsic gift requires to be completed by the extrinsic protection of God. Hence this gift of confirmation in grace adds something over and above the gift of perseverance, namely, something intrinsic and habitual which prevents sin, almost binding the power to preserve it from sin; on the other hand, the gift of final perseverance does not necessarily demand anything more than the conjunction of the state of grace with death.

REFUTATION OF OBJECTIONS

First objection. Final perseverance is the coincidence of grace with death. But shortly before death, the justified man with the ordinary helps can persevere for a considerable time in goodness until his death. Therefore final perseverance is not a special help.

Reply. I distinguish the major: final perseverance is the coincidence of grace with death, willed in virtue of itself by God for the efficacious purpose of glory: granted; a fortuitous and accidental coincidence: denied. I likewise distinguish the minor: for a moderately long time until the accidental conjunction of grace and death: granted; for a definite interval of time until the conjunction of habitual grace with death willed in virtue of itself by God: denied.

Second objection. To those who possess grace, glory is due. Therefore with still greater reason is the help due to them for the continuation of grace with glory.

Reply. I deny the conclusion, for, although glory is due to a man who possesses grace, as long as he remains in grace, it is not however due to him that he be invariably preserved in grace until death, since he is of an erratic, defectible nature.

Third objection. According to the Council of Trent, "God does not abandon a soul that is once justified unless He is first abandoned by it" (Denz., no. 804). But if, in order to persevere, the just man requires special help, which God denies to many of the just, He would desert him before being deserted by him. Therefore.

Reply. The sense of the major is: God does not abandon by withdrawing efficacious actual grace, unless man first resists sufficient grace. But to ask why God does not give to all the just efficacious grace, by means of which they may not neglect sufficient grace, is equivalent to asking why He permits sin in one defectible soul rather than in another, whereupon the answer, in the words of St. Augustine (*De dono perseverantiae,* chap. 9), is that "in this respect the judgment of God is inscrutable"; and further, in his commentary on St. John 6:44, "No man can come to Me, except the Father, who sent Me, draw him," he adds: "Why does He draw one and not another? Do not judge if you do not wish to err; but accept and understand: if you are not yet drawn, pray that you may be drawn." Cf. St. Thomas on John 6:44. Hence we should pray in the words of the Mass, before the Communion: "Grant me ever to adhere to Thy commandments and never permit me to be separated from Thee." [23]

Further, according to the Council of Trent (Denz., no. 806): "The gift of perseverance . . . can be possessed only by the one who is able to make him who stands, stand (Rom. 14:4), that he may persevere standing, and to raise up him who falls." Cf. below (q. 114, a. 9) on the gift of perseverance which cannot be the object of merit, but which can be obtained by virtue of humble, persevering, impetratory prayer in union with the prayer of Christ, the High Priest of the Sacrifice of the Mass. How advantageous it is, then, to celebrate or hear Mass in order to obtain the grace of a happy death, as Benedict XV declared!

This terminates the question of the necessity of grace for knowing natural and supernatural truth, for doing natural and supernatural good, for avoiding evil, and for persevering unto the end.

[23] It is obvious that the divine withdrawal of efficacious grace is a punishment, and as a punishment it presupposes at least an initial fault or resistance to sufficient grace. And on the other hand, even an initial fault presupposes the divine permission of it. To confuse this divine permission with a divine refusal or with the withdrawal of efficacious grace is to set the punishment before the fault, and this is the cruelty which is found in Calvinism, condemned at the Council of Trent.

CHAPTER III

QUESTION 110

THE GRACE OF GOD WITH RESPECT TO ITS ESSENCE

▲▲

AFTER considering the necessity of grace for our final end, St. Thomas passes to the treatment of its essence. This question is particularly concerned with habitual or sanctifying grace which, by antonomasia, is called "grace," whereby man is made pleasing to God, His child and heir. Actual grace is reducible to this habitual grace in a certain sense, as a disposition to a form or a proportionate movement within the same order and species. This actual grace is considered by itself in question 111 on the divisions of grace.

The present question (110) is divided into four articles which are arranged progressively, proceeding from the general to the particular, from the genus to the specific differences, as follows:

1. Whether grace posits something in the soul, or whether it is something existing in God outside of us.

2. Whether grace is a quality.

3. Whether grace differs from infused virtue, especially from charity.

4. Whether it resides in the essence of the soul as in a subject; this question presupposes the solution of article three.

We are therefore dealing both with the formal cause and with the quasi-material cause or subject in which grace is received.

ARTICLE I. WHETHER GRACE POSITS ANYTHING IN THE SOUL

State of the question. In the first objections, St. Thomas already set forth the arguments which were later proposed by the Lutherans and Calvinists, who hold that sanctifying grace is not a gift intrinsic to the soul, but an extrinsic designation, thanks to the imputation of the justice of Christ, out of regard for whom God loves the sinner and dissimulates his sin, as long as the sinner, with trusting faith, firmly believes and hopes that God will condone his sins to the end of his life for the sake of the merits of Christ. Hence the words of Luther: "Sin strongly, but believe still more strongly." These words are not a direct exhortation to sin, but an indirect one.

St. Thomas anticipated this pernicious doctrine to a certain extent by proposing three objections at the beginning of the article: 1) By the mere fact that a man is said to have the grace of the king, nothing is posited in him; it is only in the king that there resides an attitude of benevolence toward this man. 2) God vivifies the soul as the soul vivifies the body; but the soul vivifies the body immediately; therefore there is no medium between God who vivifies and the soul that is vivified. 3) Grace is the remission of sins; but this remission is effected according as God does not impute sin to us. Therefore grace does not posit anything in the soul. It is remarkable that the future doctrine of Protestants on grace should have been so explicitly formulated as early as the thirteenth century in such wise as to solve its difficulties.

NB

In the same way, St. Thomas, treating of the Sacrifice of the Mass (IIIa, q. 83, a. 1) under the title, "Whether in the celebration of this mystery Christ is immolated," stated an objection (as did St. Albert also in his *Sentences*) in terms almost word for word as the Protestants would later express it: "The immolation of Christ was made on the cross. But in the celebration of the Mass, Christ is not crucified; therefore neither is He immolated"; consequently the Mass is not a true sacrifice, but only a memorial of the past sacrifice.

From these examples it should be evident how excellent is this method of proposing difficulties at the beginning of any particularly fundamental question, difficulties opposed to the solution which one accepts or which, at least, seems to be proved the best. By this means, theology can more easily foresee errors and avoid them. For if the question is correctly stated, there cannot be many possible answers, but there are generally two opposite ones, affirmative and negative. And before proving the affirmative, it is profitable to examine the arguments which can be adduced in support of the negative. Thus the crux of the problem to be solved will be brought to light.

Reply. Habitual grace is a supernatural gift of God inhering in the soul.

1. Proof from Scripture. "I will pour upon you clean water" (Ezech.

36:25). (Grace is thus referred to metaphorically, in the New Testament as well: cf. John 4:13.) The following verse continues: "And I will give you a new heart, and put a new spirit within you" (Ezech. 36:26). "He hath given us most great and precious promises: that by these you may be made partakers of the divine nature" (II Pet. 1:4). "The charity of God is poured forth in our hearts, by the Holy Ghost, who is given to us" (Rom. 5:5). "Neglect not the grace that is in thee" (I Tim. 4:14). "I admonish thee, that thou stir up the grace of God which is in thee" (II Tim. 1:6). "Whosoever is born of God, committeth not sin: for His seed abideth in him" (I John 3:9). "Who also hath sealed us, and given the pledge of the Spirit in our hearts" (II Cor. 1:22). "Whosoever drinketh of this water, . . . the water . . . shall become in him a fountain of water, springing up into life everlasting" (John 4:13 f.).

As for the teaching of the Fathers, Rouet de Journel (*Enchiridion patristicum,* theological index, nos. 354–65) sums up their testimony according to the writings of each of them: the abiding, supernatural gift of habitual grace is infused in justification; sins are really removed; man is interiorly renewed; the Holy Ghost dwells in him; he is made a partaker of the divine nature, an adopted son of God, an heir to the kingdom of heaven, a friend of God; habitual grace ejects mortal sin. Man can never be certain of being just or in the state of grace. The just can merit eternal life.

Hence the Council of Trent declares (Sess. VI, can. 11, Denz., no. 821): "If anyone should say that men are justified either by the imputation of Christ's justice alone or by the remission of sins alone, exclusive of grace and charity, which are diffused in their hearts by the Holy Ghost, and that it inheres in them, or even that grace, by which we are justified, is only a favor from God: let him be anathema." Cf. also Council of Trent (Denz., nos. 799 ff., 809).[1]

2. *The theological proof* is presented by St. Thomas in the article, which should be read attentively; in it he begins with the definition of the word "grace" which, by analogy, has several meanings, even in its merely human signification. 1. Thus it means that by which someone is pleasing or gratifying to others; and in this sense it may be the beauty of the person, which is called grace of the countenance;

---

[1] *Catechismus romanus,* Pius V, Part II, no. 185: "But grace is a divine quality inhering in the soul, as a certain brilliance and light which removes all the stains from our souls and renders these souls more beautiful and dazzling."

or someone is said to be pleasing, for instance, to the king because
of the king's benevolence toward him; thus it is said that a man is in
the king's grace. 2. Grace means a gift gratuitously given to someone;
for example: I grant you this grace. 3. It also signifies gratitude or the
rendering of thanks.

In these human connotations the word "grace" is already applied
analogically. With still greater reason is it used in an analogical sense
of divine things, yet not metaphorically, but properly, as will presently
appear. 1. It is applied to the love of God toward those who are pleasing to Him; 2. to the gift gratuitously bestowed upon the just; 3. to
the thanksgiving for a benefit received. From God's benevolent love
proceeds the gratuitous gift, and thereupon, gratitude.

On this basis St. Thomas establishes the most sublime theological
argument, connecting the treatise on created grace with that on uncreated grace, or the uncreated love of God "which infuses and creates
goodness in things," as explained in Ia, q. 20, a. 2. This line of reasoning can be reduced to the following.

What makes us pleasing to God is that which is really produced in
us by the uncreated love of God for us.

But grace is what makes us pleasing to God as children and heirs.

Therefore grace is that which is really produced in us by the uncreated love of God for us.

The major is proved in Ia, q. 20, a. 2, according as the uncreated
love of God for us does not presuppose any lovableness in us, but bestows it upon us. In this respect it differs from created benevolence.
For it is briefly stated in this question of the First Part that, whereas
our love is not the cause of the goodness of things, but rather presupposes it, the love of God is the cause of the goodness of things. And
in the present article St. Thomas adds: "Hence it is clear that any
degree whatever of God's love is followed by some good caused in
the creature. But God's common love is commensurate with what is
bestowed on all created things in the natural order; the other is a
special love by which He draws the rational creature up above the
condition of nature to a participation in the divine goodness."

The minor is the nominal definition of the word "grace" with respect to us. Thus in Holy Scripture grace is said to be that by which
we are pleasing to God, "graced" (Ephes. 1:6), "justified freely by
His grace" (Rom. 3:24), His "beloved" (Ps. 107:7), not merely with
a natural love from which proceed natural benefits, such as being, life,

but with a supernatural love whereby we are called children of God, "born . . . of God" (John 1:13), "partakers of the divine nature" according to the expression of St. Peter: "He hath given us most great and precious promises: that by these you may be made partakers of the divine nature" (II Pet. 1:4). These texts are accepted by Protestants with respect to God's uncreated love for us.

Hence, in accordance with the aforesaid major, it follows that grace is in us a supernatural gift of God inhering in the soul, by which we are truly children of God, born of God, and participators in the divine nature. Thus the love of God is effective in the supernatural as it is in the natural order. And grace generally signifies this gift habitually abiding in the soul, as often referred to by St. Paul.

Nevertheless, as St. Thomas observes in concluding the body of the article, grace sometimes denotes that very eternal, uncreated love of God, so that accordingly even predestination is called grace, "in that God predestined or elected some gratuitously and not because of merit, for it is said to the Ephesians (1:5): [He] 'hath predestinated us unto the adoption of children . . . unto the praise of the glory of His grace, in which He hath graced us in His beloved Son' "; that is, unto the manifestation of the diffusion and splendor of His uncreated grace, by which we are made pleasing to God in His Son.

Thus "grace" is applied analogically both in the natural and in the supernatural orders, but analogically, in the strict sense, and not merely metaphorically.

Grace signifies	in the supernatural order	uncreated grace: God's benevolence toward us.
		grace as a gratuitous, created gift.
		gratitude.
	in the natural order	benevolence of a benefactor toward someone.
		a benefit which is not due.
		gratitude.

In the first place, with respect to us, according to the application of the word, "grace" means that which is pleasing to others, for example, beauty of countenance or mental qualities; and to this grace, by which someone is pleasing to others, corresponds benevolence in others, which is present in a different mode in God and in men. Thereafter, from benevolence there arises some benefit and, thence, gratitude for the benefit received.

But in itself, grace means in the first place that uncreated grace from which all benefits proceed. Hence St. Thomas likewise declares (Ia, q. 13, a. 6): Paternity, from our standpoint, denotes primarily an earthly father; but in itself, it applies primarily to the heavenly Father, according to Ephes. 3:14 f.: "I bow my knees to the Father of our Lord Jesus Christ, of whom all paternity in heaven and earth is named."

In all these acceptations, "grace" is applied not metaphorically (as when God is said to be angry) but properly. However, this proper meaning remains analogical; the analogous significations are such as bear a common name, and the meaning signified by the name is absolutely diverse, but under a particular aspect it is the same (under the analogy of proportionality, it is proportionately the same). Thus the notion of grace is proportionately realized in both its human and its divine applications.

CONFIRMATION FROM THE REFUTATION OF OBJECTIONS

Reply to first objection. That which in us is pleasing to our friends is presupposed by their love, and is not in us as received from them, whereas that which in us is pleasing to God is caused by the divine love.

Reply to second objection. God does not vivify the soul as the soul does the body; for the soul is the form of the body and hence vivifies it immediately; on the contrary, God is not the form of the soul, but a separate agent; hence He vivifies the soul not immediately but by a form produced in the soul, that is, by grace, which is life in first act, while the vital operations are life in second act.

Reply to third objection. As St. Augustine says (I *Retract.*, chap. 23), to grace pertains not only the remission of sins, but also reconciliation and peace; moreover, the very remission of sins is itself accomplished by sanctifying grace received into the soul, as will be clear from what follows below (q. 113, a. 2).

Other objections. According to Isa. 43:4, God proclaims: "Since thou becomest honorable in My eyes, thou art glorious: I have loved thee."

Reply. The word "since" does not here signify cause, but concomitance, for "what hast thou that thou hast not received?" Moreover, one person may be more pleasing to God inasmuch as, receiving grace with more fidelity, he performs greater works.

I insist. God loves the predestinate. But this love does not posit anything supernatural in them when they are in sin. Therefore not all the love of God posits something in the person loved.

Reply. God does not love the predestinate with a terminative efficacious love while he is in sin, but He decreed from all eternity to grant him efficacious graces at such and such a time toward his salvation.

I insist. Even if the love of God is efficacious, it suffices that it cause in man practical assistance.

Reply. This is true of the imperfect love whereby God disposes the sinner for justification, not of the perfect love whereby God loves man as a son and heir; hence man ought to participate in the divine nature, "made partaker of the divine nature."

First corollary. A threefold love of God toward us wayfarers can be distinguished and designated by the effects of each.

1. Merely natural love, which causes natural goods such as being, life, intelligence.

2. Supernatural but imperfect love, which causes in the sinner supernatural faith, hope, and practical helps.

3. Supernatural and perfect love, which communicates habitual grace by which man is made absolutely pleasing to God, His friend, a partaker of the divine nature, and an heir to the kingdom of heaven. (Cf. below, what is said of justification in opposition to Protestantism.)

Second corollary. It is already vaguely apparent from the major premise (the love of God infuses and creates goodness in things), that grace is intrinsically efficacious, that is, because God wills, and not because man wills, to render it efficacious. "It is God who worketh in you both to will and to accomplish, according to His good will." "What hast thou that thou hast not received?" (Cf. below, on efficacious grace.) From the foregoing it is evident that he who actually fulfills the commands of God is better than he who can fulfill them and, in fact, does not do so.

But no one would be in any respect better were he not more loved and assisted by God (Ia, q. 20, a. 3 f.). "What hast thou that thou hast not received?"

Therefore the grace whereby we actually fulfill the precepts of God contains more in itself than the sufficient grace whereby we can fulfill it, without however doing so in fact.

ARTICLE II. WHETHER GRACE IS A QUALITY OF THE SOUL

State of the question. Having established that habitual grace is something created inhering in the soul, we must discover to what category of created being it can be reduced, whether to the category of a quality rather than to a substance, a quantity, a relation, an action, or a passion. It seems that it is not a quality, for the following reasons.

1. Grace acts in the soul, justifying it; but a quality does not act upon its subject.

2. Grace is nobler than the soul, therefore it should not be an accident or quality, but a substance.

3. If grace were an accident or quality, it would be corrupted upon the entrance of mortal sin; this is unbecoming, since grace is the beginning of eternal life.

Note. The Nominalists, before Luther, declared that habitual grace is something ontologically natural, but something which bestows a moral right to eternal life, just as a bank note is physically, ontologically only a slip of paper, although its possession gives one a moral right to the equivalent gold.

On the contrary, certain Cartesian and Ontologist theologians said that grace and charity are the Holy Ghost Himself dwelling in the soul, as the Master of the *Sentences* might say. The Cartesians in particular maintained this, for they did not admit of a real distinction between substance and accident; hence grace could not be a real, supernatural accident distinct from the soul, but must be a substance, that is, God inhabiting it and impelling it to meritorious works availing to salvation.

Reply. St. Thomas replies to the question with a twofold conclusion regarding 1. actual grace and 2. habitual grace.

First conclusion. Actual grace is not a quality but a certain motion of the soul.

Proof. Actual grace is a gratuitous effect of God by which the soul of man is impelled by God toward something which ought to be known or willed or done. But that by which the soul is thus moved is not a permanent quality, but something transient, that is, a certain motion of the soul quite distinct both from the uncreated action of God whence it proceeds and from our action thus produced.

It should be noted that certain Molinists, misinterpreting St. Thomas, understand him thus: actual grace is a certain motion of the soul, that is, an indeliberate operation on our part which inclines toward a deliberate act, determinable by man alone.

On the contrary, when St. Thomas says that actual grace is a certain motion of the soul, he does not say it is an operation of the soul, but, as he himself wrote, it is a motion whereby "the soul is moved by God toward something which is to be known or willed or done." In other words, it is the application of the faculties that they may pass from potency to act and may elicit their operation; for an operation, even indeliberate, is vitally elicited by the faculty and not produced immediately by God alone; but under the infusion of actual grace, the soul elicits vitally even indeliberate operations. On the other hand, actual grace is not elicited by us.

Hence St. Thomas says: "The act of a mover in the moved is a motion" according to Aristotle (III *Physics*). For, as Aristotle declares, motion, inasmuch as it is produced by an agent, is called action or motion, and motion, as it is in the one moved, is "passion." But the action of a bodily agent is formally transitive and terminates in the "patient," whereas the uncreated external action of God is formally immanent and only virtually transitive. Therefore actual grace is something created, as an effect of God, according to St. Thomas (he does not say that actual grace is our action, our vital operation), and it is in us as a motion-passion received in the will, by which the will is moved to elicit its operation.

Zigliara explains this well (*Theol. nat.*, Bk. III, art. 4, § 5, p. 498) by the example of heat.

1. Heat is an action in the fire, or by the fire (formally transitive action);

2. Heat is a passion in the wood, in that the wood is heated;

3. Heat is an operation, since the wood, once heated, gives heat.

Likewise, with respect to divine motion.

1. Motion is an action in God, uncreated, formally immanent and virtually transient action.

2. Motion-passion by which the will is moved, or is made to pass from the potency of willing into the act of willing, is the completion

of causality, referred to by St. Thomas (*Contra Gentes,* Bk. III, chap. 66).

3. The operation elicited by the will, even if indeliberately, is yet vitally elicited.

St. Thomas says (*Contra Gentes,* Bk. III, chap. 66): "For the completion of the power of the secondary agent comes from the first agent." And again (*De potentia,* q. 3, a. 7 ad 7): "That which is made by God in the natural order, by which He may actually operate, is, as a mere intention He has, in a certain sense incomplete, in the way that colors exist in the air or the power of an art in the artist's instrument"; hence the power of an art is distinguished from the action which proceeds from this power. (Cf. our *Dieu,* 8th ed., p. 480, and the Salmanticenses, *De gratia,* disp. 5, dub. 1–6, on actual grace as distinct from the uncreated action of God and from our indeliberate operation.)

Objection. An immanent action elicited by us is reduced, as immanent, to the category of quality,[2] and consequently actual grace ordained toward this action may be reduced to a quality.

Reply. Certainly thus actual grace reductively belongs to the category of quality, but not as something habitual and permanent. What St. Thomas is particularly insistent upon is that actual grace is not something habitual and abiding, as a quality properly so called, but something passing in a transitory manner.

Second conclusion. Sanctifying grace is a certain supernatural quality abiding in the soul.

1. Scriptural proof. Proof from the passages of Sacred Scripture quoted in the explanation of the preceding article wherein grace is referred to as the seed of glory, a pledge, a seal, a fountain; likewise from St. Augustine, here quoted in the argument *Sed contra,* who calls it the luster of the soul. But all these expressions signify something permanent in the soul, by reason of which God abides in the soul, according to the words of John 14:23: "We will come to him, and will make Our abode with him."

Similarly the Council of Trent (Denz., no. 821) speaks of grace as diffused and inhering in the soul; again (Denz., no. 809): "It is called

---

[2] Cf. St. Thomas, *Contra Gentes,* Bk. I, chap. 100, and John of St. Thomas, *Phil. nat.,* q.4, a.4: action, which properly belongs to the category of action, is transitive action producing a correlative passion in the patient; immanent action is reducible to the category of quality.

our justice because by its inherence in us we are justified." As Gonet observes in his commentary on this article (p. 87), the Council of Trent proscribes the error of the Master of the Sentences according to whom charity is the Holy Ghost Himself dwelling in us and moving us to the act of charity.

2. *Theological proof.*

God does not provide less amply for our souls with respect to super-natural good than with respect to natural good.

But with respect to natural good He not only moves us actually, but gives us qualities or faculties, namely, principles, eliciting operations, so that these may be vital and connatural to us.

Therefore it is fitting that God should likewise not only move us to act, but should also give us a habitual principle of supernatural operation, that is, a certain quality, namely, grace itself.

Thus has He disposed all things sweetly. St. Thomas here differentiates between habitual and actual grace more decidedly than does St. Augustine, since he considers the matter more deeply from the ontological aspect, and not merely from the psychological and moral point of view.

Again in IIa IIae, q. 23, a. 2, he makes it clear that charity is something created in the soul and not, as the Master of the Sentences would have it, the Spirit Himself moving us to an act of charity. In the latter case, the soul would not produce the act of charity connaturally or meritoriously; to do so requires an infused habit elevating the will. Otherwise the supernatural order would be less perfect than the natural order. At the same time, an infused habit is, as it were, a second nature in us, so that our supernatural acts are also connatural.

Confirmation from the reply to the objections.

1. Grace, as a quality, acts in the soul not effectively but formally, justifying it or making it just, as whiteness makes a thing white and justice renders one just.

2. Grace cannot be the substance of God since it is the effect of the uncreated love of God (according to Article 1); nor can it be the substance of the soul, since it would then be something natural, would be identified with nature, from which it is to be distinguished, according to revelation. Therefore it can only be an accident and is thus inferior to the soul with respect to the mode of its being, that is, being in something else; but it is nobler than the soul according as it is a certain supernatural participation in the divine nature as it is divine,

that is, in the intimate life of God. Deity is in a certain sense above being, above unity, above life, and above knowledge, for these are contained within it formally and eminently.

Corollary. The essentially supernatural cannot be in us or in the angels otherwise than as an accident; in God alone is it substance.

Reply to third objection. Since grace is an accident, it is not that which is made or corrupted, but that by which someone is made pleasing, who may subsequently become unpleasing; in other words, grace is drawn forth from the obediential power of the soul, and after its loss nothing but the obediential power remains, that is, no repugnance to receiving a return of grace.

The present conclusion may be confirmed by showing that sanctifying grace cannot be classified under any other category of created being. 1. Not under quantity, for quantity results from the composite nature of matter. 2. It is not a relation, since relation demands a foundation, and sanctifying grace is itself the foundation of the relationship by which we are called children of God and it ordains us to glory, inasmuch as it is the seed of glory. It is likewise the foundation or root of the infused virtues, wherein there is a transcendental relationship to our supernatural object. 3. It cannot be an action, not even an immanent action, but is the radical principle of immanent actions, such as acts of charity, faith, hope. 4. It is not a passion; in this it differs from actual grace, which is in us a motion of the soul, or a motion-passion. Finally, it is evident that habitual grace does not belong to any other categories which are found only in bodies, for instance, location, position, time, habit or adornment, although metaphorically it is called the adornment of the soul.

It should be remarked that theologians generally maintain, in opposition to Ripalda and, in a certain measure, to Scotus, not only that grace is not a substance but that God, even by His absolute power, cannot produce a created, supernatural substance to which the vision of the divine essence would be natural. (Cf. *De revelatione*, I, 364, and Billuart, *De Deo,* diss. 4, a. 5, 4; Gonet, *De gratia,* disp. II, a. 3.)

This would be incompatible from the standpoint of the object, since such a substance would have an intellect of the same nature as the divine intellect, for it would be specified by the same formal object; hence it would be a created divine nature, which is repugnant by its terms as is pantheism.

It would also be inconsistent on the part of the subject, for something created cannot be essentially supernatural without being essentially related to the Deity as such and specified by it, since only the essence of God is above all created nature. But no created substance can be essentially related to the Deity and specified by it, because substance is being in itself and for itself (*in se et ad se*), that is, it has within itself its own specification and cannot be defined with reference to anything else.

On the contrary, any accident, such as a power or habit, can be essentially related to something else; thus grace, which is the seed of glory, is specified by the essence of God, of which it is a participation and toward the vision of which it ordains us. But Scotus did not understand this well, for he held that grace and the light of glory are supernatural only in fact, because God so willed it, but that He could have willed them to be natural, so that there could be a creature to whom the beatific vision would be natural.

There are several problems to be examined in connection with this article on account of the errors of the Nominalists who came after St. Thomas and prepared the way for Lutheranism.

First doubt. Is it of faith that sanctifying grace is a quality and a habit?

Reply. It is not a defined article of faith, for the Council of Trent as well as the Council of Vienne, refrained from using the words "quality" and "habit" so as not to define a question disputed among theologians. Hence it seems that the demands of faith would be satisfied by holding that sanctifying grace is a habitual gift, permanently inhering in the soul.

Second doubt. Is it, nevertheless, a certain theological conclusion that sanctifying grace is a quality and a habit, entitatively?

Reply. Assuredly, on account of the argument given by St. Thomas and commonly accepted at present. For habitual grace cannot be conceived as belonging to any other category than that of a quality, as we have said; and within this category it is reducible to a habit. For a habit is a permanent quality, difficult to dislodge (at least by any internal cause), disposing the subject to a certain state, whether for good or evil, in regard to its being (an entitative habit, such as beauty, health) or in regard to its operation (an operative habit).

But sancitfying grace is a permanent quality, as has been shown; moreover it is difficult to dislodge, as far as itself and its principles are concerned, supported as it is by the divine infusion, and indeed being in the spiritual soul the very seed of glory, or life eternal already begun; it is therefore difficult to dislodge, although accidentally, by reason of the subject and of the aberrations and caprices of its free will, it can be lost. "For we carry this treasure in fragile vessels." (Cf. *De veritate,* q. 27, a. 1–9.) [3] Finally, it disposes the subject in a good, or favorable, state toward God and for avoidance of sin. But in the following article, where habitual grace is distinguished from charity, we shall see that the former is an entitative and not an operative habit, except radically.

Third doubt. Is habitual grace a habit univocally or only by analogy, properly speaking?

Reply. It is called a habit not only metaphorically, but properly. However, in agreement with several Thomists (Gardeil, Billot, *De virt. inf.,* pp. 30, 33) it seems to us that it does not correspond univocally with habits of the natural order, by the very fact that it belongs to a higher order which surpasses all nature, created or capable of creation. Hence St. Thomas often speaks of it as a certain quality or as reducible to the genus: quality (cf. Ia IIae, q. 63, last article).

That this solution is indeed St. Thomas' teaching can be proved from four arguments.

1. He observes (Ia IIae, q. 61, a. 1 ad 1) that "virtue" is applied analogically even to the moral and intellectual virtues; hence, with still greater reason, to the supernatural virtues. Likewise, according as prudence directs the moral virtues, the notion of virtue belongs causally by priority to prudence as directing, rather than to the other moral virtues.

2. St. Thomas declares (*De veritate,* q. 14, a. 9, 2) that "belief, as it exists in the demons, is not conformable to infused faith, except equivocally"; the demons believe by acquired faith based on the evidence of miracles, forced, as it were, to accept this evidence.

3. St. Thomas maintains in several places that the infused virtues differ from the acquired inasmuch as they not only bestow the power to act rightly, but bestow it absolutely, according as they give the first upward impetus to a higher order; therefore they partake in a certain sense of the nature of a power and in a certain sense of that of a habit.

[3] St. Thomas says (*De verit.,* q. 27, a. 1 ad 9): "Although by one act of mortal sin grace may be expelled, grace is not, however, expelled easily; for it is not easy for one who possesses grace to perform such an act, on account of the inclination in a contrary direction; thus the Philosopher says in his *Ethics,* Bk. V, chap. 6, that it is difficult for the just man to commit an injustice."

4. St. Thomas states in various articles that "grace is reducible to the primary species of a quality" (habit); cf. Ia IIae, q. 110, a. 3 ad 3; *De veritate,* q. 27, a. 2 ad 7; II, d. 26, q. 1, a. 4 ad 1.

However, John of St. Thomas, commenting on *De virtutibus,* Ia IIae, disp. 16, a. 6, fol. 152, seems to hold that grace and the infused virtues are in accord univocally with the acquired virtues as classified by predicates and analogically as classified by their causative motive or regulative force.

But John of St. Thomas states in his *Cursus phil.,* dealing with the four causes, that they conform univocally in the general notion of cause, which seems to be false.

The argument which impels John of St. Thomas is that acquired virtue is logically univocal in kind, that is, in the order of logic; yet, causally, virtue is predicated of prudence in a prior sense to that of the virtues which are directed by it.

Fourth doubt. Whether habitual grace is a gift entitatively (that is, intrinsically, essentially) and supernaturally.

This is denied by Scotus (q. 1 of the introduction and 4, dist. 10, q. 8), where he says that if God so willed, He could give us grace and the light of glory as natural properties; and he maintains that the supernatural differs from the natural only on the part of the efficient cause, as sight supernaturally given to a man born blind differs from natural sight. Hence grace would not be something intrinsically and essentially supernatural; it would not be supernatural substantially or essentially, but only with respect to the mode of its production under present circumstances. Thus the distinction between the order of grace and the order of nature would not be necessary, in other words, not based upon its divine nature according to which it exceeds all nature, created or capable of creation, but would be a contingent distinction, founded upon the free will of God. This is "contingentism" and "libertism."

The Nominalists, such as Ockham, followed, maintaining that grace should be looked upon as a bank note (cf. Salmanticenses, dub. II, 3, no. 34). For as this note, of its nature, before being issued by the government, has no monetary value, but subsequently is equal to gold; so sanctifying grace intrinsically is a certain entity, lacking sufficient value to render man acceptable to God, but by the accession of an extrinsic disposition of God, or by the favor of God, without any intrinsic transformation, this entity receives a moral value, comparable to that of the bank note. Such, according to the Salmanticenses, was the teaching of Ockham, Gabriel, and a disciple of Ailly (probably Gerson), Durandus (I, d. 17, q. 1, nos. 7 and 8) and Scotus (*ibid.*, q. 2) seem to agree with them. To the same effect, Ockham declared that man can merit eternal life by a natural act, if this act is accepted by God. This is absolute contingentism. Molina retains something of this Nominalism when he says that the theological virtues are supernatural modally, but not by virtue of their formal object.

Thus the Nominalists denied the principles of traditional theology and prepared the way for Lutheranism, which holds that grace is only an extrinsic denomination; in other words, corruption remains in man, but sin is no longer imputed to him, as long as a man believes himself to be predestined. Therefore, "sin strongly, and believe even more strongly."

This is the Nominalist tendency. On the contrary, immoderate realism would tend to identify being in general with the divine being, and to identify grace with God dwelling in us, as the Master of the Sentences maintained. Toward this latter error the Cartesian and ontologistic theologians inclined, refusing to admit that habitual grace is an accident, since they denied any real distinction between substance and accident.

Against Scotus and the Nominalists what is to be said? Gonet (a. 3) states that this opinion is commonly rejected because it does not distinguish between what is intrinsically or substantially supernatural, and what is extrinsically or modally supernatural. However, this distinction is generally accepted by theologians, especially since the Council of Trent's condemnation of Protestantism, as Lichetto himself acknowledges, referring to Scotus. (Cf. Scotus, *Opera,* ed. Vives, XV, 200; and our *De revelatione,* I, 216.) Lichetto maintains, after Trent, that there are habits which of themselves are necessarily infused, such as the theological virtues. Moreover, the Church has always distinguished between the supernaturalness of miracles naturally intelligible, and the supernaturalness of grace and of mysteries which are naturally unintelligible even for the angels (Council of the Vatican). Hence even the Molinists hold that, although the theological virtues are supernatural substantially, yet they are not supernatural by virtue of their formal object; and therein lies the inconsistency of their position.

At present theologians generally agree, in opposition to Scotus and

Ripalda, that God, even by His absolute power, cannot create a supernatural substance or a substance to which the vision of the divine essence would be natural. (Cf. Council of Trent, Sess. VI, chap. 7, Denz., no. 800.) In regard to the justification of sinners: "By it we are renewed in spirit . . . ; we are indeed called just and so we are. Hence in this same justification, together with the remission of sins, man receives simultaneously the infusion of all these: faith, hope, and charity." Thus the virtues are, by their very nature, infused, not accidentally infused, as infused geometry would be. But we shall give the complete refutation of the foregoing theory of the Nominalists in the solution of the next problem.

Fifth doubt. Whether sanctifying grace is a formal and physical participation in the divine nature.

State of the question. In articles 3 and 4 of the present question, as well as in q. 112, a. 1, St. Thomas says that grace is a participation in the divine nature, and St. Thomas was speaking formally; but later, in the fourteenth and fifteenth centuries, there were great discussions between Thomists and Nominalists over that word "participation."

All Catholic theologians have certainly always held that sanctifying grace is in some sense a participation in the divine nature, on account of the express testimony of Sacred Scripture and the Fathers, to be quoted below, particularly on account of the words of St. Peter's Second Epistle (1:4): "that by these [gifts] you may be made partakers of the divine nature."

In the first place, the Nominalist definition of "participation" should be noted. The expression "to participate" means to take part; thus are distinguished the subject participating and the perfection participated. Cf. *Tabula aurea* of the works of St. Thomas, s.v. Participatio.

"Participate" means to take part; it is primarily applied to quantitative things which possess integral parts, for instance, to participate in this meal; subsequently it can be applied to qualities, for example, to participate in or partake of heat, light, whiteness, or to spiritual qualities, as a pupil participates in the knowledge of his master when he receives a share in it, or a soldier participates in the victory of his general.

Thus Plato often used this word in the philosophical order when, for instance, he stated that men participate in the idea of humanity, and bulls in the idea of bovinity; but he thought that these exemplary ideas had separate being. On the contrary, a separate man or bull cannot exist, since they would have to have bones and flesh, in other words, a common, not an individual material, and bones and flesh cannot exist without being these particular bones and flesh, as Aristotle maintained. But God is essential being, essential good, and essential truth.

It is commonly said that stones participate in being, plants and animals participate in life, men participate in intellect, and thus they are analogically like unto God with regard to being, life, and intellect respectively. Now it must be determined whether by habitual grace the just man participates in the divine nature, in the intimate life of God or in the Deity by which God is, properly speaking, God; in other words, whether he participates in the radical principle of operations which are properly divine, by which God knows and loves Himself immediately.

As the Salmanticenses here record (dub. III, no. 54), the Nominalists, consistently with their thesis, mentioned above, denied that sanctifying grace is a physical and formal participation in the divine nature. (Likewise Coninck, *In IIam IIae,* d. 21, no. 75, and Lessius Bk. II, *De summo bono.*)

The Nominalists declare that sanctifying grace is a moral participation, consisting in a rectitude of the will and an imitation of the sanctity and justice of God, just as those who imitate the faith of Abraham are called sons of Abraham, and those who imitate the malice of the devil are called his sons, although physically they are not born of either. In accordance with this tendency, the Protestants held that man is by grace a son of God, since he believes his sins are externally removed or no longer imputed to him. And Baius, who was a moderate Protestant, denied the strict supernaturalness of sanctifying grace, which he limited to natural, Christian virtue.[4]

Other Catholic theologians maintained that sanctifying grace is a physical participation in the divine nature, not however formal, but virtual; that is, not formal, as the light of the air is a participation in the light of the sun, but virtual, as the seed is a participation in the

---

[4] Cf. Denz., no. 1021: "The elevation and exaltation of human nature to a participation in the divine nature was due to the integrity of its primary state and accordingly is called natural and not supernatural." No. 1023: "Absurd is the opinion of those who say that man, from the beginning, was exalted by certain supernatural and gratuitous gifts above the condition of his nature, that he might seek God supernaturally by faith, hope, and charity."

procreator, by a power derived from it to produce a likeness of itself. (Cf. Gonet.)

Lastly, the Thomists hold that sanctifying grace is a physical and formal participation in the divine nature; but with respect to some secondary points they are not agreed. Cajetan, Ledesma, Martines, Gonet, and the Salmanticenses claim that it is even a physical, formal, analogical participation in the very infinity of God; others (Curiel, for example) declare that a participation in infinity is impossible. But this minor disagreement seems to be a mere matter of terminology, for John of St. Thomas and Billuart reconcile these two opinions of Thomists, as will presently be explained (cf. below: the dignity of sanctifying grace).

The more general conclusion is that sanctifying grace is a participation in the divine nature, not only moral but physical, not only virtual but formal, analogical however, imperfectly imitating as an accident what, in God, is substance.

1. This conclusion is based upon Sacred Scripture: "By whom [Christ] . . . hath given us most great and precious promises: that by these you may be made partakers of the divine nature" (II Pet. 1:4). Likewise in Sacred Scripture it is attested in various places that the just are, by grace, generated, born, reborn, of God and made sons of God; but by generation and birth, nature is communicated. "Of His own will hath He begotten us by the word of truth, that we might be some beginning of His creature" (Jas. 1:18). "He gave them power to be made sons of God . . . who are born, not of blood, nor of the will of the flesh . . . , but of God" (John 1:12 f.). What would remain of this text, according to Nominalism and Lutheranism? "Unless a man be born again of water and the Holy Ghost, he cannot enter into the kingdom of God" (John 3:5). "Whosoever is born of God committeth not sin: for His seed abideth in him" (I John 3:9). And again (*ibid.*, 5:1): "Whosoever . . . is born of God" does not sin, but the grace of God preserves him; that is, he who remains in the state of grace, as a child of God, does not sin mortally. Thus it is proved from Sacred Scripture that grace is a participation in the divine nature.

Similarly this is the obvious meaning of the Church's definitions which are thus brought together by Denzinger in his index (p. 598): "Habitual grace is distinct from actual grace (nos. 1064 ff.); it is an infused, inherent quality of the soul by which man is formally justified, made a partaker of the divine nature, regenerated, abides in Christ, puts on the new man, is made an heir to eternal life" (cf. references according to Denz., *ibid.*).[5]

2. *Theological proof.* There are two arguments in particular: a) taken from the definition of nature; b) from the essential supernaturalness of grace itself.

The first argument is stated thus: By divine nature is meant the radical principle of the divine operations by which God sees Himself intuitively and loves Himself.

But sanctifying grace imitates physically and formally this radical principle of properly divine operations, for it radically disposes man to see God intuitively and to love Him with the beatific love.

Therefore sanctifying grace is a physical and formal participation in the divine nature.

The major is based on the very definition of nature, which is the root of the properties and the radical principle of operations in any being. Thus analogically but according to the strict and not the metaphorical sense, nature is in God that which is conceived in Him as the root of the divine perfections and the radical principle of properly divine operations, which are specified by the very essence of God, seen and loved; whereas, on the contrary, the creative act proceeds, not from the divine nature, but from the divine liberty, for God does not operate outside of Himself from any necessity of nature.

The minor is clear especially with regard to grace consummated, which is called glory, from which proceeds the light of glory in the intellect and the charity of beatitude in the will. Moreover, according to St. Paul, the charity of the wayfarer never falls away, but is the same as in heaven; and faith is the substance of things hoped for. Hence grace is spoken of, in tradition, as the seed of glory, a certain beginning of eternal life, according to the words of Christ: "He that believeth in the Son, hath life everlasting" (John 3:36); "He that believeth in Me, hath everlasting life" (*ibid.*, 6:47, also 6:40 and 6:55); "Every one that . . . believeth in Me, shall not die forever" (*ibid.*, 11:26).

It is a question of grace, which establishes the adoptive sonship, which is a certain participated likeness in the sonship of the Word, for in natural filiation the whole undivided nature is communicated,

[5] With regard to the testimony of the Fathers, cf. Rouet de Journel, *Enchirid. patristicum,* index theologicus, no. 358.

essence and substance, as it is in the Father; but to us is communicated a participation in the divine nature by accidental gift.

Objections. Adversaries of this conclusion raise the following objections.

First objection. It is said in the book of Job (38:28): "Who is the father of rain? or who begot the drops of dew?" That is, God; but the rain does not participate in the nature of God; therefore neither do the other texts quoted prove anything.

Reply. The language of the book of Job is frequently poetical in style, and in this text "the father of rain" is poetically used for the creator of rain. Likewise when it asks "who begot the drops of dew," the word "begot" is taken in a broad and not a strict sense. But this is not so when it is declared of the just (II Pet. 1:4) that they are made "partakers of the divine nature."

I insist. Sacred Scripture also calls "children of God" those who lead good lives and do the will of God; for example, "Do good to them that hate you . . . that you may be the children of your Father" (Matt. 5:44 f.). "But love ye your enemies . . . and you shall be the sons of the Highest" (Luke 6:35). In these texts only a moral relationship with God is meant, and we are made His sons morally, or by imitation of His ways.

Reply. To be sure, we are also made children of God, morally, by imitation of His ways, but this moral relationship does not exclude the other but rather, indeed, presupposes it. For God first infuses grace by which we are partakers of the divine nature and are made pleasing to God and His children, by a physical participation in His nature. Then man, by meritorious acts, also becomes a child of God morally, imitating the paternal manner of acting. Thus the child of any distinguished man, if he follows the practices of his father, is said to be made his son to that extent, and this is implied by the words of Christ: "Do good to them that hate you . . . that you may be the children of your Father who is in heaven." These words presuppose that God is already a father on some other account than that of the love of enemies.

I insist. By grace we are made only adoptive sons of God. However, adoption does not communicate nature, but only a moral right to an inheritance. Therefore grace is only a moral participation in the divine nature by imitation of the divine ways.

Reply. Adoption communicates only a moral right to an inheritance in human affairs: granted; in divine things: denied. In human affairs this is true for two reasons: 1) because human adoption presupposes in the child adopted the same nature specifically as in the person adopting; it is otherwise in divine adoption; 2) because the love of the man adopting is only affective, and produces no physical effect in the child adopted, but only a moral right to an inheritance; on the contrary, "the love of God infuses and creates goodness in things."

First confirmation. Grace partakes of the divine nature as charity and the light of glory partake of the divine attributes. But charity participates strictly and physically in the divine love as divine, since it is specified by the same formal object; and the light of glory participates in the same way in the divine light as divine. Thus Christ says: "The glory which thou hast given Me, I have given to them" (John 17:22). Therefore habitual grace partakes of the divine nature as divine, that is, in the Deity itself, not only with reference to being, but to Deity as such.

Second confirmation. A cause the effects of which are real and physical is itself real and physical. But the effects of sanctifying grace, as a participation in the divine nature, are real and physical, namely, the supernatural virtues which follow upon it as properties. For, according to the Council of Trent, charity is something diffused and inhering in our hearts. The end of sanctifying grace is also something real and physical, that is, the beatific vision. Therefore sanctifying grace itself, as a participation in the divine nature, is something real and physical, not something merely moral as an imitation of the divine ways.

It must, however, be termed an analogical, not a univocal, participation, since it is something created; moreover it is an accident. The Fourth Lateran Council (Denz., no. 432), explaining the words, "Be ye perfect even as your heavenly Father is perfect," declares that it is "as if our Lord were to say: Be perfect, with the perfection of grace, as your heavenly Father is perfect, with the perfection of nature; manifestly, each in his own mode, since between the Creator and the creature such a similarity cannot be acknowledged, without acknowledging that the dissimilarity between them is even greater." Therefore it is only an analogy, not however a mere metaphor, but strictly speaking, according as grace properly ordains us to the operations of beatitude which are properly divine and have the same formal object as the uncreated operations of God Himself. Thus grace is more than a virtual participation in Deity; it is participation as a permanent form and by reason of the specifying, connatural formal object.[6] That which can be called a virtual participation in the divine nature is the instrumental power residing in the sacraments for the production of grace and likewise the actual grace which disposes one for habitual grace.

Second theological argument. Following this first argument with its confirmations, another can thus be proposed which is drawn from the essential supernaturalness of grace.

Sanctifying grace, in both men and angels, is, according to the Church, an essentially supernatural gift, exceeding any nature created or capable of being created.

But sanctifying grace cannot thus exceed any nature capable of creation unless it is a formal and physical participation in the divine nature.

Therefore sanctifying grace is a formal and physical participation in the divine nature.

It should be remarked that this argument can be inverted and proposed as a corollary of the preceding argument, to prove against the Nominalists that grace is intrinsically supernatural since it is a physical participation in the divine nature. This is done by Billuart.

But our major can be proved from the authority of the councils, for, according to the Vatican Council (Denz., 1796): "divine mysteries (among which is sanctification by grace) by their very nature so exceed the created intellect that even when transmitted by revelation and received by faith, they yet remain covered over by the veil of faith itself and enshrouded in a certain darkness, as long as we are making our way in this life toward God." Similarly with respect to the essential supernaturalness of grace, according as it surpasses the powers and merits of nature (cf. the condemnation of Pelagianism and Semi-Pelagianism by the Second Council of Orange) and according as it exceeds the requirements of our nature (cf. the condemnation of Baius, especially Denz., nos. 1021, 1023, and the reference just quoted). Moreover, the Vatican Council (Denz., no. 1813), teaching that "miracles can certainly be known" even naturally, dis-

[6] Our supernatural operations are said to be connatural inasmuch as they proceed from grace and the infused virtues as from a second nature in which we participate as in the manner of a permanent form.

tinguishes expressly between the supernaturalness of miracles, which exceeds our efficient created powers but not our cognoscitive powers, and the supernaturalness of mysteries and of grace, which exceed the powers of understanding of any intellect capable of being created. Thus without a special revelation no one is absolutely certain of being in the state of grace.

Our minor is thus proved: natures created or capable of being created have a participated likeness to God with respect to being, life, and intellect, but not with respect to Deity as such. For God exceeds all nature created or capable of being created by reason of the radical principle of properly divine operations which have God Himself for specifying object. This is the intimate life of God, belonging to God by the very strict, intimate reason of His Deity, which is in a certain sense above being, unity, life, and intellect, because it contains formally and eminently these absolutely simple perfections.

Therefore grace, according as it exceeds all nature created or indeed capable of creation, is a formal and physical participation in the divine nature, or Deity as such.

Objection. But even a stone is a certain physical participation in the divine nature inasmuch as it is substantial, and so is a plant inasmuch as it has life in first act and second act; with still greater reason the intellectual soul is a physical participation in the divine nature with respect to intellectual life at least in first act and our understanding with respect to life in second act; cf. Gardeil, O.P., *Structure de l'âme et expérience mystique,* 1927, I, 373.

Reply. The stone does not participate in the divine nature. It participates in being, being in general, not divine being; and thus it is an anological likeness of the divine being since it is being, not as being God. Likewise the plant participates in life in general, not divine life; and in the same way the rational soul participates in intellectual life in general and thus has a participated likeness of the divine intellect on the general analogical basis of intellection. In all of these there is present the common resemblance (being, life, intellect) which God and the creature share analogically.

On the other hand, sanctifying grace as such is not a participation in being in general, nor in life in general, nor in intellectuality in general, but a participation in Deity, which is found naturally only in God. Thus only grace is called a participation in the divine nature according as it is in us the radical principle of operations strictly divine, of which the formal object is (in heaven, at least) absolutely the same as the formal object of the uncreated operations of God.

All of this may be diagrammed as follows:

Being $\left\{\begin{matrix} \text{God} \\ \text{stone} \end{matrix}\right.$ life $\left\{\begin{matrix} \text{God} \\ \text{plant} \end{matrix}\right.$ intellectuality $\left\{\begin{matrix} \text{God} \\ \text{soul} \end{matrix}\right.\left|\begin{matrix} \text{Deity} \\ \text{grace} \end{matrix}\right.$

Thus the stone participates in being and has a likeness to God on the basis of being; grace, on the contrary, is directly and immediately a participation in the divine nature, not in any perfection analogically shared by God and the creature.

Therefore Deity as such cannot be partaken of except by some essentially supernatural gift. And, conversely, grace cannot be essentially supernatural unless it is a formal and physical participation in the divine nature as divine, that is, in the intimate life of God, or Deity as Deity, ordaining us to the knowledge of God as He Himself knows Himself immediately and to the love of God as He loves Himself.

Furthermore, sanctifying grace is a participation in Deity as it is in itself and not merely as it is known to us. For it is produced in our soul by an immediate infusion altogether independently of our knowledge of the Deity; and just as Deity as such is communicated to the Son by eternal generation, so Deity as such is partaken of by the just, especially by the blessed, through divine adoption.[7]

Hence, materially, grace is a finite accident, an entitative habit, but formally it is a formal participation in Deity as it is in itself, as it subsists in the three persons. Thus it is clearly evident that Deity as such in a certain sense surpasses being and intellection, since all absolutely simple perfections are identified in the eminence of Deity and can be naturally participated in, but Deity cannot be participated in naturally. (Cf. below, pp. 138 ff.: The dignity of sanctifying grace.)

First corollary. Our adoptive sonship is formally and physically a participated likeness of the eternal sonship of the Son of God. (Cf. St. Thomas on Rom. 8:29: "He . . . predestinated to be made conform-

---

[7] Cf. on this subject our article: "La grâce est-elle une participation de la Déité telle qu'elle est en soi?" *Revue thomiste,* July, 1936, pp. 470–85. The reply is in the affirmative. Thus, in this question it is not necessary to ask what the formal constituent of divine nature is according to our way of conceiving it; whether it is subsistent being itself or intelligence itself, we are concerned with Deity as it is in itself, which is in some ways above being and above intelligence, according as it eminently and formally contains these simple perfections absolutely. Cf. Cajetan *In Iam,* q.1, a.3, no. 4; q.1, a.7, no. 1; q.13, a.5, nos. 7, 10 ff.; q.39, a.1, no. 7.

able to the image of His Son"; the *Tabula aurea,* "Adoptio," 21; Ia,
q. 93, a. 4, 2; IIa IIae, q. 45, a. 6; IIIa, q. 3, a. 8; q. 23, a. 1, 2, 3, 4.)
The reason is that, just as the Father communicates to His only-
begotten Son the whole of His nature, without multiplication or division of this nature, so He communicates to us physically and
formally, by an accidental gift, a participation in this divine nature,
or in His intimate life, that we may see Him as He sees Himself immediately, although in a finite manner; for to participate is to take
a part and to leave a part; Deity is substance in God, its participation
is an accident in us.

The principal texts of Holy Scripture on the divine adoption are
the following: "For whosoever are led by the Spirit of God, they are
the sons of God. For you have not received the spirit of bondage again
in fear; but you have received the spirit of adoption of sons, whereby
we cry: Abba (Father). For the Spirit Himself giveth testimony to
our spirit, that we are the sons of God. And if sons, heirs also" (Rom.
8:14-17). "For whom He foreknew, He also predestinated to be
made conformable to the image of His Son; that He might be the
first-born among many brethren" (*ibid.,* 8:29). "God hath predestinated us unto the adoption of children through Jesus Christ unto
Himself, according to the purpose of His will" (Ephes. 1:5). "God
sent His son . . . that we might receive the adoption of sons. And
because you are sons, God hath sent the Spirit of His Son into your
hearts, crying: Abba, Father. Therefore now he is not a servant, but
a son; and if a son, an heir also through God" (Gal. 4:4-7).

St. Thomas treats of our adoptive sonship particularly in IIIa, q. 23,
a. 1, 2, 3, 4. He shows how divine adoption differs from human adoption (inasmuch as God by the gift of grace makes the man or angel
whom He adopts fit for his inheritance). He shows especially how
adoptive sonship through grace is a participated likeness of natural
sonship: as the only-begotten Son of God receives eternally the whole
divine nature from His Father, the adoptive son of God receives, in
time, a participation of the divine nature, or grace, the seed of glory,
the beginning of eternal life.

Adoption belongs to the whole Trinity, but is appropriated to the
Father as its author, to the Son as its exemplar, to the Holy Ghost as
engraving upon us the likeness of this exemplar.

Second corollary. The existence and actual possibility of grace cannot be strictly proved by reason alone, since the supernatural sub-

stantially, taken formally, is also supernatural with respect to intelligibility; truth and being are convertible. For that which is essentially supernatural has no necessary, evident connection with things of the natural order; otherwise it would be reduced to the philosophical order, as is the existence of God as author of nature.

Third corollary. Grace is nobler than all other created being, since it participates more perfectly in the divine good than any nature capable of being created. Hence St. Thomas says (below, Ia IIae, q. 113, a. 9 ad 2): "The goodness of the grace of one (man) is greater than the goodness of the nature of the whole universe." (Cf. Cajetan's Commentary on this, and Gonet.)

Confirmation. That is better which is loved more by God. But, as the Apostle says, God did all things for the sake of the elect (II Tim. 2:10), and therefore He loves the just more than all creatures of the natural order, as a father loves his son more than his fields, his house, and his cattle. (Cf. Salmanticenses.)

Fourth corollary. For perfect knowledge of the value of grace we would need to know glory itself experimentally, just as the knowledge of the value of an infant's intelligence requires a knowledge of intellectual life in its full evolution. How great, then, is the evil of mortal sin! "If thou didst know the gift of God." Thus the three orders of sensitive life, natural life, intellectual life, and the life of grace were clearly distinguished long before Pascal.

Final doubt. Whether sanctifying grace of itself alone ensures one's being formally the adopted son of God.

State of the question. Adoption is generally defined as "a gratuitous admission of a stranger into the inheritance of another." According to revelation, God adopts men as children, as is evident from the Epistle to the Romans (8:15): "You have received the spirit of adoption"; from Galatians (4:5): "that we might receive the adoption of sons"; and from Ephesians (1:5): "Who hath predestinated us unto the adoption of children through Jesus Christ." And this definition of adoption is, in fact, verified according as God gratuitously admits and elevates an alien into a beatitude which exceeds the natural requirements or rights of this person. This is generally accepted by the Fathers, especially Cyprian, Pope Leo, and Augustine.[8]

Moreover, adoptive sonship is taken either formally, as it consists

---

[8] Rouet de Journel, *Enchir. patristicum,* index theologicus, no. 359.

in a relationship, or fundamentally, as the foundation of the aforesaid relationship. We are now inquiring what this fundation is. In
the natural order natural sonship is formally the relationship, and
fundamentally it is passive generation or nature received through
generation. Hence, proportionately, the primary formal effect of
sanctifying grace is the deification of the soul; the secondary formal
effect is adoptive sonship.[9]

To the question thus stated the Nominalists replied, with Scotus
and Durandus, that through sanctifying grace we are adopted sons of
God, not on account of the very nature of grace, but because God
wished to concede this by way of an extrinsic favor.

The Thomists maintain, on the contrary, that we are adoptive sons
of God through sanctifying grace on account of its very nature, without looking for any extrinsic favor. To understand this teaching the
difference between human and divine adoption must be kept well
in mind. It is twofold: 1. Human adoption presupposes in the one
adopted the same nature specifically as in the one adopting; it is
otherwise in divine adoption. 2. The love which the man adopting
bears toward the one adopted produces no physical effect in the latter,
but only something moral and civil, that is, the right of inheritance.
On the contrary, the love of God whereby He adopts men through
grace is effective and efficacious, and by it He effects a participation
in the divine nature, or sanctifying grace. Therefore this sanctifying
grace of itself is the foundation of the relationship of adoptive sonship; just as the communication of the whole divine nature, by eternal,
quasi-passive generation of the Second Person of the Trinity, is the
foundation of the relationship of natural sonship. Hence, as sanctifying grace is not merely a moral, but also a physical and formal,
participation in the divine nature, it lays the foundation of adoptive
sonship immediately, without the need of looking for any extrinsic
favor.

Confirmation. Habitual grace is nature proportioned to the beatific
vision, that is, to the eternal inheritance. Likewise, we maintain, in
opposition to Lessius, that the divinity of the Holy Ghost intrinsically
united to us or assisting and dwelling in us does not produce, by way
of form, adoptive sonship, since the form terminating spiritual gen-

[9] This secondary effect is not present in Christ, since He is already the natural Son
of God. Cf. IIIa. q.23, a.4.

eration is that by which the generated term lives, spiritually. But God is our life not formally, but only effectively. (Cf. IIa IIae, q. 23, a. 2 ad 2, against the Master of the Sentences.)

We also hold, contrary to the opinion of Suarez, that to be the adopted son of God without habitual grace implies a contradiction. For there is required by this sonship at least an analogical conformity with God in His nature; but this is brought about only by habitual grace whereby man is spiritually begotten by God. Thus to live the divine life radically without grace implies a contradiction; without it man would have only natural justice, and not even that, since in the present state healing grace is required for the observance of the whole natural law.

RECAPITULATION: THE DIGNITY OF SANCTIFYING GRACE

Whether sanctifying grace is formally and physically a participation in infinite pure Act.

This is a disputed question among Thomists. Cajetan, Gonet, and the Salmanticenses answer in the affirmative, since it is a participation in Deity. Curiel and certain others deny it, since, as they say, the infinite as such cannot be participated in, for it is always received in a finite way. John of St. Thomas, Billuart, and also the Salmanticenses reconcile these two opinions thus: Grace participates in the nature of infinite, pure Act not adequately and subjectively (since whoever receives it does so in a finite way) but objectively and inadequately, for he participates in what is proper to God, or Deity itself, as the root of strictly divine operations which terminate objectively in the Deity itself clearly seen and loved. The disagreement is rather a matter of terms than of ideas.

John of St. Thomas says that grace is a participation in infinity objectively, as it is the likeness and splendor of the divine intellect; elevating the rational creature so that he may receive, as specifying, connatural object, God in His infinity, or rather we should say, in that He is God, according to the most eminent and proper reason of Deity. Deity as such, of which grace is a participation, in a certain sense surpasses infinity, which is a mode, as it were, of the attributes of God which are identified in the eminence of the Deity.

As Gonet declares (*De essentia gratiae,* no. 52): "The beatific vision, which is the operation of consummated grace, corresponds to God as He is the infinite being and in His essence. Therefore consummated grace participates in the divine nature as it is an infinite being," for it is the connatural principle of the beatific vision.

Sanctifying grace does not take unto itself the whole infinity of God, but infinity in a certain manner, or inadequately; that is, it has the divine essence for its connatural, immediate object; but it is not identified with this infinite object, nor does it comprehend it as God does. For this reason grace, like charity, can be increased infinitely (cf. IIa IIae, q. 24, a. 7; Gonet, *op. cit.,* for the solution of objections).

First corollary. Habitual grace is a participation in the divine nature as a nature, just as charity is a participation in divine love as being its operation. But both are participations of the intimate life of God. In contrast to natural vegetative, sensitive, or intellectual life, it is said of grace that it is a participation in the divine nature or life as divine.

Second corollary. Sanctifying grace is, through itself, directly, but secondarily, a participation in the nature of God as it is in the three persons; for the nature of God as such subsists as such in three persons and has an infinite inward fecundity by way of the divine processions. Hence from grace rises charity, which is an inclination toward God as He subsists in three persons, and also from grace, in heaven, rises the light of glory and the vision of the Trinity itself.

However, grace is not a participation in the personal divine fatherhood, since the adoptive sonship which follows from grace is a participated likeness in the eternal sonship of the Word; even by the eternal generation of the Word the divine nature is indeed communicated, but not the paternity. Therefore by divine adoption a participation of the divine nature is communicated, but not of the personal fatherhood. But from the infusion of grace there does follow the adoptive sonship which renders us like the Word, who is the image of the Father, and from grace flows that charity which produces in us a likeness to the Holy Ghost.

Third corollary. The infused virtues flow from sanctifying grace physically, as properties of the soul. (Cf. Salmanticenses.)

Fourth corollary. From the absolute power of God several kinds of sanctifying grace, essentially differing among themselves, cannot be bestowed, whatever some modern theologians may assert, for grace is a formal participation in the divine nature which is absolutely simple, nor can anything higher be conceived in which it would participate. Hence, whatever Father Billot may hold (*De Verbo incarnato,* thes. XVII, 6th ed., p. 208), not even in the most holy soul of Christ is habitual grace of a higher species than in any just man, although it is much more intense and extensive. Moreover, in Christ this habitual grace is derived from the uncreated grace of union or from the Word terminating the human nature; but considered intrinsically, habitual grace is not of a higher species in Christ than in us: it is always and everywhere a formal and physical participation of the divine nature; nor is it possible to conceive of anything higher in which it could participate than the Deity itself as such. If habitual grace in Christ were of a higher kind, so also would be His beatific vision, as Father Billot declares (*ibid.*), and then the following principle would not be observed: habit and act are specified by their formal object, for the formal object of the beatific vision of Christ is identical with that of the beatific vision of all the other blessed in heaven.

And on account of the absolute power, habitual grace, charity, and the light of glory, even in the most holy soul of Christ, could always be increased. We cannot conceive of the highest possible degree of this participation, for between any degree, even the highest, and the Deity itself, there is always an infinite distance, as there is between the incomprehensive beatific vision on the one hand, and the uncreated, comprehensive vision on the other. (Cf. IIIa, q. 10, a. 4 ad 3, and q. 7, a. 12 ad 2.)

Confirmation. If there were two graces of essentially different kinds, there would likewise be two charities of essentially different kinds and two lights of glory essentially distinct. But this is impossible, for the essential reason of charity is to tend supernaturally toward God as He is in Himself, to be loved with a love of esteem above all things, and the light of glory is terminated in God as He is. No higher specifying object can be conceived, and habits are specified by their formal object.

Fifth corollary. Hence in Adam before the fall and in Christ sanctifying grace was not of another kind than in us; but it did have other effects [10] in them, however; in fact, even in the natural order the same human species has different effects in man and in woman. Thus grace causes repentance in us, but not in Christ since He was impeccable; in us it caused adoptive sonship, but not in Christ, for

---

[10] For an accidental form (as grace) perfects the subject into which it is received according to the mode and requirements of the latter, and in a diversity of subjects it produces diverse effects occasionally differing in species Thus grace does not produce in the angels virtues which moderate the passions, as it does in us.

He was already the natural Son of God and therefore incapable of adoption. Likewise in the innocent Adam grace was the root of original justice which involves integrity of nature; this is not true in us. In the angels it does not produce the virtues of temperance and fortitude, since the angels have no passions.

By the same token, sanctifying grace remaining but one in species has nevertheless two states, that of the present life and that of heaven. In the former it requires faith and hope connaturally, but not in the latter, which, in turn, demands the light of glory and, after the resurrection, the glorification of the body. Nor is it to be wondered at, considering the diversity of these states, that the same grace is the root of different virtues.

Sixth corollary. Sanctifying grace is absolutely more perfect than charity, the light of glory, or the beatific vision, which have their source in it, as an essence is more perfect than any of its properties; for grace participates in the divine nature, under the concept of nature, not under the concept of intellectual power or intellection or love. However, the beatific vision is more perfect, under a certain aspect, than grace, as second act is more perfect than first act. Thus a tree is something more perfect than its fruit, but the tree is rendered still more perfect when it bears fruit.

Seventh corollary. Specifically, sanctifying grace is absolutely more noble than the substance of any soul, even the soul of Christ, more noble than any angelic substance created or capable of being created; accidentally, however, according to its mode of being, that is, under a particular aspect, it may be less noble. With respect to the soul of Christ, cf. *De verit.*, q. 27, a. 1 ad 6; and IIa IIae, q. 23, a. 3: "Charity is absolutely more perfect than the essence of the soul," just as the intellectual faculty, although an accident, is more noble than a stone.

Eighth corollary. Grace is, then, more spiritual and incorruptible in itself than the human soul; "we have this treasure in fragile vessels." However, sanctifying grace is absolutely less noble than the divine motherhood of the Word incarnate, for this motherhood by reason of its term belongs to the order of the hypostatic union, and this order surpasses not only the order of nature, but also the order of grace and glory.

St. Thomas says (Ia, q. 25, a. 6 ad 4): "The Blessed Virgin, because she is the Mother of God, has a certain infinite dignity deriving from the infinite good which is God; and because of this nothing better than this can be made." On this account the cult of hyperdulia is due to her (cf. IIIa, q. 25, a. 5); for, as Cajetan declares, her "dignity borders upon the confines of divinity."

Doubt. Whether actual grace disposing toward justification is a physical and formal participation of the divine nature. I reply that it is a physical, virtual, but not formal participation, as the seed is a participation in the generator as a power derived from it to produce a likeness of itself. It is not a formal participation, however, since it does not yet confer the power of eliciting connaturally supernatural operations of the order of grace. It is, as it were, a supernatural regeneration in process only, as we should say, referring to justification.

Second doubt. Whether sanctifying grace formally procures the adoptive sonship of God and whether it alone can bring about such an effect (cf. Gonet, *loc. cit.*). Adoption is usually defined as a gratuitous admission of a stranger into the inheritance of another. Thus an adopted son is distinguished from a son by nature in both human and divine applications. It is assumed as certain from faith that the just man is an adopted son of God: "That we might receive the adoption of sons" (Gal. 4:5); "You have received the spirit of adoption" (Rom. 8:15); "Who hath predestinated us unto the adoption of children through Jesus Christ" (Ephes. 1:5).

To the question as stated the reply is more commonly in the affirmative, since, just as natural sonship is a formally real relationship based on passive generation, or on nature received through generation, in like manner adoptive sonship is formally a real relationship based on a passive participation of the divine nature received through regeneration. This is true even independently of the subsequent acceptation of God, in opposition to the Nominalists, Durandus, and Scotus.

This is confirmed by the fact that no other reality can be the foundation of this real relationship: 1) not indeed the Holy Ghost, whatever Lessius may say, since He assists us as an extrinsic cause, and is not the form by which anyone is regenerated as a child of God; 2) nor charity, which presupposes habitual grace as its root, as will be more clearly demonstrated later.

First corollary. Hence, contrary to the followers of Suarez, Thomists hold that there is a contradiction implied in being the adoptive son of God without habitual grace. For this sonship requires an analogical conformity to God in the divine nature; and it implies a contradiction that the creature be conformed analogically to God in His nature without a participation of the divine nature by grace. Thus by the very fact that the just man possesses grace he is the adoptive son of God and has a right to be received into glory. (Cf. Gonet, *op. cit.*, no. 136.)

Second corollary. The adoption of man as a son is common to the three persons, in that the act of infusing grace, since it is a free, external operation, is common to the whole Trinity as omnipotence is. However, as stated in IIIa, q. 23, a. 2, active adoption is appropriated to the Father, according as adoptive sonship is a certain participated likeness in the eternal sonship. Moreover, to the extent that this adoption is brought about through grace, which is the work of divine love, it is appropriated to the Holy Ghost, the sanctifier.

Third corollary. During the time that he is in the state of grace, the reprobate is an adopted son of God; and when the predestinate is not in the state of grace, he is not an adopted son of God.

ARTICLE III. WHETHER GRACE IS IDENTICAL WITH VIRTUE, PARTICULARLY WITH CHARITY

State of the question. We are not considering whether grace is identical with the acquired virtues, nor with faith or hope, for these can be possessed in the state of mortal sin, that is, without sanctifying grace. But since the state of grace is inseparable from charity, some were of the opinion that sanctifying grace was not really distinguished from charity. According to the Master of the Sentences, as quoted in the article, they seem to be distinguished only as concepts, since, for him, both grace and charity are the Holy Ghost indwelling and moving to the act of love.

In the opinion of Durandus, they are distinguished in name only (Nominalism removes almost all real distinctions); Scotus declares them to be formally distinguished; according to certain others, they are distinguished virtually by reason of a diversity of functions. St. Thomas, those of his school, and many outside of it maintain that they are really distinct. (Cf. *De veritate,* q. 27, a. 2.)

St. Thomas' conclusion is that sanctifying grace is something beyond the infused virtues which are derived from it, just as the natural light of reason is something beyond the acquired virtues derived from that light.

1. Scriptural proof. Holy Scripture speaks of grace and of charity as of two separate things. "The grace of our Lord Jesus Christ, and the charity of God" (II Cor. 13:13). "The charity of God is poured forth in our hearts, by the Holy Ghost, who is given to us" (Rom. 5:5); but He is given to us through grace, by reason of which He dwells in us. "The grace of our Lord hath abounded exceedingly with faith and love" (I Tim. 1:14).

Likewise the Council of Vienne (Denz., no. 483) speaks of the baptized as those to whom "grace and the virtues" were imparted. The Council of Trent (Sess. VI, can. 7, Denz., no. 799) declares that "the renewal of the inner man is brought about by the voluntary acceptance of grace and the gifts"; canon 11 (Denz., 821) defines "man as not justified without grace and charity." Moreover, in this sense the mind of the Council is interpreted by the Catechism of the Council (part 2, "Baptism," chap. 38) wherein sanctifying grace is described, while not yet speaking of charity, and then (chap. 39) it is declared: "To this is added the most noble train of all the virtues, which are infused in the soul together with grace."

St. Augustine speaks in the same strain as quoted in the argument *Sed contra* (*De dono persever.,* chap. 16): "Grace precedes charity." But no reason can be adduced to explain why Holy Scripture, the Councils, and the Fathers, referring to a matter of dogma, should always understand one and the same thing under diverse names; it would be, at least, useless repetition; and since it occurs frequently, we may draw from these authorities, at least as more probable, the opinion that grace and charity are really distinct.

2. *Theological proof,* based on the definition of virtue and on a parallelism between the natural and supernatural orders.

Virtue is really distinct from the proportionate nature which it presupposes; as the acquired virtues from the nature of the soul.

But the supernatural virtues presuppose nature elevated by sanctifying grace.

Therefore the supernatural virtues, even charity, are really distinct from sanctifying grace.

The major is based on the Aristotelian definition of virtue, namely, "a disposition of a perfect thing is that which is best"; in other words, virtue presupposes a nature proportioned to itself, is a perfection of a power corresponding to that nature, and hence is really distinct from nature as already constituted. Thus the acquired virtues, such as wisdom and prudence, are really distinguished from the light of reason which they presuppose and which existed before the acquisition of these virtues.

Regarding the minor: As human virtue presupposes human nature which it disposes in the direction of its natural end, so does supernatural virtue presuppose nature elevated to supernatural being, which it disposes aptly toward its consequent supernatural end. Moreover, there is no doubt but that charity is a supernatural virtue and that it is supernaturally communicated by grace.

Therefore charity is really distinguished from sanctifying grace which it presupposes, as a habit which is immediately operative is differentiated from an entitative habit by which the essence of the soul is itself elevated, as will be made more evident in Article 4. But even here in the reply to the third objection it is declared: "Grace is reducible to the primary species of a quality [that is, of a habit]; nor is it indeed the same as a virtue, but rather a certain habit [entitative habit] which is presupposed by the infused virtues as their principle and root."

Opponents object: But the same accidental form can simultaneously elevate a nature and dispose it to operate, as heat causes wood both to be hot and to give off heat.

Reply. 1. The same accidental form cannot be received by two really distinct subjects; but the elevation of a nature must be effected in the essence of the soul, while charity, as a virtue, must be in some faculty, that is, the will. Therefore.

2. By the same token one and the same accidental form would be capable of producing the effects of all the virtues and gifts. And hence there would be no distinction between the three theological virtues, the four infused cardinal virtues, and the seven gifts, a distinction which is made by the whole of tradition on the basis of Holy Scripture itself.

3. In any order, operation follows being; especially does connatural operation presuppose a proportionate principle of being. The answer to the example of heat in the wood is: the disparity arises from the fact that heat is not a virtue in the wood, but a simple sensible quality.[11]

[11] Nor is Scotus' distinction, "formal-actual," admissible, which would be a medium between a real distinction and a rational distinction based on the reality, for there cannot be given a medium between a distinction existing before being considered by our mind and one which does not exist before being considered by the mind; there is no medium between two opposites. And the distinction which existed before being considered by our minds, however slight it may be, is nevertheless real.

Confirmation of the conclusion.

1. God hath first loved us (I John 4:10); but the effect of this love is grace; but charity is the proximate principle by which we love God.

2. Grace is a participation in the divine nature; charity is a participation in the divine will.

3. Every inclination follows upon form; but charity is an inclination of the supernatural order; therefore it presupposes the supernatural form upon which it follows.

4. God makes no less provision for the soul in the supernatural order than in the natural order; but in the natural order the faculties follow upon the essence of the soul; therefore in the supernatural order the infused virtues follow upon grace.

And what we have said applies also to the angels, since their essence is not immediately operative, and thus differs from the divine essence which alone is its own being and act.

Objection. But then faith and hope could not exist without habitual grace, as properties cannot exist without essence.

Reply. Faith and hope remain in the sinner as in a subject to which they are not connatural, but praeternatural. And they do not have the element of virtue except with grace. A sinner can indeed believe, but not so well as one ought to believe. Thus, in the natural order, heat is in fire as in a connatural subject, but in water as in a subject under compulsion, for heat is not a property of water, which is naturally cold.

However, the same effects are often attributed to both grace and charity, since they are inseparably connected. The proper effects of charity thus proceed from grace as from a root. (See Billuart for less important objections.)

ARTICLE IV. WHETHER HABITUAL GRACE IS IN THE ESSENCE OF THE SOUL AS IN A SUBJECT

State of the question. Those who say that grace is identical with charity hold grace to be attributable to the will and not immediately to the essence of the soul. Thus Scotus (II Sent., dist. 26), who adopted as his own doctrine St. Thomas' objections, as he frequently did.

St. Thomas' conclusion: Habitual grace, inasmuch as it is presupposed by the infused virtues, is in the essence of the soul as in a subject, and not in any faculty.

Proof 1. Commonly, as found in the argument *Sed contra:* "By grace we are regenerated as children of God, according to Holy Scripture." But generation has its term first in the essence and then in the powers. It is so in the natural order; why not in the supernatural order?

Proof 2. In particular, as a corollary of the preceding article, thus:

Every perfection of a rational faculty is a virtue or good operative habit.

But habitual grace is not a virtue, but is presupposed by the infused virtues (cf. preceding article).

Therefore habitual grace is not in the faculties of the soul but in the very essence of the soul presupposed by the faculties.

Hence it is a participation in the divine nature by a certain regeneration or re-creation, whereas charity is a participation by the will in divine love, and faith a participation of divine knowledge in the intellect, although all these infused habits are formally participations in the intimate life of God. But we are now considering them rather under their material aspect, that is, on the part of the subject in which they reside.

Reply to third objection. The soul is the subject of grace, since it resides in a species of intellectual nature, or in the intelligent soul, although the infused virtue of chastity is in the sensitive appetite.

Confirmation. It would be unbecoming for the essence of the soul to be less perfected supernaturally than its own faculties. The whole man would not be supernaturally complete, with respect both to being and to operation; and its radical vitality would not be elevated. Such would be the result if Scotus' teaching were true.

First corollary. Glory, taken as the root of the light of glory and of charity, is likewise in the essence of the soul; for it is grace consummated. It is also an entitative habit, for St. Thomas says in several places that habitual grace, the seed of glory, is a certain beginning of eternal life, for it is the same habit. On the contrary, infused faith, which is obscure, is not a certain beginning of the beatific vision.

Second corollary. Grace is the radical principle of merit, but charity is its proximate principle.

Third corollary. Mortal sin, being the privation of sanctifying grace, is death to the soul in the essence of the soul, and in that it is a vicious habit or act it is in the will, or in some other faculty under the command of the will.

As a complement to this question of the essence of grace, two articles in the treatise *De lege nova* (Ia IIae, q. 106, a. 1) should be read on whether the new law is written or set in the heart. The reply is as follows: "That which is most powerful in the law of the New Testament, and in which all its virtue consists, is the grace of the Holy Ghost, which is given through the faith of Christ. Therefore the new law is principally that very grace of the Holy Ghost, which is given to the faithful of Christ. . . . Hence St. Paul declares that 'the law of the spirit of life, in Christ Jesus, hath delivered me from the law of sin and of death' (Rom. 8:2). . . . Therefore it may be said that the new law is primarily a law set in the heart, but secondarily it is a written law."

Likewise the *Summa* (Ia IIae, q. 106, a. 2) declares that "the law of the Gospel (by means of what is primary in it) justifies." And in the answer to the second objection (*ibid.*), St. Thomas states: "On account of what it is of itself [as habitual grace] it gives sufficient help to avoid sin," that is, of itself it bestows the power not to sin, although as long as we are wayfarers the power to do the opposite remains in us. Again (IIIa, q. 8, a. 1, 2, 5), Christ as man merited for us all the graces we receive and He communicates them to us now as instrumental, physical cause of our divinization. (Cf. IIIa, q. 62, a. 5; q. 43, a. 2; q. 48, a. 6.)

According to IIIa, q. 62, a. 2: "Sacramental grace adds, over and above [habitual] grace generally so called and above the virtues and gifts, a certain divine help toward the attainment of the end of the sacrament." In the reply to the first objection of the same article St. Thomas maintains that "the grace of the virtues and gifts perfects the essence and powers of the soul sufficiently with respect to the general ordering of the acts of the soul (so it was in Adam before the Fall and in the angels in whom did not reside Christian grace strictly speaking, which was conferred upon men by Christ the Redeemer). But with respect to certain special effects which are demanded by a Christian life, sacramental grace is required." Thus it may also be said that in the angels and in Adam before the Fall there resided supernatural grace, as a participation of the divine nature, but not however as Christian grace proceeding from Christ the Redeemer and forming souls in the image of Christ crucified.

Sacramental grace is not a new infused habit really distinct from habitual grace, but it adds over and above ordinary grace a certain right to actual graces to be received at the appropriate time and corresponding to the special end of the sacraments; for example, the grace of holy orders confers the right to the actual graces necessary to celebrate Mass. And this moral right is a relationship which requires a real basis; the real basis is sacramental grace, properly speaking, inasmuch as it is really permanent in the soul. And the more probable opinion, as Thomists assert, is that it is a special mode and a special force of sanctifying grace, which overflow into the acts of the virtue. (Cf. St. Thomas, *De veritate,* q. 27, a. 5 ad 12.) Thus we speak of priestly charity, of priestly prudence. John of St. Thomas, the Salmanticenses, Contenson, Hugon, Merkelbach, and several other Thomists accept this explanation.

Accordingly, as sanctifying grace is the principle of the sanctification of the just, whether men or angels, so is the sacramental grace of baptism the principle of Christian sanctification, and the sacramental grace of holy orders the principle of sanctification of priests, who are the ministers of Christ.

We must now compare habitual grace with the graces *gratis datae* and with actual graces.

CHAPTER IV

QUESTION III

THE DIVISIONS OF GRACE

HAVING arrived at a definition of sanctifying grace, we must now consider the divisions of grace. As a matter of fact, at the beginning of this treatise, when we were establishing our terminology, we enumerated the various significations of created grace which may be reduced to the following outline.

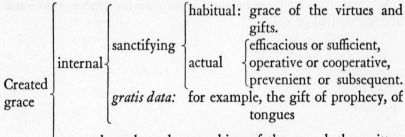

Created grace — internal — sanctifying — habitual: grace of the virtues and gifts.

actual — efficacious or sufficient, operative or cooperative, prevenient or subsequent.

gratis data: for example, the gift of prophecy, of tongues

external: such as the preaching of the gospel, the written divine law, miracles, the example of Christ and the saints, opportunities of doing good or avoiding evil.

In the present question St. Thomas examines the basis of these principal traditional divisions. He does so in five articles. The first and the last two deal with the graces *gratis datae* as compared with sanctifying grace; the second and third are concerned with the division into operative and cooperative grace, prevenient and subsequent grace, this latter division being the occasion for a discussion of efficacious and sufficient grace.

ARTICLE I. WHETHER GRACE IS PROPERLY DIVIDED INTO SANCTIFYING GRACE AND GRACE *GRATIS DATA*

State of the question. This article endeavors to explain the text of I Cor. 12:8-10, wherein St. Paul enumerates nine graces *gratis datae:*

"To one indeed, by the Spirit, is given the word of wisdom: and to another, the word of knowledge, according to the same Spirit; to another faith in the same spirit; to another the grace of healing in one Spirit: to another the working of miracles; to another prophecy; to another the discerning of spirits; to another diverse kinds of tongues; to another interpretation of speeches"; and further (*ibid.,* 12:31 and 13:1 f.): "I show unto you yet a more excellent way. If I speak with the tongues of men and of angels, and have not charity, I am become as sounding brass or a tinkling cymbal. And if I should have prophecy and should know all mysteries and all knowledge, and if I should have all faith so that I could remove mountains, and have not charity, I am nothing." (Cf. St. Thomas on this Epistle.) From this contrast has arisen the traditional division between the graces *gratis datae,* also called *charismata,* and sanctifying grace. The statement of the question will be more manifest from the problems raised at the beginning of the article.

Reply. St. Thomas shows the appropriateness of this traditional twofold division.

1. In the argument *Sed contra,* on the authority of St. Paul who attributes both characteristics to grace, namely, that of making us pleasing ("He hath graced us," Ephes. 1:6) and that of being a gratuitous gift (Rom. 11:6). Hence grace may be differentiated according to whether it possesses but one of these notes, that is, being a free gift (and every grace is gratuitous) or both notes, not only that of being given freely, but also that of making us pleasing.

Grace, or a gratuitous gift $\begin{cases} \text{which renders pleasing} \\ \text{which does not render pleasing} \end{cases}$

This is explained more clearly in the answer to the third objection: "Sanctifying grace adds something beyond the reason of graces *gratis datae,* . . . that is, it makes man pleasing to God. And therefore grace *gratis data,* which does not have this effect, retains merely the generic name," just as brute beasts are called "animals"; the name of the genus is applied to the least distinguished member. Hence this division is between an affirmation and a negation. In other words, grace in general is defined as a supernatural gratuitous gift bestowed by God upon a rational creature; and grace thus defined is divided according to whether it renders him pleasing or does not. Thus grace *gratis data* is not opposed, strictly speaking, to the other, in the sense that it cannot be the object of merit, for neither can the first sanctifying grace be merited, nor the last, that is, final perseverance, nor efficacious actual grace to persevere in good acts throughout the course of life. Nevertheless, as stated in the body of the article, grace *gratis data* is granted over and above the merits of the person. (Cf. below, q. 114.)

2. By a theological argument the appropriateness of the aforesaid divisions is proved from a consideration of the ends.

Since grace is ordained to the end that man may be restored to God, grace is twofold according to the twofold restoration to God.

But the restoration to God is twofold, thus: 1. uniting man himself to God immediately, and this is effected by sanctifying grace; 2. not of itself uniting man to God, but causing him to cooperate in the salvation of others, and this is brought about by grace *gratis data.*

Therefore this traditional division is correct. In other words, the union with God is either formal or only ministerial. This division is adequate since to render pleasing and not to render pleasing are contradictory opposites to one another and there can be no middle ground between them. Grace *gratis data* is *per se* primarily ordained to the salvation of others, or "unto profit." [1] Sanctifying grace is *per se* primarily ordained to the salvation of the recipient, whom it justifies.

It should be noted that these two statements are qualified as *"per se* primarily," that is, essentially and immediately; however, grace *gratis data* may secondarily lead to the salvation of the recipient, provided, that is, it be employed by charity. Likewise, sanctifying grace may secondarily lead to the salvation of others through the example of virtue. But the primary end of each is the one assigned to it above.

Corollary. Unlike sanctifying grace, the graces *gratis datae* may sometimes be found in the wicked or sinners; for although sinners neglect their own salvation, they may procure the salvation of others and cooperate in it, after the manner of those who built Noah's ark and yet were submerged in the waters of the flood.

Thus Caiphas prophesied as one divinely inspired, saying "It is expedient . . . that one man die for the people" (John 11:50). Again, as narrated in the Book of Numbers (23:22 ff.), Balaam, although a soothsayer and idolater, received the gift of prophecy; like-

[1] Cf. I Cor. 12:7.

wise the sibyl, in spite of being a pagan. (Cf. IIa IIae, q. 172, a. 4);
with respect to prophecy (q. 178, a. 2), the wicked can perform miracles in order to confirm revealed truths; but if the gift of prophecy,
which is the highest among the graces *gratis datae,* exists in the
wicked, with still greater reason is this true of the others. Hence St.
Paul himself says: "I chastise my body, . . . lest perhaps, when I have
preached to others, I myself should become a castaway" (I Cor. 9:27).

Doubt. Whether "sanctifying grace" can be taken in a twofold
sense.

Reply. Undoubtedly. 1. Strictly, it refers to habitual grace, distinct
from the infused virtues, by which we are justified or formally rendered pleasing to God. 2. Broadly, it includes that which is ordained
to the justification of its subject, whether antecedently as stimulating
grace which disposes us for justification, or concomitantly, or consequently, as, for example, supernatural helps, the infused virtues, the
gifts, the increase of grace, and glory, which is the consummation of
grace. In the present question sanctifying grace is thus broadly taken
in contrast to grace *gratis data.* And thus the aforesaid division is adequate. Vasquez did not take this extended use of the term into account
when, in commenting on the article, he declared this division to be
insufficient since faith, hope, and actual helps could not be found
under either of its members. Hence sanctifying grace is identical here
with the "grace of the virtues and gifts with their proportionate helps,"
which St. Thomas speaks of (IIIa, q. 62, a. 1): whether sacramental
grace adds something over and above the grace of the virtues and
gifts. Indeed to sanctifying grace also belong the sacramental graces
which are the proper effects of the sacraments; for example, baptismal
grace, the grace of absolution, of confirmation, nutritive grace (cf.
p. 148 above).

Corollary. It is of great importance to determine clearly whether
infused or mystical contemplation, according as it is distinguished
from private revelations, visions, and even from words of wisdom
or knowledge, pertains to sanctifying grace and is in the normal
way to sanctity, or to the graces *gratis datae* as something extraordinary. Theologians generally teach that infused contemplation belongs to sanctifying grace, or to the grace of the virtues and gifts; it
is something not properly extraordinary but eminent, for its proceeds
not from prophecy but from the gifts of wisdom and understanding

as they exist in the perfect. Cf. IIa IIae, q. 180, on contemplative life, after he considered graces *gratis datae* in particular.[2]

Let us pass immediately to articles four and five which deal with the same material, because afterwards there will be a longer consideration of articles 2 and 3 with reference to operative and cooperative grace, sufficient and efficacious grace.

ARTICLE IV. WHETHER GRACE *GRATIS DATA* IS ADEQUATELY SUBDIVIDED BY THE APOSTLE (1 COR. 12:8–10)

State of the question. St. Paul here enumerates nine graces *gratis datae*. St. Thomas shows the appropriateness of this division. Many Thomists, Gonet among them, hold this division to be adequate; so also does Mazella. On the other hand, Medina, Vasquez, Bellarmine, Suarez, and Ripalda do not consider this division all-embracing, but maintain that St. Paul was enumerating only the principal graces. Suarez would further add to them the priestly character, jurisdiction in the internal forum, and the special assistance conferred upon the Sovereign Pontiff.

St. Thomas seems to judge the enumeration given by St. Paul to be entirely sufficient and he defends it brilliantly in a remarkable discussion both here and in his commentary on I Cor. 12 (cf. *De revelatione,* I, 209).

It should be noted that St. Thomas, treating of these graces in particular (IIa IIae, q. 171–79) in that case divides them according as they pertain either to knowledge or to speech or to action; and under the heading "prophecy" he includes all those which refer to the knowledge of divine things, except words of wisdom and knowledge. For those which pertain to prophecy are knowable only by divine revelation, whereas whatever is included under words of wisdom and science and interpretation of speeches can be known by man through his natural reason, although they are manifested in a higher mode by the illumination of divine light.

Confirmation from the refutation of objections.

1. The graces *gratis datae* exceed the power of nature, as when a fisherman is fluent in words of wisdom and science; they are thus differentiated from the natural gifts of God which likewise do not make us pleasing to God.

---

[2] We have treated this question at length elsewhere: *Christian Perfection and Contemplation; The Three Ages of the Interior Life.*

Graces *gratis datae* ordained for instructing one's neighbor in divine things

— **for possessing the fullness of knowledge of divine things**

- **faith** — regarding principles, that is, a supereminent certitude of faith, for example, in preaching.

- **utterance** — of wisdom regarding the principal conclusions known through their highest causes (as by St. Paul, St. Augustine, St. Thomas; cf. IIa IIae, q. 177, a. 1).

- **utterance** — of knowledge concerning examples and effects, (as by St. Matthew, St. James, St. Gregory the Great, St. Alphonsus Liguori).

— **for confirming the revelation of divine things**

- **operating**
  - grace of healing by which is manifested the benignity of God toward the sick.
  - performance of miracles by which is manifested God's omnipotence, for example, the sun standing still.

- **knowing**
  - prophecy regarding future contingencies; (cf. IIa IIae, q. 171 ff.).
  - discernment of spirits regarding the hidden things of the heart.

— **to facilitate the conveying of the word of God to one's hearers**

- **kinds** — of tongues, when a preacher speaks several tongues; this is a higher mode; when a preacher speaking one language is understood by all; this grace is below prophecy.

- **interpretation** — of speeches, reducible to prophecy and therefore higher than the gift of tongues; for example, Joseph interpreting Pharaoh's dream.

2. The faith of which it is a question here is not the theological virtue present in all the faithful, but a supereminent certitude of faith by which a man is rendered capable of instructing others in the things that pertain to faith.

3. The grace of healing, the gift of tongues, and the interpretation of speeches possess a certain special motivation impelling faith, according as they excite admiration or gratitude. In the grace of healing the benignity of God toward the misery of man shines forth; in the performance of miracles, such as the opening of a passage through the sea or the stopping of the sun in its course, the omnipotence of God appears.

4. Wisdom and knowledge are included among the graces *gratis datae* not because they are gifts of the Holy Ghost, but because, by means of them, a man may instruct others and vanquish his opponents. Therefore they are purposely set down in the present enumeration as utterances of wisdom or knowledge. (Cf. St. Thomas, IIa IIae, q. 45, a. 5 and on I Cor. 12, lect. 2.)

According to Thomists, in opposition to Suarez, the sacramental character and jurisdiction in the internal forum, and the assistance of the Holy Ghost do not belong to the graces *gratis datae,* but to the ministries and operations which St. Paul himself distinguishes from the graces *gratis datae.* "There are diversities of graces, but the same Spirit; and there are diversities of ministries, but the same Lord; and there are diversities of operations, but the same God."

And they are indeed distinguished, as Billuart observes, inasmuch as grace *gratis data* concerns only an act which manifests faith, whereas ministration or the ministry refers to the authority to perform some act with respect to other men, such as the apostolate, the episcopate, the priesthood, or any other dignity. An operation, moreover, is the exercise of a ministry. Thus in the Old Testament priests and prophets were differentiated.

Doubt. Whether the aforesaid graces *gratis datae* reside in man after the manner of a habit or rather as a transient movement. (Cf. Gonet, *De essentia gratiae.*)

Reply. Gonet replies: Generally they are present as transient movements, such as the gift of prophecy, the grace of healing or of prodigies, the discerning of spirits. This is evident from the fact that a prophet or wonder-worker does not prophesy or work miracles whenever he wills. (Cf. IIa IIae, q. 171, a. 2.) However, according to the same authority, faith, words of wisdom and of knowledge do exist after the manner of habits, since one who receives them uses them when he so wills.

In Christ all these graces were present as habits for two reasons. 1. On account of the hypostatic union He was an instrument united to the divinity. 2. He had supreme power, by reason of which He disposed of all creatures and hence at will He could perform miracles or cast out demons, as explained in the treatise on the Incarnation, IIIa, q. 7, a. 7 ad 1.

ARTICLE V. WHETHER GRACE *GRATIS DATA* IS SUPERIOR TO SANCTIFYING GRACE

This question is of great importance with respect to mystical theology; for example, which are higher among the works of St. Theresa, those which pertain to sanctifying grace or those pertaining to graces *gratis datae?*

State of the question. It seems that grace *gratis data* is superior: 1. because the good of the Church in general, to which graces *gratis datae* are ordained, is higher than the good of one man, to which sanctifying grace is ordered; 2. because that which is capable of enlightening others is of greater value than that which only perfects oneself; it is better to enlighten than merely to shine; and 3. because the graces *gratis datae* are not given to all Christians, but to the more worthy members of the Church, especially to the saints. However, in spite of these arguments, St. Thomas' conclusion is in the negative; and so is that of theologians generally.

The reply is: Sanctifying grace is much more excellent than grace *gratis data.*

First proof, from the authority of St. Paul, who, after enumerating the graces *gratis datae,* continues: "And I show unto you yet a more excellent way. If I speak with the tongues of men and of angels, and have not charity, I am become as sounding brass or a tinkling cymbal. And if I should have prophecy and should know all mysteries and all knowledge, and if I should have all faith so that I could remove mountains, and have not charity, I am nothing" (I Cor. 12:31–13:2). But prophecy is the highest of all the graces *gratis datae* (cf. IIa IIae, q. 171), and this is said to be below charity, which pertains to sanctifying grace. Therefore.

In his commentary on the first Epistle to the Corinthians (chap. 13),

St. Thomas thus explains the words "I am nothing," that is, with respect to the being of grace, described in Ephesians (2:10): "For we are His workmanship, created in Christ Jesus in good works"; likewise II Cor. 5:17, and Gal. 6:15.[3]

In the same place it is shown that charity surpasses all these *charismata* in three respects:

1. From necessity, since without charity, the other gratuitous gifts do not suffice.

2. From utility, since it is through charity that every evil is avoided and every good work performed. "Charity is patient, . . . beareth all things, hopeth all things, endureth all things."

3. From its permanence, for "charity never falleth away," as St. Paul declares, whether prophecies shall be made void or tongues shall cease. Hence charity is said to be the bond of perfection uniting the soul to God and gathering together all other virtues to ordain them toward God. Therefore can Augustine say: "Love and do what you will."

Second proof from theological argument.

The excellence of any virtue is higher according as it is ordained to a higher end; and the end is superior to the means.

But sanctifying grace ordains men immediately to union with his final end; and the graces *gratis datae* ordain him toward something preparatory to his final end, since by miracles and prophecies men are led to conversion.

Therefore sanctifying grace is much more excellent than grace *gratis data.*

In a word, sanctifying grace unites man immediately to God, who dwells in him; on the other hand, grace *gratis data* serves only to dispose others for union with God. This argument appears even more profound when we observe that sanctifying grace, inasmuch as it unites man immediately to God, his final supernatural end, is supernatural substantially. It is indeed the root of the theological virtues which are immediately specified by their formal supernatural object (*objectum formale quo et quod*), and it is the seed of glory, the beginning of eternal life which is essentially supernatural.

On the contrary, the graces *gratis datae* are generally supernatural

---

[3] In fact, without charity our will is turned away from God as final end. Hence we read in I John 3:14: "We have passed from death to life, because we love the brethren. He that loveth not abideth in death."

only with respect to the mode of their production, in the same way as miracles. As a matter of fact, with respect to this supernaturalness, the division of the *charismata* corresponds to the division of miracles given by St. Thomas (Ia, q. 105, a. 8); the comparison may be made as follows:

To the miraculous

> substantially, for example, to the glorification of the body, corresponds prophecy of future events of a natural order.
>
> with respect to the subject in which it resides, for example, to a nonglorious resurrection, corresponds the knowledge of the secrets of hearts, which can be known by human revelation.
>
> modally, for example, to the sudden cure of a fever, corresponds the gift of tongues, for we can acquire languages naturally, although not suddenly.

Cf. *De revelatione,* I, 205 ff.

Thus the great difference becomes evident between the supernatural substantially and the miraculous substantially; in the former "substantially" means formally, by virtue of its formal object; in the latter "substantially" means effectively, or concerning an effect the substance of which cannot be produced by a created cause in any manner or in any subject, such, for instance, as the glorification of the body.

Hence below intrinsically supernatural knowledge, such as the beatific vision or infused faith, there exist the following three kinds of effectively supernatural knowledge the object of which is intrinsically natural.

1. Effectively, with respect to the substance of cognition, such as the prophetic knowledge of future natural events taking place at a remote time. This exceeds every created intellect, not by reason of the essential supernaturalness of its object, as would be that of the Trinity, but by reason of the uncertainty or indetermination of the future, for example, the date when some war would end.

2. Effectively, with respect to the subject in which it resides, such as the knowledge of a natural object already actually existing, but removed in regard to place or exceeding the faculty of vision of this particular man, although not of all men (IIa IIae, q. 171, a. 3). Likewise the knowledge of the secrets of hearts which are known naturally by the person whose secrets they are.

3. Effectively, modally, such as the instantaneous knowledge of some human science or unknown tongue without human study. Thus the supernaturalness of prophecy is of an inferior order to the supernaturalness of divine faith. Therefore St. Thomas says (*III Sent.,* d. 24, a. 1 ad 3): "Although prophecy and faith treat of the same matter, such as the passion of Christ, they do not do so in the same way; for faith considers the Passion formally under the aspect of something which borders on the eternal, that is, according as it was God who suffered, although materially it considers a temporal event. This is not true of prophecy."

But what has been said of the supernaturalness of prophecy, the highest of all the graces *gratis datae,* can be said of all the *charismata,* as is very evident in the case of the gift of tongues, the grace of healing, the performing of prodigies, and the discernment of spirits. The same may be said of utterances of wisdom and knowledge and of the interpretation of speech, for these latter three supply in a supernatural way for what would be attained naturally by acquired theology or hermeneutics. Thus, in general, the *charismata* are supernatural modally only, and therefore sanctifying grace, which is supernatural substantially, as a participation in the divine nature, is "much more excellent," as St. Thomas declares.

Confirmation of the aforesaid conclusion from the refutation of objections.

First objection. The common good of the Church is better than the good of one man. But sanctifying grace is ordained only to the good of one, whereas grace *gratis data* is ordered to the common good of the Church. Therefore.

Reply. The major is to be distinguished: the common good which is in the Church is below the separated common good, that is, God: granted; otherwise, denied.

I distinguish the minor: sanctifying grace is ordained to the good of the individual and also to the separate common good, that is, to God to whom it unites us immediately: granted; otherwise, denied.

Hence, above the common good of the Church, which is the ecclesiastical order, there is the separate common good, which is God Himself, to whom sanctifying grace unites us immediately. Similarly, above the common good of an army, which is its order, there is the common good considered separately, namely, the good of the country.

On this account St. Thomas says later (IIa IIae, q. 182, a. 1–4) that contemplative life, which is immediately ordained to the love and praise of God, is, in an absolute sense, better, higher, and more meritorious than the active life, which is ordained toward the love of neighbor and to the common good of the Church not considered apart. Therefore did Christ say (Luke 10:42): "Mary hath chosen the best part, which shall not be taken away from her." Many moderns would do well to read this response to the first objection.

Again St. Thomas declares (IIa IIae, q. 182, a. 1 ad 1): "It not only pertains to prelates to lead the active life, but they should also excel in the contemplative life"; which St. Gregory had already expressed in the words: "Let the leader be eminent in action, and sustained in contemplation above all others."

Second objection. It is better to enlighten others than merely to be enlightened; but by the graces *gratis datae* man enlightens others; by sanctifying grace he is only enlightened himself. Therefore.

Reply. I distinguish the major: it is better than merely to be enlightened to enlighten others formally: granted; to enlighten others merely by disposing them: denied.

I distinguish the minor: that man, by grace *gratis data,* enlightens others formally: denied; by disposing them, granted; on the contrary he is formally enlightened by sanctifying grace.

For, by the graces *gratis datae* man cannot produce sanctifying grace in another, but only offer him certain disposing or preparatory factors toward justification, such as preaching to him or performing miracles. God alone directly or through His sacraments infuses sanctifying grace. Similarly, in the natural order, St. Thomas maintains, the heat by which fire acts is not more estimable than the form of fire itself.

I insist. Then St. Thomas was wrong when he said later (IIa IIae, q. 188, a. 6) that the apostolic or mixed life "proceeding from the fullness of contemplation is to be preferred absolutely to contemplation, since it is a greater thing to enlighten than merely to shine."

Reply. The apostolic life is preferred to simple contemplation inasmuch as it includes this and something more; on the contrary, grace *gratis data* does not include sanctifying grace and something more.

Third objection. That which is proper to the more perfect is better than that which is common to all. But the graces *gratis datae* are gifts proper to the more perfect members of the Church. Therefore they are higher than the grace common to all the just, as reasoning power is superior to sensation.

Reply. There is a disparity, for sensation (which is common to all animals) is ordained to ratiocination. But on the contrary the graces *gratis datae* (which are proper) are ordained to the conversion of men, in other words, to sanctifying or justifying grace.

First corollary. Sanctifying grace or the grace of the virtues and gifts belongs to the normal supernatural. But it exists in three degrees, that of beginners, proficients, and perfect; in other words, the purgative, illuminative, and unitive ways, the last being the age of maturity of the spiritual life.

Second corollary. The graces *gratis datae* belong to the extraordinary supernatural, so called not so much in relation to the Church as to the individual, for example, private revelations, visions, and internal words pertaining to prophecy.

Third corollary. Infused contemplation, proceeding from the gifts of wisdom and understanding as they exist in the perfect, is therefore not something extraordinary, like prophetic revelation, but something normal and eminent, that is, in the normal way of sanctification.

Fourth corollary. Cajetan *In IIam IIae,* q. 178, a. 2 (quoted by Father Del Prado, *De gratia et libero arbitrio,* p. 268): "It is a most pernicious error to consider the gift of God in the working of miracles to be greater than in the works of justice. And this, contrary to the popular idea and common error of humankind, which judges men who perform miracles to be saints and, as it were, gods, whereas these dull-minded people have almost no esteem whatever for just men. The complete opposite ought to be considered of high value, as it truly is." Although the sanctity of the servants of God is outwardly manifested by miracles, the saint who performs more miracles than another is not, on that account, a greater saint.

Fifth corollary. Del Prado (*op. cit.,* p. 261): "The graces *gratis datae* may exist without sanctifying grace for the manifesting of divine truth; for of themselves they do not justify. Hence St. Thomas says, commenting on I Cor. (13, lect. 1): 'It is obvious with regard to prophecy and faith, that they may be possessed without charity. But it is to be remarked here that firm faith, even without charity, produces miracles. Wherefore the apostle Matthew (7:22), in reply to those who will ask: 'Have we not prophesied in Thy name . . . and done many miracles?' declares that our Lord will reply: 'I never knew you.' For the Holy Ghost works prodigies even by the wicked, just as He speaks truth through them."

Sixth corollary. However, the graces *gratis datae* are, in the saints, also a manifestation of their sanctity (Del Prado, *ibid.*); cf. St. Thomas on I Cor. (12, lect. 2); whence it is said in Acts (6:8) that "Stephen, full of grace and fortitude, did great wonders and signs among the people."

ARTICLE II. WHETHER GRACE IS PROPERLY DIVIDED
INTO OPERATIVE AND COOPERATIVE GRACE

State of the question. This article explains the division made by St. Augustine (*De gratia et libero arbitrio,* chap. 17); it should be carefully studied, for Molina maintains (*Concordia,* q. 14, a. 13, disp. 42, p. 242) that St. Thomas misinterprets Augustine. After giving his own interpretation, Molina says: "This is manifest in the clearest light, although Augustine has been understood otherwise by St. Thomas (Ia IIae, q. 111, a. 2 and 3), by Soto and by certain others." In fact, Molina attempts to demonstrate (*ibid.,* p. 243) that Augustine cannot be interpreted in any other way, in the light of faith. Since this is a most serious charge, the question must be considered attentively.

The principal point at issue between Thomists and Molinists on this subject may be formulated thus: For Molina (*Concordia,* p. 565), Suarez,[4] and their disciples, operative actual grace urges only by moral, and not by physical, impulsion, and leads only to indeliberate acts, but never of itself alone to free choice or consent. But cooperative actual grace, according to Molina, produces, by moral impulsion, a free choice, with simultaneous concurrence, in such a way that man is determined by himself alone. Thus man and God seem to be rather two causes acting coordinately, like two men rowing a boat, than two causes of which one is subordinate, acting under the impulsion of the superior cause.

For Thomists, on the other hand, operative actual grace does not merely urge by moral impulsion, but operates physically as well, with respect to the performance of an act and sometimes even leads to free choice; that is, when man cannot move himself to this choice deliberately by virtue of a previous higher act, such as the moment of conversion to God or the acts of the gifts of the Holy Ghost, which

---

[4] *De auxiliis divinae gratiae,* Bk. III, chap. 5, no. 4; cf. Del Prado, *De gratia et libero arbitrio,* I, 228.

proceed from a special inspiration. Cooperative actual grace, moreover, is also a physical impulsion under which man, by virtue of a
previous act of willing the end, moves himself to will the means to
the end.

Let us examine: 1. the text of St. Augustine, 2. the interpretation
of Molina, 3. the article of St. Thomas referred to and also the reply
to objections (Ia IIae, q. 9, a. 6 ad 3). The teaching of St. Thomas will
be defended.

1. St. Augustine. The text of St. Augustine (*De gratia et libero
arbitrio,* chap. 17) reads thus: "God Himself works so that we may
will at the beginning what, once we are willing, He cooperates in
perfecting; therefore does the Apostle say: 'Being confident of this
very thing, that He who hath begun a good work in you, will perfect
it unto the day of Christ Jesus' (Phil. 1:6). That we should will
therefore, He accomplishes without us; but when we do will, and
so will as to do, He cooperates with us."

2. *Molina's opinion.* For Molina, operative grace is nothing more
than prevenient grace morally urging us; cooperative grace assists us.
Hence, according to Molina, "a person assisted by the help of less
grace may be converted, although another with greater help does not
become converted and continues to be obdurate." Cf. *Concordia,*
p. 565.

As Father Del Prado observes (*De gratia,* I, 226): "Molina departs
from the ways of St. Thomas in the explanation of the nature of divine
grace, operative and cooperative, and refuses to admit that the grace
of God alone transforms the wills of men or that only God opens the
heart. Consequently, whether Molina will have it or not, although it
is God who stands at the gate and knocks, it is man who begins to
open and man alone who, in fact, does open it. . . . Hence the beginning of consent, for Molina, resides in man, who alone determines
himself to will, whereas God, who stands at the gate knocking, awaits
his will." Before this beginning of consent proceeding from us alone,
Molina maintains, however, against the Semi-Pelagians, that there
are moral divine impulsions drawing us as well as the indeliberate
movement of our will, but that they are equal and even stronger in
him who is not converted.

This is corroborated by some of his well-known propositions; for
instance, in the *Concordia* under the heading "auxilium" in the index,
we read: "It may happen that with equal assistance, one of those who

are called may be converted and another not converted" (p. 51).
Furthermore, "he who is helped by the aid of less grace may be converted, although another with more does not become converted and perseveres in his obstinacy" (p. 565). Hence, as Lessius declares, "not that he who accepts does so by his freedom alone (since there was grace attracting him), but that the turning point arose from his freedom alone and thus not from a diversity of prevenient helps." (Cf. Salmanticenses, *De gratia,* tr. XIV, disp. 7.)

St. Thomas, on the contrary, referring to the words of St. Matthew (25:15), "And to one he gave five talents, and to another two, and to another one," comments: "He who makes more effort has more grace, but the fact that he makes more effort requires a higher cause." Again, with reference to the Epistle to the Ephesians (4:7), "to everyone of us is given grace, according to the measure of the giving of Christ," he repeats this observation, and similarly in Ia IIae, q. 112, a. 4, on whether grace is equal in all men.

The root of the disagreement is manifold, but the principal point of contention is the one mentioned by Molina himself in the *Concordia* (q. 14, a. 13, disp. 26, p. 152). "There are two difficulties, it seems to me, in the teaching of St. Thomas (Ia, q. 105, a. 5); the first is that I do not see what can be that impulse and its application to secondary causes, by which God moves and applies them to act. . . . Wherefore I confess frankly that it is very difficult for me to understand this impulsion and application which St. Thomas requires in secondary causes.

But, as Father Del Prado observes (*op. cit.,* p. 227): "In this article, such application and impulsion is clearly affirmed even in free secondary causes, and so, with respect to the interior act of the free will, 'the will is situated as moved only and not as moving, God alone being the Mover.' Here, as we shall presently see, physical premotion conquers, rules, and triumphs. Thence proceed the anger and the unmentioned recriminations which Molina gives vent to against the teaching of St. Thomas, under the pretense of vindicating St. Augustine."

For Molina holds (*Concordia,* disp. 42, p. 242) that according to St. Augustine (*De gratia et libero arbitrio,* chap. 17) "whatever God effects in us that is supernatural, until the moment when He leads us to the gift of justification, whether we cooperate in it by our free will or not, is called 'operative grace'; that, however, by which He

henceforth assists us to fulfill the whole law and persevere . . . is
called 'cooperative grace.' . . . And this is plainly the sense and intention of Augustine in this place when he draws a distinction between
operative and cooperative grace, which will be obvious in the clearest
light to anyone examining that chapter, notwithstanding the fact that
St. Thomas understands Augustine otherwise in the two articles
quoted (Ia IIae, q. 111, a. 2 and 3), as well as Soto (*De natura et gratia,*
Bk. I, chap. 16) and some others."

However, Molina is obliged to explain on the following page (p.
243) the words of St. Paul to the Philippians (2:13): "It is God who
works in you, both to will and accomplish," with regard to which
Augustine had said: "Therefore, that we will is brought about by
God, without us; but when we will, and so will as to act, He cooperates with us." With regard to this text, Molina says: "But neither
does Augustine mean to assert that we do not cooperate toward
willing, by which we are justified, or that it is not effected by us,
but by God alone. That certainly would be both contrary to faith
and opposed to the teaching of Augustine himself in many other
places."

Referring to these last words of Molina, Father Del Prado (*op. cit.*
I, 226) declares: "Does St. Thomas teach something contrary to faith
in drawing the distinction between operative and cooperative grace?
. . . From the lofty and profound teaching of St. Thomas propounded
in this article, wherein all is truth and brilliance, does something
follow which is contrary to the Catholic faith and the teaching of
Augustine himself? . . . Molina departs from the ways of St. Thomas
(since he will not admit that God applies and moves the will beforehand, but). . . . He holds that, while God, drawing the soul morally,
stands at the gate and knocks, it is man who begins to open, and man
alone who actually does open." In the Apocalypse (3:20) we read:
"I stand at the gate, and knock. If any man shall hear My voice, and
open to Me the door, I will come in to him, and will sup with him,
and he with Me." But man does not open it alone; he opens in fact
according as God knocks efficaciously. Otherwise how would the
words of St. Paul be verified: "What hast thou that thou hast not received?" In the business of salvation, not everything would then be
from God.

Conclusion with respect to Molina's opinion. For Molina and Suarez
and the Molinists in general, operative grace is nothing else but pre-

venient grace which urges morally, but does not really assist,[5] and only cooperative grace assists the soul.[6] Suarez himself admits this. For the beginning of consent, according to Molina, comes from man, who alone determines himself to will; while God almost waits for our consent. Indeed, for Molina, "he who is aided by the help of less grace may be converted, whereas another, with greater help, is not converted and persists in his obduracy" (*op. cit.,* p. 365).

Thus the salient point at issue, as Father Del Prado says (*op. cit.,* I, 223), is: "Whether the free will of man, when moved by the gratuitous impulsion of God to accept and receive the gift of the grace of justification, at that very instant of justification, is in a condition of being moved only, and not of moving, while God alone moves. When God stands at the gate of the heart and knocks, that we may open to Him, is it man who alone opens his heart, or God who begins to open and is the first to open and, having opened, confers upon us that we, too, may ourselves open to Him?" This is the question which St. Thomas solves in that celebrated article 2 and explains more fully below, in question 113. But Molina jumps from what precedes our justification to what follows it, and is not willing to examine the very moment when the free will of man is moved by God, through the love of charity, and from one who is averse to Him is made a convert to Him, and is intrinsically transformed by God who infuses sanctifying grace." This is the crux of the present controversy.

3. *St. Thomas' opinion.* St. Thomas rightly interprets St. Augustine (cf. Del Prado, *op. cit.,* I, 224 and 202); for Augustine declares: [7] "God, cooperating with us, perfects what He began by operating in us; because in beginning He works in us that we may have the will, and cooperates to perfect the work with us once we are willing. For this reason the Apostle says (Phil. 1:6): 'Being confident of this very thing, that He, who hath begun a good work in you, will perfect it unto the day of Christ Jesus.' That we should will is, therefore, accomplished without us; but once we are willing, and willing to such an extent that we act, He cooperates with us; however, without either His operation or His cooperation once we will, we are incapable of any good works of piety. With regard to His bringing it about that

---

[5] Cf. Suarez, *De auxiliis divinae gratiae,* Bk. III, chap. 5, no. 4.

[6] This is contrary to the answer ad 3 of the present article: "By operative grace man is aided by God to will what is good."

[7] *De gratia et libero arbitrio,* chap. 17.

we will, it is said in Philippians (2:13): 'For it is God who worketh in you, . . . to will.' But of His cooperation, when we already are willing and willingly act, it is said: 'We know that to them that love God, all things work together unto good' (Rom. 8:28)." St. Augustine reiterates this opinion in chapters 5 and 14 of the same book.

Again, writing to Boniface (Bk. II, chap. 9): "God accomplishes many good things in man which man does not accomplish (operative grace); but man does nothing good which God does not enable him to do (cooperative grace)." This is observed by the Council of Orange (c. 20, Denz., no. 193).

Moreover, according to Augustine, operative grace is not simply grace urging equally him who is converted and him who is not, for Augustine repeats in several places, with reference to predestination: "Why does He draw this man and not that? Do not judge if you do not wish to err" (*Super Joan.*, tr. 26; cf. Ia, q. 23, a. 5). This teaching of Augustine is mentioned by St. Gregory (*Moral.*, Bk. XVI, chap. 10) and by St. Bernard (*De gratia et libero arbitrio,* chap. 14); both are quoted by Del Prado (*op. cit.*, I, 203).

In article 2 of the present question there are two conclusions, one concerning actual grace and the other habitual grace.[8]

First conclusion. Actual grace is properly divided into operative and cooperative grace.

a) Council of Orange. Above and beyond the aforesaid authority of St. Augustine, this conclusion is supported by the Council of Orange (Denz., no. 177, can. 4): "It must be acknowledged that God does not wait upon our wills to cleanse us from sin, but also that we should wish to be cleansed by the infusion and operation of the Holy Ghost in us." In canon 23 it is said that God prepares our wills that they may desire the good. Again (can. 25, Denz., no. 200): "In every good work, it is not we who begin . . . but He (God) first inspires us with faith and love of Him, through no preceding merit on our part." All these texts pertain to operative grace, as does the beginning of canon 20 (Denz., no. 193), as follows: "God does many good works in man which man himself does not do." But the second part of this canon applies to cooperative grace, thus: "But man does no good works which God does not enable him to do."

[8] Operative and cooperative grace, according to St. Thomas; cf. Ia IIae, q. 111, a. 2, o., 4; a. 3, c; *II Sent.,* dist. 26, a. 5, o., 4; *De veritate,* q. 27, a. 5, 1, 2; II Cor., 6, lect. 1 (at the beginning); IIIa, q. 86, a. 4, 2; a. 6 ad 1; q. 88, a. 1, 4.

b) Theological proof.

An operation is not attributed to the thing moved, but to the mover; for example, the fact that a cart is drawn is attributed to the horse.

But in the first interior act, the will is situated as moved only, whereas God is the mover; whereas in the exterior act, ordered by the will, the will is both moved and moves.

Therefore in the first act the operation is attributed to God, and therefore the grace is termed operative; in the second act the operation is attributed not only to God, but also to the soul, and the grace is termed cooperative.

The major is clear with regard to an inanimate thing that is moved, as the cart is moved by the horse, but if the thing moved is a living thing and the operation is a vital act, it is elicited, indeed, from it. Thus, the very first act of the will is elicited vitally from it; however, the will is not said to move itself to it, properly speaking, since, as explained above (Ia IIae, q. 9, a. 3), "the will, by the very fact that it desires the end, moves itself to will those things which conduce to the end; just as the intellect, by the fact that it knows a principle, reduces itself from potency to act, with respect to the knowledge of the conclusion." To move oneself is, indeed, to reduce oneself from potency to act. Hence it is not to be wondered at that, in this act wherein the will cannot move itself by virtue of a previous efficacious act of the same order, it should be referred to as moved only, and the operation attributed to God.

The minor needs explanation. What is this interior act? It is manifold. It is that first of all by which we desire happiness in general, and for this, supernatural help is not required (cf. Ia IIae, q. 9, a. 4, c. 2); it is particularly, according to St. Thomas (*ibid.*), "that the will which previously desired evil now begins to will the good." This is explained (IIa, q. 86, a. 6 ad 1): "The effect of operative grace is justification of the wicked, as stated in Ia IIae, q. 113, a. 1–3, which [justification] consists not only in the infusion of grace and the remission of sins, but also a movement of the free will toward God, which is the act of formed faith, and a movement of the free will in relation to sin, which is the act of penance. But these human acts are present as effects of operative grace, produced in the same way as the remission of sins. Hence the remission of sin is not accomplished without an act of the virtue of penance, even if it is the effect of operative grace." These acts are therefore vital, rather are they even free, but the will does not move itself toward them, strictly speaking, by virtue of a previous efficacious act of the same order, since beforehand, a prior act of this kind did not exist.

The following synopsis, which we have already given in the introduction and which can now be explained, should be read in an ascending order, from the natural to the supernatural.

Our intellect (*means*) is moved by God

- in the supernatural order
  - 6. by special inspiration which we receive with docility, in accordance with the gifts of the Holy Ghost — operative grace
  - 5. to determining to exercise the infused virtues — cooperative grace
  - 4. to become converted to its final supernatural end — operative grace
- in the natural order
  - 3. by special inspiration, for example, poetic, philosophic, or strategic — operative motion
  - 2. to determine { this true good, this apparent good — cooperative motion
  - 1. to desire hapiness in general upon — operative motion

We explained this elsewhere (*Christian Perfection and Contemplation,* p. 285). From the same point of view Father Del Prado has made an excellent study of the present article (*op. cit.,* I, 206, 235; II, 220); and before him, Cajetan, commenting on this article, as well as Soto, Lemos, and Billuart.

Wherefore St. Thomas declares in the reply to the second objection: "Through the movement of the free will, when we are justified, we consent to the justice of God." But man does not move himself, properly speaking, to justification; he is moved to it, freely of course, but moved nonetheless; hence it is the effect of operative, not cooperative grace.[9]

[9] St. Thomas had also said, Ia IIae, q.55, a.4 ad 6: "Infused virtue is caused in us by God, without our action, not however without our consent"; and further, Ia IIae, q.113, a.3: "By infusing grace God at once moves the free will to accept the gift of grace, in those who are capable of this movement." As Del Prado rightly observes, *op. cit.,* I, 213: The will cannot strictly move itself to this first act of charity, for as a supernatural conclusion is not contained in a natural principle, neither is a super-

This operative grace given at the instant of justification is, as Father Del Prado states (*ibid.,* II, 220), a kind of introduction to all the free movements toward the good, meritorious for salvation, a quasi door into the supernatural order, and, as it were, the first step in the work of divine predestination. And this first act of charity is rather a simple willing of the final end than election, for election as such, properly so called, belongs to those things that are means to an end. Cf. IIa IIae, q. 24, a. 1 ad 3: "Charity, the object of which is the final end, should rather be said to reside in the will than in free choice." Hence operative grace includes not only vocation to the Christian life or the prompting by which God knocks at the gate (wherein our cooperation is non-existent; they precede our consent at any time whatever), but also the movement by which we are justified, freely consenting to it. Thus we read in Ezechiel (36:25 f.): "I will pour upon you clean water, and you shall be cleansed from all your filthiness. . . . And I will give you a new heart, and put a new spirit within you: and I will take away the stony heart out of your flesh, and will give you a heart of flesh." Again in the Acts of the Apostles (16:14): "whose heart [Lydia's] the Lord opened to attend to those things which were said by Paul."

Hence, when God says (Apoc. 3:20): "Behold, I stand at the gate and knock," it is not man who begins to open and separates himself from sinners. Rather, as God opened the heart of Lydia, so does He open the heart of any of the just at the instant of justification. "God begins to open, He first opens, and in doing so, confers upon us that we, too, may open to Him," as Father Del Prado so well expresses it (*op. cit.,* I, 223).

The third example of operative grace is the special inspiration we receive with docility by means of the gifts of the Holy Ghost, according to Cajetan (cf. Ia IIae, q. 68, a. 1-3), since "the gifts are certain habits by which man is perfected so as to obey the Holy Ghost promptly. . . . But man, thus acted upon by the Holy Ghost, also acts, according as it is by free choice," as stated in the same article 3,

---

natural choice contained in man's primary natural intention. In fact, before the gift of justifying grace, the will of man is turned away from God on account of mortal sin. Hence it is God who must begin to move the free will of man determinately by grace toward the initial volition of supernatural good, as stated in the famous reply to the third objection, Ia IIae, q. 9, a. 6. Similarly, Soto, *De nat. et gratia,* chap. 16. This is the true interpretation of St. Thomas given by Cajetan, Soto, Lemos, etc.; also by the Salmanticenses, disp. V, dub. VII, no. 165.

ad 2. Hence these operations proceeding from the gifts, for instance, from the gift of piety in the will, are vital, free, and meritorious, and yet the will does not, properly speaking, move itself to perform them, as it moves itself by deliberation to works of virtue in a human manner, but is specially moved by the Holy Ghost. This is well explained by St. Thomas in his Commentary on the Epistle to the Romans (8:14, lect. 3), a beautiful commentary on the present article. Regarding the words: "Whosoever are led by the Spirit of God, they are the sons of God," he writes as follows: "They are said to be led who are moved by some superior instinct: thus we say of brutes, not that they act, but that they are led or impelled to act, since they are moved by natural instinct, and not by personal movement, to perform their actions. Likewise the spiritual man is inclined to perform some act, not, as it were, mainly by the movement of his own will, but by an instinct of the Holy Ghost." This does not, however, prevent spiritual men from using their will and free choice, since what the Holy Ghost causes in them is precisely the movement of their will and free choice, according to Phil. 2:13: "For it is God who worketh in you, both to will and to accomplish."

In the explanation of the minor, we now come to the question of cooperative grace. This is conferred for good works in which our will is not only moved, but moves itself, that is, when, already actually willing the final supernatural end, it converts itself to willing the means conducive to that end. This act is said to be external, although it may be only internal, since it is commanded by the will in virtue of a previous efficacious act of the same order. Thus it is in the use of the infused virtues, by deliberation properly so called, that the act is performed in the human mode, for example, when the will commands an act of justice or religion or fortitude or temperance, by virtue of a previous act of love of God. Not only are these acts vital, free, and meritorious, but the will properly moves toward them or "determines itself to will this or that," as is said in the well-known reply to the third objection, Ia IIae, q. 9, a. 6.

It is this cooperative grace that is referred to in Sacred Scripture; indeed there is even a comparison made with operative grace; for example, in Ezech. 36:27: "And I will put My spirit in the midst of you [operative grace]: and I will cause you to walk in My commandments, and to keep My judgments, and do them [cooperative grace]."

Again in I Cor. 15:10: "But by the grace of God, I am what I am [operative grace]; and His grace in me hath not been void, but I have labored more abundantly than all they: yet not I, but the grace of God with me." This latter is cooperative grace.

The Angelic Doctor always speaks in harmony with these texts. According to him, under operative grace, the will elicits its act vitally, in fact, it freely consents to the divine motion or inspiration, but it does not strictly move itself by its own proper activity in virtue of a previous efficacious act of the same order, for this previous efficacious act is wanting at that time; for example, in justification, in the acts of the gifts of the Holy Ghost, such as the gift of piety. With respect to justification, St. Thomas declares (Ia IIae, q. 111, a. 2 ad 2): "God does not justify us without ourselves, since by the movement of free will when we are justified we consent to the justice of God. However, this movement is not the cause of grace, but its effect; hence the whole action pertains to grace." Again, he states (IIIa, q. 86, a. 4 ad 2): "It pertains to grace to operate in man, justifying him from sin, and to cooperate with man in right action. Therefore the remission of sins and of the guilt deserving of eternal punishment belongs to operative grace, but the remission of guilt which merits temporal punishment pertains to cooperative grace, that is, according as man, enduring sufferings patiently with the help of divine grace, is also absolved from the guilt of temporal punishment, . . . the first effect is from grace alone, the second from grace and free will." (See also q. 86, a. 6 ad 1.) It is previously declared (q. 85, a. 5 c.): "Penance as a habit is immediately infused by God, without any principal operation on our part, but not however without our disposing ourselves to cooperate by some acts."

Conclusion of Father Del Prado (op. cit., I, 211): By operative grace God operates in us without our acting or moving ourselves, but not without our consent. Cf. a. 2: Thus in the instant of justification and in the operation of the seven gifts. In fact, certain operative grace is even antecedent in time to our consent, such, for instance, as vocation and admonition when God stands at the gate and knocks before it is opened. Here, however, the free consent may, broadly speaking, be called cooperation on our part; but not in the strict and formal sense in which the term is used by St. Thomas in this article. On the contrary, by cooperative grace, God works in us, not only with our consent, but with our action or motion. This is the Thomistic interpretation of St. Augustine's teaching; it is eminently profound and in full conformity with faith.

Corollary. Thus the opposition between St. Thomas' doctrine and that of heresy is manifest. Of the operative actual grace by which we are justified (cf. Del Prado, *op. cit.,* I, 213) : Calvin holds that free will is moved without any action on its own part, and is merely passive. Jansen holds that free will is moved necessarily, and cannot resist even if it wills to do so; Pelagius holds that free will begins to move itself to this first volition; Molina holds 1. that free will is moved by virtuous, indeliberate impulses which, willy-nilly, are supernatural. 2. Then it begins to deliberate within itself, freely accepting them. In his first contention, Molina borders on Jansenism; in the second he does not seem sufficiently removed from Pelagius. In both respects, the opinion of Molina deviates from the teaching of St. Thomas.

As declared in the reply to the third objection, grace is not called "cooperative" in the sense that God here places Himself in the position of a secondary agent; He ever remains the principal agent. But the will also moves itself in this case "once the end is taken for granted" in the intended act, and God assists it in the pursuit of this intended end.

The second conclusion is that habitual grace can also be referred to as operative and cooperative (cf. end of article) since it has two effects: 1. it justifies the soul; this is operative grace, not effectively but formally, that is, it makes pleasing, just as whiteness makes a thing white, as stated in the reply to the first objection; 2. it is the root principle of meritorious works, which proceed from the free will; in this sense it is cooperative.

First doubt, arising from the reply to the fourth objection (cf. Del Prado, *op. cit.,* I, 228) : Whether operative and cooperative grace may be the same grace.

Reply. Yes, if it is a question of habitual grace, which is at the same time justifying (formally) and the root principle of meritorious works. This is clearly stated here in the answer to the fourth objection and in article 3 ad 2, where it is clearly a question of habitual grace, which is said to remain numerically the same in glory, where it is consummated. Cf. also *De veritate,* q. 27, a. 5 ad 1, and IIIa, q. 60, a. 2; q. 72, a. 7. Sacramental grace is a mode of habitual grace and is applied with various effects.

But if the question is about actual grace, then operative grace and cooperative grace are not one and the same numerically; for the reason is the same for actual grace and for the act of the will, of which it is the principle and beginning. But the act is twofold, interior wherein the will does not move itself, exterior wherein it does. Therefore there are likewise two actual graces, for actual grace passes and ceases with the very operation toward which it moves. John of St. Thomas and the Salmanticenses hold this opinion.

In fact sometimes, after an act proceeding from operative grace, there is not elicited an act for which cooperative grace is required, as is evident in the case of one who, immediately after absolution and justification, sins, by not performing the act of virtue which he ought to perform. In such a one, operative grace efficaciously produced justification freely accepted, but it did not produce the following act. To produce it a new actual grace is required, that is, cooperative grace, for there is a new passage from potency to act, and whatever is moved to a new supernatural act, is moved supernaturally by another.

Operative actual grace and cooperative actual grace are therefore distinct, since at times the first is given without the second or vice versa. But if the superior and inferior acts are simultaneous, as in infused contemplation which is prolonged by some discourse, or an inspiration of the gift of council which is simultaneous with an act of prudence, then perhaps it suffices that operative grace should be given, provided that, according to God's decree, it contains cooperative grace eminently; it is then more perfect than if it did not contain it.

Second doubt. Whether operative actual grace requires a twofold motion, namely, moral on the part of the object and physical on the part of the subject. (Cf. Del Prado, *op. cit.,* I, 233.)

Reply. I reply in the affirmative, together with John of St. Thomas and Father Del Prado; for operative grace first enlightens the intellect, then touches the will and causes a sudden desire for the object proposed through the representation of the intellect; and this is the inspiration that opens the heart, as the heart of Lydia was "opened to attend to those things which were said by Paul" (Acts 16:14). Hence operative grace not only excites by moral movement, but also operates physically, so that by it the heart of man is opened and led not only to indeliberate acts but sometimes to consent as well, for example, in justification or in acts of the gifts of the Holy Ghost.

Third doubt. What are the effects of operative grace in us? There are three. (Cf. Father Del Prado, *op. cit.,* I, 234.)

1. The enlightenment of the intellect and the objective pulsation of the heart: this is a moral movement prior to any consent; thereupon the acts are indeliberate, and with respect to this stage operative grace is nothing but a grace which urges.

2. The application of the free will to the holy affection or action, that it may be converted to God; this application is the complement in the secondary cause of the power to operate.

3. The very act of willing, applied to the action, namely, the very act of believing, hoping, and loving: in these acts the will does not remain passive, but elicits the acts freely. However, the will does not properly move itself to such an act as a result of a preceding act, since this act is first in the order of grace and relates to the final end. Hence, contrary to the opinion of Molina, operative grace determinately moving toward these acts is more than a mere urging, and yet liberty is safeguarded, according to St. Thomas.

Fourth doubt. Whether cooperative grace produces in us three similar effects.

Undoubtedly, for cooperative grace is also a previous movement according to a priority not of time but of causality. But these three effects are in another way, since with cooperative grace the will moves itself on account of some preceding act; thus it wills, presupposing the end already intended. On the contrary, with operative grace the will wills by tending toward the end, and the act of the will resembles that first act of the angels discussed in Ia, q. 63, a. 5, or that first act of the soul of Christ which is considered in IIIa, q. 34, a. 3. In the first instant of His conception, Christ merited not incarnation but the glory of immortality, just as an adult at the instant of justification acquires not the grace of justification but the subsequent grace.

Final corollary. We may now read again the well-known reply to the third objection of Ia IIae, q. 9, a. 6, and easily grasp its meaning: "Occasionally God moves some men especially toward willing something determinate which is good, as in those whom He moves by grace, as stated below," that is, in our article 2. This is operative grace moving determinately, but with which liberty still remains.

Operative grace does not consist in an indeliberate act, according as it depends upon God, as Ripalda would have it, since an indeliberate supernatural act presupposes operative help moving one to this act. Nor does it consist in an indeliberate act, with God's assistance, as Suarez holds, for God is not united to us in the manner of an operative power.

Again, in opposition to Alvarez and Gonet, operative grace is not a simple movement applying a previous one, for operative grace thus understood pertains to all operations of the will, indeliberate as well as deliberate, as these authors admit, whereas St. Thomas declares that operative grace, specifically so called, pertains only to the act of the will by which it is moved toward something freely, but does not move itself by discursive deliberation.

Cooperative grace is not the indeliberate act itself inclining toward deliberate consent, because cooperative grace, and not this indeliberate act, has an infallible connection with the deliberate operation to which it moves us and which, in fact, it produces, since by such grace God co-operates and influences the eliciting of the aforesaid act. But the indeliberate affection, left to itself, has no infallible connection with deliberate assent, since we often resist a sudden inspiration or inclination; therefore cooperative grace cannot consist in an indeliberate affection; but there must be added a motion which joins the indeliberate act with the deliberate act or which ensures that the deliberate act is effective. Cf. below, p. 230, the opinion of Gonzales, where it is a matter of the fundamental distinction between efficacious and sufficient grace.

ARTICLE III. WHETHER GRACE IS PROPERLY DIVIDED INTO PREVENIENT AND SUBSEQUENT GRACE

State of the question. This article is intended to explain the classical division of grace, according to Augustine, *De natura et gratia,* chap. 31, and *ad Bonifacium,* Bk. II, chap. 9, as here cited at the end of the article. These terms should be carefully defined that it may be clear wherein lay the error of the Pelagians and Semi-Pelagians, who denied the necessity of prevenient grace. According to them, generally, every internal grace was subsequent with respect to free will; only external preaching of the word was antecedent, according as the beginning of salvation came from us and not from God. Thus did they interpret the words of Apoc. 3:20: "I stand at the gate, and knock. If any man shall hear My voice, and open to Me the door, I will come in to him, and will sup with him, and he with Me."

We shall presently see that grace can never be thus termed "subsequent" with respect to free will, but only in the sense that it follows another grace or another effect of grace; cf. below, Ia IIae, q. 112, a. 2: "Whatever preparation (for grace) may be present in man is derived from the help of God moving the soul to good"; and in *IV Sent.,* d. 17, q. 1, a. 1, solut. 2 ad 2: "Our will is entirely attendant upon divine grace and in no way before hand."

Conclusion. Grace, habitual as well as actual, is properly divided into prevenient and subsequent.

Scriptural proof, in the argument *Sed contra;* namely, that the grace of God proceeds from His mercy. But it is said (Ps. 58:11): "His mercy shall prevent me," and again (Ps. 22:6): "Thy mercy will follow me." Therefore.

Likewise in the prayers of the Church; the collect *Pretiosa:* "Anticipate, O Lord, we beseech thee, our actions by Thy inspiration, and continue them by Thine assistance; that every one of our works may begin always from Thee, and through Thee be ended." The collect for the Sixteenth Sunday after Pentecost: "O Lord, we pray Thee that Thy grace may always go before and follow us." And the collect of Easter Sunday: "Grant that the vows Thou inspirest us to perform, Thou wouldst thyself help us to fulfill."

Similarly on the authority of St. Augustine, here cited in the body of the article, from *De natura et gratia,* chap. 31: "(God) precedes us that we may be healed; He follows us that, even healed, we may yet be invigorated. He precedes us that we may be called; He follows us that we may be glorified. He precedes us that we may live piously; He follows us that we may live with Him forever, since without Him we can do nothing."

Theological proof.

Grace is properly classified according to its various effects.

But there are five effects appointed to grace: 1. that the soul may be healed; 2. that it may will the good; 3. that it may efficaciously perform the good it wills; 4. that it may persevere in the good; 5. that it may attain to glory.

Therefore the grace causing the first effect is properly termed "prevenient" with respect to the second effect, and as causing the second it is called "subsequent" in relation to the first effect; and so with the rest. Thus the same act is at once prevenient and subsequent with respect to different effects.

Corollary. Thus grace is called prevenient with respect to some following act, although it is also prevenient with respect to the act toward which it moves immediately, according as it is previous to it with the priority of causality. And grace is not said to be subsequent in relation to free will, as Pelagius held, but relative to another grace or effect of grace.

As St. Thomas remarks (*De veritate,* q. 27, a. 5 ad 6): "Prevenient and subsequent grace may be understood in another way with respect to the man whom it moves; thus prevenient grace causes a man to will what is good, and subsequent grace causes him to perform the good which he has willed." As Augustine declares in the *Enchiridion,* chap. 32: "He precedes the unwilling, that he may will, and follows the willing lest he will in vain."

Reply to first objection. Since the uncreated love of God for us is eternal, it is always prevenient. (Cf. Del Prado, *op. cit.,* I, 247.)

Corollary 2. Both operative and cooperative grace, since they move toward diverse acts, may be called prevenient and subsequent.

Doubt. Whether prevenient and subsequent grace may be the same grace numerically. The solution is found in the reply to the second objection, that is, in the case of habitual grace, yes; but in that of actual grace, no, for the same reason as for operative and cooperative grace. For it is evident that the same habitual grace, numerically, is called prevenient inasmuch as, justifying us, it precedes meritorious works; it is called subsequent inasmuch as it will be consummated, thus it is called glory."

In fact, St. Thomas expressly states here in the reply to the second objection: "Subsequent grace pertaining to glory is not different numerically from prevenient grace by which we are justified now; for as the charity of the wayfarer is not made void but perfected in heaven, so also can this be said of the light of grace, for neither of them bears any imperfection in its principle."

But if it is a question of actual grace, which ceases with the very act toward which it moves immediately and of which it is the beginning, then it is multiplied along with the acts enumerated above, as we said before of operative actual grace and cooperative actual grace.

To complete this Question 111 on the division of grace, two articles must be added since the Council of Trent and the condemnation of Jansenism: 1. The distinction between exciting or stimulating grace and assisting grace, which was considered by the Council, Sess. VI, chap. 5; 2. The difference between sufficient and efficacious grace, in respect to which the Protestants and Jansenists erred.

THE DIVISION OF ACTUAL GRACE INTO STIMULATING AND ASSISTING GRACE (CF. DEL PRADO, OP. CIT., I, 243)

This division is explained at the Council of Trent, Sess. VI, chap. 5 (Denz., no. 797): "It is declared, moreover, that the beginning of this very justification in adults is received from God through Christ Jesus by prevenient grace (can. 3), that is, by His vocation, in that none are called on account of their own existing merits; that they who were turned away from God by sin, may be disposed by His stimulating and assisting grace to become converted to their own justification, freely (can. 4 and 5) assenting to and cooperating with the same grace."

According to this text, grace rousing one from the sleep of sin by moral movement, that is, by enlightenment and attraction, and grace assisting one to will the good, by the application of the will to its exercise, are included under prevenient grace, which precedes the free consent of man's will, whereby we consent to justification and may be prepared for it. Hence this prevenient grace to which the Council refers is the same as the operative grace considered by St. Thomas in article two, especially in the reply to the second objection: "God does not justify us without ourselves, since by the movement of free will, when we are justified, we consent to the justice of God. However, this movement is not the cause of grace [as the Semi-Pelagians held], but its effect; hence the whole operation belongs to grace." (Cf. Del Prado, *De gratia,* I, 228.)

Thus is corroborated our interpretation of article two, that is: operative grace is not only stimulating but assisting. Under Sess. VI, chap. 5 of the Council the same doctrine is explained as in article two of the present question (111). The Council of Trent, Sess. VI, can. 4 (Denz., no. 814) uses the term "moving grace" for assisting grace.

Doubt. Whether the prevenient grace which stimulates the intellect and assists in the application of the will is absolutely prior to our consent, or subsequent to it. How are we to understand the following text of the Apocalypse (3:20)? "Behold, I stand at the gate and knock. If any man shall hear My voice, and open to Me the door, I will come in to him."

Reply. This grace is, with respect to its efficient cause, absolutely prior to our consent, according to St. Thomas (Ia IIae, q. 111, a. 2 ad 2; q. 113, a. 8 c.). At the same instant: 1. there is an infusion of grace; 2. a movement of the free will with respect to God; 3. a movement of the free will in regard to sin; 4. the remission of sin. Similarly in the answers to the first and second objections. (Cf. Dominico Soto, *De natura et gratia,* Bk. I, chap. 16, and Del Prado, *De gratia,* I, 245.)

Corollary. Del Prado, *op. cit.* (I, 248): From the notion of operative and cooperative grace, propounded by St. Thomas in article two, it can easily be demonstrated that the gratuitous movement of God, whereby He impels us to meritorious good, is efficacious, not on account of the consent of the free will that has been moved, but on account of the will and intention of God who moves it, as St. Thomas expressly declares in the following question (112, a. 3).

Even in article two of the present question, the Angelic Doctor has already said with reference to operative grace, that "with it, our *mens* is moved and not the mover"; and, in the answer to the second objection, that the movement of the free will, when we are justified and consent to the justice of God, "is not the cause of grace, but its effect, so that the whole operation belongs to grace."

Again in the body of this second article it is declared of cooperative grace: "And since God also helps us in this (deliberate) act, both by interiorly strengthening the will that it may accomplish the act, and by exteriorly supplying the faculty to perform it, with respect to this kind of act it is called cooperative grace."

As a matter of fact, Molina would not have denied the interpretation of Augustine given by St. Thomas, were it not declared in this interpretation that grace is efficacious of itself.

CHAPTER V

The Doctrine of the Church

The question of sufficient grace and efficacious grace is here treated in four chapters according to the following summary.

Conclusion III. Its internal efficacy is properly and formally a pre-determining physical premotion.

IV. Refutation of objections.

CHAPTER VIII. EXCURSUS ON EFFICACIOUS GRACE

I. Efficacious grace and easy acts conducive to salvation.

II. Efficacious grace in relation to spirituality.

III. Efficacious grace in holy wayfarers, particularly in martyrs.

IV. Efficacious grace in those burning with intense love of God.

V. Efficacious grace in the impeccable and freely obedient Christ.

I. INTRODUCTORY REMARKS: STATE OF THE QUESTION

Terminology used. It is evident from revelation that graces are conferred by God and that some of them miss their final effect, whereas others achieve their effect. The former are called "truly sufficient" and "merely sufficient" since they give the power for a good work, but they are resisted. The latter are called "efficacious" since they really produce their effect in us, they act indeed that we may act.

From this difference the question arises: How are sufficient grace and efficacious grace distinguished from each other? In other words, is efficacious grace efficacious of itself, intrinsically, because God so wills, or is it efficacious extrinsically, that is, on account of our consent foreseen by God's knowledge?

Underlying principles from the treatise on God: statement and difficulty of the question.

After St. Thomas, in the early days of Protestantism and Jansenism, this question has been widely debated and at length; it may fittingly be explained here, for its solution is deducible from what St. Thomas has said. (Ia IIae, q. 110, a. 1; q. 111, a. 2; q. 112, a. 3.)

However, the basic principles of the solution are first enunciated in the treatise on God, Ia, q. 14, a. 8: "The knowledge of God is the cause of things inasmuch as His will is joined to it." And further, Ia, a. 19, a. 4: "The effects determined by the infinite perfection of God proceed in accordance with the determination of His will and intellect" (that is, by a decree of the divine will). Again, Ia, q. 19, a. 6 ad 1: "Whatever God wills absolutely, is done (otherwise He would not be omnipotent), although what He wills antecedently (or only conditionally) may not be done," for in this instance God permits the opposite evil for the sake of a greater good; thus He wills antecedently that all the fruits of the earth come to maturity, but He permits that many actually do not reach this maturity. It is similar in the matter of the salvation of men. St. Thomas goes on to explain this in the same article (ad 1): On consequent or unconditional will. "The will is compared to things according as they are in themselves; but in themselves they are individual. Hence we will something absolutely inasmuch as we will it considering all its individuating circumstances; this is to will consequently." Thus whatever God (omnipotent) wills absolutely is done; although what He wills antecedently may not be done.

Antecedently God wills a thing according as it is good in itself, for example, that all men be saved, that all His commands be ever fulfilled; but at the same time He permits to some extent the opposite evil for the sake of a greater good, and thus "what He wills only antecedently or conditionally is not done."

Hence it is said in psalm 134:6: "Whatsoever the Lord pleased He hath done, in heaven, in earth." And the Council of Toucy (PL, CXXVI, 123) adds: "For nothing is done in heaven or on earth, except what God either graciously does Himself or permits to be done, in His justice." That is to say, no good, here and now, in this man rather than in another, comes about unless God Himself graciously wills and accomplishes it, and no evil, here and now, in this man rather than another, comes about unless God Himself justly permits it to be done. Nevertheless God does not command the impossible, and grants even to those who do not actually observe His commandments the power of observing them.

But those who observe His commandments are better than others and would not keep them in fact, had not God from eternity efficaciously decreed that they should observe these precepts. Thus, these good servants of God are more beloved and assisted by Him than others, although God does not command the impossible of the others.

Furthermore, this very resistance to sufficient grace is an evil which would not occur, here and now, without the divine permission, and nonresistance itself is a good which would not come about here and now except for divine consequent will. Therefore, there is a real difference between sufficient grace, to which is attached the divine permission of sin and by reason of which the fulfillment of the commandments is really possible, and efficacious grace, on the other hand, which is a greater help whence follows not only the real possibility of observing the commandments, but their effective fulfillment.

Moreover, in sufficient grace, efficacious grace is offered to us, as the fruit is in the flower; but if resistance is made on account of our defectibility, then we deserve not to receive efficacious grace. For this reason Bossuet declares: "Our intellect must be held captive before the obscurity of the divine mystery and admit two graces (sufficient and efficacious) of which the former leaves our will without any excuse before God, and the latter does not permit the will to glory in itself." (*Œuvres complètes,* Paris, 1845, I, 644.)

St. Thomas states further (Ia, q. 19, a. 8): "Since the divine will is efficacious in the highest degree, it follows not only that those things are done which God wills to be done, but also that they are done in the way God wills them to be done. But God wills certain things to be done necessarily, others contingently, that there may be order among things for the completion of the universe." This is the basis of grace efficacious in itself. Again (Ia, q. 20, a. 2): "The will of God is the cause of all things, and hence, necessarily, to the extent that a thing has being or any good whatever, it is willed by God. Therefore, since loving is nothing else but wishing well to someone, it is evident that God loves all things that are, but not in the way that we do. . . . Our will is not the cause of goodness in things," including the goodness of our choices, as appears from Ia, q. 19, a. 8.

There follows from this the great principle of predilection, by which the whole treatise on grace is elucidated and which is formulated in Ia, q. 20, a. 3: "Since the love of God is the cause of the goodness of things, no one would be better than another if God did not will a greater good to one than to another." Likewise, in article 4 of the same question and also in Ia, q. 23, a. 4: "In God, love precedes election." Already it is evident that the man who, in fact, observes the commandments is better than the one who is able to do so but actually does not. Therefore he who keeps the commandments is more beloved and assisted. In short, God loves that man more to whom He grants that he keep the commandments than another in whom He permits sin.

This principle of predilection is valid for all created being, even free beings, and for all their acts, natural or supernatural, easy or difficult, initial or final; in other words, no created being would be in any respect better if it were not better loved by God. This truth is clear in the philosophical order, for it follows from the principle of causality and of the eminently universal causality of the will or love of God. In the order of grace, this principle is revealed by several scriptural texts, for instance: "I will have mercy on whom I will, and I will be merciful to whom it shall please Me" (Exod. 33:19); and "For who distinguisheth thee? Or what hast thou that thou hast not received?" (I Cor. 4:7.)

This principle of predilection presupposes, according to St. Thomas, a decree of the divine will rendering our salutary acts intrinsically efficacious (Ia, q. 19, a. 8). For, if they were efficacious on account of our foreseen consent, of two men equally loved and helped by God, one would be better in some respect. He would be better of himself alone and not on account of divine predilection. But this principle must be reconciled with another which ought to be maintained with equal firmness: "God does not command the impossible, but He teaches thee by commanding to do what thou canst and to ask what thou canst not, and He helps thee that thou mayest be able" (St. Augustine, *De natura et gratia,* chap. 43, no. 50, and the Council of Trent, Denz., no. 804). Herein lies a great mystery of reconciliation between infinite mercy, infinite justice, and supreme liberty. They are indeed reconciled in the intimate life of the Deity, but of Deity as such we have no positive or proper conception: "Deity is above being, above unity, which are contained in it formally and eminently." (Cf. *Revue thomiste,* May–June, 1937, the author's article, "Le fondement suprême de la distinction des deux grâces suffisante et efficace.")[1] These conclusions from the treatise on God are, then, presupposed in the present discussion.

This question must now be divided into two sections. First the dogmas of faith must be sought out dealing with grace which is truly, yet merely, sufficient, and with efficacious grace which nevertheless does not take away man's freedom. Secondly, we must consider the various notions of theologians with respect to the nature of sufficient grace and of efficacious grace, whether the latter is efficacious intrinsically or extrinsically, that is, on account of our foreseen consent.[2]

With the object of better determining the status of the question,

---

[1] This article will also be found in the last section of the present volume.

[2] Cf. John of St. Thomas, O.P., *Cursus theol., De gratia,* disp. XXIV; the Salmanticenses, *Cursus theol., De gratia,* disp. V, dub. 7; Lemos, O.P., *Panoplia gratiae,* Vol. IV, Part II, p. 36; Del Prado, O.P., *De gratia,* Vol. II, chaps. 1–3.

it will be well to consider the differences which exist in this matter between the opposing heresies of Pelagianism and Jansenism, and between the theological notions of Molinists and Thomists.

For the Pelagians, actual grace (such as the preaching of the gospel) is either efficacious on account of man's consent to the good, or inefficacious on account of the evil will of man.

For the Jansenists, internal actual grace is twofold: one is efficacious of itself, the other inefficacious and insufficient as well.

For Thomists, internal actual grace is twofold: one is efficacious of itself, producing of itself the virtuous act; the other is inefficacious but truly sufficient, bestowing the possibility either proximate, or at least remote, of acting virtuously.

For the Molinists, sufficient actual grace itself is either efficacious from its effect, or from our consent foreseen by mediate knowledge, or else inefficacious and merely sufficient.

2. THE DOCTRINE OF THE CHURCH ON SUFFICIENT GRACE

Grace is given which is truly yet merely sufficient: "truly" because it really confers the power; "merely" because, through the fault of the will, it fails in its effect, with respect to which it is said to be inefficacious, but sufficient. This doctrine of the Church is formulated against the Predestinationists and later, much more explicitly, against the Jansenists. (Cf. *De praedestinianismo,* Denz., nos. 316 ff., 320 ff.)

The Predestinationists, including Lucidus, a fifth-century priest, Gottschalk in the ninth century, and later revivers, taught predestination to evil, before the prevision of demerits, and consequently must have denied the existence of sufficient grace; for, according to them, those who are damned lack the power of doing good (Denz., no. 321, at the end); and those who are saved are so necessitated to the good that they cannot resist grace. "Therefore the wicked themselves are not lost because they could not be good, but because they would not," declares the Council of Valence (Denz., no. 321). Calvin followed the ways of Predestinationism (cf. *Inst.,* Bk. III, chaps. 14–21).

At first, the Jansenists denied sufficient grace. Jansen himself (*De gratia Christi,* Bk. III, chap. 1) admits no grace that is not efficacious. Quesnel (Denz., nos. 1359 ff.) and the Pistoians (Denz., no. 1521) adhere to this fully. Jansen's first proposition (Denz., no. 1092) should be cited in particular: "Some commands of God are impossible to just men who are willing and striving, according to their present powers;

moreover they lack grace which would make their observance possible to them." In other words, many just men of good will, who make an effort, are deprived of sufficient grace which gives a real power or faculty for good works commanded by God; it would follow that the wicked are punished unjustly, since they could not be good. This proposition is declared heretical.

The second proposition is closely related to the first: "In the state of fallen nature, interior graces are never resisted," that is to say, interior grace is always efficacious, which is heresy.

Likewise the third proposition of Jansen: "For meriting and demeriting in the state of fallen nature man does not require freedom from necessity; freedom from constraint is sufficient." This proposition pertains rather to efficacious grace which, according to the Jansenists, removes freedom from necessity and leaves only spontaneity. Their fourth proposition is that the Semi-Pelagian heresy consisted in maintaining that the human will can resist or obey grace. The fifth proposition declares that Christ did not die for all men.

Quesnel's propositions (Denz., nos. 1359-75) were also condemned for the same reason, that is, for denying sufficient grace and reducing all internal grace to efficacious, under which, for him, liberty from necessity would not remain. Similarly, the twenty-one propositions of the Synod of Pistoia (Denz., no. 1521) were condemned. The motive for their condemnation, as set down, is that, like the Jansenists, they hold "the interior grace of Christ is not given to him by whom it is resisted . . . but only that is properly the grace of Christ which makes us act." Hence, according to the Pistoians, the only sufficient grace which is given is external, such as preaching or good example.

However, it should be remarked that, after the condemnation of the five propositions of Jansen, several of his followers, including Arnauld (dissertation in four parts: *De gratia efficaci* and *Apologie pour les saints Pères,* Bk. IV), to avoid being held as heretics, admitted a little interior grace which might be given to certain of the just. But what is this little grace of Arnauld's? According to him, it is grace which may be given in general, but not here and now in particular; or it is sufficient for acting generally, but not sufficient with respect to such and such a precept to be fulfilled or some particular temptation to be overcome. This little grace, according to Arnauld, is remiss charity; when charity is really intense and predominant, it is truly sufficient even here and now in particular, to such an extent that man resists temptation, and hence it is efficacious.[3] This is the famous theory of little grace which certain Jansenists hit upon to avoid the condemnation of the Church. (Cf. Guillermin, *Revue thomiste,* 1902, pp. 47 ff.; Paquier, *Le Jansénisme;* and Petitot, *Revue thomiste,* September, 1910, "Pascal et la grace suffisante.") [4] It should be observed that the Augustinians admitted little grace, but not in the sense of the Jansenists; for them it is really sufficient but remiss.

Does Arnauld's explanation preserve sufficient grace? I reply: not really, but only as a matter of verbiage, for actions to be accomplished are not general but concrete and individual. Hence, if grace does not suffice for each particular precept or each individual temptation, it is simply insufficient. Therefore Arnauld does not escape from Jansen's first proposition: "Some commands of God are impossible to just men who are willing and striving, according to their present powers; moreover, they lack grace which would make their observance possible to them" here and now.

[3] This theory is similar to the doctrine of those who, following Leibnitz' idea, maintained that man is indeed free, as a class, inasmuch as his will is specified by a universal, abstract good, so to speak, surpassing any particular good; however, actually and in the concrete, here and now, our choice is never free, since nothing is willed unless it is foreknown, and nothing is preferred unless it is foreknown as more advantageous here and now. That is, the will always follows the leadership of reason and whatever is, in the judgment of reason, here and now, the stronger motive. Hence this stronger motive is always efficacious as a victorious satisfaction, and the opposite motive is not, in fact, really sufficient. Thus psychological determinism is arrived at. Man would be free in the abstract but not in the concrete. And this theory persists in a certain sense in Kant, who holds that man has liberty in the noumenal order which may be conceived, but not in the phenomenal order. But this doctrine is subjective conceptualism, to which moderate realism is opposed, declaring that the human will is specified by the universal good not only according to our abstract conception, but in reality; our will even here and now preserves its nature and capacity, which infinitely surpasses any particular, eligible good. Hence the stronger objective motive even here and now is indeed fully sufficient for choosing freely, but not for necessitating the will; in this respect it differs from the clear vision of God.

Arnauld in his theory seems to proceed in conformity with the idea of subjective conceptualism, according to which really and merely sufficient grace may be given in the abstract but not in the concrete; as if, for instance, man might be conceived but a real man could not be given in the concrete, in whom human nature would really exist with individuating conditions.

[4] Cf. *Dictionnaire de théologie catholique,* "Jansénisme," col. 388–99; "La grace suffisante," col. 431–47; "La prédestination" (J. Carreyre); also the articles "Prémotion" and "Prédestination" (Garrigou-Lagrange).

Since this proposition is condemned as heretical, it is a dogma of faith that at least grace which is truly, yet merely, sufficient is not lacking to the just; truly, since it confers a real power of acting virtuously; merely, since it is resisted and fails of its final effect. This dogma of faith had already been equivalently expressed in several councils. The Council of Orange (Denz., no. 200) declared that "all the baptized, by the help and cooperation of Christ, can and ought to accomplish whatever pertains to salvation, if they are willing to work faithfully." The Second Council of Valence maintained against Scotus Erigenus (Denz., no. 321): "Therefore the wicked themselves are not lost because they could not be good, but because they would not." And the Council of Trent (Denz., no. 804) adopts the formula: "God does not command the impossible, but by commanding He teaches thee to do what thou canst and to ask what thou canst not, and He assists thee that thou mayest be able." Therefore God confers sufficient help to enable us, not only in general, but in individual cases, to observe His commandments.

What, then, is the scriptural basis for this dogma of sufficient grace? Especially worthy of citation are the words of the Lord in Isa. 5:4: "What is there that I ought to do more to My vineyard, that I have not done to it?" For if God ought not to do anything more, then His help is truly sufficient. However, in this text it does not say: "What is there that I could do more," and we shall see that God can do more, although not bound to do so.

Again, Scripture often bears witness to graces offered or conferred whereby God calls and urges, and which are nevertheless resisted, or received in vain. Thus we read: "I called, and you refused" (Prov. 1:24); "I have spread forth My hands all the day to an unbelieving people, who walk in a way that is not good after their own thoughts" (Isa. 65:2); "Jerusalem, Jerusalem, thou that killest the prophets, and stonest them that are sent unto thee, how often would I have gathered together thy children, as the hen doth gather her chickens under her wings, and thou wouldest not! Behold, your house shall be left to you, desolate" (Matt. 23:37).[5]

Commenting on St. Matthew, St. Thomas says of the passage just

---

[5] With regard to this symbolic expression of divine truth, cf. St. Thomas, Ia, q. 1, a.9 ad 3: "It is more fitting that the divine things in the Scriptures should be presented under less dignified bodily figures."

quoted: "This is that Jerusalem of which Ezechiel (5:6) declares: 'This is Jerusalem, I have set her in the midst of the nations, and the countries round about her. And she hath despised My judgments.' They might excuse themselves saying: 'We had no one to tell us'; therefore does Jesus add: 'and stonest them that are sent unto thee,' whereupon I sent prophets and many helps and thou didst not recognize them. 'How often would I have gathered together thy children, as the hen doth gather her chickens under her wings, and thou wouldest not?' The perpetuity of His divinity is here implied, as declared explicitly in His words: 'Before Abraham was made, I am' (John 8:58). Hence Christ Himself sent the prophets, patriarchs, and angels. As often as He sent, He wished to gather the Jews together. Those who were converted to the Lord were indeed gathered, for they are united in Him; whereas sinners, who are withdrawn from unity, are dispersed. Wherefore: I wish to gather as a hen gathers her chickens under her wings. It is said that no animal is so solicitous for its young as the hen. She defends them against the hawk and endangers her own life for them, gathering them under her wings. So is Christ solicitous for us; 'surely He hath borne our infirmities' (Isa. 53:4); and likewise exposed Himself to the hawk, that is, the devil.

"*Sed contra:* the Lord willed thus to protect them, but they refused; therefore their evil will prevailed over the will of God. Hence it could be said: As often as I willed, I acted; but I invite thee, acting as I did (for instance, sending the prophets); whereupon thy will prevented My action. Or again, the fact that He sent the prophets was a sign that He wished to gather thee in, and thou wouldst not. Then follows the punishment: behold, your house shall be left to you, desolate." So speaks St. Thomas. This is the great mystery of antecedent will and the simultaneous permission of sin, but the grace was really sufficient; had there not been resistance to it, the Lord would have given greater grace.

Similarly, we read in the Acts (7:51): "You stiffnecked and uncircumcised in heart and ears, you always resist the Holy Ghost"; and in II Corinthians (6:1): "We . . . do exhort you, that you receive not the grace of God in vain"; cf. St. Thomas on this text. This is the case often when habitual grace is lost by mortal sin; likewise prevenient grace is received in vain when man does not persevere in good. However, graces of this kind are really sufficient, for through them God truly invites, but they are merely sufficient since they fail in their effect. Whence many accusations are unjustifiably adduced against us by the Molinists on the basis of these texts, to show that grace is not intrinsically efficacious; but as a matter of fact, these texts are not concerned with efficacious grace, but with merely sufficient grace, since it fails in its effect.

The aforesaid dogma of faith regarding sufficient grace is also based on I Timothy (2:4–6) where it is written: "God will have all men to be saved, and to come to the knowledge of the truth"; and "Christ Jesus . . . gave Himself a redemption for all." For if God really wills the salvation of all, He offers truly sufficient helps to all; many, however, are not saved, and thus it is evident that these helps often remain actually inefficacious or merely sufficient. Cf. St. Thomas on I Tim. 2:9, and Ia, q. 19, a. 6: Whether the will of God is always accomplished. In this article, replying to the first objection, St. Thomas maintains that God wishes all men to be saved, not by His consequent or efficacious will, but by His antecedent will, "as a just judge antecedently desires all men to live, but wills consequently that a murderer should be hanged. In the same way, God wills antecedently the salvation of all men (for this is good absolutely), but He wills consequently that some should be damned according to the requirements of justice." Further, He permits sin to happen, since it is not to be wondered at that what is defective should fail to a certain extent, that a greater good may issue from it, such as the manifestation of divine mercy and justice. With respect to this antecedent will, cf. the commentators on Ia, q. 19, a. 6 (Billuart); moreover, from this antecedent will for the salvation of all men proceeds the aggregate of sufficient graces to all adults.

It would be equally easy to find among patristic writings the aforesaid dogma of the faith on truly, yet merely, sufficient grace, in equivalent terms at least, when they declare that we need divine aid and with it are able to do good, even if we do not, so that man remains inexcusable after sin, for he could have avoided it. Thus the wicked are justly to be punished. Cf. St. Irenaeus: "They did not do good when they could have done it" (Contra haereses, Bk. IV, chap. 37, no. 9.) Commenting on the Epistle to the Hebrews (12:13), St. John Chrysostom writes: "Unless you receive heavenly aid, all your actions are in vain; but it is evident that you will attain whatever you apply yourself to, with that help, provided you are also attentive and desirous of doing so." This text affirms the existence of really sufficient grace but does not deny the existence of grace which is efficacious of itself.[6]

3. THE MIND OF ST. AUGUSTINE AND ST. THOMAS

How did they understand the aforesaid doctrine of the Church on sufficient grace?

St. Augustine, in particular, defends efficacious grace, as will be explained later; here it suffices to quote the classic words found in the book, *De dono perseverantiae,* chap. 14: "Those who are set free are most certainly set free by the help of God"; and again in the *De praedestinatione sanctorum,* chap. 8: "Grace which is not rejected by any hardheartedness, since it is bestowed, in the first place, to remove hardness of heart." Likewise in the book, *De gratia Christi,* chap. 24, he described efficacious grace: "internal, hidden, wonderful, and ineffable power by which God effects in the hearts of men not only true revelations but even upright wills."

Augustine also admitted the principle of predilection: no created being would be better in any respect if it were not better loved and assisted more by God. This principle is affirmed in various terms; for example, in the *City of God,* Bk. XII, chap. 9, referring to good and bad angels, he says: "Thus, both were created equally good, these falling on account of their bad will, and those, receiving greater help, attaining their full beatitude, from which they most assuredly would never fall." Similarly, in *De dono perseverantiae,* chap. 9, we find: "Of two adults leading lives of great wickedness, that one should be called in such a way as to follow the call, while the other is not called, or not called in that way, is in the inscrutable judgments of God."

But this principle of predilection presupposes, as we have said, that grace is efficacious of itself. For if it were efficacious on account of our foreseen consent, then, of two angels or men equally loved and assisted by God, one would be better than the other; he would be better on his own account and not as a result of divine predilection. This is contrary to St. Paul's "For who distinguisheth thee? Or what hast thou that thou hast not received?" These words of St. Paul are often quoted by Augustine.

---

[6] Cf. Rouet de Journel, *Enchir. patrist.,* theological index, nos. 310, 318, 330. God does not command the impossible; all the just can persevere if they so will, but not for long without the help of grace; on assistance *whereby* and on assistance *without which one cannot,* nos. 1556, 1850, 1954 ff.

2. Nevertheless, St. Augustine elsewhere maintains very definitely that "God does not command the impossible, but by commanding He instructs thee both to do what thou canst and to beg what thou canst not, and He assists thee that thou mayest be able" (*De natura et gratia,* chap. 43, no. 50, cited at the Council of Trent; Denz., no. 804). In this last text Augustine affirms sufficient grace without any ambiguity, and God's will that the fulfillment of His commands should be really possible to all, and, in this sense, His will that all should be saved.

Hence St. Augustine admits that before efficacious grace, in the state of fallen nature, sufficient grace is given, without which the keeping of the commandments of God would be really impossible. And it is this grace which is called truly sufficient, in opposition to the Jansenists. Likewise in the book *De correptione et gratia,* chap. 7, discounting the excuse of those who say: we did not persevere because we did not have perseverance, he declares: "Man, thou mayest persevere in that which thou hearest and holdest, if thou willest." Again in *De natura et gratia,* chap. 67: "Since God . . . recalls the hostile, teaches the believing, consoles the hopeful, encourages the loving, assists him who strives, and hears him who prays, thou art not condemned to sin because thou art ignorant against thy will, but because thou dost neglect to seek after what thou knowest not; not because thou failest to bind up the wounded members, but because thou disdainest the will to be healed." And similarly, commenting on psalm 40:5: "Do not say: I am not able to restrain, endure, and bridle my flesh; for you are assisted that you may be able."

Furthermore, St. Augustine presented the best formulated distinction between that help without which we cannot act and that help by which we infallibly act, just as later Augustinians and Thomists distinguish between sufficient grace, which gives the power to act, and efficacious grace, which infallibly imparts that action itself. This Augustinian distinction is found in *De correptione et gratia,* chap. 11, where he teaches that Adam in the state of innocence had received sufficient help with which he could persevere in good, but not efficacious help whereby he would infallibly persevere; however, both helps are conferred on the predestinate.

St. Augustine's words are as follows: "The first grace is that which enables a man to have justice if he so wills; therefore more is possible with the second, whereby it is also brought about that he does will. . . . Nor was the former by any means small, through which the power of free will was demonstrated; for the help is such that without it he would not have continued to do good; but if he wills, he may forfeit this help. The latter, however, is so far superior, that it is not enough for man to recover his lost liberty through it . . . unless it is effected that he wills. . . . In fact, it lies within us, through this grace of God received with good dispositions and perseveringly maintained, not only to be able to will but also to will actually what we will. This was not so in the first man; for he possessed one of these but not the other." (Cf. Salmanticenses, *Cursus theol., De gratia,* q. III, disp. V, dub. VIII, no. 173.) After Augustine, the older theologians generally used the expression "help without which we cannot" for what, since the condemnation of Jansenism, has been commonly referred to as sufficient grace, and "help whereby" we do good for what is now called efficacious grace.

Objection. It seems that Augustine does not mean, by the difference between "help whereby" and "help without which," the same distinction which is now understood between efficacious help and sufficient help. For in many instances he excludes "help whereby" from the state of innocence. If therefore "help whereby" were admitted to represent grace efficacious in itself, it would follow that efficacious grace was not necessary for Adam and the angels to persevere.

Reply. This question was discussed at great length in the time of the Jansenist heresy, as can easily be seen from Billuart's *Cursus theol., De gratia,* diss. II, a. 4. But from the many texts of St. Augustine quoted there it appears that the holy doctor excluded from the state of innocence the "help whereby" for being healed, but not for being assisted.[7] And he holds that grace efficacious of itself was necessary for perseverance even in the innocent Adam and in the angels. To prove this it suffices to quote the very famous passage in the *City of God,* Bk. XII, chap. 9, regarding the good and bad angels: "Thus both were created equally good, these falling on account of their bad will, and those, receiving greater help, attaining their full beatitude, from which they most assuredly would never fall."

This is affirmed by Augustine in virtue of the principle of predilection: "For who distinguisheth thee? Or what hast thou that thou hast not received?" In other words, no man or angel, in any state, would be better than another, if he were not more loved and assisted

---

[7] That is, Adam in the state of innocence required grace efficacious in itself to persevere, by reason of his dependence on God, not by reason of any weakness in himself.

by God. The angels who fell had sufficient grace, which they resisted; the others, that is, the predestinate, were more loved and assisted. This is the doctrine of predestination itself.

Moreover, as Bossuet demonstrates (*Défense de la tradition,* Bks. X and XI, chaps. 19–27), Augustine, as well as many others of the Greek and Latin Fathers, maintains, when explaining the threefold denial of Peter during our Lord's passion, that Peter could have avoided that sin, for he was not deprived of all grace; but on account of his previous movement of presumption, he lacked the efficacious help by which he later came even to martyrdom. Cf. Bossuet, *ibid.,* where several texts from Origen, Chrysostom, Augustine, and Gregory the Great are quoted and also Book XII, *De doctrina Augustini de praedestinatione,* wherein Bossuet distinguishes very well between sufficient and efficacious grace in accordance with tradition.

The whole question is briefly formulated in the proposition already quoted from the same authority: "Our intelligence must be held captive before the divine obscurity of this great mystery, confessing these two graces (sufficient and efficacious), the first of which leaves our will without an excuse before God, while the second does not allow it to glory in itself." [8] In other words, "It must be admitted (in opposition to the Jansenists) that there are two interior graces, of which one (namely, sufficient grace) leaves our soul inexcusable before God after sin, and of which the other (that is, efficacious grace) does not permit our will to glory in itself after accomplishing good works." "What hast thou that thou hast not received? For who distinguisheth thee?"·

These two propositions, thus formulated, are as two very luminous semicircles surrounding the deepest obscurity of the mystery. Above these semicircles is the mystery of the divine good pleasure, combining infinite mercy, infinite justice, and supreme liberty, which are identified in the Deity. Below, however, is the abyss of our defectibility and the gravity of mortal sin.

Finally, this doctrine of really sufficient grace distinct from efficacious grace is expressed in several texts from St. Thomas.

Cf. IIIa, q. 79, a. 7 ad 2: "The passion of Christ does indeed benefit all men, with respect to its sufficiency, the remission of sin, and the

---

[8] "Avertissement sur le livre des Réflexions morales," a brief treatise in the *Œuvres complètes,* Paris, 1845, I, 643; see also the index to Bossuet's works under "grâce, . . . résistance à la grâce."

attainment of grace and glory, but it produces its effect only in those who are united to the passion of Christ by faith and charity." Likewise IIIa, dist. 13, q. 2, a. 2; qc., 2 ad 5: "Christ satisfied for all human nature sufficiently, but not efficiently, since not all become participants in His satisfaction; but this is the result of their unfitness, not of any insufficiency in His satisfaction." Similarly in *De veritate,* q. 29, a. 7 ad 4.

Again on the First Epistle to Timothy (2:6), with reference to the words, "Christ gave Himself a redemption for all," St. Thomas explains: "For some efficaciously, but for all sufficiently, since the price of His blood is sufficient for the salvation of all; but it is not efficacious except in the elect on account of impediments." Therefore in like manner, according to St. Thomas, sufficient helps and efficacious helps are given, which may correspond for their effect to the aforesaid passion and the mode by which it benefits us. And in Ia IIae, q. 106, a. 2 ad 2: God "gives sufficient help to avoid sin"; and again on the Epistle to the Ephesians, chap. 3, lect. 2.

In certain texts of St. Thomas the term "sufficient" is not explicitly contrasted with "efficacious," and his meaning is not always clear except from the context; but in many instances we really find this explicit contrast or distinction which was already common among theologians long before Jansenism and the discussions which it aroused. Moreover, in the *Tabula aurea* of St. Thomas' works, under *"satisfactio,"* no. 36, are given eighteen quotations from the Angelic Doctor wherein he declares substantially that Christ satisfied for the whole of human nature sufficiently, but not efficaciously.

Lastly, St. Thomas evidently holds that all infused virtue gives the power to do good in the order of grace, but not the actual doing good, for which divine motion is necessary; and furthermore, the divine motion which inclines one effectively toward a good thought does not suffice to incline one efficaciously toward a pious desire nor toward agreeing to a good or proposing it, nor, for still greater reason, toward carrying out this proposal. The actual motion which inclines one to have a good thought does give the potentiality with respect to the pious desire, but not the actual desire itself, and so on through the series. The mind of St. Thomas is clear on this point and may be demonstrated by many texts quoted below.

Nor does St. Thomas merely distinguish between sufficient grace and efficacious grace; he indicates the supreme basis of this distinction when, in Ia, q. 19, a. 6 ad 1, he establishes the difference between antecedent will (or the will for universal salvation) and consequent will. We explained this in our treatise, *De Deo uno,* 1937, p. 425. According to his argument, antecedent will is concerned with the good considered absolutely and not here and now, whereas consequent will has to do with the good considered here and now. But since the good which exists in things themselves is effected only here and now, it follows from this that the antecedent will of itself alone, without the addition of the consequent will, remains inefficacious. Hence the division into these two wills is the supreme basis of the distinction between sufficient grace which proceeds from the antecedent will and grace which is efficacious of itself proceeding from the consequent will. But man, on account of his resistance to sufficient grace, deserves to be deprived of efficacious grace.

Objection. This distinction between efficacious actual grace and sufficient grace is not found in the early Councils, not even Trent, which treated of grace and free will more accurately in order to counteract Lutheranism.

Reply. Granted that these identical terms are not encountered in the pronouncements of the councils, nevertheless terms in every respect equivalent are to be found; for instance, it is a question of efficacious grace when the Council of Orange declares (chap. 9, Denz., no. 182): "Whenever we do good, God operates in us and with us in order that we may act"; and again when the Council of Trent (Sess. VI, chap. 4, Denz., no. 814) defines "free will moved and stimulated by God, as that which assents to cooperate with God who stimulates and invites." Likewise, the Council of Trent (Sess. VI, chap. 11, Denz., no. 804) refers equivalently to sufficient grace when it states that "God does not command the impossible, but by commanding He teaches thee both to do what thou canst and to ask what thou canst not, and He assists thee that thou mayest be able." It was fitting, moreover, for theologians in their disputations to avoid such complex terms as "sufficient grace and efficacious grace."

Finally, the aforesaid dogma of faith regarding grace which is truly yet merely sufficient is confirmed by theological argument. God, even in the present economy of salvation, imposes the observance of the commandments upon all most rigorously, and the delinquents who die in final impenitence will be punished by eternal torments. But God cannot impose a precept unless at the same time He supplies the necessary means for observing it, nor justly punish him who cannot avoid evil. Therefore God offers helps by which man may be sufficiently equipped to keep the commandments and avoid sin. He does not provide less in the order of grace than in the order of nature, in which latter there are truly sufficient principles, that is, faculties, which nevertheless require final application to the act. (Cf. the Salmanticenses.)

This, then, is the dogma of faith regarding truly and merely sufficient grace. Later we shall examine the various opinions of theologians on the nature of sufficient grace. Let us first consider the Church's teaching on efficacious grace.

4. THE DOCTRINE OF THE CHURCH ON EFFICACIOUS GRACE

This doctrine contains two articles: 1. efficacious grace is conferred; 2. with efficacious grace, liberty remains.

First article. Efficacious, or effective, grace is conferred which causes us to act. This is maintained especially in the condemnation of Pelagianism and Semi-Pelagianism. For the Pelagians did not precisely deny that grace confers the power of doing good, but that it bestows the very willing and acting. Against them the Second Council of Orange (can. 9, Denz., no. 182) defined: "Whatever good we do, God operates in us and with us that we may operate." Hence a certain grace is given which is effective of an operation, although it does not exclude our cooperation but rather demands it.

This is the meaning of the words of Ezechiel (36:27): "I will cause you to walk in My commandments, and to keep My judgments, and do them." And the Council of Orange quotes in the same sense (no. 177): "It is God who works in us both to will and to do." But the grace which causes us to act, whatever it achieves of willing or completing, is efficacious, not only with the efficacy of powers, in the sense that it confers real and intrinsic powers in the supernatural order (this is already given by interior sufficient grace), but it is efficacious with an efficacy of operation, or effective, since it produces the very operation with us, whatever may be the mode whereby the will and grace concur in the act.

This is confirmed by the condemnation of the pseudosynod of Pistoia (Denz., no. 1521) where it is stated that this false synod is condemned "in that it maintains that alone to be properly the grace of Jesus Christ as creates holy love in the heart and causes us to act

. . . and also that the grace whereby the heart of man is touched by the illumination of the Holy Ghost is not, strictly speaking, the grace of Christ, and that the interior grace of Christ is not really given to him who resists it." Thus the Church affirms the existence of efficacious grace while maintaining that it is not the only grace.

Moreover, this dogma of the existence of efficacious grace is confirmed by theological argument· for it is *de fide* that no act conducive to salvation can be performed without grace, and no man can persevere without grace (Council of Orange; Denz., no. 182). But experience proves that many acts conducive to salvation are performed and many men persevere in the accomplishment of salutary acts. Therefore grace is given which achieves its effect and which is therefore rightly called efficacious. We shall consider below, in explaining the Thomistic doctrine of efficacious grace, the texts of Sacred Scripture which refer to this grace.

The second point of the Church's doctrine on efficacious grace is that, with it, liberty, not only from coercion but from necessity, remains, as required for merit. Cf. Hugon, *De gratia,* p. 339. This can be drawn from the condemnation of Predestinationism (Denz., no. 317): "We have a free will for good, anticipated and assisted by grace, and we have a free will for evil, devoid of grace." Likewise in the condemnation of Calvinism by the Council of Trent (Sess. VI, chap. 7, Denz., no. 797): "freely assenting to and cooperating with the same grace"; and again (*ibid.,* can. 4, Denz., no. 814): "If anyone should say that the free will of man, moved and stimulated by God, in no wise cooperates by assenting to the encouragement and invitation of God, whereby he disposes himself and prepares to receive the grace of justification, and further, that he cannot refuse if he so wills, but, as if he were something lifeless, does not act at all, but merely keeps himself in a passive state, let him be anathema." Similarly, against the third proposition of Jansen (Denz., no. 1094) it is declared that "for meriting and demeriting, liberty is required both from constraint and from necessity."

This dogma is confirmed by the following theological argument. Faith teaches that glory is conferred upon merit. (Councils of Orange, Denz., no. 191; Trent, nos. 809, 842.) But merit is an act which proceeds from liberty and efficacious grace. Therefore the coexistence of liberty and efficacious grace is a fundamental truth. Hence St. Augustine says: "He who made thee without thy help, does not justify thee without thy help" (Sermon 15 de Verb. Apost., chap. 11, no. 13; *PL,* XXXVIII, 923).

These two dogmas on truly and merely sufficient grace and on efficacious grace are wonderfully coordinated in the proposition quoted above from Bossuet which expresses the Christian idea profoundly: "We must admit two graces of which the one leaves our will without any excuse before God, while the other does not permit it to glory in itself."

CHAPTER VI

Sufficient Grace

▪▪

IN treating this question we should always keep before our eyes the following texts.

"God does not command the impossible, but by commanding He teaches thee both to do what thou canst and to ask what thou canst not, and He helps thee that thou mayest be able" (St. Augustine, quoted at the Council of Trent, Denz., no. 804).

"Christ is the propitiation for our sins, for some efficaciously, but for all sufficiently, since the price of His blood is sufficient for the salvation of all" (St. Thomas on I Tim. 2:5, and elsewhere).

"The help of grace is twofold: one, indeed, accompanies the power; the other, the act. But God gives the power, infusing the virtue and grace whereby man is made capable and apt for the operation; whereas He confers the operation itself according as He works in us interiorly, moving and urging us to good" (St. Thomas on Ephes. 3:7).

I. VARIOUS THEOLOGICAL SYSTEMS WITH REGARD TO SUFFICIENT AND EFFICACIOUS GRACE

Generally speaking, there are two systems. The first is held by those who declare efficacious grace to be intrinsically efficacious, that is, from the very intrinsic force of grace which of itself and with us infallibly produces consent saving free will. They consequently insist upon a real distinction, before consent, between efficacious and sufficient grace. The Thomists and Augustinians accept this view; but they are divided according as they explain "intrinsically efficacious" as signifying: by moral motion only, as pleasure is victorious, which the Augustinians hold, or as signifying also: by predetermining physical premotion, saving free will however; this is the position of Thomists.[1] Cf. the synopsis.

Another general system is that of the theologians of the Society of Jesus, who deny that efficacious grace is intrinsically efficacious since, as they declare, intrinsically efficacious grace deprives man of his liberty. In this major, as Del Prado shows, they are in agreement with Protestants and Jansenists. For these heretics say that intrinsically efficacious grace takes away liberty; but grace efficaciously moving one toward the good is intrinsically efficacious; therefore freedom from necessity is not required in order to merit, but only freedom from force.

The theologians of the Society of Jesus agree with these in the major and distinguish the minor, thus: intrinsically efficacious grace takes away freedom; but freedom from necessity is required in order to merit; therefore grace is not intrinsically efficacious but only extrinsically so, that is, on account of our consent foreseen by mediate knowledge. We, on the other hand, disagree with the heretics in the major, that is, in the very basic principle by which the problem is solved: whether God can, gently and firmly, in other words, infallibly, move our will to this free act rather than to another. To this fundamental question we reply in the affirmative; the heretics, however, deny it, and with them the Molinists and Congruists.

It is clear from this how greatly Thomism differs from Calvinism and Jansenism; the difference appears in our rejection of the five propositions of Jansen; cf. Billuart, *De gratia,* diss. V, a. 2, § 2: seven differences between Thomism and Jansenism.

Two synopses are presented: the first for the systems which admit intrinsically efficacious grace, the second for those which hold grace to be extrinsically efficacious; in the third place will be added the middle ground of the eclectics.

The last opinion which practically seems to be good, theoretically has all the difficulties of both Molinism and Thomism; nor is it so easy for prayer to possess all the required conditions even for impetratory force. It should be remarked that, before Molina, almost all the traditional theologians taught that grace was intrinsically efficacious, except a few such as the very small perversely inclined

---

[1] We have expounded the Thomistic doctrine on physical premotion elsewhere at length; see *Dictionnaire de théologie catholique:* "Prémotion" (prédéterminante), "Prédestination," "Thomisme."

Not only by moral movement, but also by (causally) predetermining physical premotion [2] (Thomists).

Grace intrinsically efficacious

Through infallible moral motion alone

- By victorious delight saving free will (Augustinians, Berti, Noris).
- By sympathy between the first and the second cause, or extrinsic assistance (Scotus).
- By a multitude of aids (Thomassin). [3]

Grace extrinsically efficacious

From the consent of the will alone, foreseen by mediate knowledge.

Hence, sufficient grace is rendered efficacious by our consent, and before consent sufficient grace and efficacious grace are indistinguishable (Molina).

From the congruity or opportuneness with which grace is given, according to the prevision of mediate knowledge. However congruous grace is not infallibly efficacious of itself.

Efficacious (or congruous) grace and sufficient (or incongruous) grace do not differ in their physical being but in their moral being, by reason of their benefits (Congruists such as Suarez).

Middle ground

Intrinsically efficacious grace is for more difficult acts. Extrinsically efficacious grace is for easier acts, such as prayer, according to this opinion. So also the Congruism of the Sorbonne and Tournely. [4]

---

[2] Some writers accept indifferent physical premotion, although not predetermining physical premotion; but in that case efficacious grace would not be strictly efficacious of itself, intrinsically and, whether they will or no, they are forced to admit of *scientia media,* by that name or by another. Thus Pignataro, Cardinal Pecci, Satolli, Paquet, L. Billot.

[3] Thomassin, *De consensu Scholae de gratia,* tr. III, maintains that, if single helps may fail to produce their effect, a combination of them never does.

[4] Likewise Isambert and Lemoine, as it appears. St. Alphonsus adhered to this party, according to some, but not absolutely. Cf. St. Alphonsus, *Op. dogm.,* II, 707 ff., against the heretical so-called reformers. St. Alphonsus rejects *scientia media.*

minority among the Dominicans, among them Durandus and Catharinus, who invented Molinism before Molina. The true sense of
St. Alphonsus' doctrine is a disputed question, but Father Jansen
(*Revue thomiste,* 1903, p. 341) maintains that St. Alphonsus in no
wise favored Molinism but rather admitted intrinsically efficacious
grace for all acts conducive to salvation.

The theologians of the Society of Jesus are divided among themselves, depending on whether they are pure Molinists or Congruists
after the fashion of Suarez. Molina, at the end of the sixteenth century,
taught (cf. *Concordia,* quaest. 14, a. 13; disp. 40, pp. 230, 459):
"Whether sufficient help is efficacious or inefficacious depends on the
will of him to whom it is given. That is, no graces are given except
those sufficient in themselves, but they are made efficacious by the
consent of the human will foreseen by mediate knowledge. (Cf. *Concordia,* index under *"Auxilium,"* and the text, pp. 230, 459, 462, 565.)
Moreover, Molina holds that "One who is aided by less help from
grace can rise, while another with greater help does not rise but may
persevere in his obduracy" (p. 565). Therefore before our consent,
sufficient grace and efficacious grace do not really differ, either physically or morally. But God predestined to glory those whom He foreknew, by mediate knowledge, would consent with their innate free
will to the grace offered to all and would persevere therein, if placed
in such and such circumstances.

Hence gratuitous predestination, being gratuitous, is not peculiar
either to glory or to grace, but to favorable circumstances. For example, God decreed to place Peter in favorable circumstances where
He foresaw Peter would consent to the grace offered, and He decreed
to place Judas in circumstances where He foresaw that Judas would
not consent to the grace offered. But, according to this theory, the
grace offered to Peter is not of itself greater than the grace offered to
Judas, even if it is a question of the interior grace offered at the last
moment of their careers. It is a moral motion with simultaneous indifferent concurrence. However, the gratuity of predestination is saved
by the divine choice of circumstances. Lessius retains this teaching of
Molina.[5]

[5] Lessius, *De gratia efficaci,* chap. 18, no. 7: "That, of two men who are similarly
invited, one accepts the proferred grace and the other rejects it, it may rightly be
said to proceed from free will alone; not that he who accepts does so by his liberty
alone, but because the difference arises from free will alone and thus not from any
diversity of prevenient help." The Thomists replied straightway: this is contrary to

Molina holds (*Concordia,* pp. 546, 548) that if this doctrine had been known in the fifth century, "from the opinion of Augustine, so many of the faithful would not have been disturbed." (Cf. Salmant., *De gratia,* disp. V, dub. VII, no. 173.) This doctrine seemed an innovation to many and was a cause of displeasure, as Billuart relates (*De gratia,* diss. V, a. 6); the Thomists disputed it before Clement VIII and Paul V, as bordering on Semi-Pelagianism, and their accusation was pursued for ten years in the famous debates *de Auxiliis.* Nor were the Thomists alone in attacking this doctrine of Molina; so, even among Jesuit theologians, did St. Robert Bellarmine, *De gratia et libero arbitrio,* Bk. I, chap. 12 (cf. Del Prado, III, 373),[6] Henry Henriquez in two judgments, dated 1594 and 1597 respectively, and Mariana, *De regimine Societatis,* chap. 4. Hence the Society of Jesus, which supported Molina's defense in the *Congregationes de Auxiliis,* after more mature deliberation on the matter, moderated the system of this author and abandoned it as it stood, taking up the advocacy of the Congruism of Suarez "as more conformable with the teaching of St. Augustine and St. Thomas."

It is expressly declared in these very terms by a decree of the Most Reverend Claude Aquaviva, General of the Society of Jesus, in 1613. This very celebrated decree is quoted by the Jesuits, Tanner, de Regnon (Bañez and Molina), and by Billuart (*op. cit.*). The distinction between Molinism and Congruism appears clearly in the decree. Thus, Father Claude Aquaviva declares: "We ordain and command that in propounding the efficacy of divine grace . . . our fathers should in the future explicitly teach that between the grace which has an effect of itself, called "efficacious," and that which is termed "sufficient," the difference is not so much as regards second act, since it still

---

St. Paul's words in I Cor. 4:7: "For who distinguisheth thee? Or what hast thou that thou hast not received? And if thou hast received, why dost thou glory, as if thou hadst not received it?" Cf. Salmanticenses, *De gratia efficaci,* disp. VII, dub. I, § IV, no. 18.

[6] St. Robert Bellarmine, I *De gratia et lib. arb.,* chap. 12, where he explains the extent to which the efficacy of grace is accepted; he distinguishes three opinions of which the first is attributed to those who "regard it as within the power of man to render grace efficacious which would otherwise of itself be only sufficient." Bellarmine adds that "this opinion, a) is entirely foreign to the thought of divine Scripture itself . . . For who distinguisheth thee? b) and it is opposed to St. Augustine, who will not have efficacious grace depend on human will, but on the divine, and c) this opinion utterly destroys the basis of divine predestination which St. Augustine established so solidly from Holy Scripture." Thus St. Robert Bellarmine withdraws from Molinism to embrace Congruism.

obtains its effect by the use of free will possessed of cooperating grace, nor likewise the other, but in first act itself, which, assuming a knowledge of the conditionals, on account of God's disposition and intention of most certainly effecting good in us, by His own activity selects those means and confers them in the way and at the time when He sees the effect will be produced infallibly, whereas He would have foreseen these as inefficacious under other circumstances. Wherefore, something more is always contained, morally, in efficacious than in sufficient grace, both by reason of its benefit and with respect to first act; and thus God effects that we may act of ourselves, not so much because He gives grace by which we are able to act. The same may be said of perseverance which, without any doubt, is a gift of God."

So writes the Most Reverend General Aquaviva, whose decree was confirmed by the seventh general Congregation of the Society of Jesus, in the year 1616, at which Muzio Vitelleschi was elected presiding General. He declared that Father Aquaviva held efficacious grace to differ from sufficient grace in first act, not physically but morally, by reason of greater congruous benefits. This decree of Father Aquaviva was subsequently confirmed at the ninth general Congregation of the Society of Jesus, in 1651, under General Picolomini. At present, however, the theologians of the Society are actually free to choose either of the two opinions.

Otherwise all the theologians of the Society agree in this matter, that they should not return to the infallible, intrinsic efficacy of grace, that is, as coming from divine omnipotence. And Congruism is therefore only whitewashed Molinism, for even in the former, ultimately, grace is infallibly efficacious, not because God so wills, but because man wills it to be efficacious. Hence God is always regarded as a created cause, urging and attracting, as a friend persuades a friend to choose the good. Whereas God is in reality infinitely more powerful than my most beloved friend to persuade me, more so than the guardian angels, or the highest angels capable of being created, and God does not only move by attracting objectively, but interiorly by contact with the will from within, inasmuch as He is closer to it than it is to itself, as we shall see.

This suffices for an explanation of the system of these theologians. Let us now proceed to the proof of the Thomistic opinion: 1. with respect to sufficient grace, that is, in what sense it is to be accepted; 2. with respect to efficacious grace: whether it is efficacious intrinsically and by physical premotion not ultimately determinable by us. We shall examine the objections to both theses.

2. IN WHAT SENSE SUFFICIENT GRACE IS TO BE ACCEPTED AND HOW IT IS DIVIDED

Conclusion. Sufficient grace is that which confers upon man the power of doing good, beyond which he requires another grace, namely, efficacious, that he may do good. (Cf. Lemos, *Panoplia,* Vol. IV, Part II, p. 36; Gonet, *De voluntate Dei,* disp. IV, no. 147; John of St. Thomas, *De gratia,* d. 24; the Salmanticenses, Gotti, Billuart.)

The first part is proved, since it must be admitted that grace which gives the power to do good is given even to those who do not do good. For this is a dogma of faith defined, as we have seen, in the condemnation of the first proposition of Jansen (Denz., no. 1092). The commandments would be impossible to those who, in fact, do not keep them. (Cf. St. Thomas on the Epistle to the Ephesians, 3:7.)

The second part of the conclusion is proved as follows:

God is the first cause of salvation and of that which is peculiar to the affair of salvation.

But the salutary action, as distinct from the potentiality of doing good, is that which is peculiar to the affair of salvation.

Therefore, beyond sufficient grace, which gives the power of doing good, efficacious grace is required, which causes us to perform the good action. (Cf. Ia, q. 109, a. 1.)

Otherwise, and this is the refutation of Molinism, the greatest activity of all, namely, the passage into a free, supernatural act, would belong exclusively to the free will and not to God. Thus, what is greatest in the affair of salvation would not derive from the author of salvation; from God would proceed only the unstable sufficient grace which effects nothing but an indeliberate motion. God would wait upon our will for our consent, which seems to be contrary to the Council of Orange (Denz., no. 177): "If anyone maintains that God waits upon our will to cleanse us from sin, and does not rather acknowledge that even our willingness to be cleansed is brought about in us through the infusion and operation of the Holy Ghost, he resists the Holy Ghost Himself, who declares . . . : 'It is God who worketh in you both to will and to accomplish, according to His good will'" (Phil. 2:13).

The Molinists admit, of course, against the Semi-Pelagians, prevenient grace, but an unstable prevenient grace, no greater in one who is converted than in another who persevers in obduracy, and therefore it still remains that, according to this theory, God waits upon our consent and does not produce it. The foregoing argument is quite certain; but that its conclusiveness may appear even more clearly, let us examine the force of both the major and the minor.

The major is evident from reason according as God is the supreme, universal first cause of all being and act. Moreover it is contained in revelation: "The salvation of the just is from the Lord" (Ps. 36:39); "Salvation is of the Lord: and Thy blessing is upon Thy people" (Ps. 3:9); "The Lord is my light and my salvation, whom shall I fear?" (Ps. 26:1); "My God is . . . my protector and the horn of my salvation" (Ps. 17:3); "Attend unto my help, O Lord, the God of my salvation" (Ps. 37:23); "O Lord, Lord, the strength of my salvation: Thou hast overshadowed my head in the day of battle" (Ps. 139:8); "The Lord . . . is become my salvation" (Ps. 117:14); "Neither is there salvation in any other" (Acts 4:12); "It is the power of God unto salvation to everyone that believeth" (Rom. 1:16); "Who then shall separate us from the love of Christ? Shall tribulation or distress or famine or nakedness or danger or persecution or the sword? . . . But in all these things we overcome, because of Him that hath loved us. For I am sure that neither death nor life nor angels nor principalities nor powers nor things present nor things to come nor might nor height nor depth nor any other creature shall be able to separate us from the love of God, which is in Christ Jesus our Lord" (Rom. 8:35–39). Cf. St. Thomas' commentary on the words of our Lord, "Without Me you can do nothing" (John 15:5), and "Have confidence, I have overcome the world" (John 16:33).[7]

[7] St. Thomas, commenting on the Epistle to the Romans (8:35), "Who then shall separate us from the love of Christ?" says of these words: "All benefits are conferred upon us by God so efficaciously that no man can withstand them. However, all these aforesaid benefits tend to this end: that we should be founded and rooted in charity. . . . Many waters could not quench charity, according to the Canticle. But St. Paul enumerates the evils the endurance of which may constrain a person to abandon the charity of Christ. . . . Tribulation or distress or famine or persecution or the sword. But in all these things we overcome, because of Him that hath loved us. We overcome; that is, in all these evils we preserve charity intact, according to the words of Wisdom (10:12): 'She . . . gave him a strong conflict, that he might overcome.' And this not by our own power, but by the help of Christ, wherefore he adds: because of Him that hath loved us, that is, on account of His help, or on account of the disposition produced in us by Him, not as if we had first loved Him, but because He hath first loved us. As declared in I Corinthians (15:57):

From all of these and many other texts of Sacred Scripture it is evident that God is the author of salvation. This is the very expression of St. Paul to the Hebrews (2:10): "For it became Him, for whom are all things, and by whom are all things, who had brought many children into glory, to perfect the author of their salvation, by His passion." Hence the title often occurs in the liturgy: "O Lord, the author of salvation"; for example, in the second prayer of the Office of the Dead: "O God, bestower of pardon and author of human salvation, we beseech Thy clemency" (at least, in the Dominican rite); and again: "O God, the Creator and Redeemer of all the faithful." Our major is therefore incontrovertible; that is: "That which is peculiar to the affair of salvation ought to proceed from God, the author of salvation." [8]

The minor is equally certain: that which is peculiar to the affair of salvation is not the power to do good, but the actual consenting to the good and the good act itself. Thus our Lord says (Matt. 7:21): "Not everyone that saith to Me, Lord, Lord, shall enter into the kingdom of heaven: but he that doth the will of My Father in heaven." And in Ezechiel we read: "I will cause you to walk in My commandments, and to keep My judgments, and do them" (36:27).

Therefore the conclusion follows: Beyond sufficient grace, which gives the power of doing good, is required efficacious grace, which actuates us to perform that good. And this is admitted by all theologians except the pure Molinists, even by the Congruists who hold that, beyond sufficient grace, congruous grace is required, differing not physically but morally in first act, that is, before consent.

Moreover, Molina does not seem to observe canon 9 of the Council of Orange (Denz., no. 182): "Whatever good we do, God operates in us and with us that we may operate." Hence a certain grace is given

---

'Thanks be to God, who hath given us the victory through our Lord Jesus Christ.' 'Death is swallowed up in victory.'

"For I am sure that neither death . . . nor principalities nor powers . . . nor any other creature shall be able to separate us from the love of God, which is in Christ Jesus our Lord." St. Thomas asks: "How is it that St. Paul says he is sure that nothing can separate him from charity when 'no man knows whether he is worthy of love or of hate?' To this question answer may be made that the Apostle is not speaking of himself individually but in the person of all the predestinate, of whom he declares, on account of the certainty of predestination, that nothing can separate them from charity. . . . However, if St. Paul is speaking of himself, he could not be certain of this statement unless perhaps by revelation."

[8] Cf. P. Guillermin, O.P., "De la grâce suffisante," *Revue Thomiste*, 1902, p. 75.

which confers on us, not only the power to act, but the very act itself. Nor does Molinism seem to respect the words of the Council of Trent (Sess. VI, chap. 13, Denz., no. 806): "For, unless men themselves fall short of His grace, God as He began a good work (by sufficient grace), so does He perfect it, working both the willing and the accomplishment" (Phil. 2:13). Likewise, Denz., no. 832. For Molina, God does not effect the willing and accomplishment except by simultaneous concurrence, and therefore what is peculiar to the business of salvation does not derive from God, namely, the good determination itself, and what may be in this man rather than in another who is equally tempted and equally assisted.

There are several confirmations of the Thomistic conclusion.

First confirmation. God provides proportionately in the same way for the supernatural as for the natural order. But in the natural order the power of acting and the impulsion to act are differentiated. Therefore in the supernatural order sufficient grace, which confers the power of doing good, and efficacious grace, which causes us to do it, are likewise distinct. (Cf. Ia IIae, q. 109, a. 1.) Moreover, in the natural order, as stated in this article, however perfect a power may be, it never passes into act without the efficacy of divine motion. Therefore in the same way, grace which bestows a power, however completely sufficient it may be, never passes into act without efficacious grace.

Second confirmation. (Cf. Gotti's commentary, IX, 128.) Otherwise it would follow that those who have such sufficient grace should not pray to God for further grace, since it is supposed that for performing a good act, nothing more is required on the part of God beyond this sufficient grace.

Third confirmation. It would follow that efficacious grace would not be necessary for doing good and persevering in a good act for which sufficient grace gives the power; or else that man could render sufficient grace efficacious without any further help from God; and consequently not from grace would a doer of good be distinguished from a doer of evil, equally assisted, but rather from himself. For he would himself, without any further help on the part of God, have rendered sufficient grace efficacious, whereas another man would not have done so. This contradicts the words of St. Paul: "For who distinguisheth thee? Or what hast thou that thou hast not received?" (I Cor. 4:7.)

Therefore St. Robert Bellarmine, when he examined the opinion of those who hold that it is within the power of man to make grace efficacious, which would otherwise of itself be only sufficient, writes as follows (*De gratia et libero arbitrio,* Bk. I, chap. 12): "This theory is entirely alien to the opinion of St. Augustine and, in my judgment, even to the meaning of Holy Scripture." For St. Augustine declares in his book on the predestination of the saints (chap. 8): "Grace (manifestly efficacious grace) is not rejected by a hard heart, since of itself it softens the heart." Whenever efficacy is attributed to grace, not to the human will, Tanner expresses the same view of Molina's opinion.

Fourth confirmation. Otherwise the distinction between sufficient and efficacious grace would not be justified as given by Augustine (*De correptione et gratia,* chap. 12), between merely sufficient, inefficacious grace ("help without which we cannot," conferring the power) and efficacious, not merely sufficient, grace ("help whereby," conferring the act). This distinction, as we have seen, is based on Sacred Scripture: "For it is God who worketh in you, both to will and to accomplish according to His good will" (Phil. 2:13); "I will cause you to walk in My commandments, and to keep My judgments, and do them" (Ezech. 36:27); here it is a question of efficacious grace. On the contrary, sufficient grace is referred to when St. Stephen says: "You always resist the Holy Ghost" (Acts 7:51); and similarly: "I called, and you refused: I stretched out My hand, and there was none that regarded" (Prov. 1:24).

The division of sufficient grace

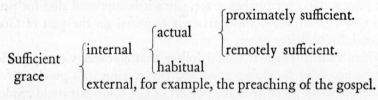

Sufficient grace is manifold and involves the following.

1. External helps, such as external revelation, the preaching of the faith, exhortation, example, miracles, salutary trials, benefits, and indeed a certain disposition of events ordained by a special providence toward salvation.

2. Internal helps, which are either permanent (such as infused habits, for instance, sanctifying grace, the virtues and gifts) or transient (such as supernatural movements which excite in us indeliberate acts, pious thoughts and aspirations). These helps are infallibly effica-

cious for producing those indeliberate acts, and sufficient for the deliberate act for which they give the proximate power. These various helps are extremely useful; it is obvious that they render our powers noble and elevated; they are truly sufficient in their order, just as the intellectual faculty is for understanding; and they really confer the proximate power. But they are called merely sufficient with respect to salutary acts which, on account of man's culpable resistance, are not performed. Indeed, as has been said, grace which is termed sufficient with respect to a perfect act, for example, contrition, is infallibly efficacious with respect to an imperfect act, such as attrition.[9]

Sufficient help is divided into remote and proximate. Proximate help is that by which a person can immediately perform a good work, such as the infused habits with respect to their acts, and with still greater reason indeliberate devout thoughts and aspirations inspired by God and inclining toward consent to the good. Remote sufficient help is that by which a person is not yet capable of the act, but can do something easier, for instance, pray, which, if he does it well, will enable him to act, for example, to overcome temptation. The Council of Trent (Sess. VI, chap. 11) indicates this difference drawn from St. Augustine: "God does not command the impossible, but by commanding He teaches thee to do what thou canst (proximately sufficient help) and to ask for what thou canst not (remotely sufficient help.)"

Furthermore, sufficient help is divided into conferred help and offered sufficient help, which we would certainly receive were there not an obstacle. Sufficient help is also either immediate and personal or mediate, for instance, conferred upon the parents for their children who are incapable of receiving personal sufficient help; thus the parents might receive from God the pious thought of the necessity of having their children baptized and not do so. Hence truly and merely sufficient help does not consist in some one, indivisible, definite thing, but in many helps, whether external or internal, permanent or transi-

[9] As Gonet states, *Clypeus,* De voluntate Dei, disp. 4, no. 14, Thomists generally agree with Alvarez, Bk. III, De auxiliis, disp. 80, that: "All help which is sufficient with respect to one act is at the same time also efficacious in the order of another act to the accomplishment of which it is ordained by an absolute decree of divine providence, so that it is sufficient absolutely (for example, with respect to contrition) and efficacious under a certain aspect"; in other words, it is efficacious with respect to an imperfect act, such as attrition, and infallibly efficacious with respect to this imperfect act.

tory, whereby a man has the proximate power of doing good or at least of praying, and nevertheless resists it.

All of this is commonly taught by Thomists; but in addition reference should be made to the opinion of Gonzalez de Albeda, O.P., in his Commentary on Ia, q. 19, a. 8, disp. 58, sect. 2, Naples, 1637, II, 85. Gonzalez holds that sufficient grace gives the ultimate completion to the power, or proximate power in readiness to consent when God calls (in fact, it impels toward second act, although it does not remove the impediments to this act); on the contrary, efficacious grace simultaneously moves toward second act and removes all impediments, and hence it is not resisted.

Thus Gonzalez still preserves a real distinction between sufficient grace, impelling toward second act, and efficacious grace, surmounting obstacles; and he explains this distinction, not as residing in our free will, but before our consent, on the part of God Himself assisting us. He says (*ibid.*): "I consider that it ought to be held without doubt that the created will, only sufficiently helped by God, possesses the ultimate fullness of active power and the prevenient concurrence of God. . . . It is otherwise, however, with the created will efficaciously assisted; for the ultimate fullness in this latter case (efficaciously assisted) establishing it finally in first act is more particular and extrinsically efficacious with greater power to incline the will to consent here and now."

Other texts of Father Gonzalez in the same connection should be consulted. We have examined this theory at length in another work.[10] Gonzalez, then, maintains the principle of predilection, namely, no one would be better than another if he were not better loved by God. Cf. below, § 4, for the value of this opinion; and the excursus on efficacious grace, chap. 1.

3. REFUTATION OF OBJECTIONS AGAINST THE THOMISTIC THESIS OF SUFFICIENT GRACE

Objection. Some have objected, declaring this grace to be useless; for that grace is useless which no one ever uses. But no one ever uses sufficient grace, as defined by Thomists. Therefore this grace is useless.

Reply. I distinguish the major: that it is useless of itself, denied,

[10] *La prédestination des saints et la grâce*, 1935, pp. 386-92.

since of itself it confers a real power which is truly useful; that it is useless accidentally, on account of a defect in man, granted; in other words, if man does not use this sufficient grace, it is not the fault of grace, but of man.

I counterdistinguish the minor: no one ever uses sufficient grace by reduplication as merely sufficient, granted, and this is so by reason of our resistance permitted by God; that no one ever uses sufficient grace specifically, in that it confers the power of doing good, denied; for we often make good use of infused habits which are in themselves sufficient. Similarly in the natural order, although the power in plants of bearing fruit may often remain ineffectual, on account of accidental defects, it is not thereby rendered useless, since in other plants it does produce fruit.

I insist. But sufficient grace as defined by Thomists is even pernicious, as the following proves. Grace by which a man is made worse is pernicious. But man is made worse by sufficient grace in the Thomistic sense, for, if he lacked it, he would not sin, whereas, possessing it, he so many times sins. Therefore this grace is pernicious. Hence some used to say: From the sufficient grace of the Thomists, deliver us, O Lord.

First reply. This argument proves too much, for in the same way it can be proved that reason is pernicious, since he who lacks it does not sin, and he who possesses it sins.

Second reply. I distinguish the major: grace by which man is made worse on account of a defect in this grace is pernicious, granted; but on account of a perverse will, denied. I counterdistinguish the minor and deny the conclusion and its consequence. For it is utterly false to say that man is made worse by sufficient grace considered in itself, since through habitual grace which is sufficient he is made pleasing to God and capable of acting supernaturally.

I insist. No one, not even the Church itself, asks God for sufficient grace in the Thomistic sense. Therefore it is not a good.

Reply. I distinguish the antecedent: no one asks for it as merely sufficient, by reduplication, since that would be asking God to permit us to decline from grace, granted. That no one asks for it taken specifically and entitatively, denied; since we ask for the power of doing good, for instance, faith, hope, and charity.

Further objection is made to the novelty of this conception. The aforesaid real distinction between sufficient and efficacious grace is not derived from St. Thomas; it was invented by Bañez to avoid censure after the condemnation of Jansenism.

Reply. We have seen that the aforesaid division is also found long before Bañez and even before St. Thomas, in Augustine, *De correptione et gratia,* chap. 12, as "help without which" conferring power, and "help whereby" producing the good act.

With respect to the term "Bañezianism," see Del Prado, *De gratia et libero arbitrio,* III, 427–59, for a discussion of whether Bañezianism is not really a farce invented by the Molinists. He replies in the affirmative and proves that this little diversion was staged by the Molinists to avoid the appearance of any opposition between Molinism and St. Thomas himself, declaring that their teaching was contrary to Bañez, not to St. Thomas. Molina himself proceeded with more straightforwardness, stating expressly (*Concordia,* p. 152) that he rejected the divine application of secondary causes as laid down by St. Thomas. And again (pp. 546, 548) he admits that he is abandoning the teaching of St. Augustine and St. Thomas on predestination, which was a source of anxiety to so many of the faithful.

Hence Cardinal Gonzales, O.P., in his philosophical work, *Theodicea,* chap. 4, a. 3, writes as follows: "Some, who strive to cast a light on the darkness, are not afraid to declare that St. Thomas is considering only simultaneous concurrence and not really physical premotion. In which matter, indeed, Molina and certain other of his disciples act more honorably and becomingly when they frankly acknowledge that, in this matter, they depart from St. Thomas." This admission is made, together with Molina, by the Coimbrian school, by Bellarmine, Tolet, and Suarez, whom I have quoted elsewhere (*God,* II, 154).

Moreover, it is clear from many texts of St. Thomas that he admitted a twofold grace: first, grace which gives the power of doing good; second, grace which makes us do good. Cf. Ia IIae, q. 106, a. 2 ad 2: "The grace of the New Testament . . . to the extent that it is sufficient of itself gives help to avoid sin but it does not confirm a man in good so that he is not able to sin . . . and hence if, after receiving the grace of the New Testament, a man should sin, he is deserving of greater punishment for not using the help given to him." Again, in his commentary on the Epistle to the Ephesians (chap. 3, lect. 2): "God gives the power by infusing virtue and grace through which man is made capable and apt for action. But He confers the action itself according as He works within us interiorly impelling and urging us toward the good . . . in the measure that His power effects in us both to will and to accomplish on account of His good will."

Likewise in Ia IIae, q. 109, a. 1: "The act of the intellect and of any created being depends upon God in two respects: 1. inasmuch as it has received from Him the form by which it operates; 2. according as it is moved to the action by Him"; and further in article two: "Man . . . requires a power superadded to his natural power on two accounts, namely, that he may be healed and, beyond this, that he may perform good works of supernatural virtue. See also *ibid.*, a. 9 and 10; and IIa IIae, q. 137, a. 4; *De perseverantia;* Ia IIae, q. 113, a. 7 and 10. At least it may be said that St. Thomas always distinguishes the infused habits, which give the power of doing supernaturally good works, and actual grace which confers the working of good itself; indeed he distinguishes between good thoughts which come from God and consent to good which presupposes greater assistance.[11]

A third objection is raised as follows. That grace is not sufficient beyond which another is required. But beyond sufficient grace in the Thomistic sense another is required. Therefore this sufficient grace of the Thomists does not suffice.

Reply. I distinguish the major: this grace is not sufficient in its own genus, denied; in every genus, granted.

[11] Cf. Ia IIae, q. 112, a. 3: "If it is in the intention of God who moves that the man whose heart He moves should attain grace, he attains it infallibly, according to the words of St. John (6:45): 'Everyone that hath heard of the Father, and hath learned, cometh to Me.'" Furthermore, St. Thomas gives the supreme basis of the distinction between efficacious and sufficient grace (Ia, q. 19, a. 6 ad 1): "Whatever God wills absolutely is done, although what He wills antecedently may not be done."

The treatise on evil (*De malo*), q. 6, a. 1 ad 3: "God moves some wills immutably on account of the efficacy of the moving power which cannot fail; but on account of the nature of the will moved, which holds itself in indifference toward various objects, necessity is not introduced, but liberty remains; just as in all things divine providence works infallibly, and yet contingent effects proceed from contingent causes, inasmuch as God moves all things proportionately, each according to its own mode"; cf. *ibid.*, ad 15.

Cf. Ia IIae, q. 10, a. 4 ad 3: "If God moves the will toward something, it is incompatible with this affirmation that the will should not be moved thereto. But it is not absolutely impossible. Hence it does not follow that the will is moved by God of necessity." Those who admit fallibly efficacious premotion, with respect to what is really effected, must reconcile their theory with this last text; "it is incompatible," and we shall see later whether such a reconciliation is possible, that is, whether fallibly efficacious premotion may be conferred with respect to what it actually produces in us, for example, with respect to the continuation of attrition or of prayer, here and now, produced in this sinner rather than in another.

I grant the minor, and distinguish the conclusion: does not suffice in its own order, denied; in every order, granted. This distinction was made long before Bañez by Ferrariensis.[12]

Explanation. This is the specifically philosophical and theological sense of the term "sufficient"; a thing is really sufficient in its own order, even though another cause may be required in another order. Thus, of the four causes, any one of which is sufficient in its own order, but requires the concurrence of the others in order actually to operate; for example, we generally say with reference to the order of final cause: this motive is sufficient for free action, and yet there does not follow an infallible choice, for which the concurrence is required of both the intelligence proposing the motive as an object and will actually willing it. Indeed, the stronger motive at the end of the deliberation seems so sufficient that the Determinists after the fashion of Leibnitz deny the liberty of indifference. In fact, however, this sufficient motive gives, on the part of the object, only a proximate potentiality, and so likewise does sufficient grace, which is either a habit of charity or of some other virtue, or an indeliberate pious aspiration toward a good conducive to salvation. And just as this motive is truly sufficient, although it may not incline one infallibly to act, so it is with this grace. We have developed this at greater length elsewhere (*God,* II, 368–79). On the contrary, the Megarians held that power does not exist without act; consequently a teacher, not actually teaching, would lose the power of teaching.

We should say nowadays that heat is sufficient to cause burning, although it must first be applied to combustible matter; and bread, similarly, is sufficient for nourishment, although it must further be masticated, swallowed, and assimilated. The intellect is sufficient for understanding, but beyond this its object must be correctly presented to it; for instance, the doctrine of St. Thomas must be presented to it correctly, and not according to the interpretation of the Molinists;

[12] Ferrariensis, commenting on the *Contra Gentes,* Bk. III, chap. 86, no. 5, says: "Any cause is said to be sufficient when it has enough power, from its own form, to be able to produce an effect without the concurrence of any other cause of its own order; just as fire is a sufficient cause of heat, for it can by itself, without the concurrence of any other particular effective cause, produce heat (presupposing, however, the influence of the first cause). On the contrary, a cause is said to be insufficient which does not possess, from its own form, sufficient power so that by itself, without the concurrence of any other cause of its own order, it can produce an effect; as when many men are rowing a boat together which no one of them could row alone, each of them is said to be an insufficient cause of the boat's being drawn."

otherwise the student will not understand although he may have sufficient intelligence. The passion of Christ is sufficient to save us, but, in addition, its merits must be applied to us, for example, in the sacrament of baptism. Hence St. Thomas says (IIIa, q. 61, a. 1 ad 3): "The passion of Christ is a sufficient cause of man's salvation, but it does not therefore follow that the sacraments are not necessary for salvation, since they operate by virtue of the passion of Christ." Again, he declares (*De malo,* q. 6, a. 1 ad 15): "Not every cause necessarily produces its effect, even if it is a sufficient cause, on account of the fact that a cause may be impeded." Thus, natural causes produce their effect only in the greater number of cases.

Therefore sufficient grace is really sufficient in its own order, since it confers the proximate power of doing good. Indeed it cannot be more sufficient; nor is the grace admitted by Molina any more sufficient, nor does it manifest the mercy of God any more. Rather, on the contrary, Molina minimizes the mercy and gifts of God by denying that efficacious is distinct from sufficient grace; for thus God is not the true author of salvation to that extent. (Cf. Bossuet, *Elévations,* eighteenth week, fifteenth elevation.)

I insist. For observing in act the divine commandments, that grace is insufficient which lacks something not in our power. But the sufficient grace of the Thomists is wanting in efficacious grace, which is not in our power. Therefore this sufficient grace of the Thomists is insufficient for the actual observance of the commandments, for which it ought to be sufficient, since God commands us not merely to be able to observe His precepts, but to observe them in fact. St. Thomas raised a similar objection to his own opinion (*De veritate,* q. 24, a. 14, objection 2).[13]

First reply. I distinguish the major: lacks something on account of our negligence, denied; otherwise, granted.

Second reply. I distinguish the major: efficacious grace is not in our

---

[13] St. Thomas in *De verit.,* q. 24, a. 14, proposes to himself the same objection: Whether free will can choose the good without grace. Second objection: "No one should be blamed for not doing what he cannot do. But a man is justly blamed if he omits doing good. Therefore by his free will man is capable of doing good (without grace)." St. Thomas replies: "to the second objection, it must be said, that man is rightly blamed for not fulfilling the commandments, since it is on account of his own negligence that he does not have the grace whereby he is enabled to keep the commandments modally; although he can observe them by his free will, substantially" with general concurrence.

power, as our own effect, granted; as a cause offered to us in sufficient grace, denied. I counterdistinguish the minor in the same way and deny the logical sequence and the conclusion.

Explanation. God, to the extent that it lies with Him, is prepared to give efficacious grace to all who have sufficient grace, and does not deny it to any man except through his own fault, at least by a priority of nature, if not antecedent in time. Hence a defect in operation by no means proceeds from an insufficiency of help, but only from negligence or a defect of free will, which resists it and sets up obstacles. Even the more rigid Thomists agree to this, such as Lemos, (*Panoplia gratiae,* Vol. IV, Bk. IV, Part II, tr. 3, chap. 2); his very words are quoted by Billuart (*De gratia sufficienti,* diss. V, a. 4).

However, the reason for this is, as Lemos himself declares (*ibid.,* chap. 6), that "God, by bestowing sufficient help, offers us, in it, efficacious grace; but since man resists sufficient grace, he is deprived of the efficacious grace which was offered to him." Likewise Alvarez, (*De auxiliis,* Bk. XI, disp. 113, no. 10, and disp. 80 ad 4); and this is entirely conformed to the teaching of St. Thomas, who says expressly (III *C. Gentes,* chap. 159): "God, to the extent that it lies with Him, is ready to give grace to all, for He wills all to be saved and come to the knowledge of the truth (I Tim., 2); but they alone are deprived of grace who present some obstacle to grace within themselves. In the same way, since the sun illuminates the world, the blame is imputed to one who shuts his eyes if some evil results therefrom, although he cannot see unless preceded by the light of the sun." St. Thomas explains this at greater length in Ia, d. 40, q. 4, a. 2, and Ia IIae, q. 112, a. 3 ad 2: "The first cause of a defect of grace lies in us, but the first cause of the bestowal of grace is in God, according to the words of Osee (13:9): 'Destruction is thy own, O Israel: thy help is only in Me.'" And again, *De veritate,* q. 24, a. 14 ad 2: "From man arises the negligence which accounts for his not having grace whereby he can keep the commandments."

Indeed, this reply is fully in accord with the Council of Trent, which declared (Sess. VI, chap. 13, Denz., no. 806): "If men did not fail His grace, God would perfect the good work, just as He began it, bringing about both the willing and the accomplishing"; also *ibid.,* chap. 11.[14]

---

[14] Council of Trent, Sess. VI, chap. 11, teaches: "The divine precepts are not impossible to any just man." Therefore the precept of finally persevering is possible to the justified man. But the same holy synod teaches, in the same session, chap. 13

Therefore the sufficient grace of the Thomists is not, as their adversaries maintain, a power, sterile in itself, from which God, according to His good pleasure, withholds the outpouring necessary for reducing it to act, but rather, in sufficient grace God offers us efficacious grace.

Doubt. How is efficacious grace offered to us in sufficient grace?

Reply. As the fruit is offered to us in the flower, although, if a hailstorm occurs, the flower is destroyed and the fruit does not appear which would have developed from the flower, under the continued influence of the sun and of the moisture in the plant, so is efficacious grace offered to us in sufficient grace, although, if resistance or sin occurs, sufficient grace is rendered sterile and efficacious grace is not given.

I insist. But this is only a metaphor.

Reply. It is not a mere metaphor, but a strictly proportionate analogy; that is, so far as in both cases an act is contained in its correlative potency. For sufficient grace is indeed the principle of a good work, virtually containing it, and would in fact accomplish it (under the continuous influence of God, as the flower under the continuous influence of the sun), did not man, by his defective liberty, resist it. Thus a good seed, consigned to the earth, bears fruit unless it is prevented by some deficiency in the soil. And hence sufficient grace is the seed of the gospel referred to by our Lord in the parable of the sower (Matt. 13:3-9): "Behold the sower went forth to sow. And while he soweth some fell by the wayside, and the birds of the air came and ate them up. And other some fell upon stony ground, where they had not much earth. . . . And others fell among thorns: and the thorns grew up and choked them. And others fell upon good ground: and they brought forth fruit, some a hundredfold, some sixtyfold, and some thirtyfold. He that hath ears to hear, let him hear." And again, in the same chapter (13:37): "He that soweth the good seed, is the Son

---

(Denz., no. 806) and canon 16, that the singular gift of perseverance, necessary for the act of persevering, is not given to all the just, and this is not in the power of man but only in that of God. Hence the Council already presupposes that there is in all the just a potency for the act of perseverance, although not in all is the efficacious help present which is required on the part of God for the act of perseverance.

The Congruists must say the same of congruous grace for persevering in act; indeed, Molina would have to declare something of the same kind with respect to the favorable circumstances in which God decrees to place those whom He has judged will persevere, according to *scientia media,* if placed in these circumstances.

of man. And the field is the world, And the good seed are the children of the kingdom." (Cf. St. Thomas' Commentary on Matthew.) Similarly, the seed of glory is habitual grace itself which, as such, is sufficient, that is, as an infused habit. Nor should it be thought that after the supernatural sowing is received into the soul, the increase derives from us and not from God. On the contrary, St. Paul says (I Cor. 3:6–9): "I have planted, Apollo watered, but God gave the increase . . . you are God's husbandry; you are God's building." And again (II Cor. 9:6–15): "He who soweth sparingly, shall also reap sparingly: and he who soweth in blessings, shall also reap blessings. . . . And God is able to make all grace abound in you; that ye always, having all sufficiency in all things, may abound to every good work. As it is written: He hath dispersed abroad, He hath given to the poor; His justice remaineth forever. And He that ministereth seed to the sower, will both give you bread to eat, and will multiply your seed, and increase the growth of the fruits of your justice; that being enriched in all things, you may abound unto all simplicity, which worketh through us thanksgiving to God. . . . Thanks be to God for His unspeakable gift." (Cf. St. Thomas' Commentary.)

I insist. Nevertheless it seems unjust that to some merely sufficient grace alone is given and to others efficacious grace besides, without which in fact the commandments are not observed.

Reply, from St. Thomas, IIa IIae, q. 2, a. 5 ad 1: "Man is held to many things which he cannot do without grace. . . . That help is in fact given to some from on high is an effect of mercy, but that it is not in fact given to others is an effect of justice, as a punishment of preceding sins or at least of original sin, as Augustine says in his book *De correptione et gratia.*" It is the absolutely free external exercise of justice and mercy, with the mystery of the intimate reconciliation of these infinite perfections in the Deity.

Hence the denial of efficacious grace is an act of justice, inasmuch as it is the punishment for preceding sin, at least with the priority of nature, that is, sin at least in its incipiency. But sin itself presupposes, not indeed as a cause, but as a condition, divine permission. Therefore the divine refusal of grace thus inflicting punishment on account of sin means something more than a simple divine permission of sin or the beginning of sin; for the permission of the incipiency of the first sin has no reason of punishment with respect to any preceding sin, and this incipiency of sin could not occur without divine permission, since if God, at that instant, were to preserve a man in good-ness, there would be no sin. But God is not bound to preserve in good forever a creature in itself deficient, and if He were held to this, no sin would ever take place. Cf. Ia IIae, q. 79, a. 1, toward the end of the body of the article: "For it happens that God does not grant help to some men for avoiding sin which, if He granted it, they would not sin; but He does all this according to the order of His wisdom and justice since He is wisdom itself and justice itself; hence it is not to be imputed to Him that a person sins, as if He were the cause of sin. In the same way, a pilot is not said to be the cause of a ship's sinking for the mere reason that he does not steer the ship, unless he re-linquishes the steering of it when he can and ought to steer it." Again, *ibid.* ad 1, and also Ia IIae, q. 109, a. 2 ad 2: "Every created thing needs to be preserved in the good proper to its nature by another; but it can, by itself, fall away from that good."

I insist. To neglect or resist sufficient grace is not to consent to it or to sin at least by a sin of omission. But in order that a man may not neglect or resist sufficient grace, efficacious grace is required. Therefore man sins because he is deprived of efficacious grace, in other words, from an insufficiency of help.

Reply. I grant the major, and the minor as well, but deny the conclusion, for the real conclusion is: "therefore, in order that a man may not sin, but consent to sufficient grace, efficacious grace is re-quired," and this is true. (Cf. *De malo,* q. 3, a. 1 ad 9.) But it is false to say that man sins because he is deprived of efficacious grace; rather, on the contrary, it should be said that he is deprived of efficacious grace because by sinning he resists sufficient grace. For a man to sin, his own defective will suffices, and resistance to sufficient grace always precedes, at least by a priority of nature (on the part of the material cause, man) the divine denial of efficacious grace; in other words, God refuses efficacious grace only to one who resists sufficient grace; otherwise there would be an injustice involved. And what on the part of God precedes this resistance is only the divine permission of sin. But this divine permission must not be confused with a denial of efficacious grace, which signifies something more; cf. *Summa,* Ia, d. 40, q. 4 a. 2: "Since God wills nothing but good, He does not will that man should lack grace (that would be a denial of efficacious grace), except to the extent that it is a good; but that he should lack grace is not a good absolutely. Hence, considered absolutely, this is not willed by God. However, it is a good for him to lack grace if he does not will to have it or if he prepares himself carelessly for receiving it, because this is just, and from this aspect it is willed by God." But God can permit sin on account of a higher good and He is not bound always to preserve in goodness what is itself defective, for it is reasonable that a thing which is in itself deficient should sometimes evince a defection.

Therefore the problem is solved according to the words of Osee (13:9) already quoted: "Destruction is thy own, O Israel: thy help is only in Me." Consult the Thomists, especially on Ia, q. 19, a. 8, concerning the divine decrees, where the objections on the grounds of insufficient help are refuted; for example, Billuart and John of St. Thomas. Moreover, all the foregoing arguments, as well as that which follows, can be thrown back upon the Congruists, or against sufficient grace in the Congruist sense.

I insist. At least the permission of the first sin is formally a denial of the efficacious grace necessary to avoid it. But, according to Thomistic teaching, it depends upon the absolute will of God that He permits the first sin in any one man or angel rather than in another whom God preserves in good.

Therefore, according to this doctrine, the denial of efficacious grace to avoid the first sin would in like manner depend upon the divine will alone, and would not be a punishment presupposing a fault, which is exceedingly severe.

Reply. I deny the major, for the notion of a denial of grace, formally, signifies more than a simple permission of sin, since it includes, in addition, the punishment due to sin which is at least incipient, which punishment is not implied in the concept of permission of sin, since this latter is entirely antecedent to the sin. Moreover, the beginning of the first sin, from the standpoint of its material cause, precedes the divine denial of efficacious grace, just as "in the order of nature, liberation from sin is prior to the consequence of justifying grace," as St. Thomas declares (Ia IIae, q. 113, a. 8). He there explains further that "on the part of the efficient cause the infusion of grace precedes the remission of sin"; indeed it precedes absolutely, since these two are effects of God and the consideration of the efficient cause prevails absolutely. Whereas, on the contrary, sin as such is a defect proceeding from a defective cause; consequently here the consideration of priority on the part of the material cause, man, prevails; hence, absolutely, the beginning of sin precedes the divine refusal to confer efficacious grace which, as a punishment, differs from the simple divine permission of sin. (Cf. above, the tract on sin, Ia IIae, q. 79, a. 1: God is not the cause of sin.)

This whole question had already been very well expounded before the time of Molina and Bañez by Ferrariensis, in his commentary on Bk. III *Contra Gentes,* chap. 161, no. 4: "Since in the reprobate four elements are found, namely, the permission of the fall into sin, the sin itself, abandonment by God who does not raise him from sin, not pouring out His grace, and the punishment, or damnation. . . . With respect to the sin, reprobation means only foreknowledge, . . . but with respect to the permission, the abandonment to sin by God, and the damnation or punishment, it signifies not only foreknowledge but also causality." (But the punishment of damnation is on account of the foreseen demerits, whereas the permission of the first sin is not.) Ferrariensis declares in the same text: "Although sin is the demeritorious cause of abandonment by God and the disposing cause of eternal punishment, the permission, which exists first in the reprobate, is not the cause of sin, for it does not invest the reprobate with anything whereby he falls into sin, since he sins with his free will, nor does it remove anything which would withhold him from sin."

Thus it appears that negative reprobation, according to Ferrariensis, precedes the foreseeing of demerits. Cf. Ia IIae, q. 79, a. 1, the end of the conclusion: "It happens that God does not grant help to some men for avoiding sin which, if He granted it, they would not commit. But He does all this according to the order of His wisdom and justice; . . . hence it is not to be imputed to Him that a person sins, as if He were the cause of sin." The universal foreseer permits for the sake of a greater good that a deficient cause should sometimes fall into defect. (Cf. Ia, q. 23, a. 3 and a. 5 ad 3.)

I insist. If an affirmation is the cause of an affirmation, a negation is the cause of negation. But the bestowal of efficacious grace is the cause of fulfilling the commandment and of nonresistance to it. Therefore the withdrawal of efficacious grace is the cause of not fulfilling the commandment, even in the beginning of the first sin.

Reply. I distinguish the major: if it is the only cause, granted; thus the presence of the pilot is the cause of the ship's safety, and his absence when he ought to be on duty is the cause of shipwreck. If there are two causes, of which the first is indefectible but not bound to prevent an evil, and the other is deficient: denied, for then this second cause alone is responsible for the defection.

St. Thomas proposed this objection to himself in *De malo,* q. 3, a. 1, objection 8: "If grace is the cause of merit, then contrariwise the withdrawal of grace is the cause of sin. But it is God who withdraws grace. Therefore God is the cause of sin."

Reply (ad 8): "God as He is in Himself communicates Himself to all according to their capacity; hence if a thing is deficient in the participation of this goodness, this is because there is to be found in the thing itself some impediment to this divine participation . . . according as [a man] keeps his back turned to a light which itself does not turn away, as Denis Dionysius says in the *Book of the Divine Names,* chap. 4."

So that a man fails on his own account and he is sufficient unto himself when it comes to failing; but he requires the divine help preserving him in good in order to persevere in it. To be preserved in goodness is a good and proceeds from the source of all good; but to fall away from goodness presupposes only a deficient cause.

Thus, with regard to this objection: it is granted that if efficacious grace were given to a man he would not sin, but it does not follow that he sins for this reason or cause of not being given efficacious grace. The permission of sin is only a condition of sin, not its cause. We must beware of confusing a cause which exerts a positive influence with an indispensible condition which does not exert an influence; otherwise there would be a vicious circle, as when it is said: I believe the Church to be infallible because God revealed this; and I believe God revealed it because it is affirmed by the Church. In the second proposition "because" is not taken in the same sense as in the first, for it does not signify the formal motive of faith, but only the indispensable condition of faith, that is, the infallible proposition of the object of faith.

Similarly, in our present case, the permission of the first sin and not being preserved in good is an indispensable condition of this sin but not its cause, for sin as such requires only a deficient cause. But on the other hand, not sinning or being preserved in good is an effect of the preserving hand of God. Cf. *De malo,* q. 3, a. 1 ad 9: "Considering the state of fallen nature, St. Augustine attributes to divine grace the avoidance of any evil whatever that he did not commit," at least that he is preserved in good by God.

In fact, the foregoing objection is found in almost the same terms in St. Thomas, Ia, d. 40, q. 4, a. 2; the third objection: "He who by his presence is the cause of the ship's safety, that is, the pilot, is by his absence the cause of the ship's danger. But God is by His presence in the soul the cause of grace. Therefore by His absence He is the cause of its obduracy."

Reply. "An effect does not follow unless all its causes work together; whereas from the defection of one of them the negation of the effect results. Therefore I say that the cause of grace as agent, is God Himself, and as recipient is the soul by way of subject and matter. . . . Nor is it essential that every defect should arise on the part of the agent; it can occur on the part of the recipient, as it does in this proposition."

Hence the major of the preceding objection, (i.e., if an affirmation is the cause of an affirmation, a negation is the cause of a negation) is valid when there is but one cause, which is bound to act, as the pilot by his presence is the cause of the ship's safety and by his absence, when he is bound to be present, the cause of its danger. But this major is not true if there are two causes of which the first is indefectible and not bound to prevent every evil and the second is deficient; for then this latter alone is the deficient cause of its own defection.

Billuart has well said: "These dialectic rules are valid to the extent that all the principles on both sides concur in the same way, not so if another principle is lacking. But in the reception of grace all the principles concur, not however in its negation. In order than an adult should receive grace, two causes must work together: God must will to infuse the grace, and man must will to receive it, since the infusion of grace is a good and a good is produced by the concurrence of all its causes; on the other hand, for man to be wanting in grace, it suffices for one cause to be in default, obviously the unwillingness of man."

Thus many of Tournely's objections are solved, as Billuart declares. Tournely held that, from the necessity of the decree and of grace efficacious in itself for individual acts of piety, the sufficient grace of the Thomists is insufficient and the commandments of God are impossible to some men. On the contrary, it is truly sufficient and in it efficacious grace is offered to us, but man himself so resists sufficient grace, by which he could observe the commandments, that he is thus deprived of efficacious grace whereby he would in fact observe them.

I insist. Franzelin thereupon makes an objection which has been recently revived; cf. Franzelin, *De Deo uno,* Rome, 1876, pp. 458 f., where he declares: "By no explanations can these two statements, affirmed by Gonet in the text cited with regard to God (tr. 4, disp. 8, no. 254), be reconciled: proposition 1. 'Unless a man or an angel previously by nature were to determine himself toward formal sin (which is foreseen by providence), he would not be predetermined by God to the material in sin.' . . . But I ask, and Gonet himself asks: 'In what medium God foresees this self-determination of the created will, by nature prior to the divine decree of predetermination (to the material in sin)?'" Gonet offers two answers of which Franzelin considers only the second, which he impugns.

Gonet's reply is that God foresees the defective determination of the will toward formal sin "in the decree denying the efficacious help to avoid sin"; but this denial has its reason in punishment, which presupposes sin, whereas the divine permission of the fault precedes it. Hence it is better expressed by many Thomists, Billuart among them, who say that God foresees the sin and its beginning in His permissive decree (cf. Father Hugon, *De Deo uno,* p. 213): "The permissive decree is a sufficient, certain, infallible medium. For if God wills to permit something, it most certainly will happen, not by causal necessity, but by logical necessity, just as, if God withholds efficacious concurrence, the good effect is not produced (however, the divine permission of sin implies the nonpreservation of the defective will in good, to which preservation God is not bound; otherwise a defective will would never fall into defect). Granting the divine permission of sin, anyone can become good, since man retains his real antecedent power; and he can avoid evil, since the omission of the decree or the permissive decree itself removes none of that real antecedent power; but as a matter of fact, if God wills to permit the evil which He is not bound to prevent, that real power will never be reduced to act. Hence, knowing His permissive decree, God infallibly recognized the deficiency, although He does not cause it.

It remains true that the divine refusal of efficacious grace signifies more than the simple permission of sin, more than the nonpreservation in good. Similarly, nonelection, which is merely negative reprobation and is prior to the foreseen demerits, as a will permitting sin, is distinguished from positive reprobation, which inflicts punishment for sin (Ia, q. 23, a. 3). Of course, the divine permission of the first sin does not have the reason of penalty, but the divine permission of the second sin is already a punishment for the first. Gonet had said as much in substance (*Clypeus,* De scientia Dei, disp. IV, a. 6, no. 195) and indeed St. Thomas himself had enunciated the principle (Ia IIae, q. 79, a. 1): "It happens that God (as universal foreseer) does not grant (efficacious) help to some men for avoiding sin which, if He granted it, they would not commit. But He does all this according to the order of His wisdom and justice."

I insist. (Cf. Gonet, *ibid.,* no. 192.) "The permissive decree cannot have an infallible connection with future sins by reason of non-preservation in good; for otherwise it would follow that the will, left to itself with only general concurrence, would be of itself determined toward evil, and this would be the heresy of the Manichaeans and Lutherans. It would also follow that the human will with general concurrence alone could not perform any morally good work, which is contrary to St. Thomas." Thus Gonet presents the objection to his own opinion according to Tournely, and the objection has recently been raised again.

Gonet's reply (*ibid.,* no. 196): Although the permissive decree may thus have an infallible connection with future sin, a consequence not of causality but of logical sequence, "it does not follow, however, that the free will of man is, of itself and by nature, determined toward evil and sin; not only because by reason of sufficient help it can do good and avoid sin (against the Jansenists), but also because it is one thing for free will to be deficient of itself and by nature and not capable of preserving itself in good according to right reason, on account of God's not preserving it by special means, and another thing for it to be of itself and by nature determined toward evil (as if it were destroyed altogether and not merely weakened).

"In the first case is signified only the deficiency and potentiality for sinning which belong to the rational creature by the very fact that he is made from nothing and is not the rule of his own operations. The second case implies further in the free will a natural determination toward evil, arising from the sin of our first parents. This is the heresy of the Lutherans."

If God were indeed bound to preserve in goodness every will which is deficient in itself, no sin would ever occur, the will of every wayfarer would already be confirmed in good, as was the will of the Blessed Virgin Mary. And since general concurrence is due to nature, but not to any particular individual, man is capable of performing certain natural good works, such as caring for his parents, governing the state. (Cf. Gonet, *ibid.,* and what precedes.)

I insist. But even if God, in this permissive decree, infallibly foresees future sin, He does not infallibly recognize which particular sin it will be.

Reply. I deny that this follows, for by the knowledge of vision God knows that at that particular time such a man so disposed will be in these circumstances, for instance, Peter in the circumstances attending the Passion; and He sees that for this man in these circumstances there are two alternatives: either to confess the faith or to commit the opposite sin. Cf. p. 236 below on the last difficulty with respect to sufficient grace and the profundity of this mystery.

4. THE OPINION OF J. GONZALEZ DE ALBEDA O.P.

J. Gonzalez de Albeda [15] maintains that sufficient grace not only gives the proximate power for a good work, but also an impulse to second act, although it does not remove the impediments to this act and, in fact, is resisted; thus it is a physical premotion, even a predetermination, but impedible, not infallible. It thus differs from efficacious grace. This opinion was accepted by Nicolai, Bancel, Massoulié, Reginaldus, and more recently by Father Guillermin.[16]

Nevertheless J. Gonzalez and these other theologians reject mediate knowledge entirely and hold that no one is better than another even through easy acts conducive to salvation unless he is more beloved and helped by God. They teach that no salutary act, even the easiest, would happen here and now unless it were willed on the part of God by consequent will and unless man were helped by infallibly efficacious grace.

Recently, in fact, Father Marin Sola [17] not only admitted the opinion of J. Gonzalez, but so extended it as to maintain that infallibly efficacious grace is not necessary for easy salutary acts, at least for their continuation. This very extended opinion of Father Marin Sola, in our judgment, can in no wise be reconciled with the principles of Thomism, as we have demonstrated elsewhere.[18] For St.

[15] *In Iam,* q. 19, a. 8, disp. 58, sect. II, Naples, 1637.
[16] *Revue Thomiste,* January and March, 1903.
[17] *Ciencia Tomista,* January, 1926.
[18] *Revue Thomiste,* November, 1925, March, 1926; and in *La prédestination des saints et la grâce,* 1936, pp. 381–93.

Thomas expressly says (Ia, q. 19, a. 6 ad 1), referring to the distinction between antecedent divine will and consequent will: "Whatever God wills absolutely is done; although what He wills antecedently may not be done." Cf. below: Excursus on efficacious grace (chap. 8).

But if the opinion of J. Gonzalez, without its being thus unduly extended, remains within the bounds proposed by its author, what judgment is to be passed on it? We reply with Lemos,[19] the Salmanticenses,[20] Billuart, Hugon,[21] and others: We cannot conceive what this physical premotion, even predetermination, is, which influences second act although the effect is not obtained but remains impedible, and not only impedible, but always impeded, while on the contrary efficacious grace is never impeded by temptation. The thing is inconceivable.

For there is no mean to be found between proximately complete power and the passage to second act accomplished in effect; nor is motion toward second act but failing in its effect comprehensible. These are the fundamental principles of the distinction between potency and act. It is likewise certain, according to St. Thomas, that no salutary act, even the easiest, would take place here and now unless it were willed by God absolutely as the object of an infallibly efficacious decree (Ia, q. 19, a. 6 ad 1). Hence sufficient grace gives a certain power, as proximate as you please, for good work, but it does not give the very act itself; this latter requires infallibly efficacious grace.[22]

However, all Thomists admit that grace which is efficacious for an imperfect act, attrition, for instance, is sufficient for a perfect act, such as contrition. Thus the efficacious grace for a pious thought is sufficient for a pious desire, and the efficacious grace for a pious desire is sufficient for consenting to good. Indeed, if a man resists sufficient grace, he deserves to be deprived of efficacious grace which is offered to him in sufficient grace as the fruit within the flower.

[19] *Panoplia,* Vol. IV, part II, p. 120, no. 119.
[20] *De gratia,* disp. VII, dub. 5, nos. 312, 318.
[21] *De gratia,* 1926, p. 211.
[22] A frequent illusion in these problems must be avoided: as a polygon inscribed within a circle, however much its sides may be multiplied, will never be the circumference, in the same way sufficient grace, however proximate, will never become grace efficacious of itself; nor will moral motion, however multiplied, ever become motion efficacious of itself. The highest of the lowest class, although it may approach the lowest of the highest class, will never be identical with it. Likewise, strong probability will never be certainty, even in the computing of probability.

5. THE OPINION OF ST. ALPHONSUS LIGUORI

See his dogmatic works, Disp. IV: The manner in which grace operates. 1. The Thomistic system and the difficulties of this system. 2. The system of Molina and the difficulties of this system. 3. Congruism, the opinion of Thomassin, of the Augustinians. 4. Our opinion set forth, that is, the opinion of Tournely, whose system I follow.

St. Alphonsus, proceeding according to the method of Tournely, sets forth correctly the doctrine of Thomists on sufficient and efficacious grace, quoting Cajetan, Alvarez, and Lemos, and rightly declares that it is based upon God's supreme dominion over created wills. Then he presents the difficulty which, as he says, the Thomistic system incurs, and says he has no intention of "examining the individual systems thoroughly, but only of touching upon them briefly and bringing out the particular difficulties into which they fall.

"The greatest difficulty of all," he says, "which the Thomistic system encounters is that, once this system is admitted, it seems unexplainable how the perfect liberty of the human will can be reconciled with the physical predetermination of efficacious grace," and he adduces in proof of this two arguments of Tournely which we have already examined: that predetermination seems to destroy liberty (Father Marin Sola does not grant this to St. Alphonsus) and that if efficacious grace is necessary for reducing potency to act, how is it to be explained that sufficient grace is really sufficient and that the fulfilling of the commandments is possible? Billuart, in his *De Deo*, d. 8, a. 4, no. 11, presents and examines at length these objections of Tournely.

We have already replied: 1. Divine motion extends even to the mode of our free choice, which it produces in us, for this mode is a modality of being and is included with the object of divine omnipotence. Ia, q. 19, a. 8: "Since the divine will is eminently efficacious, it follows not only that those things are done which God wills to be done, but also that they are done in the manner in which God wills them to be done . . . that is, either necessarily or freely." Thus St. Thomas, and again in Ia IIae, q. 10, a. 4 ad 3.[23]

2. Sufficient grace is really sufficient, in which efficacious grace is

---

[23] Ia IIae, q. 10, a. 4 ad 3: "If God moves the will toward something, it is incompatible with this affirmation that the will should not be moved thereto. But it is not absolutely impossible," for "the will is moved freely, as becomes its nature," *ibid.*, ad 1.

offered to us as the fruit in the flower; hence, as the Council of Trent declares: "Unless men themselves neglect His grace, God perfects a good work, as He began it, producing in them both the will and the accomplishment" (Denz., no. 806). This is indeed the obscurity of a mystery; but it is not the obscurity of an absurdity.

However, St. Alphonsus presents another difficulty with regard to hope. Cf. *ibid.*, p. 518, nos. 108 f., which should be read. The objection reduces itself to the following: My hope should rest, according to the Thomists, on God's help and on His promise of efficacious grace through prayer. But there is no promise on the part of God with reference to the efficacious grace necessary for me to pray and pray perseveringly. Therefore my hope is unfounded, and I cannot hope for my eternal salvation, except conditionally: provided that God grants me the efficacious grace necessary for prayer.

This objection is almost reducible to the objection which St. Thomas put to himself, IIa IIae, q. 18, a. 4, third objection: "There can be no certainty of that which may fail. But many wayfarers, possessed of hope, fail to attain beatitude. Therefore the hope of wayfarers has no certainty."

Reply. I distinguish the major: my hope inasmuch as it is certain, should rest upon the help of God and on His promise to me of efficacious grace through prayer. His promise to me, if I do not resist antecedent sufficient grace, granted; but, His promise to me absolutely, denied. For if efficacious grace were promised to me absolutely for praying well and perseveringly, by that very fact, absolutely, by way of a consequence, the grace of final perseverance would be promised to me as obtainable by this prayer. But this grace of final perseverance is not promised absolutely to any man in this life, unless by extraordinary revelation, and nevertheless all wayfarers must expect eternal life with a firm hope.

I distinguish the minor: that there is no absolute promise on the part of God assuring me of the necessary efficacious grace for prayer, granted; no conditional promise, provided I do not resist sufficient grace, denied. And I deny the logical sequence and the conclusion.

I insist. But my hope is then only conditional; yet a conditional hope is not certain. Therefore the difficulty still remains. Cf. treatise on hope, against those who place the certainty of hope in a conditioning act.

Reply. I distinguish the major. That my hope is conditional on the part of God's assistance on account of a probable insufficiency of help, denied; conditional on the part of my deficient free will, on account of my probable resistance, granted. (Cf. IIa IIae, q. 18, a. 4 ad 3.)

I distinguish the minor: conditional hope on the part of God's help is not certain, granted; on the part of deficient man, denied. Moreover, the certitude of hope is not, like the certitude of faith, a speculative certitude, but is of the practical order, and, in this order, the certitude of tending toward salvation, not really a certitude of salvation itself, of final perseverance. The act of hope proceeding from the theological virtue of hope, under the guidance of faith in God's assistance, tends certainly toward salvation, but does not know whether in fact it will actually attain salvation. Thus St. Thomas, in IIa IIae, q. 18, a. 4: "Hope tends certainly toward its end, as if participating in the certitude of faith." [24] And the Angelic Doctor adds (*ibid.,* ad 3): "That some men possessed of hope fail to attain beatitude results from a defect of free will setting up the obstacle of sin, not from any defect in the divine power or mercy on which hope depends. Hence this does not impair the certitude of hope."

St. Alphonsus, as likewise Tournely, thinks infallibly efficacious grace is not necessary for actual prayer. But in that case, we are again confronted with all the difficulties raised by Thomists against mediate knowledge. Hence, of two men, equally tempted and equally aided by sufficient grace, it may happen that one prays and the other does not; thus one man distinguishes himself in this respect from the other who does not pray; and God would remain passive in His prevision of this. Hence passivity is attributed to pure Act for the sake of dispelling the mystery of sufficient grace.

Moreover, Tournely's opinion, whether he wills it or not, sets up in the formal motive of hope not only God's help, but our effort, by which the sufficient grace for prayer is rendered efficacious. For, according to this theory, it would follow that I hope the efficacious grace of prayer will be given to me rather than to those who, with equal grace, do not pray or persevere in prayer. But the formal motive of a theological virtue can only be God or an uncreated being, and it

---

[24] As a polygon inscribed in a circle, however much its sides may be multiplied, will never be the circumference, so never in this world will the certainty of a tendency toward salvation become a certainty of salvation itself, except by a special revelation or its equivalent.

is on this account that the virtue is called theological. (Cf. Ia IIae, q. 62, a. 1 and 2.)

Moreover, it is better to trust in God than in ourselves; our salvation is much more secure in the hands of God than in our own.[25] Similarly, what the Church proposes for our belief does not pertain to the formal motive of faith, but only uncreated revelation; the proposal by the Church is only an indispensable condition. The principles of St. Thomas regarding foreknowledge, divine motion, and the formal motive of hope must be safeguarded.

Confirmation of this answer is to be found in several texts of St. Paul, St. Augustine, and St. Thomas. St. Paul writes (Rom. 9:12–20): "Not of works, but of Him that calleth it was said to her [Rebecca]: The elder shall serve the younger. As it is written: Jacob I have loved, but Esau I have hated [or loved less]. What shall we say? Is there injustice with God? God forbid. For He saith to Moses: I will have mercy on whom I will have mercy; and I will show mercy to whom I will show mercy. So then it is not of him that willeth, nor of him that runneth, but of God that showeth mercy. . . . Therefore He hath mercy on whom He will; and whom He will, He hardeneth. Thou wilt say therefore to me: Why doth He then find fault? for who resisteth His will? O man, who art thou that repliest against God? Shall the thing formed say to him that formed it: Why hast thou made me thus?" And in Rom. 8:30 f.: "Whom He predestinated, them He also called. And whom He called, them He also justified. And whom He justified, them He also glorified. What shall we then say to these things? If God be for us, who is against us?" (Cf. St. Thomas' Commentary on Rom. 9:14.) St. Augustine likewise declares in his *De dono perseverantiae,* chap. 6: "We live more securely if we give ourselves wholly to God. Moreover, we do not entrust ourselves partly to Him and partly to ourselves." We have dealt with this problem at greater length in treating of our gratuitous predestination in the treatise *The One God.*

Thereupon, in the same text, St. Alphonsus shows, as do the Thomists, that Molinism is not compatible with Scripture nor with St. Augustine nor with St. Thomas. His analysis deserves to be read.

Conclusion. The principles enunciated by St. Alphonsus in opposition to Molinism with regard to the divine decree as efficacious in it-

---

[25] Because the rectitude of God's intention is much more certain than the rectitude of our intention.

self, and to grace which man cannot render efficacious, are supremely universal, and therefore valid even for easy acts conducive to salvation. They are true of any salutary act, indeed of any act at all since it is an entity and since it is an act, for nothing moves unless efficaciously moved by God. Moreover the principle of predilection enunciated by St. Thomas is absolutely universal (Ia, q. 20, a. 3): "Since the love of God is the cause of the goodness of things, no one would be better than another if God did not will greater good to one than to another." No one is better than another even to the extent of an easy act, unless better loved and more assisted by God. Hence when one of two sinners is converted, good Christians realize that this is a special effect of God's mercy toward him.[26]

6. FINAL DIFFICULTY WITH REGARD TO SUFFICIENT GRACE AND THE DEPTH OF THIS MYSTERY

This final difficulty may be expressed thus: But no mean is offered between resistance, which proceeds from our deficiency, and non-resistance, which is already something good, proceeding from the source of every good and from efficacious grace itself. Therefore he who does not receive efficacious grace cannot help resisting sufficient grace.

Reply. I concede the antecedent but deny the consequence and the consequent. For the real consequent is as follows: Therefore he who does not receive efficacious, but only sufficient grace, although he can avoid resisting, yet does in fact resist, but freely and culpably. The divine permission of this sin is only its indispensable condition but not its cause; and the subsequent divine refusal of efficacious grace, offered within sufficient grace, is the punishment for this free resistance.

But herein lies the great mystery which is expressed in Holy Scripture in various texts: "Destruction is thy own, O Israel: thy help is only in Me" (Osee 13:9); nor is any mean between the two expressed. Again, our Lord says, speaking of the Pharisees, "He that is not with

---

[26] Furthermore, as will become more evident later, and as we demonstrated in *La prédestination des saints et la grâce*, pp. 185-90, the Congruism of the Sorbonne is an impossible middle ground between Thomism and the Molinist theory of *scientia media*, which are opposed to each other as contradictories. (God knows future possibilities infallibly, either before or not before the predetermining decrees.) Thus this Congruism has speculatively all the difficulties of Molinism for facile acts, and all the obscurities of Thomism for difficult acts.

Me, is against Me," without any middle ground; and, on the contrary, "He that is not against you, is for you" (Mark 9:39), as the Savior said to His apostles. In the same way, the angels are either very holy or very perverse; there is no mediocrity permitted them. There is a parallel in regard to men, even in the case of a single, free, voluntary act, since no free, indifferent act is conceded to an individual (Ia IIae, q. 18, a. 9), for either the act is ordained to the proper virtuous end or it is not ordained toward it, just as, on the summit of a mountain where the waters divide, every drop falls either to the right or to the left of that dividing line.

Many men, however, such as the liberals, often err by confusing the summit of the Christian life with some extreme to be avoided under pretext of moderation. Thus they tend toward a mediocre tepidity, which is a certain unstable median between the best and the worst. Accordingly they do not wish to arrive at any conclusion either for or against Christianity. They think that the salvation of this temporal world is accomplished by those who remain in this ambiguous neutrality. But this does not suffice for action, since no decision is reached. Consequently, when there is a question of acting, if men refuse to go back to Christian principles, they descend to radicalism by way of negation, thence to socialism, and finally to materialistic, atheistic communism. Christ said: "He that is not with Me, is against Me"; no middle ground is allowed, nor any neutrality with respect to God the supreme principle and final end. Thus there is no possible midway between resistance proceeding from our deficiency and nonresistance proceeding from the source of every good, since nonresistance to grace is already a certain good. Nevertheless, sufficient grace is given whereby we may avoid resisting, and therefore this resistance remains free and culpable.

This mystery is expressed by St. Prosper in replying to the second *Objectiones Vincentianae,* and his words were cited at the Council of Quierzy (Denz., no. 318) as follows: "Almighty God wills to save all men without exception (I Tim. 2:4), although not all are saved. That some are saved is, however, a gift of the Savior; whereas, that some should be lost is the just desert of those who are lost," and no median is given: "Destruction is thy own, O Israel: they help is only in Me" (Osee 13:9).

In this Council of Quierzy either proposition taken separately is clear, namely, "that some are saved is a gift of the Savior" and "that some should be lost is the just desert of those who are lost," and no middle ground is offered. But the intimate reconciliation of these two propositions is a most profound mystery; to grasp it clearly one would have to see immediately the divine essence itself and see how in the eminence of Deity are found harmonized infinite justice, infinite mercy, and supreme liberty. These three perfections are formally and eminently present in the Deity, but their intimate reconciliation will not appear clearly except in heaven. It remains for us wayfarers a very lofty chiaroscuro, for we walk in an imperfect light, above the inferior darkness of error and sin, and beneath the translucent obscurity which proceeds from a brightness too dazzling for our feeble intellects, so that "we walk by faith, and not by sight" (II Cor. 5:6).

CHAPTER VII

EFFICACIOUS GRACE

▀▀

WITH respect to efficacious grace, the following texts must always be kept in mind: "Without Me you can do nothing" (John 15:5); "It is God who worketh in you, both to will and to accomplish, according to His good will" (Phil. 2:13); "What hast thou that thou hast not received?" (I Cor. 4:7), and "No one would be better than another if he were not loved and helped more by God" (St. Thomas, Ia, q. 20, a. 3).

State of the question. As we have already said in Part One of this section, referring to the doctrine of the Church on efficacious grace: that grace is called efficacious which makes us act, according to the words of Ezechiel (36:27): "I will cause you to walk in My commandments, and to keep My judgments and do them." This manner of speaking is used by the Second Council of Orange (can. 9, Denz., no. 182): "Whatever good we do, God acts in us and with us that we may act."

It is therefore not merely a question of efficacious grace with the efficacy of power in first act, in the sense of conferring real and intrinsic powers of the supernatural order (this is true even of interior sufficient grace); but the term is applied to efficacious grace with the efficacy of operation in second act, since it produces the operation itself effectively with us. And now we must investigate whence its efficacy is derived: whether it is efficacious of itself, intrinsically, or extrinsically, that is, on account of our consent foreseen through mediate knowledge.

First conclusion. The efficacity of grace cannot be derived extrinsically, according to Catholic theologians generally, with the exception of the Molinists and Congruists.

1. *Proof from Holy Scripture,* whence it is certain that grace is given which causes us to act, which operates in us both to will and to accomplish, in a certain insuperable and inscrutable manner. Cf. Ezech. 36:26 f.: "And I will give you a new heart, and put a new spirit within you: and I will take away the stony heart out of your flesh, and will give you a heart of flesh. And I will put My spirit in the midst of you: and I will cause you to walk in My commandments, and to keep My judgments and do them." Again in Ezech. 11:19.

In the Book of Esther (13:9-11) Mardochai, praying God to convert the heart of King Assuerus who was hostile to the Jews, expresses himself thus: "O Lord, Lord, almighty king, for all things are in Thy power, and there is none that can resist Thy will, if Thou determine to save Israel. . . . Thou art Lord of all, and there is none that can resist Thy majesty." And in chapter fourteen, Queen Esther makes her prayer as follows: "Remember, O Lord, and show Thyself to us in the time of our tribulation, and give me boldness, O Lord, king of gods and of all power . . . and turn his [Assuerus'] heart to the hatred of our enemy. . . . O God, who art mighty above all, hear the voice of them that have no other hope, and deliver us from the hand of the wicked, and deliver me from my fear" (vv. 12-19), "And God changed the king's spirit into mildness" (*ibid.,* 15:11). By these words the efficacy of the divine decree and grace is evidently attributed to divine omnipotence and not to the foreseen consent of Assuerus. Hence St. Augustine, in *I ad Bonit.,* chap. 20, says in analyzing these words: "By a very hidden and efficacious power, He converted and transformed the King's heart from wrath to leniency." Similarly, in the Book of Proverbs (21:1): "As the divisions of waters, so the heart of the king is in the hand of the Lord: whitersoever He will He shall turn it," that is, the heart of the king is in the hand of the Lord as the dispersion of water in the hand of the gardener. "The souls of the just are in the hand of God" (Wisd. 3:1); "She [wisdom] gave him [Jacob] a strong conflict, that he might overcome" (*ibid.,* 10:12). Again, man in the hand of God is compared to clay in the hand of the potter: "As the potter's clay is in his hand, to fashion and order it: . . . so man is in the hand of Him that made him" (Ecclus. 33:13 f.); this entire passage, from verse ten to sixteen, should be attentively studied. The same figure is used in Isa. 29:16; 45:9; 64:8; Jer. 18:6, and Rom. 9:21. Isaias, in chapter ten, speaks of man in the hand of God as a rod, a staff, or an axe in the hand of man, wielding it as he wills. Therefore almighty God disposes of the wills of men and neither waits upon them nor subjects Himself to their desires. Again, in chapter fourteen, Isaias predicts many events to be accomplished through men, such as that the Israelites will return to their own land, and he adds: "For the Lord of hosts hath decreed, and who can disannul it? And His hand is stretched out: and who shall turn it away?" (14:27.) By the hand of God is meant His omnipotence, as in psalm 94: "In His hand are all the ends of the earth" (v. 4).

In the New Testament, too, we find: "Without Me you can do nothing" (John 15:5). Therefore grace is not rendered efficacious through our consent; rather, on the contrary, without the grace of Christ we do not consent to the good conducive to salvation. "My sheep hear My voice . . . and I give them life everlasting and they shall not perish forever, and no man shall pluck them out of My hand. That which My Father hath given Me, is greater than all; and no one can snatch them out of the hand of My Father" (*ibid.,* 10:27-29). That is to say, the souls of the just are in the hand of God, nor can the world with all its temptations nor the demon snatch the elect from the hand of God. Cf. St. Thomas' commentary on this passage. It reiterates the words of St. Paul: "Who then shall separate us from the love of Christ? Shall tribulation or distress or famine . . . or the sword? . . . But in all these things we overcome, because of [or through] Him that hath loved us. . . . For I am sure that neither death nor life . . . nor any other creature shall be able to separate us from the love of God, which is in Christ Jesus our Lord" (Rom. 8:35-39). St. Thomas comments here that either St. Paul is speaking in the person of the predestinate or, if of himself personally, then it was thanks to a special revelation.

Elsewhere St. Paul writes: "Not that we are sufficient to think anything of ourselves, as of ourselves: but our sufficiency is from God" (II Cor. 3:5). If we are not sufficient to think anything conducive to salvation of ourselves, with still greater reason is this true of giving our consent, which is primary in the role of salvation. Again, "For the word of God is living and effectual, and more piercing than any two-edged sword; and reaching unto the division of the soul and the spirit, of the joints also and the marrow, and is a discerner of the thoughts and intents of the heart. . . . All things are naked and open to His eyes" (Heb. 4:12 f.). Cf. St. Thomas' commentary: "The word of God is said to be effectual on account of the very great power and infinite effective force which it possesses. For by it are all things made: 'By the word of the Lord the heavens were established' (Ps. 32:6). . . . It effects in the innermost being of things . . . all our works. . . . In the order of causes it is to be observed that a prior cause always acts more intimately than a subsequent cause."

In Rom. 9:14–16 we read: "What shall we say then? Is there injustice in God? God forbid. For He saith to Moses: I will have mercy on whom I will have mercy; and I will show mercy to whom I will show mercy. So then it is not of him that willeth nor of him that runneth, but of God that showeth mercy" (cf. Exod. 33:19).[1] To the Philippians, St. Paul writes: "With fear and trembling work out your salvation. For it is God who worketh in you, both to will and to accomplish, according to His good will" (2:13); hence the soul should fear sin or separation from God, the author of salvation; cf. St. Thomas' commentary.

Lastly, "Who distinguisheth thee? Or what hast thou that thou hast not received? And . . . why dost thou glory, as if thou hadst not received it?" (I Cor. 4:7.) Cf. St. Thomas. According to this text, the distinction in the work of salvation between those who are converted and those who are not, between the just who persevere and those who do not, is to be sought from the part of God and not from the part of man. On the contrary, according to the system of mediate knowledge, in the work of salvation one man distinguishes himself from another, while God awaits his consent and does not determine to give grace efficacious in itself so as to produce this consent freely. In other words, if grace is not efficacious of itself, but is made efficacious by our consent upon which God waits, then man possesses something which he does not receive from God and in which he may glory, as the Pharisee did in his prayer; man has something

---

[1] It should be noted that a divine decree is referred to in the Epistle of St. Paul as a "purpose": ". . . that the purpose of God, according to election, might stand. Not of works, but of Him that calleth, it was said to her: The elder shall serve the younger. As it is written: Jacob have I loved, but Esau have I hated" (Rom. 9:11–13). "That He might show the riches of His glory on the vessels of mercy, which He hath prepared unto glory" (*ibid.*, 9:23). "To them that love God, all things work together unto good, to such as, according to His purpose, are called to be saints" (*ibid.*, 8:28); cf. II Tim. 1:9. "Who hath predestinated . . . according to the purpose of His will: unto the praise of the glory of His grace" (Eph. 1:5 f.). "In whom [Christ] we also are called by lot, being predestinated according to the purpose of Him who worketh all things according to the council of His will. That we may be unto the praise of His glory" (*ibid.*, 1:11 f.).

whereby he may distinguish himself from another, equally tempted, who, anticipated by an equal grace, does not consent to it; that is, he possesses the difference between his own consent to good conducive to salvation and the consent to evil, whereas the consent to good could, in fact, exist in the other.

2. *The Council of Orange* (Denz., no. 189): "Let no one glory in what he seems to have as if he had not received it from God" (can. 16). This is the formula of the principle of predilection, that is, no one would be better than another if he were not better loved by God. "No one has anything of his own but sin and lying" (can. 22); "Man does nothing good which God does not enable him to do" (can. 20). Cf. also the Council of Trent (Sess. VI, chap. 13, Denz., no. 806): "For unless they [men] neglect His grace, God perfects a good work as He began it, operating both to will and to accomplish" (Phil. 2:13). Likewise canon 22 (Denz., no. 832): "If anyone should say either that it is possible to persevere, without the special help of God in accepted justice, or that with it, this is impossible, let him be anathema." Concerning the mind of the Council of Trent, cf. Father del Prado, *De gratia et libero arbitrio,* II, 83-91.

3. *The Fathers,* especially St. Augustine. Thomists quote many texts of St. Augustine dealing with mediate knowledge; cf. also Del Prado, *op. cit.,* II, 67-259. It is sufficient to quote here the words of Augustine (*De gratia et libero arbitrio,* chap. 16, 32): "It is certain that we will when we will, but God causes us to will; it is certain that we act when we act, but God causes us to act, supplying most efficacious forces to the will." Therefore God confers grace, efficacious of itself, by which the hard heart is overcome and made obedient, yielding consent.

Similarly, in the *De correptione et gratia,* chap. 14: "It is not to be doubted that human wills cannot hinder the will of God, which did whatever it willed in heaven and on earth, from doing what it wills, when as a matter of fact it does what it wills, when it wills, with these very wills of men. . . . Having, beyond any doubt, the most omnipotent power of inclining human hearts to what it pleases." But this would be false if grace were rendered efficacious by our consent. Indeed, Augustine declares (*ibid.*) that "God acts within, takes hold of hearts, moves hearts, and draws men by their wills which He Himself operates within them; if, therefore, when God wills to establish rulers on earth, He has the wills of men in His power more than they have themselves, who else acts that the reproof may be beneficial and may produce amendment in the heart that receives it?"

Moreover, for Augustine, it is an inscrutable judgment of God that one man should will efficaciously and be converted, while another is not. Cf. *De dono perseverantiae,* chap. 9. But it is not inscrutable according to Molinism. Furthermore, for Augustine, it is difficult to reconcile liberty and grace; cf. *De gratia Christi,* chap. 47. But it is an easy matter for Molinism, for who, even if he is very stupid, does not understand that liberty remains with grace which depends on a command from that very liberty?

This doctrine of Augustine remains intact in his disciples, St. Prosper and Fulgentius. In fact St. Prosper, at the end of his letter to Augustine concerning the teaching of the Semi-Pelagians, beseeches St. Augustine to explain the argument against them: "I beg you to deign to reveal how free will is not impeded by this preoperative and operative grace, and whether foreknowledge is supported by a divine intention," that is, by a decree. However, St. Augustine replies that foreknowledge is dependent upon a decree. Cf. *De dono persev.,* chap. 17; *De praedest. sanctorum,* chap. 10.

4. *St. Thomas.* We shall first cite the texts from the *Summa* in proper sequence so that it may appear how this doctrine of intrinsically efficacious grace is necessarily connected with all the principles of St. Thomas' doctrine with regard to the relations between God and creatures.

Ia, q. 2, a. 3: All movement is derived from the prime mover; all created causality depends on the supreme cause, all contingent being on the first necessary being, all being on participation in essential being; and whatever is ordained toward another is from the first ordainer. These are the five ways of proving the existence of God. It is already evident that God determines and cannot be determined by another, neither in His knowledge nor in any other attribute. Whatever is outside of God, even the determination of our free will, must have a relationship of causality or dependence with respect to God. Hence our question in its entirety is reducible to this dilemma: "God either determines or is determined by another; no halfway measure is possible." This is established by the following texts of St. Thomas.

Ia, q. 6, a. 4: "Every thing is said to be good from the divine goodness as from the first exemplary, effective, and final principle of all goodness"; but the choice of salvation is a good; therefore.

Question 14, On the knowledge of God, a. 5: "Since the divine power is extended to other things, inasmuch as it is itself the first effective cause of all being, it must be that God knows other things than Himself. He sees other things not in themselves, but in Himself." But if, of two men equally tempted and equally assisted, one should be converted and not the other, this difference would not be from God. Therefore God could not know it in Himself, in His own power, contrary to the principle of St. Thomas.

Article 8: "The knowledge of God is the cause of things according as His will is joined with it," behold the decree or proposition of the divine will. Therefore the knowledge of God is the cause of the choice of salvation on our part. (Cf. ad 1.)

Article 11: "In the measure that God's knowledge is extended, His causality is extended"; so that God's knowledge extends even to individual cases.

Article 13: His knowledge is measured by eternity, which encompasses all time; thus it is applied to future things inasmuch as they are present things in eternity, but this future is not the present in eternity rather than the opposite, unless by a divine decree; otherwise God's knowledge would not be the cause of all things according as His will is joined to it, nor would God know future things in Himself, but in themselves.

Question 16, on truth, a. 7 ad 3: "That which now is, by that very fact was future before it came to be, since it existed in its cause in order that it might come to be. Hence if the cause were removed, that future thing would not come to be; for only the first cause is eternal. Wherefore it does not follow from this that it would always have been true that those things which now are, were to be future, unless in an eternal cause it was determined in the eternal that they would be future, which eternal cause indeed is God alone."

Question 19, on the will of God, a. 4: Whether the will of God is the cause of things. "God does not act (outside Himself) through any necessity of nature, but determined effects proceed from His infinite perfection according to the determination of His will and intellect." Behold the decree of the divine will.

Article 6 ad 1: "Whatever God wills absolutely is done, although what He wills antecedently may not be done."

Article 8: "Since the divine will is most efficacious, not only does it follow that those things are done which God wills should be done, but that they are done in the manner in which God wills them to be done . . . that is, either by necessity or contingency." *Ibid.,* ad 1: "If God wills this, it must necessarily be, by conditional necessity." *Ibid.,* ad 2: "From the very fact that nothing resists the will of God, it follows not only that those things which God wills are done, but that they are effected contingently or necessarily, as He so wills."

Ia, q. 20, a. 2: "The love of God infuses and creates goodness in things." *Ibid.,* a. 3: "Since the love of God is the cause of the goodness of things, nothing would be better than something else if God did not will greater good to one than to another." *Ibid.,* a. 4: "The will of God is the cause of goodness in things and so, on this account, some things are better, because God wills greater good to them. Hence it follows that He loves better things more." But of two men, equally tempted, if one does not resist grace and the other does, the first is better. Therefore he is better because God wills greater good to Him. In other words, the principle of predilection (nobody is better than another unless he is better loved by God) presupposes grace to be efficacious of itself and not from our consent. Likewise, *De providentia,* Ia, q. 22, a. 2 ad 4; a. 4.

Ia, q. 23 on predestination, a. 4, Election: "In God, love precedes election." *Ibid.,* ad 1: "If the divine communication of this or that good is considered, it is not bestowed without election, for God gives certain good things to some which He does not give to others. And thus election is looked to in the conferring of grace and glory."

Article 5. Predestination is not on account of foreseen merits, since "there is no discrepancy between what pertains to free will and what to predestination, just as there is no discrepancy between what pertains to second cause and what to first cause. Hence whatever is from free will is also by predestination." "Whatever is in man ordering him toward salvation is all included under the effect of predestination, even his own preparation for grace." Similarly the well-known reply to the third objection.

Article 6. "Predestination most certainly and infallibly attains its effect, and yet it does not impose any necessity." But this presupposes that a divine decree is intrinsically efficacious and that grace is likewise efficacious of itself.

Ia, q. 83, a. 1 ad 3: "In moving voluntary causes, God does not prevent their actions from being voluntary, but rather produces this effect in them."

Ia IIae, q. 109, a. 1: "All movements, both corporal and spiritual, are reducible absolutely to the prime mover that is God, and therefore, however perfect any corporal or spiritual nature is assumed to be, it cannot proceed to its act unless moved by God."

Ia IIae, q. 112, a. 3: "If it is in the intention of God who moves that the man whose heart He is moving should receive grace, he will receive it infallibly."

IIa IIae, q. 24, a. 11: "It is impossible that these two statements should be true at the same time: that the Holy Ghost should will to move a person to an act of charity and that that person should lose charity by sinning."

Moreover, neither St. Augustine nor St. Thomas ever admitted mediate knowledge, which was proposed by the Semi-Pelagians, on account of the conditional future merits of infants. Billuart presents further texts of St. Thomas from his other works to prove that, according to the Angelic Doctor, the use of grace itself belongs to God.

5. *Theological proof.* This argument brings together all the above-mentioned arguments of St. Thomas and is connected with the principle of predilection: "Since the love of God is the cause of goodness in things, no one would be better than another if he were not more loved by God." (Cf. Ia, q. 20, a. 3.) The argument is proposed in the following terms.

That which is greatest in the whole created order and in the supernatural in wayfarers cannot escape divine causality, otherwise God would not be the first and universal cause nor the author of salvation.

But that which is greatest in the whole created order and in the supernatural in wayfarers is the good use of grace by free determination, for this is merit or the right to eternal life. There is nothing higher in wayfaring saints than charity freely fructifying through merits.

Therefore the good use of grace by free consent is an effect of the grace of God, and it is contradictory to assert that grace is rendered efficacious extrinsically, that is, by our consent, which would thus escape divine causality. This argument is valid against the Molinists, although some admit indifferent premotion, such as L. Billot, and against the Congruists who likewise accept *scientia media.* (Cf. Bossuet, *Tr. de libre arbitre,* chap. 8, and Del Prado, *De gratia,* the whole of Book III.)

They reply that nothing escapes divine causality, since God produces an indeliberate supernatural act, but the free act is not a new entity, but a mode of the act, which the created will is capable of imposing upon it.

However, this is a vain subterfuge, for the free use of grace differs vastly from this indeliberate, nonfree act. It is really a new act, this choice itself, an act strictly meritorious, establishing the most profound separation between the bad and the good; indeed, it is the ultimate actuality of our liberty while on earth. But it is inconceivable that the very element by reason of which the saints are differentiated from the wicked should not be a real entity. In fact, for the Molinists themselves, it is something so precious that not even God can touch it; but in that case the thing which is most precious in the role of salvation is withdrawn from the causality of God. It should be evident that, just as all being depends on first being, all good on the first good, so all free determination toward good depends upon the supreme, free determination of God.

Confirmation. In the matter of salvation, two principles must be firmly maintained: all good comes from God; every defect arises from human liberty. "Destruction is thy own, O Israel: thy help is only in Me" (Osee 13:9). But these are correctly explained by the doctrine of intrinsically efficacious grace; on the contrary, the first principle is not adequately safeguarded by the opposite theory. Therefore grace is intrinsically efficacious.

Explanation. These two principles are proof for the argument, since a will which is not its own act, cannot proceed to the act by itself alone, but needs to be moved by the grace of God, and grace, by its intrinsic force, causes the good use of grace or consent. Thus the good in its entirety is from God. So the help of God is sought in the words of the Psalms: "Blessed is the man whose help is from Thee. . . . I have lifted up my eyes to the hills, to the hills whence cometh my help. . . . My help is from the Lord who made heaven and earth. . . . May He send thee help from His holy place. . . . Lord, withdraw not Thy help from me. . . . Give us help in tribulation. . . . Give glory to the Lord for He is good." Consult a Bible Concordance under "help" and "grace."

But on the other hand, the will is capable by itself alone of defection, obviously on account of its condition of creature produced out of nothingness. Therefore it fails by itself alone, but it does not perform any good by itself unaided. Hence whatever merit there may be is attributable to God as first cause, and to the will as under the premotion of God. They are two total causes, not coordinated as two men rowing a boat, but subordinated, not only in being but in causality.

Hence Molinism is a kind of dream in which the creature forgets that he is a creature. But, to be deeply aware of our creaturehood, and therefore not to consider ourselves as having being and acting except by God's help, is the fundamental basis of the virtue of humility, which is founded upon the dogmas of creation and of the necessity of grace, either habitual or actual and efficacious. It is the easiest thing in the world, however, for an intellectual creature to forget that he is a creature.

Spiritual corollaries. Many corollaries may be deduced from this principle applicable to spirituality. The more important are briefly indicated here, that this doctrine may appear alive, founded as it is in Sacred Scripture and not only in scholastic theory.

1. This doctrine leads to profound humility. For by it the following texts take on a deep significance: "Not that we are sufficient to think anything of ourselves, as of ourselves: but our sufficiency is from God" (II Cor. 3:5); "No one has anything of his own but sin and lying" (Council of Orange, can. 22); "And lead us not into temptation"; "We are unprofitable servants" (Luke 17:10); "Not to us, O Lord, not to us; but to Thy name give glory" (Ps. 113:1); "As the potter's clay is in his hand, . . . so man is in the hand of Him that made him" (Ecclus. 33:13 f.); "The mercies of the Lord that we are not consumed" (Lam. 3:22); "Thy hands have made me and formed me" (Ps. 118:73); "Thou . . . hast redeemed us to God, in Thy blood" (Apoc. 5:9); "The mercy of the Lord is above all His works." "Into Thy hands I commend My spirit" (Ps. 30:6); "What hast thou that thou hast not received?" "You have not chosen Me, but I have chosen you." (Cf. Del Prado, *op. cit.*, III, 151.) This is the basis of true mysticism, and especially of true humility. According to St. Augustine, as Del Prado notes (*ibid.*), there is no sin which another man commits, which I could not also commit, through the weakness of free will and my own frailty, and if I do not do so, not to us, Lord, not to us, but to Thy name be the glory! This ought to destroy the entire root of pharisaism in us; and hence in replying to the Pharisees, Christ often proclaimed the necessity of grace: "No

man cometh to Me unless the Father who sent Me draws him . . .
My sheep hear My voice."

2. This doctrine instils a profound sense of the necessity of prayer,
of continual, interior prayer, full of confidence. For hidden, interior,
most efficacious grace, which leads up to consent, to the overcoming
of temptation and drawing near to God must be sought. Thus the
Sacred Scripture teaches us to pray: "Have mercy on me, O Lord,
according to Thy great mercy. . . . God, be merciful to me, a sinner
. . . I am not worthy to be called Thy son . . . Father, I have sinned
against heaven and before Thee. . . . Help Thou my unbelief. . . .
Create a clean heart in me, O God: and renew a right spirit within
my bowels. . . . Convert me, Lord, to Thee, and I shall be converted."
Again, it is written: "Thy will be done on earth as it is in heaven,"
that is, give me Thy grace to perform in my actions what Thou commandest, and this perseveringly until death. Hence St. Augustine
used to say: "Lord, give what You command, and command what
You will."

The Church prays in the same way in her Missal, as St. Augustine
shows (*Epist. ad Vital.,* 217) and Bossuet in his *Défense de la tradition,* Bk. X, chap. 10: "That God may compel our rebellious wills;
that of infidels refusing to believe He may make believers.[2] That He
may apply our hearts to good works. That He may give us a good
will. That He may convert and draw us to Himself. That He may
remove our hearts of stone and give us hearts of flesh, or docile hearts.
That He may transform our wills and incline them toward good. That
He may not permit us to be separated from Him." Cf. the prayers of
the Mass before the priest's Communion.

Prayer must be continual, at least in the sense of a perpetual desire
for necessary grace, according to the admonition of Christ "that we
ought always to pray, and not to faint" (Luke 18:1); so that prayer,
the Fathers declare, should be as the breath of the soul which ceases
not any more than the respiration of the body, inhaling grace by
holy desire and exhaling the love of God, meritorious for eternal life.

Moreover this prayer should be made with complete trust like the
prayer of Queen Esther (Esther, 14), that is, with confidence that
almighty God can convert even the hardened sinner; thus holy priests

[2] Fourth Sunday after Pentecost, Secret of the Mass: "Accept, we beseech Thee, O
Lord, the offerings we lay before Thee: and, appeased thereby, constrain our rebellious wills to Thy service. Through our Lord."

have prayed, for example, in the case of criminals being led to execution, refusing to confess and blaspheming. Such great trust in prayer has obtained wonderful conversions.

3. This doctrine likewise recommends the necessity of giving thanks for every good action performed by the help of God. Therefore does St. Paul say to the Thessalonians (5:17 f.) : "Pray without ceasing. In all things give thanks"; and to the Ephesians (5:20) : "Giving thanks always for all things." In fact, this teaching leads almost normally to the prayer of contemplation wherein is considered the very profound action of God within us, mortifying and vivifying, that the soul may arrive at the perfect love of God, responding by its fiat to the entire will of God. In such contemplation, whether painful and obscure or joyful and luminous, the truth of those words of Tobias (13:1 f.) becomes apparent: "Thou art great, O Lord, forever, and Thy kingdom is unto all ages. For Thou scourgest, and Thou savest: Thou leadest down to hell, and bringest up again: and there is none that can escape Thy hand." Likewise I Kings 2:6: "The Lord killeth and maketh alive, He bringeth down to hell and bringeth back again."

The prayer of Christ in Gethsemane and the prayer of the Blessed Virgin Mary on Calvary were this very deep contemplation of the two principles enunciated by the prophet Osee (13:9) : "Destruction is thy own, O Israel; thy help is only in Me." Such profound prayer is drawn from efficacious grace, according to the text of St. Paul (Rom. 8:26–28) : "The Spirit also helpeth our infirmity. For we know not what we should pray for as we ought; but the Spirit Himself asketh for us with unspeakable groanings. And He that searcheth the hearts, knoweth what the Spirit desireth; because He asketh for the saints according to God." Whereupon he adds: "And we know that to them that love God, all things work together unto good, to such as, according to His purpose, are called to be saints." Souls that pray thus under the special inspiration of the Holy Ghost obtain whatever they ask, according to St. John of the Cross (*Dark Night,* Bk. II, chap. 20), since they ask only what the Holy Ghost inspires them to ask.

Particularly in contemplative prayer which accompanies the passive purification of the spirit does the soul derive almost an experiential knowledge of what the efficacious grace of God means. And to this grace applies what St. Paul says of the word of God (Heb. 4:12 f.): "The word of God is living and effectual, and more piercing than any two-edged sword; and reaching unto the division of the soul and the spirit, of the joints also and the marrow, and is a discerner of the thoughts and intents of the heart. . . . All things are naked and open to His eyes." But the knowledge of God founded in His causality (for the knowledge of God is the cause of things) extends even to our interior consent, since His hidden causality, at once gentle and strong, extends to this very consent. These two modalities of the divine action (sweetness and strength) are so closely connected that to minimize one of them, strength, for instance, is by that very fact to minimize the other, that is, sweetness. The grace of God is not gentle, penetrating into the very interior of free will, unless on account of its great efficacy, according to that principle of St. Thomas (Ia, q. 19, a. 8): "Since the will of God is most efficacious, not only does it follow that those things are done which God wills should be done, but also that they are done in the manner in which He wills them to be done."

4. The doctrine of intrinsically efficacious grace also leads to a high degree of the practice of the theological virtues, for it is closely identified with the sublime mystery of predestination maintained in all its loftiness, in accordance with the teaching of St. Paul (Rom. 8:28; Eph. 1:5); St. Augustine (*De praedestinatione sanctorum, De dono perseverantiae*), and St. Thomas (Ia, q. 23, a. 5). This doctrine is founded upon the word of God according to St. John (6:39): "Now this is the will of the Father who sent Me: that of all that He hath given Me, I should lose nothing; but should raise it up again in the last day."

Hence, by the foregoing principle faith in the wisdom of God is preserved in all its sublimity. "O the depth of the riches of the wisdom and of the knowledge of God! How incomprehensible are His judgments, and how unsearchable His ways! For who hath known the mind of the Lord? Or who hath been His counsellor? Or who hath first given to Him, and recompense shall be made him? For of Him and by Him and in Him are all things: to Him be glory forever" (Rom. 11:33-36). Likewise, faith in the holiness of the divine good pleasure is maintained, according to the words of St. Matthew (11:25): "I confess to Thee, O Father, Lord of heaven and earth, because Thou hast hid these things from the wise and prudent, and hast revealed them to little ones. Yea, Father, for so hath it seemed good in Thy sight." And again in St. John's Gospel (6:44), Christ says to the Pharisees: "No man can come to Me, except the Father, who hath sent Me, draw Him."

Similarly faith in divine omnipotence is observed in a high degree, in that God can convert the obdurate heart as He wills, according as He works in us both to will and to accomplish; and faith in God's supreme dominion over our wills, which are in the hand of God as clay in the hand of the potter. Again, faith is maintained in the infinite value of the prayer and merits of Christ, who merited for His elect graces which are efficacious of themselves. "The Father loveth the Son: and He hath given all things into His hands" (John 3:35); "He that believeth in Me hath everlasting life" (*ibid.,* 6:47); "I have manifested Thy name to the men whom Thou hast given me out of the world. Thine they were, and to Me Thou gavest them; and they have kept Thy word. . . . Holy Father, keep them in Thy name whom Thou hast given Me; that they may be one, as We also are. . . . Sanctify them in truth. . . . And for them do I sanctify Myself, that they also may be sanctified in truth" (*ibid.,* 17:6 ff.).

This doctrine also strengthens hope, for the formal motive of hope is not our effort, but the help of God, as is often expressed in the psalms: "In Thee, O Lord, have I hoped, let me not be confounded forever"; "But the salvation of the just is from the Lord"; "Give praise to the Lord, for He is good"; and in Proverbs (28:26): "He that trusteth in his own heart, is a fool."

Finally, charity toward God is greatly stimulated by this teaching for it is based upon the text from St. John's First Epistle (4:10): "He hath first loved us"; and He hath loved not only by conferring sufficient grace, but efficacious grace as well, reaching into our innermost being. Therefore does St. Paul write: "Who then shall separate us from the love of Christ?" (Rom. 8:35.) And Christ Himself had said: "I am come that they may have life and have it more abundantly."

Thus the doctrine of grace efficacious in itself is not merely a scholastic theory, but a living principle, founded upon Sacred Scripture. It was on this account that Benedict XIII, in his letter of November 6, 1724, to the Master General of the Order of Preachers, lauded and approved the opinions "on grace efficacious of itself and intrinsically, and on gratuitous predestination to glory, without any foreseeing of merits, which," he says, "you have taught so laudably until now, and of which your school with commendable zeal glories that they have been drawn from the holy doctors Augustine and

Thomas themselves and are in harmony with the word of God, the decrees of the Supreme Pontiffs and of the Councils and the writings of the Fathers." The *Imitation of Christ,* Bk. III, chap. 4, no. 3; chap. 55, no. 5; and chap. 58, no. 4, expresses the same opinion. And even among the theologians of the Society of Jesus, the same doctrine is accepted by Father Grou, *Spiritual Maxims* (second maxim, on grace and freedom), and by Father Billot, *De consensu B.V.M. Mysterio Incarnationis* and *De inspiratione praedeterminante secundum dona S. Sancti;* cf. also his *De virtutibus infusis,* 1905, p. 181, and *De Verbo incarnat.,* 5th ed., Th. XLI, p. 399.

Finally, the foregoing opinion is confirmed by the incongruity of *scientia media* according to which God would know our future merits before His determining decree.

Therefore our first conclusion remains firm, that grace is intrinsically efficacious. This truth is closely related to the principle of predilection, namely: "Since the love of God is the cause of the goodness of things, nothing would be better than another if God did not will greater good to one than to the other" (St. Thomas, Ia, q. 20, a. 3). No one would be better than another if he were not loved and assisted to a greater extent by God. The whole problem can be reduced to the unsolvable dilemma: "God either determines or is determined by another; no mean is possible." If God does not determine, then He is determined by our consent through foreseen *scientia media;* He is not entirely independent, but depends in some respect upon His creature.

Second conclusion. The intrinsic efficacious grace is not adequately explained by moral or objective or attracting motion, however it may be termed, that is, by a delight which takes the ascendancy or by an accumulation of moral helps.

With respect to the ascendant delight, which, saving free will, the Augustinians, such as Berti and Bellelli admitted (thereby dissenting from the Jansenists), it should be said that it is not necessary, frequently is not present, and does not move infallibly toward free choice. For truly it is often lacking; many men are converted not by the attraction of heavenly joys which surpass those of the flesh, but rather from the fear of hell. (Cf. Council of Trent, Sess. VI, chap. 6.) Besides, the saints performed many good works without any pleasure, indeed with great aridity and suffering attached to them. Hence man does not always pursue the greatest indeliberate pleasure; he chooses what seems to him better here and now, even if it is better only from the motive of obligation, without any antecedent delight. However, a superior delight follows, namely, that of having accomplished his duty, of conformity to the divine will.

Scientia media

On the part of God.

1. It withdraws from God the reason of being the first and most universal cause, since the determination of the will escapes divine causality.

2. It limits the omnipotence of God and His supreme dominion over our wills, which in some circumstances God cannot incline toward good.

3. It ascribes passivity to Pure Act, that is, the divine intelligence is measured by the determination of our free will, which it must ascertain and wait upon.

4. It implies that by physical motion God is no more the author of a good work than of an evil one.

On the part of man.

5. It destroys liberty, setting up a determinism of circumstances, by reason of which God infallibly foresees what this liberty would do if placed in such circumstances.

6. It seriously reduces the need of prayer, since it is not necessary to ask of God that we may consent to grace.

7. It diminishes notably the necessity of giving thanks, since there is no need of rendering thanks for what is paramount in the business of salvation, that is, for the determination toward good.

8. It distorts the notion of hope, since we should not rely only upon the hope of grace, but especially upon our liberty which can always render grace efficacious.

Moreover, by intrinsically efficacious grace God moves us to choice, directly and infallibly. But by merely moral motion God cannot move us directly and infallibly to choice. Therefore intrinsically efficacious grace cannot be placed in moral motion alone. The minor is proved by the argument that moral motion does not affect the will internally, but only from without, by means of the intellect, attracting it, nor is its attraction infallible. It is true that God, clearly seen everywhere as good, infallibly draws our will, according as He is perfectly adequate to its capacity, which He conquers (Ia IIae, q. 10, a. 2), but this is not true regarding moral motion which is not adequate to the capacity of our will.

The same reason holds for other conceptions of moral motion: by itself it does not satisfy or explain that the will should be moved infallibly; even should there be an accumulation of moral movements, free will would not be attracted infallibly.[3] Thus every good in this world was held out to the martyrs, and at the same time every alternative torment; their liberty remained inflexible, but it so remained in God not clearly seen, fixed on account of the physical motion of God.

Third conclusion. Intrinsic efficacious grace dispositively can be claimed, in moral motion, but strictly and formally in predetermining physical premotion. Dispositively, moral motion is required to present the good, pleasing object, but efficacious grace infallibly moving toward a choice must be the actual application of the will as to the exercise of the act which it produces in the physical order, in its own very reality. Moreover, this physical motion is previous with a priority, not of time, but of causality, since the causality of God who moves thus precedes the causality of the will which is moved. (Cf. *Contra Gentes,* Bk. III, chap. 140.)

Nor does indifferent physical premotion suffice, or toward good in general, as C. Pecci, Satolli, and Paquet maintain. There must be physical premotion in the pursuit of the divine decree. But an intrinsically efficacious divine decree extends even to the free choice of the good, for example, even to the consent of St. Paul at the moment of his conversion. Therefore divine premotion accompanying this decree is called "predetermining." (Cf. Bossuet, *Traité du libre*

[3] A multiplicity of moral motions does not change their species; it merely produces an accidental difference of degree within the same kind of motion; this does not explain that the thousandth moral motion should infallibly draw our liberty. In the same way, although the sides of a polygon inscribed in a circle may be multiplied indefinitely, it will never equal the circumference itself.

arbitre, chap. 8.) [4] Furthermore, indifferent premotion does not preserve the universality of divine causality, for that which is greatest in the matter of salvation, namely, the particular meritorious choice here and now, would escape divine causality.

Pure act, the supreme determination, must be the cause of any determination. Therefore, if physical predetermination with regard to individual acts is not admitted, that which is paramount in the role of salvation and in the whole created and supernatural order, is withdrawn from God. Indeed, if God does not determine, then He is determined by another in His knowledge; this is the highest incongruity in the theory of *scientia media.* The dilemma is insoluble.

Such premotion is called "predetermining" because, just as God's motion precedes our action in intention and causality, so does the determination of first cause, by a priority of nature, precede the determination of second cause. If the transition from potency to the final actuality of free will is not from God, who predetermines, then what is greatest in the whole supernatural order is withdrawn from God.

Hence the doctrine of grace efficacious in itself, of premotion which is not indifferent, like the doctrine of the intrinsic efficacy of divine decrees with regard to our salutary acts, is intimately connected with the principle of predilection formulated by St. Thomas, Ia, q. 20, a. 3: "Since the love of God is the cause of the goodness of things, no one would be better than another if God did not will greater good to one than to the other." In short, no one would be better than another (either by a natural or by a supernatural act, whether easy or difficult, initial or final) unless he were better loved by God. This principle allows of no exception.

In opposition to Satolli and Paquet, whose theory is unwarrantably styled "Cajetan-Thomistic," cf. Del Prado, *De gratia,* III, 496 ff. On page 501 he says: "They go astray at the very door (at the moment of arriving at the end of the journey) and part from Cajetan right at the corner of the street, that is, on cooperative motion itself." For Cajetan rejects motion which precedes by a priority of time (whereby, for instance, my will moves my arm and then the stick to send a

---

[4] We have explained this elsewhere at length: *Dict. de théol. cath.,* "Prémotion physique," what it is not, what it is, col. 31–77; and *La prédestination des saints et la grâce,* 1936, *"La grâce et son efficacité,"* pp. 257–381; refutation of objections, pp. 402–13.

stone flying), but he does not exclude physical premotion which precedes by a priority of nature only. Thus, with regard to time, before our free determination, nothing moves determinately and infallibly toward it; the predetermination is of a higher order, the order of eternity, in an eternal decree whose very premotion is its execution. (Cf. Cajetan on Ia, q. 14, a. 13, no. 17; q. 19, a. 8, no. 10; q. 20, a. 3, etc.; q. 23, a. 4; q. 105, a. 4 and 5.)

Divine motion is not a mechanical action, like the action of a man rowing a boat; it is of a higher order, to be compared rather to the influx of life-giving sap by which a plant nourishes and renders itself fruitful.[5] In fact, this infusion is proper to the eternal cause, existing beyond time, which is much closer to our will than our will is to itself; and the divine cause, moving our will from within, inclines it to self-determination through deliberation toward this particular salutary, meritorious act rather than to its contrary. Thus God actualizes our liberty, causing together with us the free mode of our choice.

As in the natural order divine motion arouses in plants the vital processes by which they spontaneously flower and fructify, so in the supernatural order efficacious grace arouses in us, not only a spontaneous love of happiness, but the love of God; and this love is free, since God is not yet clearly seen and does not yet attract us invincibly. Efficacious grace thus properly moves toward this act specified by a good which does not attract irresistibly, and in so moving toward this act it does not change its nature, which depends on its own objective specification. Thus it does not destroy, but actualizes our liberty and free mode, a mode which is real beyond question, which can be produced in us and with us by the supreme creative cause, which from on high "pours forth all being and every modality of being," excepting only evil-doing.[6] If, on the other hand, God did not predetermine, He would be determined in His knowledge by our consent through foreseen mediate knowledge.

Thus it is through efficacious grace that the prayers of the saints are heard: "Create a clean heart in me, O God: and renew a right

[5] Likewise M. J. Scheeben, *Handbuch der Katholischen Dogmatik*, Herder, 1933, Vol. II, p. 25, no. 61.

[6] Malice is outside of the adequate object of divine omnipotence, and God cannot produce it if He will; on the contrary, the free mode of our choice is a mode of being and not outside the adequate object of God's power, which is the cause of being inasmuch as it is being and also of its modality.

spirit within my bowels" (Ps. 50:12). This is best understood by the mystics, and all the more in proportion to the intimacy of their union with God.[7] Molina admits that such is the doctrine of St. Thomas; cf. *Concordia,* q. 14, a. 13, dis. 26; likewise Suarez and the Coimbran School quoted by Billuart, *De gratia,* diss. 5, a. 7, § III.

REFUTATION OF OBJECTIONS

The objections to the Thomistic teaching have been examined at length by Thomists in reference to the treatise on God, where the divine decrees are examined. They are objections either from Scripture, or from the freedom of the will, from the insufficiency of grace or from affinity with Calvinism. We have examined them in our treatise on the one God (*De Deo uno,* 1938, pp. 446–57). Attention should be drawn to the three principal objections.

From the authority of Scripture, the following texts are brought forward: "What is there that I ought to do more to My vineyard, that I have not done to it?" (Isa. 5:4); "I called, and you refused: I stretched out My hand, and there was none that regarded" (Prov. 1:24); "You always resist the Holy Ghost" (Acts 7:51). Therefore the grace of God is not efficacious intrinsically but by reason of our consent.

Reply. These texts must be reconciled with others we have cited: "As the divisions of waters, so the heart of the king is in the hand of the Lord" (Prov. 21:1); "As clay is in the hand of the potter, so are you in My hand" (Jer. 18:6); "It is God who worketh in you, both to will and to accomplish" (Phil. 2:13); "Who distinguisheth thee? Or what hast thou that thou hast not received?" (I Cor. 4:7.)

But these texts can be reconciled only by the distinction between sufficient grace which is resisted (contrary to the Jansenists, however, the existence of merely sufficient grace is defined) and efficacious grace which in fact is not resisted. Hence the foregoing texts alleged in objection refer to sufficient grace. Thus, in Isa. 5:4 it is written: "What is there that I ought to do more to My vineyard, that I have not done to it?" It does not say: "What is there that I could do more?" Hence the meaning is that God most assuredly gave the Jews suf-

[7] St. Nicholas de Flue, known in Switzerland as the "Father of his country," prayed thus: "My Lord and my God, take away from me whatever withdraws me from Thee; give me whatever leads me to Thee; take me away from myself and give me wholly unto Thee, that I may be wholly Thine." This is a very beautiful expression of the efficacy of grace in the purgative, illuminative, and unitive ways.

ficient graces by which they might be saved and, had they not resisted, they should have received efficacious graces.

Similarly, when we read in Matt. 11:21: "Woe to thee, Corozain, woe to thee, Bethsaida: for if in Tyre and Sidon had been wrought the miracles that have been wrought in you, they had long ago done penance in sackcloth and ashes." This objection is refuted in the same way by the Congruists. But the meaning of this text is that the Jews of Corozain and Bethsaida hindered the course of sufficient grace by greater obduracy and malice and set up a greater obstacle to the efficacious grace offered in sufficient grace. For a miracle or sign is an external sufficient grace, not efficacious as ordained toward conversion.

In fact, the will lacks efficacious grace because it resists sufficient grace; but if its resists sufficient grace, this is not because it lacks efficacious grace; its own deficiency suffices as a cause of such resistance. Cf. Ia IIae, q. 112, a. 3 ad 2: "The first cause of this deficiency of grace is on our part, but the first cause of the conferring of grace is on the part of God, according to the words: 'Destruction is thy own, O Israel: thy help is only in Me.'" There would indeed be a vicious circle in Thomism if of the two following propositions the second were true: Man is deprived of efficacious grace because he resists sufficient grace, and man resists sufficient grace because he lacks efficacious grace. Of course, the second statement is false; if it were true, man would sin from the insufficiency of divine help, sin would then be inevitable and would therefore no longer be sin. In truth, man does not sin on account of insufficient help or of any divine neglect, but because of his own deficiency.

Similarly, as Protestants hold, there would be a vicious circle in our faith if these two propositions were true with the same acceptation of the conjunction "because": I believe the Church to be infallible because God has revealed this; and, I believe that God has revealed this because it is infallibly proposed to me by the Church. The fact is that in these two statements the word "because" is not used in the same sense: in the first it signifies the formal motive of faith; in the second it expresses only the indispensable condition.

Likewise in our present problem, the first proposition contains the formal motive why man is deprived of efficacious grace, namely, because he resists sufficient grace. The second does not; that is, it would be erroneous to say that the motive of his resistance is because he lacks efficacious grace; he would thus be sinning on account of an insufficiency of divine help, so that God would be a defective and deficient cause. The first cause of the defect is our will so far as it is defective and deficient. God, however, is the unfailing cause, not bound to prevent the defect of sin, whereas He can, for higher reasons, permit it on account of a greater good.

Second objection. This is drawn from the Council of Trent (Sess. VI, can. 4, Denz., no. 814), which declares. "If anyone should say that free will, moved and stimulated by God, does nothing to cooperate by assenting to God's encouragement and invitation . . . or that it cannot dissent if it so wills but, like something inanimate, does not act at all and merely keeps itself passive, let him be anathema."

Reply. In this decree the doctrine of intrinsically efficacious grace is not condemned.

1. This is apparent from the subsequent declarations of Benedict XIV and Clement XII (Denz., no. 1090).

2. Among the fathers of the Council many were Thomists; in fact, Dominic Soto collaborated in the formulation of these decrees.

3. Indeed, more probably than not, the fathers of the Council referred in this canon not only to efficacious grace, but to intrinsically efficacious grace and motion, for Luther had spoken of it, declaring that: "Intrinsically efficacious grace takes away liberty." The Council anathematizes those who speak thus, so that the Council must be defining the contradictory proposition. Its intention is to declare that even intrinsically efficacious grace does not deprive man of liberty, for he can resist if he so wills. The Council does not maintain that man does, in fact, sometimes dissent, but that "he can dissent if he so wills." In other words, the contrary power remains, but under efficacious grace man never wills to resist, nor does he; otherwise the grace would not be efficacious or there would be a contradiction in terms; that is, otherwise grace would not cause us to act.

4. Had the fathers of the Council wished to condemn intrinsically efficacious grace, they ought to have said so, but they did not. Therefore it is more probable that they condemned only this conclusion of Luther's: if grace is intrinsically efficacious, it takes away free will. And in this respect the Molinists agree with him. Hence from this canon the condemnation of Molinism would follow with much more likelihood than that of Thomism. Luther held that intrinsically efficacious grace takes away free will. But grace is intrinsically efficacious.

Therefore free will is taken away. Molina maintained that intrinsically efficacious grace takes away free will. But free will remains. Therefore grace is not intrinsically efficacious.

Moreover, the Council of Trent (Sess. VI, chap. 13, Denz., no. 806) states: "Unless men themselves neglect His grace, God will complete the good work as He began it, effecting in us both to will and to accomplish." How can this declaration be reconciled with the following one of Molina: "With equal, and even less assistance, it may yet happen that one of those who are called is converted and another is not"? (*Concordia,* index under "Auxilium," pp. 51–56.) God would thus begin a good work equally in these two men, and one man, distinguishing himself, would perfect the work begun. This would be contrary to the principle of predilection: "For who distinguisheth thee?" And the Council of Orange, c. 22, corroborates: "No man has anything of his own but sin and lying."

The remaining objections may be reduced to the following: If grace is intrinsically efficacious, liberty is destroyed, since consent follows infallibly and man cannot resist. This objection is found in St. Thomas, Ia, q. 19, a. 8, objection 2. His own answer is: "From the very fact that nothing resists the divine will, it follows not only that those things which God wills to be done are done but that they are done contingently or necessarily according to how He wills them to be done."

Hence precisely because grace is most efficacious it is at the same time most gentle and respects liberty by virtue of the principle enunciated by St. Thomas, Ia, q. 19, a. 8: "For when any cause is efficacious in producing its effect, it proceeds from its cause, not only according to what it does, but also according to its manner of doing it or of being. Thus on account of a weakness in the active power of the seed it happens that a son is born unlike his father in accidental qualities which pertain to the mode of being. Since, therefore, the divine will is most efficacious, it not only follows that those things are done which God wills should be done, but also that they are done in the manner in which He wills them to be done. Now God wills that certain things be done necessarily and certain others contingently" (and freely) according as they proceed from proximate causes not determined to one end, and He moves them infallibly according to what befits their nature.

This is the basis of the Thomistic distinctions, for example, between consequential necessity and logical necessity, or between the divided sense and the composite sense. According to Aristotle, there is consequential, but not consequent, necessity in a strict syllogism of which the major is necessary and the minor contingent. For instance, there is the example from Boetius: It is necessary that what I see should really exist. But I see Peter walking. Therefore it is necessary that Peter should be walking, although contingently and freely. Likewise it is necessary that whatever God wills absolutely should be done. But God wills absolutely that the conversion of Paul should take place here and now. Therefore, by consequential necessity but not consequent necessity, Paul will be converted at that moment and his conversion will be free.

In the same way, a man who is seated may stand up, in the divided sense, but not in the composite sense; that is, while seated he has a real power of standing, but he cannot sit and stand simultaneously. These two alternatives are both possible but not concurrently; cf. Ia IIae, q. 10, a. 4 ad 3. Calvin refers to the divided sense with another meaning; according to him, under the efficacious motion of God, the real power of doing the opposite does not remain, but once this motion has been removed, the power of the opposite appears again. The Jansenists hold the same opinion. It is the like error with respect to real power as that of the Megarians who declare that a teacher does not have the power to teach except when he is actually teaching; in which case, should he be sleeping and therefore not actually seeing, he would be blind.

Objection is also contained in the condemned propositions of Quesnel: "The grace of Christ is a supreme grace without which we can in no wise confess Christ, and with which we can never deny Him" (Denz., no. 1359); "Grace is the operation of the hand of the omnipotent God, which nothing can impede or delay" (Denz., no. 1360); "When God wills to save a soul, whatever the time and place, the immutable effect will follow upon the will of God" (Denz., no. 1362.)

Reply. These propositions are condemned, as all historians grant, in the Jansenist sense as explained by the preceding propositions, that is, inasmuch as they deny the antecedent will for salvation, really yet merely sufficient grace, and freedom from necessity.

But some would retort that the Thomist doctrine of grace leads to quietism, for it would wait upon efficacious grace.

Reply. In opposition to the quietists, the Thomists firmly hold that in practice we should strive to act, when it is a question of a precept which actually obliges, and assuredly at that moment efficacious grace is offered to us at least in sufficient grace; but if by our own deficiency we resist this sufficient grace, we deserve to be deprived of efficacious grace.

Hence this doctrine does not lead to quietism, but on the contrary shows the necessity of the prayer of petition, which the quietists neglected, and recalls to mind the word of our Lord: You must pray always. Prayer is, as it were, the "breath of the soul," for at the very moment of prayer the actual grace to pray is undoubtedly received, and through prayer the soul is opened to accept new actual grace, and so on, as the lungs must ever inhale and exhale. It is evident that this Thomistic doctrine of non-necessitating predetermination is not conducive to quietism, since Bossuet, the principal adversary of Quietism, always defended it valiantly, as witnessed by his *Traité du libre arbitre,* chap. 8. Augustine had already refuted this objection with the formula: "God moves the will that it may do, not that it may do nothing," and it should act when given a precept which obliges here and now. Moreover, we should not expect a sign of the conferring of efficacious grace; we receive it without such a sign. Nor does it always remove the difficulty; in fact, the difficulty is very great in the passive state of the night of the soul. Then the soul does not operate by its own diligence alone, but under the special inspiration of God, it believes, hopes, and loves to a heroic degree.

This doctrine of grace efficacious in itself is connected with the principle of predilection: no one would be better than another were he not loved more by God. "What hast thou that thou hast not received?" We must always thank God for every good: "Not to us, O Lord, not to us; but to Thy name give glory." [8]

[8] For the solution of the objection made in logical form on the score of injuring liberty, cf. our *La prédestination des saints et la grâce,* pp. 402–13: "Brevis expositio doctrinae sancti Thomae de motione divina. Catechismus motionis." It is the work of an excellent Thomist which I appended to the aforementioned volume; it would be difficult to treat the subject with any greater accuracy or precision.

CHAPTER VIII

Excursus on Efficacious Grace

▶▶

TO complete the teaching on grace efficacious in itself we must consider in this excursus: 1. efficacious grace and facile acts conducive to salvation; 2. efficacious grace in its relation to spirituality; 3. efficacious grace in wayfaring saints, especially in the martyrs; 4. the efficacious grace of most ardent love, according to St. Theresa; 5. efficacious grace in Christ, impeccable and freely obedient, for He is the highest example of the reconciliation between grace, efficacious in itself, and free obedience in a soul confirmed in good.

I. EFFICACIOUS GRACE AND FACILE ACTS
CONDUCIVE TO SALVATION

Recent opinion. Within the past few years a new opinion has been expressed, to which we referred in the *Revue Thomiste* of November, 1925, and March, 1926, and which is alleged as conforming to the teaching of certain Thomists, especially González de Albeda, Massoulié, Bancel, and Reginaldus. It is, in fact, an unwarranted extension of their opinion.

They maintained that sufficient grace confers not only the power to do good, but also the impulse toward a good act; further, according to them, sufficient actual grace is a predetermining physical premotion, although capable of failure since it does not overcome infallibly such impediments as may arise from temptation or from the free will itself; in this respect it differs from efficacious grace. This opinion of González, Massoulié, Bancel, and Reginaldus differs from the general theory of Thomists only in this respect, that it offers a better explanation of the culpability of sinners and their real power of doing good and avoiding evil. Their opinion is presented at length in the *Revue Thomiste,* 1902, p. 654, and 1903, p. 20, by Father Guillermin,

O.P., who defended it, but understood it correctly and not as it has recently been proposed. We have already discussed this theory of González de Albeda.

According to the recent exposition, sufficient actual grace would be a fallible, predetermining, physical premotion which would incline one toward a good act, but would differ from infallible efficacious grace inasmuch as it would not always overcome the impediments which might arise. Indeed, it is held (whereas the above cited Thomists did not go so far) that frequently this impelling sufficient grace actually moves us to perform facile acts conducive to salvation, for example, to attrition or to imperfect prayer. Hence, infallibly efficacious grace is not necessary for such facile salutary acts, but only for difficult salutary acts, such as perfect contrition as distinguished from attrition. In other words, facile salutary acts presuppose only fallible divine motion and a fallible divine decree.

Critical analysis. To the mind of Thomists reading this new presentation, there immediately arises the objection: How can God know infallibly from all eternity, by a fallible decree, a free act of attrition that will occur here and now in time in the mind of this sinner? It should be remarked that this problem affects not only the predestinate, but also other men who sometimes elicit an act of attrition. The answer is that God knows infallibly this future act of attrition so far as it is already present in eternity, which encompasses all time.

However, this future act of attrition is not present in eternity, rather than the opposite act of resistance, unless by virtue of a divine decree; otherwise it would be present in eternity in the same manner as necessary truths, and we should run into fatalism. Therefore, if the divine decree regarding a future act of attrition is fallible, God can know it only fallibly. This objection is generally made to the Molinist theory of *scientia media,* and there is no escape other than by positing passivity or dependence in divine knowledge with respect to a conditioned, free future act; but no passivity can exist in Pure Act.

According to this recent opinion, with the same impelling sufficient grace, one sinner elicits an act of attrition, while another perseveres in his obduracy; hence the former receives no greater help than the latter. And so we have reverted to Molina's opinion, according to which, "equal help can cause one of those called to be converted and another not" (*Concordia,* pp. 51, 617).

But this is contrary to St. Paul (I Cor. 4:7): "For who distinguisheth thee? or what hast thou that thou hast not received?" St. Thomas declares, (Ia IIae, q. 112, a. 4): "The first cause of this diversity is to be attributed to God Himself, who dispenses the gifts of His grace in diverse ways." Again, St. Thomas comments on Matt. 25:15: "He who strives more has more grace, but the fact that he makes a greater effort demands a higher cause." The principle of predilection is thus formulated by St. Thomas (Ia, q. 20, a. 4): "Since the love of God is the cause of the goodness of things, no one would be better than another unless God willed greater good to one than to another." In other words, no one would be better than another were he not loved and helped more by God. This is the dogmatic basis of Christian humility. And as a matter of fact, when one of two hardened sinners is converted rather than the other, the faithful are accustomed to say that this was done as a special dispensation of God's mercy toward him.

If, of two sinners placed in the same circumstances and equally helped by God, one attains to an act of attrition and the other does not, the first has singled himself out. And so we are faced with an opinion in which, with regard to facile acts, we encounter all the difficulties of Molinism, as observed by Father Del Prado in his *De gratia,* III, 423.

Against this opinion there remains especially the irrefutable objection: How can God, in a fallible decree, foresee infallibly that one of two sinners, both equally assisted, will attain to attrition and the other not? At least there must be admitted for the second case a permissive decree of that resistance or defection. And therefore in the first case an infallibly efficacious positive decree (of future attrition) must be granted, without a concomitant permissive decree of actual defection, which will not take place.

Thus we return to the general doctrine of Thomists, which in fact was safeguarded by González, Massoulié, Bancel, and Reginaldus, since it is explicitly affirmed by St. Thomas when he distinguishes between antecedent and consequent will in God. Cf. Ia, q. 19, a. 6 ad 1: "The will is related to things according to what they are in themselves (inasmuch as goodness resides in things themselves); but in themselves they are individual. Hence we desire something absolutely when we will it with all the particular circumstances, here and now; that is willing consequently. (And on the other hand, antecedent will is concerned with the good taken categorically, and not here and now.) Thus it is manifest that whatever God wills absolutely is done, although what He wills antecedently may not be done." Hence even the least and most facile good does not come about here and now unless God wills it absolutely with consequent and infallibly efficacious will.

But while resistance to sufficient grace is an evil coming, not from God, but from the defective creature, nonresistance to grace is a good existing here and now, which comes from God efficaciously willing it. This is what was affirmed at the conclusion of the controversies that arose over the writings of Gottschalk at the Council of Toucy, A.D. 860 (PL, CXXVI, 123): " 'Whatsoever the Lord pleased He hath done, in heaven, in earth' (Ps. 134). For nothing is done in heaven or on earth except what He Himself graciously accomplishes or justly permits to befall." But God graciously causes attrition in one sinner and justly permits resistance in another. Thus the words of St. Paul are fully safeguarded: "For who distinguisheth thee? or what hast thou that thou hast not received?"

These metaphysical principles which are therefore absolutely universal, allowing of no exception, are not observed in the new opinion that has been proposed, although on the contrary González, Massoulié, Reginaldus, Bancel, and Guillermin retained them, as can easily be seen from their works.[1]

2. EFFICACIOUS GRACE IN RELATION TO SPIRITUALITY

The teaching of St. Thomas on efficacious grace is generally not well understood except by speculative theologians who judge everything in relation to God, the universal first cause and author of salvation, or by souls that are advancing along the ways of passive

---

[1] Cf. Guillermin, Revue Thomiste, 1903, pp. 23 ff., 27; González de Albeda, Comment. in Iam, disp. 58, sect. III (ed. 1637): "Efficacious grace is necessary for the verification of the fact that our consent is involved in the matter"; Bancel, Brevis univ. theologiae cursus, Vol. II, tr. IV, q.4, a.4. Also Massoulié, Divus Thomas sui interpres, Vol. II, diss. III, q.6, a.2, pp. 206, 213 (ed. Rome, 1709).

Indeed, González expressly says (op. cit., disp. 58, II, 97): "Of two men equally tempted, the one who consents to the Holy Ghost is always prepared by greater intrinsic prevenient grace than the one who consents to the devil." All these Thomists admit what Alvarez writes in the third Book of his De auxiliis, disp. 80: "All help which is sufficient with respect to one act is at the same time efficacious in the order of another (less perfect) act, for the effecting of which it is ordained by an absolute decree of divine providence, so that it is sufficient absolutely and efficacious under a particular aspect." Thus all Thomists admit that help which is efficacious for attrition is sufficient with regard to contrition. For all of them, facile salutary acts require infallibly efficacious help.

purgation. These souls, as it were, experience within themselves that in the affair of salvation everything comes from God; that is, in a salutary, meritorious act, its free determination cannot derive exclusively from us. This is so because man has nothing which is exclusively his own except sin and lying, as declared by the Second Council of Orange (Denz., no. 195).

As we have seen, according to St. Thomas efficacious grace is not rendered efficacious by our consent foreseen by God in such a way that the free, meritorious determination would be, as determination, exclusively our own work. Rather is efficacious grace intrinsically efficacious; that is, it moves us gently and forcibly to consent to the good, so that this consent is entirely from God's premotion, as first cause, and entirely ours as secondary, premoved cause. In other words, God produces in us and with us even the free mode of our choices.

Herein lies no contradiction, but a sublime mystery, namely, that God is more intimately present to our liberty than it is to itself. And in this it appears that "the will of God is eminently efficacious, since it follows not only that those things are done which God wills should be done, but also that they are done in the manner in which He wills them to be done. But He wills that certain things should be necessary and others contingent (and free, as well) that there may be order among things for the completion of the universe." (Ia, q. 19, a. 8). "It is God who worketh in you, both to will and to accomplish, according to His good will" (Phil. 2:13). The only thing that cannot derive from God is moral evil, which, however, He permits that from it greater good may proceed by the manifestation of His mercy and justice. Moral evil does not require an efficient cause, but rather a deficient cause. Every good thing is from God.

That it may be evident, then, how this doctrine of St. Thomas raises the mind to lofty contemplation of the action of God in the depths of our hearts, it suffices to show that this doctrine should lead to profound humility, to continual interior prayer, to the perfection of the theological virtues, and that, in point of fact, illustrious spiritual writers have accepted it. In the present excursus we shall develop by way of synthesis what we have already presented in the form of spiritual corollaries.

1. This doctrine leads to profound humility, since it follows that man has nothing exclusively his own except sin. He does no natural good without the natural help of God, no supernatural good without

supernatural grace, which not only urges and attracts but also moves him efficaciously to the performance of good. Thus the word of God is given a profound significance: "Without Me you can do nothing"; and likewise St. Paul's: "Not that we are sufficient to do anything ourselves as of ourselves, but our sufficiency is from God." And this is true even of the just who have already attained a high degree of charity, for they still require actual help in order to do good. And after they have done many and great things, they must say in all truth: "We are unprofitable servants" (Luke 17:10). That is to say, according to the thought of St. Augustine: there is no sin which another man commits of which I am not capable from the weakness of free will and my own frailty, and for the fact that I do not commit it, not to us, O Lord, but to Thy name give glory. The words of St. Paul must ever be kept in mind: "What hast thou that thou hast not received? And if thou hast received, why dost thou glory as if thou hadst not received?" St. Francis of Assisi used to repeat this to himself whenever he saw a criminal being led to execution. All these considerations profoundly understood according to St. Thomas' teaching incline the soul strongly toward true humility, "that all may be attributed to God."

2. This doctrine leads to continual interior prayer, to a profound spirit of gratitude and, in fact, to contemplative prayer.

To interior prayer, for that prayer of petition is more interior which asks of God the greater interior grace. But according to the opinion of St. Thomas, we should ask of God not only grace which will urge us to do good, but also that grace which actually moves us efficaciously toward right action and perseverance in good. We must ask for grace which will reach even unto the depths of our heart and free will, moving us, so that we may really be freed from perverse inclinations, from the lust of the flesh, the lust of the eyes, and the pride of life; for only God our Savior can deliver our souls from all of these. Nor does He injure our liberty in so acting, but rather causes it, actualizes it, and raises it above the thralldom of lower creatures. Whatever actualizes our freedom cannot injure or destroy it.

Thus only can the petitions found in Holy Scripture be understood: "Have mercy on me, O God, according to Thy great mercy. . . . O God, be merciful to me a sinner. . . . Help Thou my unbelief. . . . Create a clean heart in me, O God, and renew a right spirit in my bowels. . . . Convert me, O Lord, unto Thee, and I shall

be converted. . . . Thy will be done on earth as it is in heaven," that
is, give me efficacious grace that I may really do Thy will, or in the
words of St. Augustine: "Give, O Lord, what You command, and
command what You will."

Only thus can the prayers of the Church contained in the Missal
be profoundly understood. For the Church prays "that God may force
our rebellious wills; . . . that He may transform unbelievers who
refuse to believe into men willing to believe; . . . that He may incline our hearts to good works; . . . that He may give us a good
will; . . . that He may convert and draw us to Himself; . . . that
He may take away our hearts of stone and give us hearts of flesh, that
is, docile hearts; . . . that He may change our wills and incline them
to good."

Hence, also, the priest who attends the dying must pray for them
with great confidence, in the name of Christ, for God is not powerless
to convert even hardened sinners. For the formal motive of hope is
the merciful assistance of God. Therefore, at that moment, the priest
should bear in mind the words of Christ: "Whatsoever you shall ask
the Father in My name, that will I do: that the Father may be glorified
in the Son" (John 14:13); "Amen, amen I say to you: if you ask
the Father anything in My name, He will give it you" (John 16:23).

Moreover, this prayer must be continual for our soul is in continual
need of efficacious actual grace in order to perform any new work
conducive to salvation. This is the deep meaning of the word of God:
"Pray always," and of the expression used by the Fathers: "Prayer is,
as it were, the breath of the soul." For, by means of prayer, the soul
inhales grace, and thereupon exhales, or elicits, a meritorious act.

Likewise, according to this doctrine, thanksgiving should be rendered for every good without exception: "in all things giving thanks"
(I Thess. 5:18). We should say with all our hearts: "It is the mercy
of God that we have not been destroyed. Thy hands have made me
and formed me; and Thou hast redeemed us by Thy blood. The mercy
of God is above all His works." Furthermore, this teaching of itself
leads properly to contemplative prayer which, considering especially
the profound action of God within us, whether mortifying or vivifying
us, responds: "Thy will be done." "The Lord killeth and maketh alive,
He bringeth down to hell and bringeth back again" (I Kings 2:6).
Such passivity expressed by the word *"fiat"* is the most profound cooperation with the highest works of God. Thus did Christ pray in the

Garden of Gethsemane, thus did the Blessed Virgin utter: "Be it done unto me according to thy word" in joy on the day of the Annunciation, in suffering on Calvary.

Finally, the significance of St. Paul's words with reference to the grace necessary for prayer is fully manifest from this doctrine (Rom. 8:26 f.): "The Spirit also helpeth our infirmity. For we know not what we should pray for as we ought; but the Spirit Himself asketh for us with unspeakable groanings. And He that searcheth the hearts, knoweth what the Spirit desireth; because He asketh for the saints according to God." This is verified particularly in mystical contemplation, which is often painful and obscure, so that the soul therein recognizes how necessary grace is for praying well, just as it is for right action.

3. This teaching of St. Thomas on grace raises the theological virtues to a higher level, because it is closely connected with the very sublime mystery of predestination, in the words of St. Paul (Rom. 8:28-30): "And we know that to them that love God, all things work together unto good, to such as, according to His purpose, are called to be saints. For whom He foreknew, He also predestinated to be made conformable to the image of His Son; that He might be the first-born among many brethren. [St. Thomas understands this as referring to gratuitous predestination unto glory.] And whom He predestinated, them He also called. And whom He called, them He also justified. And whom He justified, them He also glorified." Such is the process of predestination.

This demands great faith in the wisdom of God, in the sanctity of the divine good pleasure, in His omnipotence, His supreme dominion, in the exceedingly great efficacy of the merits of Christ. Faith in the wisdom of God is thus acclaimed in the words of St. Paul (Rom. 11:33-35): "O the depth of the riches of the wisdom and of the knowledge of God! How incomprehensible are His judgments, and how unsearchable His ways! For who hath known the mind of the Lord? Or who hath been His counsellor? Or who hath first given to Him, and recompense shall be made him?" Faith in the sanctity of the divine good pleasure is magnified in accordance with the text: "Nor are your ways My ways, saith the Lord," and the words of Christ: "I confess to Thee, O Father, Lord of heaven and earth, because Thou hast hid these things from the wise and prudent, and hast revealed them to little ones. Yea, Father; for so hath it seemed good in Thy sight" (Matt. 11:25 f.); and again, Jesus said to the Pharisees: "Murmur not among yourselves. No man can come to Me, except the Father, who hath sent Me, draw him" (John 6:43 f.).

So, too, in the spirit of this teaching, faith in the divine omnipotence is extolled, whereby God can convert even the most hardened sinners to good, according to Prov. 21:1: "The heart of the king is in the hand of the Lord: whithersoever He will He shall turn it"; and Phil. 2:13: "It is God who worketh in you, both to will and to accomplish, according to His good will." Faith in the supreme dominion of God is expressed Jer. 18:6: "As clay is in the hand of the potter, so are you in My hand, O house of Israel." And St. Paul develops the same figure (Rom. 9:21–23): "Or hath not the potter power over the clay, of the same lump, to make one vessel unto honor, and another unto dishonor? What if God, willing to show His wrath, and to make His power known, endured with much patience vessels of wrath, fitted for destruction [persecutors, for example], that He might show the riches of His glory on the vessels of mercy, which He hath prepared unto glory?" So, finally, is faith in the exceedingly great merits of Christ demonstrated, in accordance with the words of St. John: "The Father loveth the Son: and He hath given all things into His hand" (3:35); "Now this is the will of the Father who sent Me: that of all that He hath given Me, I should lose nothing; but should raise it up again in the last day" (6:39); "Thine they were, and to Me Thou gavest them. . . . Those whom Thou gavest Me have I kept; and none of them is lost, but the son of perdition, that the scripture may be fulfilled" (17:6–12).

Likewise, according to this doctrine of grace a truly supernatural hope is required, that is, one founded uniquely upon this formal motive: the help of God. For we should not rely upon our own powers or free will to attain to a supernatural end, as it is written: "He that trusteth in his own heart, is a fool" (Prov. 28:26). Rather, considering our weakness, we should "with fear and trembling work out our salvation" (Phil. 2:12); and "he that thinketh himself to stand, let him take heed lest he fall" (I Cor. 10:12).

On the other hand, contemplating God, we should say to Him: "In Thee, O my God, I put my trust; let me not be ashamed" (Ps. 24:2); "Into Thy hands I commend my spirit" (Ps. 30:6). Further, we are assured, "he that trusteth in Him, shall fare never the worse" (Ecclus. 32:28); "The Lord is sweet: blessed is the man that hopeth in

Him" (Ps. 33:9); "Behold, God is my savior, I will deal confidently and will not fear" (Isa. 12:2); "Preserve me, O Lord, for I have put my trust in Thee" (Ps. 15:1); "In Thee, O Lord, have I hoped, let me never be confounded" (Ps. 30:2; 70:1); and in St. Paul's epistles: "To them that love God, all things work together unto good, to such as, according to His purpose, are called to be saints. . . . What shall we then say to these things? If God be for us, who is against us?" (Rom. 8:28–31); "I can do all things in Him who strengtheneth me" (Phil. 4:13).

In the passive purifications, the soul is frequently tempted against hope, and when all created aids fail, must hope against hope, or beyond all human hope, because of the one formal motive, the help of God. "When I am weakest then am I strong." But God helps us most efficaciously when He confers upon us, not only the grace which urges and stimulates, but grace which is efficacious in itself. Thus does the soul attain to holy abandonment in the hands of God.

Similarly, by means of this teaching on grace, charity toward God is strengthened. "In this is charity: not as though we had loved God, but because He hath first loved us, and sent His Son to be a propitiation for our sins" (I John 4:10). For our charity is based upon the divine communication of the life of grace, and the more intimately and efficaciously grace is bestowed upon us, the more we ought to love God, or to return His love. Hence, after enunciating the mystery of predestination, St. Paul adds (Rom. 8:35–39): "Who then shall separate us from the love of Christ? Shall tribulation or distress or famine . . . or persecution or the sword? . . . But in all these things we overcome, because of Him that hath loved us [that is, by the grace of Christ]. For I am sure that neither death nor life nor angels . . . nor depth nor any other creature shall be able to separate us from the love of God, which is in Christ Jesus our Lord." For Christ declares: "Those whom Thou gavest Me have I kept," and Christ can always keep our souls efficaciously: "And I give them life everlasting . . . and no man shall pluck them out of My hand" (John 10:28).

But these truths are not fully grasped except in the mystical life. Therefore it must be said that St. Thomas' sublime doctrine of grace is rejected by many precisely on account of its exceeding sublimity, but because, by really preserving the deep sense of Holy Scripture, it leads us to the highest contemplation of God, the author of salvation.

Confirmation. This doctrine of efficacious grace is accepted by great mystics and eminent spiritual writers. It is found in St. Paul, as we have already shown, and in St. Augustine, whose teaching abides in the decrees of the Second Council of Orange which defined that "no man has anything of his own but sin and lying" (chaps. 20, 22; Denz., nos. 193, 195). St. Augustine says (*De praedestin. sanct.,* chap. 5): "A haughty man may indeed say to another: 'My faith, my justice, or some other thing distinguishes me.'" To one to whom such thoughts occur, the good Doctor puts the question: "What hast thou that thou hast not received? And from whom, unless it be from Him who distinguishes thee from another, to whom He did not give what He gave to thee? But if thou hast received, why dost thou glory as if thou hadst not received? Can that be glorying in the Lord? But nothing is so contrary to this disposition as to glory in one's own merits as if in something which one was responsible for effecting, rather than the grace of God; for it is grace which distinguishes the good from the bad, not what is common to the good and the bad." "Therefore, although it might be believed that Cornelius has done something well, the whole must be attributed to God, lest anyone should be exalted" (*ibid.,* chap. 6). "This grace is exceedingly hidden; but who doubts that grace really exists? And so it is this grace, which is secretly imparted by the divine bounty to human hearts, that it may remove their hardness of heart for the first time" (*ibid.,* chap. 8). "God, in fact, does what He wills in the hearts of men" (*ibid.,* chap. 20). "We therefore assert that perseverance is a gift of God whereby one perseveres in Christ unto the end" (*De dono. persever.,* chap. 1). "Hence we ask that we may not be lead into temptation, that this may not occur. For nothing is done except what He Himself does or permits to be done. He is therefore powerful both to bend wills from evil unto good and to convert those inclined to fall, as well as to direct toward Himself an agreeable course" (*ibid.,* chap. 6).

St. Prosper and St. Fulgentius spoke in terms similar to those quoted above. With respect to the Fathers who wrote before St. Augustine on grace and predestination, consult Bossuet's *Défense de la tradition et des saints Pères,* Bk. XII, chap. 39. Pelagianism and Semi-Pelagianism had not yet arisen, and consequently the question had not yet been explicitly posed.

Together with Augustine, St. Bernard demonstrates (*De grat. et lib. arbitr.,* c. 1, no. 2) that grace saves while free will is safeguarded:

"Free will enables us to will, grace enables us to will well" (*ibid.,* chap. 6, no. 16). How do grace and free will operate? "Together, not singly; simultaneously, not in turn; not partly grace and partly free will, but they perform the whole by a single, undivided act" (*ibid.,* chap. 14, nos. 46 f.). Consequently, when God crowns our merits in heaven, He crowns His own gifts: "His gifts, which He gave to men, He divided unto merits and rewards" (*ibid.,* chap. 13, no. 43). Cf. *Dict. de théol. cath.,* article "St. Bernard" by Vacandard, col. 776 ff. St. Bonaventure speaks in similar terms (*II Sent.,* dist. 26, q. 2): "This is also the disposition of the pious, that they attribute nothing to themselves, but all to the grace of God."

In the *Following of Christ,* Bk. III, chap. 4, no. 2, we read: "Never esteem thyself to be anything on account of thy good works. . . . Of thyself thou always tendest to nothing, speedily dost thou fail, speedily art thou overcome, speedily disturbed, speedily dissolved. Thou hast not anything in which thou canst glory, but many things for which thou oughtest to abase thyself; for thou art much weaker than thou canst comprehend." *Ibid.,* chap. 8, no. 1: "I am nothing, and I knew it not. If I am left to myself, behold, I am nothing, and all weakness; but if Thou suddenly look upon me, I presently become strong, and am replenished with new joy. And truly wonderful it is that I am so quickly raised up and so graciously embraced by Thee; I who, by my own weight, am always sinking down to the lowest depths." *Ibid.,* chap. 9, nos. 2–3: "Out of Me both little and great, poor and rich, as out of a living fountain, draw living water. . . . Therefore thou must not ascribe any good to thyself, nor attribute virtue to any man; but give all to God, without whom man has nothing. I have given all, I will also have all again; and with great strictness do I require a return of thanks. This is that truth by which all vainglory is put to flight. And if heavenly grace and true charity come in, there shall be no envy nor narrowness of heart, nor shall self-love keep possession. For divine charity overcometh all, and enlargeth all the powers of the soul. If thou art truly wise, thou wilt rejoice in Me alone, thou wilt hope in Me alone; for none is good but God alone, who is to be praised above all, and to be blessed in all." *Ibid.,* chap. 55, nos. 4–5: "Without it [grace] I can do nothing; but I can do all things in Thee, when grace strengtheneth me. . . . Oh, most blessed grace, . . . come, descend upon me, replenish me early with thy consolation, lest my soul faint through weariness and dryness of mind. . . .

This alone is my strength, this alone giveth counsel and help. This is more mighty than all my enemies, and wiser than all the wise." *Ibid.,* chap. 58: "I am to be praised in all My saints; I am to be blessed above all and to be honored in each, whom I have so gloriously magnified and predestinated, without any foregoing merits of their own."

St. John of the Cross, *Spiritual Canticle,* stanza 38, no. 10: "In that day of eternity, that is, before the creation and according to His good pleasure God predestined the soul unto glory and determined the degree of glory that He would give it. From that moment this glory became a property of the soul and this in a manner so absolute that no event or accident, temporal or spiritual, can ever take it away radically, for what God has given it gratuitously will always remain its property." *Ascent of Mount Carmel,* Bk. II, chap. 5: "God determines the degree of union freely as He determines the degree of the beatific vision to each one."

St. John of the Cross declares that it depends on the good pleasure of God alone that this particular soul should be predestined to such and such a degree of glory; in other words, predestination to glory is prior to any foreseen merits. *Prière de l'âme embrasée* (Carmelite ed., I, 475): "If Thou awaitest my works, O Lord, to grant me what I ask, give them to me, effect them in me, and join thereto the sufferings Thou deignest to accept from me."

Although St. Francis de Sales does not always follow St. Thomas in this matter, he holds in the *Treatise on the Love of God,* Bk. II, chap. 12; that "Grace . . . touches powerfully but yet so delicately the springs of our spirit that our free will suffers no violence from it. . . . She acts strongly, yet so sweetly that our will is not overwhelmed by so powerful an action. . . . The consent to grace depends much more on grace than on the will, while the resistance to grace depends upon the will only. . . . If thou didst know the gift of God."

Indeed, almost all spiritual writers, dealing with souls that are being led along the passive ways are in accord with the Thomistic doctrine. (Cf. J. Grou, S.J., *Spiritual Maxims,* second maxim; L. Lallemant, S.J., *Spiritual Doctrine,* fourth principle: "Docility to the Holy Ghost," chaps. 1 and 2; J. P. de Caussade, S.J., *Self-Abandonment to Divine Providence,* Bk. III, chaps. 1 and 2.)

Let us conclude this application of the Thomist doctrine to spirituality with a quotation from Bossuet, *Elévations sur les mystères* (eighteenth week, fifteenth elevation, "Practical humility solves difficulties"): "Contradictions against Jesus Christ regarding the mystery of grace. Behold another terrible stumbling block for human pride. Man says in his heart: I have my free will; God has made me free, and I will to become a just man; I will that the stroke which decides my eternal salvation should come originally from me. Thus does he seek, on some pretext, to glorify himself. Whither are you bound, O fragile craft? You are about to strike against a reef and deprive yourself of the help of God, who assists only the humble, making them humble that He may help them. . . .

"I can. I wish to find something to cling to in my free will, that I cannot reconcile with this abandonment to grace. Proud contradictor, do you wish to reconcile these things yourself or are you willing to believe that God reconciles them? He reconciles them to such an extent that He wills, without releasing you from your action, that you should attribute the whole achievement of your salvation to Him. For He is the Savior who declares: 'there is no Savior beside Me' (Isa. 43:11). Believe firmly that Jesus Christ is the Savior, and all difficulties will vanish." [2]

This great doctrine of grace is wonderfully presented to the modern world by St. Theresa of the Child Jesus, in her way of spiritual childhood, which is suitable to all Christians, even the perfect, since they are all adopted children of God; see the last chapter of this book on the spirit of adoption of sons of God. Among the children of God, they are more truly His children who place greater trust, not in themselves, but in God and His help.[3]

---

[2] Cf. also what Bossuet says in his *Méditations sur l'Evangile,* Part II, chap. 72: Jesus Christ is always heard; the predestination of the saints. As we have already noted, he says elsewhere: "We must admit these two graces (sufficient and efficacious), of which the former leaves the will without any excuse before God, and the latter does not permit it to glory in itself." Bossuet, *Œuvres complètes,* I, 643; cf. also general index under "Grâce (résistance à la grâce)."

[3] St. Theresa of the Child Jesus says in the *History of a Soul,* chap. 9: "I read these words uttered by the Eternal Wisdom Itself: 'Whosoever is a little one, let him come to Me' (Prov. 9:4). Wishing to know further what He would do to the little one, I continued my search and this is what I found: 'You shall be carried at the breasts and upon the knees; as one whom the mother caresseth, so will I comfort you' (Isa. 66: 12 f.).

"Never have I been consoled by words more tender and sweet. Thine arms, then, O Jesus, are the lift which must raise me up even unto heaven. To get there I need not grow; on the contrary, I must remain little, I must become still less." The soul must, in fact, realize more and more that it is a child of God and that it can do

3. EFFICACIOUS GRACE IN THE SAINTS, ESPECIALLY THE MARTYRS

We shall now present eminent examples which confirm the Thomistic teaching. Our adversaries say: Efficacious grace is not efficacious of itself, nor is it a predetermining motion. To be sure, it is not the formal determination of this free act toward which it moves us, for it precedes this formal determination by a priority not of time but of nature and causality. Nevertheless, inasmuch as this efficacious motion depends on a positive, predetermining divine decree, it moves us infallibly to determine ourselves freely (often by discursive deliberation) in the same sense as this divine decree, for example, to obey here and now rather than not to obey.

Thus efficacious grace infallibly moved the Blessed Virgin Mary freely to say on the day of the Annunciation: "Behold the handmaid of the Lord; be it done unto me according to thy word." Hence the Blessed Virgin infallibly and freely uttered her fiat ordained toward the incarnation of the Word, which was the object of an eternal decree to be fulfilled infallibly. And again the Mother of God repeated her fiat on Calvary, infallibly and freely, with the highest degree of merit.

Likewise and with still greater reason, grace efficacious in itself moved the most holy soul of Christ to will freely and meritoriously to offer the sacrifice of the cross for us, as had been announced by the prophets according to an eternal decree of consequent will, to be accomplished infallibly. But if in a single case, in the soul of the Blessed Virgin Mary or in the most holy soul of Christ, grace efficacious in itself did not destroy liberty, but rather actualized it, no one can maintain that of itself it destroys or injures liberty.

In wayfaring saints, especially during the exceedingly painful passive purification or dark night of the soul, described by St. John of the Cross, temptations against faith, hope, and charity are often so vehement that a heroic act is required to resist them; hence the souls thus tried earnestly beg for the most efficacious help of God. St. John of the Cross (*Dark Night,* Bk. II, chap. 23) writes: "There is in the soul thus tried a struggle or contest between the spirit of God and

---

nothing without Him in the order of salvation; it is thus led to enter eventually into the passive ways which are the prelude to heaven.

St. Theresa of the Child Jesus further declared: "To remain little consists in not attributing anything to oneself in the practice of virtue and in recognizing that everything comes from God," who draws us to Himself and causes us to act and to merit. When He crowns our merits, it is His own gifts that He crowns.

the spirit of evil." Therefore does this soul then pray thus: "If Thou awaitest my works, O Lord, to grant me what I ask, give them to me, deign to effect in me both to will and to accomplish, together with the trials which I offer Thee according to Thy good pleasure."

Thus in particular did St. Paul of the Cross pray, he who was to walk this road of suffering for forty years, that he might become an example of the life of reparation. He wrote to a certain religious of his Order whom he directed: "In your case there will be a different sort of blade; in fact it is there already; love will be the executioner, let him do what he wills, for he is a master craftsman. When he inflicts the martyrdom, one has need of extraordinarily great assistance and strength coming from God; without that, one will not endure the thrust." (*Letters*, III, 158.) [4]

The efficacy of grace is especially evident in the martyrs, since they must traverse the path to sanctity in a short space of time by acts which are entirely heroic. In them are verified the words of St. Paul (Rom. 8:35–39): "Who then shall separate us from the love of Christ? Shall tribulation or distress or famine or nakedness or danger or persecution or the sword? (As it is written: For Thy sake we are put to death all the day long. We are accounted as sheep for the slaughter.) But in all these things we overcome, because of Him that hath loved us. For I am sure that neither death nor life nor angels nor principalities nor powers . . . nor any other creature shall be able to separate us from the love of God, which is in Christ Jesus our Lord."

In regard to this text, St. Thomas says in his Commentary on the Epistle to the Romans: "Every benefit is conferred upon us by divine Providence, and so efficaciously that nothing can withstand it. . . . In all these things we overcome, not by our own strength, but through the help of Christ. Hence it is said: 'because of Him that hath loved us,' that is, on account of His help. . . . The Apostle is speaking in the person of all the predestinate, concerning whom he declares that, in view of the certainty of their predestination, nothing can separate them from charity."

Truly, then, does the effect of grace become marvelously evident in the martyrs. It suffices to call to mind their heroic fortitude which manifests the exceedingly efficacious help of God in the midst of unendurable adversities. For the virtue of fortitude differs greatly from

---

[4] Cf. *Oraison et ascension mystique de Saint Paul de la Croix,* by Father Gaëtan du Saint Nom de Marie, Passionist, Louvain, 1930, p. 130.

the pertinacity or stubbornness of pride. Fortitude is not a virtue with the status of a virtue which is reserved for the dispositions difficult of attainment unless it is connected with other virtues, such as humility, meekness, piety; for it must come under the direction of prudence really to confirm a man in the goodness of virtue and not in the obstinacy of pride. (Cf. Ia IIae, q. 65, a. 1, 2, 3.) Moreover, in order to be heroic, fortitude must perform works exceeding the ordinary powers of men promptly, with alacrity, whenever the occasion presents itself, frequently, if need be, and constantly (Benedict XIV, *De canoni. sanct.,* Bk. III, chap. 21).

Thus did the martyrs endure the most atrocious torments. They were certainly not insensible to fear before the moment of trial; Jesus Himself began to fear and to be heavy; but they prayed and overcame their fear. They were not moved by rash impetuosity, but in tranquillity of soul and meekness of spirit, praying for their persecutors, they fulfilled their martyrdom with eagerness and constancy "rejoicing in hope, patient in tribulation" (Rom. 12:12).

However, this heroic fortitude, witnessed by all, can be explained only by grace which is efficacious of itself; indeed, it is a miracle of the moral order. For such fortitude, with the other related virtues, demands heroic acts of the principal virtues frequently repeated on the part of countless men, women, and young girls of every condition, eagerly and perseveringly carrying on amid the most intense physical and moral sufferings without the least hope of earthly reward, nay rather in spite of all worldly promises and allurements.

But heroic acts of the principal virtues cannot be performed so often nor with such alacrity and constancy, in the midst of frightful torments, by a multitude of human beings of every condition, sex, and age, without any natural motive, unless the most efficacious and, in fact, extraordinary intervention of God accompanies them. For sanctity, or a very steadfast union with God, cannot exist without efficacious help from on high, nor extraordinary sanctity without extraordinary help from God; for the order of agents must correspond to the order of ends, and only the supreme agent can move efficaciously toward the supreme end.

Lastly, the martyrs themselves declared that they were aided by efficacious divine help without which they could not have endured their torments. St. Polycarp: [5] "Leave me as I am; for He who en-

---

[5] Epistle to the Church of Smyrna, chap. 13.

abled me to endure the fire will also enable me to remain motionless on the pyre, without your precaution of lock and key." St. Felicitas while in prison experienced the severe pains of childbirth, so that one of the guards said to her: "If you suffer so much now, what will you do when you are thrown to the beasts?" But she replied confidently: [6] "Now it is I who suffer what I suffer, but then another will be in me who will suffer for me, since I am to suffer for His sake." In the same way Andronicus said to his judge: "Armed by my God I stand before thee in the faith and power of the Lord God almighty."

The Levite, Vincent, amid the most severe tortures of the rack, exclaimed: "Bestir yourself, and let loose all the intensity of your malice. You will see me able, by the power of God, to endure more torments than you yourself can inflict." As we read in the Martyrology for January 19: "In Smyrna, blessed Germanicus . . . put away by the grace of the might of God the fears of bodily weakness, and . . . provoked the wild beast prepared for him and, being devoured by the teeth of the beast, merited to be made one with the true bread, the Lord Jesus Christ, by dying for His sake."

It is enough, too, merely to recall the Office of St. Agnes martyr, in which is marvelously combined the natural weakness of this holy girl and the efficacious grace of God: "In the midst of the flames, Blessed Agnes extended her hands and prayed: 'I entreat Thee, O Father, worthy of all adoration, worship and fear, since by Thy holy Son I have escaped the threats of the sacriligeous tyrant and by an unspotted path have avoided the defilements of the flesh: behold now I come to Thee whom I have loved, whom I have sought, and for whom I have always longed.'"

Lastly, Christ had predicted this victory on the part of the martyrs: "It shall be given you in that hour what to speak" (Matt. 10:19). In their victory is likewise manifested in a wonderful manner both the free will of the martyrs who said in full liberty: "Rather to be tortured and put to death than to deny faith in God," and the efficacy of divine grace, which for three centuries continued to be the cause of this triumph. Their memory abides in Rome through the Colosseum, and no higher tribute can be paid "unto the praise of the glory of His grace" (Ephes. 1:6).

Thus are verified the words of St. Paul to the Ephesians (1:4-6): "As He chose us in Him [Christ] before the foundation of the world,

---

[6] Ruinart, *Acta martyrum*, 1731, p. 86.

that we should be holy and unspotted in His sight in charity. Who hath predestinated us unto the adoption of children through Jesus Christ unto Himself: according to the purpose of His will: unto the praise of the glory of His grace." With regard to these words St. Thomas says in his Commentary on the Epistle: "He chose us not because we should be holy nor because we were, but He chose us for this reason: that we might be holy in virtues and unspotted from vices. For He makes His choice according to both elements of justice: the withdrawal from evil and the doing of good. . . . The twofold cause of this immense benefit is indicated. One is efficient, that is, the absolute will of God: "according to the purpose of His will," and further (Rom. 9:18): "He hath mercy on whom He will; and whom He will, He hardeneth." The other cause is final, namely, that we should praise and know the goodness of God, as expressed in the words: "unto the praise of the glory of His grace."

4. THE EFFICACIOUS GRACE OF MOST ARDENT LOVE, ACCORDING TO ST. THERESA (SIXTH MANSION, CHAP. 2)

In chapter two of the sixth mansion and in her autobiography as well (chap. 29), St. Theresa speaks of the prayer of impulse in which the soul receives certain impulses from our Lord, under the stimulation of which it tends toward Him with a great vehemence of spirit. I present briefly what the mystical theologians hold in this regard.[7]

These impulses are the effect of efficacious actual grace anticipating the soul. The soul experiences them in its innermost center as at once strong and gentle. They are so delicate and subtle that they can scarcely be described by any comparison, as the mystical writers declare. They differ markedly from any sensible movement that we may induce by our own effort. For it sometimes, even frequently, happens that the soul, while thinking of nothing of the sort, suddenly feels inflamed as if by a dart from the hand of God or a thunderbolt, and although it does not perceive any audible sound, it is conscious that the wound has been made by the divine Spouse, and hears Him calling by so evident an interior sign that it cannot doubt His being present to it. It feels plainly that it is with God and nevertheless experiences pain. But this pain is sweet to it so that it wishes the pain would never

[7] Cf. Philip of the Holy Trinity, C.D., *Summa theologiae mysticae*, Brussels, 1874, III, 98: "De oratione impulsus"; Anthony of the Holy Ghost, C.D., *Directorium mysticum*, Venice, 1732, p. 156: "De oratione impulsus"; Thos. of Vallgornera, O.P., *Mystica theologia S. Thomae*, 3rd ed., 1911, II, 255-69.

cease. This delightful pain is not always equally intense; sometimes it lasts a long while, at other times it passes quickly, depending upon the good pleasure of God.

A person who is not familiar with such movements cannot recognize them. They do not resemble those vehement impulsions caused by sensible devotion, for in these latter nature has a part and, if they are not modified, they destroy health. However, these movements of which we are speaking are very different; we do not cooperate in them naturally, rather do they proceed from God. The soul feels a dart thrust into the depths of its heart and is impelled to the most ardent love of God, in obedience to whom it would gladly lose its life. It is the effect of actual grace at once exceedingly efficacious and most profound. Words are incapable of expressing the manner in which God thus wounds the soul. This pain is so exquisite that there is no delight in this life that satisfies to such an extent. The soul would wish to be forever dying of such a malady. This pain blended with joy keeps the soul beside itself, nor does it understand how such a thing can be.

Sometimes this wound is merely spiritual; sometimes it extends even to the body, to the organ of the heart. When the wound of love is not inflicted so intensely, the soul may apply a remedy to it by certain mortifications, which however are scarcely felt even when carried to the extent of shedding blood. That is, the first spiritual pain is so oppressive and penetrating that it cannot be driven out but only somewhat mitigated. Only God can apply the remedy which appears to be nothing less than death, by means of which the transpierced soul attains to immediate vision and perfect fulfillment.

When the afore-mentioned wound of love is vehemently inflicted in the interior of the heart or penetrates the very depths of the will, no remedy is of any avail to assuage that delightful pain; it racks and weakens the body to such an extent that complete ecstasy follows. However, the soul is by no means weakened, but on the contrary its vigor is greatly augmented. A sign of the divine origin of this favor is the great humility which a person experiences after the ecstasy. The soul receiving such a favor should not fear deception on the part of the demon, but rather ingratitude on its own part. Hence, rendering thanks to God, the soul should strive to submit to Him faithfully.

The value of this most efficacious profound grace is apparent from its effects. Thus the first effect of the prayer of impulse is the most complete contempt for the world, a much deeper understanding of the words of Ecclesiastes: "vanity of vanities, and all is vanity," except to love God and serve Him alone. The second effect is an intense desire for eternal things; the soul continually sighs after God. The third effect is a love of trials for the sake of God. So strong was this impulse in St. Theresa that she used to say: "Lord, either let me suffer or let me die"; nor did she ask this only on account of its merit but also because of the solace which she found in enduring pains.

There results a most ardent thirst for the living God and the almost continual exercise of heroic virtues, of the perfect imitation of Jesus Christ, and of a life of reparation for the conversion of sinners. The soul so disposes itself finally for eternal life that it has no need after death of passing through purgatory.

These effects produced in the lives of the saints render apparent the supreme efficacy of grace, arousing that which is best in them, namely, the free determination of their meritorious acts, which proceed from the infused virtues with the help of the gifts. Thus do they penetrate much more deeply the sense of our Lord's words: "Without Me you can do nothing" in the order of salvation, and those words of St. Paul: "For who distinguisheth thee? Or what hast thou that thou hast not received?" "I know both how to be brought low, and I know how to abound. . . . I can do all things in Him who strengtheneth me." That is, as St. Thomas observes in his Commentary on the Epistle to the Philippians (4:13): "I should not be able to endure these offenses unless the hand of God sustained me, according to Ezechiel (3:14): 'The hand of the Lord was with me,' and Isaias (40:31): 'They that hope in the Lord shall renew their strength, they shall take wings as eagles, they shall run and not be weary, they shall walk and not faint.'"

All this evidence confirms the doctrine according to which the grace of God is efficacious not extrinsically, on account of our foreseen consent, but of itself, intrinsically, because God wills it to be efficacious and, by it, to lead us, even through the greatest persecutions, unto life eternal.

Further confirmation from the inspiration of the Bible. Leo XIII, in his encyclical *Providentissimus Deus,* 1893 (Denz., no. 1952), thus explains the inspiration of the Bible through a movement which infallibly impels the intellect and will of the sacred writer to write freely what God wills and nothing else: "God by His supernatural power so stirred and moved them to write and so assisted them while they wrote that they might rightly conceive, will to set down faithfully, and aptly express with infallible truth all and only that which He should commend; otherwise He Himself would not be the author of the whole of Sacred Scripture." But if in this case infallibly efficacious divine motion does not destroy liberty, neither does it do so in other cases.[8]

5. EFFICACIOUS GRACE IN CHRIST, IMPECCABLE AND FREELY OBEDIENT

The question of the efficacy of grace is illustrated by what is said on the part of St. Thomas and his school by way of reconciling the free obedience of Christ with His impeccability; cf. IIIa, q. 18, a. 4. Christ was freely obedient unto the death of the cross, thus meriting our salvation, and yet He obeyed infallibly, through efficacious grace, so that He could not have sinned by disobedience; for He was not only sinless, but absolutely impeccable. Nowhere else does it appear so clearly that the predetermining divine decree with grace infallibly efficacious of itself (in respect to the heroic acts of Christ suffering for us on the cross) was simultaneous with the free will requisite for strictly meritorious acts (otherwise Christ would not have merited for us, properly speaking).

But if in one single instance grace efficacious in itself does not destroy free will, but rather actualizes and perfects it, no one can say that this grace, when given, of itself destroys our liberty. Hence this question should be carefully studied with reference to Christ Himself.

It is always advisable to have recourse to the great theological problems which are often not correctly propounded and the profundity of which always demands greater penetration. In these lofty matters, positive theology does not suffice; it gathers up certain documents of Holy Scripture and tradition, but does not furnish a deep understanding of them. Thus frequently various opinions of theologians are set forth and discussed from the historical aspect, and thereupon many writers choose from among these opinions by the eclectic system whatever subjectively appeals to them, without any objective reason. Indeed, it is said over and over again that one should proceed historically and critically; but this eclectic method does not produce a scientific theological work. It would be necessary, to begin with, to state the difficulty of the problem accurately so that its depth and sig-

[8] Cf. J. M. Vosté, O.P., *De divina inspiratione et veritate S. Scripturae*, Rome, 1932, 2nd ed., pp. 45–47, 66–68.

nificance may appear; and then, for its solution, it does not suffice to have recourse to whatever appeals to one subjectively, but rather to very certain objective principles. Otherwise the sublimity of faith is minimized, and theology is not directed toward the fruitful understanding of revealed mysteries nor toward their contemplation.

An example of this defect in method is to be found in the great problem of reconciling the free obedience of Christ with His impeccability. In the question of harmonizing two extremes difficult to reconcile, the first rule of method is this: not to deny one of the two extremes to be reconciled. Such an attempt would not solve the problem, but only do away with it. Nor have many authors been sufficiently aware of this with reference to the present question.

If Christians are asked: "Did not Christ obey the commands of His Father in perfect liberty and with real merit?" all, or almost all, reply in the affirmative. Likewise, their answer is an assent when questioned: "Was not Christ impeccable?" But frequently they do not concern themselves with the difficulty involved in reconciling these two statements which they accept as certain and utterly tenable.

The crux of the problem. However, the difficulty in such a harmonization is made manifest by the following classical objection: He who obeys freely is capable of not obeying. Hence if Christ obeyed the commands of His Father freely, He was capable of not obeying, that is, able to sin; therefore He was thoroughly sinless but not absolutely impeccable, as is generally held. On the other hand, if Christ was absolutely impeccable, He did not obey freely, with freedom from necessity or free will, but only with freedom from coercion, or spontaneity, which exists even in brute beasts. So did the Jansenists declare. According to them, "in order to merit, man does not require freedom from necessity; freedom from coercion suffices," that is, spontaneity (Denz., no. 1094). For the Jansenists and, with still greater reason, for the Calvinists, efficacious grace united with a precept does not permit of any power to do the contrary; in their opinion this power appears only at the expense of efficacious grace. This is the divided sense of Calvin which is confused in several, even recent, manuals with the divided sense of Thomists whose doctrine would thereby become heretical. Such confusion denotes an ignorance of the question, as will be made evident below.

Briefly stated, the present difficulty now to be examined is: either Christ could refrain from a commanded act and thus could sin, even if He did not in fact sin; that is, in that case He would not be impeccable although He would be sinless; or He could not refrain from a commanded act and thus would not be free in obeying with freedom from necessity, nor consequently would He merit. Hence it seems that impeccability and free obedience exclude one another in Christ. This is the antinomy to be solved.

That the difficulty may appear in a clearer light, it should be remarked that, just as Christ was not only unerring, but infallible, so was He not only sinless in fact, but absolutely impeccable *de jure,* by right, i.e., He could not sin. Christ was actually sinless i.e., *de facto,* according as efficacious grace was always given to Him. Thus those who preserve their innocence until death are saved at least from mortal sin by efficacious grace. But under this efficacious grace they never resist, although they are capable of resisting, so far as there remains in them the wretched power of sinning, which did not exist in Christ. Not only was efficacious grace always given to Him in fact, but it was due to Him *de jure,* i.e., by right, and thus not only was Jesus actually sinless, but absolutely impeccable *de jure,* by right of law of His nature, and this for three reasons.

1. By reason of the divine person of the Word, or the hypostatic union, He absolutely could not sin, either by bringing sin into contact with this union or by sin destroying the hypostatic union. For the sin would recoil upon the very person of the Word, inasmuch as actions are imputed to the person. Furthermore, all the actions of the human will of Christ were not only eminently righteous but theandric, and of infinite meritorious value by reason of the divine person of the Word.

2. Christ was absolutely impeccable by reason of the inamissible fullness of grace and charity which was, in Him, the sequel to the hypostatic union.

3. Christ was absolutely impeccable by reason of the beatific vision which He received at the instant of His conception and of the creation of His soul. Like the blessed spirits, He could not turn away from the clear vision of God nor could He love any the less God thus clearly seen.

How, then, could Christ, who was not only sinless but absolutely impeccable on three scores, freely obey the commands of His Father? It seems that He could not, since He could not disobey. In form the difficulty is thus stated formally: He who obeys freely is capable of disobeying. But Christ, who was absolutely impeccable, could not disobey. Therefore Christ did not obey freely the divine precepts whether positive or of the natural law.

At first sight, this objection appears to be thoroughly scientific, critical, and irrefutable. But, after the fashion of nominalism or empiricism, it considers only the facts and not the nature of things. It does not grasp the nature of the specifying object of free choice, which is an object not good in every respect; nor does it fathom the nature of the command and the grace which are given for the fulfillment of a free act and not for the destruction of liberty. Thus, under the appearance of keen intelligence, this beautiful sophism masks an utter misapprehension of the problem, just as in present-day existentialism, which is merely a new form of radical nominalism and absolute empiricism, there is a complete lack of understanding with regard to human life as such and its end. This failure to comprehend the higher realms of theology is known as spiritual dullness and blindness of soul, which are opposed to the gifts of wisdom and understanding. St. Thomas expressly refers to them when he treats of these gifts.

I am dwelling on this fundamental objection, which is stronger than all others that may be proposed. And it should be remarked that this objection is easier to understand than the reply to it, since the former proceeds by the inferior method of our knowledge which scarcely goes beyond sensible objects, while, on the contrary, the real reply is drawn from the sublimity of the mystery to be safeguarded, and requires great penetration and intellectual maturity.

It is indeed easy enough to see vaguely what is erroneous in this objection, but it is most difficult to set down precisely in what this error consists, just as it is easy to detect some disturbance in the movement of a clock or of a diseased heart or in the voice of a great singer, but often most difficult to discover precisely the cause of the disturbance and the effective remedy to be applied.

St. Thomas' solution. The Angelic Doctor recognized this difficulty and thus expressed it in *III Sent.,* d. 18, a. 2, objection 5: "By natural (operations, such as breathing) we do not merit because of the fact that they are determined to one end. But in Christ, free will was determined to the good (since He was impeccable); therefore He could not merit by His free will, and accordingly by no means at all, since all merit depends upon free will." Hence it seems that two fundamental truths of Christian religion are contrary one to the other;

namely, that Christ was impeccable, and that, by obeying, He freely merited our salvation. But our whole Christian life is based on the infinite value of the merits of Christ, and in particular on His heroic obedience.

St. Thomas states the same objection more succinctly and boldly in the *Summa theologica,* IIIa, q. 18, a. 4: Whether there was free will in Christ. In the third objection he says: "Free will possesses the alternative (of willing or not willing). But the will of Christ was determined to the good, since He could not sin, as declared above. Therefore in Christ there was no free will." Consequently He did not obey freely, nor did He merit, strictly speaking. It is clear from this that our adversaries did not discover this objection; it is already admirably formulated in the works of St. Thomas.

The holy doctor answers in the *Summa theologica,* as in the Commentary on the Sentences: "The will of Christ, although determined to the good, is not however determined to this or that good (for instance, to choosing Peter rather than John as His vicar). And therefore it pertained to Christ to choose, by His free will confirmed in good, as in the case of the blessed."

This was the lofty solution which many theologians subsequently failed to consider as they should have done. St. Thomas also declared in *Sent., loc. cit.:* "To be capable of sin is neither freedom of will nor a part of liberty, as St. Anselm says. And in fact this determination (that is, to moral good) is identified with the perfection of free will whereby, through the habit of grace and glory, it terminates in that to which it is naturally ordained, namely, the good."

Hence St. Thomas' solution is that Christ freely obeyed the precepts of His Father by His free will confirmed in good, in the same way as pertains to the blessed in heaven. Further, the holy doctor shows (IIIa, q. 47 ad 2) in the course of the article that Christ died through obedience, according to the words of St. John (10:18): "I have power to lay it [My life] down. . . . This commandment have I received of My Father."

Many later theologians have failed to consider these golden words attentively. In St. Thomas, however, they were highly characteristic and are verified in his opinion wherever confirmation in grace is involved. Thus after Pentecost the apostles were confirmed in grace and henceforth could not sin, at least gravely; but they obeyed the commands of God freely when something not good in every respect was commanded them, since the indifference of free will remained with regard to such an object. Likewise the Blessed Virgin Mary, confirmed in grace, freely obeyed the precepts of the Lord. In the same way the souls in purgatory, confirmed in good, can no longer sin and freely adore God whom they do not yet clearly see. And similarly, as already remarked by St. Thomas (*Sent., loc. cit.*), although the blessed in heaven do not freely love God clearly seen (since God clearly seen is an object in every respect good), they nevertheless freely obey God in the accomplishment of any particular good; and they freely pray for such and such a wayfarer rather than for another. In sum, God Himself is at the same time absolutely impeccable and utterly free to create, and to create this world rather than another. And likewise, at the opposite extreme, the demon hates God freely, not of necessity, but through his freedom confirmed in evil, as St. Thomas observes in several places.

In the mind of the Angelic Doctor, confirmation in grace, which excludes sin, in no wise excludes free obedience to the divine commands which involve an object that is not, in every respect, good. Wherefore? Because, as explained in Ia IIae, q. 10, a. 2: "If some object is proposed to the will which is universally good and is so from every aspect (such as the clear vision of God), the will tends to it of necessity (although spontaneously) if it wills anything at all; for it cannot will the opposite. But if some object is proposed to it which is not good from every possible aspect, the will does not incline to it necessarily," but freely. In short, the will retains a dominating indifference with regard to any object which is not in every respect good, for example, regarding the acceptance of the painful death of the cross for our sake. Furthermore, neither the divine command nor efficacious grace deprives the soul of this psychological liberty, since they are given precisely to actualize free will, and that which actualizes free will does not destroy it.

This was the magnificent, sublime solution offered by St. Thomas. He did not deny the impeccability of Christ nor His free obedience to commands properly so called, but found their harmonization in the lofty concept of the confirmation of free will in good. Thus did he offer a fertile understanding of the mystery and disposed it for contemplation.

St. Thomas' solution may be stated briefly as follows: an object which is not in every respect good, such as a painful death for our salvation, is chosen freely; moreover, the confirmation of free will in good does not take away free will with regard to things commanded, but rather perfects it. Such is the case with the blessed. And so, in Christ, while He was both a wayfarer and a comprehensor, there was the freedom necessary for merit when He obeyed, in the strict sense, unto the death of the cross. This most painful death was not an object in every respect good; it did not draw the will of Christ irresistibly, as a work of God clearly seen would do. Further, the command and the efficacious grace were conferred for freely accomplishing this holocaust; they therefore did not take away the liberty of this infinitely meritorious act. Hence Christ was the supreme exemplar of obedience. Thus the elements of the problem are perfectly reconciled, in spite of the obscurity of the mystery.

Nevertheless many subsequent theologians have failed to understand this sublime solution, taking another direction wherein the problem became insoluble and therefore was left unsolved; rather, by negation, did it deprive Christ of obedience in the strict sense, so that He would not have been free with respect to things commanded but only in other matters. Thus there was no longer a question of reconciliation, since one of the two extremes to be reconciled was denied.

What, then, is the source of these other solutions? Many theologians since the time of St. Thomas, notably the Molinists, began with this assumption: To preserve psychological liberty, or free will under precept and efficacious grace, it does not suffice that power to do the opposite should remain, but it is required that the will be able to unite the opposite act with the divine command and efficacious grace, or at least the omission of the command, that is, by sinning at least through omission.

The answer to this is: If this is so, that Socrates may freely sit down, it does not suffice that he be capable of standing up or of remaining seated at the same time, but it is required that he unite the very act of standing with sitting, or that he has the power to sit and to stand at the same time, which is impossible. Efficacious grace united to actual resistance would no longer be efficacious.

But even if we admit this presupposition, the problem originally proposed becomes insoluble. There could not be agreement between Christ's free obedience to the commands of His Father and His absolute impeccability. Hence, if they were commands in the strict sense, an impeccable Christ did not obey them freely, and consequently did not merit by the merit of obedience properly so called. The problem is not solved, but declared unsolvable and dismissed. Anyone who is willing to accept such a verdict while at the same time holding to the principles of St. Thomas injects the most acute dissonance into Thomism, comparable to the striking of a false note in a Beethoven symphony.

The difficulty is evidently connected intimately with the subject of efficacious grace. For it poses the question, whether under divine precept and grace efficacious of itself, in the impeccable Christ, His obedience remained free and meritorious. Does the confirming of free will in good take away free will regarding precepts? This is precisely the question to be solved.

Besides the opinion of St. Thomas and Thomists, there are two other opinions. Some authors maintain that Christ did not receive from His Father a real precept to die for our salvation. This is held by Lorca, who quotes Paludanus, and later by Petau, Franzelin, L. Billot, in his *De incarnatione,* theses 29 and 30, and, with some modification, by Father M. de la Taille: *Mysterium fidei,* elucid. 7 and 8.[9] According to this opinion, Christ was not free in things of precept, either of natural or of positive law, because it is physically impossible for a comprehensor to will not to obey. And Christ would not have been free unless He could combine disobedience with the precept. Thence arises a great disadvantage in this opinion; namely, Christ would not be the supreme exemplar of obedience "unto death, even the death of the cross."

Others, after an eclectic fashion, declare that Christ received from His Father a precept determining only the substantial element of death, but not the circumstances of time, manner, the cross, etc. This opinion is maintained by Vasquez, Disp. 74, c. 5; De Lugo, Disp. 26, sect. 7, no. 82; sect. 8, no. 102; Lessius, *De summo bono,* Bk. II, no. 185. Tournely holds that Christ could obtain a dispensation from the precept. This eclectic viewpoint agrees with the preceding one that

[9] Father de la Taille concedes to Thomists, however, that Christ had a real moral obligation to die, but, according to his view, this obligation did not arise from a command of the Father; Christ contracted it by offering Himself to the Father at the Last Supper, that He might die for us. But this does not hold for the precepts of the natural law, which do not depend on their acceptance by Christ, nor for the precept received from the Father of which Christ speaks (John 10:18) before offering Himself to the Father at the Last Supper, that He might die for us.

Christ was not free with respect to things of precept, for example, He did not freely accept the precept of dying for our sakes, but only the circumstances of His death which were not of precept. This solution does not penetrate the intellectual problem to be solved, but is only a material transposition of the elements of the problem. Moreover, the Church has always affirmed that Christ merited our salvation by His death and passion, and not merely by the circumstances of His death. Cf. Council of Trent (Denz., nos. 799 ff.).

Thomists hold, on the other hand, that Christ received from His Father a true precept, in the strict sense, to accept death for our sake, a precept determining both His death and the circumstances of His death, which Christ nevertheless freely offered on the cross; that is, He was properly free also in things strictly of precept, by a perfect liberty confirmed in good. (Cf. among Thomists, John of St. Thomas, Gonet, the Salmanticenses, Billuart, etc.; see also *Dictionnaire de théologie catholique,* article "Jésus Christ" by A. Michel, col. 1304.) I have dealt with this question at length in a recent work, *De Christo salvatore,* Turin, 1946, pp. 324–44. To a certain extent, St. Robert Bellarmine agrees with Thomists in this matter (*De justific.,* Bk. V, chap. 11), but, together with Suarez, he explains it by *scientia media,* which Thomists do not admit. Long before, St. Bernard had beautifully said of Christ: "He lost His life, lest He should lose obedience" (Sermon on the Temple soldiery, chap. 13).

Nevertheless this is a question of grave significance. For if Christ's liberty in things of precept is denied, He is no longer the exemplar of every virtue and of conformity with the divine will which issues precept. But to maintain such an opinion seems entirely thoughtless and injurious to Christ. Nor should the highest mysteries of faith be minimized for the sake of reaching an apparent clarity, which rather withdraws one from divine contemplation than disposes for it. The first thing to be considered is that faith deals with things unseen and likewise contemplation proceeding from a lively faith, illuminated by the gifts of the Holy Ghost. Hence the theological method in such matters, as it should be remarked, must not deny or minimize truths that are most certain in the present question: Christ's impeccability and His free obedience.

In these great questions some neglect the best commentators on St. Thomas, even when they are in agreement. Nevertheless they understood his teaching much more perfectly than we do. On the contrary, Leo XIII, in his encyclical *Aeterni Patris* warns: "And, lest it happen that the counterfeit supplant the genuine, and the impure instead of the pure waters be drunken down, see to it that the wisdom of Thomas be drawn from its own fountains, or from streamlets running directly from the fountain itself, which are adjudged fresh and pure by the positive and unanimous verdict of learned men." Therefore Leo XIII desired the commentaries of Cajetan and Ferrariensis to be reprinted in the Leonine edition. To attempt to reach a deep grasp of the doctrine of St. Thomas while neglecting the best commentators is like undertaking the ascent of a lofty mountain without an experienced guide, with the danger of wandering from the right path and falling into a precipice.

Proof of the Thomistic opinion. The opinion of Thomists, however, is thus proved. 1. Christ received a precept in the strict sense of the word to accept the death of the cross for our salvation. 2. Nevertheless Christ's liberty remained, as a perfect image of the impeccable liberty of God; the precept was given for the free accomplishment of the act and hence did not deprive Him of psychological liberty.

1. Christ had a real obligation of accepting death for our sake on account of the Father's precept. For we read in John 10:17 f.: "Therefore doth the Father love Me: because I lay down My life, that I may take it again. No man taketh it away from Me: but I lay it down Myself, and I have power to lay it down; and I have power to take it up again. This commandment have I received of My Father." There is no reason for saying that this is a command in the broad sense of the term. Indeed somewhat further on in St. John's Gospel (14:30 f.) after the account of the Last Supper, occur the words of our Lord: "For the prince of this world cometh, and in Me he hath not anything. But that the world may know that I love the Father: and as the Father hath given Me the commandment, so do I." It is strictly a question of a precept to die for our salvation, for the word: ἐγτελλω, ἐντολη, used to express the command of the Father in these two places is always, in the New Testament, a technical term signifying a divine command in the strict sense; cf. Matt. 5:19 and 22:36: "He therefore that shall break one of these least commandments, . . . shall be called the least in the kingdom of heaven"; "Master, which is the great commandment in the law?"

Moreover, we find in St. John (15:10): "If you keep My commandments, you shall abide in My love; as I also have kept My Father's commandments, and do abide in His love." In this text, Christ uses the same word for the precepts imposed upon Him by His Father and those which He imposed upon His apostles; but the latter were precepts strictly speaking. Thus Christ was an exemplar of perfect obedience. Furthermore, this last text is concerned not only with the precept of dying, but with all the precepts of the Father which Christ observed and in fact observed freely and meritoriously for our sake.

The thesis which affirms that Christ was not free regarding things of precept appears to be irreconcilable with the text just quoted. But many of these precepts, those, for instance, of the natural law, are antecedent to Christ's spontaneous oblation and therefore do not have their force from it, as Father de la Taille thought.

There are other texts which express Christ's free obedience to the divine precepts: "Father, if Thou wilt, remove this chalice from Me: but yet not My will, but Thine be done" (Luke 22:42). The purport of the words is almost identical in Heb. 10:7: "Behold I come: in the head of the book it is written of Me: that I should do Thy will, O God." And again in Phil. 2:8: "He humbled Himself, becoming obedient unto death, even to the death of the cross"; and Rom. 5:19: "For as by the disobedience of one man, many were made sinners; so also by the obedience of one, many shall be made just." Here it is a question of obedience properly speaking, as it is of Adam's disobedience in the strict sense. But obedience properly so called has as its formal object the command of a superior in the strict sense, not his mere counsel. It should be added that having recourse to a counsel does not help in saving Christ's liberty, for it is inconsistent with our Lord's consummate sanctity that He should be capable of omitting or neglecting the counsels of God the Father, especially counsels supported by an eternal decree and ordained for the salvation of men as well as to the greater glory of God. In fact, regardless of any precept, the death of Christ with all its circumstances remains predetermined by the absolute will of God; cf. Luke 22:22: "The Son of man indeed goeth, according to that which is determined: but yet, woe to that man by whom He shall be betrayed"; and Acts 2:23: "This same [Jesus] being delivered up, by the determinate counsel and foreknowledge of God, you by the hands of wicked men have crucified and slain." Since Christ knew this divine will, it would have been no less inconsistent for Him not to conform to it than to sin. Nor may it be held, therefore, with Tournely, that Christ could have obtained a dispensation from the precept; for thus the merit of obedience would disappear, and the argument would not hold in the case of the precepts of the natural law, which did not depend upon Christ's acceptance of them.

2. How, then, under the precept to die and under efficacious grace, did the impeccable Christ remain freely obedient? In the first place, it is certain that the human liberty of Christ is the purest image of impeccable, uncreated freedom. But God is at the same time absolutely impeccable and perfectly free, for instance, to create or not to create, or to create this world rather than another. Hence Christ, likewise, as man, has a will which was at once impeccable and free with regard to every object which is not good in every respect. Christ as God possessed liberty only in the order of good, not indeed in the order of evil; since the power of sinning or peccability, like fallibility, is a form of our defectibility, which cannot exist in perfect liberty. For liberty is defined as "the faculty of choosing the means properly ordained to the end" (Ia, q. 62, a. 8 ad 3). Hence the choice of something which deviates from the order of the end is a defect of liberty, just as it is a defect of reason to proceed while overlooking the order of principles. This is quite obvious.

In order that it may be evident that Christ's liberty is the purest image of the liberty of God, it must be emphasized that, whereas God does indeed love Himself of necessity, yet He loves His creatures freely, that His goodness may be manifested, as it is the reason for loving creatures. Similarly, Christ as man, at once a wayfarer and a comprehensor, loved God clearly seen with a necessary, although spontaneous, love; but He loved the divine goodness freely as it is the reason for loving creatures, that is, an object not in every respect good.[10]

It is true, of course, that uncreated, impeccable liberty is not subordinate to any precept, while, on the contrary, Christ as man was obliged to obey the precepts of His Father, as has been said; and it seems that a precept deprives one of liberty.

Reply. A precept indeed morally binds, that is, it takes away moral freedom with respect to the evil forbidden by it; in other words, it renders illicit the contrary act or even the contrary omission. But a

---

[10] Furthermore, as Capreolus, Ferrariensis, and Soto remark, in Christ His love of God, regulated not by the beatific vision but by infused knowledge, was free, and distinguished in its modal species from the beatific love of God known as He is.

precept does not deprive one of psychological liberty with respect to the thing commanded, since it is given precisely that the act may be accomplished freely and meritoriously. Hence, if the precept took away psychological liberty, it would destroy itself. St. Thomas speaks in equivalent terms, IIIa, q. 47, a. 2 ad 2. The fact remains that free choice is specified by the object of the precept itself; and this object, for example, a painful death accepted for our sake, is something not good under every aspect, and hence not attracting the human will infallibly.

A precept extrinsic to the will and superimposed upon it neither changes the will psychologically nor the nature of the eligible object by which free choice is specified. Rather, as has been said, the precept is given that the act of obedience may be fulfilled freely and also meritoriously, in the same way as efficacious grace itself is given. Therefore neither the precept nor the grace destroys liberty, since indifference of judgment remains regarding the aforsaid specifying object which is not in every respect good.

Refutation of the objection in form. There still remains, however, as we are told, the problem of solving the objection proposed in form as follows: He who obeys freely is capable of not obeying. But Christ who was absolutely impeccable could not disobey, that is, He did not even have the power of disobeying which we possess even when we actually do obey. Therefore Christ did not obey freely.

It is easier, as we have already observed, to understand this objection drawn from the inferior mode of our cognition, scarcely rising above sensible objects, than the solution which derives from the sublimity of the mystery to be safeguarded. The answer of Thomists is subtle, but at the same time profound, if carefully considered.

They answer: I distinguish the major; He who obeys freely is capable of disobeying either privatively, that is, by sinning at least through omission, or negatively only as, while obeying, he retains the power of not willing the object of choice commanded in some other way: granted. I counterdistinguish the minor: But the impeccable Christ could not disobey privatively, that is, by sinning: granted. That he could not disobey negatively I deny, since, while obeying, He retained the power of not willing the object of choice commanded in some other way.

This subtle distinction appears to some mere verbiage. On the contrary its significance becomes evident psychologically, for instance, when an excellent religious is obliged by obedience to accept a very difficult sacrifice. Often he is not even tempted to disobey privatively by sinning; but he sees perfectly well that the sacrifice asked of him is an object not good from every aspect and at the same time freely eligible. And so it was with Abraham in his sacrifice and with the Blessed Virgin Mary on Calvary.

However, that the profundity of the foregoing answer may be manifest, it should be recalled that there is a great difference between a simple negation and the privation of a good which is due, that is, an evil. Thus nescience, which is a mere negation, is commonly distinguished from ignorance, which is a privation, and with still greater reason from error. The Blessed Virgin Mary was nescient of many things, but not ignorant of them, strictly speaking, nor in error, since she knew all that she should know. To be ignorant, in the strict sense, is not to know that which we ought to know. I am nescient of the Chinese language, but not strictly ignorant of it.

There is another example of the distinction between negation and privation. If God had not created the world, there would not be the privation of any perfections in Him, but only their negation. For God is not better or wiser because He freely created the universe. "God is no greater for having created the universe," as Bossuet remarked, in opposition to Leibnitz. Free creation is indeed befitting, but it would not be less fitting not to create. God would not thereby have remained sterile, nor was He sterile from all eternity before He created.

What then is meant precisely by being capable of not obeying negatively as it is distinguished from the privation of obedience, or from the sin of disobedience? It is the power not to choose the object in some other way commanded according as this specifying object of choice is not good in every respect, but rather good under one aspect and not good under another.

Such, for Christ, was the death of the cross: most painful from one standpoint, and most fruitful from another. Thus Christ, so generously obedient, was capable of not obeying negatively, in the divided sense; that is, under this command and under efficacious grace, there remained in Him a power for the opposite, which was not the wretched power of sinning. Thus, He was not only sinless in fact but absolutely impeccable *de jure,* that is, by the very law of His nature, and nevertheless still free in things of precept.

In other words, there remained in Christ indifference of judgment and of will toward this eligible object; and in order that a choice should be made in fact, the liberty of Christ had to intervene; but this never failed to choose aright since, as St. Thomas said, it was "confirmed in good." That is, the freedom of Christ always intervened in favor of perfect righteousness: 1. because Christ was an impeccable divine person; 2. because He possessed an inamissible fullness of grace and charity; and 3. because He had the beatific vision, and, moreover, always received efficacious grace to obey freely and meritoriously, nor was there in His soul even the slightest inclination to privative disobedience, or sin. If Abraham, preparing to immolate his son, had not the least inclination to disobey privatively, if the same is true of the Blessed Virgin Mary on Calvary, with still greater reason is it true of Christ Himself. Thus, psychologically, there is a great difference between being capable of disobeying privatively, or sinning, and being capable of not obeying negatively, that is, of not choosing the eligible object in some other way commanded.

Hence Christ had the power of refusing death as such and as in some other respect commanded, but not death as a command. In other words, Christ obeyed freely, not in the sense that He could have done anything contrary to the precept, but in the sense that He was capable of not doing that which was in some other respect commanded. Thus freedom of exercise remained to Him. Christ was not able to divide positively, that is, as it were, He could not separate the negation of death from the command; but He could have divided the negation of death and the command precisively. Similarly, in an object which is at once true and good, the intelligence, on attaining the true, does not separate it from the good, but it does prescind from the good. Likewise the essence of an angel or of an immortal soul cannot be separated from its existence, and yet it is in reality distinct from the latter, since, as our mind considers them, the angel is not its own essence, nor is the immortal soul its own essence, in which respect they differ from God.

Again, under efficacious grace, our will can resist if it wills, but under this grace it never wills to do so. But this is unintelligible to the nominalists who consider only the fact, which in the present case is the concrete act of the will, and not its nature specified by an object not in every respect good.

Furthermore, it should be remarked that liberty of equal choice or balance is rare, that is, with regard to two equally good and eligible objects, as when a mason builds a wall of identical stones, and freely chooses any stone for the upper part of the wall and any other for the lower part. Generally liberty is present without this perfect balance; for example, when a man chooses the virtuous good in preference to a delectable but vicious good. Hence liberty is defined by St. Thomas (Ia IIae, q. 10, a. 2) as the dominating indifference of the will with regard to an object not in every respect good; he does not say, with regard to an object equally good from one aspect and not good from another. Even if the goodness of the object in one respect seems far to exceed its deficiency in another (for instance, God not yet clearly seen), liberty still remains.

Moreover, our mind does not pass from a speculative-practical judgment (I see what is better and approve) to a practico-practical judgment (I pursue the worse, judging here and now that it should be chosen), unless our will is already incipiently and actually attracted to the object which, in fact, it chooses. Thus an adulterer never abstains from his sin unless his attachment to this sin is actually removed; nevertheless as long as this attachment remains, he freely commits sin.

Likewise in the present case, Christ would never have refrained from the act of obeying unless the precept had been removed, but as long as this precept remained He obeyed freely. The eligible object specifying His choice was not in every respect good, and the superimposed precept given for the free accomplishment of the act did not destroy liberty. Similarly, confirmation in good, conferred for the perfecting of His liberty, did not destroy it, obviously. Therefore freedom from necessity remained with regard to an object not in every respect good, and hence not infallibly drawing the will.

Herein appears the vast difference between our adherence to the ontological value of the first principles of reason and Christ's adherence to the precept of dying for our sake. I have never retracted what I said against the philosophy of action: it erroneously maintains that our adherence to the ontological value of the first principles of reason is free. As St. Thomas declares (Ia IIae, q. 17, a. 6), speaking of the real value of first principles: "Assent or dissent to these is not within our power, but in the order of nature; and therefore strictly speaking, is subject to the command of nature." On the contrary, Christ freely chose to accept the death of the cross for our salvation; this object, from one aspect, was most painful, from another exceedingly noble and fruitful. Thus it was freely willed, not with a diminished liberty, but with perfect liberty, since the precept given for the free accomplishment of the act directed but did not destroy liberty. Likewise confirmation in good did not injure it, but brought it to the highest perfection.

This sublime doctrine is wonderfully expressed by St. Thomas in the classic text we have already quoted at the beginning of this discussion, IIIa, q. 18, a. 4 ad 3: 1. "The will of Christ, although determined toward the good, is not however determined toward this or that particular good. And therefore it pertains to Christ to choose by means of His free will confirmed in good, as in the case of the blessed." [11] These few words of St. Thomas are worth more than all the long dissertations which have been written subsequently by theologians who abandoned them, declaring that "Christ was not free in regard to things of precept." If this were so, Christ would not

[11] In the same way, according to St. Thomas, our will, under efficacious grace, is capable of resisting (the power of the opposite act remains), but it never does. For, as the holy doctor writes (Ia IIae, q. 10, a. 4 ad 3): "if God moves the will toward anything, it is incompatible with this assumption that the will should not be so moved (otherwise divine motion would not be efficacious). But it is not absolutely impossible," since the power of the opposite act remains.

Ia, q. 19, a. 8: "Since the divine will is most efficacious, it not only follows that those things are done which God wills should be done, but that they are done in the way God wills them to be done; but God wills that certain things should be done of necessity, others contingently." And in the answer to the second objection (*ibid.*): "From this fact that nothing resists the divine will it follows not only that those things are done which God wills should be done, but that they are done contingently or of necessity, according to His will."

De veritate, q. 22, a. 8: "Every act of the will, inasmuch as it is an act, is not only from the will as its immediate agent, but also from God as its primary agent, who impresses it even more forcibly; hence, just as the will can change its act, so to a still greater extent can God."

De malo, q. 6, a. 1 ad 3: God moves the will immutably on account of the efficacy of His moving power, which cannot fail; but because of the nature of the will moved, which is indifferent to various things, necessity is not produced and liberty remains. . . . God moves all things proportionately, each according to its mode."

Thus did St. Thomas ever interpret the words of Holy Scripture: "The heart of the king is in the hand of the Lord: whithersoever He will He shall turn it" (cf. *Contra Gentes,* Bk. III, chap. 89); "It is God who worketh in you, both to will and to accomplish, according to His good will"; "For who distinguisheth thee? Or what hast thou that thou hast not received? And if thou hast received, why dost thou glory, as if thou hadst not received it?" It is therefore not a useless process to explain the *Summa theologica* article by article; it is not enough merely to consult it, dip into it, or quote one part while neglecting another.

be the supreme exemplar of obedience in the strict sense of the word.

The absolute impeccability of Christ is therefore not irreconcilable with His liberty with regard to things of precept. Consequently neither His freedom nor His merit should be set within limits. It suffices to consider: 1. that the will of Christ is the purest image of the divine will, at once utterly impeccable and perfectly free with regard to creatures; and 2. that a precept, although it withdraws moral freedom regarding the object forbidden, does not remove psychological liberty with respect to means not necessarily and intrinsically connected, here and now, with beatitude. Indeed, every precept presupposes and affirms this psychological liberty, so far as it is ordained to the accomplishment of a free act and, were it to take away such liberty, it would destroy its own nature as a precept.

This illuminating doctrine yields a fruitful understanding of the mystery of Redemption and disposes one for the contemplation of divine things, inasmuch as this opinion, and it alone, presents Christ as the supreme exemplar of obedience to the divine commands, in the strict sense of the term. Thus, the sublimity of His words suffers no diminution: "Therefore doth the Father love Me, because I lay down My life . . . for My sheep. . . . This commandment have I received of My Father." "As the Father hath given Me commandment, so do I." "If you keep My commandments, you shall abide in My love; as I also have kept My Father's commandments, and do abide in His love." "Behold I come: . . . that I should do Thy will, O God." Thus truly and strictly "Christ was obedient unto death, even the death of the cross." May those who do not accept this opinion at least recognize its great probability and sublimity and the fact that St. Thomas himself so taught.

Corollary. But if Christ's liberty remains under grace efficacious in itself, notwithstanding the triple cause of His impeccability (the hypostatic union, His inamissible fullness of grace, and the beatific vision), with still greater reason does our liberty remain under grace efficacious of itself; with it we indeed never sin, but we possess the mournful power of sinning, which Christ did not have; under grace which is efficacious in itself our free will is capable of dissenting if it so wills, but with this grace it never does so will. That is, we cannot, of course, unite actual resistance with grace that is efficacious of itself; it would no longer be efficacious. In the same way Socrates cannot unite the act of sitting with that of standing; he cannot do both at the same time. This would be absolutely impossible and contradictory.

But for Socrates to be free to seat himself it suffices that, at one and the same time, he be capable of rising and standing erect. Similarly, that we be at liberty to follow the impulse of grace efficacious in itself, it suffices that the power to do the opposite remain in us. In other words, under efficacious grace the free will is capable of dissenting, in the divided sense. This is the meaning of the divided sense for St. Thomas and Thomists, entirely different from the divided sense of Calvin, who maintained that under efficacious grace the power to do the opposite did not remain, but that, once this grace had been removed, the power to do the opposite was restored to us. Hence it must be concluded: If in Christ, infallibly and freely obedient, grace, efficacious in itself, did not destroy His liberty, there is no basis for the statement that this grace of itself destroys our liberty. On the contrary, far from injuring it in any way, it actualizes and perfects it, causing together with us our free choice; cf. Ia, q. 19, a. 8.

So ends this excursus on efficacious grace as related to the spiritual life, in the saints, more especially the martyrs, and in the impeccable and freely obedient Christ. Let us now return to the explanation of the text of St. Thomas treating of the cause of grace.

CHAPTER IX

QUESTION 112

THE CAUSE OF GRACE

▬▬

AFTER considering the end of grace, or its necessity for our final end, the essence and divisions of grace, St. Thomas next examines its cause, particularly its efficient cause (article 1), and at the same time the disposition for grace on the part of the recipient (articles 2 and 3); this leads him to ask whether grace is equal in all men (article 4) and whether a person may know that he possesses grace (article 5).

ARTICLE I. WHETHER GOD ALONE IS THE CAUSE OF GRACE

State of the question. It refers directly to habitual grace and indirectly to actual grace, according as it is a motion toward habitual grace to which it disposes. Furthermore the question concerns only the principal efficient physical cause; because the humanity of Christ and the sacraments are instrumental causes of grace; cf. IIIa, q. 62, a. 5. The principal meritorious cause is, of course, Christ, as will be explained later, q. 114, a. 6.

The reply is: God alone can be the principal efficient cause of grace.

1. Proof from Sacred Scripture. "Who can make him clean that is conceived of unclean seed? is it not Thou who only art?" (Job 14:4); "The Lord will give grace and glory" (Ps. 83:12); cf. Isa. 43:25; Jer. 31:18; Lam. 5:21; Rom. 3:30; 8:33; II Cor. 3:5; Phil. 2:13, John 14:16. In all these texts it is declared that God alone can remit sin by justification. Cf. also the Council of Orange, can. 7, 9, 10, 14, 15, 20, 25; the Council of Trent, Sess. VI, chap. 7, on the justification of ˙nners.

2. Proof by apodictical theological argument. Nothing can, by its proper power, effectively produce anything of a higher order than its own. (Briefly: more is not produced by less.) But grace is of a higher order than any created agent since it is a participation in the divine nature. Therefore no created agent, but only God Himself, can be the principal, efficient, physical cause of grace.

Observe as to the minor that St. Thomas says: "grace surpasses every created nature," and not only, as in the case of miracles, all the powers and requirements of created nature. Grace transcends the miraculous; by the miracle of resurrection, natural life is restored supernaturally to a corpse whereas, on the other hand, grace is essentially supernatural life.

Confirmation. Just as fire alone can ignite, so God alone can deify, or bestow a participation in His intimate nature and in like manner a right to eternal life.

Objection. But a just man who already possesses grace can produce it in another.

Reply. If he possesses divine nature as he does human nature; granted; but he has only a participation in the divine nature, and thus, although he can enjoy it himself, he cannot communicate it to others, just as an adopted son cannot adopt. Nor can we produce intelligence in another unless, positing the ultimately apt disposition in the embryo for the reception of the intellectual soul, God creates it.

An angel cannot generate another angel, since an angel can be produced only by creation, that is, by God. And grace, as we shall presently see, cannot be drawn forth except from the obediential power of either a soul or an angel; but God alone can draw anything forth from the obediential power.

Reply to first objection. The humanity of Christ is the instrumental cause of the production of grace, acting, that is, by the power of God, the principal agent. Thus Christ, the head of the Church, infuses into us the grace which He obtained for us by His infinite merits. (IIIa, q. 8, a. 1.)

Reply to second objection. Likewise the sacraments cause grace only as instruments. This answer should be read; it is not limited in its application to the intentional power alone, in the sense of practically significant power.

Reply to third objection. An angel purifies, enlightens, and perfects a man by means of instruction, as does a spiritual director, not by infusing grace.

Doubt. With reference to this article Thomists ask whether grace is created or drawn forth from the obediential power of the soul. The answer generally given is that grace is neither created nor concreated but is educed from the obediential power of the soul.

1. This answer is based on many texts of St. Thomas, especially Ia IIae, q. 110, a. 2 ad 3, and q. 113, a. 9, where it is stated that "creation from the mode of operation, that is, out of nothing, is a greater work than justification; although on the part of the thing produced, justification is greater than the creation of heaven and earth." Again, in *De veritate,* q. 27, a. 3 ad 9, and the question on the virtues in general, a. 10 ad 2 and ad 13, St. Thomas teaches that supernatural habits are brought forth from the obediential power of the subject.

3. *Theological proof.* To be created is to be produced from no presupposed subject, whereas to be brought forth from the obediential power of some subject is to be produced dependently from this subject through a supernatural cause. But grace as an accident inhering in the soul is produced dependently from the substance of the soul through God, the supernatural cause. Therefore grace is not created but is brought forth from the obediential power of the soul.

The major contains its own definition both of creation and of eduction, but for a clear understanding of what is meant by eduction from the obediential power, it would be well to recall just what the obediential power is; we have treated the subject at length in *De revelatione,* I, 377. There is in any subject a passive power which is not natural, since it does not affirm an order to a natural agent, but is a passive power that affirms an order to a supernatural agent which it obeys so as to receive from it whatever it may wish to confer. Cf. IIIa, q. 11, a. 1; q. 1, a. 3 ad 3; *De virtutibus in communi,* a. 10 ad 2 and ad 13; *Compendium theol.,* chap. 104; *De potentia,* q. 6, a. 1, ad 18, and *Tabula aurea,* under "Potentia," no. 10. Thus even in the natural order the form of a statue is educed from the potentiality of the wood, inasmuch as the wood obeys the carver, or the clay the potter.

Minor. Grace is an accident inherent in the soul; therefore it depends on the substance of the soul in being, and hence likewise in becoming, inasmuch as becoming is a step toward being. Whence to be created is proper to a subsistent thing which possesses being independently of any subject. Therefore the conclusion follows.

It is conceded, however, that God, by His absolute power, could create grace independently of any subject, just as He can cause the Eucharistic accidents to exist independently of the subject; but this mode would be miraculous, and neither connatural nor according to

His ordinary power in the supernatural order, of which we are now speaking.

It cannot be said that grace is concreated as we say that the soul of the first man was concreated with his body; for in fact, as has been said, grace as an accident of the soul is made dependently upon it, whereas the intellectual soul is not educed from the potentiality of matter, like the souls in brute beasts, but is independent of matter in its becoming, just as it is intrinsically independent of it in its being and operation, whence it follows that it is immortal.

REFUTATION OF OBJECTIONS

First objection: In Sacred Scripture grace is said to be created: "Create a clean heart in me, O God" (Ps. 50:12); ". . . in Christ Jesus . . . a new creature" (Gal. 6:15); ". . . created in Christ Jesus" (Eph. 2:10).

Reply. Here is meant: created morally, not physically: morally, because it presupposes no merit; not physically because it presupposes a subject.

Second objection. It is concerned with the difficulty of rightly defining obediential power so as to safeguard at the same time both the absolute gratuitousness of grace and its conformity to the nature of the human soul.

For that which is eminently fitting to human nature cannot be absolutely gratuitous. But elevation to the vision of God is eminently fitting. Therefore it cannot be absolutely gratuitous. In other words, if grace is in conformity with, or becoming to, our nature and perfects it, it seems that the obediential power must be more than a mere non-aversion to accepting from God whatever He may will. But if this obediential power is more than a non-aversion, it is a slight entity distinct from the essence of the soul and its faculties, and hence is a positive ordination toward the life of grace and accordingly is at once something essentially natural as a property of nature, and something essentially supernatural specified by a supernatural object to be known and loved. And thus we are led to a confusion of the two orders.

Reply. We have examined this difficulty at length in our *De revelatione*, I, 399–402. The Salmanticenses also discuss it in connection with the present article.

There is certainly given to the human soul an obediential power to receive ever higher supernatural gifts, indeed, for the very hypostatic union, and even, in the most holy soul of Christ, for the greatest degree of the light of glory which God, by His absolute power, can produce. Wherefore St. Thomas declares in several places that the obediential power cannot be satisfied perfectly; for it is a capacity for receiving from God whatever He may will, and God can will and produce anything that is not contradictory. Therefore the obediential power, by its formal reason, is not a positive ordination of the nature of the human soul or its faculties toward a supernatural object, and signifies nothing more than a simple non-aversion, or capacity, to receive whatever God may will. However, by reason of its subject and materially, it is completely identified with the essence of the soul and its faculties, whether passive or active, which can be elevated to the order of grace. Hence the obediential power or capacity for being elevated regards immediately, not the supernatural object known and loved, but the supernatural agent which it obeys, that is, God who can elevate us, gratuitously and with perfect freedom.

Thus by its formal reason the obediential power signifies nothing but a non-aversion. However, God, by conferring His supernatural gifts does indeed perfect thereby the nature of the soul, raising it to a superior order. Thus these gifts of grace are, at one and the same time, completely gratuitous, in no sense due to us, and perfectly becoming to our nature, with a fitness which is not, however, natural but supernatural, at once most sublime, most profound, and gratuitous. Wherefore, with regard to the objection: that which is eminently fitting with a natural fitness cannot be gratuitous, granted; but with a supernatural fitness, denied. And this is the very mystery of the essence of grace, which is simultaneously something freely given and something which renders us pleasing.

ARTICLE II. WHETHER ANY PREPARATION OR DISPOSITION FOR GRACE IS REQUIRED ON THE PART OF MAN

State of the question. We are here concerned with the disposition toward habitual grace, for it is certain that no preparation on the part of man anticipating, so to speak, divine help, is demanded for actual grace; rather any preparation that may be found in man is produced by prevenient actual grace; cf. question 109, a. 6, above, and what is repeated here in the body of the article. With respect to the disposition for habitual grace, theologians generally agree that it is required on the part of man, but some insist that this disposition is only moral and of divine institution, not physical.

The conclusion of St. Thomas is: for habitual grace the preparation of another grace is prerequisite on the part of an adult in possession of his mental faculties. And this disposition is a motion or act of the free will in God.

First proof. By the authority of the Council of Trent, Sess. VI, chap. 6, (Denz., no. 798) and can. 9 (Denz., no. 819): "If anyone should say that by faith alone the wicked man is justified so as to mean that nothing else is required for cooperation with the grace of justification and that it is in no wise necessary to prepare or dispose himself by a movement of his will, let him be anathema." This definition is based on Holy Scripture: "Prepare your hearts unto the Lord" (I Kings 7:3) and "Turn ye to Me . . . and I will turn to you" (Zach. 1:3).

Second proof, from theological argument. A perfect and permanent form is not introduced into a subject, under ordinary providence, unless that subject is predisposed. But habitual grace is a perfect, permanent form. Therefore it is not introduced into a soul unless the soul is predisposed by the preparation which becomes its nature, that is, by a free act toward God, for man is free by nature. (This refers to adults.)

The major is always verified in the natural order, whether it is a question of substantial or of accidental form. Proportionately, and for the same reason, however, this must be true in the supernatural order. Thus the beatific vision requires that the intellect be disposed by the light of glory for union with the divine essence. Right order demands that from one extreme to the other, that is, from an utter privation to a form, the transition should only be made through certain means; hence, according to St. Thomas, no form can exist except in predisposed matter. Otherwise a monstrosity would result. And so some professors produce a monstrosity, proposing the loftiest doctrine without preliminary dispositions, so that then it is not understood and results in dangerous theory, for example, predestination as interpreted by Calvin.

Reply to first objection. St. Thomas observes that the imperfect preparation, which frequently precedes, in time, the infusion of habitual grace, is not meritorious, for habitual grace is the principle of merit. On the other hand, the preparation which is simultaneous with the infusion of habitual grace proceeds from it, and is therefore meritorious not of grace but of glory. Cf. q. 113, a. 8: The infusion of grace precedes, by nature, but not in time, this preparation, in which resides the primary act of charity and living faith.

Reply to second objection. The preparation which immediately precedes, in time, the infusion of grace, is generally made gradually, under the influence of actual grace, but it may be effected suddenly.

Reply to third objection. God, as an agent of infinite power, "requires no preparation which He does not Himself produce." And according to the usual order of providence, He produces this preparation in adults by actual grace, although He can, by His absolute power, confer habitual grace upon one who is not disposed for it, for instance, a person who is asleep, but then the sleeper does not receive it as a man, that is, not as possessed of the use of reason and free will.

Doubt. Whether acts of the free will, thus supernaturally moved by God, only dispose a man for grace morally, by divine institution, or physically, by nature, and furthermore, whether physically in the efficient or only in the predisposing sense.

The reply generally made by Thomists is that these acts dispose a man for grace, not morally only, but physically, in a predisposing way, not however an efficient way. The proof is divided into parts.

1. Not morally only, since an act of free will supernaturally moved by God is a certain beginning of the order of grace, for its relationship to habitual grace is that of motion toward its term. But a beginning is not merely a moral disposition by divine institution, but it is physical by its nature to the perfecting of motion in its term. Therefore these acts dispose not morally only, but physically toward grace.

2. Not, however, physically in an efficient sense, but only as a predisposition. First proof: from the Council of Trent, Sess. VI, chap. 7, where, in describing the causes of justification, no other efficient cause is recognized but God as principal cause and the sacraments as instrumental cause. And in the preceding chapter, the Council, referring to the act of free will, ascribes it to the disposing cause which it distinguishes from the efficient cause. Second proof: St. Thomas also makes the same differentiation in *De veritate,* q. 28, a. 8 ad 2 and ad 7: "The motion of free will is not the efficient cause of the infusion of grace; thus contrition is not the efficient cause of the remission of sins, but the power of the keys, or baptism." Thirdly, the theological argument is: Habitual grace is not an acquired but an

infused habit "which God operates in us without us," according to the words of St. Augustine in his definition of infused virtue. If, on the contrary, our acts concurred efficiently in the production of habitual grace, this grace would be called an acquired rather than an infused habit. Moreover, it is contradictory that an act should cause an active power of which it is properly and connaturally the effect; for instance, it is contradictory that the act of intellection should produce the power of intellect. But supernatural habits have the reason not only of pure habits but also of powers, that is, they confer the first connatural power in the supernatural order.

Corollary. In the same way it may be said of the increase of grace and of the infused virtues: our supernatural acts dispose for this increase not morally only (that is, meritoriously) but physically, not efficiently, however, but as predisposing; for the reason of the increase of infused habits is the same as of their original production. (Cf. IIa IIae, q. 24, a. 4, 5, 6: On the increase of charity.)

ARTICLE III. WHETHER HABITUAL GRACE IS NECESSARILY GIVEN TO A PERSON WHO PREPARES HIMSELF FOR GRACE OR DOES WHAT LIES WITHIN HIS POWER

State of the question. St. Thomas has already shown in question 109, a. 6, that man cannot prepare himself for habitual grace without actual grace, without the supernatural help of God, for the order of agents must correspond to the order of ends, and he thus generally explained the axiom: "If one does what lies in one's power (with the help of actual grace), God does not deny (habitual) grace." No preparation is required for actual grace which itself, by anticipating us, prepares us for justification. But now St. Thomas shows the infallible connection which justification has with this preparation. As we shall presently see, he does not, like Molina, have recourse to any pact entered into between Christ and the Father, by reason of which God would never refuse grace to anyone who does what in him lies by his natural powers.

The conclusion of St. Thomas is: Man's preparation for grace infallibly leads to justification, not as it proceeds from free will, but as it proceeds from God moving him efficaciously.

1. Proof from Sacred Scripture. "As clay is in the hand of the potter, so are you in My hand" (Jer. 18:6). But clay, however much it may be prepared, does not of necessity receive a form from the potter. Likewise the twenty-third and twenty-fifth canons of the Council of Orange may be cited, which declare that the will is prepared for grace by God, and the Council of Trent, Sess. VI, chap. 6 (Denz., no. 798) as follows: "Adults are disposed for justice when, excited by divine grace and assisted, receiving faith by hearing, they are freely moved toward God, believing . . . trusting . . . and they begin to love God."

2. *Theological proof,* each of the two parts being treated separately. First part: that is, such preparation, according as it is from free will, does not infallibly dispose one for grace, since the gift of God exceeds any preparation within human power, for it is of a superior order, and the order of agents corresponds to the order of ends. Moreover, as said in answer to the third objection: "Even in natural things the predisposition of the material does not of necessity obtain the form, except by virtue of the agent who causes the disposition." But, as stated in the answer to the second objection, if we cannot of ourselves prepare ourselves infallibly for grace, nevertheless "the first cause of a deficiency of grace comes from ourselves," since it is only through our own defect that we resist prevenient sufficient grace and are therefore deprived of efficacious grace.

Second part: that is, man's preparation, as it comes from God moving him efficaciously, infallibly leads to justification. This is not proved from *scientia media* or the foreknowledge of our consent if our will is placed in certain circumstances, but from the intrinsic, infallible efficacy of divine decrees and of the actual grace by which the execution of these decrees is effected.

The reason for this is that "God's intention (efficacious or a decree of justification for this man) cannot fail." And this is the teaching of St. Augustine when he says (*De dono persev.,* chap. 14): "Whoever are liberated are most certainly liberated by the beneficence of God." Cf. above, Ia, q. 19, a. 6: Whether the will of God is always accomplished: "Whatever God wills absolutely is done, although what He wills antecedently may not be done"; *ibid.,* ad 1. Hence neither St. Augustine nor St. Thomas speaks of mediate knowledge; the inventors of mediate knowledge were the Semi-Pelagians who declared: God, from all eternity, foresaw that in certain circumstances these particular men would be apt to have a beginning of faith or salvation, and He therefore decreed to give them grace on account of this natural beginning of good will. The Molinists hold some of this doctrine, but avoid heresy by having recourse to a pact between Christ and God.

Doubt. Whether it is possible to reconcile with this teaching of St. Thomas the opinion of those who maintain that "of two sinners equally tempted and equally assisted toward the continuation of attrition, at some time or other, one sets up an obstacle which the other does not, and consequently the latter receives by the mercy of God on account of the merits of Christ grace which is now efficacious for an act of perfect contrition and of justification."

Reply. Reconciliation is not possible for, according to this theory, the distinction between the two men, equally assisted, would arise not from any difference in help received, but from their free will alone; hence the man who did not himself set up an impediment would be disposing himself negatively but infallibly for justification and would thus be distinguishing himself. Infallible preparation would proceed from man, and in foreseeing this distinction God would remain passive, as a spectator, not an actor. But there cannot be passivity in pure act. Again, the divine will would be willing this difference, not before the man's faithfulness, but after it (further passivity in pure act). With respect to the foregoing distinction, God would not be predetermining but determined. Moreover, it would not be explained how, without an infallible decree, this future contingency rather than the opposite would be present in divine eternity, and would be there as a necessary, not a contingent, truth; nor would the transition be explained from a state of possibility to a state of futurition.

Finally, grace is efficacious only with regard to what it effects here and now. But with respect to what it effects here and now, it is infallibly efficacious as the consequent will of God (Ia, q. 19, a. 6 ad 1). Therefore grace is not efficacious unless it is infallibly efficacious, otherwise it would be possible for it to be efficacious sometimes with respect to something which it would not effect.

It only remains to say that grace which is termed sufficient with regard to a perfect act, for example, contrition, may be efficacious and infallibly so with regard to another act, imperfect to be sure, such as attrition. Grace which is efficacious for attrition is sufficient for contrition.

ARTICLE IV. WHETHER GRACE IS GREATER
IN ONE MAN THAN IN ANOTHER

Reply. Sanctifying grace may be greater in one man than in another, not from the standpoint of its end, but with relation to the subject participating to a greater or less degree in this gift of God; and the first reason for the diversity is on the part of God, who distributes His graces in a variety of ways.

1. Proof from Scripture. "To everyone of us is given grace, according to the measure of the giving of Christ" (Eph. 4:7); cf. St. Thomas' Commentary. Then there is the parable of the talents: "And to one he gave five talents, and to another two, and to another one, to every one according to his proper ability" (Matt. 25:15), concerning which St. Thomas writes in his Commentary: "He who makes the greater effort obtains more grace; but the fact that he makes a greater effort demands a higher cause." He says as much again in the body of the present article. And this principle is contrary to the theory of Molina as we shall presently explain. Cf. also the Council of Trent, Sess. VI, chap. 7: "We are truly called just and so we are, receiving justice into ourselves, each according to his measure, which the Holy Ghost distributes to each according as He wills (I Cor. 12:11), and according to the proper disposition and cooperation of each."

2. Theological proof, treated in parts. First part: Grace cannot be greater or less from its end, since it could not be ordained to a greater good, for it ordains us to the supernatural intuitive vision and love of God. Second part: With regard to the subject, grace is greater or less according to the subject's degree of participation in this gift of God. See the answers to the second and third objections. Third part: The primary reason for diversity is on the part of God who distributes grace in various degrees. To be sure, the proximate reason is on the part of man preparing himself, so far as he makes greater or less preparation. But since this very preparation proceeds from the motion of God, the primary reason for diversity is on the part of God, distributing His gifts variously, that the Church may be adorned with that beauty which variety produces in the universe.

Cf. ad 1 and Ia, q. 23, a. 5: "What proceeds from free will is not distinct from what proceeds from predestination, any more than what proceeds from a secondary cause is distinct from what proceeds from a primary cause." This is a reiteration of what St. Paul says in

the text here quoted, and is demanded by the principle of predilection:
"No one would be better than another were he not better loved by
God. Cf. Ia, q. 20, a. 3 and 4. "The will of God is the cause of the goodness in things, and hence they are in some respect better because God
wills greater good to them. Thus it follows that He loves better
things more."

First corollary. This doctrine is contrary to what Molina writes in
his *Concordia* (p. 565): "One who is aided by the help of less grace
may be converted, while another with greater help is not converted
and perseveres in his obduracy." Moreover, it would be opposed to
St. Thomas' teaching to hold that sometimes one person, with the
same amount of help, persists in an easy act conducive to salvation,
whereas another, equally tempted, does not persist. If this were true,
man would distinguish himself, and the lie would be given to St.
Paul's words quoted here: "To every one of us is given grace, according to the measure of the giving of Christ." We should have to say:
according to the effort made by man. It is therefore not to be wondered at that the Congruists were always eager to dissent from
Molinism in this respect, by admitting a distinction between congruous and other grace.[1]

Second corollary. Since it is true that "God resisteth the proud and
giveth His grace to the humble," an inequality of natural conditions
is frequently compensated for by an inequality of supernatural conditions, according to those words of our Lord: "I confess to Thee,
O Father, Lord of heaven and earth, because Thou hast hid these
things from the wise and prudent, and hast revealed them to little
ones." And "blessed are the poor . . . blessed are the meek . . .
blessed are they that mourn . . . blessed are they that suffer persecution." Herein appears the wonderful but deeply mysterious harmony
in the divine distribution of natural and supernatural gifts with which
the parable of the talents is concerned. Hence it sometimes happens
in a religious community that it is the humblest lay brother who has
the greatest degree of charity in his heart and is loved most by God

---

[1] Cajetan is sometimes quoted whenever he seems not to retain altogether the
last part of St. Thomas' conclusion with respect to the supernaturalness of imperfect
preparation for grace. But even if this were true, Cajetan would not deny what
St. Thomas says about the infallibility of this preparation, which comes from God;
for Cajetan maintains (Ia, q.22, a.2) that even general providence is infallible in its
own reason with respect to all that actually happens, since it depends upon the consequent will.

—a St. Alphonsus Rodriguez, S.J., or a Blessed Martin de Porres, O.P.

ARTICLE V. WHETHER MAN CAN KNOW THAT HE POSSESSES GRACE

The state of the question appears from St. Thomas' objections: It seems to be so, since: 1. the soul knows experimentally the things which are present in it; 2. the believer is certain that he has the faith; 3. a person can know certainly that he sins, therefore, with still greater reason that he is in the state of grace, for light is more perceptible than darkness; 4. the Apostle says: "But we have the mind of Christ" (I Cor. 2:16). On the other hand: "Man knoweth not whether he be worthy of love or hatred" (Eccles. 9:1); and there are many similar texts quoted below from the New Testament.

It should be observed that, with reference to the preceding texts, the Lutherans and Calvinists taught: 1. that man could know, by certain and indubitable faith, that he is in grace; 2. that the faithful, or the just man is bound to believe this of himself, otherwise he is neither just nor faithful; 3. that by this faith alone men are justified.[2]

Reply. Except by special revelation, no one can be certain that he is in grace, with an absolute certainty which excludes all fear of error, but the just man can know this only conjecturally, although indeed with very marked conjectural knowledge.

1. Proof from authority. The Council of Trent (Sess. VI, chap. 9, Denz., no. 802) declares: "No one is able to know with the certainty of faith, in which falsehood cannot be concealed, that he has obtained grace." Again (can. 13 and 14, Denz., nos. 823 f.): "If anyone should say . . . that man is bound to believe this of himself, . . . and that no one is really justified unless he believes himself to be so, let him be anathema." This definition is against the Protestants; it does not condemn the opinion of Catharinus as heretical. But as we shall see from what follows, the latter is dangerous and contrary to the general opinion of theologians. This is also true of the theory proposed by Vega.

The doctrine of the Church, however, is based upon several texts of Sacred Scripture: "There are just men and wise men, and their

---

[2] Beside the heretics, Catharinus among Catholics contends that man can be sure he has grace with absolute certainty, not immediately by faith, but mediately by theological reasoning; Vega holds that man may arrive at moral certainty which excludes all fear, like the certainty of the existence of the city of Rome in the mind of anyone who has never been to Rome.

works are in the hand of God: and yet man knoweth not whether he be worthy of love or hatred" (Eccles. 9:1). This does not refer to the wicked, for a vicious murderer can indeed know that he is worthy of hatred; it is a question of the just and wise, and hence the meaning is: no one even of the just knows whether he is worthy of love or of hatred. Again, "Be not without fear about sin forgiven" (Ecclus. 5:5); "With fear and trembling work out your salvation" (Phil. 2:12); "Neither do I judge my own self. For I am not conscious to myself of anything, yet am I not hereby justified; but He that judgeth me is the Lord. Therefore judge not before the time; until the Lord come who both will bring to light the hidden things of darkness. . . ." (I Cor. 4:3–5). (Cf. St. Thomas' Commentary on I Corinthians, chap. 4.)

In his book *De perfectione justorum* (chap. 15), St. Augustine thus explains the foregoing words of St. Paul: "However much justice a man may be endowed with, he should not consider anything in himself which he does not see may be found to be blameworthy." This is especially on account of indirectly voluntary acts by reason of which a man may be a sinner because of culpable ignorance, that is, when he acts in ignorance of what he ought and is bound to know; for example, a doctor who kills his patient because of culpable ignorance arising from his own sloth. (Cf. St. Thomas on ignorance as a cause of sin, Ia IIae, q. 76.)

It is particularly by reason of indirectly voluntary acts that Holy Scripture declares the human heart to be "unsearchable" (Jer. 17:9 and Prov. 25:3); for instance, on account of the subtlety of intellectual or spiritual pride. Therefore do we read in Job 9:21: "Although I should be simple, even this my soul shall be ignorant of," and in Ps. 18:13: "Who can understand sins?"

This is confirmed by the testimony of the saints. There is the reply of St. Joan of Arc to her judges, who asked her if she was in the state of grace: "If I am not, may God place my soul in that state!" Regarding souls that have almost attained perfection and are in the passive purification of the spirit, that is, in the sixth mansion, St. Theresa writes: "They know not whether they are worthy of love or of hate, for they see more and more clearly, in the darkness of faith, the sublimity of the sanctity of God and their own misery." This was true of the holy Curé of Ars, and of St. Thomas as well, at a time when he was almost in doubt and received from the Blessed Virgin Mary the assurance that he was in God's grace.

2. *Theological proof,* treated in its several parts.

First part: except by special revelation; for God sometimes does reveal this as He did to St. Paul, assuring him: "My grace is sufficient for thee" (II Cor. 12:9). Such was the certainty possessed by the Blessed Virgin Mary to whom the angel declared that she was "full of grace" (Luke 1:28); likewise, in the case of the paralytic and of the woman who was a sinner, to both of whom Christ said that their sins were forgiven (Matt. 9:2–7; Luke 7:37–50). But we are now dealing with the ordinary way.

Second part: Ordinarily, no just man possesses absolute certainty in this matter. The proof is as follows:

Absolute certainty is that in which no falsehood can be concealed, excluding all fear of error, such certainty as is obtained by revelation or theological reasoning or by the self-evidence of the matter. But in the ordinary way, no just man can be thus certain that he is in grace, that is, neither by general revelation, nor by theological reasoning, nor by self-evidence of the matter or experience. Therefore there can be no absolute certainty in this regard.

The major is itself a definition of absolute certainty.

The minor is proved in parts; merely natural knowledge is excluded since it cannot know supernatural grace.

a) Not by general revelation, which does not concern itself with my justification so far as it is mine.

b) Not by theological argument for the reason which is thus proved by St. Thomas in the body of the article:

To arrive at this knowledge by discursive theology one would have to know the principle of grace. But the principle of grace is God (in His intimate life), unknown because of His surpassing excellence, and the presence or absence of whom within us cannot be known with certainty, according to the words of Job 9:11: "If He come to me, I shall not see Him: if He depart I shall not understand." Therefore man cannot with certainty judge whether or not he is in the state of grace.

It should be remarked that this lack of certainty proceeds from the supernatural excellence of God and His grace and from His dwelling in inaccessible light which seems to us to be darkness, as the sun seems to the owl. Cf. ad 3: "The object or end of grace is unknown to us on account of the immensity of its light." Some may immediately object: But it is established by faith that grace will be given to one who sincerely loves God and is truly penitent. This is true, but in the ordinary way no one possesses absolute certainty that he sincerely loves God, not merely naturally but supernaturally, above all things, and that he is truly penitent. It must always be feared that some hidden sins may lie concealed in the soul, pride, for example, or presumption. "Who can understand sins?" (Ps. 18:13.)

c) Nor by the experience of grace itself or of charity (cf. ad 1); for we cannot know supernatural grace by any natural experience. And if it is a question of supernatural experience, other than a special revelation, it does not confer absolute certainty in this matter, that is, certainty excluding all fear that one's interior peace or joy may not proceed from a merely natural cause, as will presently be explained in the third part. "For the acts of the infused virtues have a very great similarity to the acts of the acquired virtues," as St. Thomas declares, *De veritate,* q. 6, a. 5 ad 3; q. 10, a. 10 ad 1 and 2.

Third part: the conclusion. This may, however, be known conjecturally and with marked conjectural knowledge. The proof is as follows:

Conjectural knowledge is that which rests upon very weighty signs and indications, yet not so solid but that, even morally speaking, it may be false.

But man has three signs of the state of grace so far as "he perceives 1. that he takes delight in God, 2. that he despises earthly things, and 3. that he is not conscious within himself of any sin."

Hence we read in the Apocalypse (2:17): "To him that overcometh, I will give the hidden manna . . . which no man knoweth, but he that receiveth it," that is, by a certain experience of sweetness. And this suffices for a man to approach the sacraments of the living.

Thus it is written in Rom. 8:16: "The Spirit Himself giveth testimony to our spirit, that we are the sons of God" by the filial affection which He inspires in us. Moreover, these signs are increased if a man is ready to die rather than offend God, and if he is humble, for "God . . . giveth grace to the humble" (Jas. 4:6). Cf. *IV Sent.,* d. 9, q. 1, a. 3; qc. 2; *Contra Gentes,* Bk. IV, chaps. 21, 22. But these signs are not absolutely certain, as St. Paul admits: "For I am not conscious to myself of anything, yet am I not hereby justified" (I Cor. 4:4).

The experience of sweetness can sometimes proceed from a natural cause or from the devil, and no one can be sure that he is truly humble; in fact, he has not begun to be humble until he fears that he is proud.

Confirmation of the conclusion. Herein appears the gentle disposition of divine providence, excluding both presumption which might arise from absolute certitude of our justice and anxiety of soul which would result from lack of a weighty conjecture which may be called certainty under a particular aspect. There is produced, on the contrary, a synchronizing of firm hope and filial fear, hope founded on the help of God who forsakes no one unless He is first forsaken, and a fear of sin or separation from God. "Permit me not to be separated from Thee!"

SOLUTION OF THE PRINCIPAL OBJECTIONS

First objection. We read in I Cor. 2:12: "Now we have received not the spirit of this world, but the Spirit that is of God; that we may know the things that are given us from God"; and again in I John 4:13: "In this we know that we abide in Him, and He in us: because He hath given us of His spirit."

Reply. The foregoing criteria do not apply to individual members of the faithful taken singly, but to the congregation of the Church, in which it is certain, with the certainty of divine faith that some members are in grace. Moreover, everyone is assured of these gifts on the part of God who promises them, although he does not know certainly that he possesses the conditions by which such gifts are merited. This is the explanation given by the Salmanticenses.

I insist. On the contrary, every just man can be certain of this, for the testimony of the Holy Ghost cannot be false. But it is written in Rom. 8:16: "The Spirit Himself giveth testimony to our spirit, that we are the sons of God"; and this especially through the gift of wisdom whereby we have an almost experimental knowledge of the presence of God in us. Therefore.

Reply. The testimony of the Holy Ghost cannot be false, but we can err by mistaking for the testimony of the Holy Ghost what is really not so. This knowledge is called "quasi-experimental," since it does not attain immediately to God Himself present within us, but to His effects, such as a filial affection for Him and works of virtue, nor can we distinguish with absolute certainty between supernatural acts and their natural counterparts. Hence, as the Salmanticenses declare: "The Holy Spirit renders testimony to our spirit, not indeed by revelation, but by producing the effects already mentioned, from which a certain moral certainty and security arise." Likewise St. Thomas comments on the Epistle to the Romans, chapter 8: "He renders testimony, not by revelation but by the effect of filial love which He produces in us." And this knowledge is not infallible.[3]

I insist. But St. John writes (13:35): "By this shall all men know that you are My disciples, if you have love one for another."

Reply. But we cannot be absolutely certain that we love our neighbor with true charity and not from cupidity or natural affection.

Final objection. But a person may possess absolute certainty of his attrition and of the validity of the absolution by which he is subsequently justified. Therefore.

Reply. Of supernatural attrition we can have and do have a valid and more probable confidence from the testimony of a good conscience, from application to good works and a prompt will to obey God. However, the heart of man is inscrutable and there is always reason for him to fear lest hidden sins lie concealed therein (on account of the indirect voluntary) or his sorrow for sin be insufficient, or some disposition be lacking for the reception of the sacrament. So Billuart maintains.

First doubt. Whether one of the faithful can have absolute certainty of at least having the faith.

Reply (ad 2). Yes, since this is not comparable to grace and charity; for "It belongs to the reason of faith that a man should be certain of those things which he believes; and this because certainty pertains to the perfection of the intellect in which knowledge and faith reside. Therefore anyone who possesses knowledge or faith is sure that he does. But the reason is not the same for grace and charity and other gifts of this sort which perfect the appetitive power." In other words, charity, first of all, does not include certainty in its reason, as faith and knowledge do, and, secondly, charity resides in the will, which is not a faculty of cognition or reflection. Many theologians, Billuart

---

[3] Cf. IIa IIae, q.97, a.2 ad 2: "Knowledge of the divine will or of goodness is twofold. One is speculative . . . whereas the other is an affective or experiential knowledge, as when a person experiences within himself the savor of divine sweetness and complacency in the divine will." Again, St. Thomas explains the words of Dionysius (*De div. nom.,* chap. 2) "patiens divina" as: "not only receiving divine knowledge into the intellect, but also enjoying union with it by the affections." We have explained this at length in *Christian Perfection and Contemplation,* p. 271.

among them, admit that a man can be certain of his hope, since he is certain of his faith, and hope follows upon faith; nor is it destroyed except by an act of despair; but a man can be certain that he has never fallen into an act of despair.

Objection is raised, however, to the absolute certainty of the existence of supernatural faith in us on the grounds that this faith might be acquired faith, such as the demons possess.

Reply. Cf. Salmanticenses, no. 17, on the present article. It is probable that one of the faithful cannot have absolute certainty of the supernatural quality of the act or habit whereby he believes. But he has twofold certainty of his faith: 1. of the object believed, at least so far as it is materially possessed, and 2. of the act of believing, abstracting however from the question of whether or not it is supernatural. For it is nowhere revealed that I have infused faith, although there is a very strong conjecture and practical certainty of it. Moreover, for a supernatural act of faith there is required in the will a pious disposition to believe, which pertains to the affective side of man.

Second doubt. Whether in the mystical state there is absolute certainty of the state of grace.

Reply. This does not belong to the essence of the mystical state, or infused contemplation, which persists even in the passive night of the soul wherein the soul thinks itself to be far from God, and feels that God is, as it were, absent from it. But, as we observed in *Christian Perfection and Contemplation,* p. 450, no. 2, according to many theologians, the altogether supreme grace conferred in the state of transforming union, in St. Theresa's seventh mansion, is equivalent to a special revelation of one's own state of grace and even of predestination. This opinion is held by Philip of the Holy Trinity and by Scaramelli. St. John of the Cross thinks that the transforming union is not bestowed without confirmation in grace and some certainty of this confirmation.

Third doubt. Whether we can have a moral certainty of the state of grace which excludes prudent doubt, or only a marked conjectural knowledge.

The reply is twofold.

1. The Salmanticenses answer (no. 8): "Except by the privilege of a special revelation, man cannot have moral certainty in the first degree but only in the second." Cf. no. 2: Moral certainty in the first

degree is that which excludes all fear of error since, for example, it is founded upon the testimony of a great number of men, such as the certainty of the existence of Rome for those who have not been to Rome. Moral certainty in the second degree does not exclude all fear of error, but does exclude prudent doubt; for instance, the certainty which we have of being baptized, or that Peter, whom we see celebrating Mass, is a priest. And there are also differences of degree within this division.

2. Gonet and some other Thomists deny that a just man can have moral certainty properly so called, of his state of grace, but hold that he can have only a marked conjectural knowledge, since moral certitude properly so called excludes all fear of error. Now a man can swear to what he knows with moral certainty, for instance, to being a priest; whereas he cannot swear that he is in the state of grace. Perhaps, as the Salmanticenses declare, the discrepancy is not so much in the matter itself as in the terminology. I agree with Gonet's opinion.

CHAPTER X

QUESTION 113

THE EFFECTS OF GRACE

▶▶

UP to this point we have considered the necessity, essence, divisions, and cause of grace; now we are to examine its effects, of which the two principal ones are: 1. the justification of the wicked, "which is the effect of operative grace," and merit, which is the effect of co-operative grace.

PART ONE: THE JUSTIFICATION OF THE WICKED, OR SINNERS

There are three parts to this question:

1. What justification is and whether an infusion of grace is necessary for it (a. 1 and 2).

2. The acts required for the justification of adult sinners (a. 3-6), that is, whether it requires a movement of the free will, or of faith or of contrition and the remission of sins.

3. The properties of justification (a. 7-10); that is, whether it is brought about instantaneously or whether there is a priority and posteriority of nature in the acts which concur toward it; whether justification is the greatest work of God; whether it is a miracle.

ARTICLE I. WHETHER THE JUSTIFICATION OF THE WICKED IS THE REMISSION OF SINS

The reply is in the affirmative; it is of faith and opposed to Protestant teaching. For Protestants contended that by justification, the sins of the sinner were not really effaced or removed, but remained in their entirety in man, being merely covered over or no longer imputed to him.

Proof from the Council of Trent, Sess. V, can. 5, (Denz., no. 792): "If anyone denies that through the grace of our Lord Jesus Christ, conferred in baptism, the guilt of original sin is remitted, or even asserts that all that is included in the true and proper reason of sin is not removed, but is only said to be erased or not imputed, let him be anathema."

This definition of the Church's faith is based on many texts of Sacred Scripture: "Blot out my iniquity . . . blot out all my iniquities. . . . Thou shalt wash me, and I shall be made whiter than snow" (Ps. 50); "I am he that blot out thy iniquities for My own sake" (Isa. 43:25); "And I will pour upon you clean water, and you shall be cleansed from all your filthiness" (Ezech. 36:25); "Behold the Lamb of God, behold Him who taketh away the sin of the world" (John 1:29); "The blood of Jesus Christ, His Son, cleanseth us from all sin" (I John 1:7); "The unjust shall not possess the kingdom of God. Do not err; neither fornicators . . . nor adulterers, nor the effeminate . . . nor extortioners, shall possess the kingdom of God. And such some of you were; but you are washed, but you are sanctified, but you are justified" (I Cor. 6:9-11). Again, St. Augustine writes, refuting two letters of Pelagius (*Ad Bonifacium,* Bk. I, chap. 12): "We hold that baptism bestows remission of sins and removes our crimes, not merely erasing them." [1]

Theological proof. Since justification is derived from justice, taken passively, it implies a motion toward justice, as calefaction imparts a motion toward heat. But the justice with which we are here concerned requires of a man not merely rectitude toward another man, but toward God, inasmuch as reason is subject to God and lower powers to reason, which rectitude excludes injustice or mortal sin. Therefore the justification of a sinner is a transmutation to the state of justice demanding the remission of sins.

This reasoning is based on the definition of motion which is from a contrary to a contrary, that is, from the *terminus a quo,* namely, the state of sin or injustice, to the *terminus ad quem,* which is the state of justice. However, justification may also be, as in Adam before the fall and in the angels, a simple generation, that is, from privation to a form. This mode of justification is appropriate to one who is not in sin, as stated in the body of the article. [2]

[1] Cf. Rouet de Journel, *Enchir. patrist.,* Theological index, nos. 354 ff., which cites evidence from many of the Fathers on this subject.

[2] From this article and the following one it appears evident that the gift of original justice was not only the integrity of nature, but included sanctifying grace as well, as its intrinsic root, from which charity flowed according to which the "highest in

Reply to second objection. It is noted that this transmutation is named from justice rather than from charity since justice demands the complete rectitude of order in general and is thus distinguished as a special virtue.

Reply to third objection. According to the words of St. Paul: "Whom He called, them He also justified" (Rom. 8:30), vocation precedes justification as it excites one to give up sin.

Confirmation of the reply by reduction *ad absurdum*. If in the justification of the wicked, sins remain and are merely covered over but not effaced, it follows:

1. that man is simultaneously just and unjust: just because justified, and unjust because he remains in habitual mortal sin, which is essentially injustice;

2. that God loves sinners as His friends;

3. that Christ is not the Lamb of God who takes away the sins of the world;

4. that He spoke a falsehood when He said: "Now you are clean" (John 15:3);

5. that God's evaluation, reputing him to be just who is in sin, must be false. These are the arguments generally proposed by theologians against the so-called Reformers.

ARTICLE II. WHETHER AN INFUSION OF GRACE IS NECESSARY FOR THE REMISSION OF GUILT, WHICH IS THE JUSTIFICATION OF THE WICKED

State of the question. In the second objection St. Thomas had already formulated the Protestant opinion according to which justification does not require an infusion of grace. The Protestants declared that man was rendered just, not by an intrinsically justifying form, but either by the justice whereby God is just or by the justice of Christ imputed extrinsically. Therefore the justification of the wicked would be an extrinsic denomination.

The reply of St. Thomas is: "The remission of guilt is inconceivable without an infusion of grace." This reply contains two elements: 1. the remission of guilt is in fact produced by an infusion of grace, and 2. it cannot be effected otherwise, even by the absolute power of God.

---

man was subjected to God." This is opposed to Father Kors' opinion, as we explained in the treatise *De Deo creatore*, pp. 431-37.

The first of these is of faith; the second is opposed to Scotus, the Scotists, and Saurez.

1. Definition of faith by the *Council of Trent* (Sess. VI, can. 10 and 11; Denz., nos. 820, 821): "If anyone should say that men are just without the justice of Christ whereby He merited our justification or by that justice itself formally, let him be anathema."

"If anyone should say that men are justified either by the sole imputation of the justice of Christ or by the remission of sins alone, excluding grace and charity which is poured forth into their hearts by the Holy Ghost and abides in them, or even that the grace whereby we are justified is only a favor from God, let him be anathema.

This article of the Church's faith is clearly based on Sacred Scripture: "Of his fullness we all have received, and grace for grace" (John 1:16); "The charity of God is poured forth in our hearts, by the Holy Ghost, who is given to us" (Rom. 5:5); "To every one of us is given grace, according to the measure of the giving of Christ" (Eph. 4:7).

Theological proof. St. Thomas shows the very impossibility of the remission of sin without the infusion of grace, thus admirably founding his argument on God's love for us.

The remission of sin is effected according as God is pacified in our regard, loving us with special benevolence. But God cannot love the sinner with a special love except by infusing grace whereby the sinner is intrinsically transformed and made pleasing to God. Therefore the remission of sin cannot be effected without an infusion of grace.

The major is self-evident, for God cannot remit the offense of the sinner unless He makes peace with him, and God makes peace with us inasmuch as He loves us with a special love. Thus nothing else can be designated wherein our peace with God consists; in other words, God makes peace with us in the matter of our offense on account of His special benevolence toward us.

The minor is based on St. Thomas' principle enunciated in Ia IIae, q. 110, a. 1, and Ia, q. 20, a. 2, to the effect that "the love of God does not presuppose goodness in us but produces it"; "the love of God infuses and creates goodness in things," since He is the author of all good. Nor are we here concerned with the general love whereby God loves and preserves the very nature of the sinner while he is in the state of sin, but rather with the special love whereby He remits or pardons the offense. This special love cannot but produce some effect in us, that is, it cannot help but make man pleasing; otherwise God's uncreated love for us would be no more effective than the love of our friends, who cannot change the interior state of our souls. Now habitual grace excludes mortal sin absolutely, which is precisely the privation of the life of grace, or the death of the soul. (Cf. ad 1.)

Reply to second objection. "God's not imputing sin to man" proceeds "from the divine love for us," and this divine love "produces an effect in us."

Reply to third objection. The cessation of actual sin does not suffice for the remission of sin, since, as has already been said, habitual sin and the liability to punishment remain.

Objection of Scotus. God can be pacified by a negative love by which He wills only not to be offended any more, just as may be done among men.

Reply. Cf. IIIa, q. 85, a. 2. The case is not parallel, for man can pardon the offense of another through a change in himself, without any change in the offender; God, however, is changeless but works a change in others. Hence the transformation is here confined to man, who at first was not pleasing to God and was then made pleasing through the effect of God's love for him.

A second theological proof may be adduced, as many theologians propose, on the basis of created grace itself.

A privation can only be removed by the opposite form, blindness, for instance, only by sight, darkness by light. But habitual sin consists essentially in the privation of sanctifying grace. Therefore, habitual sin can be removed only by the form of sanctifying grace.

Objection. The major is true of physical privation, but not of moral privation, which is the absence of a form the subject ought to have, not by the nature of things, but by divine ordination. This moral privation can be removed, not only by the introduction of the opposite form, but precisely by the fact that God's ordination is changed, determining that this form is no longer due to this subject. God would thus act if He were to withdraw man's ordination toward a supernatural end.

Reply. Although God can withdraw man's ordination toward a supernatural end, He cannot bring it about that at the time when man sinned he was not ordained to a supernatural end, for power does not extend to the past. Moreover, the voluntary privation of grace does not cease to exist in the sinner except by a retractation of his previous will.

A third theological proof on the part of man. Man does not cease to be turned away from God unless he is converted to Him by an interior transformation. But habitual mortal sin implies a habitual aversion to God. Therefore habitual mortal sin does not cease unless man is converted to God by an interior transformation.

Corollary. It follows from this that, even by absolute power, mortal sin whether actual or habitual cannot coexist with habitual grace in the same subject. This is commonly held by theologians against the Nominalists, Scotus, and Suarez. The reason is that man would be at one and the same time actually, or at least habitually, turned away from God, his last end, and habitually converted to God. For the primary formal effect of sanctifying grace is to sanctify man, to justify or "rectify" him (that is, to confer rectitude with regard to God, his last end), and thereby to make man a child of God. Whereas on the other hand, mortal sin is essentially iniquity and departure from rectitude with relation to our last end, and therefore destroys divine filiation or participation in the divine nature. But even by absolute power justice cannot be made to coexist with injustice, sanctity with iniquity and impurity, or rectitude with a turning aside from rectitude.

This would be the denial of the principle of contradiction or of identity: being is being, nonbeing is nonbeing, good is good, evil is evil, spirit is spirit, flesh is flesh. But once this supreme principle should be denied, it would give way to absolute, atheistic evolutionism the formula of which is found in the first proposition of the syllabus of Pius IX (Denz., no. 1701): "No supreme, all-wise, all-provident divine power exists distinct from the universe of things; God is the same as the nature of things and therefore subject to change, God is actually made in man . . . and God is one and the same thing with the world and, therefore, spirit with matter, necessity with liberty, truth with falsehood, good with evil, and the just with the unjust." It is to this that the opinion of the Nominalists, Scotus, and Suarez leads.

Suarez objects: The sanctification or deification of the soul is not a primary but a secondary effect of grace. But by absolute power secondary effects may be separated from a form, as risibility from rationality. Therefore by absolute power habitual grace may exist without sanctification.

Thomists answer: I deny the major. This effect, namely, sanctification, is the primary effect of sanctifying grace, for grace is essentially a participation in the divine nature and supernatural substantially; it is not, as the Nominalists claimed, something entitatively natural conferring, by divine institution, a right to glory, as a bank note confers a right to receive money. Cf. above on the essence of sanctifying grace the primary formal effect of which is to sanctify. Thus the Nominalist conception of grace would be destructive of the whole supernatural order in us since this order would become entitatively natural. This debased form of theology held by the Nominalists is indeed wretched and worthy of contempt.[3] Molina, although he taught that the act of infused faith is not specified by a higher formal object than that of acquired faith such as exists in the demons, nevertheless elsewhere deplored deep-rooted and unconscious Nominalism.

I insist. An act can coexist with the contrary habit, for instance, an act of intemperance with the habit of temperance. But habitual grace is a habit, whereas mortal sin is an act. Therefore they can coexist in the same man.

Reply. 1. This proves too much, for then even by ordinary power habitual grace might coexist with mortal sin, just as the habit of temperance may coexist in corrupt human nature with the sin of intemperance by ordinary power. But all theologians deny such a possibility by ordinary power.

2. There is a distinction to be made between acquired habits which are acquired by repeated acts and not destroyed by one sin, and the infused habits of grace and charity which are not acquired and are taken away in an instant by mortal sin which essentially includes the opposite matter of injustice and deviation from rectitude with regard to the final end.

I insist. But habitual grace resides in the essence of the soul, whereas sin lies in the will.

Reply. By the very fact that there is mortal sin, it follows that injustice and iniquity are present in the whole man; for sin destroys in the will the last disposition for habitual grace which resides in the essence of the soul and destroys as well the necessary properties of grace.

I insist. But sin does not expel grace physically, but only demeritoriously.

Reply. It does not expel grace physically, by a positive form, acting physically: granted; by its nature: denied. For iniquity, injustice, withdrawal from God, the death of the soul by its nature physically expels sanctity, approach to God, the life of the soul.

---

[3] Divine adoptive filiation follows from deification, unless a man is already the natural Son of God, which is true only of Christ.

I insist. God is not necessitated to withdraw grace from a sinner. Therefore.

Reply. God is not necessitated absolutely to do so: granted; but He is necessitated on the supposition that He permits man to fall into mortal sin, for God cannot will two contradictories simultaneously.

I insist. God does not remove His grace from those once justified, unless He is first abandoned by them, according to the Council of Trent, Sess. VI, chap. 11. Therefore sin precedes the withdrawal of grace and hence coexists with grace.

Reply. That mortal sin precedes the withdrawal of grace by a priority of time: denied; by a priority of nature on the part of the material cause: granted, as will be explained below (a. 8), just as darkness ceases in the atmosphere before the latter is illuminated, by a priority of nature but not of time.

PART TWO: THE ACTS WHICH CONCUR IN THE JUSTIFICATION OF AN ADULT SINNER

State of the question. We have already seen (q. 112, a. 2) that a certain disposition is required for the justification of an adult which is effected under the influence of prevenient actual grace. Now we are concerned with the free acts required for justification. Let us first examine the Church's definition of faith according to the Council of Trent, in opposition to the Protestants who held that only confident faith in the remission of our sins was required for justification. The Council of Trent (Sess. VI, chap. 6; Denz., no. 798) assigns six acts required for the justification of an adult sinner: 1. faith, 2. fear, 3. hope, 4. love of God, 5. repentance or contrition, and 6. the intention of receiving the sacrament instituted for the remission of sins, of beginning a new life and of keeping the divine commands, which intention is included in contrition itself. We shall see how this doctrine of the Church had already been admirably explained in the present article by St. Thomas long before the Protestant heresy.

ARTICLE III. WHETHER A MOVEMENT OF THE FREE WILL IS REQUIRED FOR THE JUSTIFICATION OF AN ADULT GUILTY OF SIN

It seems not to be, since: 1. it is not required in infants, 2. a man may be justified while asleep, and 3. grace is preserved in us without any movement of free will, so that it should also be capable of being produced in the same way.

The reply, however, is that a movement of the free will to accept the gift of grace is required for the justification of an adult guilty of sin.

1. Proof from authority. According to the Council of Trent (Sess. VI, chap. 6, can. 9; Denz., nos. 798, 819): "If anyone should say . . . that for justification . . . it is not necessary for a man to prepare and dispose himself by a movement of his will, let him be anathema." This definition is based on Sacred Scripture (I Kings 7:3): "Prepare your hearts unto the Lord," and (Zach. 1:3): "Turn ye to Me . . . and I will turn to you."

2. Theological proof. In justifying man, God moves him to justice according to the condition of his nature. But it is in accordance with the proper nature of man that he should possess free will. Therefore in one who has the use of free will, God does not produce a motion toward justice without a movement of the free will, or without the free acceptance of the gift of grace.

Reply to first objection. This is not required in infants since they do not yet have the use of free will; thus without personal consent they are freed from original sin, the guilt of which they contracted without personal consent. The same reason applies to the insane or mentally deranged who have never had the use of free will. But if a person has had the use of free will for some time and later loses it either by some infirmity or merely by sleep, he does not obtain justifying grace through baptism, in the ordinary dispensation of providence, unless he first has at least the implicit desire for the necessary sacrament; cf. treatise on baptism. By absolute power, however, a sleeping man can be justified without a previous desire for baptism.

Reply to second objection. St. Thomas makes note of two possibilities: 1. In a prophetic sleep a person may retain the use of free will; 2. without a complete movement of free will the intellect may be enlightened by the gift of wisdom, "since wisdom perfects the intellect which precedes the will." (Cf. Job 33:15.)

Reply to third objection. The preservation of grace in the soul involves no transformation of the soul from the state of injustice to the state of justice; therefore it does not require a movement of free will but "only a continuation of the divine influx." Thus the Trinity dwelling in the just soul preserves grace in it merely by the continuation of the divine presence or influx.

ARTICLE IV. WHETHER A MOVEMENT OF FAITH IS
REQUIRED FOR THE JUSTIFICATION OF
AN ADULT GUILTY OF SIN

It seems not to be so, for: 1. an act of humility or of love of God suffices: 2. natural knowledge of God on the part of the intellect is sufficient; 3. at the moment of justification a man cannot think of all the articles of faith.

The reply, however, is that an act of supernatural faith is required for the justification of an adult sinner. This is of faith.

1. Proof from authority. The Council of Trent (Sess. VI, can. 12; Denz., nos. 822, 799, 802) in opposition to the Protestants who held that confident faith alone in the remission of our sins is required, whereby we trust that our sins are remitted for the sake of Christ. According to the Council (Sess. VI, chap. 6; Denz., no. 798) faith by hearing is required of which St. Paul speaks in Rom. 10:17: "They are disposed for justice when, aroused by divine grace and aided, receiving faith by hearing (Rom. 10:17), they are freely moved unto God, believing those things to be true which are divinely revealed and promised, and this primarily: that the wicked are justified by His grace 'through the redemption, which is in Christ Jesus' (Rom. 3:24)." Again the same Council, referring to the vain confidence of heretics, declares (Sess. VI, chap. 9; Denz., no. 802): "No one is capable of knowing with the certainty of faith, in which no falsehood lies concealed, that he has obtained the grace of God." (Cf. also Denz., nos. 822 ff., 851, 922.)

Protestants, in fact, distinguished a threefold faith as follows:

Faith
- historic (or dogmatic) whereby we believe all that is contained in Holy Scripture.
- in miracles, by which miracles are brought about, believing that nothing is impossible with God. Indeed, this faith is rather a grace *gratis data.*
- in the promises
  - general, whereby we believe God has promised the remission of sins to all believers generally.
  - special, by which each one believes or surely trusts that his own sins are remitted through the merits of Christ.

They called this last form of faith "confidence," confusing faith, which resides in the intellect, with confidence, which pertains to hope and to the will; for confidence is a firm hope (cf. IIa IIae, q. 129, a. 6). The Protestants held that only this confident hope is required for justification. Some of them, however, maintained that love, contrition, and good works were necessary, not as conducing to justification but as a sign of justifying confidence.

Furthermore, many laxist propositions have been condemned; cf. Denz., no. 1173: "Faith broadly speaking, on the testimony of creatures or some similar motive, suffices for justification"; *ibid.*, no. 1172: "Only faith in one God seems to be necessary by mediate necessity, but not explicit faith in a Rewarder." Hence there is required supernatural faith at least that God exists and is a rewarder; otherwise man cannot tend toward his final supernatural end. Further condemnation follows (*ibid.*, no. 1207): "It is probable that natural attrition of an honorable kind suffices."

Supernatural contrition is necessary. It is thereupon declared that for sacramental justification, in other words, absolution, "a knowledge of the mysteries of the Trinity and the Incarnation" is required. That is, such knowledge is necessary at least with a necessity of precept; but more probably also with mediate necessity, at least directly, but not indirectly or accidentally, if these are not known on account of insufficient preaching of the gospel in some particular region. This is the opinion of the Salmanticenses, in the treatise on faith (IIa IIae, q. 2, a. 7).

The Church's belief in this matter, thus defined, is based clearly on many scriptural texts: "Preach the gospel to every creature. He that believeth [the gospel] . . . shall be saved: but he that believeth not shall be condemned" (Mark 16:15 f.); "But my just man liveth by faith" (Heb. 10:38); "But without faith it is impossible to please God. For he that cometh to God, must believe that He is, and is a rewarder to them that seek Him" (*ibid.*, 11:6). And St. Paul demonstrates this truth by Old Testament history, citing the faith of Abel, Henoch, Noe, Abraham, Isaac, Jacob, Moses, and the prophets.

However, this faith of which St. Paul speaks is faith in the revealed mysteries, for it is defined in the same Epistle (Heb. 11:1): "Now faith is the substance of things to be hoped for, the evidence of things that appear not," and one must at least believe, as he says, "that God is, and is a rewarder," that is, believe in God as author of salvation and not merely in God as author of nature, known by natural means; such belief was necessary even before Christ. This is confirmed in our Lord's words to Martha (John 11:25-27): "I am the resurrection and the life; he that believeth in Me . . . shall not die forever," and her reply: "Yea, Lord, I have believed that Thou art Christ the Son of the living God, who art come into this world." Again, St. John tells us in his Gospel (20:31): "But these signs are written, that you may believe that Jesus is the Christ, the Son of God: and that believing, you may have life in His name." That faith is justifying which Christ and His apostles preached; but they preached faith in the mysteries, not that individual, fiduciary faith whereby each one believes that his own sins are remitted.

Confirmation from tradition. From the beginning the Church, when faith is required of candidates for baptism, demanded no other faith but that by which we believe the articles of faith contained in the Creed, and not the faith by which we trust that our sins are forgiven. (Cf. on this subject with respect to the Fathers, St. Robert Bellarmine, *De justif.*, Bk. I, chap. 9.) [4]

Objection. But it is written in St. Matthew's Gospel: "And Jesus, seeing their faith, said to the man sick of the palsy: Be of good heart, son, thy sins are forgiven thee" (9:2), and further: "Be of good heart, daughter, thy faith hath made thee whole" (9:22).

Reply. Before the paralytic and the woman obtained the remission of their sins they already had faith and nevertheless they did not yet believe that their sins were forgiven. Hence when Christ said: "Thy faith hath made thee whole," He was referring to dogmatic faith, the same of which St. Paul speaks to the Romans (10:9): "If thou . . . believe . . . that God hath raised Him [the Lord Jesus] up from the dead, thou shalt be saved."

The second theological argument in the body of the article is as follows:

For the justification of adults who are in sin a movement of the soul is required freely turning toward God. But the first conversion toward God is through faith. Therefore an act of faith is required for the justification of an adult in sin.

The major is proved by what has already been said and is confirmed by Ps. 84:7: "Thou wilt turn, O God, and bring us to life."

---

[4] Cf. Rouet de Journel, *Enchir. patrist.*, Theological index, no. 362, for the opinions of the Fathers on this subject.

The minor is according to St. Paul (Heb. 11:6): "For he that cometh to God, must believe that He is, and is a rewarder to them that seek Him." It is confirmed by the principle that nothing is willed without being previously known; but a supernatural end cannot first be known by wayfarers except through faith.

Reply to second objection. Natural knowledge of God does not suffice for justification, since by it a man is not converted to God as object of (supernatural) beatitude and cause of justification. The distinction is clearly affirmed here between the two orders. Lamennais and the liberals fell into error by holding (Denz., no. 1613) that: "The eternal salvation of souls may be purchased by any profession of faith whatsoever, if their morals are required to conform to a right and honorable standard." Lammenais maintained that common sense was enough, since it was founded originally on the first revelation made to Adam. This was a confusion of the two orders, as in the case of the traditionalists. Nor does there consequently appear to have been any progress made in theology on this subject since St. Thomas, although, in founding his periodical, *l'Avenir,* Lammenais thought he was opening a new era. He passed from one extreme to the other, that is, from traditionalism to liberalism, declaring that the common traditions of all the people are sufficient.

Reply to third objection. St. Thomas determines which kind of faith is required according to St. Paul: "But to him that . . . believeth in Him that justifieth the ungodly, his faith is reputed to justice, according to the purpose of the grace of God" (Rom. 4:5). "From which it appears," as St. Thomas adds, "that for justification an act of faith is required to this extent: that a man believe God to be the justifier of men through the mystery of Christ." This text may be cited in favor of the opinion which holds that, after Christ, faith in the redemptive Incarnation is necessary even by a necessity of means for salvation, since the promulgation of the gospel. (Cf. treatise on faith, IIa IIae, q. 2, a. 7.)

The answer to the first objection will be explained below in the refutation of the error of Protestantism.

The Protestant error: faith alone suffices for the justification of an adult.

It was declared at the Council of Trent (Sess. VI, can. 9 and 19; Denz., nos. 819, 829) that neither the confident faith referred to by Protestants, nor true Christian faith alone suffices for justification.

In this respect Protestants revived an ancient heresy. Simon the Magician and, later, Eunomius misunderstood St. Paul's words concerning the merely natural or legal works of the Jews, and maintained that Christian faith alone, that is, in the articles of the Creed, sufficed for salvation, without works of charity. It was against this error of Simon the Magician, as St. Irenaeus and St. Augustine tell us, that Peter, John, James, and Jude wrote in their epistles. However, in reviving this heresy, the Lutherans and Calvinists modified it by declaring that fiduciary faith suffices for justification, whereas the older heretics had reference to the faith by which we believe all the articles of faith. The innovators insisted that their doctrine was based on certain texts of St. Paul.[5]

But the definition of the Council of Trent is clearly based on many scriptural texts. St. James asks (2:14-26): "What shall it profit, my brethren, if a man says he hath faith, but hath not works? Shall faith be able to save him? . . . So faith also, if it have not works, is dead in itself. . . . Do you see that by works a man is justified; and not by faith only? . . . Faith without works is dead." And in St. Peter's Second Epistle we read (1:10): "Labor the more, that by good works you may make sure your calling and election." St. Jude exhorts the faithful: "Keep yourselves in the love of God" (verse 21). Again St. John declares: "Little children, let no man deceive you. He that doth justice is just" (I John 3:7). And St. Paul writes: "If I should have all faith, so that I could remove mountains, and have not charity, I am nothing" (I Cor. 13:2); "For in Christ Jesus neither circumcision availeth anything nor uncircumcision, but faith that worketh

---

[5] "We account a man to be justified by faith, without the works of the law" (Rom. 3:28); "If Abraham were justified by works, he hath whereof to glory, but not before God" (Rom. 4:2); "Knowing that man is not justified by the works of the law" (Gal. 2:16); ". . . And may be found in him, not having my justice, which is of the law, but that which is of the faith" (Phil. 3:9).

It is certain that the innovators misunderstood these texts, as appears from the context. For, in the first place, St. Paul is not speaking of fiduciary faith, but of the Christian faith whereby we believe the mysteries; and in the second place, he excludes only the works of the law, or the legal obligations of the Jews, who observed the Mosaic law according to the flesh, and those merely natural works which proceed only from the powers of nature and neither from faith, nor from grace or charity. But he does not exclude the supernatural works of charity, for he himself declares to the Galatians (5:6): "In Christ Jesus neither circumcision availeth anything, nor uncircumcision: but faith that worketh by charity." (Cf. also I Cor. 13:2 and Rom. 2:13, texts to be cited below.)

JESUS I TRUST IN YOU

THE IMAGE OF THE DIVINE MERCY

The little prayer that Jesus wants associated with His image of The Divine Mercy is:

**O Blood and Water,
which gushed forth from the Heart of Jesus
as a fount of mercy for us,
I trust in You!**

He insisted that at least the shortened form of it, namely: JESUS, I TRUST IN YOU, must appear on the image.

Sister Faustina repeated this prayer every morning and often during the day to renew her act of consecration to the Divine Mercy on behalf of sinners.

All the quotations are taken from the authenticated text of the spiritual Diary of the Servant of God Sister Faustina Kowalska which bears the IMPRIMATUR of the Archbishop of Cracow, Poland, Franciszek Cardinal Macharski, dated April 18, 1979.

Imprimatur: †*Joseph F. Maguire*
February 2, 1981   *Bishop of Springfield, Mass.*

MARIAN HELPERS CENTER
CONGREGATION OF MARIANS
STOCKBRIDGE, MASS. 01263

MPI   7-173

by charity" (Gal. 5:6); "For not the hearers of the law are just before God, but the doers of the law shall be justified" (Rom. 2:13).

Christ Himself everywhere recommends good works as necessary for justification and salvation: "So let your light shine before men, that they may see your good works, and glorify your Father who is in heaven. . . . Unless your justice abound more than that of the scribes and Pharisees, you shall not enter into the kingdom of heaven" (Matt. 5:16, 20); "Every tree that bringeth not forth good fruit, shall be cut down, and shall be cast into the fire" (*ibid.,* 7:19); "If thou wilt enter into life, keep the commandments" (*ibid.,* 19.18).

Thus it becomes evident that Luther perverted Christ's doctrine radically under the pretext of a deeper understanding of it. In his sermon on the words, "God so loved the world," Luther teaches that, once justified by faith, although a man becomes a thief, murderer, adulterer, or sodomite, he still remains just; hence faith justifies without good works, indeed, even when accompanied by the worst possible works. Luther reiterates this opinion with reference to the second chapter of Galatians. Therefore he said: "Sin strongly and believe more strongly." And Protestant historians, such as Harnack, would have us believe that this represents progress in the development of dogma. (Cf. Denifle, *Luther und Luthertum.*)

The principal objection of the heretics is based upon the text of St. Paul to the Romans (4:2): "If Abraham was justified by works, he hath whereof to glory, but not before God. For what saith the scripture? Abraham believed God, and it was reputed to him unto justice [Gen. 15:6]. Now to him that worketh, the reward is not reckoned according to grace, but according to debt. But to him that worketh not, yet believeth in Him that justifieth the ungodly, his faith is reputed to justice, according to the purpose of the grace of God. . . . Blessed are they whose iniquities are forgiven, and whose sins are covered [Ps. 31:1]. Blessed is the man to whom the Lord hath not imputed sin."

Reply. This text of St. Paul is explained in the light of other texts of the Apostle by the Council of Trent (Sess. VI, chap. 8; Denz., no. 801). The meaning here is the same as in the preceding chapter of Romans (3:21 ff.): "But now without the law the justice of God is made manifest, being witnessed by the law and the prophets. Even the justice of God, by faith of Jesus Christ, unto all and upon all them that believe in Him. . . . Being justified freely [that is, not by works] by His grace, through the redemption, that is in Christ Jesus"; and again later (*ibid.*, 11:6): "If by grace, it is not now by works: otherwise grace is no more grace." Such texts are often quoted against the Pelagians and Semi-Pelagians.

Hence the reply is: St. Paul (Rom 4:5) denies only that the natural good works of pagans or the legal works of the Old Law can obtain justification for us, since justification is gratuitous, proceeding from faith in Christ the Redeemer and from grace. Therefore he declares: "To him that worketh not [that is, the natural works of the pagans or the works of the Mosaic law] yet believeth in Him that justifieth the ungodly, his faith is reputed to justice, according to the purpose of the grace of God." This text should be cited against the Pelagians and Semi-Pelagians who hold that "if one does what in one lies by natural power alone, God infallibly confers grace." (Cf. Council of Trent, Denz. no. 801, and with respect to the Fathers, cf. St. Robert Bellarmine, *De justificatione,* Bk. I, chaps. 20–25.) [6]

St. Thomas' doctrine on this subject, however, is perfectly clear, both from his answer to the first objection of the present article and from subsequent articles. Thus he maintains in his answer to the first objection of article 4: "The movement of faith is not perfect unless it is informed by charity, hence in the justification of adults guilty of sin there is a movement of charity simultaneous with the movement of faith." Therefore justification is attributed to faith as its beginning and root, not however excluding other works which dispose for it; consequently the faith which justifies is a living faith which operates through charity. The Council of Trent (Sess. VI, chap. 6; Denz., no. 798) indicates an act of love of God following acts of faith, fear, and hope.

In the reply to the first objection St. Thomas had likewise noted an act of fear; indeed he specified a kind of fear when he wrote: "However the free will is moved toward God so far as it subjects itself to Him; hence there also concurs an act of filial fear [that is, fear of sin] and an act of humility" (to the extent that man understands himself to be a sinner, as the Council of Trent declares, *ibid.*). In fact, St. Thomas mentions "an act of mercy or of love toward one's

[6] Cf. Rouet de Journel, *Enchir. patrist.,* Theological index, no. 363: Man should dispose himself for justification by faith and by acts of the other virtues. (The testimony of the Fathers on this subject.)

neighbor" according as it either follows justification, or disposes one for it, or is concomitant with it at the very moment of justification itself. Finally, the Angelic Doctor remarks that one and the same act of free will participates in several virtues so far as one imperates and the others are imperated." In article 8 he indicates the order of these acts.

A difficult problem: On the justification of a pagan child who, when he arrives at the full use of reason, does what lies in his power, with the help of actual grace, to love God above all things.

St. Thomas writes, Ia IIae, q. 89, a. 6: "When a child begins to have the use of reason, he should order his acts toward a proper end, to the extent that he is capable of discretion at that age." And again in the answer to the third objection: "The end is first in the intention. Hence this is the time when the child is obliged by the affirmative command: 'Turn ye to Me. . . .' But if the child does this, he obtains the remission of original sin." It is an excellent form of baptism of desire.

St. Thomas and Thomists reconcile this doctrine with the legitimate interpretation of the axiom: "To one who does what in him lies (with the help of actual grace), God does not deny habitual grace," and in the present case God does not deny what is necessary for justification, that is, the supernatural presentation of the truths of faith which are necessary by a necessity of means, at least that God "is, and is a rewarder" in the order of grace.

However, since this thesis is extremely difficult and very complex, demanding the refutation of numerous objections, it will be well to offer here a recapitulation of its proof while at the same time solving the principal difficulties. (Cf. especially on this subject John of St. Thomas, *De praedestinatione,* disp. 10, a. 3, nos. 40–41, and the thesis of Father Paul Angelo, O.P., *La possibilità di salute nel primo atto morale per il fanciullo infedele,* Rome, the Angelicum, 1946.)

1. Why does it not suffice, when a child begins to have the use of reason, that he wills, for example, not to lie, when the occasion arises?

Reply. Because the end is first in the intention; and the end in question is not only happiness in general, but at least some honorable good to be accomplished, as expressed in the first precept of the natural law (to live according to right reason); cf. Ia IIae, q. 94, a. 2.

2. At that moment is not the moral obligation properly so called, of loving an honorable good (living according to right reason), more

than a pleasurable or useful good, and more than sensitive life, made evident explicitly to the child?

Reply. Yes.

3. Does not the explicit knowledge of this moral obligation demand that, the next moment at least, the child know explicitly, although confusedly, that this moral obligation proceeds from the author of his nature?

Reply. Yes; at least according to St. Thomas, since right reason does not bind except as a second cause dependent upon the first and since passive ordering of the child's will toward loving an honorable good efficaciously, even at great cost, supposes the active ordination of the author of nature. Otherwise there could be a philosophical sin against right reason which would not be a sin against God. However, this has been condemned as an error (Denz., no. 1290).[7] But yet, in this instant the honorable good is known before the ultimate honorable good known confusedly, and before the ultimate basis of moral obligation, namely, the ordination proceeding from the author of nature.

4. Does the child, by loving an honorable good efficaciously and explicitly more than himself, love God, the author of nature, efficaciously but implicitly?

Reply. Yes.

5. Why in the present state cannot the child love God, the author of nature, efficaciously and implicitly more than himself, without grace which is at once healing and elevating?

Reply. Because by original sin "man follows his own exclusive good unless he is healed by the grace of God" (Ia IIae, q. 109, a. 3). And this healing grace is at the same time elevating.

6. Does it not suffice for the child to be justified that in a brief moment of time he elicits a single act of efficacious love of God, the author of nature?

Reply. Yes; but in fact this single act cannot be produced unless he is already healed by grace. He will thus be instantly justified, as St.

[7] Denz., no. 1290: "Philosophical sin or moral is a human act unbecoming to rational nature and right reason; theological, mortal sin is the transgression of the divine law. A philosophical sin, although grave, in him who either does not know God or does not think of God when he acts, is a grave sin, but it is not an offense against God nor a mortal sin dissolving friendship with God, nor is it deserving of eternal punishment." This proposition was condemned as scandalous, audacious, and erroneous.

Thomas remarked, *De veritate,* q. 24, a. 12 ad 2: "he will have grace immediately," or will be justified.

7. Why cannot this child be at the same time converted to God, the author of nature, and in the state of original sin?

Reply. Because original sin brings about directly aversion from the final supernatural end, and indirectly from the final natural end; for the natural law decrees that God is to be obeyed whatever He may command. Accordingly in the present state habitual grace cannot heal, without at the same time elevating, and being the root of infused charity.

8. But the difficulty remains with respect to the revelation of the first articles of belief. Is not a revelation, strictly speaking, required?

Reply. Yes, a revelation, strictly speaking, is required, either immediately, or mediately through the guardian angel, since there can be no justification of an adult without an act of faith based on the authority of God who reveals. But at the moment of the moral beginning of the use of reason two physical instants can be distinguished, and this revelation is given in the second of them, if the child does not set up an obstacle but, with the help of actual grace, does whatever is in his power.[8]

[8] This question has been explained more profoundly than by other Thomists in the *De auxiliis* of Alvarez, disp. 56, no. 22, and subsequently even more satisfactorily by John of St. Thomas, who writes (*De praedestinatione,* disp. 10, a.3, nos. 40–41): "This child, to whom the whole law of living according to reason is proposed, cannot accept it unless it is represented to him that the observance of the whole law is something great and for the sake of which something great is to be done which he himself cannot fully attain to; and it is the supernatural which is then implicitly proposed to him.

"And this is because, in the state of fallen nature, he cannot fulfill and accept the whole law, so as to accomplish it by his natural powers alone, but only by the help of grace, whereby eternal life is promised to those who keep the commandments; and thus the observance of the commandments cannot be separated from God, the supernatural end. . . . Hence those who, in that first instant, accept the law and fulfill the natural precept with regard to the whole law present a manifest sign of having received supernatural help, since the powers of nature do not suffice. And such persons will most assuredly be enlightened and obtain knowledge of those mysteries which are necessary for justification and salvation, either through an angel or by means of the preaching of the word, as Peter was sent to Cornelius." This whole text of John of St. Thomas should be read; he has penetrated more deeply into the subject than many other Thomists either among his predecessors or among subsequent and more recent authorities.

The words of St. Thomas must be completely safeguarded, IIa IIae, q.2, a.3: "For man to arrive at the perfect vision of beatitude, it is prerequisite that he believe in God, as a pupil in the master who instructs him." Hence belief in something above

9. In this second physical instant of the first use of reason, can the act of faith coexist with merely implicit knowledge of God?

Reply. No, the knowledge of God must be explicit, and at least vague and obscure, such as that possessed by many Christians of long standing but very poorly instructed.

10. But what are the motives of belief for this child who is unacquainted with either miracles or prophecies?

Reply. The internal motives of belief then supply for the others under divine inspiration, for instance, an experience of great peace which manifests itself as proceeding from on high.

11. Is not this divine intervention miraculous?

Reply. No, for it is produced according to the law: "To him who does what in him lies, God does not refuse grace."

But is it not extraordinary?

Reply. Yes, indeed.

Is it frequent among pagans?

Reply. It is difficult to say; probably the number of these baptisms of desire has increased since the consecration of the human race to the Most Sacred Heart of Jesus was made by Leo XIII at the beginning of the twentieth century.

12. Does God really give to pagan children at that moment sufficient grace for ordering their lives toward the proper end?

Reply. Yes.

13. Why do not the desire for faith and implicit faith in the primary objects of belief suffice?

Reply. Because implicit faith must be contained in a principle which is more universal, not of an inferior order. Thus implicit faith in the Trinity is contained in supernatural, explicit faith in God, the rewarder, but not in knowledge of an inferior order.

14. But if a child does not resist the first prevenient grace inclining him to a pious disposition to believe, will he not receive the enlightenment necessary for an act of faith?

Reply. Yes.

15. The final objection of the Nominalists is as follows: This doctrine of St. Thomas seems to be true in the abstract but not in the

---

natural reason (namely, that God is and is a rewarder in the order of salvation) has always been necessary to salvation. Cf. *ibid.*, a.8 ad 1: "At all times and with respect to all things, it has been necessary to believe explicitly in these two primary articles of faith concerning God."

concrete. In the abstract, the major, the minor, and even the consequence are valid, hence the conclusion is logically arrived at, but the mind is not convinced that the theory is true in the concrete. Many young students admit of this reaction.

Reply. This is the objection of the Nominalists or subjective conceptualists, according to whom our concepts have no certain objective value. They argue that a perfect circle does not exist in the concrete, though it may be conceived as perfect in the abstract. The answer is that, although it may be difficult to form a perfectly accurate circle, the nature of a circle truly exists so far as it corresponds to its definition. With still greater reason, according to moderate realism, the nature of intelligence and will exists in the concrete here and now in this child, and therefore the properties of deliberating intelligence and of will directed toward the final end are strictly verified in him; while a wayfarer he begins to walk rationally in the path of good or of evil. There is no doubt of these two truths: the end is first in the intention, and, if a person does what he can (with divine assistance), God does not refuse grace.

Furthermore, the Nominalists hold that the proof of free will given by St. Thomas is valid only in the abstract, since in practice the stronger motive here and now draws one, and the opposite motive is not sufficient. This is Kant's idea, at least in the phenomenal order. Likewise the Jansenists held that sufficient grace is sufficient in the abstract, but not here and now in practice. The fact remains that our will, by its nature, is free with regard to any object "not in every respect good," and that sufficient grace confers, in the concrete, here and now, the power of doing good, since potency is distinguished from act, just as the faculty of sight is distinguished from vision itself; otherwise a person who is asleep and not actually seeing would be blind. Matters must be judged according to the very nature of things, despite what may be held by Nominalism or Positivism, which is the negation of all philosophy and theology.

ARTICLE V. WHETHER THE JUSTIFICATION OF THE WICKED REQUIRES A MOVEMENT OF THE FREE WILL IN RELATION TO SIN

State of the question. It seems that charity toward God should suffice, without hatred for sin, since 1. charity covers a multitude of sins; 2. he who stretches out toward what is before should not look back upon what is behind, according to St. Paul; and 3. man cannot remember all his sins.

The reply, however, is that an act of contrition or hatred of sin is required for the justification of an adult in sin.

Proof from the declaration of the Church, particularly in view of the quotation previously cited from the Council of Trent (Sess. VI, chap. 6; Denz., no. 798): "They are disposed for justice when, aroused by divine grace and assisted . . . they are moved against sin by a certain hatred and detestation"; also canon 9. This definition is based on several scriptural texts. In the argument *Sed contra,* St. Thomas quotes Ps. 31:5: "I said I will confess against myself my injustice to the Lord: and Thou hast forgiven the wickedness of my sin."

Theological proof. The justification of sinners is a movement of the mind from the state of sin to the state of justice. But the mind cannot freely approach justice without freely withdrawing from sin by detestation of it. Therefore the justification of sinners requires not only the desire of tending toward God and justice, but the hatred of sin or injustice. Hence faith alone does not justify.

In other words, there can be no free approach to the terminus toward which one is moving without a free departure from the terminus away from which one is moving; or, there is no desire for good without flight from evil or aversion for evil, according to the words of the Psalmist: "You that love the Lord, hate evil" (96:10). Cajetan observes that from the motion of hatred for evil and the motion of affection for good there is formed, as it were, a single, complete motion of the will from evil to good. (Cf. a. 7 ad 2.)

Reply to first objection. It pertains to charity to love God and, consequently, to hate sin or offense against God; hence charity controls penitence. Cf. the treatise on penance and article 8 of the present question on the order of these acts and also of attrition and contrition.

Reply to second objection. Man ought not to look back on past sins to love them but rather to detest them.

Reply to third objection. Man should detest all the sins he has committed, including those he has forgotten, for he would hate these also if they were present to his memory.

ARTICLE VI. WHETHER THE REMISSION OF SIN SHOULD
BE NUMBERED AMONG THE REQUIREMENTS
FOR THE JUSTIFICATION OF SINNERS

State of the question. This seems not to be true, since 1. this remission is justification itself and not merely a part of it; 2. since the same thing should not be enumerated together with itself, and the infusion of grace is the same as the remission of sin.

The reply is, nevertheless, in the affirmative.

1. Proof in general. Since the remission of sin is the effect and end of justification; contrary to what Luther declared, sins are not merely covered over but forgiven. But the end toward which justification is ordained should not be omitted.

2. Specific proof. Justification is a motion of the mind from the state of sin to the state of justice. But in any motion, three elements are necessary: 1. the motion of the mover, this is the infusion of grace; 2. the movement of the moved, that is, a motion of living faith and contrition; and 3. the attainment of the end, which is the remission of sin. Therefore.

Later, in his treatise on penance (IIIa, q. 85, a. 5 c.), St. Thomas states that "Penance as a habit is immediately infused by God, without any principal operation on our part; not, however, without our cooperation in disposing ourselves by certain acts.

"From another standpoint, we may speak of penance as it consists of acts in which we cooperate toward the penance which God produces; the first and principal of these acts is the operation of God converting our hearts, according to Lam. 5:21: "Convert us, O Lord, to Thee, and we shall be converted." The second act is the movement of faith; the third is the movement of servile fear, whereby a person is drawn away from his sins through fear of punishment. The fourth act is a movement of hope, by which he resolves to amend in the hope of obtaining pardon. The fifth is a movement of charity whereby sin becomes displeasing on its own account and no longer for fear of punishment. The sixth is a movement of filial fear which voluntarily offers some amendment to God out of reverence for Him."

Reply to first objection. The justification of sinners is said to be identical with the remission of sins so far as all movement is specified by the terminus toward which it tends.

Reply to second objection. The infusion of grace and the remission of sins are the same with regard to the substance of the act, for God, by the same act, bestows grace and remits guilt; but they differ in relation to their objects, according to the distinction between guilt which is removed and grace which is infused. Thus, in natural processes, generation and corruption are differentiated, although the generation of one thing is the corruption of another. In the same way, the infusion of grace is the remission of sin.

Thus terminates this second part of question 113, that is, the consideration of the acts requisite for the justification of an adult. They are found to be: an act of living faith, that is, of faith and charity, together with acts of filial fear and hope (a. 4 c and ad 1) and an act of contrition (a. 5). All of these were subsequently defined by the Council of Trent (Sess. VI, chap. 6; Denz., no. 798) when six acts were indicated as concurring in justification: 1. faith, 2. fear of both punishment and guilt (Denz., no. 818), 3. hope, 4. love of God, 5. contrition, 6. the intention of receiving the sacraments, of beginning a new life, and of keeping the commandments, which intention is included in contrition. The fourth act is thus designated by the Council: "They begin to love God as source of all justice and, consequently, they are moved to withdraw from sin" (Denz., no. 798).

Concerning the necessity of at least a beginning of this love for justification through the sacrament, there is a well-known controversy, which is analyzed in the treatise on penance with reference to attrition and contrition. Contrition is said to be perfect if sin is displeasing principally as an offense against God; it is said to be imperfect if sin displeases principally as harmful to the sinner. Attrition is imperfect contrition (cf. Denz., nos. 898, 915). The controversy arises over the attrition necessary for justification with the sacrament, since attrition for sin committed may proceed from various motives, either natural or supernatural: 1. whether from the fact that sin is ugly in itself and revolting to right reason, 2. or because it is the cause of temporal evils, 3. or because it leads to damnation, 4. or because it deprives one of eternal glory, or 5. because it is evil and an offense against God. According to the Church, in opposition to the laxists, a natural motive does not suffice even for sacramental justification (Denz., no. 1207); attrition must be supernatural in its motivation (Denz., nos. 699, 751, 897, 1536). Perfect contrition arising from charity with the desire for the sacrament justifies even before the reception of the latter, and that not merely in case of necessity or martyrdom. The Church likewise declared that attrition without charity is not evil and may be supernatural, and that, if it is supernatural, it suffices with the sacrament of penance for justification. But it is a disputed point among theologians just what is required to make attrition supernatural, from which supernatural motive it should proceed, and whether it includes an incipient love of God, distinct from charity. According to many Thomists, it includes a love of benevolence toward God, distinct from charity, just as in faith there is a devout will to believe with reference to divine truth. We have discussed this subject at length in the treatise *De poenitentia* appended to the *De Eucharistia* (1943, pp. 360–79).

Doubt. Whether all six acts enumerated by the Council of Trent must be explicit.

Reply. The acts of faith and of love must be formal or explicit since neither in the intellect nor in the will are any more excellent or higher acts produced wherein they might be virtually contained. It seems that hope would be virtually contained in the more eminent act of charity, should a person be suddenly moved to conversion. The act of contrition, so it seems, must be explicit at least essentially, since man should regret his sin not only because it is contrary to divine goodness but also as a violation of the divine law, and this pertains formally not to charity but to penance; but accidentally a person may not think explicitly of his sins but only of loving God, and he is then justified. It suffices for the purpose of amendment to be virtual in the contrition.

The third part of the present question deals with the properties of justification, according as it takes place in an instant, including however the priority and posteriority of nature (a. 7 and 8), according as it is the greatest work of God with regard to the effect produced (a. 9), although it is not a miracle, at least ordinarily (a. 10).

ARTICLE VII. WHETHER THE JUSTIFICATION OF SINNERS TAKES
PLACE IN AN INSTANT OR SUCCESSIVELY

State of the question. It seems not to be instantaneous, since: 1. it requires an act of free will which entails previous deliberation; 2. it requires two acts, the love of God and the hatred of sin, which do not seem to be simultaneous; 3. habitual grace itself is susceptible of greater or less measure, and therefore is not received in an instant, but little by little according to its various degrees; 4. the movement of free will concurring toward justification is meritorious; therefore it cannot take place until after the infusion of grace, which is the principle of merit; 5. the same instant cannot be at once the first instant of the life of grace and the last instant of the state of sin, since these two opposites cannot coexist; but between two instants there must be an intermediate time; otherwise they would be identical.

The conclusion is, nevertheless, that the justification of sinners is effected by God instantaneously, at least so far as it signifies the infusion of habitual grace and the remission of sins, although the previous dispositions by which the sinner is prepared are ordinarily produced successively. However, these dispositions, as explained in the reply to the first objection, are the path to justification, but not the real substance of justification.

Proof from Scripture, according to which the Holy Ghost comes into the souls of men suddenly: "And suddenly there came a sound from heaven, as of a mighty wind coming" (Acts 2:2).

Nevertheless the Council of Trent (Sess. VI, chaps. 5 and 6) refers not only to the infusion of grace, but also to the antecedent dispositions by which the sinner is prepared, and, in this sense, justification is ordinarily effected successively, as St. Thomas himself here declares in the body of the article, in the answer to the first objection, in the preceding article 5 ad 3, and in q. 112, a. 2 ad 1 and 2. His teaching may be summarized as follows: Ordinarily justification including also the preceding dispositions is produced successively, for it is only under extraordinary circumstances that God sometimes bestows at the same moment of time the complete disposition and the infusion of grace, as in miraculous conversions which are utterly instantaneous, even in regard to their preparation; cf. a. 10.

Theological proof. A form is impressed upon a previously disposed subject in an instant when the agent does not require time to overcome the resistance of the subject. But justification is the impressing of habitual grace upon a previously disposed subject by God who requires no time. Therefore justification, inasmuch as it is the infusion of grace, is effected in an instant.

We are here supposing the disposition to be primary in time, not final, since justification is understood as signifying only the infusion of grace, and God almighty requires no other disposition than that which He produces and which He can also effect at the very instant when He produces grace itself, as He did in St. Paul, or gradually and successively; but this does not pertain to justification taken in the sense of the infusion of grace. What does pertain to it, as we shall see in the following article, is the final disposition through an act of living faith and contrition at the very instant of justification. Therefore justification, taken in this sense, is effected in an instant.

The major is verifiable even in the natural order, inasmuch as, once the disposition for the substantial form is present in the matter, this form, of which the specific difference is indivisible, is produced in an instant; for example, an animal either is a lion or is not a lion; and again, transparency which is predisposed can be suddenly illuminated.

The minor is clear with reference to the infusion of grace in its precise acceptation. Indeed God sometimes produces in an instant, under extraordinary circumstances, the preliminary dispositions for grace, since acts of free will can be made instantaneously.

Confirmation. (*De veritate,* q. 8, a. 9.) When there is no mean between the extremes of a change, just as there is no mean in the substantial change between being and nonbeing (for example, between the being of the form of a lion and not being), then the transition is made instantaneously. But between the extremes involved in justification, habitual grace on the one hand and deprivation of habitual grace on the other, there can be no mean; for a man either possesses habitual grace or he does not; if he does, even in the least degree, he is already justified. Therefore.

Further confirmation is found in the refutation of the objections.

Reply to first objection. The deliberation which precedes by a priority of time is the way to justification but not the substance of justification, for which there is required the final, instantaneous consent of the deliberation to detest sin and be united to God.

Reply to second objection. These two acts of hatred for sin and love of God can be simultaneous inasmuch as one is ordained to the other, for man detests sin for the reason that it is against God to whom he wishes to adhere.

Reply to third objection. Some forms can be received to a greater or less degree, such as light or grace; yet they are produced instantaneously, for even if possessed in the least degree their essence is already present. The slightest degree of habitual grace is already a participation in the divine nature.

Reply to fourth objection. The movements of living faith and of contrition are meritorious inasmuch as they proceed from habitual grace itself at the very moment of infusion. For grace begins to operate at once, just as fire immediately forces itself upward or produces light. This is a remarkable fact: life is infused simultaneously in first act and in second act.

Reply to fifth objection. There is no last instant in which guilt was present in the soul, but there is a last time; whereas there is a first instant in which habitual grace is present therein; however, throughout the preceding time, guilt was present. Hence the first nonexistence of guilt is the first existence of grace, which presents no contradiction. The text should be consulted in this regard. This question of the final instant is of great importance in the matter of the end of life.

It should be remarked that Cajetan (Ia, q. 64, a. 1, no. 18), wishing to explain the obstinacy of a damned soul by comparison with the obstinacy of the demon, declares: "I say that the soul is settled in obstinacy by the first act which it elicits in the state of separation, and that the soul then demerits, not as in life, but as having arrived at its term; as appears from what has been said above (q. 63, a. 6, no. 3), the instant of death belongs intrinsically to the state of wayfarer."

The Salmanticenses remark (*De gratia,* "de merito," disp. I, dub. IV, no. 36): "This manner of speaking of Cajetan is generally not admitted because of the testimony of several scriptural texts according to when men can merit or lose merit before death but not in death." Hence the same thing should be said of the state of wayfarer as has been said here of the state of sin: there is not the last instant of the life of the wayfarer, but the last moment of time; on the other hand, there is the first instant of life of the separated soul; and throughout the preceding time, infinitely divisible, the life of the wayfarer existed.

Hence the first nonexistence of the wayfarer's state is the first existence of the state of separated soul; and, as it seems, merit is then no longer possible, but only immediately before, since it is man who must merit and not a separated soul, for his body is given to him that he may tend toward his end, and after separation from the body his choice is rendered permanent. Thus is confirmed by revelation the Aristotelian thesis of the soul as the form of the body.

This problem is extremely difficult; cf. St. Thomas, *Contra Gentes,* Bk. IV, chaps. 92, 93, and the Commentary of Francis Silvester (Ferrariensis) who does not follow Cajetan. We have dealt with this question in the treatise *De Deo creatore,* pp. 408–12.

ARTICLE VIII. WHETHER THE INFUSION OF GRACE IS FIRST IN ORDER OF NATURE AMONG THE REQUIREMENTS FOR THE JUSTIFICATION OF SINNERS

State of the question. This question is attractive and, on the other hand, it illustrates the problem of the culpability of the sinner, according as the resistance to sufficient grace precedes, at least by a priority of nature, the refusal of divine efficacious grace.

It seems that the infusion of grace is not first in order of nature, since: 1. withdrawal from evil precedes the approach to good; therefore the remission of guilt is prior to the infusion of grace; 2. the movement of free will is a disposition for the reception of grace and therefore precedes it; 3. indeed the remission of guilt takes place before the movement of free will, for that which prevents the movement is removed before the movement can follow. Such objections are often proposed in similar questions. Many argue on the basis of priority in the order of material cause, as if the material cause were absolutely prior to any other. This would lead to materialism, and, in the present problem, to Pelagianism, which is a materialistic explanation of justification, to the extent that at least the beginning of salvation would proceed from nature.

The conclusion of St. Thomas is twofold; he explains the profound meaning of our Lord's words of Mary Magdalen (Luke 7:47): "Many sins are forgiven her, because she hath loved much. But to whom less is forgiven, he loveth less." These words seem to be opposed to each other.

First conclusion. 1. On the part of God, the agent, and absolutely, the infusion of grace is prior not by a priority of time but of nature:

2. a movement of free will toward God is produced, namely, of living faith and charity;

3. detestation for sin; and

4. the remission of guilt.

It is assumed from the preceding article that justification with respect to its essence, in the strict sense, is effected in an instant, so that the same instant is the first nonexistence of sin and the first existence of habitual grace. But there may be preceding dispositions beforehand, although not the final disposition which is produced at the very instant of justification.

Proof from common principles, from the argument *Sed contra.* Because a cause is prior to its effect; but the infusion of grace is the cause of the movement of free will toward God, of contrition, and of the remission of sin.

Proof, in particular; the body of the article should be read. In any movement there is: 1. the motion of the mover, 2. the movement of the object set in motion, and 3. the terminus toward which it is moved. But the justification of a sinner is the transmutation effected by God from the state of sin to the state of grace. Therefore it involves: 1. the motion of God infusing grace, 2. a twofold movement of free will, and 3. the end of the movement, that is, the remission of guilt.

Why does the movement of free will toward God precede contrition? Because we detest sin inasmuch as it is against God; our love of God is the cause of our contrition, which is the cause of the remission of guilt. Hence our Lord says of Mary Magdalen: "Many sins are forgiven her, because she hath loved much" (Luke 7:47); but He adds: "To whom less is forgiven, he loveth less." This is explained by St. Thomas' second conclusion which concerns the movable element or material cause.

The second conclusion refutes the first objection as follows: With regard to the movable element or the justified man, freedom from guilt is prior in order of nature to the acquisition of grace. Observe well that St. Thomas uses the terms liberation from guilt rather than remission of guilt, and acquisition of grace rather than infusion of grace, since he is here considering the matter from the standpoint of the man justified and not of God who justifies. (Consult the answer to the first objection.)

Proof. On the part of the object moved, withdrawal from the *terminus a quo* it precedes the approach to the *terminus ad quem.* For instance, with regard to the lighting up of the atmosphere, the dispelling of darkness precedes the arrival of the light, not by a priority of time but of nature, whereas on the other hand, in relation to the sun, illumination is prior by nature to the removal of darkness. Therefore, from the standpoint of man, liberation from guilt precedes the acquisition of grace, whereas, from the standpoint of God, the infusion of grace precedes the remission of guilt.

Again, St. Thomas says in answer to the second objection: "The movement of free will precedes in the order of nature the acquisition of grace for which it disposes one, but it follows the infusion of grace."

He is here referring to the final disposition which is present in the same instant as justification itself, in the strict sense; but there may be previous dispositions preceding in time, as remarked in the foregoing article (ad 1, and a. 5 ad 3; q. 112, a. 2 ad 1 and 2).

Finally in reply to the third objection: Since the end is first in the intention, free will is moved toward God as to its end before the motion to remove the impediment of sin. Thus, in the present article, St. Thomas applies with remarkable aptness the principle of Aristotle (*Met.*, Bk. V, chap. 2): "Causes are causes to each other but under different aspects"; thus there is a mutual relationship of priority without a vicious circle, since the mutual causes are not such under the same aspect, but under different aspects. Absolute evolutionism, however, perverts this principle and falls into contradiction by claiming that evolution is, of itself, creative and that God is the world or is made in the world. God makes all that are made in the world, but He was not made. There are many other applications of this principle, several of which I have indicated in *God: His Existence and His Nature,* II, 313 ff. The efficient cause is attracted by or from the end and obtains or produces the end; the matter is determined by the form and limits it; a bird bears its wings, but is borne by them; the intellect receives its object from the senses, but it passes judgment upon them; it directs the will, but is applied by the will; the final practical judgment precedes choice and is confirmed by it. Revelation is proposed by the Church and is a motive for believing in the infallibility of the Church. Again, the Word would not have become incarnate if man had not sinned, but God permitted the sin of the first man for the greater good of the Incarnation itself.[9]

First corollary. The passive purifications of the spirit are often made according to the same order, inasmuch as God, through the illumination of the gifts of intellect, purifies from all imperfection faith, hope, and charity, that the formal motive of these virtues may appear in all its purity and move the soul; and on the part of God, the purification of these virtues precedes, at least by a priority of nature, the more intense contrition.

But on the part of the purified soul the order is reversed; thus there first appears the purification of humility by a profound realization of

---

[9] Thus Peter would not have reached heaven had he not done penance, and God permitted his threefold denial so that Peter might become more humble and attain a greater degree of glory.

our misery and a hatred for sin; there follows the purification of faith, amid the overcoming of temptations against faith; then the purification of hope, surmounting the temptation to despair; and finally the purification of love or charity, described by St. Theresa in the seventh mansion.

Hence the passive purification of the spirit renews once more and much more profoundly what takes place in the justification of sinners; both of them are sanctifying, the first imperfectly, the second perfectly. God is the author of both, just as a farmer first plows a shallow furrow and then a much deeper one to extirpate stubborn weeds and roots and prepare the soil, so that the grain of wheat falling into it may bear much fruit.

Second corollary. The argument is the same in the opposite direction. To explain the culpability of the sinner it must be said conversely that in the first sin the resistance to sufficient grace absolutely precedes by a priority of nature the divine refusal of efficacious grace. St. Thomas had said in the reply to the first objection of our present article: "And since the infusion of grace and the remission of guilt are said to be on the part of God who justifies, therefore in the order of nature the infusion of grace is prior to the remission of guilt." On the other hand it must be said: "And since sin as such is a defect which of itself is reducible, not to God who is indefectible, but to the defective and deficient free will, therefore in the order of nature, at the same instant, the initial defect or voluntary heedlessness in fulfilling an obligation or resistance to sufficient grace is prior absolutely to the divine refusal of efficacious grace, which is a punishment presupposing a fault, and to the divine motion concurring in the matter of the sin. Thus the divine denial of efficacious grace, so far as it is a punishment presupposing a fault, signifies something more than the simple divine permission of the initial sin, which is the condition without which there could be no sin, but not its cause. Cf. Council of Trent, Sess. VI, chap. 11: "God by His grace does not abandon souls once justified (by the refusal of efficacious grace) unless He is first abandoned by them"; but man would not abandon God if God did not permit it; hence we must pray: "Permit me not to be separated from Thee!" We have explained this elsewhere: *God: His Existence and His Nature,* II, 371 ff., and *De Deo creatore,* pp. 346-52.

The point to be emphasized is that abandoning God is a defect pertaining to man and therefore this priority on the part of the material cause is absolute; while on the contrary, in the infusion of grace, which is the work of God, the priority on the part of the agent is absolute. (Cf. Ia IIae, q. 79, a. 1 and 2: whether God is the cause of sin and the cause of the act of sin.)

Doubt. Whether the acts of charity and contrition, which dispose finally for habitual grace, proceed from it effectively or only from the actual help communicated in a transitory way; cf. Salmanticenses, dub. 3 and 4. Billuart (*De gratia,* d. 7, a. 4, § 4) remarks that there are the three following opinions on this subject.

1. The old school of Thomists, Cajetan, Francis Silvester (Ferrariensis), Soto, Bañez, Alvarez, Godoy, the Salmanticenses, Gonet, and Serra declare that these acts proceed effectively from habitual grace by charity and penance, and they hold this answer to be more conformable to the principles of St. Thomas.

2. More recent theologians, such as Suarez, Molina, Bellarmine, and, among Thomists, John of St. Thomas, Contenson, and Philip of the Holy Trinity, maintain that they proceed from actual help distinct from habitual grace. St. Bonaventure and Scotus are quoted in support of this opinion.

3. Goudin, wishing to reconcile the two foregoing opinions, proposed that the acts proceed from grace by charity and penance, not permanently in the manner of a habit, but transiently, communicated in the same way as habitual grace in the process of being conferred.

It seems to us that the first opinion is correct as very well explained by the Salmanticenses and Gonet, *Clypeus,* with reference to the present article.

Proof from the authority of St. Thomas in this article, the argument *Sed contra* and the reply to the second objection: "The final disposition of the subject precedes the reception of a form, in the order of nature, but it follows the action of the agent whereby the subject itself is disposed. Therefore the movement of free will precedes in the order of nature [on the part of the subject] the acquisition of grace, but it follows the infusion of grace." Cf. also Ia IIae, q. 113, a. 6, 7 ad 1, and later a. 10, nonmiraculous conversion; likewise, Ia IIae, q. 112, a. 2 ad 1, where this disposition is said to be meritorious, and therefore proceeds from habitual grace which is the principle of merit; IIIa, q. 7, a. 13 ad 2; q. 9, a. 3 ad 2. In the same way, the body is organized finally only by the soul, and this organization is the disposition for receiving the soul, Ia, q. 76, a. 4 ad 1. Thus great teachers have their own peculiar language, terminology, and characteristic mannerism which finally prepare the student to receive and understand their teaching.

Theological proof. Since these acts are vitalized by supernatural life, and at the same time connatural and meritorious, as St. Thomas declares, they should therefore proceed from a faculty elevated by infused habits. Nor is there any impossibility in this; rather is it the application of the principle: causes are a cause to each other in different orders. Thus habitual grace precedes these acts under the aspect of formal cause, and follows them under the aspect of material, disposing cause. Absolutely, however, the infusion of grace and the movement (as efficient cause) precede the acts to which we refer. Cf. below, note 10.

In the same way, air will not enter a room unless a window is opened, nor can the window be opened without the air entering. So does God knock at the door of the heart and it opens, and at the same time, we open it by consenting. Actual grace suffices for a disposition which is not final, but the final disposition is effected at the very instant when the form is produced and, although as a disposition it precedes it in the genus or order of material cause, it nevertheless follows it in the genus or order of formal, efficient, and final cause. Likewise the final disposition toward a spiritual soul precedes it under the genus of material cause, and follows it under the genus of formal cause, as the property of form which inheres in a compound; when it is destroyed, death ensues, or the separation of soul from body.[10]

ARTICLE IX. WHETHER THE JUSTIFICATION OF SINNERS IS THE GREATEST WORK OF GOD

State of the question. It seems not to be so, since: 1. the glorification of the just is higher than the justification of sinners; 2. even the creation of heaven and earth is a higher thing inasmuch as the good of

---

[10] Father Henri Bouillard, S.J., in his recent book, *Conversion et grâce chez S. Thomas d'Aquin,* Paris, 1944, coming to the heart of the problem, writes (pp. 169–70): "It will be observed that St. Thomas, Ia IIae, q.113, a.8 ad 1, no longer has recourse to reciprocal causality. In the works of his youth he did so." On the contrary, as we have remarked (a.8), St. Thomas clearly resorts to reciprocal causality, as all Thomists agree. In fact, this mutual causality always comes into play when the four causes are involved. Cf. above, pp. 204 ff. Nor can we admit the opinions expressed in Father Bouillard's volume on pages 212, 219, 221, 224.

the universe is greater than the good of one justified man; and 3. creation was made from nothing.

The first conclusion, however, is that from the standpoint of the thing produced, or absolutely, justification is a greater work than creation, although not so great as glorification, since creation terminates in a good of a mutable nature in the natural order; whereas justification terminates in the eternal good of participation in the divine nature, the beginning of eternal life; and glorification terminates in the gift of glory which is greater than the gift of grace.

This conclusion is based on Holy Scripture as cited in the argument *Sed contra:* "His . . . mercies are over all His works" (Ps. 144:9). And the Church prays in her Collect: "O God who, more than in all things else, showest forth Thine almighty power by sparing and by having mercy . . ."; and Augustine comments on St. John's Gospel (chap. 14): "It is a greater work to make a just man of a sinner than to create heaven and earth."

Corollary from the answer to the second objection: "The good of grace in one man is greater than the natural good of the whole universe," greater even than all the angelic natures capable of being created taken together. For grace is of a superior order; likewise the tiniest plant or blade of grass, so far as it is living, is something more perfect than mountains of gold or silver. (Cf. Salmanticenses.)

Second conclusion. From the standpoint of the mode of action, creation is a greater work than justification, since it is a more excellent mode of operation to make something out of nothing. But this superiority with regard to the mode of operation is limited to a particular aspect, for, as St. Augustine says, absolutely "it is a greater thing to make a just man out of a sinner than to create heaven and earth. . . . Heaven and earth shall pass away, but the salvation and justification of the predestinate will remain."

Third conclusion. The justification of sinners is a greater work than glorification with respect to proportionate quantity, but not to absolute quantity. For the gift of grace exceeds the deserts of a sinner, who was worthy of punishment, more than the gift of glory does those of the just man, who is worthy of glory. Furthermore, the gift of grace exceeds human or angelic nature more than the gift of glory exceeds grace; for grace is the seed of glory, but even angelic nature is not the seed of grace. Such is the doctrine that ought to be preached; it is the basis of true mysticism. The Incarnation is a more perfect work than justification; likewise the divine maternity is immeasurably above the order of grace and glory because, by reason of its term, it belongs to the hypostatic order.

ARTICLE X. WHETHER THE JUSTIFICATION
OF SINNERS IS MIRACULOUS

State of the question. It seems to be so, since: 1. it is a greater work than other miraculous works; it is, as it were, the resurrection of the soul, surpassing that of the body; 2. the will of the sinner tends toward evil as a corpse toward corruption; 3. it is miraculous for a person to obtain wisdom from God suddenly, without any study; therefore it is equally so to attain to grace in an instant.

The first conclusion, nevertheless, is that the justification of a sinner, so far as it is ordinarily accomplished, cannot be termed miraculous, although it is a very wonderful thing.

Proof. It is said to be wonderful since it can be effected only by God. However, for a miracle, strictly speaking, it does not suffice that God alone be able to accomplish it; it must be out of the ordinary course of divine providence, such as raising of the dead or giving sight to one born blind. But justification, inasmuch as it commonly comes to pass, is within the ordinary course of supernatural providence; that is, imperfect conversion takes place first, which is the disposition for perfect conversion. The soul is naturally, by reason of its obediential power, "capable of grace," and is made "capable of God by grace." Certain immanentists misunderstood these words of St. Thomas: "the soul is naturally capable of grace"; it does not possess within itself the germ of grace but only an obediential power, as St. Thomas declares in several places; cf. ad 3.

Second conclusion. Sometimes, however, justification or conversion is miraculous, according as God, operating outside the usual order of His providence, suddenly moves a sinner to perfect conversion, without any preceding disposition in priority of time. This occurred in the conversion of St. Paul which is commemorated by the Church as a miracle for two reasons: 1. because, as St. Thomas says, St. Paul "suddenly attained to a certain perfection of justice"; 2. and because a miraculous external prostration was also added to it. The sudden conversion of Mary Magdalen is also cited by many theologians, such as Billuart, as miraculous. And in the nineteenth century such was the conversion of Father Ratisbonne in Rome.

Reply to first objection. Very many miracles, such as the resurrection of the body, are inferior to justification, with respect to the good they produce, although they possess more of the nature of a miracle. In the same way, the grace of the virtues and the gifts is higher than the graces *gratis datae,* for example, than prophecy, Ia IIae, q. 111, a. 4; cf. Salmanticenses.

THE INDWELLING OF THE MOST BLESSED TRINITY
TO WHICH JUSTIFICATION TERMINATES

We have dealt with this question at length in the treatise *De Deo Trino,* explaining St. Thomas' article, Ia, q. 43, a. 3: Whether the invisible mission of a divine person is only according to the gift of sanctifying grace. Only the principal points will be outlined here.

God is already present in all things according as He preserves them in being (Ia, q. 8, a. 3); but He is especially present in the just, according as He is in them as an object quasi-experimentally knowable and lovable, and sometimes actually known and loved. Thus Christ promises (John 14:23): "If anyone love Me, he will keep My word, and My Father will love him, and We will come to him, and will make Our abode with him." And again, St. Paul writes (Rom. 5:5): "The charity of God is poured forth in our hearts, by the Holy Ghost, who is given to us." Cf. the encyclical of Leo XIII, *Divinum illud munus,* May 9, 1897. It is a question of the special presence of the most Blessed Trinity according as, through living faith illuminated by the gift of wisdom, God is known quasi-experientially and loved, and we take delight in Him, as St. Thomas explains (Ia, q. 43, a. 3; IIa IIae, q. 45, a. 2).

But there are three different interpretations of this doctrine, the first proposed by Vasquez, the second by Suarez, and the third by the most eminent Thomists.

Vasquez holds that this special presence is not of itself real, but only affective, like the presence of a friend who is physically at a distance; God is, nevertheless, really present in us by His ordinary presence as preserving us in being. But Vasquez does not sufficiently safeguard the words of Holy Scripture on this special presence.

Suarez maintains that the most Blessed Trinity is really present in the just as object of charity, even independently of its ordinary presence; for the charity of a wayfarer demands and constitutes a presence not merely affective but real of the object which we enjoy.

The foremost Thomists, notably John of St. Thomas, declare that the charity of a wayfarer demands the affective presence and craves the real presence of the God it loves, but does not constitute that presence. Thus we love the humanity of Christ and the Blessed Virgin Mary, although they do not dwell in us. Hence a special presence of the most Blessed Trinity presupposes the ordinary presence of God preserving us in being, but it is nevertheless a real presence by a reason of its own in the sense that it is the presence of an object known and loved quasi-experientially; for a quasi-experiential knowledge has its term in a thing present, not at a distance. (Similarly accident presupposes substance but is itself a reality.) We know God quasi-experientially by the filial affection He excites in us; thus "the Spirit Himself giveth testimony to our spirit that we are the sons of God" (Rom. 8:16).

CHAPTER XI

QUESTION 114

MERIT

▀▀

AFTER considering justification, which is the effect of operative grace, we must treat of merit, which is the effect of (sanctifying) cooperative grace.[1] Merit is related to sanctifying grace in the same way as operation follows being. (Cf. above Ia IIae, q. 111, a. 2 c.)

There are two parts to this question.

1. What merit is, how divided, and what conditions it demands (a. 1-4); that is, whether man can merit anything from God, whether without grace he can merit eternal life, whether he can merit it *de condigno*, whether sanctifying grace is the principle of merit, principally by means of charity.

2. What is included under merit (a. 5-10); that is, whether man can merit the first grace for himself, or for another, whether he can merit reconversion for himself after a fall, whether he can merit an increase of grace for himself, final perseverance, and temporal goods.

ARTICLE I. WHETHER MAN CAN MERIT ANYTHING FROM GOD

State of the question. By merit is meant a good work to which a recompense is attached and constituting a right to a reward. It seems that man cannot merit anything from God: 1. because we can never repay Him adequately for what we already owe Him; "We are unprofitable servants," hence we cannot merit further gifts or reward; 2. because a man who does good profits himself, not God, and therefore God owes us no reward; 3. because God is debtor to no man;

---

[1] Cooperative actual grace is not required for all merit; for example, meritorious acts of the gifts of the Holy Ghost do not demand it. They proceed from operative actual grace, for the soul does not strictly move itself to them, but is moved by the Holy Ghost, but with free consent. (Cf. Ia IIae, q. 68, a. 1, 2, and 3; also St. Thomas on the Epistle to the Romans, 8:14.)

"who hath first given to Him, and recompense shall be made him?"
Therefore He does not owe us a reward; consequently no man can
properly merit anything from God, but only in an inaccurate sense,
for merit is a right to a reward.

It should be remarked that the Lutherans and Calvinists denied that
man could merit anything from God, and denied in particular that
he could merit eternal life. This conclusion follows from their principles, namely, that fallen man is not intrinsically justified but only
extrinsically by denomination, through imputation of the justice of
Christ, and thus all his works are evil; therefore he can merit nothing
from God, and faith alone without the works of charity justifies.

Against these heresies, it is of faith that a justified man can really
and properly merit something from God, even eternal life itself, "and
the attainment of eternal life itself provided he gives place to grace."
(Council of Trent, Denz., no. 842; cf. II Council of Orange, can. 18,
Denz., no. 191; Council of Florence, Denz., no. 714; Council of Trent,
Sess. VI, chap. 16, Denz., no. 809; can. 32, Denz., no. 842.)

From all these declarations of the Church can be drawn the following proposition which is of faith: "The good works of the just truly
and properly merit eternal life as well as the increase of grace and
glory." Indeed the Council of Trent (Sess. XIV, chap. 8; Denz., no.
904) defined the value not only of merit, but of the satisfaction resulting from the good works of the just; that is, the just, by good works
and by patiently enduring, at the same time, the sufferings inflicted
by God, satisfy for their temporal punishment; and this meritorious,
satisfactory power is derived from grace, whereby man is a son of
God and a member of Christ, by the cooperation of faith; nevertheless, these merits and satisfactions are, to a certain extent, really ours.
This last proposition is derived from the condemnation of Baius who
declared (Denz., no. 1008): "In those redeemed by the grace of Christ,
no good merit can be found which is not gratuitously conferred upon
the undeserving"; and (Denz., no. 1010): "The release from temporal
punishment, which often remains when the sin is forgiven, and the
resurrection of the body are properly to be ascribed only to the merits
of Christ." Likewise Quesnel (Denz., no. 1419): "Faith, the practice,
increase, and reward of faith, all is a gift of the sheer liberality of
God." The teaching of the Church on merit is based upon many
scriptural texts which set before us even eternal life as the reward to
be conferred upon the good works of the just.

The conclusion of St. Thomas is that man can merit something from God, not according to absolute equality, but according to the presupposition of a divine ordination.

The first, or negative, part of the proposition is thus proved by theological argument.

Since merit is a right to a reward, it cannot be in accordance with absolute equality of justice unless there is equality of justice between the parties. But between God and man there is great inequality, for they are infinitely removed from each other, and all the good in man comes from God: "Who hath first given to Him?" Therefore man cannot merit anything from God according to absolute equality of justice, that is, according to strictest justice. (This is found only in Christ for, by reason of the divine person, He was equal to the Father.) Such merit can exist only between equals. In fact, this merit according to absolute equality of justice does not exist among men between a son and his father, according as the son receives from his father that whence he merits.

This is the element of truth contained in the error of the Protestants, of Baius, and of the Jansenists; it had already been affirmed by Augustine when he declared that our merits are "the gift of God" inasmuch as they proceed from His grace.

The second, affirmative, part of St. Thomas' conclusion is proved from theological argument, supposing revelation of the fact as follows:

God deputed the power to man to do supernaturally good works for something in the way of a reward, as Sacred Scripture avers. But man can freely use this power by doing good supernaturally. Therefore man can merit something from God in accordance with the presupposition of a divine ordination. There is thus a certain parallel between the natural order and the order of grace.

Reply to first objection. Liberty is necessary for merit; that is, a meritorious act must be free, in that man gives to God what is within the range of possibility for him.

Reply to second objection. God does not seek utility from our good works, but glory, that is, the manifestation of His goodness. Rather, from our devotion to Him, the profit is ours and not His. Hence it is necessary for merit that we act with the motive of God's glory, which proceeds from our love for Him, in other words, from charity, as will be shown more explicitly below.

Reply to third objection, which should be consulted: "Since our action has no justification for merit except on the presupposition of a divine ordination, it does not follow that God is made our debtor absolutely, but His own, so far as it is due to Him that His ordination should be fulfilled." Cf. Ia, q. 21, a. 4: "A work of divine justice always presupposes a work of mercy and is based upon it. . . . And thus in any work of God whatever, mercy appears as its primary root . . . , the power of which operates more forcibly." Therefore, to avoid vainglory we should recognize that we are "unprofitable servants"; nor should we attribute our good works to ourselves or think that God is obligated to us on their account, when, as a matter of fact, He owes nothing to us but only to Himself, according to the gratuity of His ordination.

I insist. Even our action, inasmuch as it is free and prompt, comes from God and we owe it to Him; therefore neither can we merit by it.

Reply. We cannot merit by it in strict justice, as will presently be explained, I grant; but by real, proper justice, presupposing, however, the divine ordination, I deny.

OBSERVATION

From this article it is already possible to draw a definition of merit in general and the basis of its subdivisions. Merit can be defined either in the concrete or in the abstract; cf. Salmanticenses, no. 53. In the concrete, it is an action to which recompense is due in justice (cf. body of the article), or a good work which confers a right to a reward. In the abstract, it is a right to a reward (Cajetan). This is the formal reason of merit, to which is opposed the guilt demanding punishment, demerit in the abstract, or the reason on account of which sin is deserving of punishment. Thence is derived the basis for the division of merit according as this division is based on the definition of the whole to be divided according to its formal reason, so that the division may be essential rather than accidental, and through members contradictorily or contrarily opposed; cf. the laws of division in logic.

This division of merit is partly contained in our first article and partly in the sixth, which deals expressly with merit *de congruo.* But it might be well to anticipate the explanation so that the conclusion of article three may be more evident, treating as it does of merit *de condigno.* It will appear from this that merit is denominated (named), not univocally, but analogically, and first from the merits of Christ, just as demerit is denominated analogically, and first from mortal sin rather than from venial sin; cf. Ia IIae, q. 88, a. 1 ad 1. Many writers do not consider this, but seem to apply the notion of merit as if it were univocal, whereupon many difficulties arise.

According to St. Thomas and his adherents merit is divided as follows:

Merit	*de condigno* in justice	in strict justice	implies in itself absolute equality to the reward; such was the merit of Christ, inasmuch as, by reason of the divine person, He is equal to the Father.
		condign only	implies a value not equal to the reward, but proportionate to it, according to a divine ordination and promise, without which promise there would be no strict right.
	de congruo not in justice	*de congruo* strictly speaking	based on friendship, by friendly right to the reward, it presupposes the state of grace.
		de congruo broadly speaking	based on the bounty or mercy of God, it does not presuppose the state of grace, but a certain disposition for grace, or prayer as it exists in the sinner.

This demands explanation, and subsequently we shall find its basis in the articles.

Merit *de condigno* is merit based on justice according to the definition of merit: the right to a reward.

1. Merit *de condigno* in strict justice carries within it a value absolutely equal to the reward. Such was the merit of Christ alone, inasmuch as its value proceeded from the divine person by reason of which Christ is equal to the Father. Thus any act of charity on the part of Christ while still a wayfarer was of a value absolutely equal to the eternal life of all the elect. It was worth more than all the merits of men and angels taken together. Therein appears the victory of Christ, according to His own words: "I have overcome the world."

Hence Thomists commonly teach, contrary to Scotus, that the

acts of Christ were of absolutely infinite intrinsic value both for merit and for satisfaction, and that His merit was *de condigno* in strictest justice, even commutative, at the very pinnacle of right, and even superabounding, cf. IIIa, q. 46, a. 6 ad 6; q. 48, a. 1 and 2; for the charity of Christ dying on the cross was more pleasing to God than all the sins of men taken together were displeasing.

2. But merit *de condigno* which is merely condign is not defined in the same way by Thomists and by Scotus; cf. Billuart. Scotus says that the act of charity of a wayfarer is not properly and intrinsically meritorious *de condigno* for eternal life, but only so extrinsically, by divine ordination and acceptation. In fact, he accordingly holds that God can accept merely natural good works as meritorious for eternal life; in this the Nominalists agree. Herein appears the contingentism and libertism of Scotus, the root of whose theory is that, for him, habitual grace is not substantially supernatural but only extrinsically so, in the same way as the restoration of natural sight to a blind man by supernatural means.

Thomists maintain that the act of charity of a wayfarer is properly and intrinsically meritorious *de condigno* for eternal life from the very nature of charity and of grace, the seed of glory, presupposing, however, the divine ordination and promise, without which there would be no strict right to eternal life, but only a relation to it. This is a corollary of the definition of grace essentially supernatural as a physical and formal participation in the divine nature, which is opposed to Scotist and Nominalist theory. (Cf. Salmanticenses, *De gratia*, "de merito," disp. II; John of St. Thomas; Billuart.)

Merit *de congruo* is that which is not founded on justice; it is two-fold:

1. Merit *de congruo,* strictly speaking, is based on friendship or on a friendly right to a reward; it is found in works done out of charity, inasmuch as charity is analogically but properly a certain friendship between God and the just man. Thus a just man can merit the first grace for another man; a Christian mother can likewise merit *de congruo* even the very conversion of her son, as did St. Monica and as the blessed Virgin Mary merited for us *de congruo* what Christ merited for us *de condigno,* so Pius X declares in his encyclical *Ad diem illum,* February 2, 1904 (Denz., no. 3034). This merit *de congruo,* strictly speaking, is therefore based on the laws of friendship and presupposes the state of grace. (Cf. below, art. 6 c and ad 1, 2, 3.)

2. However, merit *de congruo,* broadly speaking, does not presuppose the state of grace but only a certain disposition for sanctifying grace or prayer, just as prayer may be present in a sinner in the state of mortal sin. It is therefore not based on any friendly right but only on the bounty or mercy of God who rewards it. (Cf. St. Thomas, a. 3, body of the article; *IV Sent.,* dist. 15, q. 1, a. 3, qc. 4.) Thus, by good works done outside of charity we merit something *de congruo,* in a broad sense; cf. Salmanticenses [2] and Billuart.[3] We shall presently find the basis of this division in St. Thomas' next article.

N.B. From the foregoing can be deduced a conclusion which is of the greatest moment and to which insufficient attention is paid by some writers: the term "merit" is not applied univocally but analogically, and that not only as it refers either to human affairs (such as the merit of a soldier) or to divine, but it is even applied analogically with regard to the divine referring both to merit *de condigno* and to merit *de congruo* and also to their subdivisions. It is evident from this that analogous concepts share the same name in common but the reason signified by the name is not absolutely the same in both (as in univocal concepts), but different absolutely and the same under a certain aspect (that is, either comparatively or proportionally the same). Manifestly, with respect to dignity, merit is denominated in the first place from the merits of Christ, and with respect to application of the name, it is denominated in the first place from merit in the human order, for instance, the merit of a soldier.

Merit thus refers analogically (by an analogy of proportion) but nevertheless properly and intrinsically, that is, more than metaphorically, to merit *de condigno* and also to merit *de congruo* strictly speaking. But it does not refer properly but metaphorically, or according to an analogy of extrinsic attribution, to merit *de congruo* broadly speaking; cf. Salmanticenses.

ARTICLE II. WHETHER A PERSON WITHOUT GRACE CAN MERIT ETERNAL LIFE

The reply is that neither in the state of integral nature nor in the state of fallen nature can a man by purely natural powers, or without grace, merit eternal life. This is of faith.

Proof from authority. "The grace of God life everlasting" (Rom.

---

[2] *De gratia,* tr. 16, *de merito,* disp. II, no. 9.
[3] *De gratia, de merito.*

6:23); "If I . . . have not charity, I am nothing . . . it profiteth me nothing" (I Cor. 13:2–3). Furthermore this was defined against the Pelagians and Semi-Pelagians at the Council of Orange (Denz., no. 178), which affirmed that there can be no beginning of salvation without grace. Again, the Council of Trent (Sess. VI, chap. 8; Denz., no. 801) declared "none of those things which precede justification, whether faith or works, to merit the grace of justification itself"; therefore, much less glory which is eternal life. In the same way theologians commonly distinguish salutary but not meritorious works, which precede justification, from meritorious works which presuppose it. There are also the condemned propositions of Baius (Denz., 1013, 1015), who held that the works of the just are meritorious" not from the fact that they are accomplished through grace, but because they are conformed to the law." There is a confusion of the two orders in Baius as well as in Pelagius, but by an inverse mode; for Pelagius, the optimist, the works of Christian life are not beyond the powers of nature; for Baius, the pessimist, they do not surpass the requirements of nature, hence they are not strictly supernatural; and grace, according to Baius, is reducible to integrity of nature.

Theological proof. Although the answer is revealed elsewhere, it can also be proved from more universal principles of faith. Eternal life, as essentially supernatural, exceeds the proportion of created nature and of its natural operations. But merit is a work conferring a right to a proportionate reward, on account of divine preordination (preceding article). Therefore man cannot by purely natural powers merit eternal life.

In a word, it is out of proportion with either merit *de condigno* or merit *de congruo,* properly speaking. This is true of the state of integral nature and, with still greater reason, of the state of pure nature or of fallen nature.

Confirmation for the state of corrupt or fallen nature. No one living in the state of sin can merit eternal life, unless he is first reconciled to God by the forgiveness of sin, as will be made clearer below. But sin is not forgiven except by grace, as has been said. Therefore.[4]

---

[4] The Nominalists hold that God can accept merely natural works as meritorious for eternal life; for example, dying on the battlefield in defense of one's country, a heroic, ethically good act.

Reply. This would not be merit *de condigno,* nor strictly *de congruo,* but at most *de congruo* in the broad sense; so that it would no longer be merit properly speaking. Hence this would be overturning even generally accepted nominal definitions, con-

REFUTATION OF OBJECTIONS

First objection. But a sinner can observe several commandments of the Decalogue and also hear Mass.

Reply. I distinguish: he can observe them in substance, granted; but as to mode, that is, by charity, denied.

Second objection. An evil deed merits punishment without the habit of malice; therefore a good deed merits a reward without the habit of grace.

Reply. I deny the consequence, since proportionately more is required for good and meritorious action than for doing evil; for good proceeds from an integral cause, whereas evil arises from any defect and mortal sin from any grave defect. On the other hand, a mortal sin of itself leads to the status of eternal punishment, while a good work without grace does not possess any condignity to eternal life, since the dignity of the worker is lacking.

Third objection. Man in the state of sin can satisfy by self-imposed penance; therefore he can also merit.

Reply. Admitting the premise, which is disputed, there is still a disparity in that satisfaction is estimated according to an equality between the punishment and the guilt, but merit according to the condignity of the work as well as the worker compared with the reward.

Fourth objection. Then the naturally good works which are performed before justification are useless.

Reply. They are not meritorious (cf. above, q. 109, a. 1 and 6), but in a measure they prepare the way for grace if they are performed under actual grace by a will which has begun to be converted; cf. Billuart. But works that are merely natural although ethically good neither prepare the way for grace (q. 109, a. 1 and 6), nor for still greater reason do they merit it *de congruo,* nor, accordingly, *de condigno.* However, they are not utterly useless; for they serve the purpose of preventing further sins and oppose less obstacles to grace.

---

fusing all the divisions of merit; it would especially mean confusing merit *de condigno* with merit *de congruo* in the broad sense. But the definitions generally accepted are based upon the principle that it is opposed to the nature of things for those which are of an inferior order to be ordained to supernatural goods, as if they were merits of commensurate worth. In the same way, it is incompatible with merit *de congruo* in the strict sense, for such merit is based on the laws of friendship, and the sinner is not yet a friend of God.

ARTICLE III. WHETHER A JUST MAN CAN MERIT
ETERNAL LIFE *EX CONDIGNO*

State of the question. It seems not to be so for: 1. the Apostle says (Rom. 8:18): "The sufferings of this time are not worthy to be compared with the glory to come, that shall be revealed in us"; 2. no act of the present life can be equal to eternal life.

The reply, nevertheless, is that the works of the just according as they proceed from habitual grace are properly meritorious of eternal life *de condigno*. This is a theological certainty.

1. Proof from Scripture: "Be glad and rejoice, for your reward is very great in heaven" (Matt. 5:12); "As to the rest, there is laid up for me a crown of justice, which the Lord the just judge will render to me in that day" (II Tim. 4:8); the terms "justice . . . just judge . . . render" express merit based on justice; "Blessed are they that suffer persecution for justice' sake: for theirs is the kingdom of heaven" (Matt. 5:10); in reply to Peter's question as to what reward he shall have who leaves all to follow Christ, our Lord answers that he "shall receive a hundredfold, and shall possess life everlasting" (Matt. 19:29). Again St. Matthew (20:1-16) explains this by the example of the householder who renders the daily wage of a penny to those who worked but an hour. And St. Paul affirms: "That which is at present momentary and light of our tribulation, worketh for us above measure exceedingly an eternal weight of glory" (II Cor. 4:17); "God will render to every man according to his works. To them indeed, who according to patience in good work, seek . . . incorruption, eternal life" (Rom. 2:6 f.); "For God is not unjust, that He should forget your work" (Heb. 6:10); "And do not forget to do good, and to impart; for by such sacrifices God's favor is obtained" (*ibid.,* 13:16); "all your . . . tribulations, which you endure, . . . that you may be counted worthy of the kingdom of God" (II Thess. 1:4 f.). Finally the Book of Wisdom had declared of the just: "God hath tried them, and found them worthy of Himself" (Wisd. 3:5).

2. Proof from the Council of Trent (Denz., no. 842). It is of faith that the just man can "truly merit eternal life and an increase of glory." From this it can be deduced as a theological certainty (cf. argument *Sed contra*) that the just man can merit eternal life, not merely in the true sense but also *de condigno.* In fact all theologians judge by the words quoted from Sacred Scripture by the Council of Trent, that it is here referring to merit *de condigno,* although this term is not explicitly employed. Cf. also the Councils of Orange (Denz., no. 191) and of Trent (Denz., nos. 803, 809 f.). But if the just man sins mortally before his death and perseveres in sin, he forfeits his merit.

3. *Theological proof.* Article 3 should first be read.

Merit *de condigno* is merit of which the value in justice is proportionate to the excellence of the reward, according to divine preordination. But the works of the just, inasmuch as they proceed from sanctifying grace and the movement of the Holy Ghost, are proportionate in justice to the excellence of eternal life. Therefore.

Thus the words of St. Paul cited by the Council of Trent assume a more explicit meaning: "God will render to every man according to his works" (Rom. 2:6) and "As to the rest, there is laid up for me a crown of justice, which the Lord, the just judge will render to me in that day" (II Tim. 4:8).

The major is explained above.

The minor is proved by the fact that these works are supernatural, that is, of the same order as glory; and an equality of worth is observable both from the dignity of habitual grace whereby man is made a participator in the divine nature, and accordingly can perform works worthy of God as His son and heir, and from the power of the Holy Ghost moving him, which is termed "a fountain of water, springing up into life everlasting" (John 4:14). In opposition to Scotus, it should be added that the proportion is intrinsic, based on the very essence of sanctifying grace which is essentially supernatural, intrinsically ordained toward glory, as the seed of the tree is to the tree.

Reply to first objection. Pain is not meritorious of eternal life unless it is borne from charity.

Reply to second objection. Every work of justice presupposes a work of mercy.

Reply to third objection. Habitual grace is equal to glory, not actually but virtually, as the seed of the tree, wherein is contained the whole tree in potency. Likewise dwells in man by grace the Holy Ghost, who is the sufficient cause of eternal life, wherefore He is called the pledge of our inheritance. Thus condignity remains, not according to absolute equality with the reward, but according to intrinsic proportion.

Doubt. The body of the article presents a difficulty, for St. Thomas says that the works of the just according to their substance and so far as they derive from free will (not from grace) merit glory as it were *de congruo*. This is a problem because above in q. 109, a. 1 and 6, he teaches expressly that man cannot prepare himself for grace by his merely natural powers, and therefore, with still greater reason, he cannot merit it *de congruo*. There are two interpretations (cf. Billuart).

1. According to Sylvius, by the works of the just according to substance St. Thomas does not mean works of the merely natural powers (since many surpass the powers of nature entirely as, for example, the acts of informed faith and hope); but he is referring to works proceeding from free will moved by actual grace without the infusion of sanctifying grace and charity. But these can merit glory *de congruo*.

2. The solution of John of St. Thomas is better since it distinguishes between the two kinds of merit *de congruo*, that is, merit *de congruo* strictly speaking, based on the right of friendship, and merit *de congruo* broadly speaking, based on the liberality or magnanimity of God. He affirms that merely natural works, which do not proceed from either sanctifying or actual grace, are not meritorious of eternal life by merit *de congruo* in the strict sense but only in the broad sense; not strictly because they are of an inferior order and have no proportion to glory, but broadly, that is, out of the bounty of God. Hence St. Thomas does not say "these works merit *de congruo*," but, "There is congruity because of a certain equality of proportion. For it seems congruous that if man works according to his power, God will reward him according to the excellence of His power," or according to His magnanimity. There is here a proportion of workers, not of works. This is the opinion of John of St. Thomas; cf. a. 5 below for additional explanation.

Refutation of the objections raised by Scotus; cf. Cajetan and Billuart.

First objection. God rewards the just beyond their just deserts, as is commonly said. Therefore the works of the just are not intrinsically meritorious of eternal life *de condigno*.

Reply. I grant the premise but deny the conclusion. From the fact that God rewards the works of the just beyond their due, it does not follow that the just do not merit eternal life *de condigno*, but rather that God in His liberality and mercy, which is always united to justice, adds a further degree in the perfection of vision. Thus it is also said that the punishment of the damned is short of what is due because even in their case mercy tempers somewhat the rigor of justice.

Second objection. If the works of the just were intrinsically meritorious of eternal life *de condigno,* God could not refuse them glory by His absolute power without injustice.

Reply. 1. This proves too much, for merely by His absolute power God could even annihilate the humanity of Christ and all the blessed, since there is nothing intrinsically contradictory in this. Absolute power is thus distinguished from power ordered by wisdom, whether ordinary or extraordinary. 2. As Cajetan writes: "God, who is debtor to Himself, Himself ordained [to glory] not by an additional ordination, as Scotus thought, but by grace itself, the act being meritorious from the mere fact that it proceeds from grace, . . . as He cannot act against Himself, so neither can He withdraw His reward." Cf. below, the conditions of merit. Cajetan possibly exaggerates here in the opposite direction. For a divine promise would be necessary in order that the just man should have not only an intrinsic relationship to eternal life but a strict right to it. Thomists generally hold that beyond the intrinsic worth which meritorious acts possess by reason of sanctifying grace, a promise of rendering recompense is necessary for the existence of a strict right to a reward and for God to be obliged to make a return; but it still remains true that an act proceeding from habitual grace is intrinsically worthy of eternal life.

ARTICLE IV. WHETHER GRACE IS THE PRINCIPLE OF MERIT PRINCIPALLY BY CHARITY

State of the question. It seems that some power especially infused should be the principle of any merit and labor; but charity rather diminishes the labor. Acts of faith because of their obscurity and of patience because of their difficulty seem to be far more meritorious.

Reply. Grace is the principle of merit more particularly by charity.

Proof from Scripture from the argument *Sed contra.* "He that loveth Me shall be loved of My Father: and I will love him, and will manifest Myself to him" (John 14:21); "Whosoever shall give to drink to one of these little ones a cup of cold water only in the name of a disciple (out of fraternal charity), amen I say to you, he shall not lose his reward" (Matt. 10:42); "In Christ Jesus neither circumcision availeth anything, nor uncircumcision: but faith that worketh by charity" (Gal. 5:6); "And if I should have all faith, so that I could

remove mountains, and have not charity, I am nothing . . . and if
I should deliver my body to be burned, and have not charity, it
profiteth me nothing" (I Cor. 13:2 f.).

Theological proof.

1. An act is meritorious by divine ordination according as it tends
toward a final supernatural end. But all acts of the other virtues tend
toward a final supernatural end, that is, to God loved for His own
sake efficaciously above all things, through charity; for God loved
for His own sake is the proper object of charity. Therefore. Cf. the
answers to objections 1 and 3.

Even if charity imperates the natural act of an acquired virtue, this
act is meritorious of eternal life and supernatural as to mode.

2. What we do out of love, we do with the greatest willingness. But
man merits inasmuch as he acts willingly and freely. Therefore.

If a person in the state of mortal sin elicits an act of theological
hope, the final end of this act is God loved above all things ineffica-
ciously by a love of concupiscence, and by charity alone is He loved
efficaciously above all things with a love of friendship.

Objection. But charity diminishes the difficulty, and the more
difficult a work is the more meritorious it is.

Reply to second objection. Charity diminishes the subjective difficulty which arises from a defect in the worker, but not the objective
difficulty which proceeds from the magnitude of the work. On
the contrary, charity impels us to undertake arduous labors. But
the objective difficulty on account of the magnitude of the work
pertains to the increase of merit; on the other hand, the subjective difficulty proceeding from a defect in the worker diminishes
merit.

Reply to third objection. An act of faith is not meritorious unless
faith acts through love.

Corollary. The Blessed Virgin Mary merited more by even the
easiest acts of charity than all the martyrs together in their sufferings,
because of the greater intensity of her charity.

Doubt. Whether at least the virtual influence of charity is necessary
to merit eternal life. It is a question of merit *de condigno* of eternal
life.

The generality of Thomists and many other theologians answer in
the affirmative, against Vasquez, who holds that this virtual influence
is not necessary for acts of the other virtues, even acquired, and against

Suarez who maintains that this virtual influence is not necessary for acts of the infused virtues.

Proof of the general opinion.

1. From St. Thomas in the present article, 4 c ad 1 and 3; Ia, q. 95, a. 4; *De malo,* q. 6, a. 5 ad 7. In fact, he affirms in II, d. 40, q. 1, a. 5 ad 6: "Habitual ordination of an act toward God does not suffice, since it merits nothing by being a habit but by performing an act." It is the case of a candidate who knows his subject but is mute or unable to speak.

2. The opinion is based on many texts from Sacred Scripture where, with reference to the principle of merit, this is not assigned to habitual charity alone but to its act. For example: "He that shall receive one such little child in My name, receiveth Me" (Matt. 18:5); "And every one that hath left house . . . or father or mother . . . for My name's sake, shall receive a hundredfold, and shall possess life everlasting" (*ibid.,* 19:29).

3. The principal theological argument is the one already given in the present article, 4 c and ad 1. "Charity, so far as it has the final end for its object, moves the other virtues to act, for the habit to which the end belongs always imperates the habits to which belong the means to the end." In other words, we merit to attain the final end by that whereby we tend toward it, that is, by charity at least virtually influencing us.

First confirmation. For an act to be meritorious of eternal life it must be rendered in obedience to God the rewarder. But this is done by charity virtually influencing it and not by the other virtues. Therefore there must be the love of God at least virtually influencing the act.

Second confirmation. The essential reward in heaven corresponds to the essential perfection of the way. But the Christian perfection of a wayfarer consists essentially and especially in charity, according to the words of St. Paul: "Above all these things have charity, which is the bond of perfection" (Col. 3:14). (Cf. IIa IIae, q. 184, a. 1.) Therefore the essential reward in heaven corresponds to the charity of the wayfarer. Thus the degree of merit is the degree of charity.

Objection. St. Thomas says, *De malo,* q. 2, a. 5 ad 7: "To those who possess charity, every act is either meritorious or demeritorious," since there are no indifferent acts in the individual. But according to the preceding opinion there may exist in the just man an act which is neither meritorious nor demeritorious, since there may be an act good in itself, for instance, ethically good, but without the virtual influence of charity—such as paying a debt.

Reply. In a just man all acts of virtue are under the virtual influence of charity according as the just man, not merely at the instant of justification, but often, elicits and is bound to elicit acts of charity by virtue of which all things are referred to God, as St. Thomas teaches, *De virtutibus,* q. 2, a. 11 ad 2. Therefore all the good works of the just are meritorious but not without the virtual influence of charity.

Second objection. For a work to be satisfactory, the influence of charity is not required. Therefore neither is it required for merit.

Reply. Let the premise pass (cf. treatise on penance); I deny the consequence, since more is required for merit than for satisfaction, which depends upon an equality between the punishment and the guilt, not upon an equality or proportion between the good work and the excellence of the reward.

Third objection. For prayer to possess impetratory force the influence of charity is not required, for a sinner is able to pray; therefore neither is it required for merit.

Reply. There is a disparity, for impetration of itself refers only to the order of divine mercy, but merit refers to justice. Thus a sinner in the state of mortal sin can pray and does so at times, which is a salutary act, but he cannot merit, except *de congruo* in the broad sense. (Cf. IIa IIae, q. 83, a. 15 and 16.) Therefore the conclusion stands: without the virtual influence of charity, no act of virtue, either acquired or infused, in the just man, is meritorious *de condigno* of eternal life, since charity imperates all the virtues as the will does all the faculties.

First corollary. Merit is greater or less according to whether charity influences the act more or less, proximately or remotely. Cf. treatise on charity under acts remiss in charity.

Second corollary. Subjectively at least, an easy act proceeding from greater charity is more meritorious than a very difficult act proceeding from less charity. Thus, as has been said, the Blessed Virgin Mary merited more by easy acts than all the martyrs together by their tortures.

Third corollary. All the meritorious works of Christ were of the same infinite personal value (inasmuch as they proceeded from the same divine person and from the plenitude of His charity, which did not increase) but not all were of the same objective value. Thus, objectively, His passion was of greater value than, for example, His preaching, on account of the magnitude of the work. In the same way, teaching theology for God's sake is more meritorious, objectively, than cooking for God's sake, but if the cook does his work with greater charity than the master in theology, subjectively the cook merits more than the theologian.

From the preceding four articles of St. Thomas can now be drawn the conditions necessary for merit. There are six here enumerated proceeding in order from the more general to the more particular. Thus we may construct a very clear and complete definition of a meritorious work according to remote and proximate genus and specific difference. But it is attained only at the end of the hunt or inquisition which was pursued through the foregoing articles.

A meritorious work must be: 1. free; 2. good; 3. in submission or obedience to the rewarder (this is true even for merit in the human order, such as a soldier's merit); 4. the work of a wayfarer, 5. proceeding from sanctifying grace and charity; 6. ordained by God to a promised reward. We shall explain each of these conditions briefly. They are all necessary for merit *de condigno;* in the course of the explanation it will be indicated which are not absolutely necessary for merit *de congruo.*

1. The work must be free. This is of faith against Jansenius (Denz., no. 1094), whose third proposition is condemned: "For meriting and demeriting in the state of fallen nature, freedom from necessity is not required in man; freedom from coercion suffices." The reason for this condition is that a person merits or is deserving of reward so far as he injects something of his own, and is the author of his act. But man has dominion only over free acts, which are within his power; cf. the present a. 4 and *De malo,* q. 6, a. 1, also the Salmanticenses. However, free consent to the inspiration of the Holy Ghost moving one to acts of the gifts suffices without any deliberation strictly speaking; for example, the gift of piety over and above discursive reasoning. Hence Christ would not have merited for us had He not been free in fulfilling the command of His Father; as impeccable He could not disobey privatively and yet He freely obeyed with a liberty confirmed in good.[5]

---

[5] It is certainly true that from all eternity God pre-determined the act of charity of Christ dying on the cross and the hour of Judas' betrayal, and yet both Christ's act of charity and Judas' act of treachery were free; cf. St. Thomas on John 13:1; cf. above, pp. 159 ff.

2. It must be a good work, for an evil work is deserving of punishment and an indifferent work would not suffice; it would be without relation to a reward. Moreover, there is no such thing with regard to the individual. In fact, a meritorious work must possess supernatural goodness proportioned to the supernatural reward; a work which is only ethically good does not suffice, as will be shown more explicitly in the fifth condition.

3. It must be a work done under submission or obedience to the rewarder, that is, in subordination and obedience to God; cf. Ia IIae, q. 21, a. 3; IIa IIae, q. 104, a. 3. Otherwise there would be no reason for expecting a reward from God; moreover, if our works are not referred to God they are not of the supernatural order. But an act of real charity cannot be performed except for the sake of God and, accordingly, except in subjection and reverence toward God.

4. It must be the act of a wayfarer; cf. Ia, q. 62, a. 9 ad 3. This is manifest from revelation: "In what place soever it [the tree] shall fall, there shall it be" (Eccles. 11:3); "The night cometh [that is, death] when no man can work," not meritoriously, of course (John 9:4); "Whilst we have time, let us work good" (Gal. 6:10); "For we must all be manifested before the judgment seat of Christ, that every one may receive the proper things of the body, according as he hath done, whether it be good or evil" (II Cor. 5:10); "And as it is appointed unto men once to die, and after this the judgment" (Heb. 9:27).

A reason of suitability is put forth; that is, merit is a motion and a way to a reward; therefore once the reward is obtained, the merit ceases. But this argument proves only that the blessed cannot merit the essential reward which they already possess; it does not really prove that they cannot merit an accidental reward or increase of glory; nor does it prove that the souls detained in purgatory can no longer merit.

It is admitted, however, that the term of man's pathway is death for, as St. Thomas explains (*Contra Gentes,* Bk. IV, chaps. 92-95), since man is naturally composed of soul and body, the body by its nature is united to the soul for the benefit of the soul; because matter exists for the sake of form, that is, so that the soul may tend toward and attain to its perfection. Therefore, after the separation from the body, the soul is no longer strictly wayfaring. But this is only an argument from suitability. There would be no certainty on the subject without a revelation manifesting God's will.

The difficulty regards the term of our way. Cajetan, with reference to Ia, q. 64, a. 1, no. 18, declares: "The soul is rendered inflexible by the first act which it elicits in the state of separation from the body and then demerits, not as in life, but as arrived at its term." But this opinion is generally not accepted, as the Salmanticenses remark, *De gratia,* "de merito," disp. I, dub. IV, no. 36; for, according to the testimony of Holy Scripture, men can merit and demerit before death, but not in death; and it would not be a man who merited but a separated soul. Therefore the state of wayfarer ceases with the state of union between soul and body, and before the first instant of separation between the soul and the body the time was divisible to an infinite degree, but at that instant there is no longer either wayfaring or merit. For as in matters which are measured by time, the first nonexistence of the way coincides with the first instant of the new state, that is, with the first existence of separation from the body. Otherwise, moreover, a person dying in the state of mortal sin might be saved and one dying in the state of grace might be damned; furthermore, an infant dying without baptism could be saved by an act elicited at the first instant of separation from the body. Baptism would then not be necessary for the salvation of infants nor would a limbo exist for such souls.

Vasquez teaches that the blessed can merit accidental reward, and the souls in purgatory as well; but he brings forward a text of St. Thomas in support unwarrantedly, as the Salmanticenses demonstrate. These latter hold that Elias and Enoch are in the state for meriting since they are still wayfarers.

5. It must proceed from sanctifying grace under the virtual influence of charity; cf. q. 114, a. 2. As we have said, it is of faith that the act must proceed from sanctifying grace and charity. (Council of Trent, Sess. VI, chap. 8.) "If I . . . have not charity, I am nothing . . . it profiteth me nothing" (I Cor. 13:2 f.), in the order of eternal life. This is because otherwise there would be no intrinsic proportion between a meritorious work and a supernatural reward and hence no right to the reward; in fact, man would remain in the state of mortal sin, deserving of punishment, not reward. However, merit *de congruo* broadly speaking, based on the mercy of God, may exist without this condition, in the same way as the impetrative value of the prayer of a sinner; cf. a. 3.

6. It must be a work ordained by God toward a promised reward; cf. q. 114, a. 1 ad 3: "Our action has no reason for merit except on the presupposition of a divine ordination; [wherefore] it does not follow

that God becomes our debtor absolutely [who hath first given to Him?], but rather His own, so far as it is due to Him that His ordination should be fulfilled." Again in article 2 c: "The merit of man depends on divine preordination" since "all the good in man comes from God" and man has no right before God unless he receives such a right from God. Hence without this divine ordination and promise, our good works would give us no right to a reward, since they are already due to God by several other titles, such as creation, supreme dominion, final end. Therefore, even if God had not promised us a reward, man ought to love God above all things.[6]

This doctrine is based on Holy Scripture: "The man that endureth temptation . . . when he hath been proved, . . . shall receive the crown of life, which God hath promised to them that love Him" (Jas. 1:12); "He that cometh to God, must believe that He is, and is a rewarder to them that seek Him" (Heb. 11:6). The Council of Trent (Sess. VI, chap. 16; Denz., no. 809) defines: "To those who work well unto the end, hoping in God, eternal life is offered both as the grace mercifully promised to the sons of God through Christ Jesus and as the reward faithfully rendered to their good works by the promise of the same God."

Confirmation. The good works of the blessed and of the souls in purgatory are not meritorious, because God has not ordained them to a reward. For God does not order good works to a reward outside of the state of wayfarer, although He could do so if He so willed.

This sixth condition which is required for merit *de condigno* but not really for merit *de congruo* was misinterpreted by Scotus and the Nominalists. They understood that a meritorious act possesses its condignity extrinsically and solely on account of this promise; therefore they held that God could accept a merely natural good act as meritorious *de condigno* of eternal life.

The true sense of this sixth condition, as we have already observed in agreement with the majority of Thomists, is that, beyond the intrinsic worth which every meritorious act possesses on account of sanctifying grace and charity, the promise of a reward to be rendered is necessary that there may be a strict right to the reward obliging God to render it. Thus, in the souls detained in purgatory, acts of charity

---

[6] Thus St. Thomas says at the beginning of article 4 of the present question: "A human act has the nature of meriting . . . by divine ordination whereby an act is said to be meritorious of that good toward which man is divinely ordained."

are no longer meritorious, although free, good, supernatural, and performed in obedience to God.

Cajetan, in refuting Scotus on article 4, did not perhaps advert to the possibility of the error contrary to Scotism in this matter which would be the negation of the sixth condition. Billuart examines the objections denying this condition.

Objection. Just as an evil work is of itself deserving of punishment independently of the ordination of the judge, so a work of charity possesses of itself something of worth commensurate to a reward, and that not by any divine ordination or promise. But merit is nothing other than a work of worth equal to a reward. Therefore this sixth condition is not necessary.

Reply. I deny the major: there is no comparison between a good work and an evil work; for the latter, in offending, injures the right of another by its very offense, wherefore, without any ordination of the judge, there arises an obligation to repair the injured right. On the contrary, the good work of charity is already due to God the Creator and Lord; and, for man to possess the right of exacting a recompense requires a special ordination of God; because God has no obligation except to Himself, and this by reason of His promise. Hence, if God had commanded us to do good without promise of a reward, He would not be bound to grant it to us.

Doubt. Whether God grants a reward to merits only in faithfulness to His promise, or in justice.

Reply. Not only out of faithfulness but in distributive justice, which however has something of the mode of commutative justice. For St. Paul declares: "As to the rest, there is laid up for me a crown of justice, which the Lord the just judge will render to me in that day" (II Tim. 4:8). This is because, although a simple promise produces only the obligation of faithfulness, a promise to be fulfilled by the promiser on condition of some laborious work, carries an obligation of justice. Thus "to pay the reward of labor is an act of justice" (Ia IIae, q. 21, a. 3). This is not the commutative justice which exists between equals, for man can give nothing to God which is not already His and under His dominion. But it is distributive justice whereby a superior gives to his inferiors, not equally but proportionately, each according to his worth and merit. Nevertheless it is a certain kind of commutative justice, according as God gives commensurately, and so also in imposing punishment for demerit.

WHAT IS INCLUDED UNDER MERIT (A. 6–10)

Beside eternal life, which is the essential object of merit (cf. a. 2), the question is raised in articles 5–10, which of several other objects fall under merit. The two principles that elucidate this second part of the question may be formulated thus: The just man can merit that to which his merit is ordained by God; but the principle of merit itself does not fall under merit.

By virtue of the first principle, the just man can merit for himself *de condigno:* eternal life, increase of grace and charity, and the degree of glory proportionate to this increase. This is of faith. It is explained theologically according as the merits of the just man are ordained by God to eternal life and to the spiritual progress which leads to it (a. 8). The just man can likewise merit *de congruo,* in the strict sense, the grace of conversion for another, as St. Monica did for St. Augustine (a. 6) The just man can also merit temporal goods, not for their own sake, but so far as they are useful for salvation (a. 10).

However, since the principle of merit itself does not fall under merit, man cannot merit for himself, either *de condigno* or *de congruo* in the strict sense, the first grace, whether actual or habitual. This is a truth of faith which can be explained theologically by the foregoing principle (a. 5). Moreover, the just man cannot, before he falls, merit for himself the grace of conversion, should he subsequently fall into sin; for his merits are taken away by mortal sin which follows them. In other words, the restoration of the principle of merit does not fall under merit (a. 7).

Nor can the just man merit for himself *de condigno* nor strictly *de congruo* the grace of final perseverance. This is almost of faith; it is explained theologically according as the grace of final perseverance is no other than the state of grace (or principle of merit) preserved by God at the very moment of death (a. 9).

ARTICLE V. WHETHER MAN CAN MERIT
THE FIRST GRACE FOR HIMSELF

A difficulty arises: 1. because Augustine says: "Faith merits justification," commenting on psalm 31; 2. because God does not bestow grace except on the deserving; and 3. because the first grace may perhaps be merited by subsequent works.

Reply. It is evident that no one can merit the first grace for himself, that is, neither *de condigno* nor *de congruo* properly, but only improperly speaking. This applies to the first grace, whether actual or habitual.

Proof from the definitions of the Church. This truth is of faith; cf. against the Pelagians, the Council of Orange (Denz., no. 176), can. 3–7, 9, 14–25; the definition is renewed by the Council of Trent, Sess. VI, chap. 6 (Denz., no. 798): "Therefore are we said to be justified gratuitously, since none of those things which precede justification, whether faith or works, deserves the grace of justification itself." It also appears clearly enough from these declarations that man cannot merit even the first grace for himself *de congruo* properly speaking; for it is defined against the Pelagians and Semi-Pelagians that no one can by merely natural powers dispose himself for grace. (Cf. Council of Orange, can. 3–7, 14–25.)

This doctrine of the Church is manifestly based upon many scriptural texts; especially are cited: "Being justified freely by His grace" (Rom. 3:24; 4:4); "And if by grace, it is not now by works" (*ibid.,* 11:6); in fact, almost the entire dogmatic portion of this Epistle; also I Cor. 12:13; II Cor. 3:5; Eph. 2:5–10; Phil. 2:13; II Tim. 1:9; John 15:16; I John 4:10–19.

Theological proof with respect to merit *de condigno.*

Grace of itself exceeds the proportion of nature. But merit *de condigno* is a good work proportionate to a reward and conferring a right to the reward in justice. Therefore natural good works cannot merit *de condigno* the first grace, either actual or habitual.

Confirmation. Before justification man is in the state of mortal sin, which is an impediment to meriting grace. And after justification he cannot merit the first grace which is the principle of merit, whereas the recompense is the term of the work. The principle of merit cannot fall under merit.

This reason would also be valid for the angels since the whole argument is based on the distinction between the orders of nature and grace. This distinction is eminently clear for St. Thomas. In fact, he himself declares, *Contra Gentes,* Bk. I, chap. 3: "That there are some divine ideas which completely exceed the capacities of human reason, appears most evident"; that is, because neither the human nor the angelic mind can know naturally the divine essence according to its reason of Deity, or in its intimate life, nor, accordingly, love it. Hence we have demonstrated [7] that the existence in God of the order of truth and supernatural life can be firmly established; indeed St. Thomas says that it appears most evident. Therefore this supernatural order surpasses not only the powers but the requirements of both our nature and that of angels, and, consequently, natural merits as well. In a word, the formal object of the divine intelligence cannot be attained naturally by any intellect created or capable of creation. But supernatural mysteries pertain by their nature primarily to this formal object. Therefore they are something in God naturally inaccessible to us and to the angels.

REFUTATION OF OBJECTIONS

Reply to first objection. In the instant of justification the very act of living faith follows the infusion of grace. This act of living faith is thus meritorious of eternal life, in the same way as an act of contrition; but it does not merit the first grace from which it proceeds. Furthermore, an act of dead faith is salutary but not meritorious.

Reply to second objection. "God does not confer grace except upon the deserving, not however that they were deserving beforehand, but because He Himself makes them worthy by grace"; and this supernatural disposition cannot be meritorious with respect to the first grace.

Reply to third objection. Grace itself imparts its own good use; hence the principle of merit is such that it cannot fall under subsequent merit; whereas, on the contrary, a soldier can merit his arms before they are given to him, in view of subsequent merits, for arms do not confer but rather await their own good use by the activity of the soldier. (Cf. Ia, q. 23, a. 5.)

Corollary. Not even *de congruo* properly can a man merit the first grace for himself.

Proof. Before justification man in the state of sin is not a friend of God but His enemy. But merit *de congruo* properly is based upon a right of friendship, that is, the worker must be pleasing to the rewarder and just; in other words, there is required a fitness in the worker, not merely in the work. Therefore.

This statement seems more conformable to Sacred Scripture and the Council of Trent according to which the sinner is justified gratuitously. However, man can merit *de congruo* the first grace broadly speaking, by good works preceding justification and by

---

[7] Cf. *De revelatione*, Vol. I, chap. 11.

prayers. Thus, says Augustine, the publican was heard after his humble prayer. For merit *de congruo* in the broad sense does not demand fitness in the worker, but only in the work; it is founded on God's liberality or, like the impetratory power of prayer, upon the divine mercy. (Cf. Salmanticenses, *De merito,* disp. II, no. 9.)

ARTICLE VI. WHETHER THE JUST MAN CAN MERIT THE FIRST GRACE FOR ANOTHER

It seems so, for St. James writes in his Epistle (5:16): "Pray for one another, that you may be saved. For the continual prayer of a just man availeth much."

The precise answer of St. Thomas is: not *de condigno;* but he can well do so *de congruo* even properly speaking.

The first part of his reply is based on the scriptural text: "If Moses and Samuel shall stand before Me, my soul is not toward this people" (Jer. 15:1); and yet Moses and Samuel were of the greatest merit before God.

The theological argument is the following. Grace conferred on a mere man is especially ordained to his own sanctification, but not to the sanctification of others. It differs in this respect from the capital grace which existed in Christ, the Redeemer of all (IIIa, q. 8, a. 2). But our work has the reason of merit *de condigno* on account of the moving force of divine grace, according to the ordination and extention of this grace in justice. Therefore no one but Christ, not even the Blessed Virgin Mary, can merit *de condigno* the first grace for another. The text should be consulted.

The second part of St. Thomas' answer, that is, regarding merit *de congruo* properly speaking is in the affirmative. It is based on several scriptural texts: "The continual prayer of a just man availeth much" (Jas. 5:16); and the reference to prayer for the brethren which obtains their conversion (I John 5:16). Thus the prayer of St. Stephen, the first martyr, obtained the conversion of Paul. Likewise St. Monica procured the conversion of Augustine by her prayers and good works. In these texts it is not a question of the prayer of the sinner, but of the prayer of the just man which is at once impetratory and meritorious, meritorious of itself *de condigno* and for others *de congruo,* inasmuch as the just man is a friend of God. Similarly, the Blessed Virgin Mary merited for us *de congruo* what Christ merited *de condigno;* cf. Denz., no. 3034, encycl. of Pius X.

The argument is formulated as follows: Merit *de congruo* properly speaking is based on the right of friendship. But between the just man and God there exists the friendship of charity. Therefore it is properly fitting that God should fulfill the desire and prayer of the just man for the salvation of another, as long as there is no impediment of excessive obstinacy on the part of that other; and this merit *de congruo* is higher in proportion to the degree of charity which the just man possesses. It reaches its climax in the Blessed Virgin Mary. The text of St. Thomas should be read.

REFUTATION OF THE OBJECTIONS

First objection. Thus the living faith of one is availing for others, according to merit *de congruo* even properly speaking.

Second objection. "The impetration of prayer rests on mercy; but merit *de condigno* rests on justice. Wherefore by praying much man impetrates from the divine mercy what he does not in fact merit according to justice." These words are deserving of particular attention. Cf. Daniel here quoted. (On the other hand, whatever Christ obtains He also merits *de condigno*.)

Cf. reply to the third objection which applies this to alms given to the poor. St. Thomas' beautiful interpretation deserves to be read: "The poor receiving alms are said to receive others into eternal dwellings." Thereby is also explained the true devotion to the Blessed Virgin Mary as advocated by St. Grignon de Montfort, according to which we offer to her whatever of our works is communicable to others. Thus we also offer to Mary our incommunicable merits *de condigno* for the purpose of having them safeguarded by her and augmented by her prayers, and also, in the case of mortal sin, that she may obtain the grace for us, not of any sort of attrition whatever, but of fervent contrition, so as to recover these merits in the same degree and proportionately to the fervor of our contrition; cf. IIIa, q. 89, a. 2.

Moreover, we offer to the Blessed Virgin whatever is communicable to other souls, on earth or in purgatory, of our good works, such as merit *de congruo,* prayers and satisfactions, so that she may distribute these communicable goods to the souls who need them most and especially to those for whom we ought to pray on account of a relationship of blood or vocation or in gratitude, and of whose present necessities we are often ignorant at the moment. Thus do we enter more profoundly into the mystery of the Communion of Saints.

ARTICLE VII. WHETHER THE JUST MAN CAN MERIT HIS
OWN RESTORATION AFTER A FALL

State of the question. The problem is not whether a man who has already fallen can merit his own restoration; it is already established by article 5 that he cannot, since fallen man cannot merit the first grace or justification. The meaning of the present article is: whether, at the time when a man is just, he can merit from God that, should he happen to fall into mortal sin, the grace of contrition would be given to him.

The question is disputed among theologians. Some, including Bellarmine, *De justificatione,* Bk. V, answer affirmatively, according to Ps. 70:9: "When my strength shall fail, do not Thou forsake me." Many others, St. Thomas among them, deny it; cf. Gonet. The three objections in the statement of the question show that the Angelic Doctor was not unaware of what could be said in favor of the contrary opinion.

The arguments in behalf of the affirmative are as follows:

1. The just man seems to be able to merit what can be justly asked of God, namely, to be restored after a fall.

2. The just man can merit for others *de congruo* properly speaking restoration after a fall; with still greater reason can he do so for himself.

3. A man who was once in grace merits eternal life for himself by perhaps heroic good works which he has done; but he cannot attain to it unless he is restored after a fall.

These arguments do not distinguish adequately between merit properly speaking, whether *de condigno* or *de congruo,* and merit improperly or broadly speaking.

The reply is in the negative, neither *de condigno* nor *de congruo* properly.

Proof from Scripture: "If the just man turn himself away from his justice, and do iniquity . . . all his justices which he hath done, shall not be remembered" (Ezech. 18:24).

Theological proof with respect to merit *de condigno.* Merit *de condigno* depends on the motion of divine grace. But this motion is interrupted by mortal sin. Therefore merit *de condigno* does not extend to benefits following sin, for the mortal sin would take away the merit.

Confirmation. Since all the merits of the just are suspended by subsequent mortal sin, the just man could not merit a reward to be conferred upon one who was unworthy; but a fallen man is unworthy. Accordingly, if the just man merited this restoration for himself *de condigno,* after sinning he would obtain it infallibly, and so all the just would be predestined, as it were, finally to be restored to grace.

Proof of the second part, that is, of merit *de congruo* properly speaking. Merit *de congruo* properly speaking is based on a right of friendship and demands fitness not only in the work but in the worker. But the just man has no right in friendship to restoration after a fall, since by mortal sin the friendship of God is withdrawn and so also are merits *de congruo* in the proper sense. Therefore.

Reply to first objection. Nevertheless he may well merit to obtain this by prayer, or by merit *de congruo* in the broad sense, founded not on justice but on mercy. A man may thus very profitably pray that, should he fall, he may rise again. So does the Psalmist pray (70:9): "When my strength shall fail, do not Thou forsake me."

Reply to second objection. The just man remaining in grace can merit properly *de congruo* the restoration of another, since he himself remains in grace. Cf. the last part of the body of the article. But if he falls into mortal sin, he deprives himself of his merits *de condigno* and *de congruo.*

Reply to third objection. "By an act of charity the just man merits absolutely eternal life, but by a subsequent mortal sin he sets up an impediment against the preceding merit so that he does not receive its effect." This answer should be read. St. Thomas' opinion was sustained by the Council of Trent (Denz., no. 842), which declared that the just man "merits eternal life and the attainment of eternal life itself, provided, however, that he dies in grace," that is, if he does not lose his merits by mortal sin.

ARTICLE VIII. WHETHER MAN CAN MERIT AN INCREASE OF GRACE OR CHARITY

State of the question. There are three difficulties: If the just man merits an increase of grace, after receiving it he can expect no other reward. Nothing acts beyond its species; hence grace and charity, which are the principle of merit, cannot merit greater grace. In consequence, an increase of charity would be obtained by any act of charity, even remiss, which would be remarkable.

The reply is in the affirmative even for merit *de condigno;* and this is of faith.

Proof from the Council of Trent (Sess. VI, can. 32; Denz., no. 842): "If anyone should say . . . he who is justified by good works, which are done by him through the grace of God and the merit of Jesus Christ (of whom he is a living member), does not really merit an increase of grace, eternal life, and the attainment of eternal life itself (provided, however, that he dies in grace), and also an increase of glory: let him be anathema." This definition is based upon many scriptural texts, for example: "By doing the truth in charity, we may in all things grow up in Him who is the head, even Christ" (Eph. 4:15); also Phil. 1:9 and Rom. 6:19; Augustine, commenting on chapter 5 of St. John's Gospel, writes: "Charity merits increase, that being increased, it may also merit to be perfected."

Theological proof. Whatever the motion of grace extends to falls under merit *de condigno.* But the motion of grace extends, not only to the term, which is eternal life, but to the entire progress by means of increasing grace and charity. Therefore. Thus is explained the text of Prov. 4:18: "The path of the just, as a shining light, goeth forward and increaseth even to perfect day," that is, to glory.

Reply to first and second objections. This increase does not exceed the power of the pre-existing grace.

Reply to third objection. "By any act of charity, even remiss, a man merits an increase of grace and eternal life; but just as eternal life is not bestowed immediately, so the increase of grace is not given forthwith (if the meritorious act was remiss) but when man becomes sufficiently disposed for this increase of grace." Suarez holds that even remiss acts obtain an increase of grace at once, and this for the reason that he does not give adequate consideration to the necessity for the prerequisite disposition; cf. *supra,* q. 112, a. 2; also Billuart, *ibid.,* and the treatise on charity (its increase), IIa IIae, q. 24, a. 6.

Just as a certain disposition (without merit, however) is prerequisite in an adult for justification, such that sanctifying grace is bestowed in greater or less degree according to the fervor of this disposition, so likewise is a disposition required for an increase of sanctifying grace. Should the meritorious act not be remiss, but more intense than the habit from which it proceeds, then, at the same time, there is moral merit and, as it were, a physical disposition for an increase to be obtained at once. For instance, if a person who possesses the virtue of charity in the measure of three talents should, under actual grace, elicit a fervent, meritorious act at the level of four talents, he would immediately obtain an increase of the virtue of charity in that measure. But if, possessing the virtue of charity in the measure of three talents, he performs a remiss, meritorious act at the level of two, there is, thus far, moral merit *de condigno,* but not the physical disposition, so to speak, for immediately obtaining an increase of charity. It will be forthcoming when he performs a more fervent act, or even perhaps, as Cajetan somewhere indicates, at the time of Eucharistic Communion, according as it is the disposition for receiving the proper effect of the Sacrament, according to the disposition, whether final or prior, of even remiss acts of charity.

Suarez disagrees with St. Thomas, inasmuch as he holds that every act of charity, even remiss, immediately obtains an increase which is the object of merit. St. Thomas' doctrine seems to be true, however, since a disposition is required for the increase of grace in the same way as for its infusion in an adult. But at the moment of infusion the disposition was without merit, whereas at the moment of the increase there must be a disposition with merit or with the Sacrament. By a similar analogy in the order of nature, an acquired friendship is increased only by more intense acts; remiss acts maintain but do not increase it.

Corollary. In the path of virtue, not to progress is to retrogress, as is commonly said; but on the other hand, not to retrogress is to progress. If a man does not commit a mortal sin in the course of a year, he has assuredly made progress thereby during that year. However, there is not much encouragement in remarking that "not to retrogress is to progress," so that the saints spoke quite otherwise.

ARTICLE IX. WHETHER A MAN CAN MERIT THE GIFT OF FINAL PERSEVERANCE FOR HIMSELF

State of the question. Final perseverance, as has been said (q. 109, a. 10), signifies continuance in grace until death, or the conjunction of the state of grace with death. It is the grace of a happy death. The Pelagians attributed it to the powers of nature alone. The Semi-Pelagians held that it could fall under merit.

In the three objections which are presented at the beginning of the article, St. Thomas brings out the difficulty of the question: 1. We can obtain this gift by prayer; why not by merit? 2. We can merit eternal life, the reason of which is impeccability; why cannot the just man merit for himself not sinning before death? 3. We can merit an increase of grace; why not simple perseverance in grace, which is less than an increase?

The reply, nevertheless, is in the negative. St. Thomas' conclusion is: The perseverance of glory falls under merit but not perseverance during life. This is at least theologically quite certain, according to all theologians, with respect to merit *de condigno,* as Hervé rightly declares in his *Manuale,* p. 217

This is proved from Sacred Scripture, which indicates clearly enough that none of the just has a right in justice to final perseverance, but that anyone is capable of falling. "Then shall many be scandalized . . . and many false prophets shall rise, and shall seduce many. And because iniquity hath abounded, the charity of many shall grow cold. But he that shall persevere to the end, he shall be saved (Matt. 24:10–13); "There shall arise false Christs . . . and shall show great signs and wonders, insomuch as to deceive (if possible) even the elect" (*ibid.,* 24:24); the gift of final perseverance is, then, the special gift of the elect. Again, "many are called, but few chosen" (*ibid.,* 20:16; 22:14); "Wherefore he that thinketh himself to stand, let him take heed lest he fall" (I Cor. 10:12); "Wherefore, my dearly beloved, . . . with fear and trembling work out your salvation. For it is God who worketh in you, both to will and to accomplish, according to His good will" (Phil. 2:12); it is not written: "according to our merits," but, "according to His good will." These last two texts are quoted by the Council of Trent in relation to the gift of final perseverance (Denz., no. 806).

Furthermore, texts can be cited to prove the gratuity of predestination to glory. And conversely, from the fact that the grace of final perseverance conferred only upon the elect does not proceed from foreseen merits, it follows that predestination to glory does not proceed from foreseen merits, any more than the first grace, the beginning of salvation. "Whom He predestinated, them He also called. And whom He called, them He also justified. And whom He justified, them He also glorified" (Rom. 8:30); in this text vocation, justification, and glorification are effects of predestination. "In whom [Christ] we also are called by lot, being predestinated according to the purpose of Him who worketh all things according to the counsel of His will" (Eph. 1:11); "I will have mercy on whom I will have mercy; and I will show mercy to whom I will show mercy" (Rom. 9:15; cf. Exod. 33:19); "So then it [divine election] is not of him that willeth, nor of him that runneth, but of God that showeth mercy" (Rom. 9:16); "Who hath first given to Him, and recompense shall be made him?" (*ibid.*, 11:35); "What hast thou that thou hast not received?" (I Cor. 4:7.)

The Councils likewise affirm the gratuity of the gift of final perseverance. Several of the preceding scriptural texts are quoted by the Second Council of Orange, which declared against the Semi-Pelagian contention that this gift fell under merit (can. 10; Denz., no. 183): "Even those reborn and restored to health must always implore the help of God that they may attain to a good end and may persevere in good works." If this must always be implored, it is not a thing the attainment of which is assured by previous merits.

Again, the Council of Trent (Sess. VI, chap. 13; Denz., no. 806) declares with reference to perseverance, "that a certain gift cannot be had from anyone, unless it be from Him who is able to make him who stands stand, that he may stand perseveringly, and to raise him who falls"; cf. Rom. 14:4 ff. Nevertheless the fact that a man merits, although it derives principally from God, is not said to proceed from God alone, but also from man by his merits. It is likewise defined by the Council of Trent (Denz., no. 826): "If anyone should say with absolute and infallible certainty that he will receive that great gift of perseverance to the end, unless he learns this by special revelation, let him be anathema." (Also Denz., no. 832.)

Among the Fathers, Augustine in his *De dono perseverantiae* sums up the patristic tradition and shows by many arguments that final perseverance is not bestowed on merits as a reward in justice, but may only "be obtained by supplicating prayers." [8]

St. Thomas presents two arguments. The first is indirect, in the argument *Sed contra,* which should be read. If the gift of final perseverance fell under merit, every just adult, according as he has meritorious works, would obtain it infallibly; that is, he would obtain preservation from sin. But not all the just obtain this gift; "the charity

---

[8] Cf. Rouet de Journel, *Enchir. patrist.,* Theological Index, nos. 320 f., for the testimony of the Fathers on this subject.

of many grows cold." Hence the supposition is false. As Billuart explains, this indirect argument is based on the truth that whatever a person merits, especially *de condigno,* he obtains from God infallibly, unless the merit itself is taken away by sin. Wherefore if anyone were to merit perseverance *de condigno,* he would obtain it infallibly, since he would thus merit not to have his merits taken away, and God would not permit him to fall into sin.

Someone might raise the further objection against this: perhaps this great gift of final perseverance cannot be merited *de condigno* by ordinary merits, but only by very excellent merits or by an accumulation of a great number of merits, and so it is not obtained by all the just.

Reply. If man merited eternal life and increase of grace by any meritorious work, there would be no reason why he should not likewise merit perseverance if it fell under merit.

The second argument is direct and specific, in the body of the article, which should be read. The principle of merit does not fall under merit; it would be its own effect. But the gift of final perseverance, according as it is the continuous production of the state of grace, is the principle of merit; in other words, the gift of final perseverance is nothing but the state of grace (that is, the principle of merit) preserved by God at the moment of death. Therefore it cannot fall under merit, especially *de condigno.*

The major is self-evident. The minor is proved as follows: the gift of final perseverance consists in a divine motion preserving the state of grace first bestowed. But this preservative motion is the principle of merit, since it is the same entitatively as the first production of grace. Cf. Ia, q. 104, a. 1 ad 4: "The preservation of a thing by God is not effected by any new action, but by a continuation of the action which confers being . . . in the same way, the preservation of light in the atmosphere is by the continuous influence of the sun." Therefore, just as no one can merit his own preservation, for preservation is not an act distinct from creation, which does not fall under merit; so neither can anyone merit perseverance in the state of grace, since it is nothing but the preservation of grace, not distinguished from its first production, which does not fall under merit. Hence Augustine demonstrates, against the Semi-Pelagians, that like the beginning of salvation, so final perseverance cannot fall under merit, since it is the principle of merit.

Confirmation. For merit *de condigno,* which is a strict right, the promise of God to render a reward for a work is required. But nowhere does God promise perseverance to those who do good works; on the contrary, the Scriptures often declare that even the just must work out their salvation in fear and trembling and that he who stands should take heed lest he fall. Therefore.

God often raises certain sinners after repeated falls; often, but not always; and this is the mystery of predestination.

REFUTATION OF OBJECTIONS

The twofold objection involved in the second and third is reducible to the following. He who can merit what is greater, can also merit what is less. But the just man can merit *de condigno* eternal life and the increase of grace, which are greater than final perseverance. Therefore the just man can merit *de condigno* final perseverance.

Reply. I distinguish the major; he who can merit what is greater, can also merit what is less, other things being equal: granted; other things not being equal, denied. But there is a disparity since, whereas both eternal life and perseverance in it and increase of grace are the terms of meritorious acts, the gift of perseverance is not; it is the continuation of the production of the state of grace. The principle of merit does not fall under merit.

I insist. He who can merit the end can merit the means necessary to attain it. But final perseverance is the necessary means for attaining to eternal life. Therefore.

Reply. I deny the major in its universal application; it suffices that the means are obtainable in another way than by merit. Or else, I distinguish the major as before: the just man can merit the means which are the term of merit: granted; those which are the principle of merit: denied.

I insist. Then the just man cannot merit *de condigno* eternal life either.

Reply. The just man merits eternal life absolutely, but before the end of life he can deprive himself of merit by mortal sin. Thus he merits "the attainment of eternal life, provided that he dies in grace," as the Council of Trent declares (Sess. VI, chap. 16, and can. 32; Denz., no. 842); but he cannot merit perseverance in the state of grace.

Three problems remain.

1. Whether efficacious grace can be merited *de condigno.* Thomists

answer in the negative, at least according as efficacious grace preserves us in the state of grace and prevents us from sinning mortally, for the principle of merit does not fall under merit. (Cf. Salmanticenses and John of St. Thomas.)

Confirmation. If anyone were to merit efficacious grace *de condigno* or infallibly, he would likewise thereby merit further efficacious graces and so on to the grace of final perseverance, which would thus fall under merit *de condigno,* contrary to what has been proved. Billuart writes: "Even if [that is, assuming, not granting] the just man should merit by the present good work efficacious help for the next work, he will still not obtain it infallibly except so far as he perseveres in grace; but he cannot merit persevering in grace, since this gift derives from the principle of merit, as has been said. . . . Moreover, nowhere is it established or revealed that efficacious help is presented as the reward of merit; it is to this help that St. Augustine refers when he says: 'to whom it is given, it is given in mercy; to whom it is not given, it is withheld in justice.' "

2. Whether final perseverance falls under merit *de congruo* properly speaking. This is a disputed question; cf. Hugon, *De gratia,* pp. 423 ff., and Billuart. It is answered negatively as being the more probable opinion, contrary to that of St. Robert Bellarmine, Suarez, and Ripalda; cf. Zubizarreta, *Syn., no.* 1052. Final perseverance does not fall under merit *de congruo* properly speaking: 1. for this merit is based upon the right of friendship, that is, the friendship of charity, and thus the principle of merit *de congruo,* in the proper sense, (namely, perseverance in the state of grace, or charity) would fall under merit, which is impossible; 2. since merit *de congruo* strictly speaking infallibly obtains a reward for the man himself, according as God does not refuse a man what is due to him according to the laws of friendship, and thus it would follow that nearly all the just would persevere, as stated in the argument *Sed contra.*

3. Whether the gift of perseverance falls under merit *de congruo* broadly speaking, as based on the liberality of mercy of God.

Reply to first objection, which should be read: in the affirmative; thus it can be obtained by humble, devout, confident, persevering prayer. Hence Benedict XV used to say that the celebration of Mass for the intention of obtaining this supreme gift was eminently proper, inasmuch as the celebration of Mass is the most sublime prayer of Christ Himself ever living to make intercession for us. True devotion to the Blessed Virgin Mary is likewise a sign of predestination since it inclines us to say frequently: "Holy Mary . . . pray for us . . . now and at the hour of our death. Amen"; and thus, many times a day we ask for the grace of a happy death.[9]

ARTICLE X. WHETHER TEMPORAL GOODS FALL UNDER MERIT

The reply is in the affirmative, to the extent that they are useful to salvation. If, however, they are considered in themselves, they do not fall absolutely under merit, which aims only at eternal life and those things which are conducive to it. But they do fall under a sort of merit from a particular aspect, according to a certain fitness based on the benignity of God. Thus, in the *City of God,* Bk. V, chap. 15, St. Augustine remarks that a temporal reward was rendered to the Romans on account of certain good customs which they observed.

So terminates the treatise on grace, intimately bound up with St. Thomas' principle (Ia, q. 20, a. 3) that "the love of God is the cause of goodness in things; nor does it presuppose, but rather imposes goodness in us." Therefore grace is a living manifestation of this uncreated love which demands a return of love and of gratitude, according to the words of St. John's First Epistle (4:19): "Let us therefore love God, because God first loved us."

[9] Since final perseverance can be obtained by prayer made in the proper way, that great promise made by the Sacred Heart to St. Margaret Mary seems to refer to this manner of impetration; that is, final perseverance will be given to those who receive Holy Communion on the first Fridays of nine consecutive months.

CHAPTER XII

▄▄

I. Whether Sanctifying Grace Is a Formal Participation in Deity as It Is in Itself

(We here reprint an article which appeared in the *Revue Thomiste,* 1936.)

"GRACE, which is an accident, is a certain participated likeness of the divinity in man" (St. Thomas, IIIa, q. 2, a. 10 ad 1).

This question has been put to us in connection with recent debates [1] and with reference to what we recently wrote in the *Revue Thomiste* on the subject of Deity.[2] More precisely, the question was formulated as follows: Is grace a participation in Deity as it is in itself and as seen by the blessed, or only in Deity as imperfectly known by us? This latter aspect could be further differentiated: Is it a question of Deity as imperfectly known by the philosopher, or as known by the theologian-wayfarer?

State of the question. In order to grasp better the sense of the terms, let us recall what we have discussed elsewhere [3] at greater length. The Deity as it is in itself remains naturally unknowable, and even cannot be known except by the immediate vision of the blessed. But among the divine perfections which it contains formally in its eminence, which we know by natural means, is there not one which

---

[1] Cf. *Revue Thomiste,* July and September, 1929, pp. 381–99, Father A. Gardeil's reply to Father Menéndez Rigada, O.P.; see also A. Gardeil, *La structure de l'âme et l'expérience mystique,* I, 386–90.

[2] *Revue Thomiste,* November, 1934 and February, 1935 (double issue), "Cajetan," pp. 311–18; and March, 1936: "La possibilité de la grâce est-elle rigoureusement démonstrable?" See also: *Le sens du mystère,* pp. 224–33.

[3] *God, His Existence and His Nature,* Part II, chap. I, pp. 3–32.

has priority over the others, from which the others can be deduced, as the properties of man are deduced from his rationality?

The controversy on this subject, relative to the formal constituent of the divine nature according to our imperfect mode of knowledge, is well known. Even the Thomists themselves are not in complete accord on this point. Some maintain that this formal constituent is subsistent being itself, according to the words of Exod. 3:14: "I am who am," because all the divine attributes are deducible therefrom. Others hold that it is subsistent intellection (*intelligere subsistens*). We have explained elsewhere [4] why we accept the first solution, on account of the text from Exodus, of the radical distinction between subsistent being and created being, and because all the divine attributes are deducible from it. Does not St. Thomas accordingly delay treating of the divine intelligence until question fourteen of the First Part, after he has deduced several attributes from subsistent being itself? [5]

Whatever may be the issue of this discussion, it remains true for all Thomists that Deity as it exists in itself is superior to all the absolute perfections which it contains in its eminence (*formaliter eminenter*).

This is evident from the fact that these perfections, which are naturally capable of participation by creatures, such as being, life, intelligence, are naturally knowable in a positive way, whereas Deity is not: it is the great darkness which the mystics speak of. It designates the very essence of God, that which is proper to Him, His intimate life. It is the object of the beatific vision itself, and, before that vision, it is the "obscurity from above" which proceeds from a light too intense for the weak eyes of our souls.

From this it can be inferred that subsistent being itself contains only in implicit act the attributes which are progressively deducible from it, but Deity as such contains them in explicit act, since, when it is seen, there is no longer any need of deducing these attributes. Deity can thus be represented as the apex of a pyramid the sides of which would represent subsistent being, subsistent intellection, subsistent

[4] *Ibid.*

[5] The alternative opinion is consequently forced to distinguish in God general perfections anterior to His specific perfection as if He belonged to a genus. This seems to be an abuse of our imperfect mode of cognition. Furthermore, when St. Thomas affirms, Ia, q.3, a.4, that God is subsistent being itself, he supposes it to be already demonstrated that God is not a body but pure spirit (Ia, q.3, a.1 and 2); it is therefore a question of purely spiritual being itself, the pure spirituality (or absolute immateriality) of which is the basis of intellection, as will be affirmed in Ia, q.14, a.1.

love, mercy, justice, omnipotence, that is, all the attributes formally contained in the eminence of Deity. To adopt a less far-fetched symbolism, Deity in relation to the perfections inhering in its eminence is somewhat like whiteness in relation to the seven colors of the rainbow, with this difference: the seven colors are only virtually present in the whiteness, whereas the absolute perfections (being, intelligence, love, etc.) are in Deity formally and eminently.[6]

Thereupon the question presents itself: Is grace a participation in the divine nature (or in Deity), the intimate life of God as it is in itself, or only in the divine nature as it is imperfectly conceived by us as subsistent being or subsistent intellection?

The theologians who have written on this subject generally concede that grace is a participation in Deity as it is in itself, objectively (inasmuch as it disposes us radically to see it). But some add that it is not so intrinsically or subjectively, for Deity is infinite and hence, as such, cannot be participated in subjectively. Furthermore, they declare that Deity is the intimate life of God, none other than the Trinity of the divine persons. Now grace cannot be a subjective participation in the Fatherhood, the Sonship, the Spiration which constitute the intimate life of God. These theologians deduce therefrom that grace is subjectively a participation in the divine nature as imperfectly conceived by us, as one (not as triune) and as subsistent intellection.[7]

It is at once evident that this viewpoint can be interpreted in two ways, according to whether it refers to the divine nature imperfectly known by the philosopher or to the divine nature imperfectly known

[6] Cf. Cajetan, *In Iam,* q. 1, a. 3, no. 4; a. 7, no. 1; q. 13, a. 5, no. 7, 10 ff.; q. 39, a. 1, no. 7. We have presented this traditional conception elsewhere under various forms. Cf. *God,* pp. 3 ff.; 225 ff.; *De revelatione,* I, 8, 316, 347. *Le sens du mystère et le clair-obscur intellectuel,* pp. 206–33. *La prédestination des saints et la grâce,* pp. 121, 247–49, 254 f., 374–76. To see things in God, in the Word, by the beatific vision, is like seeing them in a more or less dazzling whiteness. To attain to them by the infused light of faith is like seeing them in whiteness shadowed by a veil (under the aspect of Deity known obscurely). To consider them from the point of view of being is like seeing them under the aspect of the first color in the rainbow: violet; the viewpoint of intelligence or of love corresponds to other colors. Furthermore the coloring varies markedly according to whether it is seen naturally as by the angels in the mirror of spiritual things or by the human mind in that of sensible things; cf. Ia, q. 12, a. 4.

[7] Let us remark at the outset that subsistent intellection (even subjectively) is no less infinite than subsistent being itself and that consequently it is possible to speak only of a subjective participation, inadequate but imitative and analogical (cf. Gardeil, *Structure,* I, 390); this can also be admitted in regard to Deity as such, as we shall have occasion to say at the conclusion of this article.

beneath the light of essentially supernatural revelation by the theologian, who knows God, not only under the nature of being and first being, but also under the nature of Deity, already known obscurely by the attributes of God, author of grace (as supernatural Providence) and, above all, by the mystery of the Trinity. (Before the revelation of this mystery of the Trinity, under the Old Testament, the supernatural providence of God, author of salvation, was known.)

Basis of a solution. To the question thus stated, we reply that, according to traditional teaching, sanctifying grace in itself is intrinsically (and not merely in an objective, extrinsic manner) a formal, analogical (and, of course, inadequate) participation in the Deity as it is in itself, superior to being, intelligence, and love, which it contains in its eminence or formally and eminently. As Cajetan says, Ia, q. 39, a. 1, no. 7: "The Deity is prior to being and all its differences; for it is above being and beyond unity, etc." The reasons which we are about to indicate are presented in progressive order, beginning with the most general.

1. There can be no question of a participation in the divine nature merely as conceived by the philosopher. He does, in fact, know God as first being and first intelligence, inasmuch as He is author of nature, but not as God, author of grace. This is the basis of the distinction between the proper object of natural theology or theodicy (a branch of metaphysics): God under the reason of being and as author of nature, and the proper object of sacred theology: God under the nature of Deity (at least obscurely known) and as author of grace. This is the classical terminology employed by the great commentators on St. Thomas, Ia, q. 1, a. 3, 7; cf. Cajetan, Bañez, John of St. Thomas, the Salmanticenses, Gonet, Gotti, Billuart, etc. Nowadays several writers make use of this classical terminology from force of habit, without apparently having pondered very deeply the difference between the proper object of theodicy, or natural theology, and that of theology properly so called. Nevertheless St. Thomas has expressed this difference in very precise terms, Ia, q. 1, a. 6: "Sacred doctrine properly treats of God under the aspect of highest cause, for it considers Him not only to the extent that He is knowable through creatures (as the philosophers knew Him) but also with respect to what He alone knows of Himself which is communicated to others by revelation." This is what later theologians referred to as "God, not under the general reason of being, but under the essential, intimate

reason of Deity, or according to His intimate life." Hence in the question which engages our attention, we are not concerned with the divine nature only as it is imperfectly conceived by the philosopher.

2. Moreover, only God can produce grace in an angel or in the very essence of the soul, and He does so independently of the conception which the philosopher or theologian holds regarding the divine nature, and independently of any natural effect which might be the source of these imperfect conceptions. Grace thus assimilates us immediately to God as such in His intimate life; it is therefore a formal, analogical participation in the Deity as it is in itself.

In the natural order, a stone has an analogical likeness to God inasmuch as He is being, the plant inasmuch as He is living, man and angel inasmuch as He is intelligence. Sanctifying grace, which is far superior to the angelic nature, is an analogical likeness to God inasmuch as He is God, or to His Deity, to His intimate life, which is not naturally knowable in a positive way. This is why, above the kingdoms of nature (mineral, vegetable, animal, human, angelic), there is the kingdom of God: the intimate life of God and its formal participation by the angels and the souls of the just.

Therefore to know perfectly the essence or quiddity of grace, one would have to know the light of glory of which it is the seed, just as one must know what an oak is to know the essence of the germ contained in an acorn. But it is impossible to know perfectly the essence of the light of glory, essentially ordered to the vision of God, without knowing the divine essence immediately by intuition.

Hence St. Thomas declares, in demonstrating that only God can produce grace, Ia IIae, q. 112, a. 2: "It must be that God alone should deify, communicating a fellowship in the divine nature by a certain participated likeness, just as it is impossible for anything but fire to ignite." The word "deify" shows that grace is a participation in the divine nature, not according to the reason of being or intelligence merely, but by the essential, intimate reason of Deity.

3. But in that case, it will be objected, grace would have to be intrinsically a (subjective) participation in the intimate life of God. Now this is none other than the Trinity of the divine persons. There would therefore be in grace a participation in the fatherhood, the sonship and the spiration, which theory is a departure from traditional teaching.

The answer to this objection is that, according to traditional teaching, and particularly that of St. Thomas, the adoptive sonship of the children of God, *ex Deo nati,* is a certain likeness to the eternal sonship of the Word. In fact we find explicitly in IIIa, q. 3, a. 5 ad 2: "Just as by the act of creation divine goodness is communicated to all creatures by way of a certain similitude, so by the act of adoption a similitude of natural sonship is communicated to men, according to the words of Rom. 8:29: 'Whom He foreknew . . . to be made conformable to the image of His Son.'" And further (*ibid.,* a. 2 ad 3): "Adoptive sonship is a certain likeness of eternal sonship; just as all the things that were made in time are, as it were, likenesses of those which were from all eternity. Man however is likened to the eternal splendor of the Son by the brightness of grace, which is attributed to the Holy Ghost. And hence adoption, although common to the whole Trinity, is appropriated to the Father as its author, to the Son as its exemplar, to the Holy Ghost as imprinting this likeness of the exemplar upon us."

Likewise St. Thomas again in his commentary on Rom. 8:29 thus explains the words "to be made conformable to the image of His Son": "He who is adopted as son of God is truly conformed to His Son, first, indeed, by a right to participate in His inheritance . . . ; secondly, by sharing His glory (Heb. 1:3). Hence by the fact that He enlightens the saints with the light of wisdom and grace, He makes them conformable to Himself. . . . Thus did the Son of God will to communicate to others a conformity with His sonship, that He might not only be the Son, Himself but also the first-born of sons. And so He who is the only-begotten by eternal generation (John 1:18), . . . is, by the conferring of grace, the first-born of many brethren. . . . Therefore we are the brothers of Christ because He has communicated a likeness of sonship to us, as is here said, and because He assumed the likeness of our nature."

St. Thomas speaks similarly in his commentary on St. John's Gospel (1:13), explaining the words, "who are born of God." "And this is fitting, that all who are sons of God by being assimilated to the Son, should be transformed through the Son. . . . Accordingly the words, 'not of blood, etc.,' show how such a magnificent benefit is conferred upon men. . . . The Evangelist uses the preposition '*ex*' speaking of others, that is, of the just: '*Ex Deo nati sunt*'; but of the natural Son, he says '*De Patre est natus.*'" Why? Because, as explained in the same commentary, the Latin preposition 'de' indicates either the material, efficient, or consubstantial cause (The smith makes a little knife of [de] steel); the Latin preposition 'a' always refers to the efficient cause, and the preposition 'ex' is general, indicating either the material or efficient cause, but never the consubstantial cause.

Now the objection raised was that grace cannot be intrinsically a (subjective) participation in the Deity or the intimate life of God, for that is none other than the Trinity of persons in which there is no participating. The participation is in the divine nature as one.

From what has just been explained, the reply may be made as follows: True, the participation is in the divine nature as one, however not merely such as conceived by the philosopher, but such as it is in itself, in the bosom of the Trinity. It is not only a question of the unity of God, author of nature, but of that absolutely eminent, naturally unknowable unity which is capable of subsisting in spite of the Trinity of persons. We are concerned with the unity and identity of the nature communicated by the Father to the Son and by Them to the Holy Ghost. Therein lies the meaning of the traditional proposition which we have just read in St. Thomas: "Adoptive sonship is a certain likeness of eternal sonship." So has it always been understood.

From all eternity God the Father has a Son to whom He communicates His whole nature, without dividing or multiplying it; He necessarily engenders a Son equal to Himself, and gives to Him to be God of God, Light of Light, true God of true God. And from sheer bounty, gratuitously, He has willed to have in time other sons, adopted sons, by a filiation which is not only moral (by external declaration) but real and intimate (by the production of sanctifying grace, the effect of God's active love for us). He has loved us with a love that is not only creative and preserving, but vivifying, which causes us to participate in the very principle of His intimate life, in the principle of the immediate vision which He has of Himself and which He communicates to His Son and to the Holy Ghost. It is thus that He has predestinated us to be conformable to the image of His only Son, that this Son might be the first-born of many brethren (Rom. 8:29). The just are accordingly of the family of God and enter into the cycle of the Holy Trinity. Infused charity gives us a likeness to the Holy Ghost (personal love); the beatific vision will render us like the Word, who will make us like unto the Father whose image He is. Then the

Trinity which already dwells in us as in a darkened sanctuary, will abide in us as in an illuminated, living sanctuary, where It will be seen unveiled and loved with an inamissible love.

The only Son of God receives the divine nature eternally, not merely as it is conceived by the philosopher (as being itself or even as subsistent intellection), but as it is in itself (under the reason of the Deity clearly perceived). Consequently He received the unity of that nature, not only as conceived by the philosopher, but as it is capable of subsisting in spite of the Trinity of persons really distinct one from another. He receives with Deity the essential intellection common to the three persons, which has for its primary object the Deity itself known comprehensively. He also receives essential love, not only as known by the philosopher, but that essential love which, remaining numerically the same, belongs to the three persons, since they love one another by one sole, identical act, just as they know one another by the same, identical intellection.

Now according to traditional teaching, as we have just seen, sanctifying grace makes us children of God by an analogical, participated likeness to the eternal sonship of the Word. Hence, in us, it is a participation in Deity as it is in itself, not only under the nature of being or under the nature of intellection, but under the nature of Deity, and not only a participation in Deity as known obscurely by the theologian through created concepts, but as it is in itself and seen as it is by the blessed.

Such is the true sense of these assertions, admitted by all theologians. But their profundity does not always receive sufficient attention. The mineral already resembles God analogically as being, the plant and animal as living, man and angel as intelligent; but the just man by grace resembles God precisely inasmuch as He is God, according to His very Deity or His intimate life as it is in itself. Thus the just man penetrates, beyond the human kingdom of reason, beyond the angelic kingdom, into the kingdom of God; his life is not merely intellectual but deiform, divine, theological: "it is deified," according to St. Thomas, Ia IIae, q. 112, a. 1.

That is truly the formal aspect of the life of grace, what is proper to it, unique, significant, and interesting. Thereby it is a formal, although inadequate and analogical, participation in the divine nature as it is in itself, or of Deity as such. This is found above all in consummate, inamissible grace received into the essence of the soul, and also in the light of glory received into the intellect by the beatified soul, and in the charity received into its will.

4. It is, then, materially (in the theological sense of the term) that grace is a finite accident (an entitative habit received into the essence of the soul), that infused faith is an operative habit received into our intellect, and charity an operative habit received into our will. All of this is true by reason of the receptive subject. But these habits are a formal participation in the intimate life of God; otherwise they would not dispose us to see it as it is in itself by an immediate vision that will have the same formal object (*objectum formale quod et quo*) as the uncreated vision which God, one in three persons, has of Himself.

This distinction of what grace is either materially or formally, is similar to the one that is generally made in the natural order between intelligence and the created mode whereby it exists in us and in the angels, as a faculty (accident) distinct from the substance of the soul or of the angel, distinct also from the act of intellection. This is quite true and does not prevent intelligence as such from being an analogical perfection, the formal notion of which does not imply any imperfection, and which, consequently, is to be found properly and formally in God as subsistent intellection. In the same way, the perfection of wisdom is distinguished from its created mode whereby, in us, wisdom is measured by things, whereas in God it is the measure and cause of things.

From the same more or less material standpoint, when sanctifying grace is compared to faith and charity, it may be said that grace is a participation in the Deity as a nature, faith a participation in the Deity or intimate life of God as knowledge, and charity a participation in that intimate life as love. But it is always a question of formal participation in the intimate life of God or in the Deity in its eminent unity, not such as it is known by the philosopher, but as it is in itself in the Trinity.

5. Moreover, sanctifying grace cannot be an objective participation in the Deity as it is in itself (and dispose us radically to immediate vision) without being intrinsically specified by it, that it, without having an essential (or transcendant) relationship to the Deity as it is in itself.[8] Hence, in his reply to Father Menéndez Rigada, Father

---

[8] Cf. Salmanticenses, *Curs. theol.,* on the quiddity and perfection of habitual grace, disp. 4, dub. 4, no. 72. "If it is a question of (inadequate, analogical) participation by

Gardeil [9] recognizes, with reference to the passage from the Salmanticenses which we have just indicated in a note, that "it does not seem
possible for the intuition of the divine persons to originate in sanctifying grace, if the latter is not a kind of exemplary participation in
the divine nature inasmuch as it subsists in the divine persons. For, as
the Salmanticenses declare (*loc. cit.*), the inclination toward an object should originate in some participation in the object aimed at."
Yes, for there is here, not an accidental, but an essential (or transcendant) relationship between grace and Deity seen immediately.
This argument clarifies the last problem which we are about to propose.

6. In the light of what immediately precedes, it is apparent that
subsistent intellection (*intelligere subsistens*), even considered subjectively, is no less infinite than subsistent being, or than Deity as it
is in itself. Granted that sanctifying grace can be a participation in
the divine nature as intellection, one should admit that it can be a
participation in Deity as it is in itself.[10]

If it is objected: but Deity as it is in itself is, like subsistent being,
infinite and therefore cannot be participated in subjectively or intrinsically, the reply in the words of Father Gardeil is as follows: [11]
"That would be true if a participation could be adequate, but it could
be only imitative and analogical." The Salmanticenses (*op. cit.,* no.
64) are in accord: "Therefore in the mind of St. Thomas it is perfectly consistent for grace to participate, that is, to imitate, the whole
being as to its essence and infinity, although it does not correspond
to it adequately in all its predicables but only partially."

---

formal imitation, we grant that grace participates in the divine nature as subsisting
in three persons. . . . With the divine being . . . it includes internal fecundity
and the procession of the persons; it cannot but imply this perfection in exemplary
being, imitable by means of grace. Especially is this true since grace inclines us connaturally to the vision of God in Himself and therefore not merely as one but also
as triune; wherefore even radically it possesses a certain mode of extension and
perfection whereby it attains intuitively . . . even to the divine persons. . . . But
such an inclination and perfection would not correspond to sanctifying grace did it
not participate and find its exemplar in the divine nature as subsisting in three persons . . . , for the inclination toward an object should be said to arise from a certain
participation in that object appertaining to it."

[9] *Revue Thomiste* July–September, 1929, p. 390.

[10] St. Thomas also says, IIa IIae, q. 24, a. 7: "According to the reason of its own
species, charity has no term of increase; for it is a certain participation in infinite
charity which is the Holy Ghost."

[11] *Structure,* I, 390.

Deity is thus identified with subsistent being itself (inasmuch as it contains being and the other absolute perfections formally and eminently), whereas in us the formal, analogical participation in Deity takes the form of an accident. This is the more or less material, not formal, aspect of sanctifying grace, just as in the natural order there is a difference between the perfection of intelligence and the created mode whereby it is in us a faculty distinct from the substance of the soul and the act of intellection.

Conclusion. For these various reasons, of which the first are more general and are presupposed according to our mode of cognition, we consider sanctifying grace to be a formal, analogical participation in Deity as it is in itself. Two important corollaries follow from this:

1. It can be seen manifestly, as we have established elsewhere,[12] that reason alone is incapable (for instance, by the natural, conditional, inefficacious desire to see God) of demonstrating precisely the possibility of grace, the possibility of a formal, analogical participation in the Deity or intimate life of God which would be, materially, a finite accident of our souls. Of this possibility reason can give a proof of suitability, but not an apodictic proof, for, of itself, reason cannot know the Deity or intimate life of God positively. "This possibility of grace," as is commonly taught, "is neither proved nor disproved apodictically, but it is urged by reason, defended against those who deny it, and held with a firm faith."

2. With regard to the problem of the formal constituent of the divine nature, according to our imperfect mode of understanding, the solution which identifies it with subsistent intellection rather than with being itself is not confirmed by the sequence: grace would be a participated likeness, not of subsistent being but of subsistent intellection. This question of the philosophically formal constituent is of no importance here for the definition of grace, which is in reality a participated likeness in Deity, superior to both being and intellection which are contained in its eminence, that is, formally and eminently.

The doctrine we have just presented is found in St. Thomas, Ia, q. 13, a. 9: "This name of God is not communicable to any man according to the fullness of its meaning, but something of it is so by a kind of likeness, so that they may be called 'gods' who participate by such a likeness in something of the divinity, according to the words

[12] *Revue Thomiste*, March, 1936.

of psalm 81: 'I have said: You are gods.' " And the answer to the first
objection: "The divine nature is not communicable except by the
participation of likeness." Likewise IIIa, q. 2, a. 6 ad 1. Cf. Salmanticenses, *De gratia,* disp. IV, the quiddity and perfection of habitual grace, dub. IV, nos. 62, 63, 70–72, where the participation by
formal, analogical imitation is very well defined; also John of St.
Thomas and Gonet, quoted in the same place.

NOTE

SUPERNATURAL AND NATURAL BEATITUDE

In his volume entitled *Surnaturel* (*Etudes historiques,* 1946), p.
254, Father H. de Lubac, having examined certain texts of St. Thomas
on the distinction between the natural and the supernatural, writes as
follows: "At any rate, nothing in his works declares the distinction
which a certain number of Thomistic theologians would later con-
coct between 'God the author of the natural order' and 'God the object of supernatural beatitude.' . . . Nowhere, explicitly or implicitly,
does St. Thomas refer to a 'natural beatitude.' " It is evident that
Father de Lubac has never explained the *Summa theologica* article
by article.

St. Thomas says, Ia, q. 23, a. 1, Whether men are predestined by
God: "It pertains to providence to ordain a thing to its end. But the
end toward which created things are ordained by God is twofold.
One, which exceeds the proportion and faculty of created nature, is
eternal life, which consists of the divine vision and which is beyond
the nature of any creature as is shown above (Ia, q. 12, a. 4). The other
end, however, is proportioned to created nature, such, that is, as a
creature can attain to by the power of its nature."

Again in the *De veritate,* q. 14, a. 2: "The final good of man, which
first moves the will as to its final end, is twofold. One good is proportioned to human nature, since natural powers are sufficient to attain
it; this is the happiness of which the philosophers have spoken. It is
either contemplative, consisting in the act of wisdom, or active, consisting first in the act of prudence and accordingly in the acts of the
other moral virtues. The other good of man exceeds the proportion of
human nature, since natural powers do not suffice to attain it, nor
even to conceive or desire it; but it is promised to man by the divine
bounty alone." The whole article should be read; it affirms that "in
human nature itself there is a certain beginning of this good which

is proportioned to nature," and further that infused "faith is a certain beginning of eternal life."

St. Thomas also declares, Ia IIae, q. 62, a. 1: "The beatitude or happiness of man is twofold. One sort is proportioned to human nature, that which man can attain by the principle of his nature. But the other is a beatitude surpassing human nature, to which man can attain only by divine power, by means of a certain participation in divinity, according to the words of St. Peter's Second Epistle (1:4): 'By these [the promises of Christ] . . . you may be made partakers of the divine nature.' " St. Thomas speaks similarly with reference to angels, Ia, q. 62, a. 2.

He even affirms, *II Sent.,* dist. 31, q. 1, a. 1 ad 3: "In the beginning when God created man, He could also have formed another man of the slime of the earth and have left him in his natural condition; that is, he would have been mortal, passible, and have experienced the struggle of concupiscence against reason; this would not have been derogatory to human nature, since it follows from the principles of nature. Nor would any reason of guilt or punishment be attached to this defect, since it would not be caused voluntarily." This is indeed evident for, if sanctifying grace and likewise the gift of integrity and immortality are gratuitous or not due (as defined against Baius), it follows that the merely natural state (that is, without these gratuitous gifts) is possible both from the part of man and from that of God.

Is sanctifying grace a permanent gift in the just, like the infused virtues? Of recent years an opinion has been expressed according to which sanctifying grace is not a form or a permanent, radical principle of supernatural operations, but rather a motion.[13] It is nevertheless certain that the infused virtues, especially the three theological virtues, are, within us, permanent principles of supernatural operations and meritorious as well; and it is no less certain that sanctifying or habitual grace is the permanent root of these infused virtues. It is not therefore merely a transitory motion, nor even a motion unceasingly renewed in the just man as long as he preserves friendship with God. The Fathers always referred to the theological virtues and to sanctifying grace which they presuppose as their radical principle.

The Council of Trent leaves no room for doubt on this point. Denzinger in his *Enchiridion* sums up the definitions and declarations of

---

[13] Cf. Henri Bouillard, *Conversion et grâce chez S. Thomas d'Aquin,* Paris, 1941.

the Church very correctly in the formula: "Habitual or sanctifying grace is distinct from actual grace (nos. 1064 ff.); it is an infused, inherent quality of the soul, by which man is formally justified (nos. 483, 792, 795, 799 ff., 809, 821, 898, 1042, 1063 ff.), is regenerated (nos. 102, 186), abides in Christ (nos. 197, 698), puts on a new man (no. 792), and becomes an heir to eternal life (nos. 792, 799 ff.).[14]

II. The Principle of Predilection and Efficacious Grace

"Since the love of God is the cause of the goodness of things, nothing would be better than another were it not better loved by God" (St. Thomas, Ia, q. 20, a. 3).

One of the greatest joys experienced by the theologian who, for long years, has read and explained each day the *Summa theologica* of St. Thomas, is to glimpse the sublime value of one of those prin-

---

[14] Father Bouillard (*op. cit.,* p. 212) writes: "Grace is conceived by St. Thomas as a form, that is, not only as an inherent quality but as a principle of operation inclining the soul to produce certain determined actions. Evidently the notions used by St. Thomas are simply Aristotelian notions applied to theology." They are human notions such as those of nature, essence, constituent form. Moreover, it is the Council of Trent which itself declares that sanctifying grace is the formal cause of justification; by not maintaining this, one denies it and no longer preserves the meaning of the Council's affirmation. Father Bouillard says (p. 220): "Notions change but affirmations abide." What an illusion! An affirmation which unites two notions by the verb "to be" cannot abide if the two notions change and remain forever unstable. One might as well insist on using a grappling hook to fasten the waves of the ocean. If, for example, the notion of transubstantiation changes, and is no longer maintained in its ontological sense, which transcends phenomena, the affirmation: "The real presence depends on transubstantiation" cannot abide. And if one continues to speak of "the real presence," it will no longer be such as conceived by tradition and the councils. The examples we have used are well known; they are not of our selection.

Father Bouillard writes (p. 219): "A theology that is not abreast of the times would be a false theology," and he adds (p. 224): "By renouncing Aristotelian physics, modern thought has given up the notions . . . which had no meaning except in terms of the former." The reader is led to conclude that a theology which still makes use of the notion of form is no longer abreast of the times and is therefore false. We should thus be led to change even the notion and definition of truth and thus return to Modernism by asserting that truth is not the agreement of the judgment with extra-mental reality and its immutable laws, but the agreement of thought with the demands of a perpetually evolving human life. Thus the nature of theology and of dogma itself are changed; cf. Denz., nos. 2058, 2025, 2079, 2080. In line with the same tendency, some would change the notion of original sin so that it would no longer depend upon a single fault committed by Adam at the beginning of humanity's history, but upon the personal faults of men in the course of centuries which have rebounded on humanity as a whole. Thus we revert to Modernism; and it is a more serious matter to return to a condemned error than to fall into it for the first time.

ciples, often invoked but not sufficiently contemplated, which by their simplicity and elevation form, as it were, the great leitmotivs of theological thought, containing in themselves virtually entire treatises. The great St. Thomas formulated them especially toward the end of his comparatively short life, when his contemplation had reached that height and simplicity which one associates with the intellectual vision of the higher angels, who encompass within a very few ideas vast regions of the intelligible world, metaphysical landscapes, so to speak, composed not of colors but of principles, and illumined from above by the very light of God.

Among these very lofty, very simple principles upon which the contemplation of the Angelic Doctor paused with delight, there is one to which sufficient attention is not generally paid and yet which contains in its virtuality several of the most important treatises. It is the principle which we find thus formulated, Ia, q. 20, a. 3: "Since the love of God is the cause of the goodness of things, none would be better than another, were it not better loved by God." In article 4 of the same question, the same principle is thus stated: "If some beings are better than others it is because they are better loved by God." In short: no creature is better than another unless it is better loved by God. This may be called the principle of predilection, for principles derive their names from their predicates.

This is the principle against which all human pride ought to dash itself. Let us examine: 1. its bases, necessity, universality, 2. its principal consequences according to St. Thomas himself, and 3. by what other principle it should be balanced so as to maintain in all their purity and elevation the great mysteries of faith, particularly those of predestination and the will for universal salvation.

THE BASIS, NECESSITY, AND UNIVERSALITY OF
THE PRINCIPLE OF PREDILECTION

This principle, "no creature is better than another unless better loved by God," seems at the outset to be manifestly necessary in the philosophical order. If the love of God is, in fact, the cause of the goodness of creatures, as St. Thomas affirms in the first text quoted, no one can be better than another except for the reason that it has received more from God; this greater goodness in it, rather than in another, obviously comes from God.

As will be seen, this principle of predilection is a corollary of the principle of efficient causality: "Every contingent being or good requires an efficient cause and, in the final analysis, depends upon God the first cause." It is also a corollary of the principle of finality: "Every agent acts for an end"; consequently the order of agents corresponds to the order of ends,[15] the first agent produces every good in view of the supreme end, which is the manifestation of His goodness, and hence it is not independently of Him or of His love, that one being is better than another, the plant superior to the mineral, the animal to the plant, man to the animal, one man to another, either in the natural order or in the order of grace.

It is also apparent from reason alone that this principle is absolutely universal, valid for every created being from a stone to the highest angel, and not merely applicable to their substance, but to their accidents, qualities, actions, passions, relations, etc., for whatever is good in them and better in one than another, whether it is a question of physical, intellectual, moral, or strictly spiritual values.

The principle of predilection is also supported by revelation under various aspects in both the Old and New Testaments; it is even applied therein to our free, salutary acts. Our Lord tells us: "Without Me you can do nothing" [16] in the order of salvation. St. Paul explains this by saying: "It is God who worketh in you, both to will and to accomplish, according to His good will"; [17] "Who distinguisheth thee? Or what hast thou that thou hast not received? And if thou hast received, why dost thou glory, as if thou hadst not received it?" [18] The principle in question is contained in many other texts cited by the Council of Orange: [19] "Unto you it is given for Christ, not only to believe in Him, but also to suffer for Him"; [20] "Being confident of this very thing, that He, who hath begun a good work in you, will perfect it unto the day of Christ Jesus"; [21] "By grace you are saved through faith, and that not of yourselves, for it is the gift of God"; [22] "Now concerning virgins . . . I give counsel, as having obtained mercy of the Lord, to be faithful." [23] Again we find: "Do not err,

[15] Ia IIae, q. 109, a. 6.
[16] John 15:5.
[17] Phil. 2:13.
[18] I Cor. 4:7.
[19] Denz., no. 199.
[20] Phil. 1:29.
[21] Ibid., 1:6.
[22] Eph. 2:8.
[23] I Cor. 7:25; I Tim. 1:13.

therefore, my dearest brethren. Every best gift, and every perfect gift, is from above, coming down from the Father of lights, with whom there is no change, nor shadow of alteration"; [24] "No man can say the Lord Jesus, but by the Holy Ghost"; [25] "Not that we are sufficient to think anything of ourselves, as of ourselves: but our sufficiency is from God." [26]

That is clearly the principle of predilection or of the source of what is better. St. Augustine often expresses it in commenting on the scriptural texts which we have just quoted together with several others from the Epistle to the Romans (chapters 8, 9, and 11). He applies it not only to men but to angels, regarding whom there is no question of the fact of original sin (by title of infirmity, *titulus infirmitatis*) but only of right, of the dependence (*titulus dependentiae*) of the creature upon the Creator, both in the natural order and in the order of grace. He observes that those angels who attained supreme beatitude received greater aid than the others, *"amplius adjuti."* [27]

St. Thomas discerned an equivalent formula of the principle of the origin of superiority in the Council of Orange and the scriptural texts cited by it. He writes, in fact, with reference to predestination, in rendering an account of the condemnation of the Semi-Pelagians who attributed the beginning of salvation to man and not to God: "But opposed to this is what the Apostle says (II Cor. 3:5), that we are not sufficient to think anything of ourselves, as of ourselves. However no principle can be found anterior to thought. Hence it cannot be said that any beginning exists in us which is the cause of the effect of predestination." [28] The reader is no doubt acquainted with the texts of the Council of Orange (can. 4; cf. Denz., nos. 177–85): "If anyone holds that God waits upon our will to cleanse us from sin, and does not admit that even our willing to be cleansed is brought about by the infusion and operation of the Holy Ghost, he resists the Holy Ghost Himself . . . and the salutary preaching of the Apostle: 'It is God who worketh in you, both to will and to accomplish, according to His good will' (Phil. 2:13)." Canon 9 on the help of God asserts: "It pertains to the category of the divine when we both think rightly and restrain our steps from falsehood and injustice; for whatever

[24] Jas. 1:17.
[25] I Cor. 12:3.
[26] II Cor. 3:5.
[27] *De civitate Dei*, Bk. XII, chap. 9.
[28] Ia, q.23, a.5.

good we may do, God operates in us and with us to enable us to operate"; and canon 12 on the quality in which God loves us: "God so
loves us according to the quality we shall have by His gift, and not
as we are by our own merit." This text taken from the fifty-sixth
Sentence of St. Prosper summarizes the one preserved in the *Indiculus
de gratia Dei,* a collection of anterior statements by the Holy See
wherein we read (Denz., nos. 133–4): "No one uses his free will well
except through Christ"; "All the desires and all the works and merits
of the saints should be referred to the glory and praise of God, for no
one pleases Him otherwise than by what He Himself has bestowed."
This is essentially the principle of the origin of superiority in a formula
almost identical with the one which St. Thomas was to give later
(Ia, q. 20, a. 4). The same *Indiculus* preserves the following (Denz.,
nos. 135, 137, 139, 141, 142): "God so works in the hearts of men and
in the free will itself, that a devout thought, holy counsel and every
movement of good will is from God, since we can do some good
through Him without whom we can do nothing (John 15:5)"; and
likewise, no. 139: "The most devout Fathers taught the beginnings
of good will, the growth of commendable desires, and perseverance
in them to the end is to be referred to the grace of Christ . . .";
"Hearkening to the prayers of His Church, God deigns to draw
many souls from every kind of error, and once they are rescued from
the power of darkness He transports them into the kingdom of the
Son of His love (Col. 1:13), that from vessels of wrath He might
fashion vessels of mercy (Rom. 9:22). All this is regarded as of
divine operation to such an extent that gratitude may always be referred to God as effecting it."

The end of this famous Indiculus is well-known: "Let us acknowledge God to be the author of all good dispositions and works . . .
Indeed, free will is not taken away but rather liberated by this help
and gift of God . . . He acts in us, to be sure, in such wise that nothing interior is to be withdrawn from His work and regard; this we
believe to satisfy adequately, whatever the writings taught us according to the aforesaid rules of the Apostolic See" (Denz., no. 142). Is
this not equivalent to saying: "In the affair of salvation everything
comes from God"? "Nothing interior is to be withdrawn," as the
last text quoted declares. If, then, one man is better than another, especially in the order of salvation, it is because he has been loved more
by God and has received more. This is the meaning of: "What hast

thou that thou hast not received?" quoted by the Council of Orange (Denz., nos. 179, 199). The sense in which the same Council speaks of God the author of every good, whether natural or supernatural, is explained by the definition contained in canon 20: "Nothing of good can exist in man without God. God does many good things in man which are not done by man; but man does nothing good which God does not grant it to him to do" (Denz., no. 193); and canon 22: "No one has anything of his own but lying and sin. But if a man possesses anything of truth and justice it comes from that fountain for which we should thirst in this desert, so that, refreshed, as it were, by a few drops from it, we may not faint on the way." Cf. in the *Histoire des Conciles* of C. J. Héfèle, translated, corrected, and augmented with critical notes by Dom. H. Leclercq, Vol. II, Part II, pp. 1085-1110, the passages from St. Augustine and St. Prosper from which these canons of the Council of Orange are drawn, as confirmed by Boniface II; the most interesting, of course, are those concerning the beginning of salvation and final perseverance ("persevering in good works") for both of which they affirm the necessity of a special, gratuitous grace (Denz., nos. 177 f., 183). But the grace of final perseverance is that of the elect.

The Semi-Pelagians, reducing predestination to a foreknowledge of merits, held that from the height of His eternity God desires equally the salvation of all men and that He is therefore rather the spectator than the author of the fact that one man is saved rather than another. Is this true or not? Such was the profound question which confronted thinkers at the time of the Semi-Pelagian heresy, as anyone will recognize who reads St. Augustine and St. Prosper.

But did the Council of Orange leave it unanswered? It asserted the principle of predilection, affirming, as everyone admits, the necessity and gratuity of grace which is not granted to all in the same manner, and demonstrating that in the work of salvation everything, from beginning to end, is from God, who anticipates our free will, supports it, causes it to act without doing it any violence, lifts it up often, but not always; and therein lies the very mystery of predestination. So true is this that, henceforth, to avoid Semi-Pelagianism it will always be necessary to admit a certain gratuity in predestination.[29]

---

[29] At least gratuitous predestination to certain relatively favorable circumstances in which, according to divine prevision, the elect will consent to good. That is Molina's opinion.

Is not the incontrovertible principle of all this teaching that all good without exception comes from God, and that if there is more good in one man than in another, it cannot be so independently of God? "For who distinguisheth thee? Or what hast thou that thou hast not received?" This text, according to St. Augustine, should cause us to admit that there is no sin committed by any other man that I am not capable of committing under the same circumstances, as a result of the weakness of my free will or of my own frailty (the apostle Peter denied his Master thrice); and if, in fact, I have not fallen, if I have persevered, it is no doubt because I have labored and struggled; but without divine grace I should have accomplished nothing. Such was the thought of St. Francis of Assisi at the sight of a criminal condemned to death. St. Cyprian had said (*Ad Querin.,* Bk. III, chap. 4, *PL,* IV, 734): "We should glory in nothing, when nothing is our own." St. Basil asserts (Hom. 22 *De humilitate*): "Nothing is left to thee, O man, in which thou canst glory . . . for we live entirely by the grace and gift of God." And St. John Chrysostom adds (Serm. 2, in *Ep. ad Coloss., PG,* LXII, 312): "In the affair of salvation everything is a gift of God."

THE PRINCIPAL APPLICATIONS OF THE PRINCIPLE OF PREDILECTION, ACCORDING TO ST. THOMAS

St. Thomas deduces therefrom, in the first place, the reason for the inequality of creatures, Ia, q. 47, a. 1: "The distinction and multitude of things is from the design of the first agent who is God; for He brought creatures into existence in order to communicate His goodness to them and be represented by them. And since He cannot be adequately represented by one creature, He produced a multitude of diverse creatures"; and article 2: "And unequal . . . because a formal distinction [which is paramount] always requires inequality." By creation God willed to manifest His goodness, but it could not be sufficiently represented by one creature, which would be too deficient and limited for that. Hence He desired many and these unequal and subordinate one to another, for the mere material multiplication of individuals of the same species is much less representative of the richness of divine goodness than a multiplicity of species, hierarchically arranged as are numbers. Leibnitz remarked that there would be no satisfaction in having a thousand copies of the same edition of Virgil in one's library. But among these unequal creatures, one is better than another only because it has received more from God.

St. Thomas draws from the same principle the reason why grace is not equal in all men, Ia IIae, q. 112, a. 4: "It cannot be said," he remarks, "that the primary reason for this inequality arises from the fact that one man has prepared himself better than another to receive grace, for this preparation does not pertain to man except so far as his free will is moved by God. Hence the primary reason for this difference must be found in God who dispenses the gifts of His grace in diverse ways, so that the beauty and perfection of the Church may come forth from these different degrees." God sows a more or less choice divine seed in souls according to His good pleasure with the beauty of His Church in view.

St. Thomas also deduces from this principle of the origin of superiority that if one man prepares himself better than another for justification it is because, in the last analysis, he received more help from a stronger actual grace. In fact the holy doctor states in his commentary on St. Matthew (25:15) with reference to the parable of the talents: "He who strives harder receives more grace, but the fact that he does strive requires a higher cause." Again on the Epistle to the Ephesians (4:7), with respect to the words, "To every one of us is given grace, according to the measure of the giving of Christ," St. Thomas comments: "This difference is not owing to fate or chance or merit, but to the giving of Christ, that is, to the extent to which Christ measured it out to us. . . . For, as it is in the power of Christ to give or not to give, so also is it to give more or less."

The principle of the origin of superiority is so evident that all theologians would accept it, did it not imply as a consequence that grace, which is followed by its effect, is infallibly efficacious of itself and not on account of our consent. Yet this consequence is manifest, as many texts of St. Thomas show. If, in fact, actual grace followed by consent to the good were not infallibly efficacious of itself but only through the consent which follows it, there would be the possibility that of two men equally aided by grace one would become better than the other by his consent; he would become better without having been loved and aided more by God.

This reason is put forth by all Thomists.[30] It rests on the principle

[30] For example, Billuart in his *Cursus theologiae,* the treatise on grace, diss. V, a.6, where he explains the words of St. Paul (I Cor. 4): "Who distinguisheth thee? Or what hast thou that thou hast not received?" writes: "If grace is not by itself efficacious

of which we are speaking and is affirmed equivalently in several texts
of St. Thomas. It is found clearly stated particularly in the distinction
which he establishes between consequent divine will (which bears
upon every good, easy or difficult, which will come to pass here and
now) and antecedent divine will (bearing on the good separated
from the particular circumstances without which nothing comes to
pass); cf. Ia, q. 19, a. 6 ad 1: "What we will antecedently we do not
will absolutely but under a particular aspect; for the will is applied to
things as they are in themselves, and in themselves they are individual.
Hence we will a thing absolutely to the extent that we will it taking
into account all the particular circumstances, which means willing
it consequently. . . . And thus it is evident that whatever God wills
absolutely comes to pass, although what He wills antecedently may
not." If it happens, then, that Peter becomes here and now better

of our consent, but waits for it from us and is rendered efficacious by it, man has
something which he does not receive and in which he can glory and distinguish
himself from another who, anticipated by equal grace, does not consent; namely, his
consent to grace which he does not derive from grace but from himself."

Wherefore it can be understood why the true disciples of St. Thomas have always
refused to admit this fundamental assertion of Molinism which is thus expressed in
Molina's *Concordia*, p. 51: "It may happen that a person anticipated and called with
greater help by far is not converted on account of his free will, while another with
far less is converted." Again, p. 565 and in the Index of the same work, under
"Auxilium," p. 617, we read: "With equal help it may happen that one of those called
is converted and the other is not"; p. 618: "A person aided by less help from grace
may rise while another with more help does not, but continues in his obduracy."
Most astonishing of all, Molina, *ibid*. p. 565, claims to find the denial of the principle of the origin of what is better in the Council of Trent. Immediately after
the text we have just quoted, he adds: "For it is of faith that it rests with the faculty
of free will of a person to consent to God who urges and invites, as defined in the
Council of Trent, Sess. VI, chap. 5 and can. 4." He speaks as if the Council had
declared that, under efficacious grace, free will not only can resist but sometimes
does in fact resist, that is, sins under the very influence of efficacious grace.

Molina's proposition is retained by Lessius, *De gratia,* chap. 18, no. 7, in the famous
text often quoted: "The fact that, of two persons similarly called, one accepts the
proferred grace and the other rejects it, is rightly said to proceed from free will alone,
not that he who accepts does so by his free will alone, but because this difference
arises only from free will so as not to depend upon any diversity in their prevenient
helps." What then becomes of "Who distinguisheth thee? Or what hast thou that
thou hast not received?" It should be remarked that the congruists themselves must
adhere to this, for, since congruous grace is not efficacious of itself, it may happen
that, with equal congruous graces, one man consents to good and the other does not.
In numerous treatises written during the past three centuries on these questions we
find the same denial of the principle of predilection: "No created being is better
than another unless it is loved more by God." And yet it is an obvious corollary of
the principles of causality and finality.

than another man, whether by a facile or a difficult act, this is because from all eternity God has so willed by consequent will.

St. Thomas adds that this consequent will is expressed in time by a grace which is efficacious of itself; cf. Ia IIae, q. 112, a. 3: "The intention of God cannot fail, according to the affirmation of Augustine in the book *De dono perseverantiae,* chap. 14, that those who are liberated are most certainly liberated by the beneficence of God. Hence if it is in the designs of God who moves, that the man whose heart He moves should obtain grace, he will infallibly obtain it, according to the words of John 6:45: 'Everyone that hath heard of the Father, and hath learned, cometh to Me.' "

This proposition of St. Thomas is manifestly very different from an apparently similar one of Quesnell,[31] for the latter denies freedom from necessity and admits only freedom from coercion; moreover, he denies sufficient grace and considers every actual grace intrinsically efficacious.

Many other texts of St. Thomas on the intrinsic efficacy of grace might be cited. They are well known, quoted and explained in all the treatises on grace written by Thomists.[32] This conception of the intrinsic efficacy of grace is in no way contradictory of the traditional definition of free will, which recent historical works have set in increasingly clear relief: "the faculty of choosing the means in view of an end to be attained," [33] so that to deviate from the true end is an abuse of liberty.

Intrinsically efficacious grace is opposed only to a new definition of free will [34] which disregards the specifying object of the free act (an object not good in every respect), a definition which will not withstand metaphysical analysis and which is unmindful of the truth that free will is applied not univocally but analogically to God and to

---

[31] Cf. Denz., no. 1362: "When God wills to save a soul, whatever may be the time or place, the undoubted effect follows the will of God." The sense of this proposition is determined by the preceding one: "Grace is nothing else but the omnipotent will of God commanding and effecting what it commands," as well as by the others who deny free will (freedom from necessity) and sufficient grace.

[32] See, for example, Ia, q. 19, a.8 c and ad 2; q.22, a.4 ad 3; Ia IIae, q.10, a.4; q.109, a.1; IIa IIae, q.24, a.11; *Contra Gentes,* Bk. III, chap. 89; *De malo,* q.6, a.1 ad 3; *De veritate,* q.22, a.8; *In Ep. ad Eph.,* chap. 3, lect. 2.

[33] Ia, q.62, a.8 ad 3; q.83, a.4.

[34] A faculty which, presupposing all the prerequisites for acting (even divine motion and the last practical judgment), can either act or not act, even in the composite sense.

man, according to a reason not absolutely but proportionately the same,[35] so that the free will of man, not only as an entity but also as such under the idea of free entity (*sub ratione liberi arbitrii*) depends on God, who is not merely first being, but first intelligence and first liberty. Freedom is a perfection in God, and we can participate in it only analogically.

As a matter of fact, the human will can resist efficacious grace if it so wills, as the Council of Trent declares, but as long as the will is under efficacious grace, it never wills to resist. Under efficacious actual grace it never sins, for the grace which is termed efficacious is that which is followed by its effect: consent to good. As St. Thomas explains, in the same way, a man who is seated can stand up, he has the real, proximate power to do so; but as long as he remains seated he never does stand up, since by virtue of the principle of contradiction, he cannot be both seated and standing.

The new definition of liberty: "a faculty which, assuming all the prerequisites for acting, can either act or not act,"—if understood in the sense: under efficacious divine motion and after the final salutary, practical judgment, the free will not only can resist but at times actually does—such a definition is contrary to the principle of predilection which is a corollary of the principles of causality and finality.

By what other principle should that of predilection be balanced? By the following: God never commands the impossible. St. Thomas, great contemplative even more than able dialectician, recognizes that the Christian doctrine of predestination and grace rises like a summit above the two opposing chasms of Pelagianism and predestinationism. He understands that, on undertaking the ascent of that peak, one must deviate neither to right nor to left, neither toward a rigid doctrine which restricts the will for universal salvation and limits sufficient grace nor toward a contrary doctrine which denies the intrinsic efficacy of grace. He perceives, too, that one must not come to a halt halfway up the slope at one of those eclectic combinations which would admit grace to be intrinsically efficacious for difficult acts conducive to salvation and not intrinsically efficacious for facile acts conducive to salvation. Such a solution may appear simple in practice, but speculatively it disregards the necessity and universality of principles with relation to divine causality, principles which thereupon lose all their value; and it adds to the obscurity of the doctrine

[35] *De veritate,* q.2, a.11.

admitted for difficult acts the insoluble difficulties of that which is admitted for facile acts. St. Thomas sees in such eclectic combinations nothing but a quite human clarity, merely apparent and without basis, substituted for the higher obscurity of the mystery, the loftiness of which is thus minimized. Assuredly he does not look upon this as an insoluble question which it is useless to fathom, but rather as an object of loving contemplation, "the terrible but sweet mystery of the love of predilection in God: 'Who is like to Thee, among the strong, O Lord? who is like to Thee, glorious in holiness, terrible and praise-worthy, doing wonders?' (Exod. 15:11)."

Incapable of stopping halfway as does eclecticism, St. Thomas as-pires to climb straight toward the summit. But at a certain height the trail ends, the path has not yet been blazed, as St. John of the Cross indicates on the illustration representing the Ascent of Carmel. St. Thomas perceives clearly that here on earth no one can attain to that culminating point where it will be granted him to see the intimate reconciliation of the will for universal salvation with gratuitous pre-destination. Thus he preserves all the loftiness of the mystery and does not seek to substitute for its sublime obscurity any vain human clarity. But without seeing the summit (faith regards what is not seen), he succeeds in determining where it is to be found by means of higher principles which mutually balance one another. He formulates these very lofty, very simple principles with such great lucidity that they only bring out in clearer relief the superior obscurity of the in-accessible mystery located in its true site, there where it must be con-templated in the cloud of faith, and not elsewhere. It is one of those most beautiful chiaroscuros which have ever attracted and riveted the contemplation of great theologians. The masters of former times de-lighted in such vistas, painted not with pigments but with principles, wherein the luminous circle surrounding the mystery expresses so powerfully the grandeur of faith; vistas so manifestly surpassing those of the greatest painters or the most beautiful musical conceptions of Beethoven or Bach. And just as these great artists understood that har-mony is destroyed by a discordant commingling of sharps and flats, so did those great masters of theology strive no less to avoid the jarring dissonance produced in such difficult questions by a sharp which would tend toward predestinationism or a flat which would incline toward the opposite error.

The principles which produce equilibrium here are, on the one hand, that of predilection: "no creature is better than another unless it is better loved by God," a simple interpretation of the words of Christ: "Without Me, you can do nothing," and of those of St. Paul: "It is God who worketh in you, both to will and accomplish, according to His good will"; "Who distinguisheth thee? Or what hast thou that thou hast not received?" This principle is immutable, and together with it that other: "All that God wills by consequent will comes to pass, without liberty being thereby destroyed."

On the opposite slope of the invisible, inaccessible peak, so as to determine the point where it rises and where the blessed contemplate it in heaven, must be recalled the principle of St. Augustine quoted by the Council of Trent (Denz., no. 804): "God does not command the impossible, but by commanding He teaches thee both to do what thou canst and to ask what thou canst not." This formula is sacrosanct.

Invoking several passages of St. Paul, St. Augustine,[36] St. Prosper,[37] and St. John Damascene, the Angelic Doctor gives us the principle

[36] In quoting the restricted interpretation given by St. Augustine of St. Paul's text: "[God] will have all men to be saved," too often the texts which counterbalance this interpretation are forgotten. It would be wronging St. Augustine not to quote with reference to predestination and the will for universal salvation the classic passage from his *De natura et gratia,* chap. 43, which the Council of Trent itself cites (Sess. VI, chap. 11, Denz., no. 804) against the Protestants to show that God does not command the impossible. Assuredly, if St. Augustine understood at one time in a restricted sense the text of St. Paul, "[God] will have all men to be saved," it was with reference to the efficacious or consequent divine will. But he had no intention of denying (as later Protestants and Jansenists would do) what was subsequently to be called antecedent will. It is very evident that St. Augustine cannot be accused of teaching that God commands the impossible by not granting sufficient grace. Sin would then become inevitable, so that it would no longer be sin and could not deserve punishment from God. Such aberrations never entered the mind of St. Augustine. On the contrary, he affirms in several texts often cited by theologians against the Jansenists what was later to be termed the antecedent will for the salvation of all men and the corresponding sufficient grace; cf. *De spiritu et littera,* chap. 33. St. Augustine never retracted these texts; had he done so he would have had to assert that God commands the impossible. But, as the Council of Trent observes, he clearly said quite the opposite, especially in his *De natura et gratia,* chap. 43, no. 50; chap. 26, no. 29.

[37] Cf. St. Prosper on the second Vincentian objection. St. Prosper did not therefore abandon, as we are sometimes led to believe, the teaching of his master when he affirmed the will of universal salvation. Without deviating from the doctrine of his master, St. Prosper may well declare that positive reprobation presupposes the prevision of demerits, for a punishment is only inflicted on account of a sin. He may also concede to his adversaries without any difficulty that the divine permission of the sin of final impenitence is a chastisement for preceding sins. Did not St. Augustine affirm several times that the gift of final perseverance is granted to some out of mercy and is not granted to others in justice on account of preceding sins?

of the will for universal salvation ("God . . . will have all men to be saved," I Tim. 2:4) in an admirable and very profound formula which echoes the most beautiful psalms in praise of the mercy of God. He writes (Ia, q. 21, a. 4): "Every work of divine justice presupposes a work of mercy or of sheer bounty, and finds therein its basis. If, in fact, God owes something to His creature, it is by virtue of a preceding gift. If He owes a reward to our merits, it is because He has first given us the grace to merit; if He owes it to Himself to give us the grace necessary for salvation, it is because, from pure liberality in the first place, He has created us and called us to the supernatural life. . . . Divine mercy is thus the root, as it were, or the principle of all the divine works; it penetrates them with its virtue and governs them. In the capacity of primary source of all gifts, it is mercy which has the strongest influence, and it is for this reason that it surpasses justice, which takes second place. This is why, even with regard to things due to the creature, God in His superabundant liberality gives more than justice requires, *"et propter hoc etiam ea, quae alicui creaturae debentur, Deus ex abundantia suae bonitatis largius dispensat quam exigat propitio rei."* (See also Ia, q. 21, a. 2 ad 3.)

St. Thomas also affirms in the very question dealing with predestination: "God does not deprive anyone of what is his due."[38] "He gives help sufficient to avoid sin";[39] "Those to whom efficacious help is not given are denied it in justice, as punishment for a previous sin, . . . those to whom it is granted receive it in mercy."[40] This is the echo of the psalms relating to divine mercy, particularly Ps. 135: "Praise the Lord, for He is good: for His mercy endureth forever. Praise ye the God of gods: for His mercy endureth forever." Likewise Ps. 117: "Give praise to the Lord, for He is good."

How is this mercy, principle of all the works of God, reconcilable with the divine permission of evil and of the final impenitence of many? Why does it sometimes raise up the sinner, but not always? Therein lies a mystery surpassing the natural powers of any intelligence created or capable of being created, and beyond them not only because of its essential supernaturalness, as in the case of the Trinity, but also by the contingency resulting from dependence on the sovereign liberty of God:[41] "If efficacious grace is refused to many," says

[38] Ia, q.23, a.5 ad 3.
[39] Ia IIae, q.106, a.2 ad 2.
[40] IIa IIae, q.2, a.5 ad 1.
[41] Ia, q.23, a.5 ad 3.

St. Thomas following St. Augustine, "it is in justice, as the result of a sin [permitted, of course, by God, but of which He was in no sense the cause]; if this same grace is granted to others, it is out of mercy." [42] It is fitting that these two divine perfections should be manifested, as St. Paul declares; [43] there is consequently involved here the cooperation of infinite justice, infinite mercy, and also of supreme liberty, eminently wise in its good pleasure, which is in no way a caprice. Obviously each of these divine perfections herein involved exceeds the natural powers of any intelligence created or capable of being created. None among them may be limited, just as in the mystery of the Cross and Passion of the Savior neither infinite justice nor infinite mercy may be restricted; they are reconciled in the uncreated love of God and in the love of Christ delivered up for our sake. The apparently contradictory aspects of a mystery must not be restricted for the sake of a better understanding of them. Rather must one, as it were, soar above this apparent contradiction by the contemplation of faith. This is why St. Paul exclaims: "O the depth of the riches of the wisdom and of the knowledge of God! How incomprehensible are His judgments, and how unsearchable His ways!" (Rom. 11:33.)

To acknowledge this mystery which is at the topmost point of the peak we have just been describing, of that summit which can never be seen from here below, one must cling to it in pure faith, as Holy Scripture frequently urges us to do. Let us recall, for example, the hymn of thanksgiving uttered by the elder Tobias (Tob. 13): "Thou art great, O Lord, forever, and Thy kingdom is unto all ages. For Thou scourgest and Thou savest: Thou leadest down to hell, and bringest up again: and there is none that can escape Thy hand. . . . There is no other almighty God besides Him. He hath chastised us for our iniquities: and He will save us for His own mercy. See then what He hath done with us, and with fear and trembling give ye glory to Him: and extol the eternal King of worlds in your works."

Theology, as the Council of the Vatican asserts,[44] is essentially ordained to the contemplation of revealed mysteries; infused faith, entirely divine and essentially supernatural, is, in spite of its ob-

---

[42] IIa IIae, q.2, a.5 ad 1; also Ia, q.23, a.5 ad 3.

[43] Rom. 9:22: "What if God, willing to show His wrath, and to make His power known, endured with much patience vessels of wrath, fitted for destruction, that He might show the riches of His glory on the vessels of mercy, which He hath prepared unto glory"; (where is the injustice?)

[44] Denz., no. 1796.

scurity, eminently superior to it, especially faith which is enlightened by the gifts of wisdom and understanding. It becomes increasingly evident, then, that this obscurity does not derive from absurdity or incoherence, but from a light too intense for our feeble gaze. We begin to realize that, with reference to these great mysteries of pre-destination, of grace, and also of the will for universal salvation, we should read above all the great theologians who were at the same time great contemplatives.[45] We come to understand better and better why, in the passive purification of the soul described by the great spiritual writers, St. John of the Cross in particular, the light of the gift of understanding removes little by little the false lucidity of eclectic combinations which stop halfway, and set the soul in the presence of the real mystery without diminishing its sublimity. We finally grasp the reason for St. Theresa's remark: "The more obscure a mystery is the more devotion I have to it," obscure, that is, with the translucent darkness which gives us a presentiment of the very object of the contemplation of the blessed. Above all, we attain to a growing realization of the fact that what is most obscure in these mysteries is what is most divine, most elevated, most lovable; and if we cannot yet cling to them in vision, we do so by faith and by love.

The mystery involved here, whence proceeds the principle of the origin of superiority to which this principle leads, is the incomprehensible mystery of the love of predilection in God. "No created being would be better than another were it not better loved by God" (Ia,

---

[45] One might have gained an idea of what the spirit of theology ought to be from hearing an old theologian of Asturias, Father N. Del Prado, who was still teaching in the university some years ago; his soaring flight sometimes reminded one of the eagles of his native province. He was an eminent metaphysician who viewed the whole treatise on the one God in this single principle: "In God alone essence and existence are identical." He was, moreover, a man of great faith and used to pray before giving his lectures. Their material documentation might not always be very complete—one did not go to him for that; but he possessed the spirit of theology for which he entertained the greatest esteem, although he considered faith far superior to it. He understood that theology was ordained to the contemplation of mysteries, and it was such a joy for him to explain the *Summa theologica* of St. Thomas wherein he always found the most sublime, comprehensive, simple principles, that he probably would not have minded living another hundred or two hundred years here on earth in order to explain it to generations of students. He was a contemplative theologian who realized that the spirit of theology is drawn from prayer, from psalmody, from meditation more than from a documentation which combines the texts of the masters without throwing upon them the light of the higher principles which those same masters have formulated. He never wearied of repeating these principles; they were the themes of his teaching.

q. 20, a. 3); "What hast thou that thou hast not received?" (I Cor. 4:7); "He [God] chose us in Him [Christ] before the foundation of the world, that we should be holy and unspotted in His sight in charity.[46] Who hath predestinated us unto the adoption of children through Jesus Christ unto Himself: according to the purpose of His will: unto the praise of the glory of His grace, in which He hath graced us in His beloved Son" (Eph. 1:4-6). We can understand that these words, "unto the praise of the glory of His grace," ought to become the delight of contemplatives, expressing as they do with extraordinary splendor the principle of predilection which manifestly dominates all the problems of sanctifying and actual grace in every degree.

III. The Ultimate Basis of the Distinction Between Sufficient and Efficacious Grace

(By way of recapitulation, we here reprint this article which appeared in French in the *Revue Thomiste,* May, 1937.)

"Whatsoever the Lord pleased He hath done" (Ps. 134:6). "God does not command the impossible" (St. Augustine and Council of Trent, Sess. VI, chap. 11).

We dealt with this subject in a book which appeared in 1936: *La prédestination des saints et la grâce;* cf. especially pp. 257-64; 341-50; 141-44. In the present article we wish to stress a higher principle admitted by all theologians wherein the Thomists find the ultimate basis of the distinction between sufficient and efficacious grace.

The problem. It is certain from revelation that many actual graces bestowed by God do not produce the effect (or at least the entire effect) toward which they are ordered, whereas others do. The former are called sufficient and purely sufficient; they confer the power of doing good without carrying over efficaciously to the act itself. Man resists their attraction; but their existence is absolutely certain, regardless of what the Jansenists maintain. Otherwise God would command the impossible, which would be contrary to His mercy and His justice. Sin, moreover, would be inevitable; hence it would no longer really be sin and consequently could not be justly punished by God. In this sense we say that Judas, before sinning, could really, at the time and

---

[46] As many interpreters observe, although the Vulgate joins the words "in charity" to verse four, it seems preferable to translate thus the Greek of St. Paul.

place, have avoided the crime he committed; the same is also true of the unrepentant thief before he expired beside our Lord.

The other actual graces which are termed efficacious not only convey the real power of observing the commandments; they cause us to observe them in fact, as in the case of the good thief in contrast with the other. The existence of efficacious actual grace is affirmed in numerous passages of Scripture, such as: "I will give you a new heart, and put a new spirit within you: and I will take away the stony heart out of your flesh, and will give you a heart of flesh. And I will put My spirit in the midst of you: and I will cause you to walk in My commandments, and to keep My judgments, and do them" (Ezech. 36:26 f.); "Whatsoever the Lord pleased He hath done" (Ps. 134:6), that is, all that He wills, not conditionally but absolutely, He accomplishes even the free conversion of man, as in the case of King Assuerus at the prayer of Esther (Esther 13:9; 14:13); "And God changed the king's spirit into mildness" (*ibid.,* 15:11). The infallibility and efficacy of a decree of God's will are obviously based in these texts upon His omnipotence and not upon the foreseen consent of King Assuerus. In the same sense the Book of Proverbs declares (21:1): "As the divisions of waters, so the heart of the king is in the hand of the Lord: whithersoever He will He shall turn it"; likewise Ecclus. 33:24-27. Jesus Himself declares: "My sheep hear My voice: and I know them, and they follow Me. And I give them life everlasting: and they shall not perish forever, and no man shall pluck them out of My hand" (John 10:27); and again: "Those whom Thou gavest Me have I kept; and none of them is lost, but the son of perdition, that the scripture may be fulfilled" (*ibid.,* 17:12). St. Paul writes with the same purport to the Philippians (2:13): "For it is God who works in you, both to will and to accomplish, according to His good will."

The Second Council of Orange, opposing the Semi-Pelagians, quotes several of these scriptural texts and refers to the efficacy of grace in the following terms (Denz., no. 182): "Whatever good we do, God works in us and with us so that we may work." There is therefore a grace which not only gives the real power of doing good (which exists in one who sins), but which is effectual in the act, although it does not exclude our free cooperation but arouses and induces it in us. St. Augustine explains these same scriptural texts when he says: "God converts and transforms the heart of the king . . . from wrath into mildness by His most secret and efficacious power" (*I ad Bonifatium,* chap. 20).

Hence a great majority of the ancient theologians, Augustinians, Thomists, Scotists, have allowed that the grace termed efficacious is so of itself, because God wills it and not because we will it by a consent foreseen in the divine prevision. God is not merely the spectator of what distinguishes the just man from the sinner; He is the author of salvation. It is true that these ancient theologians are divided on the secondary question of explaining how grace is efficacious of itself; some have recourse to the divine motion known as physical premotion, others to a predominating delight or some similar attraction. But all admit that the grace called efficacious is so of itself.

Molina, on the contrary, maintained that it is extrinsically efficacious on account of our consent which was foreseen by God through mediate knowledge. This mediate knowledge has always been rejected by Thomists who accuse it of attributing passivity to God with respect to our free determinations (possible in the future, and then future) and of leading to determinism regarding circumstances (so far as, by examining these, God would foresee infallibly what a man would choose). Thus the very being and the goodness of man's free and salutary choice would derive from him and not from God, at least in the sense in which Molina writes: "It may happen that, with equal help, one of those called will be converted and not the other. Indeed, even with less help one man may rise while another with greater help does not, but perseveres in his obduracy." [47]

The opponents of Molinism reply that there would thus be a good, that of salutary free choice, which would not proceed from God, the source of all good. How then can the words of Jesus be sustained (John 15:5): "Without Me you can do nothing" in the order of salvation, and those words of St. Paul: "For who distinguisheth thee? Or what hast thou that thou hast not received? And if thou hast received, why dost thou glory, as if thou hadst not received it?" (I Cor. 4:7.) It would in fact come to pass that of two sinners placed in the same circumstances and equally aided by God, one would be converted and not the other; man would distinguish

---

[47] *Concordia,* pp. 51, 565, and the Index under *"Auxilium."* Lessius adds: "Not that he who accepts does so by his free will alone, but because this difference arises only from free will so as not to depend upon any diversity in their prevenient helps" (*De gratia efficaci,* chap. 18, no. 7).

himself and become better than another without greater assistance from God, without having received more, contrary to the text of St. Paul.

The Molinists do not fail to press the question further: If in order to act effectually one requires, in addition to sufficient grace, a grace which is efficacious of itself, does the former truly convey a real power of acting? It does so, the Thomists reply, if it is true that a real power of acting is distinct from the action itself; if it is true, as Aristotle maintained against the Megarians, that an architect who is not actually building still has the real power to do so; if it is true that a man who is asleep still has a real power of seeing: from the fact that he is not exercising his sight at the moment it does not follow that he is blind. Moreover, if a sinner did not resist sufficient grace, he would receive the efficacious grace proferred in the former, as the fruit is in the flower. If he refuses, he deserves to be deprived of this further help.

Our adversaries insist that St. Thomas himself did not distinguish explicitly between grace efficacious of itself and grace which merely conveys the power of doing good. It is an easy matter to cite many texts of the Angelic Doctor wherein he makes this distinction; for instance: "The help of God is twofold: God gives a faculty by infusing power and grace through which man is made able and apt to operate. But He confers the very operation itself inasmuch as He works in us interiorly moving and urging us to good, . . . according as His power works in us both to will and to accomplish according to His good will" (*In Ep. ad Ephes.,* chap. 3, lect. 2); likewise, Ia IIae, q. 109, a. 1, a. 2, a. 9, 10; q. 113, a. 7, 10, and elsewhere. He also writes: "Christ is the propitiation for our sins, for some efficaciously, for all sufficiently, since the price of His blood is sufficient for the salvation of all, but possesses efficacy only in the elect, on account of an impediment" (*In Ep. ad Tim.,* 2:6). God often removes this impediment, but not always. Therein lies the mystery. "God deprives no one of what is his due" (Ia, q. 23, a. 5 ad 3); "He gives sufficient help to avoid sin" (Ia IIae, q. 106, a. 2 ad 2). As for efficacious grace, "if it is given to one sinner, that is through mercy; if it is denied to another, that is in justice" (IIa IIae, q. 2, a. 5 ad 1).

Thomists analyze these texts as follows: Every actual grace which is efficacious of itself with regard to an imperfect salutary act such as attrition, is sufficient with regard to a more perfect salutary act such as contrition.[48] This is manifestly the sense of St. Thomas' doctrine, and, according to him, if a man actually resists the grace which confers the power of doing good, he deserves to be deprived of that which would effectually cause him to do good.[49] But St. Thomas not only distinguished between these two graces; he indicated the ultimate basis of the distinction.

ANTECEDENT AND CONSEQUENT DIVINE WILL

Thomists generally affirm that the distinction between efficacious and sufficient grace is based, according to St. Thomas, on the distinction between consequent will and antecedent will, as explained by him (Ia, q. 19, a. 6 ad 1). From the will known as consequent proceeds efficacious grace, and from the antecedent will, sufficient grace.

In this connection, St. Thomas writes: "The will is applied to things in accordance with what they are in themselves; but in themselves they are individual. Hence we will a thing absolutely inasmuch as we will it taking into consideration all the particular circumstances; this is willing consequently. . . . And thus it is evident that whatever God wills absolutely comes to pass." As the psalms tell us, "Whatsoever the Lord pleased He hath done" (Ps. 134:6).

The object of the will is the good. But goodness, unlike truth, resides formally not in the intellect but in the thing itself, which exists only here and now. Therefore we will absolutely, purely and simply, whatever we will as it must be realized here and now. This is consequent will, which is always efficacious in God, for all that God wills (unconditionally) He accomplishes.

If, on the contrary, the will regards what is good in itself independent of circumstances, not here and now, it is the antecedent (or conditional) will, which in itself and as such is not efficacious, since the good, natural or supernatural, facile or difficult, is realized only here and now. That is why St. Thomas says in the same place a few lines before: "In its primary signification and considered absolutely, a thing may be good or evil, which, however, when considered in connection with something else that effects the consequent estimate of it, may become quite the contrary; just as it is a good thing for a man

[48] Cf. Alvarez, *De auxiliis*, Bk. III, disp. 80; Gonet, *Clypeus thom.*, "De voluntate Dei," disp. 4, no. 147; Del Prado, *De gratia et libero arbitrio*, III, 423.

[49] Cf. Ia IIae, q. 79, a. 3: "According to His own discretion, God does not send the light of grace to those in whom He finds an obstacle."

to live, . . . but if it is added with regard to a particular man that he is a murderer, . . . it is a good thing for him to be executed."

Thus during a storm at sea, a merchant would wish (conditionally) to save his merchandise, but he is willing in fact to cast the merchandise into the sea to save his life (Ia IIae, q. 6, a. 6). Thus likewise does God will antecedently that all the fruits of the earth come to maturity, although for the sake of a higher good He permits that all do not do so. Again, in the same way, God wills antecedently the salvation of all men, although He permits sin and the loss of many in view of a higher good of which He alone is judge. Hence St. Thomas concludes in the text quoted: "It is thus evident that whatever God wills absolutely comes to pass, although what He wills antecedently may not."

It nevertheless remains true that God never commands the impossible, and that by His will and love He renders the keeping of the commandments possible to all, in the measure in which they are known and can be known. "He gives sufficient help to avoid sin" (Ia IIae, q. 106, a. 2 ad 2). In fact, He gives to each even more than strict justice demands (Ia, q. 21, a. 4). So does St. Thomas reconcile the antecedent divine will which St. John Damascene speaks of, with omnipotence which must not be lost sight of.

THE ULTIMATE PRINCIPLES ON WHICH THE DISTINCTION BETWEEN THE TWO WILLS AND THE TWO GRACES RESTS

But is there not a higher, simpler principle from which the distinction may be derived between the two divine wills, one of them always efficacious, the other conditional and the source of sufficent grace? Is there not a universally accepted principle whence proceeds the notion of consequent and antecedent will, which we have just reviewed, and which would justify them in a higher light before the eyes of those who might remain unconvinced?

The principle we are seeking is precisely the one upon which this entire article of St. Thomas is based (Ia, q. 19, a. 6). It is expressed in the psalms in the words (134:6): "Whatsoever the Lord pleased He hath done." That is, God brings to pass all that He wills purely and simply, with an unconditional will. This is the will known as consequent, the principle of grace efficacious in itself. The enunciation of this principle is completed by the formula: "For nothing is done in heaven or on earth unless God either graciously brings it about or permits it to happen in His justice." In other words, nothing happens without God's willing it if it is a good or permitting it if it is an evil.[50] So does the Church teach universally, and accordingly it is acknowledged that there is in God a conditional will, termed antecedent, which regards a good the privation of which is permitted by God for the sake of a higher good. Thus He permits that in certain cases His commandments are not kept, and He does so for the sake of that higher good, the manifestation of His mercy or of His justice.

To this principle must be added another which is also universally received, was frequently invoked by St. Augustine,[51] and was quoted by the Council of Trent, Sess. VI, chap. 11: God never commands the impossible. The fulfillment of His commands is really possible, in the measure in which they can be known. Hence it is evident that the antecedent divine will is the source of a sufficient grace which renders the accomplishment of the precepts really possible, without causing them to be fulfilled here and now.

From these two revealed principles is derived, as can be seen, the distinction between the two divine wills, the one always efficacious, called consequent, the other conditional and the source of sufficient grace. Herein lies the ultimate basis, then, of the distinction between the two kinds of grace which we are considering.

There is no exception to the universal principle: All that God wills (purely, simply, and unconditionally) comes to pass, without thereby violating our liberty, for God moves it strongly and sweetly, actualizing rather than destroying it. He wills efficaciously our free consent, and we do consent freely. The sovereign efficacy of divine causality extends even to the free mode of our acts (Ia, q. 19, a. 8). This supreme maxim is thus explained by St. Thomas (*ibid.*, a. 6): "Since the divine will is the most universal cause of all things, it is impossible for it not to be fulfilled," when it is a question of unconditional will. The reason for this is that no created agent can act without the concurrence of God, or fail without His permission. Hence this principle amounts to a declaration of what is generally taught by the Church: No good is brought about here and now (in one man rather than in another)

[50] Cf. Council of Toucy, A.D. 860, PL, CXXVI, 123; see Héfèle, *Histoire des Conciles* (French transl.), IV, 197-229.

[51] Cf. St. Augustine, *De natura et gratia,* chap. 43, no. 50 (*PL,* XLIV; 271): "God does not command the impossible, but by commanding He teaches thee to do what thou canst and to ask for what thou canst not do."

unless God has willed it positively and efficaciously from all eternity; and no evil, no sin, takes place here and now (in one man rather than in another) unless God has permitted it. The simpler formula is frequently used: Nothing takes place without the will of God if it is a good, or the permission of God if it is an evil. Equivalent definitions are found in the Councils, for example, that of Trent (Denz., no. 816).[52]

This very sublime and absolutely universal principle is repeated by many writers without any perception of what it implies. But it implies precisely, as we have just seen, the basis of the distinction between the two kinds of grace we are discussing, grace efficacious in itself and grace which is merely sufficient, which man resists, but which he would not resist without divine permission.

Hence in the ninth century, in order to terminate the discussions with regard to Gottschalk's opinion and to grant to the Augustinian bishops what they were asking, and at the same time maintaining the divine will for universal salvation and the responsibility of the sinner, the synodal letter approved by the Council of Toucy in 860 began in the following terms:[53] "God did all that He willed in heaven and on earth. For nothing is done in heaven or on earth unless He either graciously accomplishes it or permits it to happen in His justice." That is to say that every good, natural or supernatural, easy or difficult, initial or final, comes from God, and that no sin takes place, nor does it take place in one man rather than in another, without divine permission. This extremely general principle very evidently contains innumerable consequences. St. Thomas saw in it the equivalent of the principle of predilection which he thus formulated (Ia, q. 20, a. 3): "Since the love of God is the cause of the goodness of things, nothing would be better than something else did not God will a greater good to one than to another." No one would be better than another were he not more loved and helped by God. This is the equivalent of St. Paul's: "For who distinguisheth thee? Or what hast thou that thou hast not received?" (I Cor. 4:7.)

[52] "If anyone should say that it is not within the power of man to make his ways evil, but that God operates in bad works as well as good, not merely by permitting them, but even strictly and by Himself, in such wise that the betrayal of Judas is no less His own work than the vocation of Paul, let him be anathema."

[53] Cf. PL, CXXVI, 123. Cf. Denz., 17th ed., p. 145, no. 320.

CONSEQUENCES OF THIS PRINCIPLE

This truth is one of the foundations of Christian humility, resting on the dogmas of creation out of nothing and of the necessity of grace for every salutary act. The same principle of predilection contains virtually the doctrine of gratuitous predestination, for, as St. Thomas shows so clearly (Ia, q. 23, a. 5), since the merits of the elect are the effect of their predestination, they cannot be its cause. This great truth leads the saints, when they see a criminal mounting the scaffold, to say within themselves: "If that man had received all the graces I have received, he would perhaps have been less unfaithful than I; and had God permitted in my life all the faults He permitted in his, I should be in his place and he in mine." Such humility in the saints is manifestly the consequence of the principle: "Nothing happens unless God wills it, if it is a good, or permits it, if it is an evil."

In fact, whatever there is of being and of action in the sin, apart from the moral disorder it contains, all proceeds from God, first cause of all being and all action, as St. Thomas demonstrates so well (Ia IIae, q. 79, a. 2). The divine will cannot will, either directly or indirectly, the disorder which sin contains (*ibid.*, a. 1), nor can divine causality produce it. That disorder is outside the adequate object of God to much greater extent than sound is outside the object of the sense of sight. Just as we cannot see a sound, so God cannot be the cause of the disorder which lies in sin; but He is the cause of the being and action which it contains. There is nothing more precise and more "precisive," if we may so speak, than the formal object of a faculty.[54] Thus, although goodness and truth are not actually distinct in any reality, the intelligence attains to it only as true and the will only as good. In the same way, the effect of gravity in our bodily organism must not be confused with that of electricity or of heat; each of these causes produces its own effect in us, not that of any other. Likewise God is the cause of being and action in sin, but not of its moral disorder. Thus is verified once more the principle: nothing real is effected without God's will, nor any evil without His permission.

It is apparent, therefore, that theology should not only labor to deduce new conclusions following from its principles, but should also

---

[54] Hence the theological formula: "The divine causality necessary for the physical act of sin prescinds entirely from malice."

return to the first principles of faith so as to clarify conclusions which do not seem certain to those who do not recognize their connection with the prime verities.

To revert to the distinction between grace efficacious in itself and sufficient grace, it must be said, according to the generally accepted principle we have just recalled that, if of two sinners placed in the same circumstances, as were the two thieves who died with our Lord, one is converted, that is because God willed it efficaciously from all eternity for his salvation, and if the other continues in his impenitence, this does not happen without the just permission of God.

It is clear that if one of these two sinners should be converted, it will be as a result of a special mercy which causes him to merit before death and subsequently will crown its own gifts by rewarding him. But if a just man never sins mortally from the time of his first justification in baptism, that is the result of an even greater bounty on the part of God, who has preserved him thus efficaciously in good when He could have permitted his fall. This simple observation demonstrates the gratuity of predestination.

Such manifestly are the ultimate principles of the distinction between grace efficacious of itself which causes one to do good and sufficient grace which gives the power to do good. If a man resists the latter, as we have said, he deserves to be deprived of the former, which is offered to him in sufficient grace, as the fruit in the flower. Resistance or sin falls upon sufficient grace like hail upon a tree in blossom, which gave promise of a rich yield of fruit. The Lord in His mercy often lifts up the sinner; but He does not always do so, and therein lies the mystery.

Molina, refusing to admit that efficacious grace is so intrinsically, or of itself, maintained that it is efficacious only on account of our consent foreseen from all eternity through mediate knowledge. Thus there is a good, namely, that of our free, salutary determination, which comes about without God's having willed it efficaciously, contrary to the principle: "Whatsoever the Lord pleased He hath done; nothing is done unless He either graciously does it or permits it to happen in His justice."

Molina, nevertheless, attempts to preserve this universally accepted principle. But he succeeds only in retaining it in an indirect, extrinsic way by asserting that God from all eternity has seen, through mediate knowledge, that if Peter were placed in given circumstances with such and such sufficient grace, he would in fact be converted; and thereupon, since He had the intention of saving him, He willed to place him in these favorable circumstances rather than in others wherein he should have been lost. Thus the supreme principle which we have invoked, as well as that of predilection, would be degraded to a condition of relativity. It is no longer intrinsically true of itself but only on account of circumstances extrinsic to the salutary determination.

In fact, for Molina it remains true, contrary to the principle of predilection, that of two sinners placed in the same circumstances and equally aided by God, one may be converted and not the other. "A person who is aided by the same or even less help can rise from sin, while another with greater help does not rise but remains in his obduracy." [55] One of the two is converted without having received any more, contrary, so it seems, to the words of St. Paul: "Who distinguisheth thee? Or what hast thou that thou hast not received?" (I Cor. 4:7.)

THE PROBLEM

One objection remains, which St. Paul himself poses: "Thou wilt say therefore to me: Why doth He then find fault? for who resisteth His will?" (Rom. 9:19.) We know the Apostle's answer: God can prefer whom He wills without thereby being unjust (*ibid.*, 14-24), and the hymn to divine wisdom whose designs are impenetrable: "O the depth of the riches of the wisdom and of the knowledge of God! How incomprehensible are His judgments, and how unsearchable His ways! . . . Who hath been His counsellor? Or who hath first given to Him, and recompense shall be made him?" (*ibid.* 11:33-35.) St. Augustine makes the same reply: "Why does He draw this man and not that one? Do not attempt to judge if you do not wish to err." [56] St. Thomas adds that predestination cannot have as its cause the merits of the elect since these are the effect of predestination, which consequently is gratuitous or dependent upon the divine good pleasure (Ia, q. 23, a. 5).

Not infrequently an effort is made to answer the foregoing problem more specifically than either St. Paul, St. Augustine, or St. Thomas did. But is not the significance of the mystery sacrificed to an inferior

---

[55] Molina, *Concordia*, pp. 51, 565.
[56] *In Joannem*, tr. 26.

sort of clarity which it does not contain? From this standpoint one comes back, in spite of oneself, to the position of Molina, for instance, by the statement which recently appeared as follows: "Herein lies the mystery of predestination: Since from all eternity God knew that Judas would not profit by the sufficient graces which He willed to give him, why did He not will to give him, as he did to the good thief, graces with which He knew that he would correspond?" That is indeed the language of the Molinists and, willy-nilly, it presupposes the theory of mediate knowledge, which posits a passivity in the foreknowledge regarding the free determination a man would take, were he placed in given circumstances, and which he will take if he is in fact so placed. There is the dilemma: God either determines or is determined; there is no middle ground.

If, on the contrary, one attempts to safeguard the generally accepted principle: "Nothing happens which God has not either efficaciously willed if it is a good, or permitted if it is an evil," it does not suffice to affirm, as in the formula quoted above, that God knew what would happen, that the good thief would consent to the sufficient grace and that Judas would resist it. It must be held that: in one case, God permitted the final impenitence of Judas (had He not permitted it, it would not have happened, and God would not have been able to foresee it infallibly) and He would not have permitted it if He had willed efficaciously to save Judas. In the other case, God willed efficaciously the conversion of the good thief because He willed efficaciously to save him (gratuitous predestination to glory). [57] This is the conclusion which proceeds from the generally accepted principles.

If a good which ought to happen does not happen (such as the conversion of Judas), it must be concluded that God had not efficaciously willed it to happen actually, although He may have willed the possibility of its happening (antecedent will) and that Judas should have the real power to be converted, without being so in fact. (Thus a man who is asleep and not actually seeing still has the real

[57] Thomists have recently been reproached with positing a succession in God because they admit predestination before foreseen merits. Clearly they admit of no such succession since they recognize but one act of will in God by which He efficaciously wills the merits of the elect in order to save them. As St. Thomas says, Ia, q.19, a.5: "Therefore He wills this to be as means to that, but He does not will this." The principle of predilection: "No one would be better than another were he not better loved by God," manifestly leaves all temporal succession out of consideration.

power of sight.) If, on the contrary, a good actually comes to pass (such as the conversion of Peter), it must be concluded that from all eternity God had efficaciously willed (by consequent will) that it should in fact take place, and in Peter rather than in Judas.[58]

It follows, therefore, that no one would be better than another (all other things being equal), were he not better loved efficaciously and aided more by God (consequent will); although the other (less loved) could, of course, have received and often may, under other circumstances, have received greater graces. Thus Judas received the grace of the apostolate which many of the elect have never received. Hence no one would be better than another were he not loved more by God through consequent will. This is the meaning of the divine predilection upon which predestination is based (cf. St. Thomas, Ia, q. 23, a. 4). Bañez says no more than St. Thomas on the subject, and it is quite apparent that the epithet of "Bañezianism" to designate classical Thomism is only a poor attempt at humor, as Father N. Del Prado demonstrates (De gratia, 1907, III, 427–67: Whether Bañezianism is not really a farce invented by the Molinists). Molina spoke more frankly and admitted that his doctrine did not coincide with that of St. Thomas.

As for negative reprobation, according to the Angelic Doctor, it consists precisely in the divine permission of sins which in fact will not be remitted and especially of the sin of final impenitence.[59] To

[58] It is clear that the canon of the Council of Trent, "Free will moved and urged by God is capable of dissenting if it so wills," is not a condemnation of the doctrine of grace efficacious in itself. The Thomist, Dominic Soto, and several Augustinians collaborated in the formulation of that canon, all of whom admitted in precise terms the intrinsic efficacy of grace. The latter, far from doing violence to our liberty, actualizes it, allowing the power of resistance to remain, but not actual resistance. This is what St. Thomas says, for example, in Ia IIae, q. 10, a. 4 ad 3, and in many other texts. No one can be seated and standing at the same time, but a person who is seated has a real power to stand; in the same way a person who chooses such and such a particular good has the real power to refuse it freely. Real power is distinct from act, the power of resistance differs from actual resistance. In his book, De gratia, 1943, p. 199, Msgr. P. Parente confuses the divided sense of Calvin with that of Thomists. Calvin declared: "Under efficacious grace the power of the contrary does not remain; it only reappears subsequently. Thomists hold nothing of the kind. Msgr. Parente proposes a solution intermediate between Thomism and Molinism; he forgets that no middle ground is possible between these two contradictory propositions: God knows free future contingencies either before or not before His decree. God either determines or is determined; there is no middle view.

[59] Ia, q. 23, a. 3: "Reprobation includes the will to permit a person to fall into sin [negative reprobation] and to inflict the punishment of damnation for the sin [positive reprobation]."

this one cannot make answer, as has recently been done, that the permission of sin is general with regard to elect and reprobates alike; it is clear that we are here dealing with the will to permit sin which will not be forgiven.[60]

CONCLUSION

Hence it is apparent that the ultimate bases of the distinction between grace efficacious in itself and sufficient grace, as well as between consequent divine will and antecedent will, is to be found in these two principles: "Nothing happens which God has not either willed efficaciously if it is a good, or permitted if it is an evil"; and "God never commands the impossible, but renders the fulfillment of His commands really possible when He imposes them and to the extent to which He imposes them and to which they can be known."

If the true meaning of each of the terms of these two principles is well weighed, especially the opposition that exists between "efficaciously willed" and "permitted," it can be seen that there is a real difference between efficacious grace, the result of the intrinsically efficacious will of God, and merely sufficient grace, the result of His antecedent will accompanied by the divine permission of sin. In the first case, God confers the free, salutary action. In the second, He gives the real power to act, but not to act efficaciously. In sufficient grace, we cannot repeat too often, efficacious grace is offered, as the fruit in the flower, as act in potency. But if anyone resists sufficient grace, he deserves to be deprived of the efficacious help which he would have received had it not been for this resistance.

Therein lies a great mystery, as St. Paul acknowledges (Rom. 9:14-24; 11:33-36). He reminds us that, without being unjust, God can show preference for whom He will. No one has first given unto Him that he should receive a recompense in return. "O the depth of the riches of the wisdom and of the knowledge of God! . . . who hath been His counsellor? Or who hath first given to Him, and recompense shall be made him?"

---

[60] Nor can it be said: God is not the cause of sin and yet He foresees it infallibly; therefore He can infallibly foresee a salutary act without being its cause. Clearly, nothing positive can exist outside of God without having a relationship of causality or dependence with regard to Him. God is thus the cause of all the being and all the goodness of a good act; He is also the cause of the being of an evil act, but not of its disorder. Such disorder is only permitted, and it is in His permissive decree that God knows it.

What does appear manifestly in the midst of this chiaroscuro is that the question here posed involves the reconciling of infinite justice, infinite mercy, and supreme liberty within the eminence of Deity. If the grace of perseverance is granted to one, it is out of infinite mercy; if it is not granted to another, that is in just punishment for his faults. Each of these divine perfections is infinite, and their intimate reconciliation in the eminence of Deity or in the inner life of God can be seen only in the immediate vision of the divine essence.

The principles which we have just enunciated and which balance one another give us an inkling about the location of the summit toward which they converge, but the peak remains hidden from our sight. Only in heaven shall we behold the intimate reconciliation of these two truths: "Whatsoever the Lord pleased He hath done" (Ps. 134:6), and "God does not command the impossible." He who receives from God the real power to observe the commandments does not always do so in fact. If he observes them, he is obviously better in that respect. And this is a sign that he has received more.

We must therefore conclude with Bossuet: "Let us learn to control our intelligence so as to admit these two graces [sufficient and efficacious] of which the one leaves the will without any excuse before God and the other does not allow it to glory in itself." [61] Sufficient grace leaves us without any excuse before God because, as we have said, in it efficacious grace is offered to us; but by the very fact that a man resists this divine attention, he deserves to be deprived of the efficacious help which was virtually offered to him. Resistance to grace is an evil which derives from us alone; nonresistance is a good which would not come to pass here and now, had not God willed it from all eternity with a consequent or efficacious will.

But to arrive at a clear understanding of this doctrine, one must avoid several confusing misconceptions that are frequent among those who read the explanation of it for the first time. It would be an error to think that some receive only efficacious graces and others only sufficient graces. We all receive both of these helps. Even those who are in the state of mortal sin occasionally receive an efficacious grace to make an act of faith or of hope; but they often also resist the sufficient grace which inclines them toward conversion. Faithful

---

[61] Bossuet, *Œuvres complètes*, 1845, I, 644, and general index under *"Grâce"*; also *La défense de la tradition*, Bk. XI, chaps. 19-27.

servants of God frequently receive sufficient graces which they do not resist and which are followed by efficacious graces.

The various degrees of sufficient grace must also be carefully considered. First of all, sufficient grace is far from always being sterile or merely sufficient; it is rendered sterile by our resistance. But if this is not forthcoming, sufficient grace, followed by efficacious help, fructifies like a flower which produces, under the action of the sun, the fruit which it is intended to yield.

Moreover, sufficient graces are most varied in kind. There are, in the first place, the exterior graces such as the preaching of the gospel, good example, wise direction. Then there is the interior habitual or sanctifying grace received in baptism which confers the radical power of acting meritoriously. There are the infused virtues and the gifts of the Holy Ghost, which are so many principles bestowing the proximate power of supernatural action. There are interior actual graces, graces of light which produce good thoughts, graces of attraction which cause an impulse toward the good, inclining us to a salutary consent to good without causing us as yet to produce it.[62] Thus it is that, as we have said above, the grace which produces attrition in us efficaciously is sufficient with regard to contrition.

Sufficient grace, which renders possible the fulfillment of duty, may therefore go very far in the order of this real possibility. But however far it may go in this order of proximate power to produce a given salutary act, for instance, contrition, it remains distinct from the efficacious grace which will cause us to produce freely, here and now, this particular act of contrition. The latter would not in fact have been produced had it not been willed eternally by the consequent will of God.[63]

[62] Father Norbert Del Prado presents a clear exposition of these various degrees of sufficient grace in his great work, *De gratia et libero arbitrio*, 1907, II, 5-23. It is apparent from what is said in those pages that grace which is efficacious in itself with relation to an imperfect act is sufficient with relation to a more perfect act which should follow. The assistance which leads efficaciously to a good thought is sufficient for a good movement of the will; that which produces this good movement in us is sufficient with relation to a good consent.

[63] We have shown elsewhere (*La prédestination des saints et la grâce*, pp. 387-89) that the Thomists, González, Bancel, Guillermin, who conceded as much as possible to sufficient grace, maintained this point of doctrine which is essential to Thomism: as St. Thomas affirms, Ia, q. 19, a. 4, "Effects determined by the infinite perfection of God proceed according to the determination of His will and intelligence." That is the divine decree. As can be seen, this terminology is much earlier than Duns Scotus, in spite of what several writers maintain today.

A cursory reading of this doctrine may leave one unaware of how far sufficient grace can go within us. Sometimes it urges us with insistence not to resist God's will in a certain respect, manifested repeatedly by a superior or a spiritual director. It may happen that for a year or two or even more all the circumstances continue to confirm what is being asked of us in God's name. And yet the soul continues to allow itself to be deceived by self-love and by the enemy of all good; it resists the light over a period of months, in spite of all the prayers that are said for it and all the Masses offered for its intention. The prayers and Masses obtain for it graces of light which produce good thoughts in it, graces of attraction which elicit transitory impulses toward the good. But these sufficient graces are blocked by a resistance which may even go so far as obduracy of the heart. Then is fulfilled the text of the Apocalypse (3:19): "Such as I love, I rebuke and chastise. Be zealous therefore, and do penance. Behold, I stand at the gate, and knock. If any man shall hear My voice, and open to Me the door, I will come in to him, and will sup with him, and he with Me."

"Behold, I stand at the gate, and knock," says the Lord. The soul often resists; it does so by itself; the evil comes only from the soul. When it ceases to resist and at least hearkens to Him who knocks, it is already He, the Lord, who gives it to the soul to listen with docility. And if it really stops resisting, it will be led from grace to grace even to divine intimacy.

If the soul ceases its resistance, efficacious grace ever sweeter and stronger will be given it; sweetly and strongly will this grace gradually penetrate its will, as the beneficial warmth penetrates little by little a cold body which has been frozen stiff. Then the soul becomes more and more aware that all the resistance came from itself alone; that the nonresistance is itself a good proceeding from the author of all good; and that the soul must ask it of Him in that prayer which the priest repeats every day at Mass before the Communion, a prayer by which he begs for the efficacious grace which leads one to the good: "Lord, make me always adhere to Thy commandments and never suffer me to be separated from Thee." Grant, Lord, not only that I may have the power of observing Thy commandments, but that I may in fact observe them; and never permit me to be separated from Thee.

Undoubtedly, he who keeps the commandments is better than he who, although really able to keep them, does not do so. He who is thus rendered better should thank the sovereign goodness for it. The distinction between the two helps, sufficient and efficacious, which we have been speaking of, is a basis for the act of thinksgiving which will last throughout eternity. As St. Augustine says repeatedly in his *De praedestinatione sanctorum,* the elect will sing forever the mercy of God and will see how this infinite mercy is perfectly reconciled with infinite justice and sovereign liberty.[64]

IV. THE BAÑEZIAN COMEDY AND CONTEMPORARY SYNCRETISM

Any consideration of the renewal of Thomistic studies in the past hundred years must take into account the great names of the eminent Jesuits Kleutgen, Cornoldi, Liberatore, and more recently, Louis Billot and G. Mattiussi, who labored so admirably throughout their lives to lead minds back to an understanding of the works of St. Thomas. They were great admirers and often penetrating interpreters of the Angelic Doctor. Only in heaven will it be known what great friends he has had among the sons of St. Ignatius. We experience a particular joy in sincerely rendering this testimony.[65]

It is to be regretted that the same elevation of mind is not found in

[64] Will the theology of the future produce many discoveries with regard to this question? We doubt it very strongly; the problem has been examined for centuries by the greatest minds. In any case, the theology of the future must always keep in mind the supreme principle: "Whatsoever the Lord pleased He hath done" (Ps. 134:6); for nothing is done in heaven or on earth unless God either graciously does it Himself or justly permits it to be done. The first cause of evil assuredly resides in us; a deficiency proceeds from defectibility; but it would not happen without the permission of evil, allowed by God for a higher good of which He alone is judge. God remains the first cause and last end of every good without exception. Nothing positive or good can exist outside of God without a relationship of causality or dependence with respect to Him; otherwise the very proofs of His existence (based on this relationship of causality) are jeopardized. God is most certainly, according to reason as well as faith, the author of all good without exception.

[65] We were personally acquainted with a Jesuit theologian, a man of keen intelligence and wit, now some years deceased, who used to say to us in substance: "I was a professor in a Catholic institution where my colleague was a Dominican who was somewhat timid about his Thomism. I used to tell him: 'If things go on this way, when it comes to the problem of grace, I shall be teaching the Thomism and you the Molinism. If I were a Dominican I should teach your great doctrines of grace without any hedging. Do not let my being here embarrass you. Properly understood, there is in your conception something very sublime which deserves a hearing. Do not be afraid to quote the texts of St. Thomas in which your school maintains that he himself clearly taught that grace is infallibly efficacious of itself and not through our foreseen consent.'"

several authors who in the past few years have taken to applying the epithet of "Bañezian" to real Thomists. It is an ill-natured witticism to which the best theologians of the Society of Jesus would never stoop. This designation of "Bañezian" referring to genuine Thomists is even adopted by certain authors as if it were an accepted term. We are thereby reminded of the chapter, "De Comoedia banneziana," which is to be found in a work by Father N. Del Prado, O.P., *De gratia et libero arbitrio* (Fribourg, 1907, III, 427–66).

This latter work, out of print for several years, brought the sum of 6,000 lire before the last war, so we are informed, and must be even more valuable today. In the chapter referred to, pp. 457 ff., the author recalls that Dr. John Ude of Graz, who had received from his professors in Rome the conviction that classical Thomism was an invention of Bañez, undertook to write a book entitled: *Doctrina Capreoli de influxu Dei in actus voluntatis humanae* (Graz, Istria, 1904). He professed to show that the doctrine defended by Bañez was nowhere to be found in the early commentators on St. Thomas. But what was his surprise when, in Capreolus himself, he came upon the doctrine of predetermining divine decrees and causally predetermining premotion! In the first part of his book he still speaks in behalf of Molinism, but subsequently (*op. cit.,* pp. 162, 182, 197–203, 215, 216, 259) he is obliged to conclude that Capreolus [66] had certainly taught what Bañez declared and that this doctrine is St. Thomas' own, as has been demonstrated by Fathers Dummermuth [67] and Del Prado.

[66] Cajetan expresses the same thought on Ia, q.14, a.13, no. 17: "We say that [divine] ideas represent something merely naturally, for instance the quiddity of things; and something not merely naturally, but naturally on account of a free supposition, that is, the existence of things and contingent relationship. For they represent the former before every act of the divine will, but the latter presupposing the free determination of the divine will to the other side of the contradiction." Again on Ia, q.19, a.8, no. 10, Cajetan writes: "Since that [divine] willing is most efficacious, both the thing willed and the modes willed are produced," that is, even the free mode of our choice. Cf. Cajetan also on Ia, q.20, a.3 and 4; q.23, a.4; q.105, a.4 and 5. Again he says, commenting on Matt. 4:21: "It is not to be wondered at that all of these [apostles called in this chapter of Matthew] should have followed Jesus immediately; since by an interior operation Jesus was moving their hearts to leave all things and follow Him. For no spirit ever resists such an internal attraction or ever will resist it. Thus are produced willing followers, workers, martyrs, etc." That is indeed Bañezianism before Bañez, and it is clearly to be found in St. Thomas himself. One need only open one's eyes to see it undeniably; it is a question of scientific honesty.

[67] *S. Thomas et doctrina praemotionis physicae,* 1886; *Defensio doctrinae S. Thomae.* . . . Reply to Father V. Frinz, S.J., 1895.

We have proved the point at great length elsewhere,[68] and shall quote in the present article several texts of St. Thomas. It suffices to recall for the moment the two following: "If God moves the will toward anything, it is incompatible with this position that the will should not be moved toward it. However, it is not absolutely impossible. Hence it does not follow that the will is moved by God of necessity" (Ia IIae, q. 10, a. 4 ad 3). God actualizes liberty in the will and even the free mode itself whereby it directs itself toward any good conducive to salvation, safeguarding under this very movement the power (not the act) of choosing a contrary object. Likewise, "The intention of God cannot fail. . . . Hence if it is in the intention of God who moves that the man whose heart He moves should receive [sanctifying] grace, he will infallibly receive it" (Ia IIae, q. 112, a. 3 c; cf. also IIa IIae, q. 24, a. 11, and *Contra Gentes,* Bk. III, chaps. 91, 92, 94).

It is absolutely certain that, according to St. Thomas, God knows in a comprehensive manner all that He is, all that He can do, all that He wills and accomplishes, all that He permits, and that thus, without any passivity or dependence with regard to our free determinations, He knows all that is knowable. "The knowledge of God is the cause of things and is in no way caused by them" (Ia, q. 14, a. 5, 8). Without any doubt the Molinist theory of *scientia media* has no foundation in St. Thomas. It is quite certain, according to him, Ia, q. 19, a. 8, that God willed efficaciously from all eternity the free acts of Christ the Redeemer, Mary's fiat, the conversion of Mary Magdalen, of the good thief, and of Saul. And it is for this reason that these acts rather than their contraries are present to Him from all eternity (Ia, q. 14, a. 3), and that they took place infallibly in time, in a free manner, because He had efficaciously willed that they should happen freely (Ia, q. 19, a. 8). "God," says Bossuet, "wills from eternity all the future exercise of human liberty so far as it is good and real. What can be more absurd than to say that it does not exist for the reason that God wills it to exist" (*Traité du libre arbitre,* chap. 8)?

Texts from St. Thomas abound proving that this is indeed his teaching; they are well known. Not to take into account these texts, often quoted by Thomists, is to proceed unscientifically. The only opposition offered is to dismiss the case. This is done by that well-known theologian of distinction who adheres, in spite of every argu-

---

[68] *Dict. théol. cath.,* "Prémotion," especially col. 44–56; *La prédestination des saints et la grâce,* 1936, pp. 294–96, 296–310, 310 f., 333–41, 362–74.

ment, to the Molinist theory of *scientia media*. His answer to us was: "Even if the doctrine of predetermining decrees is in St. Thomas, we will have none of it." At least he had the merit of being outspoken. He would have been greatly surprised had he been told that he was indulging in pragmatism which could easily lead to a revision of the traditional definition of truth so as to define it, not as that which is, but as that which pleases us and which we wish to say and to hear others say.

But the subject deserves a more forthright discussion. It is objected: for a man to be free under efficacious grace, it is not enough for him to retain, under that grace, the power of resisting; he must be able to accommodate the grace with actual resistance. If that is the case, genuine Thomists have always replied with St. Thomas himself, then, for Socrates to be sitting down freely, it does not suffice that he meanwhile retains the power to rise, but he must be able to accommodate those two contrary positions and be at the same time seated and standing, which is impossible. In the same way, efficacious grace to which resistance was made in fact would no longer be efficacious.

But our adversaries have no wish to hear such an answer. And so they continue in certain of their works to call real Thomists "Bañezians." In order to hold on to the title of Thomists themselves without being challenged they deprive the true intellectual sons of St. Thomas of that right. And readers who lack keenness of perception or who are misinformed allow themselves to be taken in. Suppose someone tried to deprive the true descendants of the Bourbon line of their name: would not the cry of injustice be raised? The case is a parallel one.[69]

Bañezianism is then described after a fashion which no real Thomist would accept, and this description finds its way subsequently into

[69] Others no longer wish to be called Thomists. Father Gaston Fessart in *Etudes*, November, 1945, p. 270, speaks of the "blissful somnolence which safeguards that 'canonized' Thomism—which is also, as Péguy used to say, 'buried'; while the thoughts [of the Existentialists] go on living, dedicated in its name to contradiction." Can this be interpreted to mean that Leo XIII was mistaken in urging the study and development of St. Thomas' teaching? In Gunther's day, Hegelianism was also spoken of as a living system in comparison with a dead Thomism. This it was that led the great Jesuit, Kleutgen, to write *Die Theologie des Vorzeit*, 1860, and *Die Philosophie der Vorzeit*, 1866. One reverts quickly to Modernism by forgetting the words of Pius X (*"Pascendi"*): "But we warn teachers that they view this matter rightly: one cannot depart from Aquinas even slightly, especially in questions of metaphysics, without great detriment." One assumes a great responsibility in leaving such warnings unheeded.

the works of authors who attempt to advance matters by a reconciliation of the two contradictorily opposed doctrines, and who express
themselves in a way of which Msgr. P. Parente is typical. In his *De
creatione universali* (1943, p. 139), in the belief that he is accurately
reporting the doctrine of the Thomists, labeled "Bañezians," he writes:
"When the will acts under the impulse of God, it cannot deviate
toward anything else *in the composite sense;* but it can do so *in the
divided sense.* Evidently, *as long as the divine motion continues, the
will is not free, that is, it cannot* [70] fail to desire that to which it is
determined by God (composite sense); but it could if it prescinded
from that motion (divided sense). Similarly a person who sits down,
while he is seated, cannot stand, but he does not relinquish the power
of standing, in the divided sense, that is, after he has been seated."
The same author expresses himself in similar terms in his *Antro-
pologia supernaturalis,* 1943, p. 194.

This is the divided sense as Calvin understood it, and it is easy to
understand that it should be rejected. But why not seek the correct
meaning of this term from the Thomists themselves? [71] We affirm
that God actualizes liberty in us, so that there no longer remains a passive or potential indifference, but rather an actual, dominating indifference with which our will, specified by the universal good, directs
itself toward such and such a particular good which is commanded
(toward an object not in every respect good), while preserving under
this divine motion the power (not the act) of choosing the contrary.
Thus Socrates, while seated, is able to stand, but he cannot be at the
same time seated and standing. In the same way, a person with his
eyes closed does not see at that moment, but he retains the real faculty
of sight; he is not blind. Potency is really distinct from act and can
exist without it. Likewise under grace which is infallibly efficacious
of itself, the will is able to resist (the opposite power remains); but
under that grace it never does resist in fact, just as it never happens
that while Socrates is seated he is standing. Efficacious grace which a
man would resist in fact would no longer be efficacious.

The composed sense of Calvin, declared by him to be unattainable,
is our divided sense, which we maintain is real. As for the divided
sense of Calvin, it is heretical. According to him, freedom and the

---

[70] The italics are ours, indicating the phrases which we cannot accept.

[71] Billuart explains this very well against Calvin, *Cursus theol., De Deo uno,* Diss.
VIII, a.4, 11. He refutes the objections regarding the injury done to freedom. See
also our *De Deo uno,* pp. 449 ff.

power to resist do not remain under efficacious grace, but only reappear later. Thomists have never sustained such a theory; if they had, they would have completely misunderstood the teaching of their Master. They understand the divided sense in exactly the same way as St. Thomas.[72]

Another doctrine which they do not hold is attributed to Thomists when it is said: "Thomists add that God bestows sufficient grace in such wise that to those who make good use of it He may grant efficacious grace; but according to their opinion, the good use of sufficient grace depends upon efficacious grace. Therefore the matter is left unexplained." [73] What Thomists maintain is this: If a man resists sufficient grace, then he deserves to be deprived of efficacious grace, and it is clear that the latter is not necessary to resist the former. Culpable resistance falls upon sufficient grace (in which efficacious grace is offered) like hail upon a tree in blossom, which promised much fruit; but the fruit will certainly not develop.

As for the disorder of sin, God who condemns it, permits it without being its cause. This divine permission is only a condition *sine qua non.* The disorder proceeds solely from the defective and deficient created will and in no sense from God, who absolutely cannot produce it; for this disorder is outside the adequate object of His will and omnipotence, just as sound is beyond the range of the sense of sight, or truth outside the adequate object of the will. "Nothing is more precise than the formal object of any power." Hence the divine motion toward the physical act of the sin (as being and as action) prescinds from its malice. Again with regard to this last point, the authentic Thomistic teaching is often rendered utterly unrecognizable in the unscientific presentations that are made of it. All that would be necessary would be to cite the two articles of St. Thomas (Ia IIae, q. 79, a. 1, 2); Thomists hold no other view.

THE NEW SYNCRETISM

What is the substance of the new syncretism proposed by Msgr. P. Parente? He rejects Thomism and the Molinist theory of *scientia media,* as well as that of simultaneous concurrence, while admitting a

[72] Cf. *De veritate,* q.6, a.4 ad 8; Ia IIae, q.10, a.4 ad 3. St. Thomas also declares (*De veritate,* q.23, a.5): "For there is no incompatibility in this: God wills a man to be saved but he is capable of being damned; however, there is incompatibility in this: God wills a man to be saved and he is damned."

[73] P. Parente, *Anthropol. supern., De gratia.*

non-predetermining premotion. He is seeking an intermediate position. The question is whether such a position is possible between two contradictory propositions. God knows certainly all future contingencies either before or not before His predetermining decree; is any middle ground possible?

1. The new syncretism rejects what it refers to as rigid Thomism or Bañezianism, that is, the doctrine of predetermining divine decrees and the divine motion derived from them. What is its objection to this teaching? We are told in the *De creatione universali,* p. 144: "It does not seem possible to preserve human liberty if the will of man is said to be and is determined by God toward one object. Nor will it help to have recourse to composite and divided sense, since the question concerns freedom, not before or after divine motion (in the divided sense), but during that motion (in the composite sense). Therefore if in this latter sense the will, inasmuch as it is determined to one object, is not free, it never will be free, since without this motion it never has the power to act."

We have just seen that this interpretation of divided sense, attributed to Thomists, is by no means their own; more than that, it is heretical. Under efficacious grace a man can resist, but he does not do so in fact; grace would then no longer be efficacious. Moreover, we hold that by grace efficacious in itself God infallibly moves the will to determine itself freely in the direction of the commandment; this motion is thus a causal predetermination distinct from the formal determination of the act to which it is ordained. God determines to one object in the sense that He determines us to obey rather than not to obey.[74]

[74] Msgr. Parente also departs from Thomism in a diametrically opposite direction when it occurs to him to assert that in the beatified soul the love of God seen face to face is free. This is a confusion of the consciously spontaneous (freedom from force) with the free (freedom from necessity). This, however, is a familiar distinction if only on account of the condemnation of Jansenism; cf. Denz., no. 1094. St. Thomas declares, on the contrary, in two texts frequently quoted: "God alone [clearly seen] fully satisfies the will and moves it sufficiently as an object" (Ia, q.105, a.4); "But the will can be moved as by an object, by any good; not however sufficiently and efficaciously, except by God [clearly seen]" (*ibid.*). And again: "If some object is proposed to the will which is good universally and from every aspect, the will tends to it of necessity if it wills at all, for it could not will the opposite" (Ia IIae, q.10, a.2). That is, with reference to God clearly seen and lovable beyond all things, indifference of judgment and will does not remain, nor the power to choose the opposite. On the contrary, these do remain with regard to an object which is not in every respect good. If the love of God in the blessed were not only spontaneous but free, the discussion between Thomists and Molinists on free acts would never have taken place, for spontaneity would have sufficed to constitute liberty. This is evident.

2. The new syncretism also rejects Molinism; cf. Msgr. Parente, *De creatione universali,* p. 144: "If a creature is said to be moved primarily by itself to its operation, a twofold absurdity follows, namely, the creature determines God and its passes from potency to act independently of God. . . . Moreover, reasoning, both theological and philosophical, here demands not coordination but subordination." Furthermore, Msgr. Parente writes with respect to mediate knowledge (*De Deo uno,* 1938, p. 247): "Again this whole Molinistic theory simply abounds in obscurity as not a few Molinists acknowledge. For it is difficult to see how anything may be regarded as real (in the future) to the divine mind while withdrawn from the divine will. However it may be explained, this is imputing a certain determinism to God Himself. But if the futurity of free acts as dependent with respect to circumstances is urged overmuch, then we fall into determinism of circumstances. . . . In recent times no theologians have made any advance in the direction of reconciliation. Thus L. Janssens, *De Deo uno,* Vol. II, declares that the medium of knowledge of all future contingencies is the divine essence to the extent that it is eternal, or the eternity of God itself, to whom all things are present. But this opinion, if it prescinds from the divine volition, either does not explain enough, or reverts to the theory of those who hold that God draws His knowledge from His own creatures."

Mediate knowledge is then rejected by the new syncretism because God would be determined in His foreknowledge by a free determination (future contingency) which would not derive from Him. Thus far, this is a refutation of misinterpreted Thomism by means of Molinism, and of Molinism by means of Thomism.

But at this point, if the new theory refuses to come back to predetermining decrees, which it has discarded, how will it solve the inevitable dilemma: God either determines or is determined; there is no midway between the two? If He does not determine, then He is determined by a determination which does not come from Him but is imposed upon Him, since He knows it infallibly without its being derived from Him; for example, if the good thief, crucified on Calvary beside Jesus, had the help of sufficient grace, he would be converted, while the other in the same circumstances and with equal grace would not.

3. The new syncretism considers that it has solved the difficulty by

declaring that our free, salutary determination comes from God mediately by way of our deliberation. Cf. Parente, *De creatione universali,* p. 158. "In a free act a twofold element must be distinguished, that of its exercise and that of its specification. The first in the actuating of the will is in the line of efficient causality which is to be ascribed to God immediately; the other is the determination of the act from the standpoint of the object, in the line of formal causality which is immediately from the intellect, and mediately from God." The same author writes (*De gratia,* p. 208): "Physical predetermination is rejected; and premotion is admitted even in the supernatural order. Likewise the motion of exercise is distinguished from the motion of specification; the former is attributed immediately to God, the latter mediately to God and immediately to the intellect proposing the object under a favorable light." Again, (*ibid.,* p. 204): "Then the will, of which the adequate object is the Highest Good, is directed spontaneously and *infallibly* toward a particular object in which a certain nature of the Highest Good is reflected." How could the word "infallibly," which we have italicized, ever be justified? [75]

CRITICAL ANALYSIS OF THIS SYNCRETISM

To anyone who has spent a lifetime in the study of these problems under their various aspects, it is easily apparent that this new syncretism, like its predecessor, seeks an impossible mean between two contradictory propositions, between the predetermining decrees of genuine Thomists and the *scientia media* of the Molinists: God knows future contingencies infallibly, either before or not before His predetermining decree. If the new syncretism does not return to predetermining decrees, which it has discarded, it is led perforce to *scientia media* presented under another name and must reply to all the difficulties it raises. The exigencies of the principle of contradiction must not be forgotten. [76]

We shall here formulate the objections which we have already presented in the *Acta Academiae romanae S. Thomae,* 1939-40, pp.

---

[75] The italics are ours; this adverb *"infallibly"* is in no sense justified. God alone seen face to face attracts the will infallibly, not the object of a precept proposed to man as wayfarer. The good thief was not infallibly drawn by the object which the other thief rejected.

[76] They were forgotten recently by a writer who affirmed that integral truth is a polyhedron; it contains the thought of St. Thomas, Scotus, etc. This amounts to saying that it includes a goodly number of contradictory propositions.

35-37. They seem to us absolutely irrefutable. The only reply they have ever received was a dismissal of the case; this is hardly scientific.

1. This syncretism maintains that God is the cause of our free determination mediately only through the judgment of our intelligence which deliberates. Assuredly there will never be a free choice without a foregoing judgment; but at the end of the deliberation it depends on our free will (which accepts or rejects the right direction of the intelligence) that such and such a practical judgment should be the final one. (See no. 21 of the twenty-four Thomistic theses approved by the Sacred Congregation of studies.) Thereupon, since the new syncretism admits that God moves the will, as to exercise, toward this choice, in the case of a salutary choice does God will efficaciously that it should be a salutary volition rather than a nolition, an impious refusal or a culpable omission? If so, then God by moving the will toward this choice efficaciously and infallibly as to exercise, brings it about, together with the will, that such and such a salutary practical judgment should be the final one. In that case we are dealing with genuine Thomism and are presupposing the predetermining divine decrees from which this motion as to exercise derives.

2. Otherwise, by this motion in respect to exercise required for a salutary choice as well as for the contrary refusal, God would not cause the good act to any greater extent than the evil act, and He would not be even the mediate nor, above all, the infallible cause of the salutary choice as to specification; for the precept which comes from Him does not draw the will infallibly; even under the aspect of a good it did not infallibly attract the good thief who obeyed, while the other disobeyed.

3. Accordingly, God would not be the cause of what is best in the merits of the saints nor of what was best in the merits of Christ and His holy Mother. This is contrary to the words of St. Paul: "For who distinguisheth thee? Or what hast thou that thou hast not received? And if thou hast received, why dost thou glory as if thou hadst not received it?" Therefore does St. Thomas often repeat: "Whatever of reality and perfection there is in our salutary acts derives from God, the source of every good." In other words, as stated in Ia, q. 20, a. 3 and 4: "Since the love of God is the cause of the goodness of things, one thing would not be better than another if God did not will greater good to one than to the other." "Thus some things are better for the reason that God loves them better." This is the principle of predilec-

tion which clarifies the whole doctrine of predestination: No one would be better than another were he not loved and helped more by God. "What hast thou that thou hast not received?"

4. Finally, God in His foreknowledge would be passive or dependent with respect to our free salutary determination which would not derive from Him and which, at least as possible in the future, would impose itself upon Him infallibly since He would know it infallibly. Thus we are back again, whether we will or not, at mediate knowledge under another name, with all the difficulties which flow from it. The dilemma that cannot be solved ever reappears: God either determines or is determined; there is no middle course. Every theory that denies the predetermining divine decrees—call it mediate knowledge or not—comes to grief when it strikes against this dilemma.

We must therefore return to certain and revealed principles. Even in the psalms we find, as Hincmar observed at the Council of Toucy in 860,[77] terminating the controversy raised by the writings of Gottschalk: "Whatsoever the Lord pleased He hath done, in heaven, in earth" (Ps. 134:6). Hincmar added: "For nothing is done in heaven or on earth except what He graciously does or permits to be done in His justice." This means that every good, whether easy or difficult, natural or supernatural, comes from God, and that no sin takes place, or takes place in one man rather than in another, without a divine permission. This extremely general principle obviously implies a multitude of consequences. Thomists see in it the equivalent of the principle of predilection: "No one would be better than another were he not loved and aided more by God." This last principle must be balanced by that other formulated by St. Augustine [78] and cited by the Council of Trent (Denz., no. 804): "God does not command the impossible, but by commanding He teaches thee both to do what thou canst and to ask what thou canst not"; this is the Augustinian affirmation of the will for universal salvation.

According to these principles, what answer does the Christian mind offer to the following questions: Did God from all eternity efficaciously will the free acts of Christ the Redeemer, Mary's fiat consenting to her motherhood of the Savior, the conversions of Mary Magdalen, of the good thief, of Saul? Did God will efficaciously all that is good in each of these acts, especially what is best in them: their free determina-

[77] PL, CXXVI, 123.
[78] De natura et gratia, chap. 43, no. 50; PL, XLIV, 271.

tion which distinguishes them from evil acts and whereby the just man is distinguished from the sinner?

The Christian mind replies to these questions in the affirmative: Yes, God from all eternity efficaciously willed these salutary acts which took place in time; He efficaciously willed their free determination wherein a good act is distinguished from sin. Otherwise God would not be the source of all good, and what is best in the merits of the saints would not derive from Him; "in the affair of salvation, not everything would come from God, that is, not the origin of the free, salutary determination." St. Augustine repeatedly affirms this doctrine, basing it upon the words of Jesus: "Without Me you can do nothing" in the order of salvation, and on those of St. Paul: "What hast thou that thou hast not received?"

Did St. Thomas preserve this teaching, so simple in its sublimity, which becomes more and more the object of the contemplation of the saints above and beyond all controversy? To be convinced of the Angelic Doctor's adherence to this doctrine, it suffices to read in order the articles of the *Summa* relating to these questions.

According to St. Thomas, God is omniscient because He knows in a comprehensive manner all that He is, all that He can do (all possibilities), all that He wills and does (all that has been, is, and will be, as far as it is real and good), and all that He permits (all sins, their kind, number, and the exact moment when they occur); this includes all that is knowable. Nothing positive, nothing good, can in fact exist outside of God, without a relationship of causality or of dependence with respect to Him; and sin would not happen if God did not permit it—that is a condition *sine qua non*—and if He did not permit it to happen under a given form and at a given time. Thus the Pharisees were powerless to put our Lord to death before "His hour" had come, the hour predetermined by God with an infallible predetermination, but not necessitating the free acts of the Savior or of His persecutors, and moreover predicted by the prophets. This is traditional teaching in all its lofty simplicity and all its strength. Does St. Thomas retain it? Assuredly he does. Otherwise, as Bossuet says with reference to Molina's mediate knowledge, "all idea of a first cause is thrown into confusion." [79]

[79] Moreover Thomists by no means multiply the determination of future conditional contingents, outside of the conditional prophecy termed "threatening." With this exception it suffices to distinguish between simple possibles and futures properly so called, which will exist effectually in time. Furthermore, Thomists cer-

St. Thomas writes (Ia, q. 14, a. 8): "The knowledge of God is the cause of things inasmuch as His will is united to it." He has just observed: "Since the intelligible form confronts two opposite alternatives (whether to produce it or not) and since the same knowledge relates to opposites, it would not produce a determined effect unless it were determined in one direction by the will."

Again (*ibid.,* a. 13): "But the knowledge of God is measured by eternity which encompasses the whole of time"; hence it attains intuitively to all futurities as presents, without any dependence in relation to them; nor does it know them any better when they take place in time. But the conversion of St. Paul would not be infallibly present to God from all eternity had He not willed it efficaciously. Otherwise it would be present to Him not as a contingent truth but as a necessary truth. This is manifest, provided one is willing to understand it. And the presence of future contingencies in eternity is not the medium of foreknowledge but the condition of its being intuitive and not subsequently perfected when the future comes to pass in time, as in the case of a prophet who sees his prediction accomplished.

Ia, q. 19, a. 4: "The will of God is the cause of things, and determined effects proceed from His infinite perfection according to the determination of His will and intellect." And in God, as in man, "the free will, accepting the direction of the intellect, does whatever is final in the practical judgment," provision being made for virtually distinguishing several decrees in God; cf. *ibid.,* ad 4. That is the decree of the divine will. In the same question, St. Thomas concludes the answer to the first objection of article 6: "Whatever God wills absolutely is done, although what He wills antecedently may not be done." Thus from all eternity God willed antecedently Peter's fidelity during the Passion, at the same time permitting his denial; but He willed absolutely that Peter should be converted, and infallibly he is converted. In the same way from all eternity God willed absolutely and efficaciously to save the good thief (predestination to glory), and for this reason He also willed to grant him the efficacious grace of a happy death, and the good thief was converted.

Ibid., a. 8: "The divine will imposes necessity on some things willed

tainly do not suppress the mystery of the divine knowledge of vision by holding it to be based upon an infallible decree, for we do not know the content of that knowledge and, before the events take place, we cannot differentiate between what therein depends not upon the conditional divine will but upon the divine will termed consequent or absolute and efficacious.

but not on all. . . . This depends on the efficacy of the divine will. For when any cause would be efficacious in acting, the effect follows the cause, not only with respect to what is done but even according to the mode of doing or being. . . . To certain effects God adapted contingent causes." God moves creatures according to their condition; His motion is not passively determined by us, but He moves our will to determine itself by deliberation in the direction of the commandments. *Ibid.* ad 2: "From the very fact that nothing resists the divine will, it follows not only that those things are done which God wills should be done, but also that they are done contingently or necessarily as He so wills." He actualizes human liberty. He willed efficaciously that the good thief should be converted freely. What could be more absurd than to say that it cannot happen because God willed it?

Ia, q. 20, a. 3, 4: "No one would be better than another were he not better loved by God." Ia, q. 23, a. 5: "Whatever there is in man ordaining him to salvation is wholly included under the effect of predestination, even the preparation for grace. And likewise, Ia, q. 105, a. 4: "It is proper to God to move the created will, but most of all by inclining it interiorly."

Ia IIae, q. 10, a. 4 ad 3: "If God moves the will toward anything, it is incompatible with this position that the will should not be moved thereto. But it is not absolutely impossible. Hence it does not follow that the will is moved by God of necessity. Ia IIae, q. 112, a. 3: "Since the intention of God cannot fail, according to Augustine, those who are rendered free by the beneficence of God are most certainly rendered free. Hence if it is in the intention of God who moves that the man whose heart He moves should receive [sanctifying] grace, he will infallibly receive it." Bañez has said no more than this. Many other texts might be cited, particularly *Contra Gentes,* Bk. III, chaps. 91, 92, 94; *De veritate,* q. 22, a. 8, 9; *De malo,* q. 6, a. 1 ad 3; *Comment. in Perihermenias,* Bk. I, lect. 14, etc. To the mind of St. Thomas what could have appeared more absurd than the claim that by actualizing liberty in us God destroys it?

REFUTATION OF THE OBJECTIONS

The new syncretism holds that in St. Thomas the determination to one always necessitates. This is true of a faculty which by its very nature is determined to one. In that case it is necessitated to act only in that direction; man cannot use his sight for hearing but only for seeing. But it is not true of the motion, efficacious in itself, whereby God actualizes our liberty, infallibly leading our will, specified by the universal good, to determine itself toward some particular good, toward obeying some commandment rather than disobeying it.

St. Thomas says in fact, Ia IIae, q. 10, a. 4: "Since the will, then, is an active principle not determined to one but applying itself indifferently to many objects, God so moves it that He does not determine it to one of necessity, but that its motion remain contingent, not necessary, except in those things to which it is moved naturally." In this sentence the expression "not . . . of necessity" should be emphasized, for the negative refers to "of necessity" and not to "He . . . determines it to one." Throughout this question in fact, in the preceding articles, St. Thomas writes: "God does not move of necessity" in the sense of: "God moves, but not of necessity." Obviously, efficacious, salutary divine motion infallibly leads the will to determine itself to obey a given command rather than to disobey it. The proof is that in this very article 4 (ad 3) we read: "If God moves the will toward anything, it is incompatible with this position that the will should not be moved thereto." The text is clear to anyone who reads it without any preconceived idea. Moreover it is certain that efficacious grace which was resisted in fact would no longer be efficacious.

Msgr. Parente has attempted to show [80] by several texts of St. Thomas that the determination to one always necessitates. But the texts presented refer to determination to one of a faculty which, like that of seeing, is determined by its very nature to one act; they do not refer to the divine motion which actualizes freedom and produces in it even the free mode (which is of its essence), leading the will infallibly to determine itself to obey a given precept rather than to disobey.

To make this evident it suffices to quote in full the texts presented. *De malo,* q. 6, a. 1 ad 3: "God moves a certain will immutably [or infallibly] on account of the efficacy of His moving power which cannot fail; [81] but because of the nature of our will which applies itself indifferently to various objects, necessity is not introduced and liberty remains. So also in all things divine providence operates infallibly, and yet from contingent causes effects proceed contingently

---

[80] *Acta Pont. Acad. Romanae S. Thomae,* 1939–40, pp. 38–40.

[81] St. Thomas does not say: "On account of the divine prevision of our future contingent consent."

inasmuch as God moves things proportionately, each according to its mode." He actualizes freedom by leading it infallibly to meritorious obedience as He causes the tree to blossom; and just as the tree spontaneously produces its natural flowers, the just man freely obeys in a meritorious way under the grace which causes him to obey.

Without any more justification, we are confronted with the text *De potentia,* q. 3, a. 7 ad 13: "The will is said to have dominion over its act, not to the exclusion of the first cause, but since the first cause does not so act in the will as to determine it of necessity, as it determines nature. And therefore the determination of the act is left in the power of the reason and the will." Assuredly, since God by His efficacious, infallible motion leads us to free self-determination through deliberation to obey a given commandment rather than to disobey it; and when the just man obeys thus, it can be said that God had willed it so, efficaciously, from all eternity, even if it is a question of a facile act. It remains true, as St. Thomas says, *De veritate,* q. 22, a. 8, that "just as the will can change its act into another, so, to a much greater extent, can God," and *Contra Gentes,* Bk. III, chap. 91, no. 3: "A man always chooses what God operates in his will." Do we not read in Prov. 21:1: "The heart of the king is in the hand of the Lord: whithersoever He will He shall turn it"?

The testimony of Father Congar O.P., in the *Revue des sciences phil. et théol.,* 1934, pp. 369 ff., is also invoked. But it must not be forgotten that he concludes as we do: "Nothing can free us from the unavoidable dilemma: God either determines or is determined. God 'determines all things and is not determined by any' (St. Thomas, *III Sent.,* dist. 27, q. 1, a. 2 ad 1)." [82]

Finally it is objected that St. Thomas has never spoken of non-necessitating divine predetermination. It suffices to reply that he spoke of it clearly with reference to the divine decree by which Providence determined the hour of Christ's passion: "The Son of man indeed goeth, according to that which is determined" (Luke 22:22); cf. Acts 3:18. St. Thomas in his Commentary on St. John's Gospel (2:4), "My hour is not yet come," says in fact: "The hour of His passion is here meant, not as of necessity, but as determined by divine providence." Likewise (*ibid.,* 7:30): " 'They sought to apprehend Him and no man laid hands on Him, because His hour was not yet

[82] See in this same article by Father Congar the texts of St. Thomas regarding predetermination which he quotes.

come,' not of fatal necessity but as prescribed by the whole Trinity."
And again (*ibid.*, 13:1; 17:1): "Not the hour of fatal necessity but of
His ordination and good pleasure . . . determined by providence."

All these texts are manifestly concerned with a predetermining, infallible divine decree bearing upon the hour of Jesus and thereby even
upon the free act which He was to perform infallibly by willing to
die for our salvation. Herein is also concerned the permissive decree
referring to the sin of Judas, of Caiphas, of Herod, of Pilate, of all
those who, until that hour, were powerless to do any harm to our Lord.

Not to admit this teaching, especially with respect to the positive
predetermining decrees relating to salutary acts, is to affirm that what
is best in the merits of the just, the free determination which distinguishes them from sinful acts, does not derive from God. And thus,
of two men in the state of grace one of whom performs a meritorious
act and the other sins mortally, that which comes from God in both
cases would be only their faculties, habitual grace, the infused virtues,
the commandment, actual grace which draws them morally (but not
infallibly) after the manner of an object, and the motion as to exercise, from which the sinful refusal can proceed just as well as the meritorious volition. Then, what is best in the merits of the just, even in
those of Christ and His holy Mother,—their meritorious, free determination in its first beginning—would not derive from God, contrary to the words of St. Paul: "What hast thou that thou hast not
received?"

St. Thomas' teaching is quite otherwise. As Scheeben has justly
remarked,[83] the efficacious divine motion which the Angelic Doctor
speaks of, is not to be compared to the influence of a mechanical
order whereby one man assists another to row a boat, nor to that of
a qualitative order by which heat revives life, but to the vital influence in a plant, for example, of the parent stem upon the branches
causing them to blossom and fructify, and even more to the influence
of the human will, enlightened by the intelligence, upon the hand,
directing it as it writes. Moreover the handwriting varies in excellence; sometimes it becomes scarcely legible on account of the
tremor brought on by old age. Then the will of the writer is not
responsible for the defective result; no more is God for the disorder
of sin which proceeds from the evil disposition of the defective and
deficient will. Excluding the faults in the penmanship, all that is

[83] *Handbuch der Katholischen Dogmatik*, 1933, Vol. II, no. 63.

written proceeds from the hand as proximate cause and all, at the same time, from the writer as higher cause. This, however, is only an analogy to sustain the imagination and aid the intelligence. Thus our will, with the infused virtues, is secondary cause of whatever in the effect does not exceed its powers when set in operation, and it is instrumental cause of whatever exceeds its powers, as would be the case under a special inspiration of the Holy Ghost received through the gifts, as inspiration to which the just man freely consents. Let us also remark the teaching of Leo XIII that liberty remains under the motion which constitutes biblical inspiration.[84]

Once the Thomistic doctrine has been accepted, the more faithful the soul is the more it grasps, as Scheeben says, "its mystical profundity." It has less confidence in itself, more in the efficacy of grace; and this increases its generosity and docility to the Holy Ghost. Thus the saints even enter upon the ways known as passive, wherein merit certainly does not diminish, when God acts more and more in them, substituting, through inspiration received with docility, His own very sublime, very simple thought for their complicated ratiocination, His strength for their weakness. The saints realize then that God must become for them another self, as it were, more intimate than their own; and they finally reach the point of declaring with St. Paul: "I live now, not I, but Christ liveth in me." The influence of efficacious grace thus actualizes their liberty more and more; far from destroying it, grace vitalizes, transforms, and establishes it in good.

If the objection is raised: "But I wish to find something to cling to in my free will, and I cannot reconcile it with that abandonment to

---

[84] In the encyclical *Providentissimus*, 1893 (Denz., no. 1952), it was declared: "God by His supernatural power so stirred and moved them [the inspired writers] to write and so assisted them while they wrote that they might rightly conceive, will to set down faithfully, and aptly express with infallible truth all and only that which He should command; otherwise He Himself would not be the author of the whole of Sacred Scripture." It has not been sufficiently observed that here is an infallibly efficacious divine motion influencing not only the mind of the sacred writers but their free will as well: "that they might . . . will to set down faithfully." And, far from destroying their freedom, this motion actualizes it so that they may freely will to write what God wills and that alone, and may write infallibly in a manner conformed to truth. The text is clear. But if in one instance efficacious divine motion actualized freedom without doing any violence to it, this is possible in many another case. The difference between the inspired writers and us when we write is that God does not permit an error of judgment in them, whereas He sometimes does so in us; but in both cases freedom remains. Moreover, when God moves us efficaciously toward a salutary choice, He does not allow a practical error in the final judgment accepted by this salutary choice. Cf. J. M. Vosté, O.P., *De divina inspiratione et veritate sacrae scripturae*, 2nd ed., 1932, pp. 38, 66–68.

grace." Bossuet replies: "Proud contradictor, do you wish to reconcile these things or rather to believe that God reconciles them? He reconciles them in such a way that He wills, without releasing you from your action, that you attribute to Him ultimately the entire work of your salvation. For He is the Savior who has said: 'There is no savior besides Me' (Isa. 43:11). Believe firmly that Jesus Christ is the Savior, and all the contradictions will vanish." [85] This confidence in God, the author of grace, produces peace in abandonment. It goes so far as to declare with St. Paul: "When I am weak, then am I strong"; for then I no longer put my trust in self, but in God the author of salvation.

Such has been the teaching of the greatest Thomists. To indulge the liberty of disdaining them they must first have been understood; one cannot afford to remain in ignorance of all that the question involves; one must not confuse the divided sense of St. Thomas and his true disciples with that of Calvin, which is manifestly heretical. It is a source of regret for us to have been obliged to call attention to this confusion.[86]

The important thing is to hold firmly to the principle that the best part of our salutary, meritorious actions (their free determination) comes from God, that the just man does not distinguish himself by himself from the sinner: "For who distinguisheth thee? Or what hast thou that thou hast not received?" (I Cor. 4:7.) We must ever return to the principle set forth by the Council already quoted which put an end to the discussions aroused by the writings of Gottschalk: " 'Whatsoever the Lord pleased He hath done, in heaven, in earth' (Ps. 134:6). For nothing is done in heaven or on earth unless He either graciously does it (that is, a good) or permits it to be done in justice (that is, an evil permitted for the sake of a greater good)." At such heights as these we find peace. The best spiritual writers have always spoken thus, particularly when dealing with the free act of love of God which the Lord Himself causes to spring forth from our hearts. This efficacy of grace was especially manifest in the martyrs, giving them the fortitude to resist the most frightful torments.[87]

---

[85] *Elévations sur les mystères,* 18th week, 15th elevation.

[86] Msgr. Parente is under much happier inspiration in his apologetic conferences, *Dio e l'uomo,* 1946. Except for pages 253–58 wherein he again discusses Bañezianism, he shows clearly that man is not completely himself until he finds God, his last end, and he presents quite vividly the richness contained in the mysteries of Christianity.

[87] If the freedom of Christ obeying the precepts of His Father remained in spite of His impeccability, that is, even though He could not sin by disobedience, our free-

CONCLUSION

The essence of Molinism and of the theories related to it is to be found in a definition of created liberty which implies the denial of the intrinsic efficacy of the divine decrees and of grace and which requires the admission of mediate knowledge in spite of its manifest disadvantages. The opponents of Molinism refuse to accept this definition of free will which, in their estimation, is begging the question.

The definition referred to as formulated by Molina, *Concordia,* p. 10, is as follows: "Free will is the faculty which, given all the requirements for acting, can either act or not." According to Molina this definition does not mean that, under efficacious grace, liberty preserves the power to resist without ever willing, under this grace, to resist actually; it means that grace is not efficacious of itself but only through our consent foreseen by mediate knowledge. As Molina says, *ibid.,* p. 318: "It was not in the power of God to foresee anything else by His mediate knowledge; however the divine foresight would have been otherwise had the choice of the created liberty been different." Thus the divine foresight depends on the choice which a man would make and will make, supposing him to be placed in given circumstances. Hence there is passivity or dependence in God, according to the unsolvable dilemma: God either determines or is determined; there is no middle ground. Moreover man distinguishes himself; it is hard to see how the words of St. Paul are safeguarded: "What hast thou that thou hast not received?"

On the contrary it must be affirmed that every good comes from God, and especially what is best in our salutary, meritorious acts, the free determination which distinguishes an act of obedience from one of disobedience, by which our love of God is distinguished from indifference or hatred. "Convert us to Thee, O Lord, and we shall be converted." Such should be our prayer.

V. Habit and Act Are Specified by Their Formal Object: the Universality of This Principle

State of the question. All Scholastics recognize this teaching of Aristotle which St. Thomas expresses in the following terms: "Just as every natural thing has its species from its form, so every action has

---

dom remains under efficacious grace which actualizes our free will instead of destroying it, leaving in us still the unhappy power of sinning by disobedience.

its species from its object, just as motion from its term" (Ia IIae, q. 18, a. 2). The reason for this, as explained in Ia IIae, q. 54, a. 2, is that "whatever is said to be ordained toward something is distinguished according to the distinguishing marks of that toward which it is ordained." But operative powers, operative habits, and operations themselves, or acts, are said to be ordered (by a transcendental relationship) to an object. Therefore they are specifically distinguished according to the distinguishing marks of their objects; in other words, they derive their species and unity essentially from an object. This principle is invoked very frequently in the treatises on grace and on the virtues. Hence special attention should be given to it.

The foregoing principle, which Thomists have always upheld, was nevertheless assailed by Scotus, Durandus, the Nominalists, Molina, Lugo, and many others. In fact, its universality has but recently been denied. Some writers have held that "the generally admitted principle, 'an act is specified by its formal object,' is not generally valid." It is indeed valid, so they maintain, "where the formal object differs specifically; then, the corresponding act differs specifically. For instance, the mode of operation with respect to the same material object varies according as it is visible (seeing), true (understanding), or good (willing). . . . Likewise the formal object of human intellection (the intelligible in sensible objects) differs from the formal object of angelic intellection (the created intelligible in itself), and these from the formal object of divine intellection (the uncreated intelligible); further human, angelic, and divine intellection are essentially diverse in their ontological perfection. . . .

"Therefore in this example a difference in mode of operation can be concluded from a difference of formal object, and ultimately a difference of ontological perfection.

"If it were generally valid that any difference of ontological perfection was based on a difference in mode of operation with respect to the material object, it would follow that a different ontological perfection would necessarily require a different formal object. But this is not true. For the act of seeing in an irrational animal and that in a man (supposing the man not to have attained the use of reason yet) differ essentially in their ontological perfection; but their mode of operation or of reaching their object does not so differ and hence their formal object is also held to be the same. The statement is therefore not generally valid, that wherever there is diversity of ontological

perfection there is also diversity of operation and of formal object." [88]
In the same way, the formal object of infused faith would not be distinct from the object of acquired faith in the truth of the Gospel confirmed by miracles.

Having read this explanation of the foregoing principle, many Thomists conclude: then, if the commonly admitted principle, "acts are specified by their formal object," is not generally valid, it must be incorrectly formulated. It should not be stated generally that acts are specified by their formal object, but only that certain acts, not all, are specified by their formal object. In other words, if a difference of formal objects is given, then there is indeed a specific difference in the acts; but the converse is not true, that is, not every specific difference in acts corresponds to a difference in formal objects. It must therefore be discovered whether the aforesaid principle is universal for Aristotle, St. Thomas, and their disciples, or whether "it is not generally valid."

Most assuredly a person would not preserve the sense of the proposition, men are rational animals, were he to say: all rational animals are indeed men, but not all men are rational animals. Similarly it may be asked whether it is true to say: all acts formally, as they are acts, are specified by their formal object, for instance, sight as sight, hearing as hearing; although from another aspect, that is, not as acts but as properties of such and such a nature, they may have another specification, for example, sight, not as sight, but as leonine, equine, or aquiline, or even sight as it is in a man rather than in a child or in a woman.

Cajetan had already said when explaining this principle, *In Iam,* q. 77, a. 3, no. 6: "Keep in mind here that we can speak of the powers of the soul from two standpoints; from one aspect inasmuch as they are powers (ordained to an act and an object), and it is with this that we are entirely concerned at present; from the other aspect inasmuch as they are properties of such and such a nature; to this we are not referring. For from this standpoint they differ according to the diverse natures in which they reside, as Averroes remarks, I *De anima,* comment. 53: The members of a man are different specifically from those of a lion." Herein perhaps lies the solution of the problem.[89] Let us first consider whether the foregoing principle is

[88] Thus H. Lennerz, S.J., *De virtutibus theologicis* (MS) Rome, 1930, p. 179.

[89] It should therefore be noted from the start, with respect to the meaning of our principle, that we are concerned with acts formally as they are acts. In other words, the meaning is: "Acts formally as acts, are specified by their formal object," although

universal for Aristotle and St. Thomas, in other words, whether it is really a principle.

THE UNIVERSALITY OF THIS PRINCIPLE ACCORDING TO ARISTOTLE AND ST. THOMAS

In his *De anima* Aristotle had already thus distinguished sensation from intellection: sensation is ordered to perceiving sensible qualities, sight to visible color, hearing to sound; whereas intellection is ordered to intelligible being. And it is utterly impossible for even the highest sense faculty to attain to intelligible being or to the reasons of the essence of things. This is the basis of the demonstration of the spirituality and immortality of the rational soul. Again, Aristotle distinguished intellect ordained to the true from appetite ordained to the appetible, and rational appetite specified by the universal good from sense appetite ordained toward a sensible good which is not universal.

By the same principle, Aristotle distinguished various sciences, as can easily be observed in the sixth book of the *Metaphysics,* chap. 1, so far as speculative science is ordered only to cognition of truth, practical science to works. Likewise there are three principal speculative sciences (physics, mathematics, and metaphysics),—each specified by its object. Physics by mobile being according to the first degree of

they may have another specification, not as acts, but as properties of such and such a nature. St. Thomas himself says, Ia IIae, q.63, a.4: "The health of a man is not the same in kind as that of a horse, on account of their different natures, to which they are ordered." Likewise the infused virtues as properties of grace are distinguished from the acquired virtues; but, as the Angelic Doctor observes in the same article, they are also distinguished inasmuch as they are habits by the formal object toward which they are ordained.

It is evident that the principle, "Powers, habits, and acts are specified by their formal objects," considers powers formally as powers, habits as habits, acts as acts; not as properties of such and such a nature. Thus as properties of a particular nature the members of a lion differ in kind from those of a man, the eyes of a lion from those of a man, etc. But our principle is not concerned with this distinction. Again, all the faculties of the human soul are human as properties of our nature, but formally as faculties they are specified by different formal objects and are thus various faculties, not merely one.

Cf. Cajetan *In Iam,* q.77, a.3, no. 4: "The maxim that powers are differentiated by their acts and objects can be understood in a fourfold sense. . . . The true meaning is that a power as such is said to be and is directed toward its act. . . . Powers by their essences are essentially ordered toward their acts; . . . by order I mean not a predicamental relationship but a transcendant one." Similarly with regard to acts. Hence the meaning of the axiom is: "Acts as they are acts, formally, are specified by their formal objects." St. Thomas always speaks formally, not materially.

abstraction, that is, from singular matter; mathematics by quantity according to the second degree of abstraction, that is, from sensible matter; and metaphysics by being as being according to the third degree of abstraction, that is, from all matter. Similarly, in the *Ethics* Aristotle distinguishes four cardinal virtues, and likewise the virtues annexed to them and their acts, according to their objects; for example, prudence as right reason applied to practice.

Hence this principle is given by Aristotle as entirely universal: acts are specified by their objects; not indeed by their material object around which many acts converge, just as the various senses round about the same sensible body, but by their formal objects.[90] Nowhere has Aristotle set any limit to the universality of this principle rightly formulated regarding an act not materially but formally as it is an act, a habit as a habit, or a power as a power.

St. Thomas recognized the universality of this principle no less than Aristotle. In fact, he penetrated its doctrine even more deeply, and more clearly saw its extension and universal application to supernatural acts. From this principle, that "powers, habits, and acts are specified by their formal object," St. Thomas deduces that, both in angels and in the human soul, essence is really distinct from operative power inasmuch as essence is ordained to being, operative power to an act and its object, Ia, q. 54, a. 3; q. 77, a. 1. He likewise deduces from this that there are several faculties in the soul specified by diverse objects. Thus, enunciating the universality of our principle, he says, Ia, q. 77, a. 3: "A power inasmuch as it is a power is ordained to an act. Hence the reason or nature of a power must be drawn from the act to which it is ordained, and consequently the nature of a power is diversified as the nature of the act is diversified. But the nature of an act is diversified according to the diverse nature of the object. For every act is that of either an active or a passive power. However, the object is related to the act of a passive power as principle and moving cause; thus color is the principle of vision inasmuch as it moves the organ of sight. But the object is related to the act of an active power as term and end; thus the object of an augmentative virtue is perfect measure which is the end of the increase. And from these two, that is, from the principle and from the term or end, the act receives its

---

[90] In fact, an act is specified first by the formal object *by which* (*quo*) the formal object (*quod*) is attained, as sight is specified by light through which colors are made visible in act.

species. For calefaction differs from refrigeration according as the former proceeds from something hot, that is actively so, to the production of heat, but the latter from something cold to the production of cold. Hence necessarily powers are diversified according to their acts and objects." It is therefore universally true to declare that every act, formally as an act, is specified by its formal object.

St. Thomas also applies this principle to the specific differentiation of operative habits; cf. Ia IIae, q. 54, a. 2: "Habits must be ordained to something. But whatever is said to be ordained to something is differentiated according to the differences in the thing to which it is so ordained. Now a habit is a certain disposition ordained to two objects, namely to the nature and the operation following upon that nature." Operation is then specified by its object.

St. Thomas again insists upon the universality of this principle when he declares, with reference to infused faith and the loss of it by the denial of one single article of the creed, IIa IIae, q. 5, a. 3: "The species of any habit depends on the formal reason of the object; which being withdrawn, the species of the habit cannot survive." He does not say that certain operative habits and certain acts are specified by their object, but all of them; the principle is entirely universal, otherwise it would not be a principle.

Thereupon St. Thomas demonstrates from this universal principle that the infused moral virtues are distinct in species from the correlative acquired moral virtues. For he says, Ia IIae, q. 63, a. 4: "It is manifest that the mode which is imposed upon such desires by the rule of human reason has a different reason from that which is imposed by a divine rule. Consider the matter of taking food. . . . Thus it is evident that infused and acquired temperance differ in kind," according to the "specific, and formal reasons of the objects," as declared in the same article.

Again, St. Thomas distinguishes between infused faith and acquired faith as it exists in the demons, of whom it is said that they "believe and tremble" (Jas. 2:19). For he writes in *De veritate,* q. 14, a. 9 ad 4: "The demons do not assent with their wills to the things which they are said to believe, but impelled by the evidence of signs by which they are convinced of the truth of what the faithful believe; although these signs do not cause what is believed to appear in such wise that they could thence be said to have a vision of what is believed. Hence the term 'belief' is used equivocally of the faithful and of demons;

nor does faith in the latter proceed from any infused light of grace as in the faithful." It is a question of "believing" as it is an act, and of faith as it is a habit.

It is evident that for St. Thomas infused faith and this acquired faith of the demons are differentiated in kind even formally as habit and as act and, consequently, on the part of their formal object. For he says, IIa IIae, q. 5, a. 3: "The species of any habit [or act] depends on the reason of its formal object; which being withdrawn, the species of the habit cannot survive." But as has been said: "the term 'belief' is used equivocally of the faithful and of demons"; therefore these two acts have not the same formal object, but only the same material object. The faithful believe revealed mysteries on account of the authority of God who reveals them, that is, of God the author of grace; whereas the demons know naturally God the author of nature and believe in revelation on account of the evidence of signs, as said previously. Thus they attain to revealed mysteries materially, that is to say, not formally according as they are essentially supernatural mysteries of the intimate life of God, but to the extent that they are utterances of God confirmed by evident miracles, in the same way that God reveals even the natural truths of religion or future contingencies of the natural order, such as the end of a war, for example.

Likewise, explaining the words of St. Paul (I Cor. 2:14): "The sensual man perceiveth not these things that are of the Spirit of God; for it is foolishness to him, and he cannot understand," the Angelic Doctor likewise declares: "Just as sense perception cannot estimate the things which pertain to the intellect and similarly neither sense nor human reason can judge of those things which pertain to the Spirit of God, so it remains that such things are estimated only by the Holy Ghost" (Commentary on I Cor. 2:14, lect. 3). And further, on Matt. 13:14, concerning the words: "By hearing you shall hear, and shall not understand: and seeing you shall see, and shall not perceive," St. Thomas says: "From the withdrawal of grace it follows that the mind is not enlightened from on high to see rightly." We have quoted elsewhere innumerable analagous texts of St. Thomas.[91]

Moreover, St. Thomas thus shows that, on the part of the formal object, prophecy itself is inferior to infused faith, for he writes (*III Sent.*, dist. 24, q. 1, a. 1 ad 3): "Although prophecy and faith deal with

[91] *De revelatione* (2 vol. ed.), I, 470–81, 180 ff.

the same matter, such as the passion of Christ, they do not do so under the same aspect; for faith considers the Passion formally with respect to its underlying eternal truth, inasmuch as it was God who suffered, although it nevertheless considers the temporal aspect materially. But prophecy does just the opposite"; that is, prophecy considers the temporal aspect formally and what is eternal materially.

In the same way acquired faith in the truth of the Gospel, confirmed by miracles, attains only materially to that which is formally attained by infused faith. All the commentators of St. Thomas' school agree on this principle.[92] Just as a dog hears human speech materially, that is with regard to what is sensibly perceptible in it, so the demon hears the word of God materially, that is, with regard to what is naturally knowable in it.

This interpretation receives strong confirmation by reason of the end toward which infused faith is ordered. For infused faith would be useless if its formal object (*quo et quod*) were already attained by acquired faith. Moreover, if acquired faith could attain to the formal object of infused faith, then, contrary to what St. Thomas affirms, Ia IIae, q. 63, a. 4, acquired temperance could also attain to the formal object of infused temperance, at least since the external presentation of Christian revelation; again, the natural good will to which the Pelagians referred could, under the same conditions, attain to the formal object of infused charity. But in that case, of what good would be infused faith, infused temperance, infused charity, or any of the infused virtues? They would be useless *de jure,* although, in a measure, useful *de facto,* since it is declared by the Councils: "for believing and hoping, etc. as is necessary to salvation." But why should they be necessary for believing "as is necessary for salvation" if the formal object of infused faith and likewise of charity can be attained without these infused virtues? As Lemos, the Salmanticenses, John of St. Thomas, and, indeed, Suarez declare, once the foregoing principle is withdrawn, the whole structure of philosophy and theology falls into ruins.[93]

---

[92] These texts are quoted, *ibid.,* I, 469–514.

[93] These are among the texts quoted, *ibid.,* I, 492 ff. In the famous discussions of the Congregatio de Auxiliis, May 7 and 28, 1604, before Clement VIII, Father Lemos, O.P., said of the opinion mentioned above, admitted by Molina: "By this system he would overturn faith as well as philosophy; faith, certainly, because thus God is feared and loved by the powers of nature, as the end is supernatural; philosophy indeed, since, in this way, the formal object of a superior habit is attained by inferior

Hence neither Aristotle nor St. Thomas nor the Thomists have set any limits to the universality of our principle. Never have they asserted that "it was not generally valid," but on the contrary they have taught that it extended to all acts. Since St. Thomas, however, many theologians (such as Durandus, Scotus, the Nominalists, Molina, Lugo and several others) have held that infused faith does not have a formal object which is inaccessible to acquired faith; and yet it differs specifically from acquired faith. They are thus led to deny the universality of our principle, "habit and act are specified by their formal object," although, according to St. Thomas, this principle clarifies all the problems of faculties, habits, and acts, as can easily be seen from innumerable texts of his, or by consulting those at least which are cited in the *Tabula aurea* of his works under the heading: "Objectum," nos. 2–6.

---

powers." (Cf. Serry, *Historia Congreg. de Auxiliis,* Bk. III, chaps. 35–6, p. 406.) On May 29, 1604, the fifty-fourth session solved the problem proposed according to the interpretation of the Thomists as presented by Lemos. (Cf. Serry, *ibid.,* p. 410; also Lemos, *Panoplia gratiae,* Bk. IV. nos. 24 f.)

Again, the Salmanticenses, *De gratia,* tr. 19, disp. III, dub. 3; IV, no. 60, examine the opinion of Molina and de Lugo according to which "a difference of activating principle alone suffices for acts to differ in kind, even though they attain the same formal object." They reply by "denying the antecedent, for if it were true, as our adversaries contend, nothing in true philosophy but would waver in regard to species and the distinction of powers and habits; we should be compelled to establish new bases such as were not taught by Aristotle, Master Thomas, or the leaders of other schools. Although younger writers would easily grant this, lest we might have any leader among the ancients, the result would indeed be to the highest detriment to true wisdom; wherefore it is essential in this respect to hinder their proclivity with all our powers."

In fact, Suarez himself, in spite of his special theory of active, obediential power, asserts with regard to the necessity of the interior grace of faith: to say this grace "is required only that the assent may be more perfect with respect to being, although from the standpoint of the object it would not be necessary, comes very close to the declaration of Pelagius that grace is required only for greater facility. Furthermore it seems merely to be an escape contrived so as to elude the testimony of the councils and the Fathers" (*De gratia,* Bk. II, chap. 1, no. 17). But Suarez does not observe this principle when he recognizes in our nature an active obediential power for supernatural objects. In this connection John of St. Thomas says, Ia, q. 12, disp. XIV, a.2, no. 11: "Such an affirmation of active obediential power gives rise to all those inconsistencies which are strongly refuted in matters of grace." An obediential power which should be active (not only materially as it resides in an active power such as the will, but formally), would be at the same time essentially natural as a property of our nature and essentially supernatural as specified by a supernatural object. Thus elevating grace would not be absolutely necessary.

WHETHER THE UNIVERSALITY OF THE PRECEDING PRINCIPLE
CAN BE DENIED OR DEMANDS LIMITATION

The reply is in the negative, since this principle deals with power, habit, and act according as they are formally power, habit, and act and according as they are essentially ordained to their object by a transcendental relationship. This fundamental reason is admirably expressed by St. Thomas, Ia, q. 77, a. 3, when he says: "Power, inasmuch as it is a power, is ordained to an act. . . . But the nature or reason of an act is diversified according to the diverse reason or nature of the object"; and again toward the end of the body of the article: "It is not simply any difference in the objects which diversifies the powers of the soul, but that particular difference to which the power directly relates and therefore the sensitive power of color, that is, sight, is one thing and the sensitive power of sound, that is, hearing, is quite another."

Commenting on this article, Cajetan (no. 4) offers the following profound explanation: "The basis of this is what has previously been accepted in the text, that is, power, according to that which is, is to or for this act and is the act; in other words, power according to its entity is not an absolute thing, separated from its act and object. . . . But powers and habits by their essences are essentially ordained toward acts in such wise that they are unintelligible without them. . . . Their differences are derived from ordination to their acts, an ordination which, I say, is not that of a predicamental but of a transcendental relationship. And this is the primary and ultimate root of the solution, both in the present matter and in similar matters, such as motion, prime matter, action and passion, habit, etc. Once this is established, the whole text is clear."

But if act, formally taken as act, is specified by its formal object, this is universally true of every act ordained toward an object; just as, if man, formally as he is man, is a rational animal, then this is universally true of all men without exception, although the exercise of reason may be impeded in certain cases. A universal is a single note capable of inhering in many things, and the nature of the universal is prior in conception to its universality. In the same way, the necessity of any principle is prior in conception to its universal extension.

Thus the sense of sight in a lion, formally taken as an act, does not differ specifically from the sense of sight in a child, for both are essentially ordained toward sensible light and color visible in act by that light, and by these are they specified. If there are certain differences in these two senses of sight, so far as they are acts, such differences are accidental and material on the part of the disposition of the organ, somewhat as there are accidental differences in the sense of sight among men, so that some are nearsighted, others farsighted, etc. There is also a certain material difference between the eyesight of men and of women.

How, then, are we to solve the objection cited above: "The act of seeing of an irrational animal and that of a man (supposing him not yet possessed of the use of reason) differ essentially in their ontological perfection; but their mode of operation or of attaining their object does not so differ, and hence the formal object is also held to be the same. . . . Therefore the principle is not generally valid which asserts that wherever there is a difference of ontological perfection, there is also a difference of operation and of formal object."

Cajetan had already answered this objection, *In Iam,* q. 77, a. 3, no. 5, as follows: "Keep in mind that the powers of the soul may be considered from two aspects; from one standpoint, inasmuch as they are powers, and the present discussion refers to this alone; from another, inasmuch as they are properties of a given nature, and we do not refer to this aspect here [this would not be speaking formally but materially]. For they are thus distinguished according to the diversity of the natures in which they inhere, as Averroes remarks (I *De anima,* comm. 53) : 'The members of a man are different in kind from the members of a lion.' "

St. Thomas speaks in similar terms, Ia IIae, q. 63, a. 4 c: "Soundness of body in a man is not of the same kind as in a horse because of the diverse natures to which they are ordained." Thus, as a property of such and such a nature the faculty of vision in a lion is different from that of a horse or an eagle, just as their members are; the shoulder, for instance, or the leg. But from that standpoint the faculty is no longer being considered formally as an operative power, act, and habit. Similarly, in man the two superior faculties are termed human inasmuch as they are properties of his soul; but as faculties they are distinguished on the basis of their objects and are therefore two and not one. St. Thomas himself made this distinction in classifying habits, Ia IIae, q. 54, a. 2. His classification may thus be presented:

Habits are specified

- **as form passively received** — from a proximate active principle by which they are produced, inasmuch as the action of an agent is like to itself
  - infused habits from the intimate life of God, in which they are a participation.
  - acquired habits
    - of knowledge from demonstrative principles.
    - of moral virtue by an act.

- **as disposing habit**
  - **for a nature** — by a nature to which they are suited or not suited
    - infused habits by the divine nature in which they participate.
    - acquired habits
      - good ones, according to their suitability to human nature.
      - bad ones, according to their unsuitability to human nature.
  - **for an operation** — by the object of the operation
    - infused habits by an essentially supernatural object.
    - acquired habits by an object accessible to nature.

Does it not follow that infused virtues are specifically distinguished from acquired only on the part of the radical principle from which they proceed, and not on the part of their object? In other words, are not these principles of specification more than merely distinct, separable in fact?

By no means; for virtues, as they are operative habits essentially ordered toward operation, are specifically differentiated, in the same way as the operations themselves, by their formal object. Therefore

St. Thomas says (Ia IIae, q. 63, a. 4), of acquired and infused temperance that they differ "according to the specific, formal reasons of their respective objects" according as the former is directed by a human, the latter by a divine rule. And the Angelic Doctor's meaning is that, athough a man may know the gospel historically, as confirmed by miracles, and the rule of temperance it contains, he nevertheless cannot attain to this superior rule merely by acquired temperance. For if this were possible, infused temperance would be usless except for acting with greater facility, as the Pelagians contended.

However, if acquired and infused temperance are specifically distinguished on the part of their formal object, in like manner acquired faith in the truth of the gospel confirmed by miracles is distinguished from infused faith formally as a habit and as an act by reason of its object. Otherwise infused faith would be useless, were its formal object already accessible to acquired faith. Finally, the formal object of charity, presupposing external revelation, would be accessible to natural good will, as the Pelagians maintained. As we have seen, these untenable consequences have been recognized by Thomists and even by Suarez.

Thus, even by reading the Gospel, "the sensual man perceiveth not these things that are of the Spirit of God; for it is foolishness to him, and he cannot understand" (I Cor. 2:14). On the other hand, as St. Thomas shows, IIa IIae, q. 2, a. 2, c and ad 1, the believer, by means of infused faith, with one and the same act [94] believes God revealing and in God revealed. That is, through infused faith he adheres to God revealing as formal motive, and by the same act, on account of this motive he believes in God revealed, for example, in the triune God and in God incarnate. Nor is this a vicious circle. Its opponents declare it to be so: "If the authority of God revealing is believed, it is believed either on account of another revelation and thus *ad infinitum,* or on its own account, whence results a vicious circle and reasonable credibility is lacking."

We answer (*De revelatione,* I, 507), with Cajetan, the Salmanticenses, and many other Thomists: The authority of God revealing is believed on its own account without any vicious circle resulting, just as light is visible of itself, just as evidence is self-evident, just as human speech manifests itself and what it affirms simultaneously.

---

[94] Not by three acts, as Suarez maintains.

For divine revelation in revealing the Trinity reveals itself. And although divine revelation thus believed is obscure, it does not lack rational credibility from signs confirming the revelation.

Our opponents insist: If infused faith had a specific formal object, it would fall under experience.

We reply (*ibid.*, p. 509): It does in fact fall under experience in a certain sense, but not clearly, just as the spirituality of our intelligence and its specific distinctness from the imagination are not clearly manifest experientially, or again the specific difference between the will and the sensitive appetite. Thus, as St. Thomas shows, Ia, q. 87, a. 1, and *De veritate,* q. 10, a. 8, every man "perceives that he has a soul according as he observes that he feels and knows," but from this experiential knowledge the spirituality of the soul is not clearly evident, so that some men are materialists. Metaphysical analysis is required to prove the spirituality of the soul.

With still greater reason, experience does not render clearly manifest the essential supernaturalness of the formal motive of faith, nor differentiate distinctly between the supernatural act of faith and concomitant natural acts. As St. Augustine says, "The school in which God is heard and teaches is far removed from the senses. We see many coming to the Son, for we see many believing in Christ; but where and how they heard this from the Father and learned it, we did not see. This grace is exceedingly hidden." [95] Hence the believer cannot discern clearly whether he is acting from a purely supernatural motive, so that he is not entirely certain of the supernaturalness of his faith, although he may have grounds for strong conjecture. Furthermore St. Thomas says of prophets: "Sometimes the prophet's attitude before that which he knows by prophetic instinct [and not by perfect prophecy] is such that he cannot fully discern whether he thought of it with some divine instinct or with his own mind." [96] Therefore the essential supernaturalness of an act of infused faith and its motive, like the spirituality of the soul, is not known with certainty except through metaphysical analysis by virtue of the principle, that acts are specified by their formal object.

If infused faith did in fact make use of infused species, its distinctness from acquired faith would be clearly evident experientially; and some seem to consider that infused faith which would make use

[95] *De praedestinatione sanctorum, PL,* XLIV, 970.
[96] IIa IIae, q. 171, a. 5.

of infused species would be specifically different from infused faith which uses species abstracted from sensible objects.

However, speaking formally, our infused faith is certainly not specifically distinct from the infused faith which wayfaring angels had with infused species. This difference of species with respect to the thing present is only a material difference, and the infused faith of wayfaring angels was specified by the same formal object (*quo et quod*) as our faith. They believed God to be triune on the authority of God revealing; God the author of grace, of course, not merely of nature.

Therefore the commonly admitted principle, "powers, habits, and acts are specified by their formal object," is generally, indeed universally, valid; otherwise it would not be a metaphysical principle. Moreover, if it were not valid generally or universally, it would have no validity at all but would have to be rejected, since it would not be true of potency formally as it is potency, nor of habit formally as it is habit, nor of act formally as it is act. If, on the contrary, this commonly admitted principle is precisely formulated by Aristotle and St. Thomas, it is true of potency formally as such, and likewise of habit and act, and is accordingly universal with metaphysical universality, without any exception, just as the principle, that "an act is multiplied and limited by the power into which it is received." [97] More concisely, St. Thomas writes: "Just as a natural thing derives its species from its form, so does an act from its object, as a movement from its term." [98] "For whatever is said to be ordained toward something is distinguished according to the distinction of that to which it is ordained." [99]

Observations. P. C. Boyer, S.J., proposed the following objection to me: "I certainly agree with the thesis expounded. However, I should like to propose a problem which occurs among the writings of Cajetan on Ia IIae, q. 54, a. 2, where the great commentator concedes that habits as forms are distinguished according to the diversity of their active principles; from which it follows that two habits having the same formal object could differ specifically.

"It may be said, if you will, that this difference is material, not

[97] Hence in his work, *Tria principia,* Reginaldus presented the whole of St. Thomas' teaching under these three principles: 1. Being and analogue; 2. God is pure act; 3. Powers, habits, and acts are specified by their formal object.

[98] Ia IIae, q. 18, a. 2.

[99] *Ibid.,* q. 54, a. 2.

formal. But with this difference, whatever it may be, how can the argument be safeguarded by which the thesis is demonstrated: an act is specified by its formal object? For the argument is based on the proportion between a power and its own act; but here we have two powers (two habits) with the same act and yet they differ specifically. If they so differ, do they not have a difference of proportion to their own act? And why, then, can it not be concluded that a natural act and a supernatural act of love are distinct in species only because they proceed from principles differing in species?"

Reply. Cajetan concedes that habits as forms are distinguished according to the diversity of their active principles; for example, infused prudence inasmuch as it is infused by God and acquired prudence inasmuch as it is acquired by a repetition of acts. But it does not follow from this that two habits with the same formal object can differ specifically. If infused prudence had the same formal object as acquired prudence, it would only be accidentally infused, but not necessarily infused (like infused geometry). The specification of a habit as a form is essentially connected with its specification by its object; they cannot be separated in an operative habit. By no means do we have two habits with the same act, unless it were a question of a habit accidentally infused; and when infusion is accidental it does not specify, as is obvious in the case of geometry accidentally infused.

The natural and supernatural acts of love differ therefore specifically, both on the part of their eliciting principles and on the part of their formal objects toward which the eliciting principles are ordered (cf. Ia IIae, q. 63, a. 4). Cajetan affirms this positively with reference to Ia IIae, q. 54, a. 2: "Since habits are both forms and habits, and each may share the differences of the other, that is, their own respective forms and habits, and there may not remain with distinction of the former a lack of distinction in the latter; wherefore in the proposition the distinctions of both concur, that is, of the acts and of the formal objects. . . . Nor is it necessary in adducing the one always to adduce the other." We do not say that the formal difference is material; whatever would be a material distinction would hold only with respect to the subject, as, for instance, the difference between infused faith in men and in angels who make use of infused species.

P. M. Brown, O.P., professor at the Angelicum, has made this excellent observation: With entire approval of what has been said, there may perhaps present itself here a certain application (not new but rarely called to mind) of this doctrine in sacred theology, which may be helpful in solving a problem frequently discussed among theologians. For it is known that in the theology of the sacraments there is great dispute over the matter and form of certain of the sacraments. Some theologians assert that in this matter the only criterion for the solution should be liturgical history which teaches us what the usage was at the beginning with regard to matter and to form; otherwise they think there would be an admission that the specific nature or substance of the sacrament was subject to change, which is impossible. Whatever of great moment may be said of liturgical history with regard to the elucidation of the question, it seems worthy of remark that, in the case of at least some of the sacraments, their specification or constitution in their own specific nature should be considered in the same way as the specification of other intentionals as act, habit, and faculty. Accordingly the specific nature (which is given by the final formative actuality) is constituted by its ordination toward that grace (and, in some, toward that character) for the conferring of which the sacrament is ordained. This specific nature can be conceived as remaining the same, even presupposing the power conferred upon the Church of determining the so-called form or matter of the sacrament.

VI. The Supernaturalness of Faith and Its Infallible Certainty

In recent times there has been a re-examination of the problem of the supernaturalness and infallible certainty of infused faith.[100] In particular, the question is asked: Whether, according to St. Thomas, believers adhere supernaturally and infallibly to the formal motive of faith, that is, to the authority of God revealing and, thereupon, to the mysteries revealed, by an adherence which vastly surpasses the rational knowledge of the motives of credibility, or the conclusion of all apologetic arguments, whence arises at least a moral certainty of revelation *ipso facto*.

The question is not one of minor importance; it concerns that faith which is "the gift of God," that strong certitude of faith for which

<hr>

[100] Cf. Father Teresio of St. Agnes Zielinski, O.C.D., *De ultima resolutione actus fidei,* 1942; Father Anselm Stolz, O.S.B., *Manuale theologiae dogmaticae,* 1941, fasc. I, pp. 39, 41; fasc. IV, pp. 26–30. We have examined these two works at length with reference to this subject in *Angelicum,* October, 1942, pp. 312–23.

the martyrs suffered indomitably. Christ frequently spoke of this faith, declaring: "He that believeth in Me, hath everlasting life," [101] that is, incipiently, so far as "faith is the substance of things to be hoped for" [102] and a certain beginning of eternal life. Concerning it, St. John says in his First Epistle (5:4): "This is the victory which overcometh the world, our faith"; it should therefore be strong against all errors, seductions, sophistries, temptations, persecutions. This must be stressed particularly today, for nothing can resist the exceedingly pernicious errors of materialism and atheism which are disseminated among all nations today unless it be the Christian, Catholic faith. It is obvious that Protestantism, succumbing under its own errors, is inadequate to the task. But in order to resist effectively, the faith of Catholics must be strong and deep. St. Paul thus characterizes it: "When you had received of us the word of the hearing of God, you received it not as the word of men, but (as it is indeed) the word of God, who worketh in you that have believed." [103] And therefore he gives warning elsewhere: "But though we, or an angel from heaven, preach a gospel to you besides that which we have preached to you, let him be anathema." [104]

State of the question. We shall present briefly the two contrary opinions. Although all theologians admit that Christian faith, in spite of its obscurity, is firmly established in certainty, not all of them explain this certainty in the same way. There are two schools of thought in particular: the one does not hold that the believer knows infallibly, by this very infused faith itself, the formal motive of faith; the other has affirmed and defended this opinion for centuries as the apple of its eye.

First opinion. In the Middle Ages numerous theologians, especially the Nominalists and their satellites, maintained that infused faith resolves itself into acquired faith whereby we believe the Church to be ruled by the Holy Ghost and that the motives of this faith are the signs of revelation, particularly miracles which are naturally recognizable. Thus Durandus, *III Sent.,* dist. 24, q. 1, qc. 3; Gabriel Biel, *III Sent.,* dist. 23, q. 2, and thereafter several others.[105] In fact, the

---

[101] John 5:24; 6:40, 47-55.

[102] Heb. 11:1.

[103] I Thess. 2:13.

[104] Gal. 1:8.

[105] Such as the Scotists, Nominalists, Molina, Ripalda, de Lugo, Franzelin, Billot (who, however, justly denies that faith is discursive), Bainvel, van Noort, Harent

same opinion is now held by many apologists and even theologians who rather consider the act of faith externally without investigating the inner nature of infused faith. They assert that the believer naturally knows the fact of revelation from the manifest signs by which it is confirmed, especially miracles and prophecies fulfilled, and they even know naturally that God does not err nor can He err. And this suffices for the certainty of Christian faith based on divine testimony thus confirmed.

Criticism. The great commentators on St. Thomas, such as Capreolus, Cajetan, Ferrariensis, Bañez, Lemos, Alvarez, John of St. Thomas, the Salmanticenses, Gonet, Billuart, Gotti, and more recent Thomists have always rejected this opinion.[106] They recognize that the certainty of infused faith does indeed resolve itself materially and intrinsically into the evidence of miracles and other signs, but its formal, intrinsic resolution should be reducible to something higher. In the same way, metaphysical certainty of first principles does indeed resolve itself materially and extrinsically into sensible evidence, but formally and intrinsically it is resolved into something higher of the intellectual order. Otherwise the supernatural certainty of essentially infused faith would be greatly diminished, for it would be reduced to an inferior certainty of the natural order.

This difficulty presents itself at once: Few indeed are the faithful who saw the miracles with their own eyes or who could have examined them with sufficient care to enable them to judge of their supernautral origin. Hence the majority of the faithful have naturally only a moral certainty of the signs of Christian revelation through the medium of human testimony often known in an uncritical way.

Therefore, as many other theologians declare, if the certainty of Christian faith were ultimately based upon this moral certitude of the

---

(*Dict. théol. cath.*, "foi"), and many others. I presented these opinions in *De revelatione*, I, chap. 14, a.3. For Scotus in particular (*III Sent.*, d.31, no. 4), a natural act and a supernatural act of faith may have the same formal object. Likewise for him (*III Sent.*, d.23, q.1, no. 8) infused faith is not necessary on account of the supernaturalness of the object, for the formal object of theological faith does not exceed acquired faith; and infused faith resolves itself into acquired faith by which we believe the Church to be true on account of certain signs.

[106] I quoted these texts of Thomists in *De revelatione*, 3d ed., Vol. I, chap. 14, a.3, pp. 484–97. See especially Capreolus on *III Sent.*, dist. 24, q.1, a.3, 2.4; Cajetan on IIa IIae, q.1, a.1, nos. 10 f.; Ferrariensis, *Contra Gentes*, Bk. III, chap. 40, §3; and Bk. I, chap. 6; Bañez on IIa IIae, q.1, a.1; John of St. Thomas, *De gratia*, disp. 20, a.1, no. 7; *De fide*, q.1, disp. II, a.2, 3.

fact of revelation confirmed by various signs, such certitude of faith would not be solid and infallible, but only hypothetical; that is, supposing it to be certain, in another way, on the word of another, that God Himself revealed the Trinity, the redemptive Incarnation, and the infallibility of the Church in propounding these mysteries; supposing, of course, that the preaching of these mysteries does not proceed from any natural evolution of the religious sense in the subconscious mind of the prophets and of Christ, as affirmed by the Modernists, according to whom the assent of faith ultimately depends upon a mass of probabilities (Denz., no. 2079). Thus the certainty of faith would not be absolutely infallible since it would be resolved into a moral certainty of the fact of revelation.

To this the aforementioned theologians reply that natural knowledge, morally certain of the fact of revelation and of the motive of Christian faith, is not the cause but only an indispensable condition of the certainty of faith, which therefore can still be something higher and more solid. Moreover, the moral certainty of the fact of revelation already referred to is confirmed by grace whence the will to believe is derived, assuming that there are sufficient signs of divine revelation.

This answer is judged inadequate by many theologians, especially by Thomists, since the knowledge of the formal motive of faith is more than an indispensable condition of the infallible certainty of faith; it pertains to its cause, for the formal motive of faith does not move one to believe infallibly in the redemptive Incarnation or the Trinity, for example, except as it is known and infallibly certain. That is, unless the mind of the believer adheres infallibly to this motive, as St. Thomas repeats often in the texts to be cited below. Similarly in metaphysics, if the principles of causality and of finality were not certain metaphysically, but only physically or morally, the conclusion deduced from these principles would not be metaphysically certain. Hence moral certainty of the fact of revelation does not suffice even when confirmed by grace and the will to believe. Further, in this case infused faith would not be an essentially supernatural virtue, since its formal, specifying motive could be known and be attained naturally. In other words, infused faith would then be no more supernatural than prudence naturally acquired and thereafter confirmed by grace. It would be no more supernatural than a rational judgment of credibility confirmed by grace.

Second opinion. Therefore Thomists, and Suarez as well to a certain extent, hold a distinctly opposite opinion, namely, that infused faith is essentially supernatural and is specified by the essentially supernatural formal motive of the authority of God revealing, to which believers adhere supernaturally and infallibly with an adherence that is not discursive but quite absolute and firm and which greatly surpasses the already at least morally certain conclusion of apologetics, that is, the conclusion regarding the evident credibility of the mysteries of faith or the fact of revelation confirmed by certain signs. This opinion is defended by St. Thomas, St. Bonaventure, and by Thomists, classical as well as contemporary, such as Capreolus, Cajetan, Cano, Bañez, Lemos, Alvarez, John of St. Thomas, the Salmanticenses, Gonet, Gotti, Billuart, Lepidi, Zigliara, Gardeil, Del Prado, Szabo, Scheeben, and recently even by several theologians of the Society of Jesus, including Fathers Mattiussi, Petazzi, De la Taille, Rozwadowski, and Boyer.[107]

Explanation and proof of the Thomistic opinion. Two points must first be considered. 1. What precisely is the formal motive of infused faith in its essence? 2. How does the mind of the believer adhere to this motive, according to the opinion we are discussing? To begin with, it should be observed that Thomists aim at considering the act of faith not merely as it is a fact of interior experience, but its nature and the nature of the infused virtue of faith; whereas, on the contrary, the Nominalists never consider the nature of things in themselves, for they consider it to be unknowable and base their reasoning only on facts. Thus in the present case, they never consider the very nature of the infused virtue of faith nor the principle which would elucidate the whole question, to wit, habit and act are specified by their respective formal objects *quo et quod,* that is, by the formal object toward which they are essentially and immediately ordained or primarily and *per se.*

1. What precisely is the motive of faith *per se* as directly infused?

a. We are not here concerned with the motives of credibility as found particularly in miracles which are knowable naturally and which, if true, most certainly confirm the fact of revelation and thereby establish the evident credibility of the mysteries of faith.

---

[107] Many texts from St. Thomas, St. Bonaventure, and Thomist writers are quoted in favor of this opinion in *De revelatione,* Vol. I, chap. 14, a.3, pp. 467–97.

b. Nor are we concerned with the formal motive of faith whereby only the natural truths of religion would be believed as revealed by God, such as the existence of Providence in the natural order descending even to particulars or the immortality of the soul. God could indeed thus have revealed only the natural truths of religion, confirming this revelation by miracles. Such a revelation would be supernatural only with respect to the mode of its production, not with respect to its substance or essence, that is, not on the part of its specifying object. Accordingly God would then intervene only as author and ruler of nature, for as such, God can perform miracles (raise the dead, for instance) to confirm the revelation of any religious truths of the natural order. In that case, revelation would be ordained merely to the attainment of natural beatitude, that is, not to the beatific or immediate vision of the divine essence but to the mediate knowledge of God reflected in His creatures and the rational love of God above all things. And for those who were capable of arriving at a philosophical demonstration of these natural truths of religion, faith, as thus conceived, would not be necessary for salvation. In other men, not grasping such a demonstration, faith would be infused accidentally, as we speak of infused geometry or the infused gift of tongues.

c. We are concerned with the formal motive of faith *per se* or essentially infused by which we believe the essentially supernatural mysteries of the most holy Trinity, the redemptive Incarnation, the Eucharist, the life of grace, and eternal life. This faith, essentially infused, was present in the wayfaring angels and in them, as in us, it was essentially supernatural.

But what is this formal motive? According to the Vatican Council (Denz., no. 1789), it is the authority of God revealing, or as St. Thomas says, IIa IIae, q. 1, a. 1, it is "first truth," namely, first truth revealing or in speaking according as it presupposes the first truth in understanding, which is itself ontologically based on first truth in essence. Briefly, this formal motive is the authority of God revealing, who can neither deceive nor be deceived.

But it is not only a question of God the author of nature, for instance, of the nature of the human soul, nor merely a word about God the author of miracles, since He can perform these inasmuch as He is author and ruler of nature. It is strictly a question of God author of grace and glory, for we are now speaking of God who revealed the essentially supernatural mysteries of the most holy Trinity, the redemptive Incarnation, and eternal life; and the order of agents should correspond to the order of ends. God as author of nature cannot reveal the essentially supernatural mysteries of His intimate life. In short, we are here concerned with supernatural revelation not only with respect to its mode of production but with respect to its substance, that is, by virtue of its speculative object. For, when God reveals the supernatural mysteries of the life of grace and glory, He intervenes not only as Creator and Lord, but properly as adoptive Father of angels and men, calling them to a participation in His own inner life. Hence the formal motive of essentially infused faith is the authority of God the heavenly Father revealing the mysteries of the kingdom of God.

Such revelation is involved in the words of Christ: "I confess to Thee, O Father, Lord of heaven and earth, because Thou hast hid these things from the wise and prudent, and hast revealed them to little ones" (Matt. 11:25); "Blessed art thou, Simon Bar-Jona: because flesh and blood hath not revealed it to thee, but My Father who is in heaven" (Matt. 16:17); "Although I give testimony of Myself, My testimony is true: for I know whence I came, and whither I go" (John 8:14). Again, St. Paul says: "But to us God hath revealed them, by His Spirit. For the Spirit searcheth all things, yea, the deep things of God" (I Cor. 2:10), that is, even the essentially supernatural mysteries of the intimate life of God, which vastly exceed the natural knowledge of all men and angels, not merely created but capable of being created.

2. How, according to the Thomistic opinion, does the mind of the believer adhere to this formal motive of infused faith?

Reply. Essentially supernatural divine revelation as proceeding from God the author of grace is that by which and what (*quo et quod*) we believe [108] supernaturally or infallibly believed with the mysteries, although under a lower aspect, the fact of revelation, together with the miracles by which it is confirmed, is known naturally with at least moral certitude so far as it is supernatural with respect to mode.

Bases of the Thomistic opinion. Let us see whether this answer is

---

[108] This formula, "Divine revelation is that by which we believe and that which we believe," is classic among commentators on St. Thomas. Cf. Cajetan on IIa IIae, q. 1, a. 1, no. 11. It is also found in Bañez, John of St. Thomas, the Salmanticenses, Gonet, Billuart, etc.

based on principles enunciated by St. Thomas and in his own words. There are three particular arguments, as follows:

1. by reason of the absolute infallibility of faith;
2. by reason of the essential supernaturalness of the motive of faith;
3. by reason of the essential supernaturalness of infused faith *per se.*

The first argument by reason of the absolute infallibility of faith is reducible to this: The fact of revelation is not merely proposed with moral certitude by history recounting the preaching and miracles of Christ; it is proposed infallibly by the Church, which has defined this revelation to be strictly supernatural, not proceeding naturally from the subconscious minds of the prophets, and confirmed, not by deceitful tricks drawn from myths, but by miracles in the strict sense, concerning which the Church pronounces final judgment with a certainty superior to any natural certainty (Denz., nos. 1785, 1813, 2078). But whatever is thus infallibly transmitted by the Church is to be supernaturally believed by all. Therefore the faithful should believe revelation supernaturally at the same time as the revealed mysteries; that is, they must believe simultaneously in God revealing and God revealed; otherwise they would not possess, with regard to the mysteries revealed, absolutely infallible certainty essentially superior to all natural certainty, as the certainty of infused faith is, according to St. Thomas (IIa IIae, q. 4, a. 8). In spite of the obscurity of mysteries, the certitude of faith should exclude all deliberate doubt, even amid violent temptations or the tortures of martyrdom, and it does so since it proceeds from the infused virtue of faith which, under efficacious actual grace, perfects the intellect so that, as St. Thomas declares, "the intellect tends infallibly toward its object" (*ibid.,* a. 5).

If the formal motive of faith were known merely naturally, through the medium of human testimony, the certainty of faith would be infallible only hypothetically but not absolutely; that is, on the supposition that it is really God Himself who revealed these mysteries, or more specifically, supposing it to be certain from some other way that the revelation of the mysteries proceeded from God and not naturally from the subconscious of the prophets or of Christ, in accordance with the evolution of the religious sense, as the Modernists declared. Then the words of St. Paul would not be infallibly verified: "When you had received of us the word of the hearing of God, you received it not as the word of men, but (as it is indeed) the word of God, who worketh in you that have believed" (I Thess. 2:13).

Then the formal motive of faith does not move us unless it is known and it does not move us infallibly unless it is infallibly united to our intellect, producing its formal effect therein. Just as the musical sense responds to the beauty of a symphony that is heard, so does infused faith respond to the word of God contained in the Gospel according as it utterly surpasses human speech. Hence we read in St. John's First Epistle (5:10): "He that believeth in the Son of God, hath the testimony of God in himself."

Confirmation. Human reason can err, not in natural cognition of first principles, but in forming conclusions, and is all the more apt to do so the more remote the conclusions are from the principles. For it is not always easy to distinguish a true miracle from a diabolical fraud: "There shall arise false Christs and false prophets, and shall show great signs and wonders, insomuch as to deceive (if possible) even the elect" (Matt. 24:24). Nor is it always easy to verify the historical authenticity of the narrative in which the miracles are reported. In fact such investigation is not possible to great numbers of the faithful who know the signs of revelation only from the testimony of their pastors or parents. On the other hand, the Church, like the prophets of former times, judges infallibly of the existence of revelation and proposes it as doctrine, just as she proposes her own infallibility, otherwise confirmed by miracles and manifestly worthy of belief.

According to St. Thomas there is no incompatibility between knowing naturally a fact of revelation as it is supernatural modally, and simultaneously believing supernaturally in revelation under a higher aspect, as it is supernatural substantially or essentially, in the same way as the supernatural mysteries themselves. For the supernaturalness of the mysteries exceeds natural cognition and transcends the supernaturalness of naturally knowable miracles. Thus for St. Thomas (IIIa, q. 55, a. 2 ad 1 and 2, and a. 5 c, ad 2 and 3), the apostles, at the same time, knew naturally the resurrection of Christ as man, visibly restored to life as miraculous, just as they recognized the resurrection of Lazarus, and supernaturally believed in it as the mystery of the self-resurrection of the Word incarnate.

This first argument from the absolute infallibility of faith is confirmed by many texts of St. Thomas especially where he speaks of the certainty of infused faith which cannot be subjected to falsehood.

Cf. IIa IIae, q. 1, a. 3: "Nothing comes under any power or habit or even act except by means of the formal reason or aspect of the object. Thus, color can be seen only through light, nor can a conclusion be known except through the medium of demonstration. But it has already been said that the formal reason of the object of faith is the First Truth (revealing); hence nothing can come under faith except as it comes under first truth, under which no falsehood can stand." *Ibid.*, q. 4, a. 8: "As to the cause of certainty, faith is more certain than any cognition of natural wisdom, knowledge or understanding of first principles, since faith rests on divine truth, whereas the three forms of cognition just mentioned depend upon human reason. . . . Thus faith is absolutely more certain than they are [in us], but under a certain aspect it is less certain, that is, in relation to us [on account of the obscurity of the object which we do not attain to so completely as to an evident object]." Cf. *De revelatione*, I, 469–81, for several other texts from St. Thomas.

The second argument is taken from the essential supernaturalness of the motive of faith as follows: That which is essentially supernatural cannot formally as such be known naturally, not even by the highest angels created or capable of being created, since it pertains to the order of God's intimate life which surpasses any natural cognition, even that of angels, just as the proper object of the divine intellect exceeds the proper object of any created intellect. Otherwise the pantheistic confusion of the nature of divine and created intellects would result; by its nature the created intellect would already be a formal participation in the divine nature or Deity in the same way as sanctifying grace; there would be a confusion of the two orders. Wherefore whatever is supernatural essentially is supernatural cognoscitively; for truth and being are convertible.

But the formal motive of *per se* infused faith is essentially supernatural, as has been said; for it is the authority of God revealing and indeed of God the author of grace and glory, since only as such can God reveal the essentially supernatural mysteries of the Trinity, the redemptive Incarnation, and eternal life, which utterly transcend the natural truths of religion knowable by natural means. Therefore this formal motive of infused faith, formally as such, cannot be known naturally even by the angels but supernaturally only. Hence the faithful adhere to it supernaturally and most firmly at the same time as to the mysteries. This formal motive of faith is no less supernatural and inaccessible to nature than the formal motive of infused hope or charity.

This is affirmed in many texts from St. Thomas which I have quoted elsewhere; only the principal ones will be indicated here. IIa IIae, q. 5, a. 1: Whether the angel in his first state had faith. *Reply:* "In the object of faith there is something formal, as it were, that is first truth existing above all natural cognition, and something material, namely, that to which we assent by adhering to first truth. With respect therefore to the first of these, faith generally resides in all who have a knowledge of God, not yet attaining to future beatitude, by adhering to first truth. But with respect to those things which are proposed materially for belief, some are believed by one person which are manifestly known by another. Hence the wayfaring angels possessed infused faith.

Likewise IIa IIae, q. 6, a. 1: Whether faith is infused in man by God [or acquired after learning about revelation confirmed by miracles, as the Pelagians held; and further whether the beginning of faith is infused, contrary to the Semi-Pelagians]. The answer to the doctrine of both Pelagians and Semi-Pelagians is as follows: "It is false because, when a man is raised above his nature by assenting to the truths of faith, this must needs be in him from a supernatural principle moving him interiorly, which principle is God"; similarly in the answer to the third objection. Again, commenting on the First Epistle to the Corinthians with reference to the words, "The sensual man perceiveth not these things that are of the Spirit of God; for it is foolishness to him, and he cannot understand" (2:14), St. Thomas declares: "Just as sense perception cannot examine into matters which pertain to the intellect, and neither sense nor human reason can judge of those things which are of the Spirit of God, so there remain some things of a kind which are examined only by the Holy Ghost. . . . Therefore a man is said to be spiritual: in one sense with respect to his intellect, illuminated by the Spirit of God . . . , in another sense with respect to the will, inflamed by the Spirit of God." In the same way, the beauty of a Beethoven symphony is not perceived by a person lacking in musical sense, even if he learns in some other way that this particular symphony is very beautiful in the judgment of experts. For there must be a proportion between the object known and the cognitive faculty. Hence anything essentially supernatural, such as the formal motive of infused faith which is the revelation of the heavenly Father, formally as such cannot be known naturally; just as the formal motive of infused hope or charity cannot be attained without these infused virtues.

The third argument is drawn from the essential supernaturalness of *per se* infused faith. It is revealed that faith is "the gift of God" (Eph. 2:8) so far as it is "the substance of things to be hoped for" (Heb. 11:1), as it were, a certain beginning of eternal life; Christ frequently said: "He that believeth in Me, hath everlasting life" (John 6:47; cf. *ibid.,* 40, 55); and the Vatican Council defined as follows (Denz., no. 1789): "The Catholic Church professes this faith, which is the beginning of human salvation (cf. no. 801), to be indeed a supernatural virtue by which, under the inspiration and help of God's grace, we believe whatever is revealed by Him to be true, not on account of the intrinsic truth of the matter perceived by the light of natural reason, but on account of the authority of God Himself revealing, who can neither deceive nor be deceived"; and canon 2: "For according to the testimony of the Apostle, faith is the substance of things to be hoped for, the evidence of things that appear not" (Heb. 11:1). Hence *per se* infused faith is an essentially supernatural virtue.

But habit and act are specified by their respective formal objects (*quod et quo*) of the same order. Therefore the formal object (*quo*) or formal motive by which *per se* infused faith is specified is of the same essentially supernatural order. Accordingly this formal motive can be attained only by faith, as light whereby colors are seen is known only by sight; for light is that by which we see and what we see. Analogously, revelation is that by which one believes and what one believes, or is believed with the revealed mysteries, when the believer "by one and the same supernatural act believes God [revealing] and in God [revealed]" according to the very words of St. Thomas, IIa IIae, q. 2, a. 2.

Otherwise, if the formal motive of faith could be attained without grace, infused faith would be unnecessary except for believing more easily and firmly, as the Pelagians held. Moreover, faith would then be no more supernatural than acquired prudence or temperance, which in the just man are under the dominion of charity and are ordained by it to a supernatural end; but they remain acquired virtues, essentially natural and not infused.

Lastly, if the formal motive of infused faith could actually be attained without grace, without the infused light of faith, the formal motive of hope and even charity could likewise be attained by natural good will; and thus infused faith and charity would not be necessary for salvation, as the Pelagians declared, and they would be of no higher order than the natural and ineffectual desire of seeing God in His essence, referred to by St. Thomas, Ia, q. 12, a. 1.[109]

The true doctrine of tradition is far superior to the foregoing. It is thus expressed in the language of apologetics by Father Lacordaire who was speaking, as it were, from experience about converts to the faith: "What takes place within us when we believe is a phenomenon of superhuman, interior light. I do not say that exterior things (such as miracles) do not act upon us as rational motives of certitude; but the act itself of this supreme certitude of which I am speaking affects us directly as a luminous phenomenon, nay more as a translucent phenomenon (above rational evidence). . . . We are affected by a light . . . which is translucent (the infused light of faith). . . . Otherwise what proportion would there be between our adherence, which would be natural, rational, and an object which surpasses nature and reason? . . .

"A convert will tell you: 'I read, I reasoned, I desired, but I did not attain to it. Then one day—I cannot explain how—I was no longer the same: I believed; and what happened at the moment of final conviction was totally different in nature from what preceded. . . .' Recall the episode of the two disciples on the way to Emmaus." [110] "Thus a sympathetic intuition sets up a bond between two men in a single moment which logic would not have produced in the course of many years. So at times does a sudden illumination enlighten the genius." [111] "There may be a scholar who studies Catholic teaching without rejecting it bitterly; he may even say frequently: 'You are fortunate to have the faith; I wish I had your faith, but I just cannot believe.' But some day this scholar gets down on his knees; conscious of man's wretchedness, he raises his hands to heaven, saying: 'From the depths of my misery, O my God, I have cried unto Thee.' At that moment something takes place within him, the scales fall from his eyes, a mystery is accomplished, and he is a changed man. He has

---

[109] Cf. what we wrote on this subject in *Angelicum*, 1942, fasc. 4, pp. 315-19.
[110] *Conférences de Notre Dame*, 17th Conf., pp. 343, 353.
[111] *Ibid.*, p. 346.

become meek and humble of heart; now he can die, for he is master of truth." [112] A mystery has indeed been accomplished: the infusion of the light of faith which is "the gift of God." "There is at the same time an inarticulate certitude which does not come from reasoning, nor from history or literature or science, the certitude which a poor laborer or a child may possess more and better than a scholar." [113] I confess to Thee, O Father, Lord of heaven and earth, because Thou hast revealed these things to little ones.

As a matter of fact, this Thomistic opinion is admitted at least implicitly by all theologians inasmuch as they hold infused faith to be not only hypothetically but absolutely infallible and essentially supernatural. Assuredly whatever is proposed infallibly by the Church as revealed by God should be infallibly and supernaturally believed by the faithful. But the Church proposes not only the mysteries revealed but also the fact that they are truly revealed by God and not the result of any natural evolution of the religious sense in the subconscious of the prophets. Therefore revelation itself is infallibly believed together with the mysteries in one and the same act, although from a lower aspect these may be known naturally from miracles but in a manner that is not infallible, since it demands a long, complicated process of reasoning wherein our intellect is subject to error and which not all believers are capable of.

Finally it ought to be carefully observed that, should there be an admixture of error in the presentation of revealed doctrine, for example, on account of the ignorance of a preacher, then, by virtue of the infused light of faith, the mind of the believer adheres only to the divine word and does so infallibly. But to the errors mingled with it the imagination and intellect of the believer adhere in no sense by the infused light of faith but in a merely natural, human erroneous way, correcting it thereafter as much as possible. Wherefore the infused light of faith and the divine word are intimately and infallibly connected. Just as a magnet attracts iron but not wood even if the dust of iron and wood are mingled together, so does the virtue of infused faith adhere to the divine word alone, not to the errors accidentally mixed with it.

First objection. Then one must admit with Suarez that belief is first in the veracity of God, secondly in revelation, thirdly in the

[112] *Ibid.*, p. 363.
[113] *Ibid.*

Trinity or the Incarnation. But it is impossible to believe with divine faith in the veracity of God before believing in revelation.

Reply. All Thomists, from the time of Capreolus, reply: Revelation is believed together with the mysteries in one and the same act. St. Thomas himself says, IIa IIae, q. 2, a. 2 ad 1: "By these three: believing God, believing in a God, and believing in God, different acts are not signified." Thus by one and the same supernatural, infallible act we believe God revealing and in the triune God revealed, and this in an order which vastly surpasses the rational conclusion of apologetic argument.

Second objection. But the demons also believe in the supernatural mysteries of the Trinity and the redemptive Incarnation without infused faith, which they lost, but only by acquired faith. The latter therefore, although not essentially supernatural, can attain to these supernatural mysteries.

Reply. Thomists generally reply: The demons attain to supernatural mysteries and the formal motive of infused faith only materially, not formally so far as they are supernatural. They attain to them as something declared by God (like the natural truths of religion) and confirmed by miracles; wherefore "they believe and tremble" as if compelled by the evidence of miracles and not formally on account of the authority of the heavenly Father. Consequently St. Thomas says of them: "They see many manifest indications whence they perceive the doctrine of the Church to be from God. . . . Their faith is, so to speak, forced upon them by the evidence of signs. . . . Hence the faith residing in the demons is not a gift of grace, but they are all the more constrained to believe on account of the perspicacity of their natural intellects" (IIa IIae, q. 5, a. 2 ad 1 and 2). In the same way a person who lacks musical sense hears a Beethoven symphony materially as far as the sounds are concerned, but does not perceive its beauty.

Third objection. One who believes may occasionally undergo a prompting to doubt, but not one who understands the first principles of reason or a conclusion clearly demonstrated. Therefore infused faith is not more certain than any natural certitude.

Reply. St. Thomas answers, IIa IIae, q. 4, a. 8: "Faith is absolutely more certain than clear, natural knowledge, but relatively it is less certain. Thus certitude may be regarded in two ways: in one way on the part of the cause of certainty, wherefore that which has a more certain cause is said to be more certain. And in this respect faith is more certain than the three preceding, since it rests upon divine truth, whereas these three (that is, the understanding of principles, knowledge, and wisdom) depend upon human reason.

"In another sense certitude may be regarded from the standpoint of the subject, and thus that is said to be more certain which is more fully grasped by man's intellect. In this respect, because the articles of faith are beyond the mind of man, whereas the objects of the aforementioned three are not, faith is, from this standpoint, less certain. But since anything is judged absolutely by its cause, but relatively according to a disposition on the part of the subject, it follows that faith is more certain absolutely but the others are more certain relatively, that is, with respect to us." At one and the same time the infused virtue of faith and its formal motive produce their formal effect in our mind. Hence faith is more certain in itself and in us, but not to us, according as an obscure object is not grasped so completely as a clear object. Thus any certain metaphysical principle, such as the principle of causality, may be less certain relatively for some men who are not inclined toward metaphysics than the formal existence of colors outside the mind; and yet the former is more certain absolutely as to itself, for the extra-mental existence of colors is proved by this principle.

Conclusion. Our conclusion can be expressed in these words of St. Thomas, which are generally admitted by Catholic theologians: "The believer holds the articles of faith absolutely by his adherence to first truth, for which man stands in need of being assisted by the [infused] habit of faith," IIa IIae, q. 2, a. 2. "We believe God [revealing] and in God [revealed] in one and the same act," just as we see light and colors with the same sight, the light as that by which we see and that which we see simultaneously with the colors.

The Church proposes infallibly not only the revealed mysteries, but the truth that they are revealed by God and did not proceed from the subconscious minds of the prophets. Therefore the faithful infallibly believe in both simultaneously with a certitude which surpasses the natural certitude of a conclusion in apologetic argument. This is generally expressed by Thomists briefly as follows: "First truth revealing is at the same time that by which we believe and what we believe, that is, infallibly believe together with the mysteries." Thus revelation is revealed by itself just as light manifests itself while showing forth colors. Therefore the certitude of our faith resolves it-self formally and intrinsically into uncreated revelation as infallibly believed, and only materially and extrinsically into the evidence of the signs of revelation, particularly miracles. Similarly in the natural order metaphysical certitude of the real validity of first principles does indeed resolve itself materially and extrinsically into sensible evidence or sensation, but formally and intrinsically into the in-tellectual evidence of the truth of those principles as laws governing extra-mental being. Otherwise superior certitude would be reducible to the inferior as in sensationalism or empiricism for which the Nominalists of the Middle Ages, such as Ockham and Nicholas of Utrecht, prepared the way.

In this question as in others the profound investigations of sacred theology find their way back to the higher certainties of the teaching of faith expressed in Sacred Scripture, which in its eminent simplicity surpasses all the ratiocination with regard to the nature of faith itself and the manner in which it attains to its formal object (*objectum formale quo*) or motive. This very intimate, sublime, and highly sim-plified manner whereby infused faith attains to its formal motive is gradually purified more and more of every imperfect element in the passive purification of the spirit, called by St. John of the Cross the dark night of the soul. In this dolorous darkness the formal motive of faith, that is, first truth revealing, is more and more detached from every other secondary and inferior motive which is then dolorously carried away, for instance, from the harmony of the supernatural mysteries with truths about God naturally known or our own aspira-tions. This harmony is no longer amply apparent in the course of such purification, but it still remains certain that even the very obscure mysteries of eternal punishment and gratuitous predestination are revealed by God, and that it would be a grave sin of infidelity de-liberately to entertain a doubt about them.

Then the formal motive of infused faith, the authority of God re-vealing, shines forth in this dark night in all its loftiness, above every secondary motive accessible to natural reason and at that time en-shrouded by a mist. In other words, first truth revealing appears as a star of the first magnitude in this night of the spirit; and therefore infused faith is purified of every imperfection and, soaring above all temptations and indeliberate vacillations, the human intellect finds an immutable stronghold in this authority of God revealing, to which it adheres infallibly beyond all discursive reasoning, always entreating the bestowal of actual grace for a still firmer salutary and meritorious adherence. Then, as the best directors of souls thus purified affirm, is not the time for rereading one's apologetics, but for the most humble, confiding prayer.

There is a similar passive purification of hope and charity, the formal motives of which are likewise increasingly detached from every inferior motive in which sentimentality or unconsciously inordinate self-love were mingled. The formal motives of the three theological virtues: first truth revealing, omnipotence assisting, and infinite goodness lovable above all things for its own sake, are thus, as it were, the three highest stars in the dark night of the spirit, when these three theological virtues reach the heroic degree, as perfecting virtues or in perfected souls, to which St. Thomas refers in Ia IIae, q. 61, a. 5.

Thus the mystical experience of the saints confirms the assertion of theologians as follows: The formal motive of any theological virtue cannot be anything created; it cannot be a miracle or any truth naturally known. It is a perfection of the uncreated God belonging to His intimate life which accordingly surpasses all the natural cognitive faculties of any intellect created or capable of being created.

VII. The Spirit of Adoption of Sons of God

At the end of this tract on grace, by way of recapitulation, it is fitting that we should examine from the point of view of spirituality what is meant by the spirit of adoption of sons of God, inasmuch as this adoption is accomplished by sanctifying grace which is "the grace of the virtues and gifts." "The Spirit Himself giveth testimony to our spirit, that we are the sons of God" (Rom. 8:16). This is especially apparent in the liturgy of Pentecost.

The time of false peace in which we are living shows by contrast the magnitude and necessity of these graces. It is a difficult, sorry time, yet one which teaches many practical lessons if we meditate in our hearts before God. This false and merely external peace finds no place in minds or hearts or wills. It is full of deceptions and thus provokes a lively desire for true peace both interior and exterior such as only God can give.

The present state of things contains the proof by *reductio ad absurdum* of the existence of God and the truth of Christianity. The

Lord is allowing men to see what they are capable of doing alone when they try to work without divine assistance: "Without Me you can do nothing." This sad situation manifestly arises from the fact that many nations have repudiated Christian principles. They descended first to liberalism which refuses to come to any conclusion either for or against Christian truth, so that it is inadequate to effect any action and merely indulges in protracted discussions *ad infinitum*. When action became necessary, many nations then plunged from liberalism into radicalism by way of negation. Subsequently several peoples arrived at socialism and finally at materialistic, atheistic communism. The downward course was accelerated, as in the gravitation of a falling body, and it is not to be wondered at that this descent should lead to increasingly complex, insoluble problems, since minds no longer recognize true principles.

Amid the general confusion, God safeguards and directs His Church, offering and bestowing upon us graces for a meritorious reaction against error and evil. How are we to rise once more after such a decline? How recover unity of thought and life amid the diversity and complexity of insoluble problems? It is clear that for such a restoration we must return more and more to Christian principles; especially must priests and religious live their lives in accordance with them. The Holy Ghost and His seven gifts are given to us for this end. St. Thomas affirms that under difficult circumstances we stand in need of these seven gifts that we may be docile to the inspirations of the Holy Ghost, conferred to aid the virtues, which are too human in their mode of operation and lack sufficient promptitude in the service and love of God.

In difficult circumstances such as present-day conditions, Christian faith must not only be a firm supernatural adherence to revealed supernatural truths, not only must it be rendered living by charity informing it, but it must be illuminated by the gift of knowledge so as to recognize more keenly the vanity of earthly things and the ineffectualness of human expedients. Our faith should also be enlightened by the gift of understanding so as to penetrate through dogmatic formulas into the mysteries themselves of the Incarnation and Redemption, by which the just man should live, in such a way that these mysteries may be in us the very truths of life inspiring all our actions.

Our hope, in avoiding presumption, should become an increasingly certain tendency toward salvation. Toward this end, "the Spirit Himself giveth testimony to our spirit, that we are the sons of God." Our charity likewise should grow under the light of the gift of wisdom whereby we judge of all things connaturally with respect to God as our last end and as loved efficaciously above all things. Especially in more difficult situations is it essential that Christian prudence should be perfected by the gift of counsel, religion by piety, fortitude by the gift of fortitude, and chastity by that of filial love.

What great spiritual treasures, what sources of energy! But how are we to draw from these seven gifts the power to live in that unity demanded by the interior life amid such diversity of virtues to be practiced and complexity of faults to be avoided? There are more than thirty virtues which must be cultivated; and almost any one of them is either between or above two opposing vices. With the infused virtues we also possess these seven gifts. They are present in us as long as we are in the state of grace, since they are connected with charity in accordance with which the Holy Ghost is given to us. These seven gifts are for us as the seven sails of a ship, capable of receiving the impulsion of a favorable wind.

But in us the gifts are often like furled sails so that they cannot spread or yield to the force of the wind. The seven gifts are tied and knotted by a host of venial sins, scarcely conscious, which fasten our souls to external things and to our own egotism. Then our course is not directed by the Holy Ghost, but by ourselves, by our reason which clings to its own judgment unconformed to the judgment of God; it is directed by our will, tenacious of self-will, inordinate self-love and caprice. Hence, although in the state of grace, we hardly live under the inspiration of the Holy Ghost. Thus we confuse merely natural simplicity, which depends on our temperament, with supernatural simplicity which is completely different, and we likewise confuse our impulsiveness with the inspirations of the gift of counsel. And this procedure assuredly does not suffice to resist the profound errors of the present day nor to re-ascend after such a descent, nor to discover the unity of life amid the multiplicity and complexity of insoluble questions, without the grace of God.

To this end it is essential that we live deeply according to some very simple, sublime, and fruitful truth such as that we are the adopted sons of God. This is the spirit of Pentecost. St. Paul says to the Romans (8:14–16): "Whosoever are led by the Spirit of God, they are the sons of God. For you have not received the spirit of bondage again in fear; but you have received the spirit of adoption of sons, whereby we cry: Abba (Father). For the Spirit Himself giveth testimony to our spirit, that we are the sons of God." And, as St. Thomas remarks, He gives this testimony by the filial affection toward God which He awakens in us through special inspiration, for "not of blood, nor of the will of the flesh, nor of the will of man, but of God" are we born, by the grace of adoption. This is the spirit of adoption of all the seven gifts whereby the unity of life is preserved amid the complexity of problems in the upward return to God. But this fundamental truth must be a vital truth in us, not merely preserved in the memory but directing all our activity.

A certain excellent missioner from Mesopotamia recently described to me how he had arrived at this conviction. "I happened one day," he said, "to enter an Arab village which had been destroyed by some enemy tribe, and from one of the almost ruined houses a little boy of six emerged and said to me: 'They killed my father and mother and all my brothers and sisters: I am all alone. But I am a Christian; be so kind as to take me with you, Father, to the mission.'" The missioner interrogated the boy to see if he was really a Christian. The boy replied correctly to the first questions in the catechism. So the missioner was moved to pity and adopted him, taking him to the mission where he was educated and became a splendid Christian. But whenever he saw the boy going about, he would say to himself: "I adopted this boy and must fulfill my obligations toward him as adoptive father. Now I understand better that I, too, am an adoptive son of God who, when I was destitute, bestowed upon me grace, a participation in the divine nature, and the seed of glory or eternal life. I should therefore ever live more and more as an adopted son of God."

This is the simple, sublime, practical, and most fruitful truth whereby we can and ought to live profoundly through faith illuminated by the gifts with great spontaneity and unity of life. This is the truth which Christ desired to impress upon the minds of His apostles when they were disputing among themselves, which of them was greatest. He warned them: "Amen I say to you, unless you be converted and become as little children, you shall not enter into the kingdom of heaven" (Matt. 18:3). Pride, ambition, detraction can impede our entrance therein forever.

To live as a son of God according to the spirit of adoption, the

Christian's attitude toward God must be that of a child toward his parents; indeed the distance between God and us is immeasurably greater than between parents and their children. Now a child usually possesses certain native qualities: simplicity devoid of duplicity, a consciousness of his weakness disposing him to humility; moreover he firmly believes whatever his mother tells him, especially when she speaks to him of God; he also has absolute confidence in her and loves her with all his heart more than all her flattering caresses. The true adoptive son of God possesses these qualities with respect to God and through them lives willingly by the seven gifts in great unity of thought and love, in spite of the multiplicity of virtues to be practiced, and vices to be avoided.

The child of God is simple, devoid of duplicity. Why? Because his glance turns directly to God. Thus are verified the words of Scripture: "If thy eye be single, thy whole body shall be lightsome" (Matt. 6:22). If your intention is simple, pure, and straightforward, without any duplicity, your entire life will be luminous, like the candid face of a child. Thus the simple soul always looks toward God and tends to see God in all persons and events. Whatever may occur, that soul recognizes that it is willed by God or at least permitted for the sake of a greater good. In this simplicity, which is eminently superior to simplicity of nature or temperament, there is frequent exercise of the gift of wisdom, the highest of all the gifts.

Like the child, an adoptive son of God is also conscious of his weakness. He feels that of himself he is nothing. Through the gift of knowledge he clearly understands the words of our Lord: "Without Me you can do nothing" in the order of sanctification and salvation. He is so inclined toward humility that he does not indulge in unnecessary self-examination, does not speak of himself, nor seek the esteem of others in his regard. Moreover, since he feels his weakness, he is inclined to seek continually the help and direction of God his Father, as a little child looks to his mother for help. Thus is the spirit of prayer rendered more perfect.

Faith, too, is greatly increased. As the child firmly believes what his mother tells him, the son of God relies completely on divine revelation. Jesus has declared this to be true, whether immediately in the Gospel or through His Church: that suffices; there is no room for doubt. And what is the result? How blessed a one for the soul! Just as a mother delights in instructing her little one more and more as she finds him more eager to learn, so does Christ our Lord gladly manifest the deep simplicity of the mysteries of faith to the humble who hear them with great faith. Therefore He said: "I confess to Thee, O Father, Lord of heaven and earth, because Thou hast hid these things from the wise and prudent, and hast revealed them to little ones." Thus faith becomes penetrating, delectable, contemplative, radiant, practical, the source of manifold excellent counsel. So does the spirit of faith grow with the frequent exercise of the gifts of understanding, wisdom, and counsel.

Even if God permits the dark night to overtake him, the child of God traverses it, his hand in that of his Father, as a little one holds his mother's, knowing that she will take care of him. As a consequence, hope increases and becomes firm confidence, since it rests upon God's love for us, His promises, His omnipotence, and the infinite merits of the Redeemer. Hope is therefore ever more certain in accordance with the certainty of the tendency toward eternal life. As the little child trusts his mother with the greatest assurance, knowing her love for him, so does the son of God entrust himself most securely to God, never doubting the fidelity of Him who said: "Ask and you shall receive."

Nor should our frailty discourage us. As the little one assures himself: "Because of my weakness my mother always watches over me," so the child of God recognizes that Christ ever watches over the poor and weak who invoke Him. The Holy Ghost, too, willed to be called "the father of the poor." Confidence thus remains intact even in the gravest hours, when the Son of God says to His heavenly Father in the words of St. Theresa: "Lord, Thou knowest all things, Thou canst do all things, and Thou lovest me." I recently met a certain lady of the Polish aristocracy who was deported to the northernmost part of Siberia. As she entered the prison she felt the sustaining presence of God, which never ceased as long as she remained in that prison. When she was liberated, however, the presence of God was no longer sensible, although she retained the memory of this exceptional assistance of God.

Finally, charity increases greatly if we live as true children of God. This way is not a special one for certain souls only; it is the ordinary way which all the sons of God should follow. Each one should ask himself: "Which dominates in me: the man of self-love, the egotist, or the son of God?" The little child loves his mother with all his heart and lives by her. Likewise the true son of God loves God more and more for His own sake, because of the infinity of His perfections in which we participate. The real child of God is not self-seeking, but loves God Himself more than his own personal perfection, more than the consolations of prayer. His is a generous love which asks itself: "What can I do to please God and help my neighbor on the way of eternal salvation?"

Then the adoptive son of God, seeking Him in all things, often receives the inspirations of the gifts of counsel and of fortitude amid great difficulties. All seven gifts operate freely in him; they are no longer bound but completely unfurled under the inspiration of the Holy Ghost. This supernatural life of the child of God, in its simplicity and humility, and in the exercise of the theological virtues, vastly surpasses the natural activity of the most intelligent, efficient people who depend on their own powers and disregard the words of our Lord: "Without Me you can do nothing" in the order of sanctification and salvation.

We should therefore ask for this spirit of adoption, this simplicity, humility, faith, confidence, and radiating charity. So will the Holy Spirit give more and more testimony to our spirit that we are sons of God. He renders this testimony by the filial affection toward God the Father which He arouses in us. He will also bestow that peace which the world cannot give, that interior peace which is the tranquillity of order, elevating the soul and restoring unity of thought and contemplation even amid the diversity of extremely complex questions which present themselves at the present day, questions that remain insoluble without this light from above. This supernatural peace is the fruit of the gift of wisdom: "Blessed are the peacemakers, for they shall be called the children of God." This is a beginning in us of eternal beatitude.

May the Blessed Virgin Mary, deign to make use of these imperfect pages to lead many souls to such sanctity, that our life may be unto the praise of the glory of the grace of God!

APPENDIX

WHETHER AVERSION FROM THE SUPERNATURAL END CANNOT EXIST WITHOUT AVERSION FROM THE NATURAL END

In classical Thomism as understood by Capreolus, Cajetan, Ferrariensis, Bañez, Alvarez, Lemos, John of St. Thomas, Gonet, Godoy, the Salmanticenses, Billuart, Gotti, Del Prado, and others, it is generally admitted that fallen man cannot be directly averted from his final supernatural end without at the same time being at least indirectly averted from God, his final natural end and the author of nature. Why? Because even the natural law prescribes that God is to be obeyed whatever He commands whether in the natural or in a higher order. From this principle Thomists generally deduce the following conclusions which are rejected by many only because of insufficient grasp of the foregoing principle.

1. Fallen man cannot by his natural powers alone, without restorative grace, love God the author of nature above all things with an effectively efficacious love. This is the express opinion of St. Thomas, Ia IIae, q. 109, a. 3, where he says that, in contrast to the state of incorrupt nature, "man in the state of fallen nature requires for this the help of grace which heals nature," since, "on account of the corruption of nature, the rational appetite of the will seeks an individual good unless it is healed by grace." A weakened power cannot exercise toward God the very efficient act of a healthy power unless it is healed. With still greater reason, fallen man cannot observe the whole of the natural law without healing grace. (Cf. Ia IIae, q. 109, a. 4.)

2. In the state of fallen nature not yet restored, man has less strength to perform a moral good than he would have had in the state of pure nature. Why? Because now man is born with original sin, that is, directly averted from his supernatural end and indirectly averted from his final natural end; whereas, on the contrary, in the state of pure nature he would not have been born directly turned away from his final natural end, but capable of either conversion or aversion in regard to it. St. Thomas affirms this explicitly enough in treating of the "wounds inflicted upon the whole of human nature by the sin of our first parents," especially the wound of malice in the will

whereby the natural inclination to virtue is diminished. (Cf. Ia IIae, q. 85, a. 3; q. 82, a. 1 ad 1.)

3. As the Angelic Doctor asserts, Ia IIae, q. 89, a. 6, with regard to an unbaptized child: "When he begins to have the use of reason . . . the first thing that occurs to a man as subject for thought is to deliberate about himself. And if he directs himself to the proper end, he obtains through grace the remission of original sin. Again, ad 3: "For the first thing that occurs to a man who attains to discretion is to consider himself as that toward which he should order other things as to an end. For the end is first in intention. And therefore this is the time when he becomes obligated by the positive command of God, who says: 'Turn ye to Me . . . and I will turn to you' (Zach. 1:3)." In the *De veritate,* q. 24, a. 12 ad 1, St. Thomas also writes: "As soon as an adult receives the use of free will, if he prepares himself for grace he will have grace"; that is, if he does what in him lies with the help of actual grace, God does not refuse habitual grace nor, accordingly, faith and charity; and He therefore manifests the revealed truths which are entirely necessary for salvation, at least that God is and is a rewarder. This is an admirable form of baptism of desire, without miracle but with the very special help of God and the guardian angle. Then the child should efficaciously love God the author of nature above all things, and this cannot be done without healing grace. But if he does what he can under actual grace, according to St. Thomas, he is justified. Many theologians, however, deny this last conclusion of St. Thomas and Thomists regarding the justification of an unbaptized child. Yet it is not easy to reject it or destroy the principles upon which this conclusion is based. (Cf. above, pp. 197 ff.)

4. The fourth consequence of the principle enunciated above is that in the limbo of children the souls of infants who died before receiving baptism, although they do not strictly suffer from the loss of supernatural happiness, yet do not have absolute, perfect natural happiness since they remain indirectly averted from their final natural end on account of unforgiven original sin. But they have "a certain natural beatitude"; cf. *De malo,* q. 5, a. 3; and they are exempt from any pain of the senses which is inflicted in punishment for a personal conversion to a transitory good; cf. *De malo,* q. 5, a. 2. In the supplement to the *Summa,* q. 89, a. 5 ad 3, we read: "Even

children who die before attaining maturity will appear at the last general judgment, not to be judged but to witness the glory of the Judge." Cf. Hugon, *De novissimis,* 1927, p. 813. There are other consequences of the foregoing principles.[114]

Is it certain that this basic principle is found in the works of St. Thomas? Beyond any doubt, if the texts cited are carefully studied, especially Ia IIae, q. 109, a. 3: "In the state of fallen nature man requires the help of grace healing nature in order that he may love God naturally [as author of nature] above all things." And again, IIa IIae, q. 10, a. 1 ad 1: "It is not proper to human nature to have infused faith. But it is proper to human nature for the mind of man not to reject the interior instinct and exterior preaching of truth. Hence unbelief is accordingly contrary to nature." All sin which is directly opposed to the supernatural end is at least indirectly against God as natural end and author of nature, since the natural law already prescribes that God is to be obeyed whatever He commands, whether in the natural order or in a higher order.

The conclusion is therefore contrary to naturalism and laicism: He who withdraws from his supernatural end most assuredly cannot perfectly attain to his natural end. In the present economy of salvation there is a necessary connection between the two orders. As a matter of fact, every man is either in the state of grace or in the state of sin, and if he is in sin, he is directly averted from his final supernatural end and indirectly from his final natural end. St. Thomas comments on Matt. 12:30: "God is the natural end toward which all things tend; therefore he who is not with God must be separated from Him." Naturalism is, after all, contrary to nature, since it is against God toward whom all nature tends.

Hence Christ declared: "He that is not with Me, is against Me: and he that gathereth not with Me, scattereth" (Matt. 12:30). But on the other hand He assured the apostles: "He that is not against you, is for you" (Mark 9:39). Accordingly, those who are already sincerely seeking God do so by the help of grace, as if God were to say to them: "You would not be seeking me sincerely if in some measure you had not already found Me." "Not that we are sufficient to think anything [salutary] of ourselves, as of ourselves: but our sufficiency is from God" (II Cor. 3:5).

[114] The Salmanticenses, *De gratia,* on Ia IIae, q. 109, disp. II, dub. IV, nos. 144-57.

INDEX

Abraham's obedience, 299

Absolute certainty; *see* Certainty, absolute

Absolute supernatural, 7

Absolute will of God; *see* Consequent will

Absolution, faith required for, 335

Accident essentially related to substance, 122

Act specified by object, 464-80: differentiating acquired and infused virtues, 469-71, 475; Cajetan on, 473

Action, philosophy of, 301

Actual grace
divisions of, 150
a motion, 117
necessary to just man, 97-99
not formal participation in divine nature, 142
operative and cooperative, 163-77
twofold, 175
twofold motion for operative, 175

Adam before the fall: justification a simple generation in, 326; not Christian grace in, 148; sanctifying grace in, 140; sufficient and efficacious grace in, 194 and note

Adoption of sonship
appropriated to the three persons, 404
different from human adoption, 135, 137
established by grace, 114, 116, 129
formally procured by grace, 142
gratuitous, 136 and note
Nominalist theory of, 137, 331 note
participated likeness, 134, 405
predestinate in sin and, 143
qualities of child for, 500-503
reprobate and, 143
Scriptural texts on, 135
secondary formal effect of grace, 137
spirit of, 497-503
and supernatural revelation, 486

Aeterni Patris (encyclical), 295

Agnes, St., 282

Ailly, Nominalist disciple of, 125

Albeda, González de; *see* González de Albeda

Albert, St.: on the Mass, 111

Almsgiving, 388

Alphonsus Liguori, St., 182
difficulty about hope, 233
difficulty of Thomism, 232
divine decrees, 235
opinion of, 205, 232-36
reply to objections of, 232
scientia media rejected by, 204 note, 235

Alvarez
aversion from supernatural and natural ends, 504
justification of pagan child, 343 note
operative grace, 177
procession of acts in justification, 357
quoted by St. Alphonsus, 232
sufficient and efficacious grace, 220, 432 note
supernaturalness of faith, 482, 484

Analogous concepts, 123, 369, 403

Andronicus, grace of martyrdom, 282

Angelo, O. P.: thesis on justification of pagan child, 341

Angels
baptism of desire and guardian, 505
effects of grace in, 140 note, 141
essence and existence distinct in, 300
essence distinct from operative power in, 468
faith of wayfaring, 478, 485, 490
first act of, 176
grace according to rank, 90
grace naturally unintelligible to, 125
infused species in, 478
intelligence in, 407
justification a simple generation in, 326

Divisions of Grace

Created grace
- internal
  - Sanctifying
    - habitual – virtues / gifts
    - actual
      - effic – suffic
      - oper – coop
      - praev – subs.
  - gratis data : prophecy, tongues, etc
- external : Gospel, example etc.